Dictionary
French – English
English – French

Dictionnaire
Français – Anglais
Anglais – Français

Berlitz Publishing
Union, NJ · Munich · Singapore

Edited by the Berlitz Editorial Staff

Cover photo by ID Image Direkt CD-ROM GmbH, Germany

© 2004 Berlitz Publishing/APA Publications GmbH & Co. Verlag KG
Singapore Branch, Singapore

Berlitz Publishing
95 Progress Street
Union, NJ 07083
USA

Printed in Singapore
ISBN 981-246-127-2

Contents

Table des matières

Preface

In selecting the vocabulary and phrases for this dictionary, the editors have had the traveller's needs foremost in mind. This book will prove a useful companion to casual tourists and business travellers alike who appreciate the reassurance a small and practical dictionary can provide. It offers them—as well as beginners and students—all the basic vocabulary they will encounter and have to use, giving the key words and expressions to allow them to cope in everyday situations.

Like our successful phrase books and travel guides, these dictionaries— created with the help of a computer data bank— are designed to slip into your pocket or purse, and thus have a role as handy companions at all times.

Besides just about everything you normally find in dictionaries, there are these Berlitz bonuses:

- simplified pronunciation after each foreign-word entry, making it easy to read and enunciate words whose spelling may look forbidding

- a unique, practical glossary to simplify reading a foreign restaurant menu and to take the mystery out of complicated dishes and indecipherable names on bills of fare

- useful information on how to tell the time and how to count, on conjugating irregular verbs, commonly seen abbreviations and converting to the metric system, in addition to basic phrases.

While no dictionary of this size can pretend to completeness, we are confident this dictionary will help you get most out of your trip abroad.

Berlitz Publishing

Préface

En choisissant les mots et expressions de ce dictionnaire, nos rédacteurs se sont souciés des besoins essentiels de l'étudiant et du voyageur. Cet ouvrage s'avérera indispensable aux touristes, globe-trotters, hommes ou femmes d'affaires qui apprécient l'appoint qu'apporte un dictionnaire pratique et de format réduit. Il leur offre le vocabulaire qu'ils seront amenés à rencontrer et à utiliser; il leur propose des mots-clés et des expressions leur permettant de faire face aux situations de tous les jours.

A l'instar de nos manuels de conversation et de nos guides de voyage déjà fort appréciés, nos dictionnaires — réalisés grâce à une banque de données sur ordinateur — sont conçus pour se glisser dans une poche ou dans un sac, assumant ainsi leur rôle de compagnons à tout moment.

Ce dictionnaire présente:

• une transcription phonétique facilitant la prononciation de chaque entrée

• un lexique pratique visant à faciliter la lecture du menu dans un restaurant et révélant les mystères de plats jusqu'alors inconnus

• des informations précieuses sur la façon d'exprimer le temps, de compter, sur les verbes irréguliers, sur les abréviations courantes, en plus des expressions usuelles.

Aucun dictionnaire de ce format ne peut prétendre être exhaustif, mais le but principal de cet ouvrage est de permettre à son utilisateur d'affronter avec confiance un voyage à l'étranger.

Berlitz Publishing

French-English

Français-Anglais

Introduction

The dictionary has been designed to take account of your practical needs. Unnecessary linguistic information has been avoided. The entries are listed in alphabetical order, regardless of whether the entry word is printed in a single word, contains an apostrophe, or is in two or more separate words. When an entry is followed by sub-entries such as expressions and locutions, these, too, have been listed in alphabetical order.

Each main-entry word is followed by a phonetic transcription (see Guide to Pronunciation). Following the transcription is the part of speech of the entry word whenever applicable. When an entry word may be used as more than one part of speech, the translations are grouped together after the respective part of speech.

French feminine headwords are shown as follows:

campeur ... *m*, **-euse** *f* camper
descendant... *m*, **-e** *f* descendant
électeur ... *m*, **-trice** *f* voter
citoyen ... *m*, **-ne** *f*

The feminine forms of these headwords are: **campeuse** (pl ~s), **descendante** (pl ~s), **électrice** (pl ~s), **citoyenne** (pl ~s).

The feminine or plural forms of French adjectives have been supplied whenever they diverge from the standard rule for the word-ending in question. Similarly, the plural forms of nouns are given when not in accordance with the rules for the particular word-ending.

Whenever an entry word is repeated in irregular forms, or in subentries, a tilde (~) is used to represent the full entry word.

In irregular feminine and plural forms, a hyphen is used to represent the part of the main-entry word that precedes the relevant word-ending.

An asterisk (*) in front of a verb indicates that the verb is irregular. For details, refer to the lists of irregular verbs.

Abbreviations

adj	adjective	*num*	numeral
adv	adverb	*p*	past tense
Am	American	*pl*	plural
art	article	*plAm*	plural (American)
conj	conjunction	*pp*	past participle
f	feminine	*pr*	present tense
fpl	feminine plural	*pref*	prefix
m	masculine	*prep*	preposition
mpl	masculine plural	*pron*	pronoun
n	noun	*v*	verb
nAm	noun (American)	*vAm*	verb (American)

Guide to Pronunciation

Each main entry in this part of the dictionary is followed by a phonetic transcription which shows you how to pronounce the words. This transcription should be read as if it were English. It is based on Standard British pronunciation, though we have tried to take account of General American pronunciation also. Below, only those letters and symbols are explained which we consider likely to be ambiguous or not immediately understood.

The syllables are separated by hyphens, and stressed syllables are printed in *italics*.

Of course, the sounds of any two languages are never exactly the same, but if you follow carefully our indications, you should be able to pronounce the foreign words in such a way that you'll be understood. To make your task easier, our transcriptions occasionally simplify slightly the sound system of the language while still reflecting the essential sound differences.

Consonants

g	always hard, as in **g**o
ñ	as in Spanish se**ñ**or, or like **ni** in o**ni**on
r	pronounced in the back of the mouth
s	always hard, as in **s**o
zh	a soft, voiced **sh**, like **s** in plea**s**ure

The sign (') indicates a so-called aspirate h. It means that no liaison (*les huttes*—lay 'ewt) nor elision (*la hutte*—lah 'ewt) should be made.

Vowels and Diphthongs

aa	long **a**, as in c**a**r
ah	a short version of **aa**; between **a** in c**a**t and **u** in c**u**t
ai	like **air**, without any **r**-sound
eh	like **e** in g**e**t
er	as in oth**er**, without any **r**-sound
ew	a "rounded **ee**-sound". Say the vowel sound **ee** (as in s**ee**), and while saying it, round your lips as for **oo** (as in s**oo**n), without moving your tongue; when your lips are in the **oo** position, but your tongue in

the **ee** position, you should be pronouncing the correct sound

igh	as in s**igh**
o	always as in h**o**t (British pronunciation)
ur	as in f**ur**, but with rounded lips and no **r**-sound

1) A bar over a vowel symbol (e.g. $\overline{\text{ew}}$) shows that this sound is long.
2) Raised letters (e.g. **oo**^{ee}, ^{y}**ur**) should be pronounced only fleetingly.
3) French contains nasal vowels, which we transcribe with a vowel symbol plus **ng** (e.g. **ahng**). This **ng** should *not* be pronounced, and serves solely to indicate nasal quality of the preceding vowel. A nasal vowel is pronounced simultaneously through the mouth and the nose.
4) French vowels (i.e. not diphthongs) are relatively short and pure. Therefore, you should try to read a transcription like **oa** without moving tongue or lips while pronouncing the sound.

A

à (ah) *prep* to; at, on

abandonner (ah-bahn͞g-do-*nay*) *v* desert

abat-jour (ah-bah-*zhoor*) *m* lampshade

***abattre** (ah-*bahtr*) *v* knock down; kill; dishearten

abbaye (ah-bay-*ee*) *f* abbey

abcès (ah-*psay*) *m* abscess

abeille (ah-*bay*) *f* bee

abîme (ah-*beem*) *m* abyss

abîmer (ah-bee-*may*) *v* *spoil

abolir (ah-bo-*leer*) *v* abolish

abondance (ah-bawn͞g-*dahn͞gss*) *f* abundance; plenty

abondant (ah-bawn͞g-*dahn͞g*) *adj* abundant; plentiful

abonné (ah-bo-*nay*) *m* subscriber

abonnement (ah-bon-*mahn͞g*) *m* subscription

abord: d'abord (dah-*bawr*) at first

abordage (ah-bor-*daazh*) *m* collision

aboutir à (ah-boo-*teer*) end at; result in

aboyer (ah-bwah-*ʸay*) *v* bark, bay

abréviation (ah-bray-vʸah-sʸawn͞g) *f* abbreviation

abri (ah-*bree*) *m* shelter; cover

abricot (ah-bree-*koa*) *m* apricot

abriter (ah-bree-*tay*) *v* shelter

abrupt (ah-*brewpt*) *adj* steep

absence (ah-*psahn͞gss*) *f* absence

absent (ah-*psahn͞g*) *adj* absent

absolu (ah-pso-*lew*) *adj* total, sheer

absolument (ah-pso-lew-*mahn͞g*) *adv* absolutely

absorber (ah-psor-*bay*) *v* absorb

***abstenir** (ah-pster-*neer*): **s'~ de** abstain from

abstraction faite de (ahp-strahk-sʸawn͞g feht der) apart from

abstrait (ahp-*stray*) *adj* abstract

absurde (ah-*psewrd*) *adj* absurd; foolish

abus (ah-*bew*) *m* abuse, misuse

académie (ah-kah-day-*mee*) *f* academy; **~ des beaux-arts** art school

accélérateur (ahk-say-lay-rah-*tūr*) *m* accelerator

accélérer (ahk-say-lay-*ray*) *v* accelerate

accent (ahk-*sahn͞g*) *m* accent, stress

accepter (ahk-sehp-*tay*) *v* accept

accès (ahk-*say*) *m* access; approach, entrance, admittance

accessible (ahk-say-*seebl*) *adj* accessible; attainable

accessoire (ahk-say-*swaar*) *adj* additional

accessoires (ahk-say-*swaar*) *mpl* accessories *pl*

accident (ahk-see-*dahn͞g*) *m* accident; **~ d'avion** plane crash

accidenté (ahk-see-dahn͞g-*tay*) *adj* hilly; uneven

accidentel (ahk-see-dahn͞g-*tehl*) *adj* accidental

acclamer (ah-klah-*may*) *v* cheer

accommodation (ah-ko-mo-dah-sʸawn͞g) *f* accommodation

accompagner (ah-kawn͞g-pah-*ñay*) *v* accompany

accomplir (ah-kawn͞g-*pleer*) *v* accomplish; perform, achieve

accomplissement (ah-kawn͞g-plee-*smahn͞g*) *m* fulfilment, accomplishment

accord (ah-*kawr*) *m* settlement, agreement; approval; **d'accord!** all right!; okay!; ***être d'accord** agree; ***être d'accord avec** approve of

accorder (ah-kor-*day*) *v* grant; tune; **s'accorder avec** match

accoster (ah-ko-*stay*) *v* dock

accoucher (ah-koo-*shay*) *v* have a

baby, be delivered (of, **de**)

accouchement (ah-koosh-*mahng*) *m* childbirth, delivery

accoutumé (ah-koo-tew-*may*) *adj* accustomed

accrocher (ah-kro-*shay*): **s'~** *hold on

accueil (ah-*kur^{ee}*) *m* reception; welcome

accueillir (ah-kur-^yeer*) *v* welcome

accumulateur (ah-kew-mew-lah-*tūrr*) *m* battery

accumuler (ah-kew-mew-*lay*): **s'~** increase

accusation (ah-kew-zah-*s^yawng*) *f* charge

accuser (ah-kew-*zay*) *v* accuse; charge

achat (ah-*shah*) *m* purchase; **~ à tempérament** hire purchase; ***faire des achats** shop

acheter (ahsh-*tay*) *v* *buy, purchase

acheteur (ahsh-*tūrr*) *m*, **-euse** *f* buyer, purchaser

achever (ahsh-*vay*) *v* finish; complete, accomplish

acide (ah-*seed*) *m* acid

acier (ah-*s^yay*) *m* steel; **~ inoxydable** stainless steel

acné (ahk-*nay*) *f* acne

acompte (ah-*kawngt*) *m* down payment; instal(l)ment

à-coup (ah-*koo*) *m* tug

*acquérir (ah-kay-*reer*) *v* acquire; *buy

acquisition (ah-kee-zee-*s^yawng*) *f* acquisition, purchase

acquittement (ah-keet-*mahng*) *m* acquittal

acte (ahkt) *m* act, deed

acteur (ahk-*tūrr*) *m* actor

actif (ahk-*teef*) *adj* active

action (ahk-*s^yawng*) *f* action, deed; share; **actions** stocks and shares

activité (ahk-tee-vee-*tay*) *f* activity; work

actrice (ahk-*treess*) *f* actress

actualité (ahk-twah-lee-*tay*) *f* current events; **actualités** news; newsreel

actuel (ahk-*twehl*) *adj* present; topical

actuellement (ahk-twehl-*mahng*) *adv* nowadays

adapter (ah-dahp-*tay*) *v* adapt; **~ à** suit

addition (ah-dee-*s^yawng*) *f* addition; bill

additionner (ah-dee-*s^yo-nay*) *v* add

adéquat (ah-day-*kwah*) *adj* adequate; appropriate, proper; sufficient

adhérer à (ah-day-*ray*) join

adieu (ah-*d^yur*) *m* parting

adjectif (ah-jehk-*teef*) *m* adjective

*admettre (ahd-*mehtr*) *v* acknowledge, admit; **en admettant que** supposing that

administratif (ahd-mee-nee-strah teef) *adj* administrative

administration (ahd-mee-nee-strah-*s^yawng*) *f* administration

administrer (ahd-mee-nee-*stray*) *v* run; administer

admiration (ahd-mee-rah-*s^yawng*) *f* admiration

admirer (ahd-mee-*ray*) *v* admire

admission (ahd-mee-*s^yawng*) *f* admission; entry

adolescent (ah-do-leh-*sahng*) *m* teenager

adopter (ah-dop-*tay*) *v* adopt

adorable (ah-do-*rahbl*) *adj* adorable

adorer (ah-do-*ray*) *v* worship

adoucir (ah-doo-*seer*) *v* soften

adoucisseur d'eau (ah-doo-see-*sūrr* doa) water softener

adresse (ah-*drehss*) *f* address

adresser (ah-dray-*say*) *v* address; **s'adresser à** address

adroit (ah-*drwah*) *adj* skil(l)ful; smart

adulte (ah-*dewlt*) *m/f* adult, grown-up; *adj* adult, grown-up

adversaire (ahd-vehr-*sair*) *m/f* opponent

aération (ah-ay-rah-$s^y aw\overline{ng}$) f
ventilation

aérer (ah-ay-*ray*) v ventilate, air; **aéré**
airy

aéroport (ah-ay-ro-*pawr*) m airport

affaire (ah-*fair*) f business, matter,
case; affair, concern; deal; **~ de cœur**
affair

affairé (ah-fay-*ray*) adj busy

affaires (ah-*fair*) fpl business;
belongings pl; **chiffre d'affaires**
turnover; ***faire des ~ avec** *deal with

affamé (ah-fah-*may*) adj hungry

affecter (ah-fehk-*tay*) v affect

affection (ah-fehk-$s^y aw\overline{ng}$) f affection;
ailment

affectueux (ah-fehk-*twur*) adj
affectionate

affiche (ah-*feesh*) f placard, poster

affiler (ah-fee-*lay*) v sharpen

affilier (ah-fee-$l^y ay$): **s'~ à** join

affirmatif (ah-feer-mah-*teef*) adj
affirmative

affirmer (ah-feer-*may*) v affirm; state

affliction (ah-fleek-$s^y aw\overline{ng}$) f grief

affligé (ah-flee-*zhay*) adj sad

affluent (ah-flew-$ah\overline{ng}$) m tributary

affranchir (ah-frah$\overline{ng}$-*sheer*) v stamp

affreux (ah-*frur*) adj dreadful, frightful

affronter (ah-fraw$\overline{ng}$-*tay*) v face

afin de (ah-*fa$\overline{ng}$* der) to, in order to;
afin que so that

Africain (ah-free-*ka$\overline{ng}$*) m African

africain (ah-free-*ka$\overline{ng}$*) adj African

Afrique (ah-*freek*) f Africa; **~ du Sud**
South Africa

after-shave (ahf-terr-*shehv*) m
aftershave lotion

agacer (ah-gah-*say*) v irritate, annoy

âge (aazh) m age

âgé (ah-*zhay*) adj aged, elderly; **le plus
~** eldest; **plus ~** elder

agence (ah-*zhah$\overline{ng}$ss*) f agency

agenda (ah-zha$\overline{ng}$-*dah*) m diary

agenouiller: (ahzh-noo-$^y ay$): **s'~**
*kneel

agent (ah-*zhah$\overline{ng}$*) m agent; **~ de
police** policeman; **~ de voyages**
travel agent; **~ immobilier** house
agent

agir (ah-*zheer*) v act

agitation (ah-zhee-tah-$s^y aw\overline{ng}$) f
excitement, fuss; disturbance, unrest

agiter (ah-zhee-*tay*) v agitate; stir;
agité restless

agneau (ah-*ñoa*) m lamb

agrafe (ah-*grahf*) f staple

agrandir (ah-grah$\overline{ng}$-*deer*) v extend;
enlarge

agrandissement (ah-grah$\overline{ng}$-dee-
smah$\overline{ng}$) m enlargement; extension

agréable (ah-gray-*ahbl*) adj pleasing,
pleasant, agreeable; enjoyable

agréer (ah-gray-*ay*) v accept

agrément (ah-gray-*mah$\overline{ng}$*) m pleasure

agressif (ah-gray-*seef*) adj aggressive

agricole (ah-gree-*kol*) adj agricultural

agriculteur (ah-gree-kewl-*tūrr*) m
farmer

agriculture (ah-gree-kewl-*tēwr*) f
agriculture

aide (ehd) f help, assistance, aid; m/f
helper

aider (ay-*day*) v help, aid

aigle (aigl) m eagle

aiglefin (ehgl-*fa$\overline{ng}$*) m haddock

aigre (aigr) adj sour

aigu (ay-*gew*) adj (f -guë) acute; sharp;
keen

aiguille (ay-$gwee^y$) f needle; spire;
travail à l'aiguille needlework

aiguiser (ay-gee-*zay*) v sharpen

ail (igh) m (pl ails, aulx) garlic

aile (ehl) f wing

ailleurs (ah-$^y \overline{urr}$) adv elsewhere;
d'ailleurs moreover, besides

aimable (ay-*mahbl*) adj kind

aimer (ay-*may*) v like, *be fond of,

love; fancy; **aimé** beloved; **~ mieux** prefer

aine (ehn) f groin

aîné (ay-*nay*) adj elder

ainsi (ang-*see*) adv so, thus

air (air) m air; tune; ***avoir l'air** look

airbag (air-*bahg*) m airbag

airelle (ay-*rehl*) f blueberry

aisance (eh-*zahngss*) f ease

aise (aiz) f leisure, ease

aisé (ay-*zay*) adj well-to-do

ajournement (ah-zhoor-ner-*mahng*) m delay

ajourner (ah-zhoor-*nay*) v adjourn, *put off, postpone

ajouter (ah-zhoo-*tay*) v add

ajuster (ah zhew-*stay*) v adjust

alarmer (ah-lahr-*may*) v alarm

album (ahl-*bom*) m album; **~ de collage** scrapbook

alcool (ahl-*kol*) m alcohol; **réchaud à ~** spirit stove

alcoolique (ahl-ko-*leek*) adj alcoholic

alentours (ah-lahng-*toor*) mpl surroundings pl; vicinity

alerte (ah-*lehrt*) f alarm; adj smart

Algérie (ahl-zhay-*ree*) f Algeria

Algérien (ahl-zhay-r'*ang*) m Algerian

algérien (ahl-zhay-r'*ang*) adj Algerian

algue (ahlg) f alga; seaweed

alimentation (ah-lee-mahng-tah-s'*awng*) f nourishment

alimenter (ah-lee-mahng-*tay*) v *feed

aliments (ah-lee-*mahng*) mpl foodstuffs pl; **~ surgelés** frozen food

allaiter (ah-lay-*tay*) v nurse

allée (ah-*lay*) f avenue

Allemagne (ahl-*mahñ*) f Germany

Allemand (ahl-*mahng*) m, **-e** f German

allemand (ahl-*mahng*) adj German

*aller (ah-*lay*) v *go; **~ chercher** collect, pick up; **aller et retour** round trip Am; **~ prendre** *get; **bien ~** suit; **s'en ~** *go away; depart

allergie (ah-lehr-*zhee*) f allergy

alliance (ah-l'*ahngss*) f alliance; wedding ring

allié (ah-l'*ay*) m associate; **Alliés** Allies pl

allier (ah-l'*ay*): **s'~** ally

allocation (ah-lo-kah-s'*awng*) f allowance

allocution (ah-lo-kew-s'*awng*) f speech

allonger (ah-lawng-*zhay*) v lengthen; dilute

allumage (ah-lew-*maazh*) m ignition

allumer (ah-lew-*may*) v *light; switch on, turn on

allumette (ah-lew-*meht*) f match

allure (ah-*lewr*) f pace

alors (ah-*lawr*) adv then

alouette (ah-*lweht*) f lark

alphabet (ahl-fah-*bay*) m alphabet

alpinisme (ahl-pee-*neezm*) m mountaineering

alternatif (ahl-tehr-nah-*teef*) adj alternate

alternative (ahl-tehr-nah-*teev*) f alternative

altitude (ahl-tee-*tewd*) f altitude

aluminium (ah-lew-mee-n'*om*) m aluminium

amande (ah-*mahngd*) f almond

amant (ah-*mahng*) m, **-e** f lover

amateur (ah-mah-*tūrr*) m amateur

ambassade (ahng-bah-*sahd*) f embassy

ambassadeur (ahng-bah-sah-*dūrr*) m, **-drice** f ambassador

ambiance (ahng-b'*ahngss*) f atmosphere

ambigu (ahng-bee-*gew*) adj (f **-guë**) ambiguous

ambitieux (ahng-bee-s'*ur*) adj ambitious

ambre (ahngbr) m amber

ambulance (ahng-bew-*lahngss*) f

ambulance

âme (aam) f soul

amélioration (ah-may-l^{y}o-rah-s^{y}aw$\overline{n}g$) f improvement

améliorer (ah-may-l^{y}o-ray) v improve

amende (ah-mahngd) f fine, penalty

amener (ahm-nay) v *bring; lower, *strike

amer (ah-mair) adj bitter

Américain (ah-may-ree-ka$\overline{n}g$) m American

américain (ah-may-ree-ka$\overline{n}g$) adj American

Amérique (ah-may-reek) f America; ~ **latine** Latin America

ami (ah-mee) m friend

amiante (ah-m^{y}ah$\overline{n}gt$) m asbestos

amical (ah-mee-kahl) adj friendly

amie (ah-mee) f friend

amitié (ah-mee-t^{y}ay) f friendship

ammoniaque (ah-mo-n^{y}ahk) f ammonia

amnistie (ahm-nee-stee) f amnesty

amoncellement (ah-maw$\overline{n}g$-sehl-mah$\overline{n}g$) m heap

amont: en ~ (ah$\overline{n}g$-nah-maw$\overline{n}g$) upstream

amorce (ah-mors) f bait

amortir (ah-mor-teer) v *pay off

amortisseur (ah-mor-tee-sü$\overline{r}$) m shock absorber

amour (ah-m$\overline{oo}$r) m love; **mon ~** sweetheart

amoureux (ah-moo-rur) adj in love

ample (ah$\overline{n}gpl$) adj detailed; full

ampoule (ah$\overline{n}g$-pool) f blister; light bulb; ~ **de flash** flash bulb

amulette (ah-mew-leht) f charm

amusant (ah-mew-zah$\overline{n}g$) adj funny, entertaining

amuse-gueule (ah-mewz-gurl) m appetizer

amusement (ah-mewz-mah$\overline{n}g$) m entertainment, amusement

amuser (ah-mew-zay) v entertain, amuse

amygdales (ah-mee-dahl) fpl tonsils pl

amygdalite (ah-mee-dah-leet) f tonsillitis

an (ah$\overline{n}g$) m year; **par ~** per annum

analogue (ah-nah-log) adj similar

analyse (ah-nah-leez) f analysis

analyser (ah-nah-lee-zay) v analyse; *break down

analyste (ah-nah-leest) m analyst

ananas (ah-nah-nah) m pineapple

anarchie (ah-nahr-shee) f anarchy

anatomie (ah-nah-to-mee) f anatomy

ancêtre (ah$\overline{n}g$-saitr) m ancestor

anchois (ah$\overline{n}g$-shwah) m anchovy

ancien (ah$\overline{n}g$-s^{y}a$\overline{n}g$) adj ancient; former

ancre (ah$\overline{n}g$kr) f anchor

âne (aan) m donkey

anéantissement (ah-nay-ah$\overline{n}g$-tee-smah$\overline{n}g$) m destruction

anémie (ah-nay-mee) f anaemia

anesthésie (ah-neh-stay-zee) f anaesthesia

anesthésique (ah-neh-stay-zeek) m anaesthetic

ange (ah$\overline{n}gzh$) m angel

Anglais (ah$\overline{n}g$-glay) m Englishman; **les ~** the English

anglais (ah$\overline{n}g$-glay) adj English

Anglaise (ah$\overline{n}g$-glays) f Englishwoman

angle (ah$\overline{n}ggl$) m angle

Angleterre (ah$\overline{n}g$-gler-tair) f England; Britain

angoisse (ah$\overline{n}g$-gwahss) f anguish

anguille (ah$\overline{n}g$-geey) f eel

animal (ah-nee-mahl) m animal; ~ **familier** pet

animateur (ah-nee-mah-tü$\overline{r}$) m, **-trice** f entertainer

animer (ah-nee-may) v enliven; **animé** busy, active, crowded

anneau (ah-*noa*) m ring
année (ah-*nay*) f year; **~ bissextile** leap year
annexe (ah-*nehks*) f annex
annexer (ah-nehk-*say*) v annex
anniversaire (ah-nee-vehr-*sair*) m anniversary, birthday; jubilee
annonce (ah-*nawngss*) f announcement; advertisement; **~ publicitaire** commercial
annoncer (ah-nawng-*say*) v announce
annuaire (ah-*nwair*) m annual; **~ téléphonique** telephone directory; telephone book Am
annuel (ah-*nwehl*) adj yearly, annual
annulation (ah-new-lah-s^y*awng*) f cancellation
annuler (ah-new-*lay*) v cancel
anonyme (ah-no-*neem*) adj anonymous
anorak (ah-no-*rahk*) m anorak
antenne (ahng-*tehn*) f aerial
antérieur (ahng-tay-r^y*ürr*) adj prior, previous
antérieurement (ahng-tay-r^yurr-*mahng*) adv formerly
antialcoolique (ahng-tee-ahl-ko-*leek*) m teetotaller
antibiotique (ahng-tee-b^yo-*teek*) m antibiotic
anticiper (ahng-tee-see-*pay*) v anticipate
antigel (ahng-tee-*zhehl*) m antifreeze
antipathie (ahng-tee-pah-*tee*) f dislike, antipathy
antipathique (ahng-tee-pah-*teek*) adj nasty; unpleasant
antiquaire (ahng-tee-*kair*) m/f antique dealer
antique (ahng-*teek*) adj antique, ancient
antiquité (ahng-tee-kee-*tay*) f antique; **Antiquité** antiquity; **antiquités** antiquities pl

anxiété (ahng-ks^{y}ay-*tay*) f anxiety
août (oo) August
***apercevoir** (ah-pehr-ser-*vwaar*) v perceive
aperçu (ah-pehr-*sew*) m glimpse
apéritif (ah-pay-ree-*teef*) m drink, aperitif
apeuré (ah-pur-*ray*) adj afraid
apogée (ah-po-*zhay*) m height, zenith; peak
***apparaître** (ah-pah-*raitr*) v appear
appareil (ah-pah-*ray*) m appliance, apparatus, machine; aircraft; **~ à jetons** slot machine; **~ de chauffage** heater; **~ photographique** camera
apparemment (ah-pah-rah-*mahng*) adv apparently
apparence (ah-pah-*rahngss*) f appearance; semblance, look
apparent (ah-pah-*rahng*) adj apparent
apparenté (ah-pah-rahng-*tay*) adj related
appartement (ah-pahr-ter-*mahng*) m flat; apartment Am, suite
***appartenir** (ah-pahr-ter-*neer*) v belong
appel (ah-*pehl*) m call, cry; appeal; **~ interurbain** trunk-call; **~ téléphonique** telephone call
appeler (ah-*play*) v call, cry; **s'appeler** *be called
appendice (ah-pang-*deess*) m appendix
appendicite (ah-pang-dee-*seet*) f appendicitis
appétissant (ah-pay-tee-*sahng*) adj appetizing
appétit (ah-pay-*tee*) m appetite
applaudir (ah-ploa-*deer*) v clap
applaudissements (ah-ploa-dee-*smahng*) mpl applause
application (ah-plee-kah-s^y*awng*) f application; diligence
appliquer (ah-plee-*kay*) v apply;

s'appliquer à apply

apporter (ah-por-*tay*) *v* *bring; fetch

appréciation (ah-pray-s*y*ah-s*y*aw*n̄g*) *f* appreciation

apprécier (ah-pray-s*y*ay) *v* appreciate; judge

*apprendre (ah-*prahn̄gdr*) *v* *learn; *teach; ~ **par cœur** memorize

apprenti (ah-prahn-*tee*) *m*, **-e** *f* apprentice

apprivoiser (ah-pree-vwah-*zay*) *v* tame; **apprivoisé** tame

approbation (ah-pro-bah-s*y*aw*n̄g*) *f* approval

approche (ah-*prosh*) *f* approach

approcher (ah-pro-*shay*) *v* approach

approprié (ah-pro-pree-*ay*) *adj* appropriate, adequate, convenient; proper, suitable

approuver (ah-proo-*vay*) *v* approve; consent

approvisionner en (ah-pro-vee-z*y*o-*nay*) furnish with

approximatif (ah-prok-see-mah-*teef*) *adj* approximate

approximativement (ah-prok-see-mah-teev-*mahn̄g*) *adv* approximately

appuyer (ah-pwee-*y*ay) *v* press; **s'appuyer** *lean

âpre (aapr) *adj* harsh

après (ah-*pray*) *adv* afterwards; *prep* after; ~ **que** after; **d'après** according to

après-demain (ah-pray-der-*mang*) *adv* the day after tomorrow

après-midi (ah-pray-mee-*dee*) *m/f* afternoon

apte (ahpt) *adj* apt

aptitude (ahp-tee-*tewd*) *f* faculty

aquarelle (ah-kwah-*rehl*) *f* watercolo(u)r

Arabe (ah-*rahb*) *m* Arab

arabe (ah-*rahb*) *adj* Arab

Arabie Séoudite (ah-rah-bee say-oo-*deet*) Saudi Arabia

araignée (ah-ray-*ñay*) *f* spider; **toile d'araignée** spider's web

arbitraire (ahr-bee-*trair*) *adj* arbitrary

arbitre (ahr-*beetr*) *m* umpire

arbre (ahrbr) *m* tree

arbuste (ahr-*bewst*) *m* shrub

arc (ahrk) *m* bow

arcade (ahr-*kahd*) *f* arcade

arc-en-ciel (ahr-kahn̄g-s*y*ehl) *m* rainbow

arche (ahrsh) *f* arch

archéologie (ahr-kay-o-lo-*zhee*) *f* arch(a)eology

archéologue (ahr-kay-o-*log*) *m/f* arch(a)eologist

archevêque (ahr-sher-*vehk*) *m* archbishop

architecte (ahr-shee-*tehkt*) *m* architect

architecture (ahr-shee-tehk-*tēwr*) *f* architecture

archives (ahr-*sheev*) *fpl* archives *pl*

ardoise (ahr-*dwaaz*) *f* slate

arène (ah-*rehn*) *f* bullring

arête (ah-*reht*) *f* ridge; fishbone, bone

argent (ahr-*zhahn̄g*) *m* silver; money; ~ **comptant** cash; ~ **liquide** cash; **en ~** silver

argenterie (ahr-zhahn̄g-*tree*) *f* silverware

argentin (ahr-zhahn̄g-*tang*) *adj* Argentinian

Argentine (ahr-zhahn̄g-*teen*) *f* Argentina

argile (ahr-*zheel*) *f* clay

argument (ahr-gew-*mahn̄g*) *m* argument

argumenter (ahr-gew-mahn̄g-*tay*) *v* argue

armateur (ahr-mah-*tūrr*) *m* shipowner

arme (ahrm) *f* weapon, arm

armée (ahr-*may*) *f* army

armer (ahr-*may*) *v* arm

armoire (ahr-*mwaar*) *f* cupboard

armure (ahr-*mewr*) f arm(o)ur

arôme (ah-*roam*) m aroma

arqué (ahr-*kay*) adj arched

arracher (ah-rah-*shay*) v extract

arrangement (ah-rahngzh-*mahng*) m settlement

arranger (ah-rahng-*zhay*) v arrange; settle

arrestation (ah-reh-stah-*s^{y}awng*) f arrest

arrêt (ah-*reh*) m stop

arrêter (ah-ray-*tay*) v stop; arrest; **s'arrêter** halt; pull up

arriéré (ah-r^{y}ay-*ray*) adj overdue

arrière (ah-r^y*air*) m rear; **en ~** backwards, back; behind

arrivée (ah-ree-*vay*) f coming, arrival

arriver (ah-ree-*vay*) v arrive; happen

arrondi (ah-rawng-*dee*) adj rounded

arrondissement (ah-rawng-dee-*smahng*) m district

art (aar) m art; **arts et métiers** arts and crafts

artère (ahr-*tair*) f artery; thoroughfare

artichaut (ahr-tee-*shoa*) m artichoke

article (ahr-*teekl*) m article; item; **articles d'épicerie** groceries pl; **articles de toilette** toiletry

articulation (ahr-tee-kew-lah-*s^{y}awng*) f joint

artificiel (ahr-tee-fee-*s^{y}ehl*) adj artificial

artisan (ahr-tee-*zahng*) m craftsman

artisanat (ahr-tee-zah-*nah*) m handicraft

artiste (ahr-*teest*) m/f artist

artistique (ahr-tee-*steek*) adj artistic

ascenseur (ah-sahng-*surr*) m lift; elevator Am

ascension (ah-sahng-*s^{y}awng*) f climb; ***faire l'ascension de** ascend

Asiatique (ah-z^{y}ah-*teek*) m Asian

asiatique (ah-z^{y}ah-*teek*) adj Asian

Asie (ah-*zee*) f Asia

asile (ah-*zeel*) m asylum

aspect (ah-*spay*) m aspect; appearance, look

asperge (ah-*spehrzh*) f asparagus

asphalte (ah-*sfahlt*) m asphalt

aspirateur (ah-spee-rah-*turr*) m vacuum cleaner; **passer l'aspirateur** hoover; vacuum Am

aspirer (ah-spee-*ray*) v aspire; **~ à** pursue, aim at

aspirine (ah-spee-*reen*) f aspirin

assaisonner (ah-say-zo-*nay*) v flavour

assassinat (ah-sah-see-*nah*) m assassination, murder

assassiner (ah-sah-see-*nay*) v murder

assécher (ah-say-*shay*) v drain

assemblée (ah-sahng-*blay*) f assembly, meeting

assembler (ah-sahng-*blay*) v assemble; join

assentiment (ah-sahng-tee-*mahng*) m consent

*asseoir (ah-*swaar*): **s'~** *sit down

assez (ah-*say*) adv enough; fairly, pretty, rather, quite

assidu (ah-see-*dew*) adj diligent

assiette (ah-*s^{y}eht*) f plate, dish

assigner (ah-see-*ñay*) v allot; **~ à** assign to

assistance (ah-see-*stahngss*) f assistance; attendance

assistant (ah-see-*stahng*) m assistant

assister (ah-see-*stay*) v assist, aid; **~ à** attend, assist at

association (ah-so-s^{y}ah-*s^{y}awng*) f society, club, association

associé (ah-so-*s^{y}ay*) m, **-e** f associate, partner

associer (ah-so-*s^{y}ay*) v associate

assoiffé (ah-swah-*fay*) adj thirsty

assortiment (ah-sor-tee-*mahng*) m assortment

assurance (ah-sew-*rahngss*) f insurance; **assurance-vie** f life insurance; **assurance-voyages** *f* travel insurance

assurer (ah-sew-*ray*) *v* insure, assure; **s'assurer de** ascertain; secure

asthme (ahsm) *m* asthma

astronomie (ah-stro-no-*mee*) *f* astronomy

astucieux (ah-stew-*s*ʸ*ur*) *adj* clever

atelier (ah-ter-*l*ʸ*ay*) *m* workshop

athlète (ah-*tleht*) *m/f* athlete

athlétisme (ah-tlay-*teezm*) *m* athletics *pl*

Atlantique (aht-lah*n̄g*-*teek*) *adj, n* Atlantic

atmosphère (aht-mo-*sfair*) *f* atmosphere

atomique (ah-to-*meek*) *adj* atomic

atroce (ah-*tross*) *adj* horrible

attacher (ah-tah-*shay*) *v* fasten, attach; tie; **attaché à** attached to

attaque (ah-*tahk*) *f* fit, attack; hold-up; stroke

attaquer (ah-tah-*kay*) *v* attack, assault

***atteindre** (ah-*ta*ñ*gdr*) *v* attain, reach

attendre (ah-*tah*ñ*gdr*) *v* wait; expect, await; **en attendant** in the meantime

attente (ah-*tah*ñ*gt*) *f* waiting; expectation

attentif (ah-tah*n̄g*-*teef*) *adj* attentive, careful

attention (ah-tah*n̄g*-*s*ʸ*aw*ñ*g*) *f* attention, consideration; notice; ***faire ~** *pay attention, look out; beware; ***faire ~ à** attend to, mind; **prêter ~ à** mind

atterrir (ah-tay-*reer*) *v* land

attestation (ah-teh-stah-*s*ʸ*aw*ñ*g*) *f* certificate

attirer (ah-tee-*ray*) *v* attract

attitude (ah-tee-*tewd*) *f* attitude; position

attouchement (ah-toosh-*mah*ñ*g*) *m* touch

attraction (ah-trahk-*s*ʸ*aw*ñ*g*) *f* attraction

attrait (ah-*tray*) *m* attraction; **attraits** charm

attraper (ah-trah-*pay*) *v* *catch; contract

attribuer à (ah-tree-*bway*) assign to

aube (ōab) *f* dawn

auberge (oa-*behrzh*) *f* inn, hostel; roadhouse; roadside restaurant; **~ de jeunesse** youth hostel

aubergine (oa-behr-*zheen*) *f* eggplant

aucun (oa-*kur*ñ*g*) *adj* no; *pron* none

audace (oa-*dahss*) *f* nerve

audacieux (oa-dah-*s*ʸ*ur*) *adj* bold

au-dessous (oa-der-*soo*) *adv* beneath; **~ de** below

au-dessus (oa-der-*sew*) *adv* over; **~ de** above; over

audible (oa-*deebl*) *adj* audible

auditeur (oa-dee-*tūrr*) *m*, **auditrice** *f* auditor, listener

augmentation (oag-mah*n̄g*-tah-*s*ʸ*aw*ñ*g*) *f* increase, rise; **~ de salaire** rise; raise *Am*

augmenter (oag-mah*n̄g*-*tay*) *v* increase

aujourd'hui (oa-zhoor-*dwee*) *adv* today

auparavant (oa-pah-rah-*vah*ñ*g*) *adv* formerly

auprès de (oa-*pray* der) near

auriculaire (oa-ree-kew-*lair*) *m* little finger

aurore (oa-*rawr*) *f* dawn

aussi (oa-*see*) *adv* too, also; as; **~ bien** as well; **~ bien que** as well as; both … and

aussitôt (oa-see-*toa*) *adv* at once; **~ que** as soon as

Australie (oa-strah-*lee*) *f* Australia

australien (oa-strah-*l*ʸ*a*ñ*g*) *adj* Australian

autant (oa-*tah*ñ*g*) *adv* as much

autel (oa-*tehl*) *m* altar

auteur (oa-*ürr*) *m* author

authentique (oa-tah$\overline{\text{ng}}$-*teek*) *adj* authentic, original, genuine

auto (oa-*toa*) *f* automobile

autobus (oa-toa-*bewss*) *m* bus

autocar (oa-toa-*kaar*) *m* coach

auto-école (oa-toa-ay-*kol*) *f* driving school

automatique (oa-toa-mah-*teek*) *adj* automatic

automatisation (oa-toa-mah-tee-zah-s^y*awng*) *f* automation

automne (oa-*ton*) *m* autumn; fall *Am*

automobile (oa-toa-mo-*beel*) *f* motorcar

automobiliste (oa-toa-mo-bee-*leest*) *m/f* motorist

autonome (oa-to-*nom*) *adj* autonomous; independent

autonomie (oa-to-no-*mee*) *f* self-government

autoradio (oa-toa-rah-d^y*oa*) *m* car radio

autorisation (oa-to-ree-zah-s^y*awng*) *f* authorization; permission

autoriser (oa-to-ree-*zay*) *v* allow; license; ~ **à** allow to

autoritaire (oa-to-ree-*tair*) *adj* authoritarian

autorité (oa-to-ree-*tay*) *f* authority

autoroute (oa-toa-*root*) *f* motorway; highway *Am*

auto-stop (oa-toa-*stop*): ***faire de l'auto-stop** hitchhike

auto-stoppeur (oa-toa-sto-*pürr*) *m*, **-euse** *f* hitchhiker

autour (oa-*toor*) *adv* about; around; ~ **de** around, about; round

autre (*öatr*) *adj* other; different; **entre autres** among other things

autrefois (oa-trer-*fwah*) *adv* formerly

autrement (oa-trer-*mahng*) *adv* otherwise, else

Autriche (oa-*treesh*) *f* Austria

Autrichien (oa-tree-sh^y*ang*) *m* Austrian

autrichien (oa-tree-sh^y*ang*) *adj* Austrian

autruche (oa-*trewsh*) *f* ostrich

aval: en ~ (ah$\overline{\text{ng}}$-nah-*vahl*) downstream

avalanche (ah-vah-*lah$\overline{\text{ng}}$sh*) *f* avalanche

avaler (ah-vah-*lay*) *v* swallow

avance (ah-*vah$\overline{\text{ng}}$ss*) *f* lead; advance; **à l'avance** in advance; **d'avance** before; in advance

avancement (ah-vah$\overline{\text{ng}}$-*smah$\overline{\text{ng}}$*) *m* advance

avancer (ah-vah$\overline{\text{ng}}$-*say*) *v* advance

avant (ah-*vah$\overline{\text{ng}}$*) *prep* before; *adv* before; ~ **que** before; **en ~** forward; ahead, onwards

avantage (ah-vah$\overline{\text{ng}}$-*taazh*) *m* profit, advantage, benefit

avantageux (ah-vah$\overline{\text{ng}}$-tah-*zhur*) *adj* advantageous; cheap

avant-dernier (ah-vah$\overline{\text{ng}}$-dehr-n^y*ay*) *adj* last but one

avant-hier (ah-vah$\overline{\text{ng}}$-t^y*air*) *adv* the day before yesterday

avant-saison (ah-vah$\overline{\text{ng}}$-seh-*zaw$\overline{\text{ng}}$*) *f* off-peak season

avec (ah-*vehk*) *prep* with

avenir (ah-*vneer*) *m* future

aventure (ah-vah$\overline{\text{ng}}$-*tewr*) *f* adventure

avenue (ah-*vnew*) *f* avenue

averse (ah-*vehrs*) *f* shower; downpour

aversion (ah-vehr-s^y*awng*) *f* aversion, dislike

avertir (ah-vehr-*teer*) *v* warn, caution; notify

avertissement (ah-vehr-tee-*smahng*) *m* warning

aveugle (ah-*vurgl*) *adj* blind

aveugler (ah-vur-*glay*) *v* blind

aviation (ah-v^yah-s^y*awng*) *f* aviation

avion (ah-v^y*awng*) *m* aeroplane; plane;

aircraft; airplane *Am*; ~ **à réaction** jet

avis (ah-*vee*) *m* advice; notice

avocat (ah-vo-*kah*) *m* solicitor, attorney, lawyer, barrister

avoine (ah-*vwahn*) *f* oats *pl*

*****avoir** (ah-*vwaar*) *v* *have

avoisinant (ah-vwah-zee-*nahng*) *adj* neighbo(u)ring

avortement (ah-vort-*mahng*) *m* abortion

avoué (ah-voo-*ay*) *m* solicitor

avouer (ah-voo-*ay*) *v* admit

avril (ah-*vreel*) April

B

babeurre (bah-*burr*) *m* buttermilk

bâbord (bah-*bawr*) *m* port

bac (bahk), **baccalauréat** (bah-kah-loa-ray-*ah*) *m* school-leaving certificate

bactérie (bahk-tay-*ree*) *f* bacterium

bagage (bah-*gaazh*) *m* baggage; luggage; ~ **à main** hand luggage; hand baggage *Am*

bague (bahg) *f* ring; ~ **de fiançailles** engagement ring

baguette (bah-geht) *f* stick, rod; stick of bread; baton; ~ **magique** magic wand

baie (bay) *f* berry; bay, creek

baigner (bay-*ñay*)*v*: **se** ~ bathe

baignoire (bay-*ñwaar*) *f* bath (tub); groundfloor box

bail (bigh) *m* (pl baux) lease

bâiller (bah-*ʸay*) *v* yawn

bain (bang) *m* bath; ~ **turc** Turkish bath; **bonnet de** ~ bathing cap; **caleçon de** ~ bathing trunks

baiser (bay-*zay*) *m* kiss

baisse (behss) *f* drop, decline

baisser (bay-*say*) *v* lower

bal (bahl) *m* (pl ~s) ball

balai (bah-*lay*) *m* broom

balance (bah-*lahngss*) *f* scales *pl*

balancer (bah-lahng-*say*) *v* *swing; rock

balançoire (bah-lahng-*swaar*) *f* swing; seesaw

balayer (bah-lay-*ʸay*) *v* *sweep

balbutier (bahl-bew-*sʸay*) *v* falter

balcon (bahl-*kawng*) *m* balcony; circle

baleine (bah-*lehn*) *f* whale

balle (bahl) *f* ball; bullet

ballet (bah-*lay*) *m* ballet

ballon (bah-*lawng*) *m* football, ball; balloon

balustrade (bah-lew-*strahd*) *f* rail

bambin (bahng-*bang*) *m* tot, toddler

bambou (bahng-*boo*) *m* bamboo

banane (bah-*nahn*) *f* banana

banc (bahng) *m* bench; ~ **d'école** desk

bande (bahngd) *f* bunch, gang; tape, strip; **bandes dessinées** comics *pl*

bandit (bahng-*dee*) *m* bandit

banlieue (bahng-*lʸur*) *f* suburb

bannière (bah-*nʸair*) *f* banner

banque (bahngk) *f* bank

banquet (bahng-*kay*) *m* banquet

baptême (bah-*tehm*) *m* christening, baptism

baptiser (bah-tee-*zay*) *v* christen, baptize

bar (baar) *m* bar

baratiner (bah-rah-tee-*nay*) *v* talk rubbish

barbe (bahrb) *f* beard

baril (bah-*ree*) *m* cask, barrel

bariton (bah-ree-*tawng*) *m* baritone

barman (bahr-*mahn*) *m* barman; bartender

baromètre (bah-ro-*mehtr*) *m* barometer

baroque (bah-*rok*) *adj* baroque

barque (bahrk) *f* boat

barrage (bah-*raazh*) *m* dam

barre (baar) *f* rod, bar, rail; helm; counter

barreau (bah-*roa*) *m* bar

barrière (bah-r*y*air) *f* barrier; fence

bas¹ (bah) *adj* (f ~se) low; **en ~** down; downstairs; **en ~ de** under, below; **vers le ~** downwards, down

bas² (bah) *m* stocking; **~ élastiques** support hose

bas-côté (bah-koa-*tay*) *m* aisle

bascule (bah-*skewl*) *f* weighing machine

base (bahz) *f* basis, base

baser (bah-*zay*) *v* base

basilique (bah-zee-*leek*) *f* basilica

baskets (bah-*skeht*) *mpl* tennis shoes, plimsolls *pl*

basse (bahss) *f* bass

bassin (bah-*sang*) *m* pelvis, basin

bataille (bah-*tigh*) *f* battle

bateau (bah-*toa*) *m* boat; **~ à moteur** motor boat; **~ à rames** rowing boat; **~ à vapeur** steamer; **~ à voiles** sailing boat; **bateau-citerne** *m* tanker

bâtiment (bah-tee-*mahng*) *m* building; building trade

bâtir (bah-*teer*) *v* *build; construct

bâton (bah-*tawng*) *m* stick; **bâtons de ski** ski sticks; ski poles *Am*

*battre (bahtr) *v* slap; *beat; shuffle; **se ~** *fight

bavard (bah-*vaar*) *adj* talkative

bavardage (bah-vahr-*daazh*) *m* chat

bavarder (bah-vahr-*day*) *v* chat

beau (boa) *adj* (bel; f belle) beautiful; fair, pretty, lovely, handsome

beaucoup (boa-*koo*) *adv* much; far; **~ de** much; many; **de ~** by far

beau-fils (boa-*feess*) *m* son-in-law

beau-frère (boa-*frair*) *m* brother-in-law

beau-père (boa-*pair*) *m* father-in-law; stepfather

beauté (boa-*tay*) *f* beauty; **produits de ~** cosmetics *pl*

beaux-arts (boa-*zaar*) *mpl* fine arts

beaux-parents (boa-pah-*rahng*) *mpl* parents-in-law *pl*

bébé (bay-*bay*) *m* baby

bec (behk) *m* beak; nozzle

bêche (behsh) *f* spade

beige (baizh) *adj* beige

beignet (bay-*ñay*) *m* doughnut

Belge (behlzh) *m* Belgian

belge (behlzh) *adj* Belgian

Belgique (behl-*zheek*) *f* Belgium

belle-fille (behl-*feey*) *f* daughter-in-law

belle-mère (behl-*mair*) *f* mother-in-law; stepmother

belle-sœur (behl-*sūrr*) *f* sister-in-law

bénédiction (bay-nay-deek-s*y*awng) *f* blessing

bénéfice (bay-nay-*feess*) *m* profit, benefit

bénéficiaire (bay-nay-fee-s*y*air) *m/f* payee

bénéficier de (bay-nay-fee-s*y*ay) profit by

bénir (bay-*neer*) *v* bless

béquille (bay-*keey*) *f* crutch

berceau (behr-*soa*) *m* cradle; **~ de voyage** carrycot

béret (bay-*ray*) *m* beret

berge (behrzh) *f* embankment

berger (behr-*zhay*) *m* shepherd

besogne (ber-*zoñ*) *f* work

besoin (ber-*zwang*) *m* need; want; ***avoir ~ de** need

bétail (bay-*tigh*) *m* cattle *pl*

bête (beht) *f* beast; *adj* silly, dumb; **~ de proie** beast of prey

bêtise (bay-*teez*) *f* stupidity; blunder; nonsense

béton (bay-*tawng*) *m* concrete

betterave (beh-*traav*) *f* beetroot, beet

beurre (burr) *m* butter

biberon (bee-*brawng*) *m* feeding (*Am* nursing) bottle; tippler

Bible (beebl) *f* bible

bibliothèque (bee-blee-o-*tehk*) *f* library

bicyclette (bee-see-*kleht*) *f* cycle, bicycle

bien (b^yang) *adv* well; **bien!** well!; all right!; **~ que** though, although; **biens** *mpl* goods *pl*, possessions

bien-être (b^yang-*naitr*) *m* welfare; comfort

bientôt (b^yang-*toa*) *adv* soon; shortly

bienveillance (b^yang-vay-*^yahngss*) *f* goodwill

bienvenu (b^yang-*vnew*) *adj* welcome

bière (b^yair) *f* beer; ale

bifteck (beef-*tehk*) *m* steak

bifurcation (bee-fewr-kah-s^y*awng*) *f* fork, road fork

bifurquer (bee-fewr-*kay*) *v* fork

bigorneau (bee-gor-*noa*) *m* winkle

bigoudi (bee-goo-*dee*) *m* curler

bijou (bee-*zhoo*) *m* (pl ~x) jewel; gem; **bijoux** jewellery, jewelry *Am*

bijoutier (bee-zhoo-t^y*ay*) *m* jewel(l)er

bikini (bee-kee-*nee*) *m* bikini

bilan (bee-*lahng*) *m* balance

bile (beel) *f* gall, bile

bilingue (bee-*langg*) *adj* bilingual

billard (bee-^y*aar*) *m* billiards *pl*

bille (beey) *f* marble

billet (bee-^y*ay*) *m* ticket; **~ de banque** banknote; **~ de quai** platform ticket; **~ gratuit** free ticket

biologie (bee-o-lo-*zhee*) *f* biology

biscotte (bee-*skot*) *f* rusk

biscuit (bee-*skwee*) *m* biscuit; cookie *Am*; cracker *Am*

bistrot (bee-*stroa*) *m* pub

bizarre (bee-*zaar*) *adj* funny, odd, strange

blague (blahg) *f* joke; **~ à tabac** tobacco pouch

blaireau (bleh-*roa*) *m* shaving brush

blâme (blaam) *m* blame

blâmer (blah-*may*) *v* blame

blanc (blahng) *adj* (f blanche) white; blank

blanchisserie (blahng-shee-*sree*) *f* laundry

blé (blay) *m* corn; wheat; grain

blesser (blay-*say*) *v* injure, *hurt, wound; offend

blessure (blay-*sewr*) *f* wound; injury

bleu (blur) *adj* (pl bleus) blue; *m* bruise

bloc (blok) *m* block

bloc-notes (blok-*not*) *m* pad, writing pad

blond (blawng) *adj* fair

blonde (blawngd) *f* blonde

bloquer (blo-*kay*) *v* block

bobine (bo-*been*) *f* spool; **~ d'allumage** ignition coil

bœuf (burf) *m* ox; beef

bohémien (bo-ay-m^y*ang*) *m* Bohemian

***boire** (bwaar) *v* *drink

bois (bwah) *m* wood; forest; **~ d'œuvre** timber; **en ~** wooden

boisé (bwah-*zay*) *adj* wooded

boisson (bwah-*sawng*) *f* drink, beverage; **~ non alcoolisée** soft drink; **boissons alcoolisées** spirits

boîte (bwaht) *f* box; can, tin; **~ à ordures** dustbin; trash can *Am*; **~ à outils** tool kit; **~ aux lettres** letterbox; mailbox *Am*; **~ d'allumettes** matchbox; **~ de couleurs** paintbox; **~ de nuit** nightclub; **~ de vitesse**

gearbox

boiter (bwah-*tay*) v limp

boiteux (bwah-*tur*) adj lame

bol (bol) m basin; bowl

Bolivie (bo-lee-*vee*) f Bolivia

Bolivien (bo-lee-v*y*a͞ng) m Bolivian

bolivien (bo-lee-v*y*a͞ng) adj Bolivian

bombarder (bawng-bahr-*day*) v bomb

bombe (bawngb) f bomb

bon[1] (bawng) adj good; enjoyable, nice; kind

bon[2] (bawng) m voucher; ~ **de commande** order form

bonbon (bawng-*bawng*) m sweet; candy *Am*

bond (bawng) m jump

bondé (bawng-*day*) adj crowded

bondir (bawng-*deer*) v *leap

bonheur (bo-*nurr*) m happiness

bonjour! (bawng-*zhoor*) hello!

bonne (bon) f maid; housemaid; ~ **d'enfants** nurse

bonne-maman (bon-mah-*mahng*) f grandmother

bonnet (bo-*nay*) m cap; **gros ~** bigwig, *Am* big shot

bon-papa (bawng-pah-*pah*) m grandfather

bonsoir! (bawng-*swaar*) good evening!

bonté (bawng-*tay*) f kindness

bord (bawr) m edge; brim, verge, border; **à ~** aboard; ~ **de la mer** seaside; seashore; ~ **de la rivière** riverside; ~ **de la route** roadside; wayside; ~ **du trottoir** curb

bordel (bor-*dehl*) m brothel

borne routière (born roo-t*y*air) f milestone

borné (bor-*nay*) adj narrow-minded

bosquet (bo-*skay*) m grove

bosse (boss) f dent, lump

botanique (bo-tah-*neek*) f botany

botte (bot) f boot

bottin (bo-*tang*) m telephone directory

bouc (book) m goat; ~ **émissaire** scapegoat

bouche (boosh) f mouth

bouchée (boo-*shay*) f bite

boucher[1] (boo-*shay*) m, **-ère** f butcher

boucher[2] (boo-*shay*) v stop up

boucherie (boo-*shree*) f butcher's shop

bouchon (boo-*shawng*) m cork; stopper

boucle (bookl) f buckle; curl; loop; ~ **d'oreille** earring

boucler (boo-*klay*) v curl; **bouclé** curly

boudin (boo-*dang*) m black pudding, *Am* blood sausage

boue (boo) f mud; slush

bouée (boo-*ay*) f buoy; ~ **de sauvetage** lifebelt

boueux (boo-*ur*) adj muddy

bouger (boo-*zhay*) v move; stir

bougie (boo-*zhee*) f candle; ~ **d'allumage** sparking plug

***bouillir** (boo-*y*eer) v boil

bouilloire (boo-*y*waar) f kettle

bouillotte (boo-*y*ot) f hot-water bottle

boulanger (boo-lahng-*zhay*) m, **boulangère** f baker

boulangerie (boo-lahng-*zhree*) f bakery

boule (bool) f ball

bouleau (boo-*loa*) m birch

boulevard (bool-*vaar*) m boulevard

bouleversé (bool-vehr-*say*) adj upset

boulon (boo-*lawng*) m bolt

boulot (boo-*loa*) m job

bouquet (boo-*kay*) m bunch, bouquet

bouquin (boo-*kang*) m book

bourdon (boor-*dawng*) m great bell; bumblebee; **faux ~** drone

bourg (bo͞or) m town

bourgeois (boor-*zhwah*) adj bourgeois, middle-class

bourgeon (boor-*zhawng*) *m* bud

bourré (boo-*ray*) *adj* chock-full

bourse (boors) *f* purse; ~ **des valeurs** stock exchange; ~ **d'études** scholarship

boussole (boo-*sol*) *f* compass

bout (boo) *m* end; tip

bouteille (boo-*tay*) *f* bottle

boutique (boo-*teek*) *f* boutique; shop

bouton (boo-*tawng*) *m* button, knob; ~ **de col** collar stud; **boutons de manchettes** cuff links *pl*

boutonner (boo-to-*nay*) *v* button

boutonnière (boo-to-n'*air*) *f* buttonhole

bowling (boa-*leeng*) *m* bowling; bowling alley

boxer (bok-*say*) *v* box

bracelet (brah-*slay*) *m* bracelet; bangle; **bracelet-montre** *m* wristwatch; ~ **pour montre** watchstrap

braconner (brah-ko-*nay*) *v* poach

braguette (brah-*geht*) *f* fly

branche (brahngsh) *f* branch

brancher (brahng-*shay*) *v* connect; plug in

branchie (brahng-*shee*) *f* gill

branlant (brahng-*lahng*) *adj* unsteady

bras (brah) *m* arm; **bras-dessus brasdessous** arm-in-arm

brasse (brahss) *f* breaststroke; ~ **papillon** butterfly stroke

brasser (brah-*say*) *v* brew

brasserie (brah-*sree*) *f* brewery

brave (brahv) *adj* brave, courageous; good

brèche (brehsh) *f* breach; gap

bref (brehf) *adj* (f **brève**) brief

Brésil (bray-*zeel*) *m* Brazil

brésilien (bray-zee-l'*ang*) *adj* Brazilian

bretelles (brer-*tehl*) *fpl* braces *pl*; suspenders *plAm*

breton (brer-*tawn*) *adj* Breton

brevet (brer-*vay*) *m* patent

bricoler (bree-ko-*lay*) do odd jobs; potter

bridge (breej) *m* bridge

brillant (bree-'*ahng*) *adj* bright; brilliant

briller (bree-'*ay*) *v* *shine; glow

brin d'herbe (brang dehrb) blade of grass

brindille (brang-*deey*) *f* twig

brioche (bree-*osh*) *f* bun

brique (breek) *f* brick

briquet (bree-*kay*) *m* cigarette lighter, lighter

brise (breez) *f* breeze

briser (bree-*zay*) *v* *break; **brisé** broken

Britannique (bree-tah-*neek*) *m* Briton

britannique (bree-tah-*neek*) *adj* British

broche (brosh) *f* brooch; spit

brochet (bro-*shay*) *m* pike

brochette (bro-*sheht*) *f* skewer; pin

brochure (bro-*shewr*) *f* brochure

brocoli (bro-ko-*lee*) *m* broccoli

broder (bro-*day*) *v* embroider

broderie (bro-*dree*) *f* embroidery

bronchite (brawng-*sheet*) *f* bronchitis

bronze (brawngz) *m* bronze; **en ~** bronze

bronzer (brawng-*zay*) *v* bronze; tan

brosse (bross) *f* brush; ~ **à cheveux** hairbrush; ~ **à dents** toothbrush; ~ **à ongles** nailbrush

brosser (bro-*say*) *v* brush

brouette (broo-*eht*) *f* wheelbarrow

brouillard (broo-'*aar*) *m* fog, mist

brouiller (broo-'*ay*) *v* mix; mix up; *sow discord

bruit (brwee) *m* noise

brûler (brew-*lay*) *v* *burn

brûlure (brew-*lewr*) *f* burn; **brûlures d'estomac** heartburn

brume (brewm) *f* mist; haze

brumeux (brew-*mur*) *adj* misty; hazy, foggy

brun (brurng) *adj* brown

brunette (brew-*neht*) *f* brunette

brusque (brewsk) *adj* sudden; rude

brut (brewt) *adj* gross

brutal (brew-*tahl*) *adj* brutal

bruyant (brwee-*y*ahng) *adj* noisy

bruyère (brwee-*y*air) *f* heather; moor

bûche (bewsh) *f* log

bûcher (bew-*shay*) *v* labo(u)r

budget (bew-*jay*) *m* budget

buffet (bew-*fay*) *m* buffet

buisson (bwee-*sawng*) *m* bush, scrub

bulbe (bewlb) *m* bulb

bulgare (bewl-*gaar*) *adj* Bulgarian

Bulgarie (bewl-gah-*ree*) *f* Bulgaria

bulle (bewl) *f* bubble

bulletin météorologique (bewl-tang may-tay-o-ro-lo-*zheek*) weather forecast

bureau (bew-*roa*) *m* office; bureau; desk, agency; ~ **de change** exchange office; ~ **de l'emploi** employment exchange; ~ **de poste** post-office; ~ **de renseignements** information bureau; ~ **des objets trouvés** lost property office; ~ **de tabac** tobacconist's; ~ **de voyages** travel agency; **employé(e) de** ~ clerk; **heures de** ~ business hours

bureaucratie (bew-roa-krah-*see*) *f* bureaucracy

bus (bewss) *m* bus

buste (bewst) *m* bust

but (bew) *m* purpose, aim; goal

butte (bewt) *f* mound

C

ça (sah) *pron* that

cabane (kah-*bahn*) *f* cabin

cabaret (kah-bah-*ray*) *m* cabaret

cabine (kah-*been*) *f* cabin, booth; ~ **de pont** deck cabin; ~ **d'essayage** fitting room; ~ **téléphonique** telephone booth

cabinet (kah-bee-*nay*) *m* lavatory; cabinet; study; ~ **de consultations** surgery

câble (kahbl) *m* cable

cacahuète (kah-kah-*weht*) *f* peanut

cachemire (kahsh-*meer*) *m* cashmere

cacher (kah-*shay*) *v* *hide

cachet (kah-*shay*) *m* stamp; capsule

cactus (kahk-*tewss*) *m* cactus

cadavre (kah-*daavr*) *m* corpse

cadeau (kah-*doa*) *m* present, gift

cadenas (kahd-*nah*) *m* padlock

cadet (kah-*day*) *adj* junior

cadre (kaadr) *m* frame; setting; cadre

café (kah-*fay*) *m* coffee; café, public house, saloon

caféine (kah-fay-*een*) *f* caffeine

cafétéria (kah-fay-tay-*r*y*ah*) *f* cafeteria

cafetière (kahf-*r*y*air*) *f* coffee-pot

cage (kaazh) *f* cage

cahier (kah-*y*ay) *m* notebook; ~ **de croquis** sketch-book

cahoteux (kah-o-*tur*) *adj* bumpy

caille (kigh) *f* quail

caillou (kah-*y*oo) *m* (pl ~x) pebble

caisse (kehss) *f* crate; pay desk, cashier *Am*; ~ **d'épargne** savings bank

caissier (kay-*s*y*ay*) *m* cashier

caissière (keh-*s*y*air*) *f* cashier

calamité (kah-lah-mee-*tay*) *f* calamity,

disaster

calcium (kahl-s^yom) m calcium

calcul (kahl-kewl) m calculation; ~ **biliaire** gallstone

calculatrice (kahl-kew-lah-treess) f calculator

calculer (kahl-kew-lay) v reckon; calculate

caleçon (kahl-sawng) m drawers; briefs pl, shorts plAm, pants pl; underpants plAm; ~ **de bain** swimmingtrunks

calendrier (kah-lahng-dree-ay) m calendar

câliner (kah-lee-nay) v cuddle

calmant (kahl-mahng) m tranquillizer

calme (kahlm) adj calm, quiet

calmer (kahl-may) v calm down

calomnie (kah-lom-nee) f slander

calorie (kah-lo-ree) f calorie

camarade (kah-mah-rahd) m/f comrade; ~ **de classe** classmate

cambrioler (kahng-bree-o-lay) v burgle

cambrioleur (kahng-bree-o-lurr) m, **-euse** f burglar

caméra (kah-may-rah) f camera; ~ **vidéo** video camera

camion (kah-m^yawng) m lorry; truck Am; ~ **de livraison** delivery van

camionnette (kah-m^yo-neht) f pick-up van

camomille (kah-mo-meey) f camomile

camp (kahng) m camp; ~ **de vacances** holiday camp

campagne (kahng-pahñ) f countryside, country; campaign

camper (kahng-pay) v camp

campeur (kahng-purr) m, **-euse** f camper

camping (kahng-peeng) m camping; **terrain de** ~ camping site

Canada (kah-nah-dah) m Canada

canadien (kah-nah-d^yang) adj Canadian

canal (kah-nahl) m canal; channel

canapé (kah-nah-pay) m sofa, couch

canard (kah-naar) m duck

canari (kah-nah-ree) m canary

cancer (kahng-sair) m cancer

candidat (kahng-dee-dah) m, **-e** f candidate

candidature (kahng-dee-dah-tewr) f application

caniche (kah-neesh) m poodle

canif (kah-neef) m penknife

caniveau (kah-nee-voa) m gutter

canne (kahn) f cane; walking stick; ~ **à pêche** fishing rod

cannelle (kah-nehl) f cinnamon

canoë (kah-no-ay) m canoe

canon (kah-nawng) m gun

canot (kah-noa) m canoe; dinghy; ~ **automobile** motorboat

cantine (kahng-teen) f canteen

caoutchouc (kah-oo-choo) m rubber; ~ **mousse** foam rubber

cap (kahp) m cape; course

capable (kah-pahbl) adj capable; able; **être ~ de *be able to

capacité (kah-pah-see-tay) f ability; capacity

cape (kahp) f cape

capitaine (kah-pee-tehn) m captain

capital (kah-pee-tahl) m capital; adj capital

capitale (kah-pee-tahl) f capital

capitalisme (kah-pee-tah-leesm) m capitalism

capitulation (kah-pee-tew-lah-s^yawng) f capitulation

capot (kah-poa) m bonnet; hood Am

caprice (kah-preess) m fancy; whim

capsule (kah-psewl) f capsule

capture (kahp-tewr) f capture

capturer (kahp-tew-ray) v capture

capuchon (kah-pew-shawng) m hood

car¹ (kaar) *conj* for

car² (kaar) *m* coach

caractère (kah-rahk-*tair*) *m* character

caractériser (kah-rahk-tay-ree-*zay*) *v* characterize; mark

caractéristique (kah-rahk-tay-ree-*steek*) *f* feature, characteristic, quality; *adj* characteristic, typical

carambolage (kah-rahng-bo-*laazh*) *m* cannon; *Am* carom; collision, crash

caramel (kah-rah-*mehl*) *m* caramel; toffee

caravane (kah-rah-*vahn*) *f* caravan; trailer *Am*

carburateur (kahr-bew-rah-*tūrr*) *m* carburettor

cardigan (kahr-dee-*gahng*) *m* cardigan

cardinal (kahr-dee-*nahl*) *m* cardinal; *adj* cardinal

carence (kah-*rahngss*) *f* shortage; want

cargaison (kahr-gay-*zawng*) *f* cargo

carillon (kah-ree-ʸ*awng*) *m* chimes *pl*

carnaval (kahr-nah-*vahl*) *m* (pl ~s) carnival

carnet (kahr-*nay*) *m* notebook; ~ de chèques chequebook; checkbook *Am*

carotte (kah-*rot*) *f* carrot

carpe (kahrp) *f* carp

carré (kah-*ray*) *m* square; *adj* square

carreau (kah-*roa*) *m* tile; pane; à carreaux chequered

carrefour (kahr-*fōōr*) *m* junction; crossroads

carrière (kah-rʸ*air*) *f* career; quarry

carrosse (kah-*ross*) *m* carriage; coach

carrosserie (kah-ro-*sree*) *f* motor body *Am*

cartable (kahr-*tahbl*) *m* satchel

carte (kahrt) *f* card; map; menu; ~ d'abonnement season ticket; ~ de crédit credit card; charge card *Am*; ~

de jeu playing card; ~ des vins wine list; ~ de visite visiting-card; ~ d'identité identity card; ~ marine chart; ~ postale card, picture postcard, postcard; ~ routière road map; ~ verte green card

cartilage (kahr-tee-*laazh*) *m* cartilage

carton (kahr-*tawng*) *m* cardboard; carton; en ~ cardboard

cartouche (kahr-*toosh*) *f* cartridge; carton

cas (kah) *m* case; instance, event; au ~ où in case; ~ d'urgence emergency; en aucun ~ by no means; en ~ de in case of

cascade (kah-*skahd*) *f* waterfall

case (kaaz) *f* section

caserne (kah-*zehrn*) *f* barracks *pl*

casino (kah-zee-*noa*) *m* casino

casque (kahsk) *m* helmet

casquette (kah-*skeht*) *f* cap

casse-croûte (kah-*skroot*) *m* snack

casse-noix (kah-*snwah*) *m* nutcrackers *pl*

casser (kah-*say*) *v* *break; **cassé** broken

casserole (kah-*srol*) *f* pan

casse-tête (kah-*steht*) *m* puzzle

cassette (kah-*seht*) *f* casket; cassette

cassis (kah-*seess*) *m* blackcurrant

castor (kah-*stawr*) *m* beaver

catacombe (kah-tah-*kawngb*) *f* catacomb

catalogue (kah-tah-*log*) *m* catalogue

catarrhe (kah-*taar*) *m* catarrh

catastrophe (kah-tah-*strof*) *f* calamity, disaster

catégorie (kah-tay-go-*ree*) *f* category; sort

cathédrale (kah-tay-*drahl*) *f* cathedral

catholique (kah-to-*leek*) *adj* catholic; Roman Catholic

cause (kōaz) *f* cause, reason; à ~ de because of; for, on account of

causer (koa-*zay*) v cause; chat
causette (koa-*zeht*) f chat
caution (koa-s*ʸawng*) f bail, security, guarantee; **sujet à ~** untrustworthy
cavalier (kah-vah-*lʸay*) m horseman; rider
cave (kahv) f cellar; wine cellar
caverne (kah-*vehrn*) f cavern
caviar (kah-*vʸaar*) m caviar
cavité (kah-vee-*tay*) f cavity
ce (ser) adj (cet; f cette, pl ces) that; this
ceci (ser-*see*) pron this
céder (say-*day*) v *give in; indulge
ceinture (sang-*tewr*) f belt; **~ de sécurité** safety belt; seat belt
cela (ser-*lah*) pron that
célébration (say-lay-brah-s*ʸawng*) f celebration
célèbre (say-*lehbr*) adj famous
célébrer (say-lay-*bray*) v celebrate
célébrité (say-lay-bree-*tay*) f fame, celebrity
céleri (sehl-*ree*) m celery
célibataire (say-lee-bah-*tair*) m bachelor; adj single
cellule (seh-*lewl*) f cell
celui-là (ser-lwee-*lah*) pron (f celle-là, pl ceux-là, celles-là) that
cendre (sahngdr) f ash
cendrier (sahng-dree-*ay*) m ashtray
censure (sahng-*sewr*) f censorship
cent (sahng) num hundred; **pour ~** percent
centigrade (sahng-tee-*grahd*) adj centigrade
centimètre (sahng-tee-*mehtr*) m centimeter Am, centimetre
central (sahng-*trahl*) adj central; **~ téléphonique** telephone exchange
centrale (sahng-*trahl*) f power station
centraliser (sahng-trah-lee-*zay*) v centralize
centre (sahngtr) m center Am, centre;

~ commercial shopping centre; mall; **~ de la ville** town centre; **~ de loisirs** recreation centre
cependant (ser-pahng-*dahng*) conj however; but, yet, only
céramique (say-rah-*meek*) f ceramics pl
cercle (sehrkl) m circle, ring; club
céréale (say-ray-*ahl*) f grain; corn
cérémonie (say-ray-mo-*nee*) f ceremony
cérémonieux (say-ray-mo-*nʸur*) adj formal
cerf (sair) m stag, hart
cerise (ser-*reez*) f cherry
certain (sehr-*tang*) adj certain; **certains** pron some
certificat (sehr-tee-fee-*kah*) m certificate; **~ médical** health certificate
cerveau (sehr-*voa*) m brain
ces (say) adj these; those
cesser (say-*say*) v cease; discontinue, quit, stop
c'est-à-dire (say-tah-*deer*) conj that is (to say), namely
ceux-là (sur-*lah*) pron (f celles-là) those
chacun (shah-*kurng*) pron everyone; anyone
chagrin (shah-*grang*) m sorrow; grief
chaîne (shehn) f chain; **~ de montagnes** mountain range
chair (shair) f flesh; **~ de poule** goose flesh
chaire (shair) f pulpit
chaise (shaiz) f chair; **~ longue** deck chair
chalet (shah-*lay*) m chalet
chaleur (shah-*lurr*) f heat; warmth
chambre (shahngbr) f room; **~ à air** inner tube; **~ à coucher** bedroom; **~ d'ami** spare room, guest room; **~ d'enfants** nursery; **~ et petit déjeuner**

bed and breakfast; **~ forte** vault

chameau (shah-*moa*) *m* camel

champ (shahng) *m* field; **~ de blé** cornfield; **~ de courses** racecourse; **sur-le-champ** immediately

champagne (shahng-*pahñ*) *m* champagne

champignon (shahng-pee-*ñawng*) *m* mushroom, toadstool

champion (shahng-*pʸawng*) *m*, **-ne** *f* champion

chance (shahngss) *f* luck; fortune; chance

chanceux (shahng-*sur*) *adj* lucky

chandail (shahng-*digh*) *m* jersey, jumper, sweater

change (shahngzh) *m* change; **bureau de ~** money exchange

changement (shahngzh-*mahng*) *m* change; variation, alteration

changer (shahng-*zhay*) *v* vary, change, alter; exchange, switch; **~ de vitesse** change gear; **~ en** turn into; **se ~** change

chanson (shahng-*sawng*) *f* song; **~ populaire** folk song

chant (shahng) *m* song, singing

chantage (shahng-*taazh*) *m* blackmail

chanter (shahng-*tay*) *v* *sing; ***faire ~** blackmail

chanteur (shahng-*tūrr*) *m*, **-euse** *f* singer; vocalist

chantier (shahng-*tʸay*) *m* building site; yard; roadwork, **~ naval** (shahng-tʸay nah-*vahl*) shipyard

chanvre (shahngvr) *m* hemp

chaos (kah-*oa*) *m* chaos

chaotique (kah-o-*teek*) *adj* chaotic

chapeau (shah-*poa*) *m* hat

chapelain (shah-*plang*) *m* chaplain

chapelet (shah-*play*) *m* beads *pl*

chapelle (shah-*pehl*) *f* chapel

chapitre (shah-*peetr*) *m* chapter

chaque (shahk) *adj* each; every

charbon (shahr-*bawng*) *m* coal; **~ de bois** charcoal

charcuterie (shahr-kew-*tree*) *f* delicatessen; butcher's shop

chardon (shahr-*dawng*) *m* thistle

charge (shahrzh) *f* charge

chargement (shahr-zher-*mahng*) *m* cargo, load, charge, freight

charger (shahr-*zhay*) *v* charge; load; **chargé de** in charge of; **se ~ de** *take charge of

charité (shah-ree-*tay*) *f* charity

charmant (shahr-*mahng*) *adj* graceful; glamorous

charme (shahrm) *m* charm, glamour

charmer (shahr-*may*) *v* charm, enchant

charnière (shahr-*nʸair*) *f* hinge

charrette (shah-*reht*) *f* cart

charrue (shah-*rew*) *f* plough

chasse (shahss) *f* chase; hunt

chasser (shah-*say*) *v* chase; hunt

chasseur (shah-*sūrr*) *m* hunter; bellboy

châssis (shah-*see*) *m* chassis

chaste (shahst) *adj* chaste

chat (shah) *m* cat

château (shah-*toa*) *m* castle

chatouiller (shah-too-*ʸay*) *v* tickle

chaud (shoa) *adj* hot; warm

chaudière (shoa-*dʸair*) *f* boiler

chauffage (shoa-*faazh*) *m* heating; **~ central** central heating

chauffer (shoa-*fay*) *v* heat; warm

chauffeur (shoa-*fūrr*) *m* chauffeur; **~ de taxi** cab driver

chaussée (shoa-*say*) *f* causeway; carriageway; roadway *Am*

chaussette (shoa-*seht*) *f* sock

chaussure (shoa-*sēwr*) *f* shoe; **chaussures** footwear; **chaussures de basket** plimsolls *pl*; **chaussures de gymnastique** gym shoes; sneakers *plAm*; **chaussures de ski** ski boots;

chaussures de tennis tennis shoes

chauve (shoāv) *adj* bald

chaux (shoa) *f* lime

chef (shehf) *m* chief; manager, boss; chieftain; **~ cuisinier** chef; **~ d'Etat** head of state; **~ d'orchestre** conductor

chef-d'œuvre (sheh-*dūrvr*) *m* masterpiece

chemin (sher-*manḡ*) *m* lane; **à michemin** halfway; **~ de fer** railroad *Am*; railway; **~ du retour** way back

chemineau (sher-mee-*noa*) *m* tramp

cheminée (sher-mee-*nay*) *f* chimney; fireplace; hearth

chemise (sher-*meez*) *f* shirt; vest; **~ de nuit** nightdress

chemisier (sher-mee-*z*ʸ*ay*) *m* blouse

chêne (shehn) *m* oak

chenil (sher-*nee*) *m* kennel

chèque (shehk) *m* cheque, check *Am*; **~ de voyage** traveler's check *Am*, traveller's cheque

cher (shair) *adj* dear; expensive

chercher (shehr-*shay*) *v* *seek, search; hunt for, look up, look for; *aller ~ fetch

chère (shair) *f* fare

chéri (shay-*ree*) *m* darling, sweetheart

cheval (sher-*vahl*) *m* horse; **~ de bois** wooden horse; **~ de course** racehorse; **cheval-vapeur** *m* horsepower; **monter à ~** *ride

chevalier (sher-vah-*l*ʸ*ay*) *m* knight

chevelu (sher-*vlew*) *adj* hairy

cheveu (sher-*vur*) *m* hair; **coupe de cheveux** haircut

cheville (sher-*veey*) *f* ankle

chèvre (shaivr) *f* goat

chevreau (sher-*vroa*) *m* kid

chevreuil (sher-*vrur*ᵉᵉ) *m* roebuck

chez (shay) *prep* at; to; with; **~ soi** home

chic (sheek) *adj* (f ~) smart

chichi (shee-*shee*) *m* fuss

chien (sh*ʸanḡ*) *m* dog; **~ d'aveugle** guide dog

chienne (sh*ʸ*ehn) *f* bitch

chiffon (shee-*fawnḡ*) *m* cloth; rag

chiffre (sheefr) *m* figure; digit, number

Chili (shee-*lee*) *m* Chile

chilien (shee-*lʸanḡ*) *adj* Chilean

chimie (shee-*mee*) *f* chemistry

chimique (shee-*meek*) *adj* chemical

Chine (sheen) *f* China

chinois (shee-*nwah*) *adj* Chinese

chirurgien (shee-rewr-*zhʸanḡ*) *m* surgeon

chlore (klawr) *m* chlorine

choc (shok) *m* shock

chocolat (sho-ko-*lah*) *m* chocolate

chœur (kūr) *m* choir

choisir (shwah-*zeer*) *v* *choose; pick, select; **choisi** select

choix (shwah) *m* choice; pick, selection

chômage (shoa-*maazh*) *m* unemployment; **en ~** unemployed

chômeur (shoa-*mūrr*) *m*, **-euse** *f* unemployed worker

chope (shop) *f* mug

choquer (sho-*kay*) *v* shock

chose (shoāz) *f* thing; **quelque ~** something

chou (shoo) *m* (pl ~x) cabbage; **chou-fleur** cauliflower; **choux de Bruxelles** Brussels sprouts *pl*

chouchou (shoo-*shoo*) *m* pet

choucroute (shoo-*kroot*) *f* sauerkraut

chouette (shweht) *f* owl; *adj* fine, splendid

chrétien (kray-*tʸanḡ*) *adj* Christian; *m*, **-ne** *f* Christian

chronique (kro-*neek*) *adj* chronic

chronologique (kro-no-lo-*zheek*) *adj* chronological

chuchotement (shew-shot-*mahnḡ*) *m* whisper

chuchoter (shew-sho-*tay*) v whisper

chute (shewt) f fall

cible (seebl) f target; mark

ciboulette (see-boo-*leht*) f chives pl

cicatrice (see-kah-*treess*) f scar

cidre (seedr) m cider

ciel (s^yehl) m (pl cieux) heaven; sky

cigare (see-*gaar*) m cigar

cigarette (see-gah-*reht*) f cigarette

cigogne (see-*goñ*) f stork

cil (seel) m eyelash

ciment (see-*mahng*) m cement

cimetière (seem-t^yair) m graveyard, cemetery, churchyard

cinéma (see-nay-*mah*) m cinema; pictures; movie theater Am, movies Am

cinq (sangk) num five

cinquante (sang-*kahngt*) num fifty

cinquième (sang-k^yehm) num fifth

cintre (sangtr) m coat hanger, hanger

cirage (see-*raazh*) m shoe polish

circonstance (seer-kawng-*stahngss*) f circumstance; condition

circuit (seer-*kwee*) m circumference; circuit

circulation (seer-kew-lah-s^yawng) f circulation; traffic

cire (seer) f wax; **musée des figures de ~** waxworks pl

cirque (seerk) m circus

ciseaux (see-*zoa*) mpl scissors pl; **~ à ongles** nail scissors pl

citation (see-tah-s^yawng) f quotation

cité (see-*tay*) f city

citer (see-*tay*) v quote

citoyen (see-twah-^yang) m, **-ne** f citizen

citoyenneté (see-twah-^yehn-*tay*) f citizenship

citron (see-*trawng*) m lemon

civil (see-*veel*) m civilian; adj civilian, civil

civilisation (see-vee-lee-zah-s^yawng) f civilization

civilisé (see-vee-lee-*zay*) adj civilized

civique (see-*veek*) adj civic

clair (klair) adj clear; plain, light, serene

clairière (kleh-r^yair) f clearing

claque (klahk) f slap; smack, blow; **donner une ~** smack

claquer (klah-*kay*) v slam

clarifier (klah-ree-f^yay) v clarify

clarté (klahr-*tay*) f light, clearness

classe (klahss) f class; form; **~ moyenne** middle class; **~ touriste** tourist class

classer (klah-*say*) v classify; assort, grade, arrange, sort

classique (klah-*seek*) adj classical

clavecin (klahv-*sang*) m harpsichord

clavicule (klah-vee-*kewl*) f collarbone

clavier (klah-v^yay) m keyboard; range

clé (klay) f key; wrench; **~ à écrous** spanner, wrench Am; **~ de la maison** latchkey

clémence (klay-*mahngss*) f mercy; grace

client (klee-*ahng*) m client; customer

clientèle (klee-ahng-*tehl*) f customers pl

clignotant (klee-ño-*tahng*) m indicator

climat (klee-*mah*) m climate

climatisation (klee-mah-tee-zah-s^yawng) f air conditioning

climatisé (klee-mah-tee-*zay*) adj airconditioned

clinique (klee-*neek*) f clinic

cliquer (klee-*kay*) v click

cloche (klosh) f bell

clocher (klo-*shay*) m steeple

cloison (klwah-*zawng*) f partition; wall

cloître (klwaatr) m cloister

cloque (klok) f blister

clos (kloa) *adj* closed; shut

clôture (kloa-*tewr*) *f* fence

clou (kloo) *m* nail

clown (kloon) *m* clown

club (klurb) *m* club; ~ **automobile** automobile club; ~ **de golf** golfclub

cocaïne (ko-kah-*een*) *f* cocaine

cochon (ko-*shawng*) *m* pig; ~ **de lait** piglet; ~ **d'Inde** guinea pig

cocktail (kok-*tehl*) *m* cocktail

code (kod) *m* code; ~ **postal** zip code *Am*

cœur (kurr) *m* heart; core; **par** ~ by heart

coffre (kofr) *m* chest; boot; trunk *Am*; **coffre-fort** safe

cognac (ko-*ñahk*) *m* cognac

cogner (ko-*ñay*) *v* bump; ~ **contre** knock against

cohérence (koa-ay-*rahngss*) *f* coherence

coiffeur (kwah-*furr*) *m* hairdresser; barber

coiffeuse (kwah-*furz*) *f* dressing table

coiffure (kwah-*fewr*) *f* hairdo

coin (kwang) *m* corner

coïncidence (koa-ang-see-*dahngss*) *f* concurrence

coïncider (koa-ang-see-*day*) *v* coincide

col (kol) *m* collar; mountain pass

coléoptère (ko-lay-op-*tair*) *m* bug

colère (ko-*lair*) *f* anger; temper, passion; **en** ~ angry

coléreux (ko-lay-*rur*) *adj* hot-tempered

colis (ko-*lee*) *m* parcel, package

collaboration (ko-lah-borah-*s^{y}awng*) *f* cooperation

collant (ko-*lahng*) *adj* sticky; close-fitting, (skin)tight; clinging

collants (ko-*lahng*) *mpl* tights *pl*; panty hose

colle (kol) *f* glue, gum

collectif (ko-lehk-*teef*) *adj* collective

collection (ko-lehk-*s^{y}awng*) *f* collection; ~ **d'art** art collection

collectionner (ko-lehk-s^{y}o-*nay*) *v* gather

collectionneur (ko-lehk-s^{y}o-*nurr*) *m*, **-euse** *f* collector

collège (ko-*laizh*) *m* college

collègue (ko-*lehg*) *m* colleague

coller (ko-*lay*) *v* paste, *stick

collier (ko-*l^{y}ay*) *m* necklace; collar, beads *pl*

colline (ko-*leen*) *f* hill

collision (ko-lee-z^{y}awng) *f* collision; crash; **entrer en** ~ collide, crash

Colombie (ko-lawng-*bee*) *f* Colombia

colombien (ko-lawng-b^{y}ang) *adj* Colombian

colonel (ko-lo-*nehl*) *m* colonel

colonie (ko-lo-*nee*) *f* colony

colonne (ko-*lon*) *f* column; pillar; ~ **de direction** steering column

coloré (ko-lo-*ray*) *adj* colo(u)rful

coma (ko-*mah*) *m* coma

combat (kawng-*bah*) *m* struggle; fight, combat, contest, battle

*combattre (kawng-*bahtr*) *v* *fight; combat, battle

combien (kawng-b^{y}ang) *adv* how much; how many

combinaison (kawng-bee-nay-*zawng*) *f* combination; slip

combiner (kawng-bee-*nay*) *v* combine

comble (kawngbl) *m* roof; height; *adj* full

combler (kawng-*blay*) *v* fill up; overload

combustible (kawng-bew-*steebl*) *m* fuel

comédie (ko-may-*dee*) *f* comedy; ~ **musicale** musical

comédien (ko-may-d^{y}ang) *m*, **-ne** *f* comedian

comestible (ko-meh-*steebl*) *adj* edible

comique (ko-*meek*) *m* comedian; *adj* comic, humorous

comité (ko-mee-*tay*) *m* committee

commandant (ko-mahn̄g-*dahn̄g*) *m* commander; captain

commande (ko-*mahn̄g*d) *f* order; **fait sur ~** made to order

commandement (ko-mahn̄gd-*mahn̄g*) *m* order

commander (ko-mahn̄g-*day*) *v* command; order

comme (kom) *conj* as; like; since; **~ si** as if

commémoration (ko-may-mo-rah-*s^yawn̄g*) *f* commemoration

commencement (ko-mahn̄g-*smahn̄g*) *m* beginning

commencer (ko-mahn̄g-*say*) *v* *begin; commence, start

comment (ko-*mahn̄g*) *adv* how; **n'importe ~** anyhow

commentaire (ko-mahn̄g-*tair*) *m* comment

commenter (ko-mahn̄g-*tay*) *v* comment

commerçant (ko-mehr-*sahn̄g*) *m*, **-e** *f* merchant; trader, shopkeeper

commerce (ko-*mehrs*) *m* commerce; business, trade; **~ de détail** retail trade; *faire du ~** trade

commercial (ko-mehr-*s^yahl*) *adj* commercial

***commettre** (ko-*mehtr*) *v* commit

commission (ko-mee-*s^yawn̄g*) *f* committee, commission; errand, message

commode (ko-*mod*) *f* chest of drawers; bureau *Am*; *adj* convenient, easy, handy

commodité (ko-mo-dee-*tay*) *f* comfort

commotion (ko-moa-*s^yawn̄g*) *f* shock; **~ cérébrale** concussion

commun (ko-*murn̄g*) *adj* common; ordinary

communauté (ko-mew-noa-*tay*) *f* community

communication (ko-mew-nee-kah-*s^yawn̄g*) *f* communication; information; connection; **~ locale** local call; *mettre en ~** connect

communiqué (ko-mew-nee-*kay*) *m* communiqué

communiquer (ko-mew-nee-*kay*) *v* communicate; inform

communisme (ko-mew-*neesm*) *m* communism

commutateur (ko-mew-tah-*tūrr*) *m* switch

compact (kawn̄g-*pahkt*) *adj* compact

compact-disc (kawn̄g-*pahkt* deesk) *m* compact disc; **lecteur de ~** compact disc player

compagne (kawn̄g-*pah*-ñe) *f* companion

compagnie (kawn̄g-pah-*ñee*) *f* company; society; **~ de navigation** shipping line

compagnon (kawn̄g-pah-*ñawn̄g*) *m* companion

comparaison (kawn̄g-pah-ray-*zawn̄g*) *f* comparison

comparer (kawn̄g-pah-*ray*) *v* compare

compartiment (kawn̄g-pahr-tee-*mahn̄g*) *m* compartment; **~ fumeurs** smoking compartment

compassion (kawn̄g-pah-*s^yawn̄g*) *f* compassion

compatir (kawn̄g-pah-*teer*) *v* sympathize

compatissant (kawn̄g-pah-tee-*sahn̄g*) *adj* sympathetic

compatriote (kawn̄g-pah-tree-*ot*) *m/f* fellow countryman

compensation (kawn̄g-pahn̄g-sah-*s^yawn̄g*) *f* compensation

compenser (kawn̄g-pahn̄g-*say*) *v* compensate for; *make good

compétence (kawn̄g-pay-*tahn̄gss*) *f*

capacity

compétent (kawng-pay-*tahng*) *adj*
qualified; expert

compétition (kawng-pay-tee-s*y*awng)
f competition

compiler (kawng-pee-*lay*) *v* compile

complémentaire (kawng-play-mahng-*tair*) *adj* further

complet[1] (kawng-*play*) *adj* (f -plète)
whole, complete; total, utter; full up

complet[2] (kawng-*play*) *m* suit

complètement (kawng-pleht-*mahng*)
adv completely

complexe (kawng-*plehks*) *m* complex;
adj complex

compliment (kawng-plee-*mahng*) *m*
compliment

complimenter (kawng-plee-mahng-*tay*) *v* compliment

compliqué (kawng-plee-*kay*) *adj*
complicated

complot (kawng-*ploa*) *m* plot

comportement (kawng-por-ter-*mahng*) *m* behavio(u)r

comporter (kawng-por-*tay*) *v* imply;
se ~ behave

composer (kawng-poa-*zay*) *v*
compose

compositeur (kawng-po-zee-*tūrr*) *m*,
-trice *f* composer

composition (kawng-po-zee-s*y*awng)
f composition; essay

composter (kawng-po-*stay*) *v* punch
(*a ticket*)

compote (kawng-*pot*) *f* stewed fruit;
en ~ stewed; to *or* in a pulp

compréhension (kawng-pray-ahng-s*y*awng) *f* understanding; insight

***comprendre** (kawng-*prahngdr*) *v*
*understand; *see; comprise,
include, contain

comprimé (kawng-pree-*may*) *m* tablet

compris (kawng-*pree*) *adj* inclusive;
tout ~ all in

compromis (kawng-pro-*mee*) *m*
compromise

comptable (kawng-*tahbl*) *m*
accountant

compte (kawngt) *m* account; ~ **en
banque** bank account; ~ **rendu**
report; minutes; **en fin de** ~ at last;
rendre ~ de account for; **se rendre ~**
realize; *see

compter (kawng-*tay*) *v* count; ~ **sur**
rely on

compteur (kawng-*tūrr*) *m* meter

comptoir (kawng-*twaar*) *m* counter

comte (kawngt) *m* count; earl

comté (kawng-*tay*) *m* county

comtesse (kawng-*tehss*) *f* countess

concéder (kawng-say-*day*) *v* grant

concentration (kawng-sahng-trah-s*y*awng) *f* concentration

concentrer (kawng-sahng-*tray*) *v*
concentrate

concept (kawng-*sehpt*) *m* idea

conception (kawng-seh-ps*y*awng) *f*
conception

concernant (kawng-sehr-*nahng*) *prep*
concerning; as regards, about,
regarding

concerner (kawng-sehr-*nay*) *v*
concern; **en ce qui concerne** as
regards, regarding

concert (kawng-*sair*) *m* concert

concession (kawng-seh-s*y*awng) *f*
concession

concessionnaire (kawng-seh-s*y*o-*nair*) *m* distributor

concierge (kawng-s*y*ehrzh) *m/f*
concierge; janitor

concis (kawng-*see*) *adj* concise

***conclure** (kawng-*klēwr*) *v* finish;
conclude

conclusion (kawng-klew-z*y*awng) *f*
conclusion, end; issue

concombre (kawng-*kawng*br) *m*
cucumber

concorder (kawng-kor-*day*) *v* agree

*concourir (kawng-koo-*reer*) *v*
compete

concours (kawng-*koor*) *m* contest

concret (kawng-*kray*) *adj* (f -crète)
concrete

concurrence (kawng-kew-*rahngss*) *f*
rivalry

concurrent (kawng-kew-*rahng*) *m*
competitor; rival

condamnation (kawng-dah-nah-
s^y*awng*) *f* condemnation; sentence

condamné (kawng-dah-*nay*) *m*
convict

condamner (kawng-dah-*nay*) *v*
sentence

condition (kawng-dee-s^y*awng*) *f*
condition; term

conducteur (kawng-dewk-*türr*) *m*
driver; conductor

*conduire (kawng-*dweer*) *v* conduct,
guide; *drive; carry, *take; se ~ act

conduite (kawng-*dweet*) *f* conduct;
lead

confédération (kawng-fay-day-rah-
s^y*awng*) *f* confederation

conférence (kawng-fay-*rahngss*) *f*
conference; lecture; ~ de presse
press conference

confesser (kawng-fay-*say*) *v* confess

confession (kawng-feh-s^y*awng*) *f*
confession

confiance (kawng-f^y*ahngss*) *f*
confidence; faith, trust; digne de ~
reliable, trustworthy; *faire ~ trust

confiant (kawng-f^y*ahng*) *adj* confident

confidentiel (kawng-fee-dahng-s^y*ehl*)
adj confidential

confier (kawng-f^y*ay*) *v* confide

confirmation (kawng-feer-mah-
s^y*awng*) *f* confirmation

confirmer (kawng-feer-*may*) *v*
confirm; acknowledge

confiserie (kawng-fee-*zree*) *f*
sweetshop; candy *Am*; candy store
Am

confiseur (kawng-fee-*zürr*) *m*, -euse *f*
confectioner

confisquer (kawng-fee-*skay*) *v*
confiscate

confiture (kawng-fee-*tewr*) *f* jam

conflit (kawng-*flee*) *m* conflict

confondre (kawng-*fawng*dr) *v*
confuse; *mistake

*être conforme (aitr kawng-*form*)
correspond

conformément à (kawng-for-may-
mahng) in accordance with,
according to

confort (kawng-*fawr*) *m* comfort

confortable (kawng-*for*-tahbl) *adj*
comfortable; cosy, cozy *Am*

confus (kawng-*few*) *adj* confused;
embarrassed

confusion (kawng-few-z^y*awng*) *f*
confusion; disorder, muddle

congé (kawng-*zhay*) *m* vacation

congélateur (kawng-zhay-lah-*türr*) *m*
deep-freeze

congelé (kawng-*zhlay*) *adj* frozen

congratuler (kawng-grah-tew-*lay*) *v*
congratulate

congrès (kawng-*gray*) *m* congress

conifère (ko-nee-*fair*) *m* conifer

conjecture (kawng-zhehk-*tewr*) *f*
conjecture, guess

conjoint (kawng-*zhwang*) *adj* joint

conjointement (kawng-zhwangt-
mahng) *adv* jointly

connaissance (ko-nay-*sahngss*) *f*
knowledge; acquaintance

connaisseur (ko-nay-*sürr*) *m*
connoisseur

*connaître (ko-*naitr*) *v* *know; connu
well-known

connotation (ko-no-tah-s^y*awng*) *f*

connotation

conquérant (kawng-kay-*rahng*) *m* conqueror

*conquérir (kawng-kay-*reer*) *v* conquer

conquête (kawng-*keht*) *f* conquest

consacrer (kawng-sah-*kray*) *v* devote

conscience (kawng-s*ʸahngss*) *f* conscience; consciousness

conscient (kawng-s*ʸahng*) *adj* conscious; aware

conscrit (kawng-*skree*) *m* conscript

conseil (kawng-*say*) *m* advice; counsel, council; board; **donner des conseils** advise

conseiller (kawng-say-*ʸay*) *v* advise; recommend; *m* councillor; counsellor

consentement (kawng-sahngt-*mahng*) *m* consent, approval

*consentir (kawng-sahng-*teer*) *v* consent, agree

conséquence (kawng-say-*kahngss*) *f* consequence; result

conséquent: par ~ (pahr kawng-say-*kahng*) consequently

conservateur (kawng-sehr-vah-*tūrr*) *adj* conservative

conservation (kawng-sehr-vah-s*ʸawng*) *f* preservation

conservatoire (kawng-sehr-vah-*twaar*) *m* music academy

conserver (kawng-sehr-*vay*) *v* preserve

conserves (kawng-*sehrv*) *fpl* tinned food, canned food *Am*; ***mettre en conserve** preserve

considérable (kawng-see-day-*rahbl*) *adj* considerable; extensive

considération (kawng-see-day-rah-s*ʸawng*) *f* consideration; respect

considérer (kawng-see-day-*ray*) *v* consider; **~ comme** regard as

consigne (kawng-*seeñ*) *f* deposit; left

luggage office; checkroom, baggage check *Am*

consister (kawng-see-*stay*) v: **~ en** consist of

consoler (kawng-so-*lay*) *v* comfort

consommateur (kawng-so-mah-*tūrr*) *m* consumer

consommation (kawng-so-mah-s*ʸawng*) *f* consumption; drink

consommer (kawng-so-*may*) *v* consume

conspiration (kawng-spee-rah-s*ʸawng*) *f* plot

conspirer (kawng-spee-*ray*) *v* conspire

constant (kawng-*stahng*) *adj* constant; even

constater (kawng-stah-*tay*) *v* note, notice; certify

constipation (kawng-stee-pah-s*ʸawng*) *f* constipation

constituer (kawng-stee-*tway*) *v* constitute

constitution (kawng-stee-tew-s*ʸawng*) *f* constitution

construction (kawng-strewk-s*ʸawng*) *f* construction; building

*construire (kawng-*strweer*) *v* construct

consulat (kawng-sew-*lah*) *m* consulate

consultation (kawng-sewl-tah-s*ʸawng*) *f* consultation

consulter (kawng-sewl-*tay*) *v* consult

contact (kawng-*tahkt*) *m* contact; touch

contacter (kawng-tahk-*tay*) *v* contact

contagieux (kawng-tah-*zhʸur*) *adj* contagious

conte (kawngt) *m* tale; **~ de fées** fairytale

contempler (kawng-tahng-*play*) *v* view

contemporain (kawng-tahng-po-*rang*) *m* contemporary; *adj* contemporary

conteneur (kawng̅t-*nürr*) *m* container

*contenir (kawng̅t-*neer*) *v* contain; restrain

content (kawng̅-*tahng̅*) *adj* glad; pleased, happy

contenu (kawng̅-*new*) *m* contents *pl*

contester (kawng̅-teh-*stay*) *v* dispute

continent (kawng̅-tee-*nahng̅*) *m* continent

continental (kawng̅-tee-nahng̅-*tahl*) *adj* continental

continu (kawng̅-tee-*new*) *adj* continuous

continuel (kawng̅-tee-*nwehl*) *adj* continual; continuous

continuellement (kawng̅-tee-nwehl-*mahng̅*) *adv* all the time, continually

continuer (kawng̅-tee-*nway*) *v* continue; carry on, *keep on, *keep, *go on, *go ahead

contour (kawng̅-*toor*) *m* outline, contour

contourner (kawng̅-toor-*nay*) *v* by-pass

contraceptif (kawng̅-trah-sehp-*teef*) *m* contraceptive

contradictoire (kawng̅-trah-deek-*twaar*) *adj* contradictory

*contraindre (kawng̅-*trang̅dr*) *v* compel

contraire (kawng̅-*trair*) *adj* opposite; *m* reverse, contrary; **au ~** on the contrary

contralto (kawng̅-trahl-*toa*) *m* contralto

contraste (kawng̅-*trahst*) *m* contrast

contrat (kawng̅-*trah*) *m* agreement, contract

contravention (kawng̅-trah-vahng̅-*s*ᵧ*awng̅*) *f* ticket

contre (kawng̅tr) *prep* against; versus

contrecœur: à ~ (ah kawng̅-trer-*kürr*) reluctantly

*contredire (kawng̅-trer-*deer*) *v* contradict

*contrefaire (kawng̅-trer-*fair*) *v* counterfeit

contrefait (kawng̅-trer-*fay*) *adj* deformed

contremaître (kawng̅-trer-*maitr*) *m* foreman

contribution (kawng̅-tree-bew-*s*ᵧ*awng̅*) *f* contribution

contrôle (kawng̅-*trōal*) *m* control; inspection; **~ des passeports** passport control

contrôler (kawng̅-troa-*lay*) *v* control; check

contrôleur (kawng̅-troa-*lürr*) *m* ticket collector

controversé (kawng̅-troa-vehr-*say*) *adj* controversial

contusion (kawng̅-tew-*z*ᵧ*awng̅*) *f* bruise

contusionner (kawng̅-tew-z*ᵧ*o-*nay*) *v* bruise

*convaincre (kawng̅-*vang̅gkr*) *v* convince; persuade

convenable (kawng̅-*vnahbl*) *adj* proper; fit

*convenir (kawng̅-*vneer*) *v* fit, suit

conversation (kawng̅-vehr-sah-*s*ᵧ*awng̅*) *f* conversation; discussion, talk

convertir (kawng̅-vehr-*teer*) *v* convert

conviction (kawng̅-veek-*s*ᵧ*awng̅*) *f* conviction; persuasion

convulsion (kawng̅-vewl-*s*ᵧ*awng̅*) *f* convulsion

coopérant (koa-o-pay-*rahng̅*) *adj* cooperative

coopératif (koa-o-pay-rah-*teef*) *adj* cooperative

coopération (koa-o-pay-rah-*s*ᵧ*awng̅*) *f* co-operation

coopérative (koa-o-pay-rah-*teev*) *f* cooperative

coordination (koa-or-dee-nah-

coordonner (koa-or-do-*nay*) *v* coordinate

copain (ko-*pang*) *m* pal

copie (ko-*pee*) *f* copy; carbon copy

copier (ko-*pʸay*) *v* copy

copine (ko-*peen*) *f* pal; girlfriend

coq (kok) *m* cock; ~ **de bruyère** black grouse

coquelicot (ko-klee-*koa*) *m* poppy

coquetier (kok-*tʸay*) *m* eggcup

coquillage (ko-kee-*ʸaazh*) *m* seashell

coquille (ko-*keey*) *f* shell; ~ **de noix** nutshell

coquin (ko-*kang*) *m* rascal

corail (ko-*righ*) *m* (pl coraux) coral

corbeau (kor-*boa*) *m* raven

corbeille à papier (kor-bay ah pah-*pʸay*) wastepaper basket

corde (kord) *f* rope; cord; string

cordial (kor-*dʸahl*) *adj* hearty, cordial; warm

cordon (kor-*dawng*) *m* cord; string

cordonnier (kor-do-*nʸay*) *m* shoemaker

coriace (ko-*rʸahss*) *adj* tough

corne (korn) *f* horn

corneille (kor-*nay*) *f* crow

cornichon (kor-nee-*shawng*) *m* gherkin; colloquial nitwit

corps (kawr) *m* body

corpulent (kor-pew-*lahng*) *adj* corpulent; stout

correct (ko-*rehkt*) *adj* correct; right

correction (ko-rehk-*sʸawng*) *f* correction

correspondance (ko-reh-spawng-*dahngss*) *f* correspondence; connection

correspondant (ko-reh-spawng-*dahng*) *m* correspondent

correspondre (ko-reh-*spawngdr*) *v* correspond

corrida (ko-ree-*dah*) *f* bullfight

corridor (ko-ree-*dawr*) *m* corridor

corriger (ko-ree-*zhay*) *v* correct

***corrompre** (ko-*rawngpr*) *v* corrupt; bribe; **corrompu** corrupt

corruption (ko-rew-*psʸawng*) *f* corruption; bribery

corset (kor-*say*) *m* corset

cortège (kor-*taizh*) *m* procession

cosmétiques (ko-smay-*teek*) *mpl* cosmetics *pl*

costume (ko-*stewm*) *m* suit; costume; ~ **national** national dress

côte (*koāt*) *f* coast; rib; chop

côté (koa-*tay*) *m* side; way; **à** ~ next-door; **à** ~ **de** next to, beside; **de** ~ aside, sideways; **de l'autre** ~ **de** across; **passer à** ~ pass by

coteau (ko-*toa*) *m* hillside

côtelette (ko-*tleht*) *f* chop, cutlet

coton (ko-*tawng*) *m* cotton; **en** ~ cotton

cou (koo) *m* neck

couche (koosh) *f* layer; nappy; diaper *Am*; **fausse** ~ miscarriage

coucher (koo-*shay*) *v*: **se** ~ *lie down

couchette (koo-*sheht*) *f* couchette, bunk

coucou (koo-*koo*) *m* cuckoo

coude (kood) *m* elbow

***coudre** (koodr) *v* sew

couler (koo-*lay*) *v* flow, stream

couleur (koo-*lūrr*) *f* colo(u)r; ~ **à l'eau** watercolo(u)r; **de** ~ colo(u)red

couloir (koo-*lwaar*) *m* corridor

coup (koo) *m* blow; bump, tap, push, knock; ~ **de feu** shot; ~ **d'envoi** kickoff; ~ **de pied** kick; ~ **de poing** punch; ~ **de téléphone** call; **jeter un** ~ **d'œil à** glance at

coupable (koo-*pahbl*) *adj* guilty; **déclarer** ~ convict

coupe (koop) *f* cup

coupe-papier (koop-pah-*pʸay*) *m* paper knife, letter opener *Am*

couper (koo-*pay*) *v* *cut; *cut off

couple (koopl) *m* couple; ~ **marié** married couple

coupon (koo-*pawng*) *m* coupon

coupure (koo-*pewr*) *f* cut

cour (koor) *f* court; yard

courage (koo-*raazh*) *m* courage

courageux (koo-rah-*zhur*) *adj* courageous; plucky; brave

couramment (koo-rah-*mahng*) *adv* fluently

courant (koo-*rahng*) *m* current, stream; undercurrent; *adj* frequent, current; ~ **alternatif** alternating current; ~ **continu** direct current; ~ **d'air** draught, draft *Am*; ***mettre au** ~ inform

courbatures (koor-bah-*tewr*) *fpl* sore muscles

courbe (koorb) *f* bend, curve; *adj* curved

courbé (koor-*bay*) *adj* curved

courber (koor-*bay*) *v* *bend; bow

courgette (koor-*zheht*) *f* courgette, zucchini *Am*

*courir (koo-*reer*) *v* *run

couronne (koo-*ron*) *f* crown

couronner (koo-ro-*nay*) *v* crown

courrier (koo-*r^{y}ay*) *m* mail

courroie (koo-*rwah*) *f* strap; ~ **de ventilateur** fan belt

cours (koor) *m* course; lecture; ~ **accéléré** crash course; ~ **du change** foreign exchange rate

course (koors) *f* race; ride; ~ **de chevaux** horserace

court (koor) *adj* short; ~ **de tennis** tennis court

court-circuit (koor-seer-*kwee*) *m* short circuit

courtier (koor-*t^{y}ay*) *m* broker

courtois (koor-*twah*) *adj* courteous

cousin (koo-*zang*) *m* cousin

cousine (koo-*zeen*) *f* cousin

coussin (koo-*sang*) *m* cushion

coût (koo) *m* cost

couteau (koo-*toa*) *m* knife; ~ **de poche** pocketknife

coûter (koo-*tay*) *v* *cost

coûteux (koo-*tur*) *adj* expensive

coutume (koo-*tewm*) *f* custom

couture (koo-*tewr*) *f* seam; **sans** ~ seamless

couturière (koo-tew-*r^{y}air*) *f* dressmaker

couvent (koo-*vahng*) *m* convent; nunnery

couvercle (koo-*vehrkl*) *m* top, lid, cover

couvert (koo-*vair*) *m* cutlery; cover charge; *adj* overcast

couverture (koo-vehr-*tewr*) *f* blanket; cover

*couvrir (koo-*vreer*) *v* cover

crabe (krahb) *m* crab

cracher (krah-*shay*) *v* *spit

crachin (krah-*shang*) *m* drizzle

craie (kray) *f* chalk

*craindre (krangdr) *v* fear, dread

crainte (krangt) *f* fear, dread

cramoisi (krah-mwah-*zee*) *adj* crimson

crampe (krahngp) *f* cramp

crampon (krahng-*pawng*) *m* clamp

cran (krahng) *m* guts

crâne (kraan) *m* skull

crapaud (krah-*poa*) *m* toad

craquement (krahk-*mahng*) *m* crack

craquer (krah-*kay*) *v* crack

cratère (krah-*tair*) *m* crater

cravate (krah-*vaht*) *f* necktie, tie

crawl (kroal) *m* crawl

crayon (kreh-^{y}*awng*) *m* pencil; ~ **à bille** Biro; ~ **pour les yeux** eyebrow pencil

création (kray-ah-s^y*awng*) *f* creation

créature (kray-ah-*tewr*) *f* creature

crèche (krehsh) *f* nursery

crédit (kray-*dee*) *m* credit

créditer (kray-dee-*tay*) v credit
créditeur (kray-dee-*tūrr*) m creditor
crédule (kray-*dewl*) adj credulous
créer (kray-*ay*) v create; design
crème (krehm) f cream; adj cream; ~ à
  raser shaving cream; ~ **capillaire** hair
  cream; ~ **de beauté** face cream; skin
  cream; ~ **de nuit** night cream; ~
  fraîche crème fraîche; ~ **glacée** ice
  cream; ~ **hydratante** moisturizing
  cream
crémeux (kray-*mur*) adj creamy
crêpe (krehp) f pancake
crépi (kray-*pee*) m roughcast
crépuscule (kray-pew-*skewl*) m dusk,
  twilight
cresson (kreh-*sawng*) m watercress
creuser (krur-*zay*) v *dig
creux (krur) adj hollow
crevaison (krer-vay-*zawng*) f
  puncture; flat
crevasse (krer-*vahss*) f crack, fissure
crever (krer-*vay*) v *burst; die; **crevé**
  punctured
crevette (krer-*veht*) f shrimp; prawn; ~
  rose prawn
cri (kree) m shout, yell, scream, cry;
  pousser des cris shriek
cric (kreek) m jack
cricket (kree-*keht*) m cricket
crier (kree-*ay*) v cry; shout, scream
crime (kreem) m crime
criminalité (kree-mee-nah-lee-*tay*) f
  criminality
criminel (kree-mee-*nehl*) m criminal;
  adj criminal
crique (kreek) f inlet, creek
crise (kreez) f crisis; ~ **cardiaque** heart
  attack
cristal (kree-*stahl*) m crystal; **en** ~
  crystal
critique (kree-*teek*) f criticism; review;
  m/f critic; adj critical
critiquer (kree-tee-*kay*) v criticize

crochet (kro-*shay*) m hook; *faire du ~
  crochet
crocodile (kro-ko-*deel*) m crocodile
*croire (krwaar) v believe; guess
croisement (krwahz-*mahng*) m
  crossing
croisière (krwah-z[y]*air*) f cruise
croissance (krwah-sah*ngss*) f growth
*croître (krwaatr) v increase
croix (krwah) f cross
croque-monsieur (krok-mer-s[y]*ur*) m
  toasted ham and cheese sandwich
croustillant (kroo-stee-[y]*ahng*) adj
  crisp
croûte (kroot) f crust
croyable (krwah-[y]*aabl*) adj credible
croyance (krwah-[y]*ahngss*) f belief
cru (krew) adj raw
cruche (krewsh) f pitcher; jug
crucifier (krew-see-f[y]*ay*) v crucify
crucifix (krew-see-*fee*) m crucifix
crucifixion (krew-see-fee-ks[y]*awng*) f
  crucifixion
crudités (krew-dee-*tay*) fpl crudités
cruel (krew-*ehl*) adj cruel; harsh
crustacé (krew-stah-*say*) m shellfish
Cuba (kew-*bah*) m Cuba
cubain (kew-*bang*) adj Cuban
cube (kewb) m cube
*cueillir (kur-[y]*eer*) v pick
cuillère (kwee-[y]*air*) f spoon;
  tablespoon; ~ **à thé** teaspoon
cuillerée (kwee-[y]er-*ray*) f spoonful
cuir (kweer) m leather; **en** ~ leather
*cuire (kweer) v cook; ~ **au four** bake
cuisine (kwee-*zeen*) f kitchen
cuisinier (kwee-zee-n[y]*ay*) m cook
cuisinière (kwee-zee-n[y]*air*) f cooker;
  stove; ~ **à gaz** gas cooker
cuisse (kweess) f thigh
cuit (kwee) adj cooked
cuivre (kweevr) m brass, copper
cul-de-sac (kewd-*sahk*) m cul-de-sac
culotte (kew-*lot*) f panties pl; **culottes**

courtes short trousers *pl*

culpabilité (kewl-pah-bee-lee-*tay*) *f* guilt

culte (kewlt) *m* worship

cultiver (kewl-tee-*vay*) *v* cultivate; *grow, raise; **cultivé** cultured

culture (kewl-*tewr*) *f* culture

cupide (kew-*peed*) *adj* greedy

cupidité (kew-pee-dee-*tay*) *f* greed

cure (kewr) *f* cure

cure-dent (kewr-*dahng*) *m* toothpick

cure-pipe (kewr-*peep*) *m* pipe cleaner

curieux (kew-r^y*ur*) *adj* inquisitive, curious

curiosité (kew-r^{y}o-zee-*tay*) *f* curiosity; sight

curry (kur-*ree*) *m* curry

cycle (seekl) *m* cycle

cycliste (see-*kleest*) *m* cyclist

cygne (seeñ) *m* swan

cylindre (see-*langdr*) *m* cylinder; **tête de ~** cylinder head

cystite (see-*steet*) *f* cystitis

D

dactylographier (dahk-tee-loa-grah-f^y*ay*) *v* type

daltonien (dahl-to-n^y*ang*) *adj* colo(u)r-blind

dame (dahm) *f* lady

damier (dah-m^y*ay*) *m* check; **à damiers** chequered

Danemark (dahn-*mahrk*) *m* Denmark

danger (dahng-*zhay*) *m* risk, danger

dangereux (dahng-*zhrur*) *adj* dangerous; risky

danois (dah-*nwah*) *adj* Danish

dans (dahng) *prep* into, inside, in, within

danse (dahngss) *f* dance; **~ folklorique** folk dance

danser (dahng-*say*) *v* dance

date (daht) *f* date

datte (daht) *f* date

davantage (dah-vahng-*taazh*) *adv* more

de (der) *prep* of; out of, from, off; about; with

dé (day) *m* thimble

déballer (day-bah-*lay*) *v* unwrap, unpack

débarquer (day-bahr-*kay*) *v* disembark, land

débarrasser (day-bah-rah-*say*) *v*: **se ~ de** *get rid of

débat (day-*bah*) *m* debate; discussion

*débattre (day-*bahtr*) *v* discuss

débit (day-*bee*) *m* debit

déboucher (day-boo-*shay*) *v* uncork

debout (der-*boo*) *adv* standing up, up

déboutonner (day-boo-to-*nay*) *v* unbutton

débrancher (day-brahng-*shay*) *v* disconnect

débrouiller (day-broo-^{y}*ay*): *v*: **se ~ avec** *make do with

début (day-*bew*) *m* start, beginning; **au ~** at first

débutant (day-bew-*tahng*) *m* learner, beginner

débuter (day-bew-*tay*) *v* *begin

décaféiné (day-kah-fay-ee-*nay*) *adj* decaffeinated

décalage (day-kah-*laazh*) *m* shifting; gap, discrepancy

décapsuleur (day-kah-psew-*lurr*) *m* bottle opener

décédé (day-say-*day*) *adj* dead, deceased

décembre (day-sah$\overline{ng}$br) December

décence (day-*sah$\overline{ng}$ss*) *f* decency

décent (day-*sah$\overline{ng}$*) *adj* decent

déception (day-seh-ps^y*aw$\overline{ng}$*) *f* disap**décerner** (day-sehr-*nay*) *v* award

*décevoir (day-*svwaar*) *v* disappoint

déchaînement (day-shehn-*mah$\overline{ng}$*) *m* outbreak

décharger (day-shahr-*zhay*) *v* discharge; unload

déchets (day-*shay*) *mpl* scraps, waste

déchirer (day-shee-*ray*) *v* rip, *tear

déchirure (day-shee-*r$\overline{ew}$r*) *f* tear

décider (day-see-*day*) *v* decide

décision (day-*see-z^{y}aw$\overline{ng}$*) *f* decision

déclaration (day-klah-rah-s^y*aw$\overline{ng}$*) *f* declaration, statement

déclarer (day-klah-*ray*) *v* declare, state

décliner (day-klee-*nay*) *v* slope

décollage (day-ko-*laazh*) *m* take-off

décoller (day-ko-*lay*) *v* *take off

décolorer (day-ko-lo-*ray*) *v* fade; bleach

déconcerter (day-kaw$\overline{ng}$-sehr-*tay*) *v* discomfort; confound

décontracté (day-kaw$\overline{ng}$-trahk-*tay*) *adj* easy-going

décoration (day-ko-rah-s^y*aw$\overline{ng}$*) *f* decoration

décorer (day-ko-*ray*) *v* decorate

découper (day-koo-*pay*) *v* carve; *cut up; *cut out

décourager (day-koo-rah-*zhay*) *v* discourage

découverte (day-koo-*vehrt*) *f* discovery

*découvrir (day-koo-*vreer*) *v* discover; uncover

*décrire (day-*kreer*) *v* describe

déçu (day-*sew*) *adj* disappointed

dédain (day-*da$\overline{ng}$*) *m* contempt; scorn

dedans (der-*dah$\overline{ng}$*) *adv* in; inside

dédier (day-d^y*ay*) *v* dedicate

dédommagement (day-do-mahzh-*mah$\overline{ng}$*) *m* indemnity

*déduire (day-*dweer*) *v* infer, deduce; deduct

défaillant (day-fah-^{y}*ah$\overline{ng}$*) *adj* faint

*défaire (day-*fair*) *v* *undo

défaite (day-*feht*) *f* defeat

défaut (day-*foa*) *m* fault

défavorable (day-fah-vo-*rahbl*) *adj* unfavo(u)rable

défectueux (day-fehk-*twur*) *adj* faulty, defective

défendre (day-*fah$\overline{ng}$dr*) *v* defend

défense (day-*fah$\overline{ng}$ss*) *f* defence, defense *Am*; ~ de doubler no overtaking; ~ no passing *Am*; ~ de fumer no smoking; ~ d'entrer no entry

défi (day-*fee*) *m* challenge

défiance (day-f^y*ah$\overline{ng}$ss*) *f* mistrust, distrust

déficience (day-fee-s^y*ah$\overline{ng}$ss*) *f* deficiency

déficit (day-fee-*seet*) *m* deficit

défier (day-f^y*ay*) *v* challenge; defy

définir (day-fee-*neer*) *v* determine, define

définition (day-fee-nee-s^y*aw$\overline{ng}$*) *f* definition

dégât (day-*gah*) *m* waste

dégel (day-*zhehl*) *m* thaw

dégeler (day-*zhlay*) *v* thaw

dégoût (day-*goo*) *m* disgust

dégoûtant (day-goo-tah$\overline{ng}$) *adj* disgusting, revolting

dégoûté (day-goo-*tay*) *adj* fed up with

degré (der-*gray*) *m* degree

déguisement (day-geez-*mah$\overline{ng}$*) *m* disguise

déguiser (day-gee-*zay*) *v*: se ~ disguise

dehors (der-*awr*) *adv* outside, outdoors; out; en ~ de out of

déjà (day-*zhah*) *adv* already

déjeuner (day-zhur-*nay*) *m* lunch; **petit ~** breakfast

delà: au ~ de (oa der-*lah* der) past, beyond

délabré (day-lah-*bray*) *adj* dilapidated

délai (day-*lay*) *m* time limit; **dans les plus brefs délais** as soon as possible

délégation (day-lay-gah-s^y*awng*) *f* delegation

délégué (day-lay-*gay*) *m*, **-e** *f* delegate

délibération (day-lee-bay-rah-s^y*awng*) *f* deliberation; discussion

délibérer (day-lee-bay-*ray*) *v* deliberate; **délibéré** deliberate

délicat (day-lee-*kah*) *adj* tender, delicate; gentle; critical

délicatesse (day-lee-kah-*tehss*) *f* delicacy

délice (day-*leess*) *m* delight

délicieux (day-lee-s^y*ur*) *adj* delightful, delicious, wonderful, lovely

délinquant (day-lang-*kahng*) *m*, **-e** *f* criminal

délivrance (day-lee-*vrahngss*) *f* delivery

délivrer (day-lee-*vray*) *v* deliver

demain (der-*mang*) *adv* tomorrow

demande (der-*mahngd*) *f* demand; application, request

demander (der-mahng-*day*) *v* ask, beg; **se ~** wonder

démangeaison (day-mahng-zhay-*zawng*) *f* itching

démanger (day-mahng-*zhay*) *v* itch

démarche (day-*mahrsh*) *f* walk, gait; step, move

déménagement (day-may-nahzh-*mahng*) *m* move

déménager (day-may-nah-*zhay*) *v* move

démence (day-*mahngss*) *f* madness

dément (day-*mahng*) *adj* mad

demeure (der-*murr*) *f* home

demeurer (der-mur-*ray*) *v* stay; live

demi (der-*mee*) *adj* half

demi-heure (der-mee-*urr*) *f* **une ~** half an hour

demi-pension (der-mee-pahng-s^y*awng*) *f* part board

démission (day-mee-s^y*awng*) *f* resignation

démissionner (day-mee-s^{y}o-*nay*) *v* resign

demi-tour (der-mee-*toor*) *m* half-turn, U-turn; **faire demi-tour** turn back

démocratie (day-mo-krah-*see*) *f* democracy

démocratique (day-mo-krah-*teek*) *adj* democratic

démodé (day-mo-*day*) *adj* out of date, old-fashioned

demoiselle (der-mwah-*zehl*) *f* miss

démolir (day-mo-*leer*) *v* demolish

démolition (day-mo-lee-s^y*awng*) *f* demolition

démonstration (day-mawng-strah-s^y*awng*) *f* demonstration

démontrer (day-mawng-*tray*) *v* *show, demonstrate, prove

dénier (day-n^y*ay*) *v* deny

dénomination (day-no-mee-nah-s^y*awng*) *f* denomination

dénouer (day-*nway*) *v* untie

dense (dahngss) *adj* dense

dent (dahng) *f* tooth

dentelle (dahng-*tehl*) *f* lace

dentier (dahng-t^y*ay*) *m* false teeth, denture

dentifrice (dahng-teh-*freess*) *m* toothpaste

dentiste (dahng-*teest*) *m/f* dentist

dénudé (day-new-*day*) *adj* naked

dénutrition (day-new-tree-s^y*awng*) *f* malnutrition

déodorant (day-o-do-*rahng*) *m* deodorant

départ (day-*paar*) *m* departure

département (day-pahr-ter-*mahng*) *m* division, department

dépasser (day-pah-*say*) *v* *overtake; pass

dépêcher (day-pay-*shay*): **se ~** hurry

dépendant (day-pahng-*dahng*) *adj* dependent

dépendre de (day-*pahng*dr) depend on

dépense (day-*pahng*ss) *f* expense, expenditure

dépenser (day-pahng-*say*) *v* *spend

dépit: en ~ de (ahng day-*pee* der) in spite of

déplacement (day-plah-*smahng*) *m* moving

déplacer (day-plah-*say*) *v* move

*déplaire (day-*plair*) *v* displease

déplaisant (day-play-*zahng*) *adj* unpleasant

déplier (day-plee-*ay*) *v* unfold

déployer (day-plwah-*ay*) *v* expand

déposer (day-poa-*zay*) *v* deposit

dépôt (day-*poa*) *m* deposit; warehouse, depot

dépression (day-preh-*s*^{y}*awng*) *f* depression

déprimer (day-pree-*may*) *v* depress; **déprimé** down; blue; low

depuis (der-*pwee*) *prep* since; *adv* since; **~ que** since

député (day-pew-*tay*) *m/f* deputy; Member of Parliament

déraisonnable (day-ray-zo-*nahbl*) *adj* unreasonable

dérangement (day-rahngzh-*mahng*) *m* trouble; disturbance; **en ~** broken, out of order

déranger (day-rahng-*zhay*) *v* disturb, upset, trouble

déraper (day-rah-*pay*) *v* slip, skid

dermatologue (dehr-mah-to-*log*) *m/f* dermatologist

dernier (dehr-*n*^{y}*ay*) *adj* last; past

dernièrement (dehr-n^{y}ehr-*mahng*) *adv* lately

derrière (deh-*r*^{y}*air*) *prep* after, behind; *m* bottom

dès que (day ker) as soon as

désaccord: *être en ~ (aitr ahng day-zah-*kawr*) disagree

désagréable (day-zah-gray-*ahbl*) *adj* nasty, disagreeable, unpleasant, unkind

désagrément (day-zah-gray-*mahng*) *m* inconvenience

*désapprendre (day-zah-*prahng*dr) *v* unlearn

désapprouver (day-zah-proo-*vay*) *v* disapprove

désastre (day-*zahstr*) *m* disaster

désastreux (day-zah-*strur*) *adj* disastrous

désavantage (day-zah-vahng-*taazh*) *m* disadvantage

descendance (day-sahng-*dahng*ss) *f* origin

descendant (day-sahng-*dahng*) *m*, **-e** *f* descendant

descendre (day-*sahng*dr) *v* descend; *get off

descente (day-*sahng*t) *f* descent

description (day-skree-*ps*^{y}*awng*) *f* description

désenchanter (day-zahng-shahng-*tay*) *v* disillusion

désert (day-*zair*) *m* desert; *adj* desert

déserter (day-zehr-*tay*) *v* desert

désespérer (day-zeh-spay-*ray*) *v* despair; **désespéré** desperate; hopeless

désespoir (day-zeh-*spwaar*) *m* despair

déshabiller (day-zah-bee-*y*^{y}*ay*) *v*: **se ~** undress

déshonneur (day-zo-*nurr*) *m* disgrace, shame

désigner (day-zee-*ñay*) *v* designate;

appoint

désinfectant (day-zang-fehk-*tahng*) *m* disinfectant

désinfecter (day-zang-fehk-*tay*) *v* disinfect

désintéressé (day-zang-tay-ray-*say*) *adj* unselfish

désir (day-*zeer*) *m* desire, wish

désirable (day-zee-*rahbl*) *adj* desirable

désirer (day-zee-*ray*) *v* want, desire, wish, long for

désireux (day-zee-*rur*) *adj* eager, anxious

désobligeant (day-zo-blee-*zhahng*) *adj* disagreeable

désodorisant (day-zo-do-ree-*zahng*) *m* deodorant

désoler (day-zo-*lay*) *v* grieve; **désolé** sorry

désordonné (day-zor-do-*nay*) *adj* disorderly, untidy

désordre (day-*zordr*) *m* disorder, mess

désormais (day-zawr-*may*) *adv* from now on, henceforth

désosser (day-zo-*say*) *v* bone

dessein (day-*sang*) *m* design

desserrer (day-say-*ray*) *v* loosen

dessert (day-*sair*) *m* dessert, sweet

dessin (day-*sang*) *m* sketch, drawing; pattern; **dessins animés** cartoon

dessiner (day-see-*nay*) *v* sketch, *draw

dessous (der-*soo*) *adv* underneath; **en ~** below; **en ~ de** beneath

dessus (der-*sew*) *m* top; **au-dessus de** on top of; **sens ~ dessous** upside-down

destin (day-*stang*) *m* destiny; fate

destinataire (day-stee-nah-*tair*) *m* addressee

destination (day-stee-nah-*s*ʸ*awng*) *f* destination

destiner (day-stee-*nay*) *v* destine

destruction (day-strewk-*s*ʸ*awng*) *f* destruction

détachant (day-tah-*shahng*) *m* cleaning fluid, stain remover

détacher (day-tah-*shay*) *v* unfasten, detach

détail (day-*tigh*) *m* detail; **commerce de ~** retail trade

détaillant (day-tah-ʸ*ahng*) *m*, **-e** *f* retailer

détaillé (day-tah-ʸ*ay*) *adj* detailed

détailler (day-tah-ʸ*ay*) *v* retail

détecter (day-tehk-*tay*) *v* detect

détective (day-tehk-*teev*) *m* detective

***déteindre** (day-*tangdr*) *v* fade

détendre (day-*tahngdr*) *v*: **se ~** relax

détente (day-*tahngt*) *f* relaxation

détention (day-tahng-*s*ʸ*awng*) *f* detention

détenu (dayt-*new*) *m* prisoner

détergent (day-tehr-*zhahng*) *m* detergent

déterminer (day-tehr-mee-*nay*) *v* determine, define; **déterminé** *adj* definite; resolute

détester (day-teh-*stay*) *v* dislike, hate

détour (day-*tōōr*) *m* detour

détourner (day-toor-*nay*) *v* divert; hijack

détresse (day-*trehss*) *f* distress; misery

détritus (day-tree-*tewss*) *m* litter, garbage, rubbish

***détruire** (day-*trweer*) *v* destroy, wreck

dette (deht) *f* debt

deuil (dur^(ee)) *m* mourning

deux (dur) *num* two; **les ~** either, both

deuxième (dur-z^ʸ*ehm*) *num* second

deux-pièces (dur-p^ʸ*ehss*) *m* two-piece

dévaluation (day-vah-lwah-*s*ʸ*awng*) *f* devaluation

dévaluer (day-vah-*lway*) *v* devalue

devant (der-*vahng*) *prep* in front of, ahead of, before

dévaster (day-vah-*stay*) *v* destroy

développement (day-vlop-*mahng*) *m* development

développer (day-vlo-*pay*) *v* develop

*devenir (der-*vneer*) *v* *become, *go, *get

déviation (day-v*y*ah-s*y*-*awng*) *f* diversion, detour

dévier (day-v*y*ay) *v* deviate

deviner (der-vee-*nay*) *v* guess

devise (der-*veez*) *f* slogan, motto

dévisser (day-vee-*say*) *v* unscrew

devoir (der-*vwaar*) *m* duty

*devoir (der-*vwaar*) *v* *be obliged to, *be bound to, *have to; need to, *should, *ought to, *shall; owe

dévorer (day-vo-*ray*) *v* devour

dévouement (day-voo-*mahng*) *m* devotion

diabète (d*y*ah-*beht*) *m* diabetes

diabétique (d*y*ah-bay-*teek*) *m/f* diabetic

diable (d*y*aabl) *m* devil

diagnostic (d*y*ahg-no-*steek*) *m* diagnosis

diagnostiquer (d*y*ahg-no-stee-*kay*) *v* diagnose

diagonale (d*y*ah-go-*nahl*) *f* diagonal; *adj* diagonal

diagramme (d*y*ah-*grahm*) *m* graph, diagram

dialecte (d*y*ah-*lehkt*) *m* dialect

diamant (d*y*ah-*mahng*) *m* diamond

diapositive (d*y*ah-po-zee-*teev*) *f* slide

diarrhée (d*y*ah-*ray*) *f* diarrh(o)ea

dictée (deek-*tay*) *f* dictation

dicter (deek-*tay*) *v* dictate

dictionnaire (deek-s*y*o-*nair*) *m* dictionary

diesel (d*y*ay-*zehl*) *m* diesel

dieu (d*y*ur) *m* god

différence (dee-fay-*rahngss*) *f* difference, contrast

différent (dee-fay-*rahng*) *adj* different

différer (dee-fay-*ray*) *v* delay; vary, differ

difficile (dee-fee-*seel*) *adj* difficult, hard

difficulté (dee-fee-kewl-*tay*) *f* difficulty

difforme (dee-*form*) *adj* deformed

digérer (dee-zhay-*ray*) *v* digest

digestible (dee-zheh-*steebl*) *adj* digestible

digestif (dee-zheh-*steef*) *adj, m* digestive

digestion (dee-zheh-st*y*-*awng*) *f* digestion

digne (deeñ) *adj* dignified; ~ **de** worthy of

digue (deeg) *f* dike, dam

diluer (dee-*lway*) *v* dissolve, dilute

dimanche (dee-*mahngsh*) *m* Sunday

dimension (dee-mahng-s*y*-*awng*) *f* size, extent

diminuer (dee-mee-*nway*) *v* decrease, lessen, reduce

diminution (dee-mee-new-s*y*-*awng*) *f* decrease

dinde (dangd) *f* turkey

dîner (dee-*nay*) *v* dine, *have dinner; *m* dinner

diphtérie (deef-tay-*ree*) *f* diphtheria

diplomate (dee-plo-*maht*) *m* diplomat

diplôme (dee-*ploam*) *m* certificate, diploma

*dire (deer) *v* *tell, *say

direct (dee-*rehkt*) *adj* direct

directement (dee-rehk-ter-*mahng*) *adv* straight away, straight

directeur (dee-rehk-*turr*) *m* manager, director; ~ **d'école** headmaster, head teacher

direction (dee-rehk-s*y*-*awng*) *f* management, direction, leadership; way; **indicateur de** ~ indicator, blinker *Am*

directive (dee-rehk-*teev*) *f* directive

directrice (dee-rehk-*trees*) *f* director; ~

d'école headmistress, head teacher

dirigeant (dee-ree-*zhahng*) m, **-e** f leader, ruler

diriger (dee-ree-*zhay*) v direct; head, conduct, *lead; manage

discerner (dee-sehr-*nay*) v distinguish

discipline (dee-see-*pleen*) f discipline

discours (dee-*skoor*) m speech

discret (dee-*skray*) adj (f discrète) discreet, reserved; unobtrusive

discussion (dee-skew-*s^yawng*) f discussion, argument, deliberation; dispute

discuter (dee-skew-*tay*) v discuss, argue, deliberate

*disjoindre (deess-*zhwangdr*) v disconnect

disloqué (dee-slo-*kay*) adj dislocated

*disparaître (dee-spah-*raitr*) v vanish, disappear

disparu (dee-spah-*rew*) adj lost; m missing person

dispensaire (dee-spahng-*sair*) m health center Am, health centre

dispenser (dee-spahng-*say*) v exempt; **~ de** discharge of

disperser (dee-spehr-*say*) v scatter

disponible (dee-spo-*neebl*) adj available; obtainable; spare

disposé (dee-spoa-*zay*) adj inclined, willing

disposer de (dee-spoa-*zay*) dispose of

dispositif (dee-spoa-zee-*teef*) m apparatus

disposition (dee-spoa-zee-*s^yawng*) f disposal

dispute (dee-*spewt*) f argument

disputer (dee-spew-*tay*) v argue; **se ~** dispute, quarrel

disque (deesk) m disc; record

dissertation (dee-sehr-tah-*s^yawng*) f essay

dissimuler (dee-see-mew-*lay*) v *hide, conceal

*dissoudre (dee-*soodr*) v dissolve; **se ~** dissolve

dissuader (dee-swah-*day*) v dissuade from

distance (dee-*stahngss*) f way, distance, space

distinct (dee-*stang*) adj distinct, separate

distinction (dee-stangk-*s^yawng*) f distinction, difference

distinguer (dee-stang-*gay*) v distinguish

distraction (dee-strahk-*s^yawng*) f diversion; inadvertence

distrait (dee-*stray*) adj absent-minded

distribuer (dee-stree-*bway*) v distribute, *deal

distributeur (dee-stree-bew-*turr*) m distributor; **~ de billets** ticket machine; **~ d'essence** fuel pump Am; **~ de timbres** stamp machine; **~ automatique** cash dispenser, ATM

distribution (dee-stree-bew-*s^yawng*) f distribution

district (dee-*stree*) m district

divers (dee-*vair*) adj various, several; miscellaneous

diversion (dee-vehr-*s^yawng*) f diversion

divertir (dee-vehr-*teer*) v entertain, amuse

divertissant (dee-vehr-tee-*sahng*) adj entertaining

divertissement (dee-vehr-tee-*smahng*) m pleasure, fun, entertainment, amusement

divin (dee-*vang*) adj divine

diviser (dee-vee-*zay*) v divide; **~ en deux** halve

division (dee-vee-*z^yawng*) f division; department

divorce (dee-*vors*) m divorce

divorcer (dee-vor-*say*) v divorce

dix (deess) num ten

dix-huit (dee-*zweet*) *num* eighteen

dix-huitième (dee-zwee-*t*^y*ehm*) *num* eighteenth

dixième (dee-*z*^y*ehm*) *num* tenth

dix-neuf (deez-*nurf*) *num* nineteen

dix-neuvième (deez-nur-*v*^y*ehm*) *num* nineteenth

dix-sept (dee-*seht*) *num* seventeen

dix-septième (dee-seh-*t*^y*ehm*) *num* seventeenth

dock (dok) *m* dock

docteur (dok-*tūr*) *m* doctor

document (do-kew-*mahng*) *m* document, certificate

doigt (dwah) *m* finger

domaine (do-*mehn*) *m* field

dôme (dōam) *m* dome

domestique (do-meh-*steek*) *adj* domestic; *m/f* domestic, servant

domestiqué (do-meh-stee-*kay*) *adj* tame

domicile (do-mee-*seel*) *m* domicile

domicilié (do-mee-see-*l*^y*ay*) *adj* resident

domination (do-mee-nah-*s*^y*awng*) *f* domination

dominer (do-mee-*nay*) *v* dominate; prevail; **dominant** leading

dommage (do-*maazh*) *m* mischief, damage; **dommage!** what a pity!

don (dawng) *m* faculty, talent; donation, gift

donateur (do-nah-*tūr*) *m*, **-trice** *f* donor

donation (do-nah-*s*^y*awng*) *f* donation

donc (dawngk) *conj* therefore; so

données (do-*nay*) *fpl* data *pl*

donner (do-*nay*) *v* *give; donate; **étant donné** que given that

dont (dawng) *pron* of which; of whom

doré (do-*ray*) *adj* gilt

***dormir** (dor-*meer*) *v* *sleep; **~ trop longtemps** *oversleep

dortoir (dor-*twaar*) *m* dormitory

dos (doa) *m* back

dose (dōaz) *f* dose

dossier (do-*s*^y*ay*) *m* file, record

douane (dwahn) *f* Customs *pl*; **droit de ~** Customs duty

douanier (dwah-*n*^y*ay*) *m* Customs officer

double (dōobl) *adj* double

doubler (doo-*blay*) *v* pass *Am*

doublure (doo-*blēwr*) *f* lining

doucement (doos-*mahng*) *adv* gently; softly; smoothly; carefully

douceurs (doo-*sūr*) *fpl* sweets

douche (doosh) *f* shower

doué (doo-*ay*) *adj* talented, gifted

douleur (doo-*lūr*) *f* ache, pain; sorrow, grief; **sans ~** painless; **douleurs** labo(u)r

douloureux (doo-loo-*rur*) *adj* painful; distressing

doute (doot) *m* doubt; ***mettre en ~** query; **sans ~** doubtless, probably

douter (doo-*tay*) *v* doubt; **~ de** doubt

douteux (doo-*tur*) *adj* doubtful; unreliable

douve (dōov) *f* moat

doux (doo) *adj* (f douce) mild; smooth, gentle

douzaine (doo-*zehn*) *f* dozen

douze (dōoz) *num* twelve

douzième (doo-*z*^y*ehm*) *num* twelfth

dragon (drah-*gawng*) *m* dragon

drainer (dray-*nay*) *v* drain

dramatique (drah-mah-*teek*) *adj* dramatic

dramaturge (drah-mah-*tewrzh*) *m* dramatist; playwright

drame (drahm) *m* drama

drap (drah) *m* sheet

drapeau (drah-*poa*) *m* flag

dresser (dray-*say*) *v* *draw up; train

drogue (drog) *f* drug

droguerie (dro-*gree*) *f* hardware shop; hardware store *Am*

droit (drwah) *m* right, law, justice; *adj* right, straight; erect, upright; ~ **administratif** administrative law; ~ **civil** civil law; ~ **commercial** commercial law; ~ **de douane** Customs duty; ~ **de stationnement** parking fee; ~ **de vote** right to vote; ~ **d'importation** duty; ~ **pénal** criminal law; **droits** duties *pl*; **tout** ~ straight ahead

droite: de ~ (der drwaht) right-hand

drôle (drōal) *adj* humorous, funny, queer

dû (dew) *adj* (f due; pl dus, dues) due

duc (dewk) *m* duke

duchesse (dew-*shehss*) *f* duchess

dune (dewn) *f* dune

dupe (dewp) *f* victim

duper (dew-*pay*) *v* cheat

dur (dēwr) *adj* hard

durable (dew-*rahbl*) *adj* permanent, lasting

durant (dew-*rahng*) *prep* during

durée (dew-*ray*) *f* duration

durer (dew-*ray*) *v* continue, last

duvet (dew-*vay*) *m* down

dynamo (dee-nah-*moa*) *f* dynamo

E

eau (oa) *f* water; ~ **courante** running water; ~ **de mer** sea water; ~ **dentifrice** mouthwash; ~ **de Seltz** soda water; ~ **douce** fresh water; ~ **gazeuse** sparkling mineral water; ~ **glacée** iced water; ~ **minérale** mineral water; ~ **oxygénée** hydrogen peroxide; ~ **potable** drinking water

eau-de-vie (oa-der-*vee*) *f* brandy; spirits

eau-forte (oa-*fort*) *f* etching

ébène (ay-*behn*) *f* ebony

éblouissant (ay-bloo-ee-*sahng*) *adj* glaring

éblouissement (ay-bloo-ee-*smahng*) *m* glare

ébrécher (ay-bray-*shay*) *v* chip

écaille (ay-*kigh*) *f* scale

écarlate (ay-kahr-*laht*) *adj* scarlet

écarter (ay-kahr-*tay*) *v* *spread, part; remove; **écarté** out of the way

ecclésiastique (ay-klay-z^yah-*steek*) *m* clergyman

échafaudage (ay-shah-foa-*daazh*) *m* scaffolding

échange (ay-*shahngzh*) *m* exchange

échanger (ay-shahng-*zhay*) *v* exchange

échantillon (ay-shahng-tee-^y*awng*) *m* sample

échappement (ay-shahp-*mahng*) *m* exhaust

échapper (ay-shah-*pay*) *v* escape; **s'échapper** slip

écharde (ay-*shahrd*) *f* splinter

écharpe (ay-*shahrp*) *f* scarf

échec (ay-*shehk*) *m* failure; **échec!** check!; **échecs** chess

échelle (ay-*shehl*) *f* ladder; scale

échiquier (ay-shee-k^y*ay*) *m* checkerboard *Am*

écho (ay-*koa*) *m* echo

échoppe (ay-*shop*) *f* booth

échouer (ay-*shway*) *v* fail

éclabousser (ay-klah-boo-*say*) *v* splash

éclair (ay-*klair*) *m* flash; lightning

éclairage (ay-kleh-*raazh*) *m* lighting

éclaircir (ay-klehr-*seer*) *v* clarify

éclaircissement (ay-klehr-see-*smahng*) *m* explanation

éclairer (ay-klay-*ray*) *v* illuminate

éclat (ay-*klah*) *m* glow; glare; chip

éclatant (ay-klah-*tahng*) *adj* bright, gay

éclater (ay-klah-*tay*) *v* *burst

éclipse (ay-*kleeps*) *f* eclipse

éclisse (ay-*kleess*) *f* splint

écluse (ay-*klēwz*) *f* sluice, lock

écœurant (ay-kur-*rahng*) *adj* repellent

école (ay-*kol*) *f* school; ~ **maternelle** kindergarten; ~ **secondaire** secondary school; ***faire l'école buissonnière** play truant

écolier (ay-ko-*l^yay*) *m* schoolboy

écolière (ay-ko-*l^yair*) *f* schoolgirl

économe (ay-ko-*nom*) *adj* economical

économie (ay-ko-no-*mee*) *f* economy; **économies** savings *pl*

économique (ay-ko-no-*meek*) *adj* economic

économiser (ay-ko-no-mee-*zay*) *v* economize

économiste (ay-ko-no-*meest*) *m* economist

écorce (ay-*kors*) *f* bark

écossais (ay-ko-*say*) *adj* Scotch; Scottish

Ecosse (ay-*koss*) *f* Scotland

écouler (ay-koo-*lay*): **s'**~ flow

écouter (ay-koo-*tay*) *v* listen

écouteur (ay-koo-*tūrr*) *m* earpiece

écran (ay-*krahng*) *m* screen

écraser (ay-krah-*zay*) *v* mash; overwhelm; **s'écraser** crash

***écrire** (ay-*kreer*) *v* *write; **par écrit** in writing, written

écriture (ay-kree-*tēwr*) *f* handwriting

écrivain (ay-kree-*vang*) *m*, **-e** *f* writer

écrouler (ay-kroo-*lay*): **s'**~ collapse

Ecuadorien (ay-kwah-do-*r^yang*) *m* Ecuadorian

écume (ay-*kewm*) *f* froth, lather

écureuil (ay-kew-*rur^{ee}*) *m* squirrel

eczéma (ehg-zay-*mah*) *m* eczema

édification (ay-dee-fee-kah-*s^yawng*) *f* construction

édifice (ay-dee-*feess*) *m* construction

édifier (ay-dee-*f^yay*) *v* construct

éditeur (ay-dee-*tūrr*) *m* publisher

édition (ay-dee-*s^yawng*) *f* edition; ~ **du matin** morning edition

éditrice (ay-dee-*trees*) *f* publisher

édredon (ay-drer-*dawng*) *m* eiderdown

éducation (ehr-*tsee*-oong) *f* education

éduquer (ay-dew-*kay*) *v* educate

effacer (ay-fah-*say*) *v* wipe out

effectif (ay-fehk-*teef*) *adj* effective

effectivement (ay-fehk-teev-*mahng*) *adv* as a matter of fact

effectuer (ay-fehk-*tway*) *v* effect

effet (ay-*fay*) *m* result; consequence, effect; **en** ~ indeed

efficace (ay-fee-*kahss*) *adj* effective; efficient

effilocher (ay-fee-lo-*shay*): **s'**~ fray

effondrer (ay-fawng-*dray*): **s'**~ collapse

efforcer (ay-for-*say*): **s'**~ try hard, endeavour

effort (ay-*fawr*) *m* effort, strain

effrayé (ay-fray-*^yay*) *adj* frightened, afraid

effrayer (ay-fray-*^yay*) *v* frighten; scare

effronté (ay-frawng-*tay*) *adj* bold; impertinent

égal (ay-*gahl*) *adj* even, level, equal

également (ay-gahl-*mahng*) *adv* as well, likewise, equally, also

égaler (ay-gah-*lay*) *v* equal

égaliser (ay-gah-lee-*zay*) *v* level, equalize

égalité (ay-gah-lee-*tay*) *f* equality

égards (ay-*gaar*) *mpl* consideration

égarer (ay-gah-*ray*) *v* mislay

égayer (ay-gay-*^yay*) *v* cheer up

église (ay-*gleez*) f chapel, church

égocentrique (ay-go-sahng-*treek*) adj self-centred

égoïsme (ay-go-*eesm*) m selfishness, ego(t)ism

égoïste (ay-go-*eest*) adj ego(t)istic, selfish

égout (ay-*goo*) m drain, sewer

égratignure (ay-grah-tee-*ñewr*) f graze, scratch

Egypte (ay-*zheept*) f Egypt

égyptien (ay-zhee-ps*ʸ*ang) adj Egyptian

élaborer (ay-lah-bo-*ray*) v elaborate

élan (ay-*lahng*) m vigour; moose

élargir (ay-lahr-*zheer*) v widen

élasticité (ay-lah-stee-see-*tay*) f elasticity

élastique (ay-lah-*steek*) adj elastic; m elastic, rubber band

électeur (ay-lehk-*turr*) m, **-trice** f voter

élection (ay-lehk-s*ʸ*awng) f election

électricien (ay-lehk-tree-s*ʸ*ang) m electrician

électricité (ay-lehk-tree-see-*tay*) f electricity

électrique (ay-lehk-*treek*) adj electric

électronique (ay-lehk-tro-*neek*) adj electronic

élégance (ay-lay-*gahngss*) f elegance

élégant (ay-lay-*gahng*) adj smart, elegant

élément (ay-lay-*mahng*) m element

élémentaire (ay-lay-mahng-*tair*) adj primary

éléphant (ay-lay-*fahng*) m elephant

élevage (ehl-*vaazh*) m breeding

élévation (ay-lay-vah-s*ʸ*awng) f rise

élève (ay-*laiv*) m/f pupil, scholar

élever (ehl-*vay*) v *bring up, rear, raise; *breed

éliminer (ay-lee-mee-*nay*) v eliminate

*élire (ay-*leer*) v elect

elle (ehl) pron she

elle-même (ehl-*mehm*) pron herself

éloge (ay-*lozh*) m praise

éloigner (ay-lwah-*ñay*) v remove; **éloigné** distant, far-away, remote

élucider (ay-lew-see-*day*) v elucidate

émail (ay-*migh*) m (pl émaux) enamel

émaillé (ay-mah-*ʸay*) adj enamelled

émancipation (ay-mahng-see-pah-s*ʸ*awng) f emancipation

emballage (ahng-bah-*laazh*) m packing

emballer (ahng-bah-*lay*) v pack up, pack

embargo (ahng-bahr-*goa*) m embargo

embarquement (ahng-bahr-ker-*mahng*) m embarkation

embarquer (ahng-bahr-*kay*) v embark

embarras (ahng-bah-*rah*) m fuss

embarrassant (ahng-bah-rah-*sahng*) adj awkward, embarrassing; puzzling

embarrasser (ahng-bah-rah-*say*) v embarrass

embêtant (ahng-bay-*tahng*) adj annoying

emblème (ahng-*blehm*) m emblem

embouchure (ahng-boo-*shewr*) f mouth

embouteillage (ahng-boo-teh-*ʸaazh*) m traffic jam, jam

embrasser (ahng-brah-*say*) v kiss

embrayage (ahng-breh-*ʸaazh*) m clutch

embrouiller (ahng-broo-*ʸay*) v muddle

émeraude (aym-*road*) f emerald

émerveiller (ay-mehr-vay-*ʸay*): **s'~** marvel

émetteur (ay-meh-*turr*) m transmitter

*émettre (ay-*mehtr*) v utter; transmit; *broadcast

émeute (ay-*murt*) f riot

émigrant (ay-mee-*grahng*) m emigrant

émigration (ay-mee-grah-s*ʸ*awng) f emigration

émigrer (ay-mee-*gray*) v emigrate

éminent (ay-mee-*nahng*) *adj* outstanding

émission (ay-mee-*s*ʸ*awng*) *f* issue; transmission, broadcast

emmagasiner (ahng-mah-gah-zee-*nay*) *v* store

emmener (ahng-mer-*nay*) *v* *take along

émoi (ay-*mwah*) *m* emotion

émotion (ay-moa-*s*ʸ*awng*) *f* emotion

émoussé (ay-moo-*say*) *adj* dull, blunt

*émouvoir (ay-moo-*vwaar*) *v* move

empêcher (ahng-pay-*shay*) *v* prevent

empereur (ahng-*prurr*) *m* emperor

empiéter (ahng-pʸay-*tay*) *v* trespass

empire (ahng-*peer*) *m* empire

emploi (ahng-*plwah*) *m* use; job, employment; **solliciter un ~** apply

employé (ahng-plwah-ʸ*ay*) *m*, **-e** *f* employee; **~ de bureau** clerk

employer (ahng-plwah-ʸ*ay*) *v* use; employ

employeur (ahng-plwah-ʸ*urr*) *m*, **-euse** *f* employer

empoisonner (ahng-pwah-zo-*nay*) *v* poison

emporter (ahng-por-*tay*) *v* *take away

empreinte digitale (ahng-prangt dee-zhee-*tahl*) fingerprint

emprisonnement (ahng-pree-zon-*mahng*) *m* imprisonment

emprisonner (ahng-pree-zo-*nay*) *v* imprison

emprunt (ahng-*prurng*) *m* loan

emprunter (ahng-prurng-*tay*) *v* borrow

en (ahng) *prep* in; by; *pron* of it

encaisser (ahng-kay-*say*) *v* cash

enceinte (ahng-*sangt*) *adj* pregnant

encens (ahng-*sahng*) *m* incense

encercler (ahng-sehr-*klay*) *v* circle, encircle

enchanté (ahng-shahng-*tay*) *adj* enchanted; delightful; **~ de** delighted at, with

enchantement (ahng-shahngt-*mahng*) *m* spell

enchanter (ahng-shahng-*tay*) *v* delight; bewitch

enchanteur (ahng-shahng-*turr*) *adj* (f -teresse) glamorous

enclin (ahng-*klang*) *adj* inclined

encore (ahng-*kawr*) *adv* again; still; yet; **~ que** though; **~ un** another; **~ un peu** some more

encourager (ahng-koo-rah-*zhay*) *v* encourage

encre (ahngkr) *f* ink

encyclopédie (ahng-see-klo-pay-*dee*) *f* encyclop(a)edia

endive (ahng-*deev*) *f* chicory

endommager (ahng-do-mah-*zhay*) *v* damage

endormir (ahng-dor-*meer*) *v* send to sleep; numb; deaden; bore; lull

endormi (ahng-dor-*mee*) *adj* asleep

endosser (ahng-do-*say*) *v* endorse

endroit (ahng-*drwah*) *m* spot

endurer (ahng-dew-*ray*) *v* endure, sustain; *go through

énergie (ay-nehr-*zhee*) *f* energy; power; **~ nucléaire** nuclear energy

énergique (ay-nehr-*zheek*) *adj* energetic

énerver (ay-nehr-*vay*) *v* *get on someone's nerves; **s'énerver** *get excited

enfance (ahng-*fahngss*) *f* childhood

enfant (ahng-*fahng*) *m* child, kid

enfer (ahng-*fair*) *m* hell

enfermer (ahng-fehr-*may*) *v* lock up, *shut in

enfiler (ahng-fee-*lay*) *v* thread

enfin (ahng-*fang*) *adv* at last

enfler (ahng-*flay*) *v* *swell

enflure (ahng-*flewr*) *f* swelling

enfoncer (ahng-fawng-*say*) *v*: **s'~** *sink

engagement (ahng-gahzh-*mahng*) *m* engagement

engager (ahng-gah-*zhay*) v engage;
  s'engager engage
engourdi (ahng-goor-*dee*) adj numb
engrais (ahng-*gray*) m fertilizer
énigme (ay-*neegm*) f mystery, riddle,
  puzzle, enigma
enjeu (ahng-*zhur*) m stake
enlacement (ahng-lah-*smah*) m
  embrace
enlever (ahngl-*vay*) v remove; *take
  away
ennemi (ehn-*mee*) m, **-e** f enemy
ennui (ahng-*nwee*) m annoyance,
  trouble; nuisance
ennuyer (ahng-nwee-*y*ay) v annoy,
  bore
ennuyeux (ahng-nwee-*y*ur) adj
  annoying; dull, unpleasant, boring
énorme (ay-*norm*) adj tremendous,
  immense, huge, enormous
enquête (ahng-*keht*) f inquiry; enquiry
enquêter (ahng-kay-*tay*) v investigate,
  enquire
enragé (ahng-rah-*zhay*) adj mad
enregistrement (ahngr-zhee-strer-
  mahng) m recording
enregistrer (ahngr-zhee-*stray*) v book;
  record
enrhumer (ahng-rew-*may*): **s'~** catch a
  cold
enroué (ahng-roo-*ay*) adj hoarse
enrouler (ahng-roo-*lay*) v *wind
enseignement (ahng-sehn-*mahng*) m
  education; teaching
enseigner (ahng-say-*ñay*) v *teach
ensemble (ahng-*sahngbl*) adv
  together; m whole
ensoleillé (ahng-so-lay-*y*ay) adj sunny
ensorceler (ahng-sor-ser-*lay*) v
  bewitch
ensuite (ahng-*sweet*) adv then,
  afterwards
entailler (ahng-tah-*y*ay) v carve
entasser (ahng-tah-*say*) v pile

entendre (ahng-*tahngdr*) v *hear
entente (ahng-*tahngt*) f agreement
enterrement (ahng-tehr-*mahng*) m
  burial
enterrer (ahng-tay-*ray*) v bury
enthousiasme (ahng-too-z*y*ahsm) m
  enthusiasm
enthousiaste (ahng-too-z*y*ahst) adj
  enthusiastic
entier (ahng-t*y*ay) adj whole, complete,
  entire
entièrement (ahng-t*y*ehr-*mahng*) adv
  wholly, completely, entirely,
  altogether
entonnoir (ahng-to-*nwaar*) m funnel
entourer (ahng-too-*ray*) v encircle;
  surround
entracte (ahng-*trahkt*) m interval,
  intermission
entrailles (ahng-*trigh*) fpl entrails, guts
entrain (ahng-*trang*) m zest
entraînement (ahng-trehn-*mahng*) m
  training
entraîner (ahng-tray-*nay*) v drill
entraîneur (ahng-treh-*nürr*) m coach
entrave (ahng-*traav*) f impediment
entraver (ahng-trah-*vay*) v impede
entre (ahngtr) prep between, among,
  amid
entrée (ahng-*tray*) f way in, entry,
  entrance; appearance; **~ interdite** no
  admittance
entrepôt (ahng-trer-*poa*) m depository
***entreprendre** (ahng-trer-*prahngdr*) v
  *undertake
entrepreneur (ahng-trer-prer-*nürr*) m,
  -euse f contractor
entreprise (ahng-trer-*preez*) f
  enterprise; business, company,
  undertaking
entrer (ahng-*tray*) v enter, *go in
entre-temps (ahng-trer-*tahng*) adv
  meanwhile, in the meantime
***entretenir** (ahng-trer-*tneer*) v

maintain; support

entretien (ahng-trer-t*y*ang) m upkeep, maintenance; conversation

*****entrevoir** (ahng-trer-vwaar) v glimpse

entrevue (ahng-trer-vew) f interview

envahir (ahng-vah-eer) v invade

enveloppe (ahng-vlop) f envelope

envelopper (ahng-vlo-pay) v wrap

envers (ahng-vair) prep towards; **à l'envers** inside out

envie (ahng-vee) f longing, desire; envy; *****avoir ~ de** *feel like; fancy, desire

envier (ahng-v*y*ay) v grudge, envy

envieux (ahng-v*y*ur) adj envious

environ (ahng-vee-rawng) adv about

environnant (ahng-vee-ro-nahng) adj surrounding

environnement (ahng-vee-ron-mahng) m environment

environs (ahng-vee-rawng) mpl environment

envisager (ahng-vee-zah-zhay) v consider

envoyé (ahng-vwah-*y*ay) m envoy

*****envoyer** (ahng-vwah-*y*ay) v *send; dispatch

épais (ay-pay) adj (f ~se) thick

épaisseur (ay-peh-surr) f thickness

épaissir (ay-pay-seer) v thicken

épargner (ay-pahr-ñay) v save

épaule (ay-pool) f shoulder

épave (ay-paav) f wreck

épée (ay-pay) f sword

épeler (eh-play) v *spell

épice (ay-peess) f spice

épicé (ay-pee-say) adj spicy, spiced

épicerie (ay-pee-sree) f grocer's; **~ fine** delicatessen

épicier (ay-pee-s*y*ay) m, **-ière** f grocer

épidémie (ay-pee-day-mee) f epidemic

épier (ay-p*y*ay) v peep

épilepsie (ay-pee-leh-psee) f epilepsy

épinards (ay-pee-naar) mpl spinach

épine (ay-peen) f thorn; **~ dorsale** backbone, spine

épingle (ay-pangl) f pin; **~ à cheveux** hairpin; **~ de sûreté** safetypin

épingler (ay-pang-glay) v pin

épisode (ay-pee-zod) m episode

éplucher (ay-plew-shay) v peel; clean; examine closely, sift

éponge (ay-pawngzh) f sponge

époque (ay-pok) f period; **de l'époque** contemporary

épouse (ay-pooz) f wife

épouser (ay-poo-zay) v marry

épouvantable (ay-poo-vahng-tahbl) adj terrible

épouvante (ay-poo-vahngt) f horror

époux (ay-poo) m husband

épreuve (ay-prurv) f test, experiment; print

éprouver (ay-proo-vay) v experience; test

épuiser (ay-pwee-zay) v exhaust; use up; **épuisé** sold out

Equateur (ay-kwah-turr) m Ecuador

équateur (ay-kwah-turr) m equator

équilibre (ay-kee-leebr) m balance

équipage (ay-kee-paazh) m crew

équipe (ay-keep) f shift, team, gang; soccer team

équipement (ay-keep-mahng) m outfit, gear, equipment

équiper (ay-kee-pay) v equip

équitable (ay-kee-tahbl) adj right; reasonable

équitation (ay-kee-tah-s*y*awng) f riding

équivalent (ay-kee-vah-lahng) adj equivalent

équivoque (ay-kee-vok) adj ambiguous

érable (ay-rahbl) m maple

érafler (ay-rah-flay) v scratch

ériger (ay-ree-zhay) v erect

errer (ay-ray) v err; wander

erreur (eh-*rūrr*) *f* error; mistake

erroné (eh-ro-*nay*) *adj* mistaken

érudit (ay-rew-*dee*) *m* scholar

éruption (ay-rew-*ps*y*awñg*) *f* rash

escale (eh-*skahl*) *f* port of call; stop; call

escalier (eh-skah-*l*y*ay*) *m* staircase; stairs *pl*; ~ **de secours** fire escape; ~ **roulant** escalator

escalope (eh-skah-*lop*) *f* escalope

escargot (eh-skahr-*goa*) *m* snail

escarpé (eh-skahr-*pay*) *adj* steep

escorte (eh-*skort*) *f* escort

escorter (eh-skor-*tay*) *v* escort

escrime: *faire de l'escrime (fair der leh-*skreem*) fence

escroc (eh-*skroa*) *m* swindler

escroquer (eh-skro-*kay*) *v* swindle

escroquerie (eh-skro-*kree*) *f* swindle

espace (eh-*spahss*) *m* space; room

espacer (eh-spah-*say*) *v* space

Espagne (eh-*spahñ*) *f* Spain

espagnol (eh-spah-*ñol*) *adj* Spanish

espèce (eh-*spehss*) *f* species; breed

espérance (eh-spay-*rahñgss*) *f* expectation

espérer (eh-spay-*ray*) *v* hope

espièglerie (eh-sp*y*eh-gler-*ree*) *f* piece of mischief, prank

espion (eh-sp*y*awñg*) *m* spy

esplanade (eh-splah-*nahd*) *f* esplanade

espoir (eh-*spwaar*) *m* hope

esprit (eh-*spree*) *m* spirit; soul, mind; ghost

esquisse (eh-*skeess*) *f* sketch

esquisser (eh-skee-*say*) *v* sketch

essai (ay-*say*) *m* trial, essay; **à l'essai** on approval

essayer (ay-say-y*ay*) *v* try; attempt, test; try on

essence (ay-*sahñgss*) *f* essence; petrol, fuel; gasoline *Am*, gas *Am*

essentiel (ay-sahñg-s*y*ehl*) *adj* capital; essential

essentiellement (ay-sahñg-s*y*ehl-*mahñg*) *adv* essentially

essieu (ay-s*y*ur*) *m* axle

essor (ay-*sawr*) *m* rise

essuie-glace (ay-swee-*glahss*) *m* windscreen wiper, windshield wiper *Am*

essuyer (ay-swee-y*ay*) *v* wipe; dry

est (ehst) *m* east

estampe (eh-*stahñgp*) *f* print; engraving

estimation (eh-stee-mah-s*y*awñg*) *f* estimate

estime (eh-*steem*) *f* esteem; respect

estimer (eh-stee-*may*) *v* consider, esteem, reckon; value, estimate

estomac (eh-sto-*mah*) *m* stomach

estropié (eh-stro-p*y*ay*) *adj* crippled

estuaire (eh-*stwair*) *m* estuary

et (ay) *conj* and

étable (ay-*tahbl*) *f* stable

établir (ay-tah-*bleer*) *v* establish; found; **s'établir** settle down

étage (ay-*taazh*) *m* floor, stor(e)y; apartment *Am*

étagère (ay-tah-*zhair*) *f* shelf

étain (ay-*tañg*) *m* pewter, tin

étal (ay-*tahl*) *m* stall

étalage (ay-tah-*laazh*) *m* shop-window

étaler (ay-tah-*lay*) *v* display

étang (ay-*tahñg*) *m* pond

étape (ay-*tahp*) *f* stage

Etat (ay-*tah*) *m* state; **Etats-Unis** United States; the States

état (ay-*tah*) *m* state; condition; ~ **d'urgence** emergency

et cætera (eht-say-tay-*rah*) etcetera

été (ay-*tay*) *m* summer; **en plein** ~ in midsummer

*éteindre (ay-*tañgdr*) *v* *put out; switch off; extinguish

étendre (ay-*tahñgdr*) *v* expand, *spread, enlarge; extend

étendu (ay-tah$\overline{ng}$-*dew*) *adj* broad, extensive; comprehensive

éternel (ay-tehr-*nehl*) *adj* eternal

éternité (ay-tehr-nee-*tay*) *f* eternity

éternuer (ay-tehr-*nway*) *v* sneeze

Ethiopie (ay-t^{y}o-*pee*) *f* Ethiopia

éthiopien (ay-t^{y}o-p^{y}a$\overline{ng}$) *adj* Ethiopian

étincelle (ay-ta$\overline{ng}$-*sehl*) *f* spark

étiqueter (ay-teek-*tay*) *v* label

étiquette (ay-tee-*keht*) *f* tag, label

étoffes (ay-*tof*) *fpl* drapery

étoile (ay-*twahl*) *f* star

étole (ay-*tol*) *f* stole

étonnant (ay-to-*nah$\overline{ng}$*) *adj* astonishing

étonnement (ay-ton-*mah$\overline{ng}$*) *m* astonishment, wonder, amazement

étonner (ay-to-*nay*) *v* amaze; astonish

étouffant (ay-too-*fah$\overline{ng}$*) *adj* stifling

étouffer (ay-too-*fay*) *v* choke

étourdi (ay-toor-*dee*) *adj* dizzy, giddy

étourneau (ay-toor-*noa*) *m* starling

étrange (ay-*trah$\overline{ng}$zh*) *adj* strange; quaint, curious, queer

étranger (ay-trah$\overline{ng}$-*zhay*) *m*, **-ère** *f* foreigner, alien, stranger; *adj* foreign, alien; **à l'étranger** abroad

étrangler (ay-trah$\overline{ng}$-*glay*) *v* choke, strangle

être (aitr) *m* being; creature; **~ humain** human being

*être (aitr) *v* *be

*étreindre (ay-*tra$\overline{ng}$dr*) *v* hug, embrace

étreinte (ay-*tra$\overline{ng}$t*) *f* grip; hug

étroit (ay-*trwah*) *adj* narrow, tight

étude (ay-*tewd*) *f* study

étudiant (ay-tew-d^y*ah$\overline{ng}$*) *m* student

étudiante (ay-tew-d^y*ah$\overline{ng}$t*) *f* student

étudier (ay-tew-d^y*ay*) *v* study

étui (ay-*twee*) *m* case; **~ à cigarettes** cigarette case

Europe (ur-*rop*) *f* Europe

Européen (ur-ro-pay-*a$\overline{ng}$*) *m*, **-ne** *f* European

européen (ur-ro-pay-*a$\overline{ng}$*) *adj* European

eux (ur) *pron* them; **eux-mêmes** *pron* themselves

évacuer (ay-vah-*kway*) *v* evacuate, clear

évaluer (ay-vah-*lway*) *v* evaluate; appreciate, estimate

évangile (ay-vah$\overline{ng}$-*zheel*) *m* gospel

évanouir (ay-vah-*nweer*): **s'~** faint

évaporer (ay-vah-po-*ray*) *v* evaporate

évasion (ay-vah-z^y*aw$\overline{ng}$*) *f* escape

éveillé (ay-vay-^{y}*ay*) *adj* clever

éveiller (ay-vay-^{y}*ay*): **s'~** wake up

événement (ay-vehn-*mah$\overline{ng}$*) *m* event; occurrence

éventail (ay-vah$\overline{ng}$-*tigh*) *m* fan

éventuel (ay-vah$\overline{ng}$-*twehl*) *adj* possible, eventual

évêque (ay-*vehk*) *m* bishop

évidemment (ay-vee-dah-*mah$\overline{ng}$*) *adv* of course

évident (ay-vee-*dah$\overline{ng}$*) *adj* obvious, evident; self-evident

évier (ay-v^y*ay*) *m* sink

éviter (ay-vee-*tay*) *v* avoid

évolution (ay-vo-lew-s^y*aw$\overline{ng}$*) *f* evolution

évoquer (ay-vo-*kay*) *v* call to mind; evoke

exact (ehg-*zahkt*) *adj* just, precise, exact

exactement (ehg-zahk-ter-*mah$\overline{ng}$*) *adv* exactly

exactitude (ehg-zahk-tee-*tewd*) *f* correctness

exagérer (ehg-zah-zhay-*ray*) *v* exaggerate

examen (ehg-zah-*ma$\overline{ng}$*) *m* examination; checkup

examiner (ehg-zah-mee-*nay*) *v* examine

excéder (ehk-say-*day*) *v* exceed

excellent (ehk-seh-*lah$\overline{ng}$*) *adj* excellent

exceller (ehk-say-*lay*) *v* excel

excentrique (ehk-sahng-*treek*) *adj* eccentric

excepté (ehk-sehp-*tay*) *prep* except

exception (ehk-sehp-s^y*awng*) *f* exception

exceptionnel (ehk-sehp-s^{y}o-*nehl*) *adj* exceptional

excès (ehk-*say*) *m* excess; **~ de vitesse** speeding

excessif (ehk-say-*seef*) *adj* excessive

excitation (ehk-see-tah-s^y*awng*) *f* excitement

exciter (ehk-see-*tay*) *v* excite

exclamation (ehk-sklah-mah-s^y*awng*) *f* exclamation

exclamer (ehk-sklah-*may*) *v* exclaim

***exclure** (ehk-*sklewr*) *v* exclude

exclusif (ehk-sklew-*zeef*) *adj* exclusive

exclusivement (ehk-sklew-zeev-*mahng*) *adv* solely, exclusively

excursion (ehk-skewr-s^y*awng*) *f* trip, excursion; day trip; tour

excuse (ehk-*skewz*) *f* excuse, apology

excuser (ehk-skew-*zay*) *v* excuse; **excusez-moi!** sorry!; **s'excuser** apologize

exécuter (ehg-zay-kew-*tay*) *v* execute

exécutif (ehg-zay-kew-*teef*) *m* executive; *adj* executive

exécution (ehg-zay-kew-s^y*awng*) *f* execution

exemplaire (ehg-zahng-*plair*) *m* copy

exemple (ehg-*zahngpl*) *m* instance, example; **par ~** for instance, for example

exempt (ehg-*zahng*) *adj* exempt; **~ de droits** duty-free; **~ d'impôts** tax-free

exempter (ehg-zahng-*tay*) *v* exempt

exemption (ehg-zahng-ps^y*awng*) *f* exemption

exercer (ehg-zehr-*say*) *v* exercise; **s'exercer** practise

exercice (ehg-zehr-*seess*) *m* exercise

exhiber (ehg-zee-*bay*) *v* exhibit

exhibition (ehg-zee-bee-s^y*awng*) *f* exhibition

exhorter (ehg-zor-*tay*) *v* urge

exigeant (ehg-zee-*zhahng*) *adj* particular

exigence (ehg-zee-*zhahngss*) *f* requirement

exiger (ehg-zee-*zhay*) *v* demand, require

exile (ehg-*zeel*) *m* exile

exilé (ehg-zee-*lay*) *m* exile

existence (ehg-zee-*stahngss*) *f* existence

exister (ehg-zee-*stay*) *v* exist

exotique (ehg-zo-*teek*) *adj* exotic

expédier (ehk-spay-d^y*ay*) *v* dispatch, despatch, *send off, *send; ship

expéditeur (ehk-spay-dee-*turr*) *m* sender; shipper; forwarding agent

expédition (ehk-spay-dee-s^y*awng*) *f* expedition; consignment

expeditrice (ehk-spay-dee-*trees*) *f* sender

expérience (ehk-spay-r^y*ahngss*) *f* experience; experiment; ***faire l'expérience de** experience

expérimenter (ehk-spay-ree-mahng-*tay*) *v* test; experiment with; **expérimenté** experienced

expert (ehk-*spair*) *adj* skilled; *m* expert

expirer (ehk-spee-*ray*) *v* breathe out, expire

explicable (ehk-splee-*kahbl*) *adj* explicable, explainable

explication (ehk-splee-kah-s^y*awng*) *f* explanation

explicite (ehk-splee-*seet*) *adj* explicit

expliquer (ehk-splee-*kay*) *v* explain

exploitation (ehk-splwah-tah-s^y*awng*) *f* exploitation; concern; **~ minière** mining development

exploiter (ehk-splwah-*tay*) *v* exploit

explorer (ehk-splo-*ray*) *v* explore

exploser (ehk-sploa-*zay*) *v* explode

explosif (ehk-sploa-*zeef*) *m* explosive; *adj* explosive

explosion (ehk-sploa-z^y*awng*) *f* explosion, blast

exportation (ehk-spor-tah-s^y*awng*) *f* exports *pl*, exportation, export

exporter (ehk-spor-*tay*) *v* export

exposer (ehk-spoa-*zay*) *v* exhibit, *show

exposition (ehk-spoa-zee-s^y*awng*) *f* display, exposition, exhibition, show; exposure; ~ **d'art** art exhibition

exprès[1] (ehk-*spray*) *adv* on purpose

exprès[2] (ehk-*sprehss*) *adj* express; special delivery

expression (ehk-spreh-s^y*awng*) *f* expression

exprimer (ehk-spree-*may*) *v* express

expulser (ehk-spewl-*say*) *v* expel

exquis (ehk-*skee*) *adj* delicious; exquisite; select

extase (ehk-*staaz*) *m* ecstasy

exténuer (ehk-stay-*nway*) *v* exhaust

extérieur (ehk-stay-r^y*ur*) *m* exterior, outside; *adj* external, exterior; **vers l'extérieur** outwards

externe (ehk-*stehrn*) *adj* outward

extincteur (ehk-sta$\overline{ng}$k-*tur*) *m* fire extinguisher

extorquer (ehk-stor-*kay*) *v* extort

extorsion (ehk-stor-s^y*awng*) *f* extortion

extrader (ehk-strah-*day*) *v* extradite

***extraire** (ehk-*strair*) *v* extract

extrait (ehk-*stray*) *m* excerpt

extraordinaire (ehk-strah-or-dee-*nair*) *adj* extraordinary, exceptional

extravagant (ehk-strah-vah-gah$\overline{ng}$) *adj* extravagant

extrême (ehk-*strehm*) *adj* extreme, utmost; *m* extreme

exubérant (ehg-zew-bay-rah$\overline{ng}$) *adj* exuberant

F

fable (fahbl) *f* fable

fabricant (fah-bree-*kah$\overline{ng}$*) *m* manufacturer

fabriquer (fah-bree-*kay*) *v* manufacture

façade (fah-*sahd*) *f* façade

face (fahss) *f* front; **en ~ de** facing, opposite

fâcher (fah-*shay*) *v* annoy; **fâché** cross

facile (fah-*seel*) *adj* easy

façon (fah-*saw$\overline{ng}$*) *f* way; **de la même ~** alike; **de toute ~** anyway; at any rate

façonner (fah-so-*nay*) *v* model

facteur (fahk-*tur*) *m* factor; postman

facture (fahk-*tewr*) *f* invoice, bill

facturer (fahk-tew-*ray*) *v* bill

facultatif (fah-kewl-tah-*teef*) *adj* optional

faculté (fah-kewl-*tay*) *f* faculty

faible (fehbl) *adj* feeble, weak; small, slight; faint

faiblesse (feh-*blehss*) *f* weakness

faïence (fah-^{y}*ah$\overline{ng}$ss*) *f* crockery

faillite: en ~ (ah$\overline{ng}$ fah-^{y}*eet*) bankrupt

faim (fa$\overline{ng}$) *f* hunger

***faire** (fair) *v* *do; *make; cause to, *have

faisable (fer-*zahbl*) *adj* feasible

faisan (fer-*zah$\overline{ng}$*) *m* pheasant

fait (fay) *m* fact; **de ~** in fact; **en ~** as a matter of fact, in effect

falaise (fah-*laiz*) *f* cliff

*falloir (fah-*lwaar*) v need, *must

falsification (fahl-see-fee-kah-*s*^{y}*awng*) f fake

falsifier (fahl-see-*f*^{y}*ay*) v forge

fameux (fah-*mur*) adj famous

familial (fah-mee-*l*^{y}*ahl*) adj of the family

familiariser (fah-mee-l^{y}ah-ree-*zay*) v familiarize, accustom

familier (fah-mee-*l*^{y}*ay*) adj familiar

famille (fah-*meey*) f family

fan (fahn) m/f fan

fanatique (fah-nah-*teek*) adj fanatical

faner (fah-*nay*) v: **se ~** fade

fanfare (fahng-*faar*) f brass band

fantaisie (fahng-tay-*zee*) f fantasy

fantastique (fahng-tah-*steek*) adj fantastic

fantôme (fahng-*tōam*) m phantom, ghost; spook

faon (fahng) m fawn

farce (fahrs) f filling, stuffing

farci (fahr-*see*) adj stuffed

fardeau (fahr-*doa*) m burden, load

farine (fah-*reen*) f flour

farouche (fah-*roosh*) adj shy

fasciner (fah-see-*nay*) v fascinate

fascisme (fah-*sheesm*) m fascism

fasciste (fah-*sheest*) m fascist; adj fascist

fastidieux (fah-stee-*d*^{y}*ur*) adj tedious, tiresome, boring

fatal (fah-*tahl*) adj (pl ~s) fatal, mortal

fatigant (fah-tee-*gahng*) adj tiring

fatigue (fah-*teeg*) f fatigue

fatiguer (fah-tee-*gay*) v tire; **fatigué** weary

faubourg (foa-*bōōr*) m outskirts pl, suburb

fauché (foa-*shay*) adj broke

faucon (foa-*kawng*) m hawk

faute (fōat) f mistake, error; fault; **donner la ~ à** blame; **sans ~** without fail

fauteuil (foa-*tur*^{ee}) m armchair, easy chair; **~ d'orchestre** orchestra seat Am; **~ roulant** wheelchair

faux (foa) adj (f fausse) false; untrue

faveur (fah-*vūrr*) f favo(u)r; **en ~ de** on behalf of

favorable (fah-vo-*rahbl*) adj favo(u)rable

favori (fah-vo-*ree*) m, **-rite** f favo(u)rite; adj favo(u)rite; **favoris** whiskers pl, sideburns pl

favoriser (fah-vo-ree-*zay*) v favo(u)r

favorite (fah-vo-*reet*) f favo(u)rite

fax (fahks) m fax; **envoyer un ~** send a fax

fédéral (fay-day-*rahl*) adj federal

fédération (fay-day-rah-*s*^{y}*awng*) f federation

*feindre (fangdr) v pretend

félicitations (fay-lee-see-tah-*s*^{y}*awng*) fpl congratulations

féliciter (fay-lee-see-*tay*) v congratulate, compliment

femelle (fer-*mehl*) f female

féminin (fay-mee-*nang*) adj feminine, female

femme (fahm) f woman, wife

fendre (fahngdr) v *split; crack

fenêtre (fer-*naitr*) f window

fenouil (fer-*noo*^{ee}) m fennel

fente (fahngt) f slot, cleft

fer (fair) m iron; **en ~** iron; **~ à cheval** horseshoe; **~ à repasser** iron

ferme (fehrm) f farmhouse, farm; adj firm, steady; steadfast

fermenter (fehr-mahng-*tay*) v ferment

fermer (fehr-*may*) v close, *shut; fasten; turn off; **fermé** closed shut; **~ à clé** lock

fermeture (fehrm-*tēwr*) f fastener; **~ éclair** zip, zipper Am

fermier (fehr-*m*^{y}*ay*) m farmer

fermière (fehr-*m*^{y}*air*) f farmer's wife

féroce (fay-*ross*) adj fierce, wild

ferraille (feh-*righ*) f scrap-iron

ferry-boat (feh-ree-*boat*) m ferryboat; train ferry

fertile (fehr-*teel*) adj fertile

fesse (fehss) f buttock

fessée (fay-*say*) f spanking

festival (feh-stee-*vahl*) m (pl ~s) festival

fête (feht) f feast

Fête-Dieu (feht-d^y*ur*) m Corpus Christi

feu (fur) m fire; ~ **arrière** taillight, rear light; ~ **de circulation** traffic light; ~ **de position** parking light

feuille (fur^{ee}) f leaf; sheet

feuilleton (fur^{ee}-*tawng*) m serial

feutre (fūrtr) m felt

février (fay-vree-*ay*) February

fiançailles (f^{y}ahng-*sigh*) fpl engagement

fiancé (f^{y}ahng-*say*) m fiancé; adj engaged

fiancée (f^{y}ahng-*say*) f fiancée, bride

fibre (feebr) f fibre

ficelle (fee-*sehl*) f twine, string

fiche (feesh) f plug

fiction (feek-s^y*awng*) f fiction

fidèle (fee-*dehl*) adj faithful, true

fier (f^{y}air) adj proud

fièvre (f^{y}aivr) f fever

fiévreux (f^{y}ay-*vrur*) adj feverish

figue (feeg) f fig

figure (fee-*gewr*) f figure; shape, form; face; appearance; court-card

se figurer (fee-gew-*ray*) imagine

fil (feel) m thread; line, yarn; ~ **de fer** wire; ~ **électrique** electric wire

file (feel) f line

filer (fee-*lay*) v *spin

filet (fee-*lay*) m net; ~ **à bagage** luggage rack; ~ **de pêche** fishing net

fille (feey) f girl; daughter; **vieille** ~ spinster

film (feelm) m film, movie; ~ **en** couleurs colo(u)r film

filmer (feel-*may*) v film

fils (feess) m son

filtre (feeltr) m filter; ~ **à air** air-filter; ~ **à huile** oil filter

filtrer (feel-*tray*) v filter

fin (fang) f finish, ending, end; issue; adj fine, thin

final (fee-*nahl*) adj (pl ~s) final

financer (fee-nahng-*say*) v finance

finances (fee-*nahngss*) fpl finances pl

financier (fee-nahng-s^y*ay*) adj financial

finir (fee-*neer*) v finish, end; **fini** finished, over

Finlandais (fang-lahng-*day*) m Finn

finlandais (fang-lahng-*day*) adj Finnish

Finlande (fang-*lahngd*) f Finland

fissure (fee-*sewr*) f crack, fissure

fixateur (feek-sah-*tūrr*) m setting lotion

fixe (feeks) adj fixed; permanent

fixer (feek-*say*) v attach; gaze, stare; ~ **le prix** price

flacon (flah-*kawng*) m flask

flamant (flah-*mahng*) m flamingo

flamme (flahm) f flame

flanelle (flah-*nehl*) f flannel

flâner (flah-*nay*) v stroll

flaque (flahk) f puddle

flash (flahsh) m flash-light

flasque (flahsk) adj limp

fléau (flay-*oa*) m plague

flèche (flehsh) f arrow

flétan (flay-*tahng*) m halibut

fleur (flūrr) f flower

fleuriste (flur-*reest*) m/f flower shop, florist

fleuve (flūrv) m river

flexible (flehk-*seebl*) adj flexible, elastic

flic (fleek) m cop, policeman

flotte (flot) f fleet

flotter (flo-*tay*) *v* float

flotteur (flo-*tūrr*) *m* float

fluide (flew-*eed*) *adj* fluid

flûte (flewt) *f* flute

foi (fwah) *f* faith

foie (fwah) *m* liver

foin (fwang) *m* hay

foire (fwaar) *f* fair

fois (fwah) *f* time; *prep* times; **à la ~** at the same time; **deux ~** twice; **une ~** once; some time; **une ~ de plus** once more

folie (fo-*lee*) *f* lunacy

folklore (fol-*klawr*) *m* folklore

foncé (fawng-*say*) *adj* dark

foncer (fawng-*say*) *v* *speed

fonction (fawngk-s^y*awng*) *f* function; office

fonctionnaire (fawngk-s^y o-*nair*) *m* civil servant

fonctionnement (fawngk-s^y on-*mahng*) *m* working, operation

fonctionner (fawngk-s^y o-*nay*) *v* work, operate

fond (fawng) *m* ground, bottom; essence; background; **à ~** thoroughly; **au ~** fundamentally; **~ de teint** foundation cream

fondamental (fawng-dah-mahng-*tahl*) *adj* fundamental, basic, essential

fondation (fawng-dah-s^y*awng*) *f* foundation

fondement (fawngd-*mahng*) *m* base

fonder (fawng-*day*) *v* found; **bien fondé** well-founded

fondre (fawngdr) *v* melt; thaw

fonds (fawng) *mpl* fund

fontaine (fawng-*tehn*) *f* fountain

fonte (fawngt) *f* cast iron

football (foot-*bol*) *m* soccer

force (fors) *f* force, power, strength; **~ armée** military force; **~ motrice** driving force

forcément (for-say-*mahng*) *adv* by

force

forcer (for-*say*) *v* force; strain

forer (fo-*ray*) *v* drill, bore

forestier (fo-reh-st^y*ay*) *m* forester

forêt (fo-*ray*) *f* forest

foreuse (fo-*rūrz*) *f* drill

forgeron (for-zher-*rawng*) *m* smith, blacksmith

formalité (for-mah-lee-*tay*) *f* formality

format (for-*mah*) *m* size

formation (for-mah-s^y*awng*) *f* formation, forming; training

forme (form) *f* shape, form; figure

formel (for-*mehl*) *adj* explicit

former (for-*may*) *v* shape, form; train, educate

formidable (for-mee-*dahbl*) *adj* fine, swell; terrific

formulaire (for-mew-*lair*) *m* form; **~ d'inscription** registration form

formule (for-*mewl*) *f* formula

fort (fawr) *adj* powerful, strong; loud

fortement (for-ter-*mahng*) *adv* tight

forteresse (for-ter-*rehss*) *f* fortress

fortuit (for-*twee*) *adj* casual, incidental

fortune (for-*tewn*) *f* fortune

fosse (foass) *f* pit

fossé (foa-*say*) *m* ditch

fou[1] (foo) *adj* (fol; f folle) crazy, mad; insane, lunatic

fou[2] (foo) *m* fool

foudre (foodr) *f* lightning

fouet (fway) *m* whip

fouetter (fway-*tay*) *v* whip

fouille (foo^ee) *f* search

fouiller (foo-^y*ay*) *v* search; *dig

foulard (foo-*laar*) *m* scarf

foule (fool) *f* crowd

fouler (foo-*lay*) *v* press; **se ~ la cheville** sprain one's ankle

foulure (foo-*lewr*) *f* sprain

four (foor) *m* oven; **~ à micro-ondes** microwave oven

fourbe (foorb) *adj* hypocritical

ourchette (foor-*sheht*) *f* fork

ourgon (foor-*gawng*) *m* luggage van; van

ourmi (foor-*mee*) *f* ant

ournaise (foor-*naiz*) *f* furnace

ourneau (foor-*noa*) *m* stove; **~ à gaz** gas stove

ournir (foor-*neer*) *v* provide, furnish, supply

ourniture (foor-nee-*tewr*) *f* supply

ourreur (foo-*rurr*) *m* furrier

ourrure (foo-*rewr*) *f* fur

oyer (fwah-*y*ay) *m* foyer, lounge; home; focus

fracas (frah-*kah*) *m* noise

fraction (frahk-s*y*awng) *f* fraction

fracture (frahk-*tewr*) *f* break, fracture

fracturer (frahk-tew-*ray*) *v* fracture

fragile (frah-*zheel*) *adj* fragile

fragment (frahg-*mahng*) *m* extract, fragment

frais[1] (fray) *adj* (*f* fraîche) fresh; chilly, cool

frais[2] (fray) *mpl* expenses *pl*, expenditure; **~ de voyage** travel(l)ing expenses

fraise (fraiz) *f* strawberry

framboise (frahng-*bwaaz*) *f* raspberry

franc (frahng) *adj* (*f* franche) open

français (frahng-*say*) *adj* French

France (frahngss) *f* France

franchir (frahng-*sheer*) *v* cross

frange (frahngzh) *f* fringe

frappant (frah-*pahng*) *adj* striking

frappé (frah-*pay*) *m* milkshake

frapper (frah-*pay*) *v* *beat; *hit, bump, tap, knock, *strike

fraternité (frah-tehr-nee-*tay*) *f* fraternity

fraude (froad) *f* fraud

frayeur (freh-*y*urr) *f* fright

fredonner (frer-do-*nay*) *v* hum

frein (frang) *m* brake; **~ à main** handbrake; **~ à pédale** foot brake

freiner (fray-*nay*) *v* slow down, curb

fréquemment (fray-kah-*mahng*) *adv* frequently

fréquence (fray-*kahngss*) *f* frequency

fréquent (fray-*kahng*) *adj* frequent

fréquenter (fray-kahng-*tay*) *v* see frequently, mix with

frère (frair) *m* brother

fret (fray) *m* freight

friction (freek-s*y*awng) *f* friction

frigidaire (free-zhe-*dair*) *m* refrigerator

frigo (free-*goa*) *m* fridge

fripon (free-*pawng*) *m* rascal

***frire** (freer) *v* fry

friser (free-*zay*) *v* curl

frisson (free-*sawng*) *m* shudder, chill, shiver

frissonnant (free-so-*nahng*) *adj* shivery

frissonner (free-so-*nay*) *v* tremble, shiver

frites (freet) *fpl* chips, *Am* French fries

froid (frwah) *m* cold; *adj* cold

froisser (frwah-*say*) *v* crease

fromage (fro-*maazh*) *m* cheese

front (frawng) *m* forehead

frontière (frawng-t*y*air) *f* border; frontier, boundary

frotter (fro-*tay*) *v* rub, scrub

fruit (frwee) *m* fruit

fugitif (few-zhe-*teef*) *m* runaway

***fuir** (fweer) *v* escape; leak

fuite (fweet) *f* flight; leak

fumée (few-*may*) *f* smoke

fumer (few-*may*) *v* smoke

fumeur (few-*murr*) *m*, **-euse** *f* smoker; **compartiment fumeurs** smoker

fumier (few-m*y*ay) *m* manure; dung; **tas de ~** dunghill

funérailles (few-nay-*righ*) *fpl* funeral

fureur (few-*rurr*) *f* anger, rage

furibond (few-ree-*bawng*) *adj* furious

furieux (few-r*y*ur) *adj* furious

furoncle (few-*rawngkl*) *m* boil

fusée (few-*zay*) *f* rocket

fusible (few-*zeebl*) *m* fuse

fusil (few-*zee*) *m* rifle, gun

fusion (few-z^y*awng*) *f* merger

futile (few-*teel*) *adj* petty, insignificant, idle

futur (few-*tewr*) *adj* future

G

gâcher (gah-*shay*) *v* mess up

gâchette (gah-*sheht*) *f* trigger

gâchis (gah-*shee*) *m* mess

gadget (gah-*jeht*) *m* gadget

gadoue (gah-*doo*) *f* muck

gages (gaazh) *mpl* wages *pl*; **donner en gage** pawn

gagner (gah-*ñay*) *v* *win; *make, earn, gain

gai (gay) *adj* jolly, cheerful, gay

gain (gang) *m* gain; **gains** earnings *pl*; winnings *pl*

gaine (gehn) *f* girdle

galerie (gahl-*ree*) *f* gallery; **~ d'art** art gallery

galet (gah-*lay*) *m* pebble

galop (gah-*loa*) *m* gallop

gamin (gah-*mang*) *m* little boy

gamine (gah-*meen*) *f* little girl

gamme (gahm) *f* scale; range

gant (gahng) *m* glove

garage (gah-*raazh*) *m* garage

garagiste (gah-rah-*zheest*) *m* garage proprietor

garantie (gah-rahng-*tee*) *f* guarantee

garantir (gah-rahng-*teer*) *v* guarantee

garçon (gahr-*sawng*) *m* boy; lad; waiter

garde (gahrd) *m* guard; *f* custody; **~ du corps** bodyguard; ***prendre ~** watch out

garder (gahr-*day*) *v* *keep; *hold

garde-robe (gahr-*drob*) *f* wardrobe; closet *Am*

gardien (gahr-d^y*ang*) *m* attendant, warden; caretaker; **~ de but** goalkeeper

gardon (gahr-*dawng*) *m* roach

gare (gaar) *f* station; depot *Am*

garer (gah-*ray*) *v* garage; **se ~** park

se gargariser (gahr-gah-ree-*zay*) gargle

gars (gah) *m* fellow

gaspillage (gah-spee-^{y}*aazh*) *m* waste

gaspiller (gah-spee-^{y}*ay*) *v* waste

gaspilleur (gah-spee-^{y}*ūrr*) *adj* wasteful

gastrique (gah-*streek*) *adj* gastric

gastro-entérite (gah-stroa-ahng-tay-*reet*) *f* gastroenteritis

gâteau (gah-*toa*) *m* cake

gâter (gah-*tay*) *v* *spoil

gauche (gōash) *adj* left; **de ~** left-hand

gaucher (goa-*shay*) *adj* left-handed

gaufre (gōafr) *f* waffle

gaufrette (goa-*freht*) *f* wafer

gaz (gaaz) *m* gas; **~ d'échappement** exhaust gases

gazeux (gah-*zur*) *adj* gaseous; aerated, fizzy

gazole (gah-*zol*) *m* diesel

gazon (gah-*zawng*) *m* lawn

géant (zhay-*ahng*) *m* giant

gel (zhehl) *m* frost

gelée (zher-*lay*) *f* jelly

geler (zher-*lay*) *v* *freeze

gémir (zhay-*meer*) *v* groan, moan

gênant (zheh-*nahng*) *adj*

inconvenient, troublesome

gencive (zhahng-*seev*) f gum

gendre (zhahngdr) m son-in-law

gêner (zhay-*nay*) v hinder; embarrass, bother; **se ~** *be embarrassed

général (zhay-nay-*rahl*) m general; *adj* universal, public, general; **en ~** as a rule, in general

généralement (zhay-nay-rahl-*mahng*) *adv* as a rule

générateur (zhay-nay-rah-*tūrr*) m generator

génération (zhay-nay-rah-*s^yawng*) f generation

généreux (zhay-nay-*rur*) *adj* liberal, generous

générosité (zhay-nay-ro-zee-*tay*) f generosity

génie (zhay-*nee*) m genius

génital (zhay-nee-*tahl*) *adj* genital

genou (zher-*noo*) m (pl ~x) knee

genre (zhahngr) m kind; gender

gens (zhahng) mpl/fpl people pl

gentil (zhahng-*tee*) *adj* friendly, kind; nice; sweet

gentillesse (zhahng-tee-*^yehss*) f politeness; **avoir la ~ de** be so kind as to

géographie (zhay-o-grah-*fee*) f geography

géologie (zhay-o-lo-*zhee*) f geology

géométrie (zhay-o-may-*tree*) f geometry

germe (zhehrm) m germ

geste (zhehst) m sign

gesticuler (zheh-stee-kew-*lay*) v gesticulate

gestion (zheh-st^y*awng*) f management, administration

gibier (zhee-*b^yay*) m game

gigantesque (zhee-gahng-*tehsk*) *adj* gigantic, enormous

gifle (zheefl) f slap in the face; box on the ear

gilet (zhee-*lay*) m waistcoat; vest *Am*

gingembre (zhang-*zhahngbr*) m ginger

gîte (zheet) m resting-place, lodging; form; vein

glace (glahss) f ice; ice cream

glacial (glah-*s^yahl*) *adj* freezing

glacier (glah-*s^yay*) m glacier

glaçon (glah-*sawng*) m icicle; ice cube; ice floe

glande (glahngd) f gland

glissade (glee-*sahd*) f slide

glissant (glee-*sahng*) *adj* slippery

glisser (glee-*say*) v *slide, glide; slip

global (glo-*bahl*) *adj* global, total, comprehensive

globe (glob) m globe

gloire (glwaar) f glory

glousser (gloo-*say*) v chuckle; giggle

gluant (glew-*ahng*) *adj* sticky

gobelet (go-*blay*) m mug, tumbler

goéland (go-ay-*lahng*) m seagull

golf (golf) m golf; **terrain de ~** golf links, golf course

golfe (golf) m gulf

gomme (gom) f gum; rubber, eraser

gondole (gawng-*dol*) f gondola

gonflable (gawng-*flahbl*) *adj* inflatable

gonfler (gawng-*flay*) v inflate

gorge (gorzh) f throat; gorge

gorgée (gor-*zhay*) f sip

gosse (goss) m kid, boy

goudron (goo-*drawng*) m tar

goulot d'étranglement (goo-lo day-trahng-gler-*mahng*) bottleneck

gourdin (goor-*dang*) m club

gourmand (goor-*mahng*) *adj* greedy

gourmet (goor-*may*) m gourmet

goût (goo) m taste; *avoir ~ de** taste

goûter (goo-*tay*) v taste

goutte (goot) f drop; gout

gouvernail (goo-vehr-*nigh*) m rudder

gouvernante (goo-vehr-*nahngt*) f

governess; housekeeper

gouvernement (goo-vehr-ner-*mahng*) *m* rule, government

gouverner (goo-vehr-*nay*) *v* rule, govern

gouverneur (goo-vehr-*nurr*) *m* governor

grâce (graass) *f* grace; pardon; ~ **à** thanks to

gracieux (grah-*s^{y}ur*) *adj* graceful; **à titre** ~ free of charge

grade (grahd) *m* grade; degree, rank

graduel (grah-*dwehl*) *adj* gradual

graduellement (grah-dwehl-*mahng*) *adv* gradually

grain (grang) *m* corn, grain

graisse (grehss) *f* grease, fat

graisser (gray-*say*) *v* grease

graisseux (greh-*sur*) *adj* greasy

grammaire (grah-*mair*) *f* grammar

grammatical (grah-mah-tee-*kahl*) *adj* grammatical

gramme (grahm) *m* gram

grand (grahng) *adj* great; tall, big, major

Grande-Bretagne (grahngd-brer-*tahñ*) *f* Great Britain

grandeur (grahng-*durr*) *f* size

grandiose (grahng-*d^{y}oaz*) *adj* superb, magnificent

grandir (grahng-*deer*) *v* *grow

grand-mère (grahng-*mair*) *f* grandmother

grand-papa (grahng-pah-*pah*) *m* granddad

grand-père (grahng-*pair*) *m* grandfather

grands-parents (grahng-pah-*rahng*) *mpl* grandparents *pl*

grange (grahngzh) *f* barn

granit (grah-*neet*) *m* granite

graphique (grah-*feek*) *adj* graphic; *m* diagram; chart

gras (grah) *adj* (f ~se) fatty, fat

gratitude (grah-tee-*tewd*) *f* gratitude

gratte-ciel (grah-*ts^{y}ehl*) *m* skyscraper

gratter (grah-*tay*) *v* scratch

gratuit (grah-*twee*) *adj* gratis, free of charge, free

grave (graav) *adj* grave; bad, severe

graver (grah-*vay*) *v* engrave

graveur (grah-*vurr*) *m* engraver

gravier (grah-*v^{y}ay*) *m* gravel

gravillon (grah-vee-*^{y}awng*) *m* grit

gravité (grah-vee-*tay*) *f* gravity

gravure (grah-*vewr*) *f* engraving; carving

grec (grehk) *adj* (f grecque) Greek

Grèce (grehss) *f* Greece

grêle (grehl) *f* hail

grenier (grer-*n^{y}ay*) *m* attic

grenouille (grer-noo^{ee}) *f* frog

grève (graiv) *f* strike; ***faire** ~ *strike

gréviste (gray-*veest*) *m/f* striker

griffe (greef) *f* claw

grill (greel) *m* steakhouse

grillade (gree-*^{y}ahd*) *f* grilled meat

grille (greey) *f* gate; grate

griller (gree-*^{y}ay*) *v* roast; grill

grillon (gree-*^{y}awng*) *m* cricket

grimper (grang-*pay*) *v* climb

grincer (grang-*say*) *v* creak

grippe (greep) *f* flu, influenza

gris (gree) *adj* grey

grive (greev) *f* thrush

grogner (gro-*ñay*) *v* grumble, growl

grondement (grawng-*mahng*) *m* roar

gronder (grawng-*day*) *v* rumble; scold

gros (groa) *adj* (f -se) big; thick, fat, corpulent, stout

groseille (groa-*zay*) *f* currant; ~ **à maquereau** gooseberry

grosse (groass) *f* gross

grossesse (groa-*sehss*) *f* pregnancy

grossier (groa-*s^{y}ay*) *adj* coarse, gross, rude

grossir (gro-*seer*) *v* increase; *put on weight

grossiste (groa-*seest*) *m* wholesale dealer
grotesque (gro-*tehsk*) *adj* ludicrous
grotte (grot) *f* cave; grotto
groupe (groop) *m* group; party
grouper (groo-*pay*) *v* group
grue (grew) *f* crane
grumeau (grew-*moa*) *m* lump
grumeleux (grewm-*lur*) *adj* lumpy
gruyère (grew-*ʸair*) *m* Swiss cheese
guêpe (gehp) *f* wasp
guère: ne ... ~ (ner ... gair) scarcely
guérir (gay-*reer*) *v* cure; heal, recover
guérison (gay-ree-*zawn͞g*) *f* recovery, cure
guérisseur (gay-ree-*sūrr*) *m* quack
guerre (gair) *f* war; **d'avant-guerre** pre-war; **~ mondiale** world war

guetter (gay-*tay*) *v* watch for
gueule (gurl) *f* mouth; **~ de bois** hangover
guichet (gee-*shay*) *m* box office; **~ de location** box office
guide (geed) *m* guidebook; *m/f* guide
guider (gee-*day*) *v* *lead
guidon (gee-*dawn͞g*) *m* handlebars *pl*
guillemets (geey-*may*) *mpl* quotation marks
guitare (gee-*taar*) *f* guitar
gymnase (zheem-*naaz*) *m* gymnasium
gymnaste (zheem-*nahst*) *m/f* gymnast
gymnastique (zheem-nah-*steek*) *f* gymnastics *pl*
gynécologue (zhee-nay-ko-*log*) *m/f* gyn(a)ecologist

H

habile (ah-*beel*) *adj* skil(l)ful; skilled
habileté (ah-beel-*tay*) *f* skill, art
habiller (ah-bee-*ʸay*) *v* dress
habitable (ah-bee-*tahbl*) *adj* inhabitable, habitable
habitant (ah-bee-*tahn͞g*) *m* inhabitant
habitation (ah-bee-tah-*sʸawn͞g*) *f* house
habiter (ah-bee-*tay*) *v* inhabit, live
habits (ah-*bee*) *mpl* clothes *pl*
habitude (ah-bee-*tewd*) *f* habit; custom; ***avoir l'habitude de** would; **d'habitude** usually
habitué (ah-bee-*tway*) *adj* accustomed; ***être ~ à** *be used to
habituel (ah-bee-*twehl*) *adj* common, habitual, ordinary
habituellement (ah-bee-twehl-*mahn͞g*) *adv* usually
habituer (ah-bee-*tway*): **s'~** *get

accustomed
hache ('ahsh) *f* axe
hacher ('ah-*shay*) *v* chop, mince
haie ('ay) *f* hedge
haine ('ehn) *f* hatred, hate
*haïr ('ah-*eer*) *v* hate
hâlé ('ah-*lay*) *adj* tanned
haleter (ahl-*tay*) *v* pant
hamac ('ah-*mahk*) *m* hammock
hameau ('ah-*moa*) *m* hamlet
hameçon (ahm-*sawn͞g*) *m* fishing hook
hanche ('ahn͞gsh) *f* hip
handicapé ('ahn͞g-dee-kah-*pay*) *adj* disabled, handicapped
hardi ('ahr-*dee*) *adj* bold
hareng ('ah-*rahn͞g*) *m* herring
haricot ('ah-ree-*koa*) *m* bean
harmonie (ahr-mo-*nee*) *f* harmony
harmonieux (ahr-mo-*nʸur*) *adj* tuneful
harpe ('ahrp) *f* harp

hasard ('ah-*zaar*) *m* chance, luck; hazard; **par ~** by chance

hâte ('aat) *f* hurry, speed, haste

hâter ('ah-*tay*) *v*: **se ~** hasten

hausse ('o͞ass) *f* rise

haut ('oa) *m* top side; *adj* high, tall; **en ~** upstairs, above, overhead; up; **vers le ~** upwards

hautain (oa-*tang*) *adj* haughty

hauteur (oa-*tu͞rr*) *f* height; ***être à la ~ de** *keep up with

haut-parleur ('oa-pahr-*lu͞rr*) *m* loudspeaker

hebdomadaire (ehb-do-mah-*dair*) *adj* weekly

héberger (ay-behr-*zhay*) *v* accommodate, put up, take in

hébreu (ay-*brur*) *m* Hebrew

hélas ('ay-*laass*) *adv* unfortunately

hélice (ay-*leess*) *f* propeller

hémorragie (ay-mo-rah-*zhee*) *f* h(a)emorrhage

hémorroïdes (ay-mo-ro-*eed*) *fpl* piles *pl*, h(a)emorrhoids *pl*

herbe (ehrb) *f* grass; herb; **mauvaise ~** weed

héréditaire (ay-ray-dee-*tair*) *adj* hereditary

hérisson ('ay-ree-*sawng*) *m* hedgehog

héritage (ay-ree-*taazh*) *m* inheritance

hériter (ay-ree-*tay*) *v* inherit

hermétique (ehr-may-*teek*) *adj* airtight

hernie ('ehr-*nee*) *f* hernia; **~ discale** slipped disc

héron ('ay-*rawng*) *m* heron

héros ('ay-*roa*) *m* hero

hésiter (ay-zee-*tay*) *v* hesitate

hétérosexuel (ay-tay-ro-sehk-*swehl*) *adj* heterosexual

hêtre ('aitr) *m* beech

heure (u͞rr) *f* hour; **à … heures** at … o'clock; **~ d'arrivée** time of arrival; **~ de départ** time of departure; **~ de pointe** rush hour; **~ d'été** summer

time; **heures de bureau** office hours; **heures de consultation** consultation hours; **heures de visite** visiting hours; **heures d'ouverture** business hours; **tout à l'heure** a short while ago; shortly; **toutes les heures** hourly

heureux (ur-*rur*) *adj* fortunate, happy

heurter ('urr-*tay*) *v* knock

hibou ('ee-*boo*) *m* (pl ~x) owl

hideux ('ee-*dur*) *adj* hideous

hier ('*air*) *adv* yesterday

hiérarchie ('ʸay-rahr-*shee*) *f* hierarchy

hippodrome (ee-po-*drom*) *m* racecourse

hirondelle (ee-rawng-*dehl*) *f* swallow

hisser ('ee-*say*) *v* hoist

histoire (ee-*stwaar*) *f* history; story; **~ d'amour** love story; **~ de l'art** art history

historien (ee-sto-rʸ*ang*) *m*, **-ne** *f* historian

historique (ee-sto-*reek*) *adj* historic; historical

hiver (ee-*vair*) *m* winter

H.L.M. (ahsh-ehl-*ehm*) *f or m* council flat

hobby ('o-*bee*) *m* hobby

hockey ('o-*kay*) *m* hockey

hollandais ('o-lahng-*day*) *adj* Dutch

Hollande ('o-*lahngd*) *f* Holland

homard ('o-*maar*) *m* lobster

hommage (o-*maazh*) *m* homage, tribute; **rendre ~** hono(u)r

homme (om) *m* man; **~ d'affaires** businessman; **~ d'Etat** statesman

homosexuel (o-mo-sehk-*swehl*) *adj* homosexual

Hongrie ('awng-*gree*) *f* Hungary

hongrois ('awng-*grwah*) *adj* Hungarian

honnête (o-*neht*) *adj* hono(u)rable, honest; fair

honnêteté (o-neht-*tay*) *f* honesty

honneur (o-*nūrr*) m hono(u)r, glory

honorable (o-no-*rahbl*) adj hono(u)rable, respectable

honoraires (o-no-*rair*) mpl fee

honorer (o-no-*ray*) v hono(u)r

honte ('*awnḡt*) f shame; ***avoir ~** *be ashamed; **quelle honte!** shame!

honteux ('*awnḡ-tur*) adj ashamed

hôpital (o-pee-*tahl*) m hospital

hoquet ('o-*kay*) m hiccup

horaire (o-*rair*) m timetable, schedule

horizon (o-ree-*zawnḡ*) m horizon

horizontal (o-ree-zawnḡ-*tahl*) adj horizontal

horloge (or-*lawzh*) f clock

horloger (or-lo-*zhay*) m watchmaker

horreur (o-*rūrr*) f horror

horrible (o-*reebl*) adj horrible

horrifiant (o-ree-f'*ahnḡ*) adj horrible

hors ('*awr*) adv out; **~ de** outside

hors d'œuvre ('or-*dūrv*) m hors-d'œuvre

horticulture (or-tee-kewl-*tewr*) f horticulture

hospice (o-*speess*) m home

hospitalier (o-spee-tah-l'*ay*) adj hospitable

hospitalité (o-spee-tah-lee-*tay*) f hospitality

hostile (o-*steel*) adj hostile

hôte (*ōat*) m host; guest

hôtel (oa-*tehl*) m hotel; **~ de ville** town hall

hôtel-Dieu (oa-tehl-*d'ur*) m general hospital

hôtesse (oa-*tehss*) f hostess; receptionist; **~ de l'air** stewardess

houblon ('oo-*blawnḡ*) m hop

housse ('*ooss*) f sleeve

hublot ('ew-*bloa*) m porthole

huile (*weel*) f oil; **~ capillaire** hair oil; **~ de table** salad oil; **~ d'olive** olive oil; **~ solaire** suntan oil

huiler (wee-*lay*) v lubricate

huileux (wee-*lur*) adj oily

huit ('*weet*) num eight

huitième ('wee-t'*ehm*) num eighth

huître (*weetr*) f oyster

humain (ew-*manḡ*) adj human

humanité (ew-mah-nee-*tay*) f mankind, humanity

humble (*urnḡbl*) adj humble

humecter (ew-mehk-*tay*) v moisten

humeur (ew-*mūrr*) f mood, spirit

humide (ew-*meed*) adj humid; wet, damp

humidifier (ew-mee-dee-f'*ay*) v damp

humidité (ew-mee-dee-*tay*) f humidity, moisture, damp

humour (ew-*mōor*) m humo(u)r

hurler ('ewr-*lay*) v yell, scream

hutte ('*ewt*) f hut

hydrogène (ee-dro-*zhehn*) m hydrogen

hygiène (ee-zh'*ehn*) f hygiene

hygiénique (ee-zh'ay-*neek*) adj hygienic

hymne (*eemn*) m hymn; **~ national** national anthem

hypermarché (ee-pehr-mahr-*shay*) m superstore, hypermarket

hypocrisie (ee-po-kree-*zee*) f hypocrisy

hypocrite (ee-po-*kreet*) m hypocrite; adj hypocritical

hypothèque (ee-po-*tehk*) f mortgage

hystérique (ee-stay-*reek*) adj hysterical

I

ici (ee-*see*) *adv* here

icône (ee-*kōan*) *f* icon

idéal[1] (ee-day-*ahl*) *adj* (pl -aux) ideal

idéal[2] (ee-day-*ahl*) *m* (pl ~s, -aux) ideal

idée (ee-*day*) *f* idea; opinion; ~ **lumineuse** brain wave

identification (ee-dahng-tee-fee-kah-s*y*awng) *f* identification

identifier (ee-dahng-tee-*f*y*ay*) *v* identify

identique (ee-dahng-*teek*) *adj* identical

identité (ee-dahng-tee-*tay*) *f* identity

idiot (ee-*d*y*oa*) *adj* idiotic; *m*, **-e** *f* fool, idiot

idole (ee-*dol*) *f* idol

idylle (ee-*deel*) *f* romance

ignorant (ee-ño-*rahng*) *adj* ignorant; uneducated

ignorer (ee-ño-*ray*) *v* ignore; overlook

il (eel) *pron* he

île (eel) *f* island

illégal (ee-lay-*gahl*) *adj* illegal

illettré (ee-leh-*tray*) *m* illiterate

illicite (ee-lee-*seet*) *adj* unlawful, unauthorized

illimité (ee-lee-mee-*tay*) *adj* unlimited

illisible (ee-lee-*zeebl*) *adj* illegible

illumination (ee-lew-mee-nah-s*y*awng) *f* illumination

illuminer (ee-lew-mee-*nay*) *v* illuminate

illusion (ee-lew-z*y*awng) *f* illusion

illustration (ee-lew-strah-s*y*awng) *f* illustration; picture

illustre (ee-*lewstr*) *adj* noted

illustré (ee-lew-*stray*) *m* comic

illustrer (ee-lew-*stray*) *v* illustrate

ils (eel) *pron* they

image (ee-*maazh*) *f* picture, image

imaginaire (ee-mah-zhee-*nair*) *adj* imaginary

imagination (ee-mah-zhee-nah-s*y*awng) *f* fancy, imagination

imaginer (ee-mah-zhee-*nay*) *v* fancy, imagine; **s'imaginer** fancy, imagine

imitation (ee-mee-tah-s*y*awng) *f* imitation

imiter (ee-mee-*tay*) *v* imitate, copy

immaculé (ee-mah-kew-*lay*) *adj* stainless, spotless

immangeable (ang-mahng-*zhahbl*) *adj* inedible

immédiat (ee-may-*d*y*ah*) *adj* immediate

immédiatement (ee-may-d*y*aht-*mahng*) *adv* at once, instantly, immediately

immense (ee-*mahngss*) *adj* immense; vast, huge

immérité (ee-may-ree-*tay*) *adj* unearned

immeuble (ee-*murbl*) *m* house; ~ **d'habitation** block of flats; apartment house *Am*

immigrant (ee-mee-*grahng*) *m*, **-e** *f* immigrant

immigration (ee-mee-grah-s*y*awng) *f* immigration

immigrer (ee-mee-*gray*) *v* immigrate

immobile (ee-mo-*beel*) *adj* motionless

immodeste (ee-mo-*dehst*) *adj* immodest

immuniser (ee-mew-nee-*zay*) *v* immunize

immunité (ee-mew-nee-*tay*) *f* immunity

impair (ang-*pair*) *adj* odd

imparfait (ang-pahr-*fay*) *adj* imperfect; faulty

impartial (ang-pahr-s*y*ahl) *adj* impartial

impasse (ang-*pahss*) *f* dead end,

blind alley; deadlock

impatient (ang-pah-s^yahng) *adj*
impatient; eager

impeccable (ang-peh-*kahbl*) *adj*
faultless

impératrice (ang-pay-rah-*treess*) *f*
empress

imperfection (ang-pehr-fehk-s^yawng) *f*
fault

impérial (ang-pay-r^yahl) *adj* imperial

imperméable (ang-pehr-may-*ahbl*) *m*
mackintosh, raincoat; *adj*
waterproof, rainproof

impersonnel (ang-pehr-so-*nehl*) *adj*
impersonal

impertinence (ang-pehr-tee-*nahngss*)
f impertinence

impertinent (ang-pehr-tee-*nahng*) *adj*
impertinent

impétueux (ang-pay-*twur*) *adj*
impetuous, fiery; raging

impliquer (ang-plee-*kay*) *v* involve,
imply

impoli (ang-po-*lee*) *adj* impolite

impopulaire (ang-po-pew-*lair*) *adj*
unpopular

importance (ang-por-*tahngss*) *f*
importance; ***avoir de l'importance**
matter; **sans ~** insignificant

important (ang-por-*tahng*) *adj*
important; considerable, big

importateur (ang-por-tah-*türr*) *m*
importer

importation (ang-por-tah-s^yawng) *f*
import; **taxe d'importation** import
duty

importer (ang-por-*tay*) *v* import

imposable (ang-poa-zahbl) *adj*
dutiable

imposant (ang-poa-*zahng*) *adj*
imposing

imposer (ang-poa-*zay*) *v* tax

impossible (ang-po-*seebl*) *adj*
impossible

impôt (ang-*poa*) *m* tax; **~ sur le chiffre
d'affaires** turnover tax; **~ sur le
revenu** income tax

impotence (ang-po-*tahngss*) *f*
impotence

impotent (ang-po-*tahng*) *adj* impotent

impraticable (ang-prah-tee-*kahbl*) *adj*
impassable

impression (ang-*preh*-s^yawng) *f*
impression; ***faire ~ sur** impress

impressionnant (ang-preh-s^yo-*nahng*)
adj impressive

impressionner (ang-preh-s^yo-*nay*) *v*
impress

imprévu (ang-pray-*vew*) *adj*
unexpected

imprimé (ang-pree-*may*) *m* printed
matter

imprimer (ang-pree-*may*) *v* print

imprimerie (ang-preem-*ree*) *f* printing
office

improbable (ang-pro-*bahbl*) *adj*
improbable, unlikely

impropre (ang-*propr*) *adj* improper,
unfit; wrong

improviser (ang-pro-vee-*zay*) *v*
improvise

imprudent (ang-prew-*dahng*) *adj*
unwise

impuissant (ang-pwee-*sahng*) *adj*
powerless

impulsif (ang-pewl-*seef*) *adj* impulsive

impulsion (ang-pewl-s^yawng) *f* urge,
impulse

inabordable (ee-nah-bor-*dahbl*) *adj*
prohibitive

inacceptable (ee-nahk-sehp-*tahbl*) *adj*
unacceptable

inaccessible (ee-nahk-say-*seebl*) *adj*
inaccessible

inadéquat (ee-nah-day-*kwah*) *adj*
inadequate, unsuitable

inadvertance (ee-nahd-vehr-*tahngss*) *f*
oversight

inattendu (ee-nah-tahng-*dew*) *adj*
unexpected

inattentif (ee-nah-tahng-*teef*) *adj*
careless

incapable (ang-kah-*pahbl*) *adj*
incapable, unable

incassable (ang-kah-*sahbl*) *adj*
unbreakable

incendie (ang-sahng-*dee*) *m* fire;
alarme d'incendie fire alarm

incertain (ang-sehr-*tang*) *adj* doubtful,
uncertain

incident (ang-see-*dahng*) *m* incident

incinérer (ang-see-nay-*ray*) *v* cremate

incision (ang-see-z^y*awng*) *f* cut

inciter (ang-see-*tay*) *v* incite

inclinaison (ang-klee-neh-*zawng*) *f*
gradient

inclination (ang-klee-nah-s^y*awng*) *f*
tendency; **~ de la tête** nod

incliné (ang-klee-*nay*) *adj* slanting

incliner (ang-klee-*nay*): **s'~** slant

***incluire** (ang-*klewr*) *v* include,
enclose; comprise, count

incompétent (ang-kawng-pay-*tahng*)
adj incompetent, unqualified

incomplet (ang-kawng-*play*) *adj* (f
-plète) incomplete

inconcevable (ang-kawng-*svahbl*) *adj*
inconceivable

inconditionnel (ang-kawng-dee-s^yo-
nehl) *adj* unconditional

inconfortable (ang-kawng-for-*tahbl*)
adj uncomfortable

inconnu (ang-ko-*new*) *adj* unknown;
m stranger

inconscient (ang-kawng-s^y*ahng*) *adj*
unconscious; unaware

inconsidéré (ang-kawng-see-day-*ray*)
adj rash

inconvénient (ang-kawng-vay-
n^y*ahng*) *m* inconvenience

incorrect (ang-ko-*rehkt*) *adj* incorrect,
inaccurate, wrong

incroyable (ang-krwah-^y*ahbl*) *adj*
incredible

inculte (ang-*kewlt*) *adj* uncultivated

incurable (ang-kew-*rahbl*) *adj*
incurable

Inde (angd) *f* India

indécent (ang-day-*sahng*) *adj* indecent

indéfini (ang-day-fee-*nee*) *adj*
indefinite

indemne (ang-*dehmn*) *adj* unhurt

indemnité (ang-dehm-nee-*tay*) *f*
compensation, indemnity

indépendance (ang-day-pahng-
dahngss) *f* independence

indépendant (ang-day-pahng-*dahng*)
adj independent; self-employed

indésirable (ang-day-zee-*rahbl*) *adj*
undesirable

index (ang-*dehks*) *m* index finger;
index

indicatif (ang-dee-kah-*teef*) *m* area
code

indication (ang-dee-kah-s^y*awng*) *f*
indication

Indien (ang-d^y*ang*) *m* Indian

indien (ang-d^y*ang*) *adj* Indian

indifférent (ang-dee-fay-*rahng*) *adj*
indifferent

indigène (ang-dee-*zhehn*) *m/f* native;
adj native

indigent (ang-dee-*zhahng*) *adj* poor

indigestion (ang-dee-zheh-st^y*awng*) *f*
indigestion

indignation (ang-dee-ñah-s^y*awng*) *f*
indignation

indiquer (ang-dee-*kay*) *v* point out,
indicate; declare

indirect (ang-dee-*rehkt*) *adj* indirect

indispensable (ang-dee-spahng-
sahbl) *adj* essential

indisposé (ang-dee-spoa-*zay*) *adj*
unwell

indistinct (ang-dee-*stang*) *adj*
indistinct, vague

individu (aṅg-dee-vee-*dew*) *m*
individual

individuel (aṅg-dee-vee-*dwehl*) *adj*
individual

Indonésie (aṅg-do-nay-*zee*) *f*
Indonesia

Indonésien (aṅg-do-nay-z^y*aṅg*) *m*
Indonesian

indonésien (aṅg-do-nay-z^y*aṅg*) *adj*
Indonesian

industrie (aṅg-dew-*stree*) *f* industry

industriel (aṅg-dew-stree-*ehl*) *adj*
industrial

inefficace (ee-nay-fee-*kahss*) *adj*
inefficient

inégal (ee-nay-*gahl*) *adj* uneven,
unequal

inéquitable (ee-nay-kee-*tahbl*) *adj*
unfair

inestimable (ee-neh-stee-*mahbl*) *adj*
priceless

inévitable (ee-nay-vee-*tahbl*) *adj*
inevitable, unavoidable

inexact (ee-nehg-*zahkt*) *adj*
inaccurate, inexact

inexpérimenté (ee-nehk-spay-ree-
mahṅg-*tay*) *adj* inexperienced

inexplicable (ee-nehk-splee-*kahbl*)
adj inexplicable

infâme (aṅg-*faam*) *adj* foul

infanterie (aṅg-fahṅg-*tree*) *f* infantry

infecter (aṅg-fehk-*tay*) *v* infect;
s'infecter *become septic

infectieux (aṅg-fehk-s^y*ur*) *adj*
infectious

infection (aṅg-fehk-s^y*awṅg*) *f* infection

inférieur (aṅg-fay-r^y*ūrr*) *adj* inferior,
bottom

infidèle (aṅg-fee-*dehl*) *adj* unfaithful

infini (aṅg-fee-*nee*) *adj* infinite, endless

infinitif (aṅg-fee-nee-*teef*) *m* infinitive

infirme (aṅg-*feerm*) *m* invalid; *adj*
invalid

infirmière (aṅg-feer-m^y*air*) *f* nurse

inflammable (aṅg-flah-*mahbl*) *adj*
inflammable

inflammation (aṅg-flah-mah-s^y*awṅg*) *f*
inflammation

inflation (aṅg-flah-s^y*awṅg*) *f* inflation

influence (aṅg-flew-*ahṅgss*) *f*
influence

influencer (aṅg-flew-ahṅg-*say*) *v*
influence

influent (aṅg-flew-*ahṅg*) *adj*
influential

information (aṅg-for-mah-s^y*awṅg*) *f*
information; enquiry

informer (aṅg-for-*may*) *v* inform;
s'informer inquire, enquire, query

infortune (aṅg-for-*tewn*) *f* misfortune

infortuné (aṅg-for-tew-*nay*) *adj*
unlucky

infraction (aṅg-frahk-s^y*awṅg*) *f*
offence, offense *Am*

infrarouge (aṅg-frah-*rōōzh*) *adj*
infrared

infructueux (aṅg-frewk-*twur*) *adj*
unsuccessful

infusion (aṅg-few-z^y*awṅg*) *f* infusion;
herb tea

ingénieur (aṅg-zhay-n^y*ūrr*) *m*
engineer

ingénu (aṅg-zhay-*new*) *adj* simple

ingérence (aṅg-zhay-*rahṅgss*) *f*
interference

ingrat (aṅg-*grah*) *adj* ungrateful

ingrédient (aṅg-gray-d^y*ahṅg*) *m*
ingredient

inhabitable (ee-nah-bee-*tahbl*) *adj*
uninhabitable

inhabité (ee-nah-bee-*tay*) *adj*
uninhabited

inhabitué (ee-nah-bee-*tway*) *adj*
unaccustomed

inhabituel (ee-nah-bee-*twehl*) *adj*
unusual, uncommon

inhaler (ee-nah-*lay*) *v* inhale

ininterrompu (ee-naṅg-teh-rawṅg-

pew) adj continuous
initial (ee-nee-*s^{y}ahl*) *adj* initial
initiale (ee-nee-*s^{y}ahl*) *f* initial
initiative (ee-nee-*s^{y}ah-teev*) *f* initiative
injecter (ang-zhehk-*tay*) *v* inject
injection (ang-zhehk-*s^{y}awng*) *f* injection
injurier (ang-zhew-*r^{y}ay*) *v* abuse, insult
injuste (ang-*zhewst*) *adj* unjust, unfair
injustice (ang-zhew-*steess*) *f* injustice
inné (ee-*nay*) *adj* natural
innocence (ee-no-*sahngss*) *f* innocence
innocent (ee-no-*sahng*) *adj* innocent
inoculer (ee-no-kew-*lay*) *v* inoculate
inoffensif (ee-no-fahng-*seef*) *adj* harmless
inondation (ee-nawng-dah-*s^{y}awng*) *f* flood
inopportun (ee-no-por-*turng*) *adj* inconvenient, misplaced
inquiet (ang-*k^{y}ay*) *adj* (f -ète) anxious; restless
inquiétant (ang-k^{y}ay-*tahng*) *adj* scary
inquiéter (ang-k^{y}ay-*tay*): **s'~** worry
inquiétude (ang-k^{y}ay-*tewd*) *f* worry; unrest
insatisfaisant (ang-sah-teess-fer-*zahng*) *adj* unsatisfactory
insatisfait (ang-sah-tee-*sfay*) *adj* dissatisfied
inscription (ang-skree-*ps^{y}awng*) *f* inscription; registration; entry
***inscrire** (ang-*skreer*) *v* enter, book; list; **s'*inscrire** check in, register
insecte (ang-*sehkt*) *m* insect; bug *Am*
insecticide (ang-sehk-tee-*seed*) *m* insecticide
insensé (ang-sahng-*say*) *adj* crazy, senseless, mad
insensible (ang-sahng-*seebl*) *adj* insensitive; imperceptible
insérer (ang-say-*ray*) *v* insert
insignifiant (ang-see-ñee-*f^{y}ahng*) *adj*

petty, insignificant, unimportant
insipide (ang-see-*peed*) *adj* tasteless
insister (ang-see-*stay*) *v* insist
insolation (ang-so-lah-*s^{y}awng*) *f* sunstroke
insolence (ang-so-*lahngss*) *f* insolence
insolent (ang-so-*lahng*) *adj* insolent, impudent, impertinent
insolite (ang-so-*leet*) *adj* unusual
insomnie (ang-som-*nee*) *f* insomnia
insonorisé (ang-so-noa-ree-*zay*) *adj* soundproof
insouciant (ang-soo-*s^{y}ahng*) *adj* carefree
inspecter (ang-spehk-*tay*) *v* inspect
inspecteur (ang-spehk-*turr*) *m* (*f* **-trice**) inspector
inspection (ang-spehk-*s^{y}awng*) *f* inspection
inspectrice (ang-spehk-*trees*) *f* inspector
inspirer (ang-spee-*ray*) *v* inspire
instable (ang-*stahbl*) *adj* unsteady, unstable
installation (ang-stah-lah-*s^{y}awng*) *f* installation
installer (ang-stah-*lay*) *v* instal(l;) furnish
instant (ang-*stahng*) *m* instant, moment; second
instantané (ang-stahng-tah-*nay*) *m* snapshot; *adj* prompt
instantanément (ang-stahng-tah-nay-*mahng*) *adv* instantly
instinct (ang-*stang*) *m* instinct
instituer (ang-stee-*tway*) *v* institute
institut (ang-stee-*tew*) *m* institute; **~ de beauté** beauty parlo(u)r
instituteur (ang-stee-tew-*turr*) *m* master, teacher, schoolteacher, schoolmaster
institution (ang-stee-tew-*s^{y}awng*) *f* institution; institute
instructeur (ang-strewk-*turr*) *m*

instructor

instructif (aṅg-strewk-*teef*) *adj* instructive

instruction (aṅg-strewk-*s⁰awṅg*) *f* instruction, direction

***instruire** (aṅg-*strweer*) *v* instruct

instrument (aṅg-strew-*mahṅg*) *m* instrument; tool, implement; ~ **de musique** musical instrument

insuffisant (aṅg-sew-fee-*zahṅg*) *adj* insufficient

insulte (aṅg-*sewlt*) *f* insult

insulter (aṅg-sewl-*tay*) *v* insult; scold

insupportable (aṅg-sew-por-*tahbl*) *adj* unbearable

insurrection (aṅg-sew-rehk-*s⁰awṅg*) *f* revolt, uprising

intact (aṅg-*tahkt*) *adj* whole, intact, unbroken

intellect (aṅg-teh-*lehkt*) *m* intellect

intellectuel (aṅg-teh-lehk-*twehl*) *adj* intellectual

intelligence (aṅg-teh-lee-*zhahṅgss*) *f* intelligence, intellect, brain

intelligent (aṅg-teh-lee-*zhahṅg*) *adj* intelligent, bright, clever

intense (aṅg-*tahṅgss*) *adj* intense; heavy

intention (aṅg-tahṅg-*s⁰awṅg*) *f* intention, purpose; ***avoir l'intention de** intend

intentionnel (aṅg-tahṅg-*s⁰o-nehl*) *adj* intentional, on purpose

interdiction (aṅg-tehr-deek-*s⁰awṅg*) *f* prohibition

***interdire** (aṅg-tehr-*deer*) *v* *forbid, prohibit

interdit (aṅg-tehr-*dee*) *adj* prohibited; ~ **aux piétons** no pedestrians

intéressant (aṅg-tay-reh-*sahṅg*) *adj* interesting

intéresser (aṅg-tay-ray-*say*) *v* interest

intérêt (aṅg-tay-*ray*) *m* interest

intérieur (aṅg-tay-*r⁰ūrr*) *m* interior,

inside; *adj* internal, inside, inner; indoor; domestic; **à l'intérieur** inside; indoors, within; **à l'intérieur de** inside; **vers l'intérieur** inwards

intérim (aṅg-tay-*reem*) *m* interim

interloqué (aṅg-tehr-lo-*kay*) *adj* speechless

interlude (aṅg-tehr-*lewd*) *m* interlude

intermédiaire (aṅg-tehr-may-*d⁰air*) *m/f* intermediary; ***servir d'intermédiaire** mediate

internat (aṅg-tehr-*nah*) *m* boarding school

international (aṅg-tehr-nah-*s⁰o-nahl*) *adj* international

interne (aṅg-*tehrn*) *adj* internal, resident

Internet (aṅg-tehr-*neht*) *m* internet

interprète (aṅg-tehr-*preht*) *m/f* interpreter

interpréter (aṅg-tehr-pray-*tay*) *v* interpret

interrogatif (aṅg-teh-ro-gah-*teef*) *adj* interrogative

interrogatoire (aṅg-teh-ro-gah-*twaar*) *m* interrogation, examination

interroger (aṅg-teh-ro-*zhay*) *v* interrogate

***interrompre** (aṅg-teh-*rawṅgpr*) *v* interrupt; **s'*interrompre** *break off

interruption (aṅg-teh-rew-*ps⁰awṅg*) *f* interruption

intersection (aṅg-tehr-sehk-*s⁰awṅg*) *f* intersection

intervalle (aṅg-tehr-*vahl*) *m* interval; space

***intervenir** (aṅg-tehr-ver-*neer*) *v* intervene, interfere

intervertir (aṅg-tehr-vehr-*teer*) *v* invert

interview (aṅg-tehr-*v⁰oo*) *f* interview

intestin (aṅg-teh-*staṅg*) *m* intestine, gut; **intestins** bowels *pl*

intime (aṅg-*teem*) *adj* intimate, cosy, cozy *Am*

intimité (ang-tee-mee-*tay*) *f* privacy

intolérable (ang-to-lay-*rahbl*) *adj* intolerable

intoxication alimentaire (ang-tok-see-kah-s^{y}awng ah-lee-mahng-*tair*) food poisoning

intrigue (ang-*treeg*) *f* intrigue; plot

introduction (ang-tro-dewk-s^{y}awng) *f* introduction

*introduire (ang-tro-*dweer*) *v* introduce

intrus (ang-*trew*) *m* trespasser

inutile (ee-new-*teel*) *adj* useless

inutilement (ee-new-teel-*mahng*) *adv* in vain

invalide (ang-vah-*leed*) *adj* disabled, handicapped

invasion (ang-vah-z^{y}awng) *f* invasion

inventaire (ang-vahng-*tair*) *m* inventory

inventer (ang-vahng-*tay*) *v* invent

inventeur (ang-vahng-*türr*) *m* inventor

inventif (ang-vahng-*teef*) *adj* inventive

invention (ang-vahng-s^{y}awng) *f* invention

inverse (ang-*vehrs*) *adj* reverse

investigation (ang-veh-stee-gah-s^{y}awng) *f* investigation, enquiry

investir (ang-veh-*steer*) *v* invest

investissement (ang-veh-stee-*smahng*) *m* investment

investisseur (ang-veh-stee-*sürr*) *m* investor

invisible (ang-vee-*zeebl*) *adj* invisible

invitation (ang-vee-tah-s^{y}awng) *f* invitation

invité (ang-vee-*tay*) *m* guest

inviter (ang-vee-*tay*) *v* invite

involontaire (ang-vo-lawng-*tair*) *adj* unintentional

iode (^{y}od) *m* iodine

Irak (ee-*rahk*) *m* Iraq

Irakien (ee-rah-k^{y}ang) *m* Iraqi

irakien (ee-rah-k^{y}ang) *adj* Iraqi

Iran (ee-*rahng*) *m* Iran

iranien (ee-rah-n^{y}ang) *adj* Iranian

irascible (ee-rah-*seebl*) *adj* quick-tempered

irlandais (eer-lahng-*day*) *adj* Irish

Irlande (eer-*lahngd*) *f* Ireland

ironie (ee-ro-*nee*) *f* irony

ironique (ee-ro-*neek*) *adj* ironical

irréel (ee-ray-*ehl*) *adj* unreal

irrégulier (ee-ray-gew-l^{y}ay) *adj* irregular, uneven

irréparable (ee-ray-pah-*rahbl*) *adj* irreparable

irrétrécissable (ee-ray-tray-see-*sahbl*) *adj* shrinkproof

irrévocable (ee-ray-vo-*kahbl*) *adj* irrevocable

irritable (ee-ree-*tahbl*) *adj* irritable

irrité (ee-ree-*tay*) *adj* angry, annoyed

irriter (ee-ree-*tay*) *v* irritate

islandais (ee-slahng-*day*) *adj* Icelandic

Islande (ee-*slahngd*) *f* Iceland

isolateur (ee-zo-lah-*türr*) *m* insulator

isolation (ee-zo-lah-s^{y}awng) *f* isolation, insulation

isolement (ee-zol-*mahng*) *m* isolation

isoler (ee-zo-*lay*) *v* isolate, insulate

Israël (ee-srah-*ehl*) *m* Israel

israélien (ee-srah-ay-l^{y}ang) *adj* Israeli

issue (ee-*sew*) *f* issue

Italie (ee-tah-*lee*) *f* Italy

italien (ee-tah-l^{y}ang) *adj* Italian

itinéraire (ee-tee-nay-*rair*) *m* itinerary

ivoire (ee-*vwaar*) *m* ivory

ivre (eevr) *adj* drunk; intoxicated

J

jadis (zhah-*deess*) *adv* formerly

jalousie (zhah-loo-*zee*) *f* jealousy

jaloux (zhah-*loo*) *adj* jealous, envious

jamais (zhah-*may*) *adv* ever; **ne ... ~** never

jambe (zhahn͞gb) *f* leg

jambon (zhahn͞g-*bawn͞g*) *m* ham

jante (zhahn͞gt) *f* rim

janvier (zhahn͞g-*v*ʸ*ay*) January

Japon (zhah-*pawn͞g*) *m* Japan

Japonais (zhah-po-*nay*) *m* Japanese

japonais (zhah-po-*nay*) *adj* Japanese

jaquette (zhah-*keht*) *f* jacket

jardin (zhahr-*dan͞g*) *m* garden; **~ potager** kitchen garden; **~ public** public garden; **~ zoologique** zoological gardens

jardinier (zhahr-dee-*n*ʸ*ay*) *m* gardener

jarre (zhaar) *f* jar

jauge (zhōazh) *f* gauge

jaune (zhōan) *adj* yellow; **~ d'œuf** yolk, egg yolk

jaunisse (zhoa-*neess*) *f* jaundice

je (zher) *pron* I

jersey (zhehr-*zay*) *m* jersey

jet (zhay) *m* cast; jet, squirt, spout

jetée (zher-*tay*) *f* jetty, pier

jeter (zher-*tay*) *v* *cast, *throw; **à ~** disposable

jeton (zher-*tawn͞g*) *m* token, chip

jeu (zhur) *m* play, game; set; **carte de ~** playing card; **~ concours** quiz; **~ de dames** draughts; checkers *plAm*; **~ de quilles** ninepins, skittles; **terrain de jeux** playground

jeudi (zhur-*dee*) *m* Thursday

jeune (zhurn) *adj* young

jeunesse (zhur-*nehss*) *f* youth

joaillerie (zhwigh-*ree*) *f* jewellery, jewelry *Am*

joaillier (zhwigh-*yay*) *m*, **-ière** *f* jewel(l)er

jockey (zho-*kay*) *m* jockey

joie (zhwah) *f* joy, gladness

*joindre (zhwan͞gdr) *v* join, connect; attach, enclose

jointure (zhwan͞g-*tewr*) *f* knuckle

joli (zho-*lee*) *adj* fine, nice, pretty, good-looking

jonc (zhawn͞g) *m* rush

jonction (zhawn͞gk-s*ʸawn͞g*) *f* junction

jonquille (zhawn͞g-*keey*) *f* daffodil

Jordanie (zhor-dah-*nee*) *f* Jordan

jordanien (zhor-dah-*n*ʸ*an͞g*) *adj* Jordanian

joue (zhoo) *f* cheek

jouer (zhoo-*ay*) *v* play; act

jouet (zhoo-*ay*) *m* toy

joueur (zhoo-*ūrr*) *m*, **-euse** *f* player

joug (zhoo) *m* yoke

jouir de (zhoo-*eer*) enjoy

jour (zhōor) *m* day; **de ~** by day; **~ de fête** holiday; **~ de la semaine** weekday; **~ ouvrable** working day; **l'autre ~** recently; **par ~** per day; **un ~ ou l'autre** some day

journal (zhoor-*nahl*) *m* newspaper, paper; diary; **~ du matin** morning paper

journalier (zhoor-nah-*l*ʸ*ay*) *adj* daily

journalisme (zhoor-nah-*leesm*) *m* journalism

journaliste (zhoor-nah-*leest*) *m/f* journalist

journée (zhoor-*nay*) *f* day

joyau (zhwah-*ʸoa*) *m* gem

joyeux (zhwah-*ʸur*) *adj* joyful, cheerful, merry, glad

juge (zhēwzh) *m* judge

jugement (zhewzh-*mahn͞g*) *m* judgment; sentence

juger (zhew-*zhay*) *v* judge

juif (zhweef) *adj* Jewish; *m* Jew

juillet (zhwee-*ʸay*) July

juin (zhwang) June
juive (zhweef) *adj* Jewish; *f* Jew
jumeaux (zhew-*moa*) *mpl* twins *pl*
jumelage (zhew-mer-*laazh*) *m* twinning
jumelles (zhew-*mehl*) *fpl* field glasses, binoculars *pl*
jument (zhew-*mahng*) *f* mare
jungle (zhawnggl) *f* jungle
jupe (zhewp) *f* skirt
jupon (zhew-*pawng*) *m* underskirt
jurer (zhew-*ray*) *v* vow, *swear; curse
juridique (zhew-ree-*deek*) *adj* legal
juriste (zhew-*reest*) *m* lawyer
juron (zhew-*rawng*) *m* curse

jury (zhew-*ree*) *m* jury
jus (zhew) *m* juice; gravy; ~ **de fruits** fruit juice
jusque (zhewsk) *prep* to; **jusqu'à** *prep* till; until; **jusqu'à ce que** till
juste (zhewst) *adj* just, righteous, right, fair; appropriate, proper, correct, exact; tight; *adv* just
justement (zhew-ster-*mahng*) *adv* rightly
justice (zhew-*steess*) *f* justice
justifier (zhew-stee-*f'ay*) *v* justify
juteux (zhew-*tur*) *adj* juicy
juvénile (zhew-vay-*neel*) *adj* juvenile

K

kaki (kah-*kee*) *m* khaki
kangourou (kahng-goo-*roo*) *m* kangaroo
Kenya (kay-*n'ah*) *m* Kenya
kilo (kee-*loa*) *m* kilogram
kilométrage (kee-lo-may-*traazh*) *m* distance in kilometres (kilometers *Am*)

kilomètre (kee-lo-*mehtr*) *m* kilometre, kilometer *Am*
kiosque (k'osk) *m* kiosk; ~ **à journaux** newsstand
klaxon (klahk-*sawng*) *m* hooter; horn
klaxonner (klahk-so-*nay*) *v* hoot; toot *Am*, honk *Am*

L

la (lah) *art* the; *pron* her
là (lah) *adv* there
là-bas (lah-*bah*) *adv* over there
labeur (lah-*būrr*) *m* labo(u)r
laboratoire (lah-bo-rah-*twaar*) *m* laboratory; ~ **de langues** language laboratory
labourer (lah-boo-*ray*) *v* plough
labyrinthe (lah-bee-*rangt*) *m* maze,

labyrinth
lac (lahk) *m* lake
lacet (lah-*say*) *m* shoelace, lace
lâche (laash) *m* coward; *adj* cowardly; loose
lâcher (lah-*shay*) *v* *let go
lagune (lah-*gewn*) *f* lagoon
laid (lay) *adj* ugly
laine (lehn) *f* wool; **en ~** wool(l)en; ~ **à**

repriser darning wool

laisse (lehss) f leash, lead

laisser (lay-say) v *let, *leave; *leave behind

lait (lay) m milk

laiterie (leh-tree) f dairy

laiteux (lay-tur) adj milky

laitier (lay-t^yay) m milkman

laiton (lay-taw$\overline{ng}$) m brass

laitue (lay-tew) f lettuce

lame (lahm) f blade; ~ **de rasoir** razor blade

lamentable (lah-mah$\overline{ng}$-tahbl) adj lamentable

lampadaire (lah$\overline{ng}$-pah-dair) m lamppost

lampe (lah$\overline{ng}$p) f lamp; ~ **de poche** torch; ~ **de travail** reading lamp; **lampe-tempête** f hurricane lamp

lance (lah$\overline{ng}$ss) f spear

lancement (lah$\overline{ng}$-smah$\overline{ng}$) m throw; launching

lancer (lah$\overline{ng}$-say) v *cast, toss, *throw; launch

lande (lah$\overline{ng}$d) f heath, moor

langage (lah$\overline{ng}$-gaazh) m language

langue (lah$\overline{ng}$g) f tongue; language; ~ **maternelle** native language, mother tongue

lanterne (lah$\overline{ng}$-tehrn) f lantern

lapin (lah-pa$\overline{ng}$) m rabbit

laque (lahk) f varnish; ~ **capillaire** hair spray

lard (laar) m bacon

lardon (lahr-daw$\overline{ng}$) m piece of larding bacon; kid, baby

large (lahrzh) adj wide, broad; generous, liberal

largeur (lahr-zh$\overline{ur}$r) f width, breadth

larme (lahrm) f tear

laryngite (lah-ra$\overline{ng}$-zheet) f laryngitis

las (lah) adj (f ~se) weary; ~ **de** tired of

latitude (lah-tee-tewd) f latitude

lavable (lah-vahbl) adj washable

lavabo (lah-vah-boa) m washbasin

lavage (lah-vaazh) m washing

laver (lah-vay) v wash

laverie automatique (lah-vree oa-toa-mah-teek) launderette

lave-vaisselle (lahv-veh-sehl) m dish washer

laxatif (lahk-sah-teef) m laxative

le[1] (ler) art (f la, pl les) the

le[2] (ler) pron (f la) him; it

leader (lee-dair) m leader

lécher (lay-shay) v lick

lèche-vitrines (lehsh-vee-treen) m windowshopping

leçon (ler-saw$\overline{ng}$) f lesson

lecteur (lehk-t$\overline{ur}$r) m, **-trice** f reader

lecture (lehk-t$\overline{ew}$r) f reading

légal (lay-gahl) adj legal, lawful

léger (lay-zhay) adj (f légère) slight, light; weak, gentle

légitime (lay-zhee-teem) adj legitimate, legal; just

légume (lay-gewm) m vegetable

lendemain (lah$\overline{ng}$d-ma$\overline{ng}$) m next day

lent (lah$\overline{ng}$) adj slow; sluggish

lentille (lah$\overline{ng}$-teey) f lens

lèpre (lehpr) f leprosy

lequel (ler-kehl) pron (f laquelle; pl lesquels, lesquelles) which

les (lay) art the; pron them

lésion (lay-z^yaw$\overline{ng}$) f injury

lessive (lay-seev) f washing, laundry

lettre (lehtr) f letter; **boîte aux lettres** letterbox, mailbox Am; ~ **de crédit** letter of credit; ~ **de recommandation** letter of recommendation; ~ **recommandée** registered letter

leur (l$\overline{ur}$r) adj their; pron them

levée (ler-vay) f collection

lever (ler-vay) v lift; ~ **du jour** daybreak; **se** ~ *rise, *get up

levier (ler-v^yay) m lever; ~ **de vitesse** gear lever

lèvre (laivr) f lip

lévrier (lay-vr^y ay) m greyhound

levure (ler-vewr) f yeast

liaison (l^y ay-zawng) f connection; affair

Liban (lee-bahng) m Lebanon

libanais (lee-bah-nay) adj Lebanese

libéral (lee-bay-rahl) adj liberal

libération (lee-bay-rah-s^y awng) f liberation

libérer (lee-bay-ray) v release; liberate

Libéria (lee-bay-r^y ah) m Liberia

libérien (lee-bay-r^y ang) adj Liberian

liberté (lee-behr-tay) f freedom, liberty

libraire (lee-brair) m/f bookseller

librairie (lee-bray-ree) f bookstore

libre (leebr) adj free

libre-service (leebr-sehr-veess) m self-service

licence (lee-sahngss) f permission, licence, license

licencier (lee-sahng-s^y ay) v fire

lien (l^y ang) m band; link

lier (lee-ay) v *bind

lierre (l^y air) m ivy

lieu (l^y ur) m spot; **au ~ de** instead of; ***avoir ~** *take place; **~ de naissance** place of birth; **~ de rencontre** meeting place

lièvre (l^y aivr) m hare

ligne (leen) f line; **~ aérienne** airline; **~ d'arrivée** finish; **~ de pêche** fishing line; **~ intérieure** extension; **~ principale** main line

ligue (leeg) f union, league

lime (leem) f file; **~ à ongles** nail file

limette (lee-meht) f lime

limite (lee-meet) f limit, boundary, bound; **~ de vitesse** speed limit

limiter (lee-mee-tay) v limit

limonade (lee-mo-nahd) f lemonade

linge (langzh) m linen

lingerie (lang-zhree) f lingerie

lion (l^y awng) m lion

liqueur (lee-kurr) f liqueur

liquide (lee-keed) m fluid; adj liquid

*lire (leer) v *read

lis (leess) m lily

lisible (lee-zeebl) adj legible

lisse (leess) adj smooth

liste (leest) f list; **~ d'attente** waiting list

lit (lee) m bed; **~ de camp** camp bed; cot Am; **lits jumeaux** twin beds

literie (lee-tree) f bedding

litige (lee-teezh) m dispute

litre (leetr) m liter Am, litre

littéraire (lee-tay-rair) adj literary

littérature (lee-tay-rah-tewr) f literature

littoral (lee-to-rahl) m sea-coast

livraison (lee-vreh-zawng) f delivery

livre[1] (leevr) m book; **~ de cuisine** cookery book; cookbook Am; **~ de poche** paperback

livre[2] (leevr) f pound

livrer (lee-vray) v deliver

local (lo-kahl) adj local

localiser (lo-kah-lee-zay) v locate

localité (lo-kah-lee-tay) f locality

locataire (lo-kah-tair) m tenant

location (lo-kah-s^y awng) f lease; **donner en ~** lease; **~ de voitures** car hire; car rental Am

locomotive (lo-ko-mo-teev) f locomotive, engine

locution (lo-kew-s^y awng) f phrase

loge (lozh) f dressing room

logement (lozh-mahng) m lodgings pl, accommodation

loger (lo-zhay) v accommodate; lodge

logeur (lo-zhurr) m landlord

logeuse (lo-zhurz) f landlady

logique (lo-zheek) f logic; adj logical

loi (lwah) f law

loin (lwang) adv away, far; **plus ~** further

lointain (lwang-*tang*) *adj* far-off, remote

loisir (lwah-*zeer*) *m* leisure

long (lawng) *adj* (f longue) long; **en ~** lengthways; **le ~ de** past, along

longitude (lawng-zhee-*tewd*) *f* longitude

longtemps (lawng-*tahng*) *adv* long

longueur (lawng-*gurr*) *f* length; **~ d'onde** wavelength

lopin (lo-*pang*) *m* plot

lors de (lor der) at the time of

lorsque (lorsk) *conj* when

lot (loa) *m* batch

loterie (lo-*tree*) *f* lottery

lotion (lo-s*y*awng) *f* lotion

louange (loo-*ahngzh*) *f* glory

louche (loosh) *adj* cross-eyed

louer (loo-*ay*) *v* hire, rent, lease; *let; praise; **à ~** for hire

loup (loo) *m* wolf

lourd (loor) *adj* heavy

loyal (lwah-*y*ahl) *adj* true, loyal

loyer (lwah-*y*ay) *m* rent

lubie (lew-*bee*) *f* whim

lubrifiant (lew-bree-f*ahng*) *m* lubrication oil

lubrification (lew-bree-fee-kah-s*y*awng) *f* lubrication

lubrifier (lew-bree-f*y*ay) *v* lubricate

lueur (lwurr) *f* gleam

luge (lewzh) *f* sleigh, sled(ge)

lugubre (lew-*gewbr*) *adj* creepy

lui (lwee) *pron* him; her; **lui-même** *pron* himself

luisant (lwee-*zahng*) *adj* glossy

lumbago (lawng-bah-*goa*) *m* lumbago

lumière (lew-m*y*air) *f* light; **~ du jour** daylight; **~ du soleil** sunlight; **~ latérale** sidelight

lumineux (lew-mee-*nur*) *adj* luminous

lundi (lurng-*dee*) *m* Monday

lune (lewn) *f* moon; **clair de ~** moonlight; **~ de miel** honeymoon

lunettes (lew-*neht*) *fpl* spectacles, glasses; **~ de plongée** goggles *pl*; **~ de soleil** sunglasses *pl*

lustre (lewstr) *m* gloss

lustrer (lew-*stray*) *v* lustre; *shine

lutte (lewt) *f* fight, combat, battle, struggle

lutter (lew-*tay*) *v* struggle; combat

luxe (lewks) *m* luxury

luxueux (lewk-*swur*) *adj* luxurious

lycée (lee-*say*) *m* (state) secondary school

M

mâcher (mah-*shay*) *v* chew

machine (mah-*sheen*) *f* engine, machine; **~ à coudre** sewing machine; **~ à écrire** typewriter; **~ à laver** washing machine

machinerie (mah-sheen-*ree*) *f* machinery

mâchoire (mah-*shwaar*) *f* jaw

maçon (mah-*sawng*) *m* bricklayer

madame (mah-*dahm*) madam

mademoiselle (mahd-mwah-*zehl*) miss

magasin (mah-gah-*zang*) *m* store; warehouse, store house; **grand ~** department store; **~ de chaussures** shoe shop; **~ de jouets** toyshop; **~ de spiritueux** off-licence, liquor store *Am*

magazine (mah-gah-*zeen*) *m* magazine

magie (mah-*zhee*) f magic

magique (mah-*zheek*) adj magic

magistrat (mah-zhee-*strah*) m magistrate

magnétique (mah-ñay-*teek*) adj magnetic

magnéto (mah-ñay-*toa*) f magneto

magnétophone (mah-ñay-to-*fon*) m tape recorder

magnétoscope (mah-ñay-to-*skop*) m video recorder

magnifique (mah-ñee-*feek*) adj splendid, gorgeous, magnificent

mai (may) May

maigre (maigr) adj thin, lean

maigrir (meh-*greer*) v slim

maille (migh) f mesh

maillet (mah-*ᵞay*) m mallet

maillot de bain (mah-ᵞoa der bañg) bathing suit, swimsuit

main (mañg) f hand; **fait à la ~** hand-made

main-d'œuvre (mañg-*dürvr*) f manpower

maintenant (mañgt-*nahñg*) adv now; **jusqu'à ~** so far

*maintenir (mañgt-*neer*) v maintain

maire (mair) m mayor

mairie (may-*ree*) f town hall

mais (may) conj but

maïs (mah-*eess*) m maize, corn Am; **~ en épi** corn on the cob

maison (may-*zawñg*) f house; home; **à la ~** at home; **fait à la ~** home-made; **maison-bateau** houseboat; **~ de campagne** country house; **~ de repos** rest home

maître (maitr) m master; **~ d'école** teacher, schoolmaster; **~ d'hôtel** head waiter

maîtresse (meh-*trehss*) f mistress; **~ de maison** mistress

maîtriser (meh-tree-*zay*) v master

majeur (mah-*zhürr*) adj major; superior, main; of age

majorité (mah-zho-ree-*tay*) f bulk, majority

majuscule (mah-zhew-*skewl*) f capital letter

mal (mahl) m (pl maux) evil, harm; mischief; ***faire du ~** harm; ***faire ~** ache; ***hurt; ~ à l'aise** uneasy; **~ au cœur** sickness; **~ au dos** backache; **~ au ventre** stomachache; **~ aux dents** toothache; **~ de gorge** sore throat; **~ de l'air** airsickness; **~ de mer** seasickness; **~ d'estomac** stomach ache; **~ de tête** headache; **~ d'oreille** earache; **~ du pays** homesickness

malade (mah-*lahd*) adj sick, ill

maladie (mah-lah-*dee*) f sickness, illness, disease; **~ vénérienne** venereal disease

maladroit (mah-lah-*drwah*) adj clumsy, awkward

Malais (mah-*lay*) m Malay

malaisien (mah-lay-z^yañg) adj Malaysian

malaria (mah-lah-r^yah) f malaria

malchance (mahl-*shahñgss*) f bad luck

mâle (maal) adj male

malentendu (mah-lahñg-tahñg-*dew*) m misunderstanding

malgré (mahl-*gray*) prep in spite of, despite

malheur (mah-*lürr*) m misfortune

malheureusement (mah-lur-rurz-*mahñg*) adv unfortunately

malheureux (mah-lur-*rur*) adj unhappy, unfortunate; miserable, sad

malhonnête (mah-lo-*neht*) adj dishonest, crooked

malice (mah-*leess*) f mischief

malicieux (mah-lee-s^yur) adj mischievous

malin (mah-*lañg*) adj (f maligne) malignant; sly; bright

malle (mahl) f trunk

mallette (mah-*leht*) f suitcase; ~ **de voyage** grip Am

malodorant (mah-lo-do-*rahng*) adj smelly

malpropre (mahl-*propr*) adj foul, unclean

malsain (mahl-*sang*) adj unsound, unhealthy

malveillant (mahl-veh-*yahng*) adj spiteful; malicious

maman (mah-*mahng*) f mum

mammifère (mah-mee-*fair*) m mammal

manche (*mahngsh*) m handle; f sleeve; **La Manche** English Channel

manchette (mahng-*sheht*) f cuff; headline

mandarine (mahng-dah-*reen*) f tangerine, mandarin

mandat (mahng-*dah*) m mandate

manège (mah-*naizh*) m riding school

mangeoire (mahng-*zhwaar*) f manger

manger (mahng-*zhay*) v *eat; m food

maniable (mah-n*y*ahbl) adj manageable

manier (mah-n*y*ay) v handle

manière (mah-n*y*air) f way, manner; **de la même ~** likewise; **de ~ que** so that

manifestation (mah-nee-feh-stah-s*y*awng) f demonstration

manifestement (mah-nee-feh-ster-*mahng*) adv apparently

manifester (mah-nee-feh-*stay*) v express; demonstrate

manipuler (mah-nee-pew-*lay*) v handle

mannequin (mahn-*kang*) m model, mannequin

manoir (mah-*nwaar*) m mansion, manor house

manquant (mahng-*kahng*) adj missing

manque (*mahngk*) m want, shortage, lack

manquer (mahng-*kay*) v fail, lack; miss

manteau (mahng-*toa*) m coat, cloak; ~ **de fourrure** fur coat

manucure (mah-new-*kewr*) f manicure

manuel (mah-*nwehl*) m textbook, handbook; adj manual; ~ **de conversation** phrase book

manuscrit (mah-new-*skree*) m manuscript

maquereau (mah-*kroa*) m mackerel

maquillage (mah-kee-*yaazh*) m make-up

marais (mah-*ray*) m marsh, swamp, bog

marbre (*mahrbr*) m marble

marchand (mahr-*shahng*) m, **-e** f merchant; tradesman, dealer; ~ **de journaux** newsagent; ~ **de légumes** greengrocer; vegetable merchant; ~ **de volaille** poulterer

marchander (mahr-shahng-*day*) v bargain

marchandise (mahr-shahng-*deez*) f merchandise; wares pl, goods pl

marche (*mahrsh*) f march; step; ***faire ~ arrière** reverse

marché (mahr-*shay*) m market; **bon ~** cheap; inexpensive; ~ **des valeurs** stock market; ~ **noir** black market; **place du ~** marketplace

marcher (mahr-*shay*) v walk, step, *go; march; ***faire ~** fool

mardi (mahr-*dee*) m Tuesday

marée (mah-*ray*) f tide; ~ **basse** low tide; ~ **haute** flood; high tide

margarine (mahr-gah-*reen*) f margarine

marge (*mahrzh*) f margin

mari (mah-*ree*) m husband

mariage (mah-r*y*aazh) m matrimony, marriage; wedding

marié (mah-r*y*ay) m bridegroom

marier: se ~ (mah-r*y*ay) marry

marin (mah-*rang*) *m* sailor; seaman

marinade (mah-ree-*nahd*) *f* marinade *f*

marine (mah-*reen*) *f* navy; seascape

maritime (mah-ree-*teem*) *adj* maritime

marmelade (mahr-mer-*lahd*) *f* marmalade

marmite (mahr-*meet*) *f* pot

Maroc (mah-*rok*) *m* Morocco

marocain (mah-ro-*kang*) *adj* Moroccan

maroquinerie (mah-ro-keen-*ree*) *f* leather goods *pl*

marque (mahrk) *f* mark; sign, brand; ~ **de fabrique** trademark

marquer (mahr-*kay*) *v* mark

marquise (mahr-*keez*) *f* awning

marrant (mah-*rahng*) *adj* funny; odd

marron (mah-*rawng*) *m* chestnut

mars (mahrs) March

marteau (mahr-*toa*) *m* hammer

marteler (mahr-ter-*lay*) *v* thump

martyr (mahr-*teer*) *m*, **-e** *f* martyr

masculin (mah-skew-*lang*) *adj* masculine

masque (mahsk) *m* mask; ~ **de beauté** face pack

massage (mah-*saazh*) *m* massage; ~ **facial** face massage

masse (mahss) *f* mass; bulk; crowd

masser (mah-*say*) *v* massage

masseur (mah-*surr*) *m* masseur

massif (mah-*seef*) *adj* massive, solid

massue (mah-*sew*) *f* club

mat (maht) *adj* mat, dull, dim

mât (mah) *m* mast

match (mahch) *m* match; ~ **de boxe** boxing match; ~ **de football** football match

matelas (mah-*tlah*) *m* mattress

matériau (mah-tay-r^y*oa*) *m* material

matériel (mah-tay-r^y*ehl*) *m* material; *adj* material; substantial

maternel (mah-tehr-*nehl*) *adj* motherly

mathématique (mah-tay-mah-*teek*) *adj* mathematical

mathématiques (mah-tay-mah-*teek*) *fpl* mathematics

matière (mah-t^y*air*) *f* matter; ~ **première** raw material

matin (mah-*tang*) *m* morning; **ce** ~ this morning

matinée (mah-tee-*nay*) *f* morning

maturité (mah-tew-ree-*tay*) *f* maturity

***maudire** (moa-*deer*) *v* curse

mausolée (moa-zo-*lay*) *m* mausoleum

mauvais (moa-*vay*) *adj* bad; wicked, ill, evil; **le plus** ~ worst

mauve (mōav) *adj* mauve

maximum (mahk-see-*mom*) *m* maximum; **au** ~ at most

mayonnaise (mah-^{y}o-*naiz*) *f* mayonnaise

mazout (mah-*zoot*) *m* fuel oil

me (mer) *pron* me; myself

mécanicien (may-kah-nee-s^y*ang*) *m* mechanic

mécanique (may-kah-*neek*) *adj* mechanical

mécanisme (may-kah-*neesm*) *m* mechanism, machinery

méchant (may-*shahng*) *adj* evil; naughty; nasty, ill

mèche (mehsh) *f* fuse

mécontent (may-kawng-*tahng*) *adj* discontented

médaille (may-*digh*) *f* medal

médecin (may-*dsang*) *m* physician, doctor; ~ **généraliste** general practitioner

médecine (may-*dseen*) *f* medicine

médiateur (may-d^{y}ah-*ūrr*) *m*, **-trice** *f* mediator

médical (may-dee-*kahl*) *adj* medical

médicament (may-dee-kah-*mahng*) *m* medicine, drug

médiéval (may-d^{y}ay-*vahl*) *adj*

mediaeval

méditer (may-dee-*tay*) *v* meditate

Méditerranée (may-dee-tay-rah-*nay*) *f* Mediterranean

méduse (may-*dēwz*) *f* jellyfish

méfiance (may-f*ʸahn̄gss*) *f* suspicion

méfiant (may-f*ʸahn̄g*) *adj* suspicious

méfier (may-f*ʸay*) *v*: **se ~ de** mistrust

meilleur (meh-*ʸūrr*) *adj* better; **le ~** best

mélancolie (may-lahn̄g-ko-*lee*) *f* melancholy

mélancolique (may-lahn̄g-ko-*leek*) *adj* melancholy

mélange (may-*lahn̄gzh*) *m* mixture

mélanger (may-lahn̄g-*zhay*) *v* mix

mêler (may-*lay*) *v* mix; **se ~ de** interfere with

mélo (may-*loa*) *m* tear-jerker

mélodie (may-lo-*dee*) *f* melody

mélodrame (may-lo-*drahm*) *m* melodrama

melon (mer-*lawn̄g*) *m* melon

membre (mahn̄gbr) *m* member, associate; limb

mémé (may-*may*) *f* granny

même (mehm) *adj* same; *adv* even; **de ~** also

mémoire (may-*mwaar*) *f* memory

mémorable (may-mo-*rahbl*) *adj* memorable

mémorandum (may-mo-rahn̄g-*dom*) *m* memo

mémorial (may-mo-r*ʸahl*) *m* memorial

menaçant (mer-nah-*sahn̄g*) *adj* threatening

menace (mer-*nahss*) *f* threat

menacer (mer-nah-*say*) *v* threaten

ménage (may-*naazh*) *m* housekeeping, household

ménagère (may-nah-*zhair*) *f* housewife

mendiant (mahn̄g-d*ʸahn̄g*) *m*, **-e** *f* beggar

mendier (mahn̄g-d*ʸay*) *v* beg

mener (mer-*nay*) *v* *take, *lead

menottes (mer-*not*) *fpl* handcuffs *pl*

mensonge (mahn̄g-*sawn̄gzh*) *m* lie

menstruation (mahn̄g-strew-ah-s*ʸawn̄g*) *f* menstruation

mensuel (mahn̄g-*swehl*) *adj* monthly

mental (mahn̄g-*tahl*) *adj* mental; **aliéné ~** lunatic

menthe (mahn̄gt) *f* peppermint, mint

mention (mahn̄g-s*ʸawn̄g*) *f* mention

mentionner (mahn̄g-s*ʸ*o-*nay*) *v* mention

*mentir (mahn̄g-*teer*) *v* lie

menton (mahn̄g-*tawn̄g*) *m* chin

menu¹ (mer-*new*) *m* menu; **~ fixe** set menu

menu² (mer-*new*) *adj* minor

menuisier (mer-nwee-z*ʸay*) *m* carpenter

mépris (may-*pree*) *m* contempt, scorn

méprise (may-*preez*) *f* mistake

mépriser (may-pree-*zay*) *v* despise, scorn

mer (mair) *f* sea

merci (mehr-*see*) thank you

mercredi (mehr-krer-*dee*) *m* Wednesday

mercure (mehr-*kēwr*) *m* mercury

merde (mehrd) *f* shit

mère (mair) *f* mother

méridional (may-ree-d*ʸ*o-*nahl*) *adj* southern, southerly

mérite (may-*reet*) *m* merit

mériter (may-ree-*tay*) *v* merit, deserve

merlan (mehr-*lahn̄g*) *m* whiting

merle (mehrl) *m* blackbird

merveille (mehr-*vay*) *f* marvel

merveilleux (mehr-veh-*ʸur*) *adj* marvel(l)ous; fine, wonderful

mesquin (meh-*skan̄g*) *adj* mean, stingy

message (meh-*saazh*) *m* message

messager (meh-sah-*zhay*) *m*
messenger

messe (mehss) *f* mass

mesure (mer-*zewr*) *f* measure; size; **en
~ able**; **fait sur ~** tailor-made

mesurer (mer-zew-*ray*) *v* measure

métal (may-*tahl*) *m* metal

métallique (may-tah-*leek*) *adj* metal

météo (may-tay-*oa*) *f* weather report;
m meteorologist

méthode (may-*tod*) *f* method

méthodique (may-to-*deek*) *adj*
methodical

méticuleux (may-tee-kew-*lur*) *adj*
meticulous

métier (may-t*y*ay) *m* trade, profession

mètre (mehtr) *m* meter, metre, metre

métrique (may-*treek*) *adj* metric

métro (may-*troa*) *m* underground;
subway *Am*

***mettre** (mehtr) *v* *put; *put on

meuble (murbl) *m* piece of furniture;
meubles furniture

meubler (mur-*blay*) *v* furnish

meunier (mur-n*y*ay) *m* miller

meurtrier (murr-tree-*ay*) *m*, **-ière** *f*
murderer

mexicain (mehk-see-*kang*) *adj*
Mexican

Mexique (mehk-*seek*) *m* Mexico

mi-bas (mee-*bah*) *m* knee-length sock

miche (meesh) *f* loaf

microbe (mee-*krob*) *m* germ

microphone (mee-kro-*fon*) *m*
microphone

microsillon (mee-kro-see-*y*awng) *m*
long-playing record

midi (mee-*dee*) *m* midday, noon

miel (m*y*ehl) *m* honey

mien: le ~ (ler m*y*ang) mine

miette (m*y*eht) *f* crumb

mieux (m*y*ur) *adv* better

mignon (mee-*ñawng*) *adj* dainty, nice,
sweet; **péché ~** little weakness

migraine (mee-*grehn*) *f* migraine

milieu (mee-l*y*ur) *m* middle, midst;
milieu; **au ~ de** among, amid; **du ~**
middle

militaire (mee-lee-*tair*) *adj* military

mille (meel) *num* thousand; *m* mile

million (mee-l*y*awng) *m* million

millionnaire (mee-l*y*o-*nair*) *m/f*
millionaire

mince (mangss) *adj* slim, thin

mine[1] (meen) *f* pit, mine; **~ d'or**
goldmine

mine[2] (meen) *f* look

minerai (meen-*ray*) *m* ore

minéral (mee-nay-*rahl*) *m* mineral

minet (mee-*nay*) *m* pussy-cat

mineur (mee-*nurr*) *m* miner; minor;
adj minor; under age

miniature (mee-n*y*ah-*tewr*) *f* miniature

mini-jupe (mee-nee-*zhewp*) *f*
miniskirt

minimum (mee-nee-*mom*) *m*
minimum

ministère (mee-nee-*stair*) *m* ministry

ministre (mee-*neestr*) *m* minister;
premier ~ Prime Minister

minorité (mee-no-ree-*tay*) *f* minority

minuit (mee-*nwee*) *m* midnight

minuscule (mee-new-*skewl*) *adj* tiny,
minute

minute (mee-*newt*) *f* minute

minutieux (mee-new-s*y*ur) *adj*
thorough

miracle (mee-*raakl*) *m* miracle,
wonder

miraculeux (mee-rah-kew-*lur*) *adj*
miraculous

miroir (mee-*rwaar*) *m* looking-glass,
mirror

misérable (mee-zay-*rahbl*) *adj*
miserable

misère (mee-*zair*) *f* misery

miséricorde (mee-zay-ree-*kord*) *f*
mercy

miséricordieux (mee-zay-ree-kor-*d*ʸ*ur*) *adj* merciful

mite (meet) *f* moth

mi-temps (mee-*tahng*) *f* half time

mixeur (meek-*sur*) *m* mixer

mobile (mo-*beel*) *adj* mobile; movable

mode¹ (mod) *f* fashion; **à la ~** fashionable

mode² (mod) *m* fashion, manner; **~ d'emploi** directions for use

modèle (mo-*dehl*) *m* model

modeler (mo-*dlay*) *v* model

modéré (mo-day-ray) *adj* moderate

moderne (mo-*dehrn*) *adj* modern

modeste (mo-*dehst*) *adj* modest

modestie (mo-deh-*stee*) *f* modesty

modification (mo-dee-fee-kah-*s*ʸ*awng*) *f* change, alteration

modifier (mo-dee-*f*ʸ*ay*) *v* change, modify, alter

moelle (mwahl) *f* marrow

moelleux (mwah-*lur*) *adj* mellow

mœurs (murrs) *fpl* morals

mohair (mo-*air*) *m* mohair

moi (mwah) *pron* me; **moi-même** *pron* myself

moindre (mwa*ngdr*) *adj* least; inferior

moine (mwahn) *m* monk

moineau (mwah-*noa*) *m* sparrow

moins (mwa*ng*) *adv* less; *prep* minus; **à ~ que** unless; **au ~** at least

mois (mwah) *m* month

moisi (mwah-*zee*) *adj* mouldy

moisissure (mwah-zee-*sewr*) *f* mildew

moisson (mwah-*sawng*) *f* harvest

moite (mwaht) *adj* moist; damp

moitié (mwah-*t*ʸ*ay*) *f* half; **à ~** half

molaire (mo-*lair*) *f* molar

mollet (mo-*lay*) *m* calf

moment (mo-*mahng*) *m* moment; while

momentané (mo-mahng-tah-*nay*) *adj* momentary

mon (maw*ng*) *adj* (f ma, pl mes) my

monarchie (mo-nahr-*shee*) *f* monarchy

monarque (mo-*nahrk*) *m* monarch, ruler

monastère (mo-nah-*stair*) *m* monastery

monde (maw*ng*d) *m* world; **tout le ~** everyone

mondial (mawng-*d*ʸ*ahl*) *adj* worldwide; global

monétaire (mo-nay-*tair*) *adj* monetary

monnaie (mo-*nay*) *f* currency; **~ étrangère** foreign currency; **petite ~** petty cash, change; **pièce de ~** coin

monopole (mo-no-*pol*) *m* monopoly

monotone (mo-no-*ton*) *adj* monotonous

monsieur (mer-*s*ʸ*ur*) *m* (pl messieurs) gentleman; mister; sir

mont (maw*ng*) *m* mount

montagne (mawng-*tahñ*) *f* mountain

montagneux (mawng-tah-*ñur*) *adj* mountainous

montant (mawng-*tahng*) *m* amount

montée (mawng-*tay*) *f* rise; ascent

monter (mawng-*tay*) *v* *rise; ascend; *get on; assemble; mount; **se ~ à** amount to

monteur (mawng-*ūrr*) *m* mechanic

monticule (mawng-tee-*kewl*) *m* hillock

montre (maw*ng*tr) *f* watch; **~ à affichage numérique** digital watch

montrer (mawng-*tray*) *v* *show; display; **~ du doigt** point

monture (mawng-*tewr*) *f* frame

monument (mo-new-*mahng*) *m* monument

moquer (mo-*kay*): **se ~ de** mock

moquerie (mo-*kree*) *f* mockery

moral (mo-*rahl*) *adj* moral; *m* spirits

morale (mo-*rahl*) *f* moral

moralité (mo-rah-lee-*tay*) *f* morality

morceau (mor-*soa*) *m* piece, part; morsel, fragment, scrap, bit, lump; ~ **de sucre** lump of sugar

mordre (mordr) *v* *bite

morphine (mor-*feen*) *f* morphine, morphia

morsure (mor-*sewr*) *f* bite

mort (mawr) *f* death; *adj* dead

mortel (mor-*tehl*) *adj* fatal; mortal

morue (mo-*rew*) *f* cod

mosaïque (mo-zah-*eek*) *f* mosaic

mosquée (mo-*skay*) *f* mosque

mot (moa) *m* word; ~ **de passe** password

motel (mo-*tehl*) *m* motel

moteur (mo-*tūrr*) *m* motor, engine

motif (mo-*teef*) *m* cause, motive; pattern

moto (mo-*toa*) *f* motor bike

motocyclette (mo-to-see-*kleht*) *f* motorcycle

mou (moo) *adj* (*f* **molle**) soft

moucher (moo-*shay*) wipe (*s.o.'s*) nose; snuff; snub

mouche (moosh) *f* fly

mouchoir (moo-*shwaar*) *m* handkerchief; ~ **de papier** tissue

*moudre (moodr) *v* *grind

mouette (mweht) *f* gull; seagull

moufles (moofl) *fpl* mittens *pl*

mouiller (moo-*ʸay*) *v* wet; **mouillé** wet, moist

moule (mool) *f* mussel

moulin (moo-*lang*) *m* mill; ~ **à paroles** chatterbox; ~ **à vent** windmill

*mourir (moo-*reer*) *v* die

mousse (mooss) *f* foam; moss

mousser (moo-*say*) *v* foam

mousseux (moo-*sur*) *adj* sparkling

moustache (moo-*stahsh*) *f* moustache

moustiquaire (moo-stee-*kair*) *f* mosquito net

moustique (moo-*steek*) *m* mosquito

moutarde (moo-*tahrd*) *f* mustard

mouton (moo-*tawng*) *m* sheep; mutton

mouvement (moov-*mahng*) *m* motion, movement

*mouvoir (moo-*vwaar*): **se** ~ move

moyen (mwah-*ʸang*) *m* means; *adj* medium, average

moyen-âge (mwah-*ʸeh-naazh*) *m* Middle Ages

moyenne (mwah-*ʸehn*) *f* mean, average; **en** ~ on the average

muet (mway) *adj* dumb, mute

mugir (mew-*zheer*) *v* roar

muguet (mew-*gay*) *m* lily of the valley; thrush

mule (mewl) *f* mule

mulet (mew-*lay*) *m* mule

multiplication (mewl-tee-plee-kah-*sʸawng*) *f* multiplication

multiplier (mewl-tee-plee-*ay*) *v* multiply

municipal (mew-nee-see-*pahl*) *adj* municipal

municipalité (mew-nee-see-pah-lee-*tay*) *f* municipality

munir (mew-*neer*): ~ **de** provide with

mur (mēwr) *m* wall

mûr (mēwr) *adj* mature, ripe

mûre (mēwr) *f* blackberry

muscade (mew-*skahd*) *f* nutmeg

muscle (mewskl) *m* muscle

musclé (mew-*sklay*) *adj* muscular

museau (mew-*zoa*) *m* snout

musée (mew-*zay*) *m* museum

musical (mew-zee-*kahl*) *adj* musical

musicien (mew-zee-*sʸang*) *m*, **-ne** *f* musician

musique (mew-*zeek*) *f* music; ~ **pop** pop music

musulman (mew-zewl-*mahng*) *adj* Moslem; *m*, **-e** *f* Moslem, Muslim

mutinerie (mew-teen-*ree*) *f* mutiny

mutuel (mew-*twehl*) *adj* mutual

myope (mʸop) *adj* short-sighted

mystère (mee-*stair*) *m* mystery

mystérieux (mee-stay-*r^yur*) *adj* mysterious

mythe (meet) *m* myth

N

nacre (nahkr) *f* mother of pearl

nager (nah-*zhay*) *v* *swim

nageur (nah-*zhūrr*) *m* swimmer

naïf (nah-*eef*) *adj* naïve

nain (na͞ng) *m* dwarf

naissance (nay-*sah͞ngss*) *f* birth

***naître** (naitr) *v* *be born

nappe (nahp) *f* tablecloth

narcose (nahr-*ko͞az*) *f* narcosis

narcotique (nahr-ko-*teek*) *m* narcotic

narine (nah-*reen*) *f* nostril

natation (nah-tah-*s^yaw͞ng*) *f* swimming

nation (nah-*s^yaw͞ng*) *f* nation

national (nah-s^yo-*nahl*) *adj* national

nationaliser (nah-s^yo-nah-lee-*zay*) *v* nationalize

nationalité (nah-s^yo-nah-lee-*tay*) *f* nationality

nature (nah-*tēwr*) *f* nature; essence

naturel (nah-tew-*rehl*) *adj* natural

naturellement (nah-tew-rehl-*mah͞ng*) *adv* naturally

naufrage (noa-*fraazh*) *m* shipwreck

nausée (noa-*zay*) *f* nausea

naval (nah-*vahl*) *adj* (pl ~s) naval

navette (nah-*veht*) *f* shuttle (service); ~ **spatiale** space shuttle; **faire la ~** commute

navigable (nah-vee-*gahbl*) *adj* navigable

navigation (nah-vee-gah-*s^yaw͞ng*) *f* navigation

naviguer (nah-vee-*gay*) *v* navigate; sail

navire (nah-*veer*) *m* ship; ~ **de guerre** man-of-war

né (nay) *adj* born

néanmoins (nay-ah͞ng-*mwa͞ng*) *adv* nevertheless

nébuleux (nay-bew-*lur*) *adj* hazy

nécessaire (nay-say-*sair*) *adj* necessary; ~ **de toilette** toilet case

nécessité (nay-say-see-*tay*) *f* need, necessity

nécessiter (nay-say-see-*tay*) *v* require

néerlandais (nay-ehr-lah͞ng-*day*) *adj* Dutch

néfaste (nay-*fahst*) *adj* fatal

négatif (nay-gah-*teef*) *m* negative; *adj* negative

négligé (nay-glee-*zhay*) *m* negligee

négligence (nay-glee-*zhah͞ngss*) *f* neglect

négligent (nay-glee-*zhah͞ng*) *adj* careless, neglectful

négliger (nay-glee-*zhay*) *v* neglect

négociant (nay-go-s^y*ah͞ng*) *m* dealer; ~ **en vins** wine merchant

négociation (nay-go-s^yah-s^y*aw͞ng*) *f* negotiation

négocier (nay-go-*s^yay*) *v* negotiate

neige (naizh) *f* snow

neiger (nay-*zhay*) *v* snow

neigeux (neh-*zhur*) *adj* snowy

néon (nay-*aw͞ng*) *m* neon

nerf (nair) *m* nerve

nerveux (nehr-*vur*) *adj* nervous

n'est-ce pas? (nehss-*pah*) *adv* isn't it

net (neht) *adj* distinct; net

nettoyage (neh-twah-^y*aazh*) *m* cleaning

nettoyer (neh-twah-^y*ay*) *v* clean; ~ **à sec** dry-clean

neuf[1] (nurf) *adj* (f neuve) new

neuf[2] (nurf) *num* nine

neutre (nūrtr) *adj* neuter; neutral

neuvième (nur-v*y*ehm) *num* ninth

neveu (ner-*vur*) *m* nephew

névralgie (nay-vrahl-*zhee*) *f* neuralgia

névrose (nay-v*rōaz*) *f* neurosis

nez (nay) *m* nose; **saignement de ~** nosebleed

ni … ni (nee) neither … nor

nickel (nee-*kehl*) *m* nickel

nicotine (nee-ko-*teen*) *f* nicotine

nid (nee) *m* nest

nièce (n*y*ehss) *f* niece

nier (nee-*ay*) *v* deny

Nigeria (nee-zhay-r*y*ah) *m* Nigeria

nigérien (nee-zhay-r*y*ang) *adj* Nigerian

niveau (nee-*voa*) *m* level; **~ de vie** standard of living; **passage à ~** level crossing

niveler (nee-*vlay*) *v* level

noble (nobl) *adj* noble

noblesse (no-*blehss*) *f* nobility

nocturne (nok-*tewrn*) *adj* nightly

Noël (no-*ehl*) Christmas, Xmas

nœud (nur) *m* knot; **~ papillon** bow tie

Noir (nwaar) *m* black

noir (nwaar) *adj* black

noisette (nwah-*zeht*) *f* hazelnut

noix (nwah) *f* nut; walnut; **~ de coco** coconut

nom (nawng) *m* name; noun; denomination; **au ~ de** in the name of, on behalf of; **~ de famille** family name, surname; **~ de jeune fille** maiden name

nombre (nawngbr) *m* number; quantity; numeral

nombreux (nawng-*brur*) *adj* numerous

nombril (nawng-*bree*) *m* navel

nomination (no-mee-nah-s*y*awng) *f* nomination, appointment

nommer (no-*may*) *v* name; nominate appoint

non (nawng) no

non-fumeur (nawng-few-mūrr)* *m* nonsmoker

nord (nawr) *m* north

nord-est (no-*rehst*) *m* north-east

nord-ouest (no-*rwehst*) *m* north-west

normal (nor-*mahl*) *adj* normal, regular

norme (norm) *f* standard

Norvège (nor-*vaizh*) *f* Norway

norvégien (nor-vay-zh*y*ang) *adj* Norwegian

notaire (no-*tair*) *m* notary

notamment (no-tah-*mahng*) *adv* namely

note (not) *f* note; mark; bill; check *Am*

noter (no-*tay*) *v* note, *write down; notice

notifier (no-tee-f*y*ay) *v* notify

notion (noa-s*y*awng) *f* notion; idea

notoire (no-*twaar*) *adj* notorious

notre (notr) *adj* our

nouer (noo-*ay*) *v* tie, knot

nougat (noo-*gah*) *m* nougat

nourrir (noo-*reer*) *v* *feed; **nourrissant** nourishing

nourrisson (noo-ree-*sawng*) *m* infant

nourriture (noo-ree-*tewr*) *f* food

nous (noo) *pron* we; ourselves, us; **nous-mêmes** *pron* ourselves

nouveau (noo-*voa*) *adj* (nouvel; f nouvelle) new; **de ~** again; **Nouvel An** New Year

nouvelle (noo-*vehl*) *f* notice; **nouvelles** news

Nouvelle-Zélande (noo-vehl-zay-*lahngd*) *f* New Zealand

novembre (no-*vahngbr*) November

noyau (nwah-*y*oa) *m* stone; nucleus

noyer (nwah-*y*ay) *v* drown; **se ~** *be drowned

nu (new) *adj* naked, nude; bare; *m* nude

nuage (nwaazh) *m* cloud; **nuages** clouds
nuageux (nwah-*zhur*) *adj* cloudy, overcast
nuance (nwahn̄gss) *f* nuance; shade
nucléaire (new-klay-*air*) *adj* atomic, nuclear
*nuire (nweer) *v* harm
nuisible (nwee-*zeebl*) *adj* harmful
nuit (nwee) *f* night; **boîte de ~** cabaret;

cette **~** tonight; **de ~** by night, overnight; **tarif de ~** night rate
nul (newl) *adj* (f nulle) invalid, void
numéro (new-may-*roa*) *m* number; act; **~ d'immatriculation** registration number; license number *Am*
nuque (newk) *f* nape of the neck
nutritif (new-tree-*teef*) *adj* nutritious
nylon (nee-*lawn̄g*) *m* nylon

O

oasis (oa-ah-*zeess*) *f* oasis
obéir (o-bay-*eer*) *v* obey
obéissance (o-bay-ee-*sahn̄gss*) *f* obedience
obéissant (o-bay-ee-*sahn̄g*) *adj* obedient
obèse (o-*baiz*) *adj* stout, corpulent
obésité (o-bay-zee-*tay*) *f* fatness
objecter (ob-zhehk-*tay*) *v* object
objectif (ob-zhehk-*teef*) *m* target, objective, object, goal; *adj* objective
objection (ob-zhehk-*s^y awn̄g*) *f* objection; ***faire ~ à** object to
objet (ob-*zhay*) *m* object; **objets de valeur** valuables *pl*; **objets trouvés** lost and found
obligation (o-blee-gah-*s^y awn̄g*) *f* bond
obligatoire (o-blee-gah-*twaar*) *adj* compulsory, obligatory
obligeant (o-blee-*zhahn̄g*) *adj* obliging
obliger (o-blee-*zhay*) *v* oblige; force
oblique (o-*bleek*) *adj* slanting
oblong (o-*blawn̄g*) *adj* (f oblongue) oblong
obscène (o-*psehn*) *adj* obscene
obscur (op-*skewr*) *adj* obscure; dim, dark

obscurité (op-skew-ree-*tay*) *f* dark
observation (o-psehr-vah-*s^y awn̄g*) *f* observation
observatoire (o-psehr-vah-*twaar*) *m* observatory
observer (o-psehr-*vay*) *v* watch, observe; notice, note
obsession (o-pseh-*s^y awn̄g*) *f* obsession
obstacle (op-*stahkl*) *m* obstacle
obstiné (op-stee-*nay*) *adj* stubborn, obstinate; dogged
obstruer (op-strew-*ay*) *v* block
*obtenir (op-ter-*neer*) *v* *get; obtain
occasion (o-kah-*z^y awn̄g*) *f* chance, opportunity; occasion; **d'occasion** second-hand
occident (ok-see-*dahn̄g*) *m* west
occidental (ok-see-dahn̄g-*tahl*) *adj* western, westerly
occupant (o-kew-*pahn̄g*) *m* occupant
occupation (o-kew-pah-*s^y awn̄g*) *f* occupation; business
occuper (o-kew-*pay*) *v* occupy; *take up; **occupé** busy, engaged, occupied; **s'occuper de** attend to, look after; *take care of, see to, *deal with
océan (o-say-*ahn̄g*) *m* ocean; **Océan**

Atlantique Atlantic; **Océan Pacifique** Pacific Ocean
octobre (ok-*tobr*) October
oculiste (o-kew-*leest*) *m*/*f* oculist
odeur (o-*durr*) *f* smell, odo(u)r
œil (ur^{ee}) *m* (pl yeux) eye; **coup d'œil** look; glance; glimpse
œuf (urf) *m* egg; **œufs de poisson** roe
œuvre (*urvr*) *m* work; **~ d'art** work of art
offense (o-*fahngss*) *f* offence, offense *Am*
offenser (o-fahng-*say*) *v* injure, *hurt, wound, offend; **s'offenser de** resent
offensif (o-fahng-*seef*) *adj* offensive
offensive (o-fahng-*seev*) *f* offensive
office (o-*fees*)* *m* office; agency; service
officiel (o-fee-s^y*ehl*) *adj* official
officier (o-fee-s^y*ay*) *m* officer
officieux (o-fee-s^y*ur*) *adj* unofficial
offre (ofr) *f* offer; supply
***offrir** (o-*freer*) *v* offer
oie (wah) *f* goose
oignon (o-*ñawng*) *m* onion; bulb
oiseau (wah-*zoa*) *m* bird; **~ de mer** seabird
oisif (wah-*zeef*) *adj* idle
olive (o-*leev*) *f* olive
ombragé (awng-brah-*zhay*) *adj* shady
ombre (*awngbr*) *f* shadow, shade; **~ à paupières** eye shadow
omelette (om-*leht*) *f* omelette
***omettre** (o-*mehtr*) *v* *leave out, omit; fail
omnibus (om-nee-*bewss*) *m* slow train
omnipotent (om-nee-po-*tahng*) *adj* omnipotent
on (awng) *pron* one
oncle (*awngkl*) *m* uncle
ondulation (awng-dew-lah-s^y*awng*) *f* wave
ondulé (awng-dew-*lay*) *adj* wavy, undulating

ongle (*awnggl*) *m* nail
onguent (awng-*gahng*) *m* ointment, salve
onze (awngz) *num* eleven
onzième (awng-z^y*ehm*) *num* eleventh
opéra (o-pay-*rah*) *m* opera; opera house
opération (o-pay-rah-s^y*awng*) *f* operation, surgery
opérer (o-pay-*ray*) *v* operate
opérette (o-pay-*reht*) *f* operetta
opiniâtre (o-pee-n^y*aatr*) *adj* obstinate
opinion (o-pee-n^y*awng*) *f* view, opinion
opposé (o-poa-*zay*) *adj* contrary, opposite
opposer (o-poa-*zay*): **s'~** oppose
opposition (o-poa-zee-s^y*awng*) *f* opposition
oppresser (o-pray-*say*) *v* oppress
opprimer (o-pree-*may*) *v* oppress
opticien (op-tee-s^y*ang*) *m*, **-ne** *f* optician
optimisme (op-tee-*meesm*) *m* optimism
optimiste (op-tee-*meest*) *m*/*f* optimist; *adj* optimistic
or (awr) *m* gold; **en ~** golden; **~ en feuille** gold leaf
orage (o-*raazh*) *m* thunderstorm
orageux (o-rah-*zhur*) *adj* thundery, stormy
oral (o-*rahl*) *adj* oral
orange (o-*rahngzh*) *f* orange; *adj* orange
orchestre (or-*kehstr*) *m* orchestra; band; **fauteuil d'orchestre** seat in the stalls
ordinaire (or-dee-*nair*) *adj* plain, simple, usual, regular, customary; common
ordinateur (or-dee-nah-*turr*) *n* computer; **~ portable** lap-top computer

ordonnance (or-do-*nahngss*)* f arrangement, layout, organisation; prescription

ordonner (or-do-*nay*) v arrange; order; **ordonné** adj tidy

ordre (ordr) m order; method; command; ~ **du jour** agenda

ordures (or-*dewr*) fpl garbage

oreille (o-*ray*) f ear

oreiller (o-ray-*yay*) m pillow; **taie d'oreiller** pillowcase

oreillons (o-reh-*yawng*) mpl mumps

orfèvre (or-*faivr*) m goldsmith; silversmith

organe (or-*gahn*) m organ

organique (or-gah-*neek*) adj organic

organisation (or-gah-nee-zah-*syawng*) f organization

organiser (or-gah-nee-*zay*) v organize

orgue (org) m (pl f) organ; ~ **de Barbarie** street-organ

orgueil (or-*guree*) m pride

orgueilleux (or-gur-*yur*) adj proud

Orient (o-*ryahng*) m Orient

oriental (o-*ryahng-tahl*) adj oriental; eastern, easterly

orienter (o-*ryahng-tay*): **s'~** orientate

originairement (o-ree-zhee-nehr-*mahng*) adv originally

original (o-ree-zhee-*nahl*) adj original

origine (o-ree-*zheen*) f origin

ornement (or-ner-*mahng*) m ornament

ornemental (or-ner-mahng-*tahl*) adj ornamental

orphelin (or-fer-*lang*) m, **-e** f orphan

orteil (or-*tay*) m toe

orthodoxe (or-to-*doks*) adj orthodox

orthographe (or-to-*grahf*) f spelling

os (oss) m (pl ~) bone

oser (oa-*zay*) v dare

otage (o-*taazh*) m hostage

ôter (oa-*tay*) v *take out; wipe

ou (oo) conj or; ~ **...** **ou** either ... or

où (oo) adv where; pron where; **n'importe ~** anywhere

ouate (waht) f cotton wool

oublier (oo-blee-*ay*) v *forget

oublieux (oo-blee-*ur*) adj forgetful

ouest (wehst) m west

oui (wee) yes

ouïe (oo-*ee*) f hearing

ouragan (oo-rah-*gahng*) m hurricane

ourlet (oor-*lay*) m hem

ours (oors) m bear

oursin (oor-*sang*) m sea urchin

outil (oo-*tee*) m tool, utensil, implement

outrage (oo-*traazh*) m outrage; offence, offense Am

outrager (oo-trah-*zhay*) v offend

outre (ootr) prep beyond, besides; **d'outre-mer** overseas; **en ~** furthermore, besides

ouvert (oo-*vair*) adj open

ouverture (oo-vehr-*tewr*) f opening; overture

ouvrage (oo-*vraazh*) m work

ouvre-boîte (oo-vrer-*bwaht*) m tin opener, can opener Am

ouvre-bouteille (oo-vrer-boo-*tay*) m bottle opener

ouvreur (oo-*vrurr*) m usher

ouvreuse (oo-*vrurz*) f usherette

ouvrier (oo-vree-*ay*) m, **-ière** f worker

***ouvrir** (oo-*vreer*) v open; unlock; turn on

ovale (o-*vahl*) adj oval

oxygène (ok-see-*zhehn*) m oxygen

P

pacifisme (pah-see-*feesm*) *m* pacifism

pacifiste (pah-see-*feest*) *adj* pacifist; *m/f* pacifist

pagaie (pah-*gay*) *f* paddle

pagaille (pah-*gigh*) *f* muddle

page (paazh) *f* page; *m* pageboy

paie (pay) *f* salary

paiement (pay-*mahng*) *m* payment; ~ **échelonné** payment by insta(l)lments

païen (pah-*^yang*) *m* pagan, heathen; *adj* pagan, heathen

paille (pigh) *f* straw

pain (pang) *m* bread; ~ **complet** wholemeal bread; **petit ~** roll

pair (pair) *adj* even

paire (pair) *f* pair

paisible (pay-*zeebl*) *adj* peaceful, quiet

paix (pay) *f* peace

Pakistan (pah-kee-*stahng*) *m* Pakistan

pakistanais (pah-kee-stah-*nay*) *adj* Pakistani

palais (pah-*lay*) *m* palace; palate

pâle (paal) *adj* pale

palmier (pahl-*m^yay*) *m* palm (tree)

palper (pahl-*pay*) *v* *feel

palpitation (pahl-pee-tah-*s^yawng*) *f* palpitation

pamplemousse (pahng-pler-*mooss*) *m* grapefruit

panier (pah-*n^yay*) *m* basket

panique (pah-*neek*) *f* panic; scare

panne (pahn) *f* breakdown; **tomber en ~** *break down

panneau (pah-*noa*) *m* panel

pansement (pahng-*smahng*) *m* bandage

panser (pahng-*say*) *v* dress

pantalon (pahng-tah-*lawng*) *m* trousers *pl*, slacks *pl*; pants *plAm*; **ensemble-pantalon** pant suit; ~ **de ski** ski pants

pantoufle (pahng-*toofl*) *f* slipper

paon (pahng) *m* peacock

papa (pah-*pah*) *m* daddy

pape (pahp) *m* pope

papeterie (pah-peh-*tree*) *f* stationer's; stationery

papier (pah-*p^yay*) *m* paper; **en ~** paper; ~ **de brouillon** rough paper; ~ **à lettres** notepaper, writing paper; ~ **à machine** typing paper; ~ **buvard** blotting paper; ~ **carbone** carbon paper; ~ **d'emballage** wrapping paper; ~ **d'étain** tinfoil; ~ **de verre** sandpaper; ~ **hygiénique** toilet paper; ~ **peint** wallpaper

papillon (pah-pee-*^yawng*) *m* butterfly

paquebot (pahk-*boa*) *m* liner

Pâques (paak) Easter

paquet (pah-*kay*) *m* parcel, packet; bundle

par (pahr) *prep* by; for

parade (pah-*rahd*) *f* parade

paragraphe (pah-rah-*grahf*) *m* paragraph

***paraître** (pah-*raitr*) *v* seem, appear

parallèle (pah-rah-*lehl*) *m* parallel; *adj* parallel

paralyser (pah-rah-lee-*zay*) *v* paralyze; **paralysé** paralyzed

parapluie (pah-rah-*plwee*) *m* umbrella

parasol (pah-rah-*sol*) *m* sunshade

parc (pahrk) *m* park; ~ **de stationnement** car park; ~ **national** national park

parce que (pahr-*sker*) as, because

parcmètre (pahrk-mehtr) *m* parking meter

***parcourir** (pahr-koo-*reer*) *v* *go through; cover

parcours (pahr-*koor*) *m* distance; route; course

par-dessus (pahr-der-*sew*) *prep* over

pardessus (pahr-der-*sew*) *m* coat, overcoat

pardon (pahr-*dawng*) *m* pardon; **pardon!** sorry!

pardonner (pahr-do-*nay*) *v* *forgive

pare-brise (pahr-*breez*) *m* windscreen, windshield *Am*

pare-choc (pahr-*shok*) *m* bumper

pareil (pah-*ray*) *adj* alike, like; **sans ~** unsurpassed

parent (pah-*rahng*) *m* relative, relation; **parents** parents *pl*; **parents nourriciers** foster parents *pl*

paresseux (pah-reh-*sur*) *adj* lazy

parfait (pahr-*fay*) *adj* perfect; faultless

parfois (pahr-*fwah*) *adv* sometimes

parfum (pahr-*furng*) *m* scent; perfume

parfumerie (pahr-fewm-*ree*) *f* perfumery

pari (pah-*ree*) *m* bet

parier (pah-*r^yay*) *v* *bet

parking (pahr-*keeng*) *m* parking lot *Am*

parlement (pahr-ler-*mahng*) *m* parliament

parlementaire (pahr-ler-mahng-*tair*) *adj* parliamentary

parler (pahr-*lay*) *v* talk, *speak

parmi (pahr-*mee*) *prep* among, amid

paroisse (pah-*rwahss*) *f* parish

parole (pah-*rol*) *f* speech

parrain (pah-*rang*) *m* godfather

part (paar) *f* part, share; **à ~** separately, apart; aside; **nulle ~** nowhere; **quelque ~** somewhere

partager (pahr-tah-*zhay*) *v* share

partenaire (pahr-ter-*nair*) *m/f* associate, partner

parti (pahr-*tee*) *m* party; side

partial (pahr-s^y*ahl*) *adj* partial

participant (pahr-tee-see-*pahng*) *m*, **-e** *f* participant

participer (pahr-tee-see-*pay*) *v* participate

particularité (pahr-tee-kew-lah-ree-*tay*) *f* particularity, characteristic

particulier (pahr-tee-kew-*l^yay*) *adj* particular, special; individual, private; peculiar; *m* private individual; **en ~** in particular

particulièrement (pahr-tee-kew-l^y*ehr-mahng*) *adv* specially

partie (pahr-*tee*) *f* part; **en ~** partly

partiel (pahr-s^y*ehl*) *adj* partial

partiellement (pahr-s^yehl-*mahng*) *adv* partly

*partir (pahr-*teer*) *v* *leave, *go away; *set out, depart, pull out; **à partir de** as from, from; **parti** gone

partisan (pahr-tee-*zahng*) *m* advocate

partout (pahr-*too*) *adv* throughout, everywhere; **~ où** wherever

*parvenir à (pahr-ver-*neer*) achieve

pas (pah) *m* step; pace; move; **faux ~** slip; **ne ... ~** not

passablement (pah-sah-bler-*mahng*) *adv* pretty, rather, fairly

passage (pah-*saazh*) *m* passage; crossing; aisle; **~ à niveau** crossing; **~ clouté** pedestrian crossing; **~ pour piétons** crosswalk *Am*

passager (pah-sah-*zhay*) *m*, **-ère** *f* passenger

passant (pah-*sahng*) *m* passer-by

passé (pah-*say*) *m* past; *adj* past; *prep* over

passeport (pah-*spawr*) *m* passport

passer (pah-*say*) *v* pass; *give; **en passant** casually; **~ à côté** pass by; **~ en contrebande** smuggle; **se ~** occur; **se ~ de** spare

passerelle (pah-*srehl*) *f* gangway

passe-temps (pah-*stahng*) *m* hobby

passif (pah-*seef*) *adj* passive

passion (pah-s^y*awng*) *f* passion

passionnant (pah-s^yo-*nahng*) *adj* exciting

passionné (pah-s^yo-*nay*) *adj*
passionate; keen

passoire (pah-*swaar*) *f* sieve; strainer

pastèque (pah-*stehk*) *f* watermelon

pasteur (pah-*stūr*) *m* clergyman;
parson, minister; rector

pastille (pah-*steey*) *f* pastille, lozenge

patauger (pah-toa-*zhay*) *v* wade

pâte (paat) *f* paste; dough, batter; pie;
~ **dentifrice** toothpaste

patère (pah-*tair*) *f* peg

paternel (pah-tehr-*nehl*) *adj* fatherly

patience (pah-s^yah<u>ng</u>ss) *f* patience

patient (pah-s^yah<u>ng</u>) *adj* patient; *m*, **-e**
f patient

patin (pah-*ra<u>ng</u>*) *m* skate

patinage (pah-tee-*naazh*) *m* skating; ~
à roulettes roller-skating

patiner (pah-tee-*nay*) *v* skate

patinette (pah-tee-*neht*) *f* scooter

patinoire (pah-tee-*nwaar*) *f* skating
rink

pâtisserie (pah-tee-*sree*) *f* cake,
pastry; pastry shop

patrie (pah-*tree*) *f* native country

patriote (pah-tree-*ot*) *m* patriot

patron (pah-*traw<u>ng</u>*) *m* master, boss

patronne (pah-*tron*) *f* mistress

patrouille (pah-*troo^{ee}*) *f* patrol

patrouiller (pah-troo-^y*ay*) *v* patrol

patte (paht) *f* paw

pâture (pah-*tēwr*) *f* pasture

paume (pōam) *f* palm

paupière (poa-p^y*air*) *f* eyelid

pause (pōaz) *f* pause; break

pauvre (pōavr) *adj* poor

pauvreté (poa-vrer-*tay*) *f* poverty

paver (pah-*vay*) *v* pave

pavillon (pah-vee-^y*aw<u>ng</u>*) *m* pavilion;
~ **de chasse** lodge

pavot (pah-*voa*) *m* poppy

payable (pay-^y*ahbl*) *adj* due

paye (pay) *f* pay

payer (pay-^y*ay*) *v* *pay; ~ comptant

*pay cash

pays (pay-*ee*) *m* country, land; ~ **boisé**
woodland; ~ **natal** native country

paysage (pay-ee-*zaazh*) *m* landscape
scenery

paysan (pay-ee-*zah<u>ng</u>*) *m* peasant

Pays-Bas (pay-ee-*bah*) *mpl* the
Netherlands

péage (pay-*aazh*) *m* toll

peau (poa) *f* skin; hide; ~ **de porc**
pigskin

péché (pay-*shay*) *m* sin

pêche[1] (pehsh) *f* peach

pêche[2] (pehsh) *f* fishing industry;
attirail de ~ fishing tackle, fishing
gear

pêcher (pay-*shay*) *v* fish; ~ **à la ligne**
angle

pêcheur (peh-*shūrr*) *m* fisherman

pédale (pay-*dahl*) *f* pedal

pédiatre (pay-*dyaatr*) *m* p(a)ediatrist

peigne (pehñ) *m* comb

peigner (pay-*ñay*) *v* comb

peignoir (peh-*ñwaar*) *m* bathrobe

***peindre** (pa<u>ng</u>dr) *v* paint

peine (pehn) *f* trouble, pains,
difficulty; penalty; **à** ~ hardly; just,
barely, scarcely; ***avoir de la** ~ grieve;
~ **de mort** death penalty

peiner (pay-*nay*) *v* labo(u)r

peintre (pa<u>ng</u>tr) *m* painter

peinture (pa<u>ng</u>-*tēwr*) *f* paint; picture,
painting; ~ **à l'huile** oil painting

peler (per-*lay*) *v* peel

pèlerin (pehl-*ra<u>ng</u>*) *m* pilgrim

pèlerinage (pehl-ree-*naazh*) *m*
pilgrimage

pélican (pay-lee-*kah<u>ng</u>*) *m* pelican

pelle (pehl) *f* spade, shovel

pellicule (peh-lee-*kewl*) *f* film;
pellicules dandruff

pelouse (per-*lōoz*) *f* lawn

pelure (per-*lēwr*) *f* peel

penchant (pah<u>ng</u>-shah<u>ng</u>) *m*

inclination

bencher (pahng-*shay*) v: **se ~** *bend down

bendant (pahng-*dahng*) prep for, during; **~ que** while

bendentif (pahng-dahng-*teef*) m pendant

pendre (pahngdr) v *hang

pénétrer (pay-nay-*tray*) v penetrate

pénible (pay-*neebl*) adj laborious; painful

pénicilline (pay-nee-see-*leen*) f penicillin

péninsule (pay-nang-*sewl*) f peninsula

pensée (pahng-*say*) f thought; idea

penser (pahng-*say*) v *think; **~ à** *think of

pensif (pahng-*seef*) adj thoughtful

pension (pahng-s^y*awng*) f guesthouse, pension, boardinghouse; board; **~ complète** room and board, full board, bed and board, board and lodging

pensionnaire (pahng-s^{y}o-*nair*) m/f boarder

pente (pahngt) f incline; ramp; **en ~** sloping, slanting

Pentecôte (pahngt-*koat*) f Whitsun, Pentecost Am

pénurie (pay-new-*ree*) f scarcity

pépé (pay-*pay*) m grandad

pépin (pay-*pang*) m pip

pépinière (pay-pee-n^y*air*) f nursery

perceptible (pehr-sehp-*teebl*) adj noticeable, perceptible

perception (pehr-seh-ps^y*awng*) f perception

percer (pehr-*say*) v pierce

*percevoir (pehr-ser-*vwaar*) v perceive; sense

perche (pehrsh) f perch, bass

percolateur (pehr-ko-lah-*tūrr*) m percolator

perdre (pehrdr) v *lose

perdrix (pehr-*dree*) f partridge

père (pair) m father

perfection (pehr-fehk-s^y*awng*) f perfection

performance (pehr-for-*mahngss*) f achievement; performance

péril (pay-*reel*) m peril

périlleux (pay-ree-^{y}*ur*) adj perilous

périmé (pay-ree-*may*) adj expired

période (pay-r^y*od*) f period; term

périodique (pay-r^{y}o-*deek*) adj periodical; m journal, periodical

périr (pay-*reer*) v perish

périssable (pay-ree-*sahbl*) adj perishable

perle (pehrl) f pearl; bead

permanent (pehr-mah-*nahng*) adj permanent

permanente (pehr-mah-*nahngt*) f permanent wave

*permettre (pehr-*mehtr*) v permit, allow; enable; **se ~** afford

permis (pehr-*mee*) m permit; permission, licence; **~ de conduire** driver's license Am, driving licence; **~ de pêche** fishing licence; **~ de séjour** residence permit; **~ de travail** work permit; labor permit Am

permission (pehr-mee-s^y*awng*) f authorization, permission; leave

perpendiculaire (pehr-pahng-dee-kew-*lair*) adj perpendicular

perroquet (peh-ro-*kay*) m parrot

perruche (peh-*rewsh*) f parakeet

perruque (peh-*rewk*) f wig

persan (pehr-*sahng*) adj Persian

Perse (pehrs) f Persia

persévérer (pehr-say-vay-*ray*) v *keep up

persienne (pehr-s^y*ehn*) f blind; shutter

persil (pehr-*see*) m parsley

persister (pehr-see-*stay*) v insist

personnalité (pehr-so-nah-lee-*tay*) f personality

personne (pehr-*son*) f person; **ne ...
personne** nobody, no one; **par ~** per
person

personnel (pehr-so-*nehl*) m
personnel, staff; *adj* personal, private

perspective (pehr-spehk-*teev*) f
perspective, prospect

persuader (pehr-swah-*day*) v
persuade

perte (pehrt) f loss

pertinent (pehr-tee-*nahng*) adj proper

peser (per-*zay*) v weigh

pessimisme (peh-see-*meesm*) m
pessimism

pessimiste (peh-see-*meest*) m/f
pessimist; *adj* pessimistic

pétale (pay-*tahl*) m petal

pétanque (pay-*tahngk*) f petanque

pétillement (pay-teey-*mahng*) m fizz

petit (per-*tee*) adj small, little; petty,
short, minor

petite-fille (per-teet-*feey*) f
granddaughter

petit-fils (per-tee-*feess*) m grandson

pétition (pay-tee-s^y*awng*) f petition

petits pois (per-tee-*pwah*)* pl peas

pétrole (pay-*trol*) m petroleum, oil;
kerosene, paraffin; **gisement de ~** oil
well

peu (pur) adj little; m bit; **à ~ près**
approximately, about; almost; **~ de**
few; **quelque ~** somewhat; **sous ~**
soon, shortly; **un ~** some

peuple (purpl) m people; nation

peur (pūrr) f fear, fright; ***avoir ~** *be
afraid

peut-être (pur-*taitr*) adv maybe,
perhaps

phare (faar) m lighthouse; headlight,
headlamp; **~ anti-brouillard** foglamp

pharmacie (fahr-mah-*see*) f pharmacy,
chemist's; drugstore *Am*

pharmacien (fahr-mah-s^y*ang*) m, **-ne** f
chemist, pharmacist *Am*

pharmacologie (fahr-mah-ko-lo-*zhee*)
f pharmacology

phase (faaz) f phase, stage

philippin (fee-lee-*pang*) adj Philippine

Philippines (fee-lee-*peen*) fpl
Philippines pl

philosophe (fee-lo-*zof*) m
philosopher

philosophie (fee-lo-zo-*fee*) f
philosophy

phonétique (fo-nay-*teek*) adj phonetic

phoque (fok) m seal

photo (fo-*toa*) f photo; **~ d'identité**
passport photograph

photocopie (fo-to-ko-*pee*) f photocopy

photographe (fo-to-*grahf*) m/f
photographer

photographie (fo-to-grah-*fee*) f
photography; photograph

photographier (fo-to-grah-f^y*ay*) v
photograph

phrase (fraaz) f sentence

physicien (fee-zee-s^y*ang*) m, **-ne** f
physicist

physique (fee-*zeek*) f physics; adj
physical

pianiste (p^yah-*neest*) m/f pianist

piano (p^yah-*noa*) m piano; **~ à queue**
grand piano

pickpocket (peek-po-*keht*)* m
pickpocket

pie (pee) f magpie

pièce (p^yehss) f piece; room, chamber;
~ de monnaie coin; **~ de rechange**
spare part; **~ détachée** spare part; **~
de théâtre** play

pied (p^yay) m foot; leg; **à ~** walking, on
foot

piège (p^yaizh) m trap

pierre (p^yair) f stone; **en ~** stone; **~ à
briquet** flint; **~ ponce** pumice stone;
~ précieuse gem; stone; **~ tombale**
tombstone, gravestone

piétiner (p^yay-tee-*nay*) v stamp

piéton (pʸay-*tawng̅*) *m* pedestrian

piètre (pʸehtr) *adj* poor

pieuvre (pʸūrvr) *f* octopus

pieux (pʸur) *adj* pious

pigeon (pee-*zhawng̅*) *m* pigeon

pignon (pee-*ñawng̅*) *m* gable

pile (peel) *f* stack; battery

pilier (pee-*lʸay*) *m* pillar

pilote (pee-*lot*) *m* pilot

pilule (pee-*lewl*) *f* pill

piment (pee-*mahng̅*)* *m* red pepper; spice

pin (pang̅) *m* pine

pince (pang̅ss) *f* pliers *pl*, tongs *pl*; tweezers *pl*; ~ **à cheveux** hairgrip; bobby pin *Am*

pinceau (pang̅-soa) *m* brush; paintbrush

pincer (pang̅-say) *v* pinch

pincettes (pang̅-seht) *fpl* tweezers *pl*

pingouin (pang̅-gwang̅) *m* penguin

ping-pong (peeng-pong) *m* table tennis

pion (pʸawng̅) *m* pawn

pionnier (pʸo-n*ʸay*) *m* pioneer

pipe (peep) *f* pipe

piquant (pee-*kahng̅*) *adj* savo(u)ry

pique-nique (peek-*neek*) *m* picnic

pique-niquer (peek-nee-*kay*) *v* picnic

piquer (pee-*kay*) *v* *sting, prick

piqûre (pee-*kēwr*) *f* shot; sting, bite

pirate (pee-*raht*) *m* pirate

pire (peer) *adj* worse; **le ~** worst

pis (pee) *adv* worse; **tant pis!** never mind!

piscine (pee-*seen*) *f* swimming pool

pissenlit (pee-sahng̅-*lee*) *m* dandelion

pistache (pee-*stahsh*)* *f* pistachio nut

piste (peest) *f* trail; track; ring; ~ **de courses** racetrack; ~ **de décollage** runway

pistolet (pee-sto-*lay*) *m* pistol

piston (pee-*stawng̅*) *m* piston; **segment de ~** piston ring

pitié (pee-*tʸay*) *f* pity; ***avoir ~ de** pity

pittoresque (pee-to-*rehsk*) *adj* picturesque, scenic

pizza (pee-*tsah*)* *f* pizza

placard (plah-*kaar*) *m* closet, cupboard

place (plahss) *f* place; seat; room; square; ~ **forte** stronghold

placement (plah-*smahng̅*) *m* investment

placer (plah-*say*) *v* place; *put, *lay; invest

plafond (plah-*fawng̅*) *m* ceiling

plage (plaazh) *f* beach; ~ **pour nudistes** nudist beach

plaider (play-*day*) *v* plead

plaidoyer (pleh-dwah-*ʸay*) *m* plea

plaie (play) *f* wound

*plaindre (plang̅dr) *v*: **se ~** complain

plaine (plehn) *f* plain, lowlands *pl*

plainte (plang̅t) *f* complaint

*plaire (plair) *v* please; **s'il vous plaît** please

plaisant (pleh-*zahng̅*) *adj* pleasant; nice, enjoyable, amusing

plaisanter (pleh-zahng̅-*tay*) *v* joke

plaisanterie (play-zahng̅-*tree*) *f* joke

plaisir (play-*zeer*) *m* pleasure; joy, delight, fun, enjoyment; **avec ~** gladly; ***prendre ~** enjoy

plan (plahng̅) *m* plan, project; map; scheme; *adj* flat, level, even; **premier ~** foreground

planche (plahng̅sh) *f* plank, board

plancher (plahng̅-*shay*) *m* floor

planétarium (plah-nay-tah-r*ʸom*) *m* planetarium

planète (plah-*neht*) *f* planet

planeur (plah-*nūrr*) *m* glider

planifier (plah-nee-*fʸay*) *v* plan

plantation (plahng̅-tah-s*ʸawng̅*) *f* plantation

plante (plahng̅t) *f* plant

planter (plahng̅-*tay*) *v* plant

plaque (plahk) f plate; sheet; ~ **d'immatriculation** registration plate; license plate Am

plastique (plah-*steek*) adj plastic; m plastic

plat (plah) m dish; course; adj flat, plane, smooth, level

plateau (plah-*toa*) m plateau; tray

plate-bande (plaht-*bahnḡd*) f flowerbed

platine (plah-*teen*) m platinum

plâtre (plaatr) m plaster

plein (planḡ) adj full; ***faire le ~** fill up; **pleine saison** high season

pleurer (plur-*ray*) v *weep, cry

***pleuvoir** (plur-*vwaar*) v rain

pli (plee) m fold; crease; ~ **permanent** permanent press

plie (plee) f plaice

plier (plee-*ay*) v fold

plomb (plawnḡ) m lead; **sans ~** unleaded

plombage (plawnḡ-*baazh*) m filling

plombier (plawnḡ-b*y*ay) m plumber

plonger (plawnḡ-*zhay*) v dive

pluie (plwee) f rain

plume (plewm) f feather; pen

plupart (plew-*paar*): (**la**) ~ most

pluriel (plew-r*y*ehl) m plural

plus (plewss) adj more; prep plus; **de ~** moreover; **le ~** most; **ne ... ~** no longer; **~ ... plus** the ... the

plusieurs (plew-z*y*ūūr) adj several

plutôt (plew-*toa*) adv fairly, pretty, rather, quite; sooner

pluvieux (plew-v*y*ur) adj rainy

pneu (pnur) m (pl ~s) tire Am, tyre; ~ **crevé** flat tyre (tire Am); ~ **de rechange** spare tyre (tire Am)

pneumatique (pnur-mah-*teek*) adj pneumatic

pneumonie (pnur-mo-*nee*) f pneumonia

poche (posh) f pocket; **lampe de ~** flashlight

pochette (po-*sheht*) f pouch

poêle (pwahl) f saucepan; m stove; ~ **à frire** frying pan

poème (po-*ehm*) m poem; ~ **épique** epic

poésie (po-ay-*zee*) f poetry

poète (po-*eht*) m poet

poids (pwah) m weight

poignée (pwah-*ñay*) f handle; handful; ~ **de main** handshake

poignet (pwah-*ñay*) m wrist

poil (pwahl) m hair

poing (pwanḡ) m fist

point (pwanḡ) m point; item; period, full stop; stitch; ~ **de congélation** freezing point; ~ **de départ** starting point; ~ **de repère** landmark; ~ **de vue** view, outlook; ~ **d'interrogation** question mark; **point-virgule** m semicolon

pointe (pwanḡt) f point; **heure de ~** peak hour

pointer (pwanḡ-*tay*) v tick off

pointu (pwanḡ-*tew*) adj pointed

pointure (pwanḡ-*tewr*)* f size

poire (pwaar) f pear

poireau (pwah-*roa*) m leek

pois (pwah) m pea

poison (pwah-*zawnḡ*) m poison

poisson (pwah-*sawnḡ*) m fish

poissonnerie (pwah-son-*ree*) f fish shop

poitrine (pwah-*treen*) f chest; bosom

poivre (pwaavr) m pepper

pôle nord (poal nawr) North Pole

pôle sud (poal sewd) South Pole

poli (po-*lee*) adj polite; civil

police (po-*leess*) f police pl; policy; **commissariat de ~** police station; ~ **d'assurance** insurance policy

policier (po-lee-s*y*ay) m policeman

poliomyélite (po-l*y*o-m*y*ay-*leet*) f polio

polir (po-*leer*) v polish

polisson (po-lee-*sawng*) *adj* naughty

politicien (po-lee-tee-s*ʸang*) *m*, **-ne** *f*
politician

politique (po-lee-*teek*) *f* politics;
policy; *adj* political

pollution (po-lew-s*ʸawng*) *f* pollution

Pologne (po-*loñ*) *f* Poland

Polonais (po-lo-*nay*) *m* Pole

polonais (po-lo-*nay*) *adj* Polish

pomme (pom) *f* apple; **~ de terre**
potato; **pommes frites** chips, French
fries *Am*

pompe (*pawngp*) *f* pump; **~ à eau**
water pump; **~ à essence** petrol
pump, gas pump *Am*

pomper (pawng-*pay*) *v* pump

pompier (pawng-*pʸay*) *m* fireman;
pompiers fire brigade, fire
department *Am*

ponctuel (pawngk-*twehl*) *adj* punctual

pondéré (pawng-day-*ray*) *adj* level-
minded

pondre (*pawngdr*) *v* *lay

poney (po-*nay*) *m* pony

pont (*pawng*) *m* bridge; deck;
pontlevis *m* drawbridge; **~ principal**
main deck; **~ suspendu** suspension
bridge

populaire (po-pew-*lair*) *adj* popular

population (po-pew-lah-s*ʸawng*) *f*
population

populeux (po-pew-*lur*) *adj* populous

porc (pawr) *m* pork

porcelaine (por-ser-*lehn*) *f* porcelain,
china

porc-épic (por-kay-*peek*) *m* porcupine

port[1] (pawr) *m* port, harbo(u)r; **~ de
mer** seaport

port[2] (pawr) *m* postage; **~ payé**
postage paid, post-paid

portatif (por-tah-*teef*) *adj* portable

porte (port) *f* door; gate; **~ coulissante**
sliding door; **~ tournante** revolving
door

porte-bagages (port-bah-*gaazh*) *m*
luggage rack

porte-bonheur (port-bo-*nūrr*) *m*
lucky charm

portée (por-*tay*) *f* reach; litter

portefeuille (por-ter-*fuʸeᵉ*) *m* wallet,
billfold *Am*

porte-manteau (port-mahng-*toa*) *m*
hat rack

porte-monnaie (port-mo-*nay*) *m*
purse

porter (por-*tay*) *v* carry, *bear; *wear;
~ sur concern; **se ~ bien** *be in good
health

porteur (por-*rūrr*) *m* bearer; porter

portier (por-*tʸay*) *m* porter, doorman,
doorkeeper

portière (por-*tʸair*)* *f* door

portion (por-s*ʸawng*) *f* helping,
portion

portrait (por-*tray*) *m* portrait

Portugais (por-tew-*gay*) *m* Portuguese

portugais (por-tew-*gay*) *adj*
Portuguese

Portugal (por-tew-*gahl*) *m* Portugal

poser (poa-*zay*) *v* place; *put, *lay,
*set

positif (poa-zee-*teef*) *m* positive; *adj*
positive

position (poa-zee-s*ʸawng*) *f* position

posséder (po-say-*day*) *v* possess, own

possession (po-seh-s*ʸawng*) *f*
possession

possibilité (po-see-bee-lee-*tay*) *f*
possibility

possible (po-*seebl*) *adj* possible

poste[1] (post) *f* post; *mettre à la **~** mail;
~ aérienne airmail; **~ restante** poste
restante

poste[2] (post) *m* station; post; **~ de
secours** first aid post; **~ d'essence**
petrol station, gas station *Am*

poster (po-*stay*) *v* post

postérieur (po-stay-r*ʸūrr*) *m* bottom;

adj subsequent

postiche (po-*steesh*) *m* hair piece

pot (poa) *m* pot

potable (po-*tahbl*) *adj* for drinking

potage (po-*taazh*) *m* soup

poteau (po-*toa*) *m* post, pole; ~ **indicateur** milepost, signpost

potelé (po-*tlay*) *adj* plump

poterie (po-*tree*) *f* pottery, crockery

pou (poo) *m* (pl ~x) louse

poubelle (poo-*behl*) *f* rubbish bin

pouce (pooss) *m* thumb

poudre (poodr) *f* powder; ~ **à canon** gunpowder; ~ **dentifrice** toothpowder; ~ **de riz** face powder; ~ **pour les pieds** foot powder; **savon en** ~ soap powder

poudrier (poo-dree-*ay*) *m* powder compact

poule (pool) *f* hen

poulet (poo-*lay*) *m* chicken

pouls (poo) *m* pulse

poumon (poo-*mawng*) *m* lung

poupée (poo-*pay*) *f* doll

pour (po͞or) *prep* for, to; ~ **que** so that

pourboire (poor-*bwaar*) *m* tip, gratuity

pourcentage (poor-sahng-*taazh*) *m* percentage

pourchasser (poor-shah-*say*) *v* chase

pourpre (poorpr) *adj* purple

pourquoi (poor-*kwah*) *adv* why; what for

pourrir (poo-*reer*) *v* rot; **pourri** rotten

***poursuivre** (poor-*sweevr*) *v* carry on, continue, pursue

pourtant (poor-*tahng*) *adv* however, yet; though

pourvu que (poor-vew ker) provided that

poussée (poo-*say*) *f* push

pousser (poo-*say*) *v* push

poussette (poo-*seht*) *f* baby carriage *Am*

poussière (poo-s^y*air*) *f* dust

poussiéreux (poo-s^y*ay-rur*) *adj* dusty

poutre (pootr) *f* beam

pouvoir (poo-*vwaar*) *m* power; authority; ~ **exécutif** executive

***pouvoir** (poo-*vwaar*) *v* *can, *be able to; *might, *may

praline (prah-*leen*) *f* chocolate

pratique (prah-*teek*) *f* practice; *adj* practical, convenient

pratiquer (prah-tee-*kay*) *v* practise

pré (pray) *m* meadow

préalable (pray-ah-*lahbl*) *adj* previous

précaire (pray-*kair*) *adj* precarious, critical

précaution (pray-koa-s^y*awng*) *f* precaution

précédemment (pray-say-dah-*mahng*) *adv* before

précédent (pray-say-*dahng*) *adj* preceding, previous, last; former

précéder (pray-say-*day*) *v* precede

prêcher (pray-*shay*) *v* preach

précieux (pray-s^y*ur*) *adj* valuable; precious

précipice (pray-see-*peess*) *m* precipice

précipitation (pray-see-pee-tah-s^y*awng*) *f* precipitation

précipité (pray-see-pee-*tay*) *adj* hasty

se précipiter (pray-see-pee-*tay*) *v* dash

précis (pray-*see*) *adj* precise; accurate

préciser (pray-see-*zay*) *v* specify

précision (pray-see-z^y*awng*) *f* precision; **précisions** points *pl*

***prédire** (pray-*deer*) *v* predict

préférable (pray-fay-*rahbl*) *adj* preferable

préférence (pray-fay-*rahngss*) *f* preference

préférer (pray-fay-*ray*) *v* prefer; **préféré** favo(u)rite

préjudiciable (pray-zhew-dee-s^y*ahbl*) *adj* harmful

préjugé (pray-zhew-*zhay*) *m* prejudice

prélever (prayl-*vay*) v impose; deduct; *withdraw

préliminaire (pray-lee-mee-*nair*) adj preliminary

prématuré (pray-mah-tew-*ray*) adj premature

premier (prer-*m*ᵞ*ay*) num first; adj foremost, primary; ~ **ministre** premier

***prendre** (prahn̄gdr) v *take; collect; v *catch; capture; ~ **garde** look out, beware; ~ **soin de** look after

prénom (pray-*nawn̄g*) m first name, Christian name

préparation (pray-pah-rah-s*ᵞawn̄g*) f preparation

préparer (pray-pah-*ray*) v prepare; arrange; cook

préposition (pray-poa-zee-s*ᵞawn̄g*) f preposition

près (pray) adv near; **à peu** ~ about; ~ **de** by, near

prescription (preh-skree-*ps*ᵞawn̄g*) f prescription

***prescrire** (preh-*skreer*) v prescribe

présence (pray-*zahn̄gss*) f presence

présent (pray-*zahn̄g*) m present; adj present; **jusqu'à** ~ so far

présentation (pray-zahn̄g-tah-s*ᵞawn̄g*) f introduction

présenter (pray-zahn̄g-*tay*) v present; introduce; **se** ~ appear; report

préservatif (pray-sehr-vah-*teef*) m condom

président (pray-zee-*dahn̄g*) m, **-e** f president, chairman

présomptueux (pray-zawn̄gp-*twur*) adj presumptuous

presque (prehsk) adv nearly, almost

presqu'île (preh-*skeel*) f peninsula

pressant (preh-*sahn̄g*) adj pressing

presse (prehss) f press

presser (pray-*say*) v press; **se** ~ hurry, rush

pression (preh-s*ᵞawn̄g*) f pressure; ~ **atmosphérique** atmospheric pressure; ~ **des pneus** tyre (tire *Am*) pressure; ~ **d'huile** oil pressure

prestidigitateur (preh-stee-dee-zhee-tah-*tūūr*) m magician

prestige (preh-*steezh*) m prestige

présumer (pray-zew-*may*) v assume

prêt (pray) m loan; adj ready; prepared

prétendre (pray-*tahn̄gdr*) v claim, pretend

prétentieux (pray-tahn̄g-s*ᵞur*) adj conceited

prétention (pray-tahn̄g-s*ᵞawn̄g*) f claim

prêter (pray-*tay*) v *lend; ~ **attention à** attend to, mind

prétexte (pray-*tehkst*) m pretence, pretext

prêtre (praitr) m priest

preuve (prūrv) f proof, evidence

prévenant (preh-*vnahn̄g*) adj considerate, thoughtful

***prévenir** (preh-*vneer*) v warn; prevent, anticipate

préventif (preh-vahn̄g-*teef*) adj preventive

prévenu (pray-*vnew*) m, **-e** f accused

prévision (pray-vee-z*ᵞawn̄g*) f forecast, outlook

***prévoir** (pray-*vwaar*) v forecast; anticipate

prier (pree-*ay*) v pray; ask

prière (pree-*air*) f prayer

primaire (pree-*mair*) adj primary

prime (preem) f premium

primordial (pree-mor-*d*ᵞ*ahl*) adj primary

prince (prahn̄gss) m prince

princesse (prahn̄g-*sehss*) f princess

principal (prahn̄g-see-*pahl*) adj principal; cardinal, chief, leading, main

principalement (prahn̄g-see-pahl-

mahng) *adv* especially, mainly

principe (prang-*seep*) *m* principle

printemps (prang-*tahng*) *m* spring; springtime

priorité (pree-o-ree-*tay*) *f* priority; ~ **de passage** right of way

prise (preez) *f* grip, clutch, grasp; capture; ~ **de vue** shot

prison (pree-*zawng*) *f* prison; jail

prisonnier (pree-zo-*n*ʸ*ay*) *m*, **-ière** *f* prisoner; *faire ~ capture; ~ **de guerre** prisoner of war

privation (pree-vah-*s*ʸ*awng*) *f* deprivation, deprival

privé (pree-*vay*) *adj* private

priver de (pree-*vay*) deprive of

privilège (pree-vee-*laizh*) *m* privilege

prix (pree) *m* price; charge, cost; award, prize; ~ **courant** *m* price list; ~ **d'achat** purchase price; ~ **de consolation** consolation prize; ~ **d'entrée** entrance fee; ~ **du voyage** fare

probable (pro-*bahbl*) *adj* probable; presumable, likely

probablement (pro-bah-bler-*mahng*) *adv* probably

problème (pro-*blehm*) *m* problem; question

procédé (pro-say-*day*) *m* process

procéder (pro-say-*day*) *v* proceed

procédure (pro-say-*dewr*) *f* procedure

procès (pro-*say*) *m* process; trial, lawsuit

procession (pro-seh-*s*ʸ*awng*) *f* procession

processus (pro-say-*sewss*) *m* process

prochain (pro-*shang*) *adj* following, next

prochainement (pro-shen-*mahng*) *adv* soon, shortly

proche (prosh) *adj* close, near; nearby; oncoming

proclamer (pro-klah-*may*) *v* proclaim

procurer (pro-kew-*ray*) *v* furnish; **se ~** obtain

prodigue (pro-*deeg*) *adj* extravagant; generous

producteur (pro-dewk-*tūrr*) *m*, **-trice** *f* producer

production (pro-dewk-*s*ʸ*awng*) *f* production; output; ~ **en série** mass production

*produire (pro-*dweer*) *v* produce; generate; **se ~** occur, happen

produit (pro-*dwee*) *m* product; produce

prof (prof) *m or f* teacher

profane (pro-*fahn*) *m* layman

professer (pro-fay-*say*) *v* confess

professeur (pro-feh-*sūrr*) *m* teacher; professor

profession (pro-feh-*s*ʸ*awng*) *f* profession

professionnel (pro-feh-*s*ʸ*o-nehl*) *adj* professional

profit (pro-*fee*) *m* profit, benefit

profitable (pro-fee-*tahbl*) *adj* profitable

profiter (pro-fee-*tay*) *v* profit, benefit

profond (pro-*fawng*) *adj* deep; low; profound

profondeur (pro-fawng-*dūrr*) *f* depth

programme (pro-*grahm*) *m* programme

progrès (pro-*gray*) *m* progress

progresser (pro-gray-*say*) *v* *get on

progressif (pro-gray-*seef*) *adj* progressive

projecteur (pro-zhehk-*tūrr*) *m* spotlight; searchlight

projet (pro-*zhay*) *m* project; scheme

prolongation (pro-lawng-gah-*s*ʸ*awng*) *f* extension

prolonger (pro-lawng-*zhay*) *v* prolong, extend

promenade (prom-*nahd*) *f* walk, stroll; promenade; ~ **en voiture** drive

promener (prom-*nay*) *v*: **se ~** go for a walk

promeneur (prom-*nūrr*) *m* walker

promesse (pro-*mehss*) *f* promise

***promettre** (pro-*mehtr*) *v* promise

promontoire (pro-mawng-*twaar*) *m* headland

promotion (pro-mo-s^y*awng*) *f* promotion

***promouvoir** (pro-moo-*vwaar*) *v* promote

prompt (prawng) *adj* prompt; fast

prononcer (pro-nawng-*say*) *v* pronounce

prononciation (pro-nawng-s^yah-s^y*awng*) *f* pronunciation

proportion (pro-por-s^y*awng*) *f* proportion

proportionnel (pro-por-s^yo-*nehl*) *adj* proportional

propos (pro-*poa*) *m* intention; **à ~** by the way; **à ~ de** regarding

proposer (pro-poa-*zay*) *v* propose

proposition (pro-poa-zee-s^y*awng*) *f* proposition, proposal

propre (propr) *adj* clean; own

propriétaire (pro-pree-*ay*-tair) *m/f* owner, proprietor; landlord

propriété (pro-pree-ay-*tay*) *f* property; estate

propulser (pro-pewl-*say*) *v* propel

prospectus (pro-spehk-*tewss*) *m* prospectus

prospère (pro-*spair*) *adj* prosperous

prospérité (pro-spay-ree-*tay*) *f* prosperity

prostituée (pro-stee-*tway*) *f* prostitute

protection (pro-tehk-s^y*awng*) *f* protection

protéger (pro-tay-*zhay*) *v* protect

protestant (pro-teh-*stahng*) *adj* Protestant

protestation (pro-teh-stah-s^y*awng*) *f* protest

protester (pro-teh-*stay*) *v* protest

prouver (proo-*vay*) *v* prove

provenance (pro-*vnahngss*) *f* origin

***provenir de** (pro-*vneer*) *v* come from

proverbe (pro-*vehrb*) *m* proverb

province (pro-*vangss*) *f* province

provincial (pro-vang-s^y*ahl*) *adj* provincial

proviseur (pro-vee-*zūrr*) *m* principal

provision (pro-vee-z^y*awng*) *f* store; provisions *pl*

provisoire (pro-vee-*zwaar*) *adj* temporary, provisional

provoquer (pro-vo-*kay*) *v* cause

prudence (prew-*dahngss*) *f* caution

prudent (prew-*dahng*) *adj* careful; cautious, wary

prune (prewn) *f* plum

pruneau (prew-*noa*) *m* prune

prurit (prew-*reet*) *m* pruritus

psychiatre (psee-k^y*aatr*) *m* psychiatrist

psychique (psee-*sheek*) *adj* psychic

psychologie (psee-ko-lo-*zhee*) *f* psychology

psychologique (psee-ko-lo-*zheek*) *adj* psychological

psychologue (psee-ko-*log*) *m/f* psychologist

public (pew-*bleek*) *m* audience, public; *adj* public

publication (pew-blee-kah-s^y*awng*) *f* publication

publicité (pew-blee-see-*tay*) *f* advertising, publicity; advertisement

publier (pew-blee-*ay*) *v* publish

puer (pway) *v* *stink

puis (pwee) *adv* then

puisque (pweesk) *conj* as

puissance (pwee-*sahngss*) *f* might, force; power, energy

puissant (pwee-*sahng*) *adj* powerful, mighty; strong

puits (pwee) *m* well; **~ de pétrole** oil well

pull(-over) (pew-lo-*vair*) *m* pullover

pulvérisateur (pewl-vay-ree-zah-*türr*) *m* atomizer

pulvériser (pewl-vay-ree-*zay*) *v* *grind

punaise (pew-*naiz*) *f* bug; drawing pin; thumbtack *Am*

punir (pew-*neer*) *v* punish

punition (pew-nee-*s^{y}awng*) *f* punishment

pupitre (pew-*peetr*) *m* desk; pulpit

pur (pewr) *adj* pure; clean; sheer, neat

pus (pew) *m* pus

pustule (pew-*stewl*) *f* pimple

putain (pew-*tang*) *f* whore

puzzle (purzl) *m* jigsaw puzzle

pyjama (pee-zhah-*mah*) *m* pyjamas *pl*

Q

quai (kay) *m* wharf, dock, quay; platform

qualification (kah-lee-fee-kah-*s^{y}awng*) *f* qualification

qualifié (kah-lee-*f^{y}ay*) *adj* qualified; *être ~ qualify; non ~ unskilled

qualité (kah-lee-*tay*) *f* quality; de première ~ first-class; first-rate

quand (kahng) *adv* when; *conj* when; n'importe ~ whenever

quant à (kahng-*tah*) as regards

quantité (kahng-tee-*tay*) *f* quantity, amount; lot

quarantaine (kah-rahng-*tehn*) *f* quarantine

quarante (kah-*rahngt*) *num* forty

quart (kaar) *m* quarter; ~ d'heure quarter of an hour

quartier (kahr-*t^{y}ay*) *m* district, quarter; bas ~ slum; ~ général headquarters *pl*

quatorze (kah-*torz*) *num* fourteen

quatorzième (kah-tor-*z^{y}ehm*) *num* fourteenth

quatre (kahtr) *num* four

quatre-vingt-dix (kah-trer-vang-*deess*) *num* ninety

quatre-vingts (kah-trer-*vang*) *num* eighty

quatrième (kah-*tr^{y}ehm*) *num* fourth

que (ker) *conj* that; as, than; *adv* how; ce ~ what

quel (kehl) *pron* which; n'importe ~ any; whichever

quelquefois (kehl-ker-*fwah*) *adv* sometimes

quelques (kehlk) *adj* some, some

quelqu'un (kehl-*kurng*) *pron* someone, somebody

querelle (ker-*rehl*) *f* dispute, row, quarrel

question (keh-*st^{y}awng*) *f* question; inquiry, query; matter, issue, problem

quêter (kay-*tay*) *v* collect

queue (kur) *f* tail; queue; *faire la ~ queue; stand in line *Am*

qui (kee) *pron* who; which, that; à ~ whom; n'importe ~ anybody

quiche (keesh) *f* quiche

quille (keey) *f* keel

quincaillerie (kang-kigh-*ree*) *f* hardware; hardware store

quinze (kangz) *num* fifteen; ~ jours fortnight

quinzième (kang-*z^{y}ehm*) *num* fifteenth

quitter (kee-*tay*) *v* *leave

quoi (kwah) *pron* what; n'importe ~ anything

quoique (kwahk) *conj* though,

although; **quoiqu'il en soit** at any rate

quote-part (kot-*paar*) f quota

R

rabais (rah-*bay*) m discount, reduction, rebate

raccourcir (rah-koor-*seer*) v shorten

racial (rah-*s^yahl*) adj racial

racine (rah-*seen*) f root

racler (rah-*klay*) v scrape

raconter (rah-kawng-*tay*) v *tell

radeau (rah-*doa*) m raft

radiateur (rah-d^yah-*turr*) m radiator

radical (rah-dee-*kahl*) adj radical

radio (rah-*d^yoa*) f wireless, radio

radiographie (rah-d^yoa-grah-*fee*) f X-ray

radiographier (rah-d^yoa-grah-*f^yay*) v X-ray

radis (rah-*dee*) m radish

radotage (rah-do-*taazh*) m rubbish

rafale (rah-*fahl*) f gust

raffinerie (rah-feen-*ree*) f refinery; **~ de pétrole** oil refinery

rafraîchir (rah-fray-*sheer*) v refresh

rafraîchissement (rah-freh-shee-*smahng*) m refreshment

rage (raazh) f rabies; rage; craze

rager (rah-*zhay*) v rage

raide (rehd) adj stiff

raie (ray) f stripe; parting

raifort (ray-*fawr*) m horseradish

rail (righ) m rail

raisin (ray-*zang*) m grapes pl; **~ sec** currant, raisin

raison (ray-*zawng*) f reason; cause; wits pl, sense; ***avoir ~** * be right; **en ~ de** for, owing to, because of

raisonnable (ray-zo-*nahbl*) adj reasonable; sensible

raisonner (ray-zo-*nay*) v reason

ralentir (rah-lahng-*teer*) v slow down

rallonge (rah-*lawngzh*) f extension cord

ramasser (rah-mah-*say*) v pick up

rame (rahm) f oar

ramener (rahm-*nay*) v *bring back

ramer (rah-*may*) v row

rampe (rahngp) f railing

ramper (rahng-*pay*) v *creep, crawl

rance (rahngss) adj rancid

rançon (rahng-*sawng*) f ransom

randonnée (rahng-do-*nay*) f tour, excursion; (long) trip; outing; hike

rang (rahng) m row, rank

rangée (rahng-*zhay*) f line

ranger (rahng-*zhay*) v sort; tidy up, *put away

râpe (raap) f grater

râper (rah-*pay*) v grate

rapide (rah-*peed*) adj quick; fast, swift, rapid; m rapids pl

rapidement (rah-peed-*mahng*) adv soon

rapidité (rah-pee-dee-*tay*) f speed

rappeler (rah-*play*) v remind; recall; **se ~** remember, recall

rapport (rah-*pawr*) m report; connection, relation; **rapports** intercourse

rapporter (rah-por-*tay*) v *bring back; report

rapprocher (rah-pro-*shay*) v *bring closer

quotidien (ko-tee-*d^yang*) adj everyday, daily; m daily

rare (raar) *adj* rare; uncommon, scarce

rarement (rahr-*mahng*) *adv* seldom, rarely

raser (rah-*zay*): **se ~** shave

raseur (rah-*zūrr*) *m* bore

rasoir (rah-*zwaar*) *m* razor; **~ électrique** electric razor; shaver

rassemblement (rah-sahng-bler-*mahng*) *m* rally

rassembler (rah-sahng-*blay*) *v* assemble; collect

rassis (rah-*see*) *adj* stale

rassurer (rah-sew-*ray*) *v* reassure

rat (rah) *m* rat

râteau (rah-*toa*) *m* rake

ration (rah-s^y*awng*) *f* ration

rauque (rōak) *adj* hoarse

ravissant (rah-vee-*sahng*) *adj* lovely, delightful, enchanting

rayé (ray-*^{y}ay*) *adj* striped

rayon (ray-*^{y}awng*) *m* beam, ray; radius; spoke

rayure (ray-*^{y}ewr*) *f* scratch

réaction (ray-ahk-s^y*awng*) *f* reaction

réalisable (ray-ah-lee-*zahbl*) *adj* feasible; realizable

réalisation (ray-ah-lee-zah-s^y*awng*) *f* realization; direction

réaliser (ray-ah-lee-*zay*) *v* realize; carry out, implement

réaliste (ray-ah-lee-*leest*) *adj* matter-of-fact

réalité (ray-ah-lee-*tay*) *f* reality; **en ~** actually; really

rébellion (ray-beh-l^y*awng*) *f* revolt, rebellion

rebord (rer-*bawr*) *m* edge, rim; **~ de fenêtre** windowsill

rebut (rer-*bew*) *m* junk, refuse

récemment (ray-sah-*mahng*) *adv* lately, recently

récent (ray-*sahng*) *adj* recent

réception (ray-seh-ps^y*awng*) *f* receipt; reception; reception office

recette (rer-*seht*) *f* recipe; **recettes** revenue

***recevoir** (rer-*svwaar*) *v* receive; entertain

recharge (rer-*shahrzh*) *f* refill

réchaud (ray-*shoa*)* *m* (portable) stove

réchauffer (ray-shoa-*fay*) *v* warm up

recherche (rer-*shehrsh*) *f* research

rechercher (rer-shehr-*shay*) *v* search for

récif (ray-*seef*) *m* reef

récipient (ray-see-p^y*ahng*) *m* container, vessel

réciproque (ray-see-*prok*) *adj* mutual

récit (ray-*see*) *m* tale; account

récital (ray-see-*tahl*) *m* (pl **~s**) recital

réclamation (ray-klah-mah-s^y*awng*) *f* claim

réclame (ray-*klahm*) *f* publicity

réclamer (ray-klah-*may*) *v* claim

récolte (ray-*kolt*) *f* crop

recommandation (rer-ko-mahng-dah-s^y*awng*) *f* recommendation

recommander (rer-ko-mahng-*day*) *v* recommend; register

recommencer (rer-ko-mahng-*say*) *v* recommence

récompense (ray-kawng-*pahngss*) *f* reward, prize

récompenser (ray-kawng-pahng-*say*) *v* reward

réconciliation (ray-kawng-see-l^{y}ah-s^y*awng*) *f* reconciliation

réconfort (ray-kawng-*fawr*) *m* comfort

reconnaissance (rer-ko-nay-*sahngss*) *f* recognition

reconnaissant (rer-ko-nay-*sahng*) *adj* thankful, grateful

***reconnaître** (rer-ko-*naitr*) *v* recognize; acknowledge; admit

record (rer-*kawr*) *m* record

***recouvrir** (rer-koo-*vreer*) *v* cover; recover

récréation (ray-kray-ah-sawng) f
recreation
rectangle (rehk-tahnggl) m rectangle;
oblong
rectangulaire (rehk-tahng-gew-lair)
adj rectangular
rectification (rehk-tee-fee-kah-
sawng) f correction
reçu (rer-sew) m receipt; voucher
***recueillir** (rer-kur-eer) v gather
reculer (rer-kew-lay) v step back; back
up
récupérer (ray-kew-pay-ray) v recover
rédacteur (ray-dahk-turr) m editor
rédiger (ray-dee-zhay) v *draw up
redouter (rer-doo-tay) v fear
réduction (ray-dewk-sawng) f
discount, reduction
***réduire** (ray-dweer) v reduce;
decrease, *cut
réduit (ray-dwee) m shed
rééducation (ray-ay-dew-kah-sawng)
f rehabilitation
réel (ray-ehl) adj real; true, factual,
actual, substantial
réellement (ray-ehl-mahng) adv really
référence (ray-fay-rahngss) f reference
réfléchir (ray-flay-sheer) v *think; ~ à
*think over
réflecteur (ray-flehk-turr) m reflector
reflet (rer-flay) m reflection
refléter (rer-flay-tay) v reflect
réforme (ray-form) f reformation
réfrigérateur (ray-free-zhay-rah-turr)
m fridge, refrigerator
refroidir (rer-frwah-deer) v cool off
refuge (rer-fewzh) m refuge
réfugié (ray-few-zhay) m, -e f refugee
refus (rer-few) m refusal
refuser (rer-few-zay) v refuse; deny,
reject
regard (rer-gaar) m look
regarder (rer-gahr-day) v look; watch,
look at; concern

régime (ray-zheem) m régime; rule,
government; diet
région (ray-zhawng) f region; area,
zone
régional (ray-zho-nahl) adj regional
règle (raigl) f rule; ruler; **en ~** in order
règlement (reh-gler-mahng) m
regulation; arrangement, settlement
régler (ray-glay) v regulate; settle
réglisse (ray-gleess) f liquorice
règne (rehñ) m reign; dominion, rule
régner (ray-ñay) v reign; rule
regret (rer-gray) m regret
regretter (rer-gray-tay) v regret
régulier (ray-gew-lay) adj regular
rein (rang) m kidney
reine (rehn) f queen
rejeter (rerzh-tay) v reject; turn down
***rejoindre** (rer-zhwangdr) v rejoin
relater (rer-lah-tay) v relate; report
relatif (rer-lah-teef) adj relative;
comparative; **~ à** with reference to,
concerning
relation (rer-lah-sawng) f connection;
relation
relayer (rer-lay-ay) v relieve
relèvement (rer-lehv-mahng) m
increase
relever (rerl-vay) v raise
relief (rer-lehf) m relief
relier (rer-lay) v link; *bind
religieuse (rer-lee-zhurz) f nun
religieux (rer-lee-zhur) adj religious
religion (rer-lee-zhawng) f religion
relique (rer-leek) f relic
reliure (rer-lewr) f binding
remarquable (rer-mahr-kahbl) adj
remarkable; noticeable, striking
remarque (rer-mahrk) f remark
remarquer (rer-mahr-kay) v notice;
remark
remboursement (rahng-boor-ser-
mahng) m repayment, refund
rembourser (rahng-boor-say) v

*repay, reimburse, refund

remède (rer-*mehd*) *m* remedy

remerciement (rer-mehr-see-*mahng*) *m* thanks *pl*

remercier (rer-mehr-s^y*ay*) *v* thank

***remettre** (rer-*mehtr*) *v* deliver; commit; hand over; remit; **se ~** recover

remise (rer-*meez*) *f* delivery

remonter (rer-mawng-*tay*) *v* *wind up

remorque (rer-*mork*) *f* trailer

remorquer (rer-mor-*kay*) *v* tow, tug

remorqueur (rer-mor-*kurr*) *m* tug

rémoulade (ray-moo-*lahd*) *f* remoulade-sauce

remplacer (rahng-plah-*say*) *v* replace

remplir (rahng-*pleer*) *v* fill; fill in; fill out *Am*

remue-ménage (rer-mew-may-*naazh*) *m* bustle

remuer (rer-*mway*) *v* stir

rémunération (ray-mew-nay-rah-s^y*awng*) *f* remuneration

rémunérer (ray-mew-nay-*ray*) *v* remunerate

renard (rer-*naar*) *m* fox

rencontre (rahng-*kawngtr*) *f* meeting, encounter; **aller à la ~** *go and *meet

rencontrer (rahng-kawng-*tray*) *v* *meet; *come across, run into, encounter

rendement (rahng-der-*mahng*) *m* profit

rendez-vous (rahng-day-*voo*) *m* appointment, date

rendre (*rahngdr*) *v* refund; *make; **~ compte de** account for; **~ visite à** call on; **se ~** surrender; *go; **se ~ compte** realize

renommée (rer-no-*may*) *f* fame

renoncer (rer-nawng-*say*) *v* *give up

renouveler (rer-noo-*vlay*) *v* renew

renseignement (rahng-sehn-*mahng*) *m* information; **bureau des**

renseignements inquiry office

renseigner (rahng-say-*ñay*) *v*: **se ~** inquire

rentable (rahng-*tahbl*) *adj* paying

rentrée (rahng-*tray*) *f* return; homecoming; re-entry

rentrer (rahng-*tray*) *v* *go home; reassemble

renverser (rahng-vehr-*say*) *v* knock down

***renvoyer** (rahng-vwah-^{y}*ay*) *v* *send back; dismiss; **~ à** refer to; postpone

répandre (ray-*pahngdr*) *v* *shed; *spill

réparation (ray-pah-rah-s^y*awng*) *f* reparation, repair

réparer (ray-pah-*ray*) *v* repair; mend; fix

répartir (ray-pahr-*teer*) *v* divide

repas (rer-*pah*) *m* meal

repassage *m* ironing

repasser (rer-pah-*say*) *v* press, iron

repentir (rer-pahng-*teer*) *m* repentance

répertoire (ray-pehr-*twaar*) *m* repertory

répéter (ray-pay-*tay*) *v* repeat; rehearse

répétition (ray-pay-tee-s^y*awng*) *f* repetition; rehearsal

répit (ray-*pee*) *m* respite

répondre (ray-*pawngdr*) *v* reply, answer

réponse (ray-*pawngss*) *f* reply, answer; **en ~** in reply; **sans ~** unanswered

reporter (rer-por-*tay*) *m* reporter

repos (rer-*poa*) *m* rest

reposant (rer-poa-*zahng*) *adj* restful

reposer (rer-poa-*zay*) *v*: **se ~** rest

repousser (rer-poo-*say*) *v* turn down; repel; **repoussant** repulsive

***reprendre** (rer-*prahngdr*) *v* resume; *take over

représentant (rer-pray-zahng-*tahng*) *m*, **-e** *f* agent

représentatif (rer-pray-zah͞ng-tah-*teef*) *adj* representative

représentation (rer-pray-zah͞ng-tah-*s*ʸ*aw͞ng*) *f* show; representation

représenter (rer-pray-zah͞ng-*tay*) *v* represent

réprimander (ray-pree-mah͞ng-*day*) *v* reprimand

réprimer (ray-pree-*may*) *v* suppress

reprise (rer-*preez*) *f* revival; round

repriser (rer-pree-*zay*) *v* darn

reproche (rer-*prosh*) *m* reproach

reprocher (rer-pro-*shay*) *v* reproach

reproduction (rer-pro-dewk-*s*ʸ*aw͞ng*) *f* reproduction

*reproduire (rer-pro-*dweer*) *v* reproduce

reptile (rehp-*teel*) *m* reptile

républicain (ray-pew-blee-*kah͞ng*) *adj* republican

république (ray-pew-*bleek*) *f* republic

répugnance (ray-pew-ñah͞ngss) *f* dislike

répugnant (ray-pew-ñah͞ng) *adj* repellent; filthy, disgusting, revolting

réputation (ray-pew-tah-*s*ʸ*aw͞ng*) *f* fame, reputation

*requérir (rer-kay-*reer*) *v* request

requête (rer-*keht*) *f* request

requin (rer-*kah͞ng*) *m* shark

requis (rer-*kee*) *adj* requisite

R.E.R. (ehr-er-*ehr*) *m* high-speed train service between Paris and the suburbs

réseau (ray-*zoa*) *m* network; ~ **routier** road system

réservation (ray-zehr-vah-*s*ʸ*aw͞ng*) *f* reservation; booking

réserve (ray-*zehrv*) *f* reserve; qualification; **de** ~ spare; ~ **zoologique** game reserve

réserver (ray-zehr-*vay*) *v* reserve; book

réservoir (ray-zehr-*vwaar*) *m* reservoir; tank; ~ **d'essence** petrol tank, gas tank *Am*

résidence (ray-zee-*dah͞ngss*) *f* residence

résident (ray-zee-*dah͞ng*) *m* resident

résider (ray-zee-*day*) *v* reside

résille (ray-*zeey*) *f* hair net

résine (ray-*zeen*) *f* resin

résistance (ray-zee-*stah͞ngss*) *f* resistance

résister (ray-zee-*stay*) *v* resist

résolu (ray-zo-*lew*) *adj* determined, resolute

*résoudre (ray-*zoodr*) *v* solve

respect (reh-*spay*) *m* respect; esteem, regard

respectable (reh-spehk-*tahbl*) *adj* respectable

respecter (reh-spehk-*tay*) *v* respect

respectif (reh-spehk-*teef*) *adj* respective

respectueux (reh-spehk-*twur*) *adj* respectful

respiration (reh-spee-rah-*s*ʸ*aw͞ng*) *f* breathing, respiration

respirer (reh-spee-*ray*) *v* breathe

resplendir (reh-splah͞ng-*deer*) *v* *shine

responsabilité (reh-spaw͞ng-sah-bee-lee-*tay*) *f* responsibility; liability

responsable (reh-spaw͞ng-*sahbl*) *adj* responsible; in charge; liable

ressemblance (rer-sah͞ng-*blah͞ngss*) *f* resemblance

ressembler à (rer-sah͞ng-*blay*) resemble

resserrer (rer-say-*ray*) *v* tighten; **se** ~ tighten

ressort (rer-*sawr*) *m* spring

ressource (rer-*soors*) *f* option; **ressources** resources *pl*; means *pl*

restant (reh-*stah͞ng*) *adj* remaining; *m* remnant, remainder

restaurant (reh-stoa-*rah͞ng*) *m* restaurant; ~ **libre service** self-service restaurant

reste (rehst) *m* rest; remnant, remainder

rester (reh-*stay*) *v* stay; remain

restituer (reh-stee-*tway*) *v* reimburse

restriction (reh-streek-*s^yawng*) *f* restriction; qualification

résultat (ray-zewl-*tah*) *m* result; issue, effect, outcome

résulter (ray-zewl-*tay*) *v*: ~ **de** result from

résumé (ray-zew-*may*) *m* résumé, summary; survey

retard (rer-*taar*) *m* delay; **en ~** overdue, late

retarder (rer-tahr-*day*) *v* delay

***retenir** (rert-*neer*) *v* reserve, book; remember; restrain

rétine (ray-*teen*) *f* retina

retirer (rer-tee-*ray*) *v* *withdraw

retour (rer-*toor*) *m* return; **voyage de ~** return journey

retourner (rer-toor-*nay*) *v* *get back; return, turn back, *go back; turn over, turn, turn round; **se ~** turn round

retracer (rer-trah-*say*) *v* trace

retraite (rer-*treht*) *f* retirement; pension

retraité (rer-tray-*tay*) *adj* retired

rétrécir (ray-tray-*seer*) *v* *shrink

rétroviseur (ray-tro-vee-*zurr*) *m* driving mirror, rear-view mirror

réunion (ray-ew-*n^yawng*) *f* meeting, assembly

réunir (ray-ew-*neer*) *v* join; reunite; **se ~** gather

réussir (ray-ew-*seer*) *v* manage, succeed; pass, *make; **réussi** successful

rêve (raiv) *m* dream

réveil (ray-*vay*) *m* alarm clock

réveiller (ray-vay-*^yay*) *v* *awake, *wake; **réveillé** awake; **se ~** wake up

révélation (ray-vay-lah-*s^yawng*) *f* revelation

révéler (ray-vay-*lay*) *v* reveal; *give away; **se ~** prove

revendication (rer-vahng-dee-kah-*s^yawng*) *f* claim

revendiquer (rer-vahng-dee-*kay*) *v* claim

***revenir** (rer-*vneer*) *v* return

revenu (rer-*vnew*) *m* earnings *pl*, income, revenue

rêver (ray-*vay*) *v* *dream

revers (rer-*vair*) *m* reverse; lapel

revirement (rer-veer-*mahng*) *m* reverse, turn

reviser (rer-vee-*zay*) *v* revise; overhaul

révision (ray-vee-*z^yawng*) *f* revision

***revoir** (rer-*vwaar*) *v* *see again; review; **au revoir!** goodbye!

révoltant (ray-vol-*tahng*) *adj* revolting

révolte (ray-*volt*) *f* revolt, rebellion

révolter (ray-vol-*tay*) *v*: ~ **se ~** revolt

révolution (ray-vo-lew-*s^yawng*) *f* revolution

revolver (ray-vol-*vair*) *m* gun, revolver

révoquer (ray-vo-*kay*) *v* recall

revue (rer-*vew*) *f* revue; review, magazine; ~ **mensuelle** monthly magazine

rez-de-chaussée (reh-dshoa-*say*) *m* ground floor

rhinocéros (ree-no-say-*ross*) *m* rhinoceros

rhubarbe (rew-*bahrb*) *f* rhubarb

rhum (rom) *m* rum

rhumatisme (rew-mah-*teesm*) *m* rheumatism

rhume (rewm) *m* cold; ~ **des foins** hay fever

riche (reesh) *adj* rich; wealthy

richesse (ree-*shehss*) *f* wealth; riches *pl*

ride (reed) *f* wrinkle

rideau (ree-*doa*) *m* curtain

ridicule (ree-dee-*kewl*) *adj* ridiculous; ludicrous

ridiculiser (ree-dee-kew-lee-*zay*) *v* ridicule

rien (r^{y}a$\overline{ng}$) *pron* nothing; nil; **ne ... ~** nothing; **~ que** only

rigoler (ree-go-*lay*) *v* laugh; have fun; be joking

rime (reem) *f* rhyme

rinçage (ra$\overline{ng}$-*saazh*) *m* rinse

rincer (ra$\overline{ng}$-*say*) *v* rinse

rire (reer) *m* laughter, laugh

***rire** (reer) *v* laugh

risque (reesk) *m* risk; chance

risquer (ree-*skay*) *v* venture, risk; **risqué** risky

rivage (ree-*vaazh*) *m* shore

rival (ree-*vahl*) *m* rival

rivaliser (ree-vah-lee-*zay*) *v* rival

rivalité (ree-vah-lee-*tay*) *f* rivalry

rive (reev) *f* bank, shore

rivière (ree-v^{y}air) *f* river

riz (ree) *m* rice

robe (rob) *f* dress; robe, frock, gown; **~ de chambre** dressing gown

robinet (ro-bee-*nay*) *m* tap; faucet *Am*

robuste (ro-*bewst*) *adj* solid, robust

rocade (ro-*kahd*) *f* bypass

rocher (ro-*shay*) *m* rock, boulder

rocheux (ro-*shur*) *adj* rocky

roi (rwah) *m* king

rôle (r$\overline{oa}$l) *m* role

roman (ro-*mah$\overline{ng}$*) *m* novel; **~ policier** detective story

romantique (ro-mah$\overline{ng}$-*teek*) *adj* romantic

rompre (raw$\overline{ng}$gpr) *v* *break

rond (raw$\overline{ng}$) *adj* round

rond-point (raw$\overline{ng}$-*pwa$\overline{ng}$*) *m* roundabout

ronfler (raw$\overline{ng}$-*flay*) *v* snore

rosaire (roa-*zair*) *m* rosary

rose (r$\overline{oa}$z) *f* rose; *adj* pink, rose

roseau (roa-*zoa*) *m* reed

rosée (roa-*zay*) *f* dew

rossignol (ro-see-*ñol*) *m* nightingale

rotation (ro-tah-s^{y}aw$\overline{ng}$) *f* revolution

rôti (roa-*tee*) *m* roast (meat)

rotin (ro-*ta$\overline{ng}$*) *m* rattan

rôtir (roa-*teer*) *v* roast

rôtisserie (ro-tee-*sree*) *f* grillroom

rotule (ro-*tewl*) *f* kneecap

roue (roo) *f* wheel; **~ de secours** spare wheel

rouge (r$\overline{oo}$zh) *adj* red; *m* rouge; **~ à lèvres** lipstick

rouge-gorge (roozh-*gorzh*) *m* robin

rougeole (roo-*zhol*) *f* measles

rougir (roo-*zheer*) *v* blush

rouille (roo^{ee}) *f* rust

rouillé (roo-^{y}ay) *adj* rusty

rouleau (roo-*loa*) *m* roll

rouler (roo-*lay*) *v* roll; *go

roulette (roo-*leht*) *f* roulette

roulotte (roo-*lot*) *f* caravan

roumain (roo-*ma$\overline{ng}$*) *adj* Rumanian

Roumanie (roo-mah-*nee*) *f* Rumania

route (root) *f* drive, road; route; **en ~ pour** bound for; **~ à péage** turnpike *Am*; **~ d'évitement** by-pass; **~ principale** thoroughfare, main road

routine (roo-*teen*) *f* routine

royal (rwah-^{y}ahl) *adj* royal

royaume (rwah-$^{yo}\overline{oa}$m) *m* kingdom

ruban (rew-*bah$\overline{ng}$*) *m* ribbon; **~ adhésif** adhesive tape, scotch tape

rubrique (rew-*breek*) *f* column

ruche (rewsh) *f* beehive

rude (rewd) *adj* rough

rue (rew) *f* street; road; **~ principale** main street; **~ transversale** side street

ruelle (rwehl) *f* alley, lane

rugir (rew-*zheer*) *v* roar

rugissement (rew-zhee-*smah$\overline{ng}$*) *m* roar

rugueux (rew-*gur*) *adj* rough

ruine (rween) *f* ruins; ruin

ruiner (rwee-*nay*) *v* ruin

ruisseau (rwee-*soa*) *m* brook, stream

rumeur (rew-*mūr*) *f* rumo(u)r

rural (rew-*rahl*) *adj* rural

rusé (rew-*zay*) *adj* cunning

russe (rewss) *adj* Russian

Russie (rew-*see*) *f* Russia

rustique (rew-*steek*) *adj* rustic

rythme (reetm) *m* rhythm; pace

S

sable (sahbl) *m* sand

sableux (sah-*blur*) *adj* sandy

sabot (sah-*boa*) *m* wooden shoe; hoof

sac (sahk) *m* bag; sack; ~ **à dos** rucksack; ~ **à glace** ice bag; ~ **à main** bag, handbag; ~ **à provisions** shopping bag; ~ **de couchage** sleeping bag; ~ **en papier** paper bag

sachet (sah-*shay*) *m* small bag; ~ **de thé** teabag

sacoche (sah-*kosh*) *f* bag

sacré (sah-*kray*) *adj* holy, sacred

sacrifice (sah-kree-*feess*) *m* sacrifice

sacrifier (sah-kree-*f*'*ay*) *v* sacrifice

sacrilège (sah-kree-*laizh*) *m* sacrilege

sage (saazh) *adj* wise; good

sage-femme (sahzh-*fahm*) *f* midwife

sagesse (sah-*zhehss*) *f* wisdom

saigner (say-*ñay*) *v* *bleed

sain (sang) *adj* healthy; wholesome, well

saint (sang) *m* saint

saisir (say-*zeer*) *v* seize; *catch, grip, *take, grasp

saison (seh-*zawng*) *f* season; **hors ~** off season; **morte-saison** *f* low season; **pleine ~** peak season

salade (sah-*lahd*) *f* salad

salaire (sah-*lair*) *m* salary, pay

salaud (sah-*loa*) *m* bastard

sale (sahl) *adj* dirty; filthy

salé (sah-*lay*) *adj* salty

saleté (sahl-*tay*) *f* dirt

salière (sah-*l*'*air*) *f* salt cellar, salt

shaker *Am*

salir (sah-*leer*) *v* soil

salive (sah-*leev*) *f* spit

salle (sahl) *f* hall; ~ **à manger** dining room; ~ **d'attente** waiting room; ~ **de bains** bathroom; ~ **de bal** ballroom; ~ **de classe** classroom; ~ **de concert** concert hall; ~ **de lecture** reading room; ~ **de séjour** living room; ~ **d'exposition** showroom

salon (sah-*lawng*) *m* sitting room; drawing room, salon; ~ **de beauté** beauty salon; ~ **de thé** tearoom

salopette (sah-lo-*peht*) *f* overalls *pl*

saluer (sah-*lway*) *v* greet; salute

salut (sah-*lew*) *m* welfare

salutation (sah-lew-tah-*s*'*awng*) *f* greeting

samedi (sahm-*dee*) *m* Saturday

S.A.M.U. (sah-*mew*) *m* mobile accident unit

sanatorium (sah-nah-to-*r*'*om*) *m* sanatorium

sanctuaire (sahngk-*twair*) *m* shrine

sandale (sahng-*dahl*) *f* sandal

sandwich (sahng-*dweech*) *m* sandwich

sang (sahng) *m* blood

sanitaire (sah-nee-*tair*) *adj* sanitary

sans (sahng) *prep* without

santé (sahng-*tay*) *f* health

sapin (sah-*pang*) *m* fir-tree

sardine (sahr-*deen*) *f* sardine

satellite (sah-tay-*leet*) *m* satellite

satin (sah-*tang*) *m* satin

satisfaction (sah-teess-fahk-s*ʸawng*) f satisfaction

*satisfaire (sah-tee-s*fair*) v satisfy; **satisfait** satisfied; content

sauce (sōass) f sauce

saucisse (soa-*seess*) f sausage

saucisson (soa-see-*sawng*) m sausage

sauf (soaf) prep but

saumon (soa-*mawng*) m salmon

sauna (soa-*nah*) m sauna

saut (soa) m jump; hop, leap; **~ à ski** ski jump

sauter (soa-*tay*) v jump; skip; ***faire ~** fry

sauterelle (soa-*trehl*) f grasshopper

sautiller (soa-tee-*ʸay*) v hop, skip

sauvage (soa-*vaazh*) adj savage; wild, fierce

sauver (soa-*vay*) v rescue, save

sauvetage (soav-*taazh*) m rescue

sauveur (soa-*vūrr*) m savio(u)r

savant (sah-*vahng*) m scientist

saveur (sah-*vūrr*) f flavour

*savoir (sah-*vwaar*) v *know; *be able to

savoir-vivre (sah-vwahr-*veevr*) m manners pl

savon (sah-*vawng*) m soap; **~ à barbe** shaving soap; **~ en poudre** soap powder

savoureux (sah-voo-*rur*) adj tasty, savo(u)ry

scandale (skahng-*dahl*) m scandal

scandinave (skahng-dee-*naav*) adj Scandinavian

Scandinavie (skahng-dee-nah-*vee*) f Scandinavia

sceau (soa) m seal

scène (sehn) f scene; stage; **metteur en ~** director; ***mettre en ~** direct

scie (see) f saw

science (s*ʸahngss*) f science

scientifique (s*ʸahng*-tee-*feek*) adj scientific

scierie (see-*ree*) f sawmill

scintillant (sang-tee-*ʸahng*) adj sparkling

scolaire (sko-*lair*) adj school-

scooter (skoo-*tair*) m scooter

scout (skoot) m scout; boy scout

sculpteur (skewl-*tūrr*) m sculptor

sculpture (skewl-*tēwr*) f sculpture

se (ser) pron himself; herself; themselves

séance (say-*ahngss*) f session

seau (soa) m bucket, pail

sec (sehk) adj (f sèche) dry

sèche-cheveux (sehsh-sher-*vur*) m hairdrier, hairdryer

sécher (say-*shay*) v dry

sécheresse (say-*shrehss*) f drought

séchoir (say-*shwaar*) m dryer

second (ser-*gawng*) adj second

secondaire (ser-gawng-*dair*) adj secondary; subordinate

seconde (ser-*gawngd*) f second

secouer (ser-*kway*) v *shake

secours (ser-*kōor*) m assistance; **premier ~** first aid

secousse (ser-*kooss*) f jolt; jerk

secret[1] (ser-*kray*) m secret

secret[2] (ser-*kray*) adj (f secrète) secret

secrétaire (ser-kray-*tair*) m/f clerk, secretary

section (sehk-s*ʸawng*) f section; stretch

sécurité (say-kew-ree-*tay*) f safety, security; **glissière de ~** crash barrier

sédatif (say-dah-*teef*) m sedative

*séduire (say-*dweer*) v seduce

séduisant (say-dwee-*zahng*) adj attractive, charming

sein (sang) m breast; bosom

seize (saiz) num sixteen

seizième (seh-z*ʸehm*) num sixteenth

séjour (say-*zhōor*) m stay

séjourner (say-zhoor-*nay*) v stay

sel (sehl) m salt; **sels de bain** bath

salts

sélection (say-lehk-s^yawng) f choice, selection

sélectionner (say-lehk-s^yo-nay) v select

selle (sehl) f saddle

selon (ser-lawng) prep according to

semaine (ser-mehn) f week

semblable (sahng-blahbl) adj alike

sembler (sahng-blay) v seem; look, appear

semelle (ser-mehl) f sole

semence (ser-mahngss) f seed

semer (ser-may) v *sow

semi- (ser-mee) semi-

sénat (say-nah) m senate

sénateur (say-nah-türr) m senator

sénile (say-neel) adj senile

sens (sahngss) m sense; reason; **bon ~** sense; **en ~ inverse** the other way round; **~ unique** one-way traffic

sensation (sahng-sah-s^yawng) f sensation; feeling

sensationnel (sahng-sah-s^yo-nehl) adj sensational

sensible (sahng-seebl) adj sensitive; considerable

sentence (sahng-tahngss) f verdict

sentier (sahng-t^yay) m path; trail; **~ pour piétons** footpath

sentiment (sahng-tee-mahng) m feeling; emotion; consciousness, sense

sentimental (sahng-tee-mahng-tahl) adj sentimental

séparation (say-pah-rah-s^yawng) f division

séparé (say-pah-ray) adj separate

séparément (say-pah-ray-mahng) adv apart

séparer (say-pah-ray) v separate; divide, part

sept (seht) num seven

septembre (sehp-tahngbr) September

septentrional (sehp-tahng-tree-o-nahl) adj northern, north

septicémie (sehp-tee-say-mee) f bloodpoisoning

septième (seh-t^yehm) num seventh

septique (sehp-teek) adj septic

sépulture (say-pewl-tewr) f burial

serein (ser-rang) adj serene

série (say-ree) f sequence; series

sérieux (say-r^yur) adj serious; m seriousness

seringue (ser-rangg) f syringe

serment (sehr-mahng) m vow, oath; **faux ~** perjury

sermon (sehr-mawng) m sermon

serpent (sehr-pahng) m snake

serpentant (sehr-pahng-tahng) adj winding

serpenter (sehr-pahng-tay) v *wind

serre (sair) f greenhouse

serrer (say-ray) v tighten; **serré** tight, narrow

serrure (say-rewr) f lock; **trou de la ~** keyhole

sérum (say-rom) m serum

serveuse (sehr-vürz) f waitress

serviable (sehr-v^yahbl) adj helpful

service (sehr-veess) m service; service charge; section; **~ à thé** tea set; **~ de table** dinner service; **~ d'étage** room service; **services postaux** postal service

serviette (sehr-v^yeht) f towel; napkin; serviette; briefcase; **~ de bain** bath towel; **~ de papier** paper napkin; **~ hygiénique** sanitary towel, sanitary napkin Am

*servir (sehr-veer) v serve; attend on, wait on; *be of use; **se ~ de** apply

serviteur (sehr-vee-türr) m servant

seuil (sur^ee) m threshold

seul (surl) adv alone; adj single, only

seulement (surl-*mahng*) *adv* only; merely

sévère (say-*vair*) *adj* strict; harsh; severe

sévir (say-*veer*) *v* rage

sexe (sehks) *m* sex

sexualité (sehk-swah-lee-*tay*) *f* sexuality

sexuel (sehk-*swehl*) *adj* sexual

shampooing (shahng-*pwang*) *m* shampoo

short (short) *m* shorts

si (see) *conj* if; whether; *adv* so; **si ... ou** whether ... or

Siamois (s^yah-*mwah*) *m* Siamese

siamois (s^yah-*mwah*) *adj* Siamese

sida (see-*dah*) *m* Aids, AIDS

siècle (s^yehkl) *m* century

siège (s^yaizh) *m* chair, seat; siege

sien: le ~ (ler s^yang) his

sieste (s^yehst) *f* siesta; nap

siffler (see-*flay*) *v* whistle

sifflet (see-*flay*) *m* whistle

signal (see-*ñahl*) *m* signal; **~ de détresse** distress signal

signalement (see-ñahl-*mahng*) *m* description

signaler (see-ñah-*lay*) *v* signal; indicate

signature (see-ñah-*tewr*) *f* signature

signe (seeñ) *m* sign; token, signal, indication; ***faire ~** *make a sign, wave

signer (see-*ñay*) *v* sign

significatif (see-ñee-fee-kah-*teef*) *adj* significant

signification (see-ñee-fee-kah-s^yawng) *f* meaning, sense

signifier (see-ñee-f^yay) *v* *mean

silence (see-*lahngss*) *m* silence; quiet

silencieux (see-lahng-s^yur) *adj* silent; *m* silencer; muffler *Am*

sillon (see-^yawng) *m* groove

similaire (see-mee-*lair*) *adj* similar

similitude (see-mee-lee-*tewd*) *f* similarity

simple (sangpl) *adj* simple; plain

simplement (sang-pler-*mahng*) *adv* simply

simuler (see-mew-*lay*) *v* simulate

simultané (see-mewl-tah-*nay*) *adj* simultaneous

sincère (sang-*sair*) *adj* honest, sincere

singe (sangzh) *m* monkey

singulier (sang-gew-*l^ay*) *m* singular; *adj* remarkable, singular, uncommon

sinistre (see-*neestr*) *adj* sinister, ominous; *m* catastrophe

sinon (see-*nawng*) *conj* otherwise

sirène (see-*rehn*) *f* siren

sirop (see-*roa*) *m* syrup

site (seet) *m* site

situation (see-twah-s^yawng) *f* situation; position, location

situé (see-*tway*) *adj* situated

six (seess) *num* six

sixième (see-z^yehm) *num* sixth

ski (skee) *m* ski; skiing; **~ nautique** water ski

skier (skee-*ay*) *v* ski

skieur (skee-*ūrr*) *m* skier

slip (sleep) *m* briefs *pl*

smoking (smo-*keeng*) *m* dinner jacket; tuxedo *Am*

S.N.C.F. (eh-sehn-say-*ehf*) *f* French national railway company

snob (snob) *adj* snooty

sobre (sobr) *adj* sober

social (so-s^yahl) *adj* social

socialisme (so-s^yah-*leesm*) *m* socialism

socialiste (so-s^yah-*leest*) *adj* socialist; *m* socialist

société (so-s^yay-*tay*) *f* community, society; company

sœur (sūrr) *f* sister

soi (swah) *pron* oneself; **soi-même** *pron* oneself

soi-disant (swah-dee-*zahng*) *adj* socalled

soie (swah) *f* silk

soif (swahf) *f* thirst

soigné (swah-*ñay*) *adj* neat; thorough

soigner (swah-*ñay*) *v* treat; nurse

soigneux (swah-*ñur*) *adj* careful

soin (swang) *m* care; ***prendre ~ de** *take care of; **soins de beauté** beauty treatment

soir (swaar) *m* night, evening; **ce ~** tonight

soirée (swah-*ray*) *f* evening

soit … soit (swah) either … or

soixante (swah-*sahngt*) *num* sixty

soixante-dix (swah-sahng-*deess*) *num* seventy

sol (sol) *m* floor; soil, earth, ground

soldat (sol-*dah*) *m* soldier

solde (sold) *m* balance; **soldes** sales, clearance sale

sole (sol) *f* sole

soleil (so-*lay*) *m* sun; sunshine; **coucher du ~** sunset; **coup de ~** sunburn; **lever du ~** sunrise

solennel (so-lah-*nehl*) *adj* solemn

solide (so-*leed*) *adj* solid; firm, sound; *m* solid

solitaire (so-lee-*tair*) *adj* lonely

solitude (so-lee-*tewd*) *f* loneliness

soluble (so-*lewbl*) *adj* soluble

solution (so-lew-*s*^{y}*awng*) *f* solution

sombre (sawngbr) *adj* somber *Am*, sombre, obscure; gloomy

sommaire (so-*mair*) *m* summary

somme (som) *f* sum; amount; *m* nap; **~ globale** lump sum

sommeil (so-*may*) *m* sleep

sommelier (so-mer-*l*^{y}*ay*) *m* winewaiter

sommet (so-*may*) *m* summit; top, peak, height; **~ de colline** hilltop

somnifère (som-nee-*fair*) *m* sleeping pill

somnolent (som-no-*lahng*) *adj* sleepy

son[1] (sawng) *adj* (f sa, pl ses) his; her

son[2] (sawng) *m* sound

songer (sawng-*zhay*) *v* *dream; **~ à** *think of

sonner (so-*nay*) *v* sound; *ring

sonnette (so-*neht*) *f* bell; doorbell

sorcière (sor-*s*^{y}*air*) *f* witch

sort (sawr) *m* fortune, lot, destiny

sorte (sort) *f* sort; **toutes sortes de** all sorts of

sortie (sor-*tee*) *f* way out, exit; **~ de secours** emergency exit

*sortir (sor-*teer*) *v* *go out

sot (soa) *adj* (f sotte) foolish, silly

sottise (so-*teez*) *f* nonsense, rubbish

souche (soosh) *f* stub

souci (soo-*see*) *m* concern, worry; care

soucier (soo-*s*^{y}*ay*) *v*: **se ~ de** care about

soucieux (soo-*s*^{y}*ur*) *adj* concerned, worried

soucoupe (soo-*koop*) *f* saucer

soudain (soo-*dang*) *adj* sudden; *adv* suddenly

souder (soo-*day*) *v* weld

souffle (soofl) *m* breath

souffler (soo-*flay*) *v* *blow

souffrance (soo-*frahngss*) *f* suffering

*souffrir (soo-*freer*) *v* suffer

souhait (sweh) *m* wish

souhaiter (sway-*tay*) *v* wish

souillé (soo-*y*^{y}*ay*) *adj* soiled, dirty

soulagement (soo-lahzh-*mahng*) *m* relief

soulager (soo-lah-*zhay*) *v* relieve

soulever (sool-*vay*) *v* lift; *bring up

soulier (soo-*l*^{y}*ay*) *m* shoe

souligner (soo-lee-*ñay*) *v* underline; stress, emphasize

*soumettre (soo-*mehtr*) *v* subject; **se ~** submit

soupape (soo-*pahp*) *f* valve

soupçon (soop-*sawng*) *m* suspicion

soupçonner (soop-so-*nay*) *v* suspect

soupçonneux (soop-so-*nur*) *adj*
  suspicious
soupe (soop) *f* soup
souper (soo-*pay*) *m* supper
souple (soopl) *adj* supple; flexible
source (soors) *f* well; fountain, source,
  spring
sourcil (soor-*see*) *m* eyebrow
sourd (sōōr) *adj* deaf
sourire (soo-*reer*) *m* smile; ~ **forcé**
  forced smile
*****sourire** (soo-*reer*) *v* smile
souris (soo-*ree*) *f* mouse
sous (soo) *prep* under
sous-estimer (soo-zeh-stee-*may*) *v*
  underestimate
sous-locataire (soo-lo-kah-*tair*) *m*
  lodger
sous-marin (soo-mah-*rang*) *adj*
  underwater
soussigné (soo-see-*ñay*) *m*
  undersigned
sous-sol (soo-*sol*) *m* basement
sous-titre (soo-*teetr*) *m* subtitle
*****soustraire** (soo-*strair*) *v* subtract
sous-vêtements (soo-veht-*mahng*)
  mpl underwear
*****soutenir** (soot-*neer*) *v* support; *****hold**
  up
souterrain (soo-teh-*rang*) *adj*
  underground
soutien (soo-t^y*ang*) *m* support; relief
soutien-gorge (soo-t^{y}ang-*gorzh*) *m*
  bra
souvenir (soo-*vneer*) *m* memory,
  remembrance; souvenir; **se**
  *****souvenir** recollect
souvent (soo-*vahng*) *adv* often; **le plus**
  ~ mostly
souverain (soo-*vrang*) *m* sovereign
spacieux (spah-s^y*ur*) *adj* spacious,
  roomy, large
sparadrap (spah-rah-*drah*) *m* adhesive
  plaster

spécial (spay-s^y*ahl*) *adj* special;
  peculiar, particular
spécialement (spay-s^{y}ahl-*mahng*) *adv*
  especially
spécialiser (spay-s^{y}ah-lee-*zay*) *v*: **se** ~
  specialize
spécialiste (spay-s^{y}ah-*leest*) *m/f*
  specialist, expert
spécialité (spay-s^{y}ah-lee-*tay*) *f*
  speciality
spécifique (spay-see-*feek*) *adj* specific
spectacle (spehk-*tahkl*) *m* spectacle;
  show; sight; ~ **de variétés** floor show,
  variety show
spectaculaire (spehk-tah-kew-*lair*) *adj*
  sensational
spectateur (spehk-tah-*ūrr*) *m*, **-trice** *f*
  spectator
spectre (spehktr) *m* spook
spéculer (spay-kew-*lay*) *v* speculate
sphère (sfair) *f* sphere
spirituel (spee-ree-*twehl*) *adj* spiritual;
  witty
spiritueux (spee-ree-*twur*) *mpl* liquor,
  spirits
splendeur (splahng-*dūrr*) *f*
  splendo(u)r
splendide (splahng-*deed*) *adj*
  splendid; wonderful, glorious,
  enchanting, magnificent
sport (spawr) *m* sport; **sports d'hiver**
  winter sports
sportif (spor-*teef*) *m* sportsman
square (skwaar) *m* square
stable (stahbl) *adj* permanent, stable;
  solid, fixed
stade (stahd) *m* stadium
stand (stahng) *m* stand; ~ **de livres**
  bookstand
standard (stahng-*daar*) *adj* standard
starter (stahr-*tair*) *m* choke
station (stah-s^y*awng*) *f* station; ~
  balnéaire seaside resort; ~ **de taxis**
  taxi rank; taxi stand *Am*; ~ **thermale**

spa

stationnaire (stah-s^yo-*nair*) *adj* stationary

stationnement (stah-s^yon-*mahng*) *m* parking; ~ **interdit** no parking

station-service (stah-s^yon-sehr-*veess*) *f* filling station, service station; gas station *Am*

statistique (stah-tee-*steek*) *f* statistics *pl*

statue (stah-*tew*) *f* statue

stature (stah-*tewr*) *f* figure

steak (stehk) *m* steak

stéréo (*stay*-ray-oa) *f* stereo

stérile (stay-*reel*) *adj* sterile

stériliser (stay-ree-lee-*zay*) *v* sterilize

stimulant (stee-mew-*lahng*) *m* impulse; stimulant

stimuler (stee-mew-*lay*) *v* stimulate

stock (stok) *m* stock; supply; *avoir en ~ stock

stop! (stop) stop!

store (stawr) *m* blind

strophe (strof) *f* stanza

structure (strewk-*tewr*) *f* structure; fabric

studio (stew-d^yoa) *m* studio; flatlet, one-room apartment

stupide (stew-*peed*) *adj* foolish, stupid

style (steel) *m* style

stylo (stee-*loa*) *m* fountain pen; ~ **à bille** ballpoint pen

subir (sew-*beer*) *v* suffer

sublime (sew-*bleem*) *adj* grand

subordonné (sew-bor-do-*nay*) *adj* subordinate

subsistance (sewb-zee-*stahngss*) *f* livelihood

substance (sewb-*stahngss*) *f* substance

substantiel (sewb-stahng-s^y*ehl*) *adj* substantial

substantif (sewb-stahng-*teef*) *m* noun

substituer (sewb-stee-*tway*) *v* substitute

substitut (sewb-stee-*tew*) *m* substitute; deputy

subtil (sewb-*teel*) *adj* subtle

suburbain (sew-bewr-*bang*) *adj* suburban

subvention (sewb-vahng-s^y*awng*) *f* subsidy; grant

succéder (sewk-say-*day*) *v* succeed

succès (sewk-*say*) *m* success; hit

succession (sewk-seh-s^y*awng*) *f* sequence

succomber (sew-kawng-*bay*) *v* succumb

succulent (sew-kew-*lahng*) *adj* tasty

succursale (sew-kewr-*sahl*) *f* branch

sucer (sew-*say*) *v* suck

sucre (sewkr) *m* sugar

sucrer (sew-*kray*) *v* sweeten; **sucré** sweet

sud (sewd) *m* south

sud-américain (sew-dah-may-ree-*kang*) *adj* Latin-American

sud-est (sew-*dehst*) *m* southeast

sud-ouest (sew-*dwehst*) *m* southwest

Suède (swehd) *f* Sweden

suédois (sway-*dwah*) *adj* Swedish

suer (sway) *v* perspire, sweat

sueur (swūrr) *f* perspiration, sweat

*suffire (sew-*feer*) *v* *do, suffice

suffisant (sew-fee-*zahng*) *adj* enough, sufficient

suffrage (sew-*fraazh*) *m* vote

suggérer (sewg-zhay-*ray*) *v* suggest

suggestion (sewg-zheh-st^y*awng*) *f* suggestion

suicide (swee-*seed*) *m* suicide

Suisse (sweess) *f* Switzerland; *m/f* Swiss

suisse (sweess) *adj* Swiss

suite (sweet) *f* sequel; series; **et ainsi de ~** and so on; **par la ~** afterwards; **tout de ~** at once, instantly

suivant (swee-*vahng*) *adj* following, next

suivre (sweevr) *v* follow; ***faire ~**
  forward

sujet (sew-*zhay*) *m* subject; issue,
  topic, theme; **~ à** liable to, subject to

superbe (sew-*pehrb*) *adj* superb

superficiel (sew-pehr-fee-*s*ʸ*ehl*) *adj*
  superficial

superflu (sew-pehr-*flew*) *adj*
  superfluous; unnecessary, redundant

supérieur (sew-pay-r*ʸūrr*) *adj*
  superior; top, upper; excellent

supermarché (sew-pehr-mahr-*shay*)
  m supermarket

superstition (sew-pehr-stee-*s*ʸ*awng*) *f*
  superstition

superviser (sew-pehr-vee-*zay*) *v*
  supervise

supervision (sew-pehr-vee-z*ʸawng*) *f*
  supervision

supplément (sew-play-*mahng*) *m*
  supplement; surcharge

supplémentaire (sew-play-mahng-
  tair) *adj* additional; extra

supplier (sew-plee-*ay*) *v* beg

supporter[1] (sew-por-*tay*) *v* *bear;
  support

supporter[2] (sew-por-*tair*) *m* supporter

supposer (sew-poa-*zay*) *v* suppose;
  guess, assume, reckon

suppositoire (sew-poa-zee-*twaar*) *m*
  suppository

supprimer (sew-pree-*may*) *v* *do away
  with

suprême (sew-*prehm*) *adj* supreme

sur (sewr) *prep* upon; on; in; about

sûr (sēwr) *adj* sure; safe, secure; **bien ~**
  naturally

surcharge (sewr-*shahrzh*) *f*
  overweight

sûrement (sewr-*mahng*) *adv* surely

surface (sewr-*fahss*) *f* surface, surface
  area

surgelé (sewr-zher-*lay*) *adj* deep- *or*
  quick-frozen

surgir (sewr-*zheer*) *v* *arise

surmené (sewr-mer-*nay*) *adj*
  overworked

surmener (sewr-mer-*nay*) *v*: **se ~**
  overwork

surnom (sewr-*nawng*) *m* nickname

surpasser (sewr-pah-*say*) *v* *outdo,
  exceed

surplus (sewr-*plew*) *m* surplus

*surprendre (sewr-*prahngdr*) *v*
  surprise; amaze; *catch

surprise (sewr-*preez*) *f* surprise

surprise-partie (sewr-preez-pahr-*tee*) *f*
  party

surtout (sewr-*too*) *adv* most of all

surveillance (sewr-veh-ʸ*ahngss*) *f*
  supervision

surveillant (sewr-veh-ʸ*ahng*) *m*
  warden, supervisor

surveiller (sewr-vay-ʸ*ay*) *v* watch;
  guard, patrol

*survenir (sewr-ver-*neer*) *v* occur

survie (sewr-*vee*) *f* survival

*survivre (sewr-*veevr*) *v* survive

suspect (sew-*spehkt*) *adj* suspicious; *m*
  suspect

suspecter (sew-spehk-*tay*) *v* suspect

suspendre (sew-*spahngdr*) *v* *hang;
  discontinue, suspend

suspension (sew-spahng-*s*ʸ*awng*) *f*
  suspension

suture (sew-*tēwr*) *f* stitch

svelte (svehlt) *adj* slender

syllabe (see-*lahb*) *f* syllable

symbole (sang-*bol*) *m* symbol

sympathie (sang-pah-*tee*) *f* sympathy

sympathique (sang-pah-*teek*) *adj* nice;
  pleasant

symphonie (sang-fo-*nee*) *f* symphony

symptôme (sangp-*tōam*) *m* symptom

synagogue (see-nah-*gog*) *f* synagogue

syndicat (sang-dee-*kah*) *m* trade
  union; **~ d'initiative** tourist office

synonyme (see-no-*neem*) *m* synonym

synthétique (sang-tay-*teek*) *adj*
  synthetic
Syrie (see-*ree*) *f* Syria
syrien (see-r^y*ang*) *adj* Syrian
systématique (see-stay-mah-*teek*) *adj*
systematic
système (see-*stehm*) *m* system; ~
  décimal decimal system; ~ **de**
  lubrification lubrication system

T

tabac (tah-*bah*) *m* tobacco; **bureau de**
  ~ tobacconist's; **débitant de** ~
  tobacconist; ~ **à rouler** cigarette
  tobacco; **tabac pour pipe** pipe
  tobacco
table (tahbl) *f* table; ~ **des matières**
  table of contents
tableau (tah-*bloa*) *m* chart; board; ~ **de**
  bord dashboard; ~ **de conversions**
  conversion chart; ~ **de distribution**
  switchboard; ~ **noir** blackboard
tablette (tah-*bleht*) *f* tablet
tablier (tah-blee-*ay*) *m* apron
tabou (tah-*boo*) *m* taboo
tache (tahsh) *f* speck, stain, spot, blot
tâche (taash) *f* duty, task
tacher (tah-*shay*) *v* stain
tâcher (tah-*shay*) *v* try
tacheté (tahsh-*tay*) *adj* spotted
tactique (tahk-*teek*) *f* tactics *pl*
taille (tigh) *f* waist; size
taille-crayon (tigh-kreh-^y*awng*) *m*
  pencil sharpener
tailler (tah-^y*ay*) *v* trim, chip; carve
tailleur (tah-^y*urr*) *m* tailor
*****taire** (tair) *v*: **se** ~ *keep quiet, *be
  silent
talc (tahlk) *m* talc powder
talent (tah-*lahng*) *m* talent; faculty,
  gift
talon (tah-*lawng*) *m* heel; counterfoil
tambour (tahng-*boor*) *m* drum; ~ **de**
  frein brake drum

tamiser (tah-mee-*zay*) *v* sift, sieve
tampon (tahng-*pawng*) *m* tampon
tamponner (tahng-po-*nay*) *v* bump
tandis que (tahng-dee ker) while;
  whilst
tangible (tahng-*zheebl*) *adj* tangible
tanière (tah-n^y*air*) *f* den
tante (tahngt) *f* aunt
tapageur (tah-pah-*zhurr*) *adj* rowdy
taper (tah-*pay*) *v* slap; ~ **à la machine**
  type
tapis (tah-*pee*) *m* carpet; rug, mat
taquiner (tah-kee-*nay*) *v* kid, tease
tard (taar) *adj* late
tarif (tah-*reef*) *m* rate
tarte (tahrt) *f* tart; flan
tartine (tahr-*teen*) *f* sandwich
tas (tah) *m* pile, lot, heap
tasse (tahss) *f* cup; ~ **à thé** teacup
taureau (toa-*roa*) *m* bull
taux (toa) *m* tariff; ~ **d'escompte**
  bankrate
taverne (tah-*vehrn*) *f* tavern
taxe (tahks) *f* tax
taxi (tahk-*see*) *m* taxi; cab; **chauffeur**
  de ~ taxi driver
taximètre (tahk-see-*mehtr*) *m*
  taximeter
tchèque (chehk) *adj* Czech
te (ter) *pron* you; yourself
technicien (tehk-nee-s^y*ang*) *m*
  technician
technique (tehk-*neek*) *f* technique; *adj*

technical

technologie (tehk-no-lo-*zhee*) f technology

*****teindre** (tang̅dr) v dye

teint (tang̅) m complexion

teinture (tang̅-*tewr*) f dye

teinturerie (tang̅-tewr-*ree*) f dry cleaner's

tel (tehl) adj such; **~ que** such as

télé (tay-*lay*) f television

télécarte (tay-lay-*kahrt*) f phonecard

télégramme (tay-lay-*grahm*) m cable, telegram

télé-objectif (tay-lay-ob-zhehk-*teef*) m telephoto lens

téléphone (tay-lay-*fon*) m telephone; phone; **coup de ~** telephone call

téléphoner (tay-lay-fo-*nay*) v phone; call, ring up; call up Am

téléski (tay-lay-*skee*) m ski lift

téléviseur (tay-lay-vee-*zūrr*) m television set

télévision (tay-lay-vee-*z*ʸ*awng̅*) f television; television set; **~ par câble** cable television; **~ par satellite** satellite television

télex (tay-*lehks*) m telex

tellement (tehl-*mahng̅*) adv such; so

téméraire (tay-may-*rair*) adj daring

témoignage (tay-mwah-*n*ʸ*aazh*) m testimony

témoigner (tay-mwah-*ñay*) v testify

témoin (tay-*mwang̅*) m witness; **~ oculaire** eye-witness

tempe (tahng̅p) f temple

température (tahng̅-pay-rah-*tewr*) f temperature; **~ ambiante** room temperature

tempête (tahng̅-*peht*) f storm; tempest, gale; **~ de neige** snowstorm, blizzard

temple (tahng̅pl) m temple

temporaire (tahng̅-po-*rair*) adj temporary

temps (tahng̅) m time; weather; **à ~** in

time; **ces derniers ~** lately; **de temps en ~** now and then, occasionally; **~ libre** spare time

tenailles (ter-*nigh*) fpl pincers pl

tendance (tahng̅-*dahng̅ss*) f tendency; *****avoir ~** *be inclined to, tend

tendon (tahng̅-*dawng̅*) m sinew, tendon

tendre[1] (tahng̅dr) adj delicate, tender

tendre[2] (tahng̅dr) v stretch; **~ à** tend to; **tendu** tense

tendresse (tahng̅-*drehss*) f tenderness

ténèbres (tay-*nehbr*) fpl dark; gloom

tennis (tay-*neess*) m tennis; **~ de table** table tennis

tension (tahng̅-s*ʸ*awng̅) f tension; stress, strain; pressure; **~ artérielle** blood pressure

tentation (tahng̅-tah-s*ʸ*awng̅) f temptation

tentative (tahng̅-tah-*teev*) f try, attempt

tente (tahng̅t) f tent

tenter (tahng̅-*tay*) v try; attempt; tempt

tenue (ter-*new*) f conduct; dress; **~ de soirée** evening dress

térébenthine (tay-ray-bahng̅-*teen*) f turpentine

terme (tehrm) m term

terminer (tehr-mee-*nay*) v finish; **se ~** expire

terminus (tehr-mee-*newss*) m terminal

terne (tehrn) adj dull, colo(u)rless

terrain (teh-*rang̅*) m terrain; grounds; **~ d'aviation** airfield; **~ de camping** camping site; **~ de golf** golf course; **~ de jeux** recreation ground

terrasse (teh-*rahss*) f terrace

terre (tair) f earth; soil, land; **à ~** ashore; **hautes terres** uplands pl; **par ~** down; **~ cuite** terracotta; **~ ferme**

terreur 126

mainland
terreur (teh-*rürr*) f terror
terrible (tay-*reebl*) adj terrible; awful,
dreadful, frightful
terrifiant (teh-ree-f'*ahng*) adj
terrifying; horrible, creepy
terrifier (teh-ree-f'*ay*) v terrify
territoire (teh-ree-*twaar*) m territory
terroir (teh-*rwaar*) m soil
terrorisme (teh-ro-*reesm*) m terrorism
terroriste (teh-ro-*reest*) m terrorist
test (tehst) m test
testament (teh-stah-*mahng*) m will
tête (teht) f head
têtu (tay-*tew*) adj head-strong,
stubborn
texte (tehkst) m text
textile (tehk-*steel*) m textile
T.G.V. (tay-zhay-*vay*) m high-speed
train
thaïlandais (tah-ee-lahng-*day*) adj
Thai
Thaïlande (tah-ee-*lahngd*) f Thailand
thé (tay) m tea
théâtre (tay-*aatr*) m theater Am,
theatre; drama; ~ **de marionnettes**
puppet-show; ~ **de variétés** variety
theatre (theater Am)
théière (tay-*'air*) f teapot
thème (tehm) m theme
théologie (tay-o-lo-*zhee*) f theology
théorie (tay-o-*ree*) f theory
théorique (tay-o-*reek*) adj theoretical
thérapie (tay-rah-*pee*) f therapy
thermomètre (tehr-mo-*mehtr*) m
thermometer
thermoplongeur (tehr-moa-plawng-
zhürr) m immersion heater
thermos (tehr-*moss*) m thermos flask,
vacuum flask
thermostat (tehr-mo-*stah*) m
thermostat
thèse (taiz) f thesis
thon (tawng) m tuna

thym (tang) m thyme
ticket (tee-*kay*) m ticket
tiède (t'*ehd*) adj lukewarm, tepid
tien: le ~ (ler t'*ang*) yours
tiers (t'*air*) adj (f tierce) third
tige (teezh) f stem; rod
tigre (teegr) m tiger
tilleul (tee-*'url*) m limetree, lime
timbre (tangbr) m stamp; tone
timbre-poste (tang-brer-*post*) m
postage stamp
timide (tee-*meed*) adj timid, shy
timidité (tee-mee-dee-*tay*) f timidity,
shyness
tirage (tee-*raazh*) m draw; issue
tire-bouchon (teer-boo-*shawng*) m
corkscrew
tirer (tee-*ray*) v *draw, pull; fire,
*shoot
tiroir (tee-*rwaar*) m drawer
tisane (tee-*zahn*) f infusion; tea
tisser (tee-*say*) v *weave
tissu (tee-*sew*) m tissue; fabric, cloth,
material
tissu-éponge (tee-sew-ay-*pawngz*) m
towel(l)ing
titre (teetr) m title; heading
toast (toast) m toast
toboggan (to-bo-*gahng*) m slide
toi (twah) pron you
toile (twahl) f linen; **grosse ~** canvas
toilettes (twah-*leht*) fpl toilet,
bathroom; washroom Am; ~ **pour
dames** ladies' room; powder room; ~
pour hommes men's room
toi-même (twah-*mehm*) pron yourself
toit (twah) m roof; ~ **de chaume** m
thatched roof
tolérable (to-lay-*rahbl*) adj tolerable
tolérer (to-lay-*ray*) v *bear
tomate (to-*maht*) f tomato
tombe (tawngb) f tomb, grave
tomber (tawng-*bay*) v *fall
tome (tom) m volume

ton[1] (tawng) *adj* (f ta, pl tes) your

ton[2] (tawng) *m* note, tone

tonique (to-*neek*) *m* tonic; ~ **capillaire** hair tonic

tonne (ton) *f* ton

tonneau (to-*noa*) *m* barrel; cask

tonnerre (to-*nair*) *m* thunder

torche (torsh) *f* torch

torchon (tor-*shawng*) *m* tea towel, kitchen towel *Am*

tordre (tordr) *v* twist; wrench

tordu (tor-*dew*) *adj* crooked

torsion (tor-*s*^{y}*awng*) *f* twist

tort (tawr) *m* wrong; harm; **avoir ~* **be wrong; *faire du ~ harm

tortue (tor-*tew*) *f* turtle

torture (tor-*tewr*) *f* torture

torturer (tor-tew-*ray*) *v* torture

tôt (toa) *adv* early

total (to-*tahl*) *adj* total; utter, overall; *m* total

totalement (to-tahl-*mahng*) *adv* completely

totalitaire (to-tah-lee-*tair*) *adj* totalitarian

touchant (too-*shahng*) *adj* touching

toucher (too-*shay*) *v* touch; affect; **hit; cash; *m* touch

toujours (too-*zhoor*) *adv* always; ever; ~ **et encore** again and again

tour (toor) *m* turn; move; *f* tower

tourisme (too-*reesm*) *m* tourism

touriste (too-*reest*) *m/f* tourist

tourment (toor-*mahng*) *m* torment

tourmenter (toor-mahng-*tay*) *v* torment

tournant (toor-*nahng*) *m* turn, curve; turning point

tourne-disque (toor-ner-*deesk*) *m* record player

tourner (toor-*nay*) *v* turn; **spin

tournevis (toor-ner-*veess*) *m* screwdriver

tournoi (toor-*nwah*) *m* tournament

tousser (too-*say*) *v* cough

tout (too) *adj* all; every; entire; *pron* everything; **du ~** at all; **en ~** altogether; ~ **à fait** quite; ~ **à l'heure** presently; ~ **au plus** at most; ~ **ce que** whatever; ~ **de suite** immediately, straight away; ~ **droit** straight on; ~ **le monde** everybody

toutefois (toot-*fwah*) *adv* still

toux (too) *f* cough

toxique (tok-*seek*) *adj* toxic

tracas (trah-*kah*) *m* bother

tracasser (trah-kah-*say*) *v* bother

trace (trahss) *f* trace

tracer (trah-*say*) *v* trace

tracteur (trahk-*tūrr*) *m* tractor

tradition (trah-dee-*s*^{y}*awng*) *f* tradition

traditionnel (trah-dee-*s*^{y}*o-nehl*) *adj* traditional

traducteur (trah-dewk-*tūrr*) *m*, **-trice** *f* translator

traduction (trah-dewk-*s*^{y}*awng*) *f* translation

*traduire (trah-*dweer*) *v* translate

trafic (trah-*feek*) *m* traffic

tragédie (trah-zhay-*dee*) *f* tragedy; drama

tragique (trah-*zheek*) *adj* tragic

trahir (trah-*eer*) *v* betray

trahison (trah-ee-*zawng*) *f* treason

train (trang) *m* train; ~ **de marchandises** goods train; freight train *Am*; ~ **de nuit** night train; ~ **de voyageurs** passenger train; ~ **direct** through train; ~ **express** fast train; ~ **local** local train

traîneau (treh-*noa*) *m* sled(ge); sleigh

traîner (tray-*nay*) *v* drag, haul

trait (tray) *m* line; trait; ~ **de caractère** characteristic; ~ **d'union** hyphen; ~ **du visage** feature

traite (treht) *f* draft

traité (tray-*tay*) *m* treaty

traitement (treht-*mahng*) *m* treatment

traiter (tray-*tay*) v treat; handle

traître (traitr) m traitor

trajet (trah-*zhay*) m way

tram (trahm) m tram; streetcar *Am*

tranche (trahn̄gsh) f slice

trancher (trahn̄g-*shay*) v *cut off; settle

tranquille (trahn̄g-*keel*) adj calm; tranquil, quiet, still

tranquillité (trahn̄g-kee-lee-*tay*) f quietness

transaction (trahn̄g-zahk-s^y*awn̄g*) f transaction, deal

transatlantique (trahn̄g-zaht-lahn̄g-*teek*) adj transatlantic

transférer (trahn̄g-sfay-*ray*) v transfer

transformateur (trahn̄g-sfor-mah-*turr*) m transformer

transformer (trahn̄g-sfor-*may*) v transform

transition (trahng-zee-s^y*awn̄g*) f transition

transparent (trahn̄g-spah-*rahn̄g*) adj transparent

transpiration (trahng-spee-rah-s^y*awn̄g*) f perspiration

transpirer (trahn̄g-spee-*ray*) v perspire

transport (trahn̄g-*spawr*) m transportation, transport

transporter (trahn̄g-spor-*tay*) v transport

travail (trah-*vigh*) m (pl travaux) work, labo(u)r, job; **~ artisanal** handwork; **~ manuel** handicraft; **travaux ménagers** housekeeping, housework

travailler (trah-vah-^{y}*ay*) v work

travailleur (trah-vah-^{y}*urr*) m, **-euse** f worker

travers: à ~ (ah trah-*vair*) through; across

traversée (trah-vehr-*say*) f passage, crossing

traverser (trah-vehr-*say*) v cross; pass through

trébucher (tray-bew-*shay*) v stumble

trèfle (trehfl) m clover; shamrock

treize (traiz) num thirteen

treizième (treh-z^y*ehm*) num thirteenth

trembler (trahn̄g-*blay*) v tremble; shiver

tremper (trahn̄g-*pay*) v soak

trente (trahn̄gt) num thirty

trentième (trahn̄g-t^y*ehm*) num thirtieth

trépasser (tray-pah-*say*) v pass away

très (tray) adv very

trésor (tray-*zawr*) m treasure; darling; **Trésor** treasury

triangle (tree-*ahn̄ggl*) m triangle

triangulaire (tree-ahn̄g-gew-*lair*) adj triangular

tribord (tree-*bawr*) m starboard

tribu (tree-*bew*) f tribe

tribunal (tree-bew-*nahl*) m court, law court

tribune (tree-*bewn*) f stand

tricher (tree-*shay*) v cheat

tricot (tree-*koa*) m knitted wear; jersey; **~ de corps** undershirt

tricoter (tree-ko-*tay*) v *knit

trier (tree-*ay*) v sort

trimestre (tree-*mehstr*) m quarter

trimestriel (tree-meh-stree-*ehl*) adj quarterly

triomphant (tree-awn̄g-*fahn̄g*) adj triumphant

triomphe (tree-*awn̄gf*) m triumph

triompher (tree-awn̄g-*fay*) v triumph

triste (treest) adj sad

tristesse (tree-*stehss*) f sorrow, sadness

trivial (tree-v^y*ahl*) adj coarse, crude

trognon (tro-ñ*awn̄g*) m core

trois (trwah) num three; **~ quarts** three-quarter

troisième (trwah-z^y*ehm*) num third

tromper (trawn̄g-*pay*) v deceive; **se ~** *be mistaken; err

tromperie (trawng-*pree*) f deceit

trompette (trawng-*peht*) f trumpet

tronc (trawng) m trunk

trône (troan) m throne

trop (troa) adv too

tropical (tro-pee-*kahl*) adj tropical

tropiques (tro-*peek*) mpl tropics pl

troquer (tro-*kay*) v swap

trottoir (tro-*twaar*) m pavement, sidewalk Am

trou (troo) m hole

trouble (troobl) adj turbid; dubious; m perturbation

troubler (troo-*blay*) v disturb

troupeau (troo-*poa*) m herd; flock

troupes (troop) fpl troops pl

trousseau (troo-*soa*) m kit

trousse de secours (trooss der ser-*koor*) first aid kit

trouver (troo-*vay*) v *find; *come across; consider

truc (trewk) m trick

truite (trweet) f trout

tu (tew) pron you

tube (tewb) m tube; ~ **de plongée** snorkel

tuberculose (tew-behr-kew-*loaz*) f tuberculosis

tuer (tway) v kill

tuile (tweel) f tile

tulipe (tew-*leep*) f tulip

tumeur (tew-*murr*) f tumo(u)r; growth

tunique (tew-*neek*) f tunic

Tunisie (tew-nee-*zee*) f Tunisia

tunisien (tew-nee-z'*ang*) adj Tunisian

tunnel (tew-*nehl*) m tunnel

turbine (tewr-*been*) f turbine

turc (tewrk) adj Turkish; **Turc** m Turk

Turquie (tewr-*kee*) f Turkey

tuteur (tew-*turr*) m guardian, tutor

tuyau (twee-'*oa*) m tube, pipe; ~ **d'échappement** exhaust

tympan (tang-*pahng*) m eardrum

type (teep) m type; guy, chap

typhoïde (tee-fo-*eed*) f typhoid

typique (tee-*peek*) adj typical

U

ulcère (ewl-*sair*) m ulcer; ~ **à l'estomac** gastric ulcer

ultime (ewl-*teem*) adj ultimate

ultra-violet (ewl-trah-v'o-*lay*) adj ultraviolet

un (urng) art (f une) a art; num one; **l'un l'autre** each other; **l'un ou l'autre** either; **ni l'un ni l'autre** neither

unanime (ew-nah-*neem*) adj unanimous

uni (ew-*nee*) adj joint; smooth

uniforme (ew-nee-*form*) m uniform; adj uniform

unilatéral (ew-nee-lah-tay-*rahl*) adj one-sided

union (ew-n'*awng*) f union

unique (ew-*neek*) adj unique; sole

uniquement (ew-neek-*mahng*) adv exclusively

unir (ew-*neer*) v unite

unité (ew-nee-*tay*) f unity; unit; ~ **monétaire** monetary unit

univers (ew-nee-*vair*) m universe

universel (ew-nee-vehr-*sehl*) adj universal; all-round

université (ew-nee-vehr-see-*tay*) f university

urbain (ewr-*bang*) adj urban

urgence (ewr-*zhahngss*) f urgency; emergency

urgent (ewr-*zhahng*) *adj* pressing, urgent
urine (ew-*reen*) *f* urine
Uruguay (ew-rew-*gay*) *m* Uruguay
uruguayen (ew-rew-gay-*y ang*) *adj* Uruguayan
usage (ew-*zaazh*) *m* usage
usager (ew-zah-*zhay*) *m* user
user (ew-*zay*) *v* use up; wear out; **usé** worn; threadbare, worn-out
usine (ew-*zeen*) *f* factory; mill, plant, works *pl*; ~ **à gaz** gasworks

ustensile (ew-stahng-*seel*) *m* utensil
usuel (ew-*zwehl*) *adj* customary
utile (ew-*teel*) *adj* useful
utilisable (ew-tee-lee-*zahbl*) *adj* usable
utilisateur (ew-tee-lee-zah-*turr*) *m* consumer
utilisation (ew-tee-lee-zah-*s y awng*) *f* utilization
utiliser (ew-tee-lee-*zay*) *v* utilize, employ
utilité (ew-tee-lee-*tay*) *f* utility, use

V

vacance (vah-*kahngss*) *f* vacancy; **vacances** holiday
vacant (vah-*kahng*) *adj* vacant, unoccupied
vacarme (vah-*kahrm*) *m* noise, racket
vaccination (vahk-see-nah-*s y awng*) *f* vaccination
vacciner (vahk-see-*nay*) *v* vaccinate
vache (vahsh) *f* cow
vaciller (vah-see-*y ay*) *v* falter
vagabond (vah-gah-*bawng*) *m* tramp
vagabonder (vah-gah-bawng-*day*) *v* tramp, roam
vague (vahg) *f* wave; *adj* vague; faint, obscure
vaillance (vah-*y ahngss*) *f* courage
vain (vang) *adj* vain; **en ~** in vain
*vaincre (vangkr) *v* *overcome; conquer, defeat
vainqueur (vang-*kurr*) *m* winner
vaisseau (vay-*soa*) *m* vessel; ~ **sanguin** blood vessel
vaisselle (veh-*sehl*) *f* crockery; dishes *pl*; ***faire la ~** wash up
valable (vah-*lahbl*) *adj* valid
valeur (vah-*lurr*) *f* value, worth; **sans ~**

worthless
valise (vah-*leez*) *f* case, bag, suitcase
vallée (vah-*lay*) *f* valley
*valoir (vah-*lwaar*) *v* *be worth; ~ **la peine** *be worth-while
valse (vahls) *f* waltz
vanille (vah-*neey*) *f* vanilla
vaniteux (vah-nee-*tur*) *adj* vain
vanneau (vah-*noa*) *m* peewit
vanter (vahng-*tay*): **se ~** boast
vapeur (vah-*purr*) *f* steam; vapo(u)r
vaporisateur (vah-po-ree-zah-*turr*) *m* atomizer
variable (vah-r y ahbl) *adj* variable
variation (vah-r y ah-s y awng) *f* variation
varice (vah-*reess*) *f* varicose vein
varicelle (vah-ree-*sehl*) *f* chickenpox
varier (vah-r y ay) *v* vary
variété (vah-r y ay-tay) *f* variety
variole (vah-r y ol) *f* smallpox
vase (vaaz) *m* vase; *f* mud *m*
vaseline (vah-*zleen*) *f* vaseline
vaste (vahst) *adj* large; wide, broad, vast; extensive
vautour (voa-*toor*) *m* vulture
veau (voa) *m* calf; veal; calf skin

végétarien (vay-zhay-tah-*r*ʸ*ang*) *m*
vegetarian

végétation (vay-zhay-tah-*s*ʸ*awng*) *f*
vegetation

véhicule (vay-ee-*kewl*) *m* vehicle

veille (*vayʸ*) *f* day before

veiller (vay-ʸ*ay*) *v* stay awake; **~ sur**
watch over

veine (vain) *f* vein

vélo (vay-*loa*) *m* bicycle, cycle

vélomoteur (vay-loa-mo-*tūrr*) *m*
motorbike *Am*, moped

velours (ver-*loor*) *m* velvet; **~ côtelé**
corduroy; **~ de coton** cotton velvet

vendable (vahng-*dahbl*) *adj* saleable

vendange (vahng-*dahngzh*) *f* vintage

vendeur (vahng-*dūrr*) *m*, **-euse** *f*
vendor; seller; sales clerk *Am*, shop
assistant

vendre (vahngdr) *v* *sell; **à ~** for sale

vendredi (vahng-drer-*dee*) *m* Friday

vénéneux (vay-nay-*nur*) *adj* poisonous

vénérable (vay-nay-*rahbl*) *adj*
venerable

Venezuela (vay-nay-zway-*lah*) *m*
Venezuela

vénézuélien (vay-nay-zway-*l*ʸ*ang*) *adj*
Venezuelan

vengeance (vahng-*zhahngss*) *f*
revenge

venger (vahng-*zhay*) *v* avenge

***venir** (ver-*neer*) *v* *come; ***faire ~**
*send for

vent (vahng) *m* wind; **coup de ~** blow

vente (vahngt) *f* sale; **~ aux enchères**
auction; **~ en gros** wholesale

venteux (vahng-*tur*) *adj* windy, gusty

ventilateur (vahng-tee-lah-*tūrr*) *m* fan,
ventilator

ventilation (vahng-tee-lah-*s*ʸ*awng*) *f*
ventilation

ventiler (vahng-tee-*lay*) *v* ventilate

ventre (vahngtr) *m* belly

venue (ver-*new*) *f* arrival

ver (vair) *m* worm

véranda (vay-rahng-*dah*) *f* veranda

verbal (vehr-*bahl*) *adj* verbal

verbe (vehrb) *m* verb

verdict (vehr-*deekt*) *m* verdict

verger (vehr-*zhay*) *m* orchard

véridique (vay-ree-*deek*) *adj* truthful

vérifier (vay-ree-*f*ʸ*ay*) *v* verify; check

véritable (vay-ree-*tahbl*) *adj* real

vérité (vay-ree-*tay*) *f* truth

vernir (vehr-*neer*) *v* varnish; glaze

vernis (vehr-*nee*) *m* varnish; lacquer; **~
à ongle** nail polish

verre (vair) *m* glass; **~ de couleur**
stained glass; **~ grossissant**
magnifying glass; **verres de contact**
contact lenses

verrou (veh-*roo*) *m* bolt

vers (vair) *m* verse; *prep* towards, at; **~
le bas** downwards; **~ le haut** up

versant (vehr-*sahng*) *m* slope

versement (vehr-ser-*mahng*) *m*
deposit, remittance

verser (vehr-*say*) *v* pour; *shed

version (vehr-*s*ʸ*awng*) *f* version

vert (vair) *adj* green

vertical (vehr-tee-*kahl*) *adj* vertical

vertige (vehr-*teezh*) *m* dizziness,
giddiness

vertu (vehr-*tew*) *f* virtue

vessie (vay-*see*) *f* bladder

veste (vehst) *f* jacket; **~ de sport** blazer

vestiaire (veh-*st*ʸ*air*) *m* cloakroom;
checkroom *Am*

vestibule (veh-stee-*bewl*) *m* hall,
lobby

veston (veh-*stawng*) *m* jacket; **~ sport**
sports jacket

vêtements (veht-*mahng*) *mpl* clothes
pl; **~ de sport** sportswear

vétérinaire (vay-tay-ree-*nair*) *m*/*f*
veterinary surgeon

***vêtir** (vay-*teer*) *v* dress

veuf (vurf) *m* widower

veuve (vūrv) f widow

via (vee-*ah*) prep via

viaduc (v^yah-*dewk*) m viaduct

viande (v^yah<u>n</u>gd) f meat

vibration (vee-brah-s^yaw<u>n</u>g) f vibration

vibrer (vee-*bray*) v vibrate; tremble

vicaire (vee-*kair*) m vicar

vice-président (vee-spray-zee-*dah<u>n</u>g*) m vice president

vicieux (vee-s^yur) adj vicious

victime (veek-*teem*) f victim; casualty

victoire (veek-*twaar*) f victory

vide (veed) adj empty; m vacuum

vider (vee-*day*) v empty

vie (vee) f life; lifetime; **en ~** alive; **~ privée** privacy

vieillard (v^yeh-^y*aar*) m old man

vieillesse (v^yeh-^y*ehss*) f age, old age

vieilli (v^yay-^y*ee*) adj ancient

vieillot (v^yeh-^y*oa*) adj quaint

vierge (v^yehrzh) f virgin

vieux (v^yur) adj (vieil; f vieille) old; aged, ancient

vif (veef) adj vivid; intense, brisk, lively

vigilant (vee-zhee-*lah<u>n</u>g*) adj vigilant

vigne (veeñ) f vine

vignoble (vee-*ñobl*) m vineyard

vigoureux (vee-goo-*rur*) adj vigorous

vigueur (vee-*gūrr*) f strength

vilain (vee-*la<u>n</u>g*) adj bad

villa (vee-*lah*) f villa; cottage

village (vee-*laazh*) m village

ville (veel) f town

vin (va<u>n</u>g) m wine

vinaigre (vee-*naigr*) m vinegar

vingt (va<u>n</u>g) num twenty

vingtième (va<u>n</u>g-t^y*ehm*) num twentieth

violation (v^yo-lah-s^y*aw<u>n</u>g*) f violation

violence (v^yo-*lah<u>n</u>gss*) f violence

violent (v^yo-*lah<u>n</u>g*) adj violent; fierce, severe

violer (v^yo-*lay*) v assault, rape

violet (v^yo-*lay*) adj violet

violette (v^yo-*leht*) f violet

violon (v^yo-*law<u>n</u>g*) m violin

virage (vee-*raazh*) m turning, bend

virer (vee-*ray*) v turn

virgule (veer-*gewl*) f comma

vis (veess) f screw

visa (vee-*zah*) m visa

visage (vee-*zaazh*) m face

viser (vee-*zay*) v aim at

viseur (vee-*zūrr*) m viewfinder

visibilité (vee-zee-bee-lee-*tay*) f visibility

visible (vee-*zeebl*) adj visible

vision (vee-z^y*aw<u>n</u>g*) f vision

visite (vee-*zeet*) f visit; call; **rendre ~ à** call on

visiter (vee-zee-*tay*) v visit

visiteur (vee-zee-*ūrr*) m visitor

vital (vee-*tahl*) adj vital

vitamine (vee-tah-*meen*) f vitamin

vite (veet) adv quickly

vitesse (vee-*tehss*) f speed; gear; **en ~** in a hurry; **indicateur de ~** speedometer; **limitation de ~** speed limit; **~ de croisière** cruising speed

vitre (veetr) f window-pane

vitrine (vee-*treen*) f showcase, shopwindow

vivant (vee-*vah<u>n</u>g*) adj alive; live

*****vivre** (veevr) v live; experience

vocabulaire (vo-kah-bew-*lair*) m vocabulary

vocal (vo-*kahl*) adj vocal

vœu (vur) m desire; vow

voici (vwah-*see*) adv here is

voie (vwah) f way; track; lane; **~ d'eau** waterway; **~ ferrée** railway line; railroad line Am

voilà (vwah-*lah*) adv there is; here you are

voile (vwahl) f sail; m veil

*****voir** (vwaar) v *see

voisin (vwah-*zañg*) *m* neighbo(u)r

voisinage (vwah-zee-*naazh*) *m* vicinity, neighbo(u)rhood

voisine (vwah-*zeen*) *f* neighbo(u)r

voiture (vwah-*tewr*) *f* car; carriage; ~ **d'enfant** pram; ~ **de sport** sports car; ~ **Pullman** Pullman

voix (vwah) *f* voice; **à haute ~** aloud

vol (vol) *m* flight; robbery, theft; ~ **charter** charter flight; ~ **de nuit** night flight; ~ **de retour** return flight

volaille (vo-*ligh*) *f* poultry, fowl

volant (vo-*lañg*) *m* steering wheel

volcan (vol-*kañg*) *m* volcano

voler (vo-*lay*) *v* *fly; *steal; rob

volet (vo-*lay*) *m* shutter

voleur (vo-*lurr*) *m* thief; robber

volontaire (vo-lawñg-*tair*) *adj* voluntary; *m* volunteer

volonté (vo-lawñg-*tay*) *f* will; willpower

volontiers (vo-lawñg-*tᵞay*) *adv* willingly, gladly

volt (volt) *m* volt

voltage (vol-*taazh*) *m* voltage

volume (vo-*lewm*) *m* volume

volumineux (voa-lew-mee-*nur*) *adj* bulky, big

vomir (vo-*meer*) *v* vomit

vote (vot) *m* vote; **droit de ~** franchise

voter (vo-*tay*) *v* vote

votre (votr) *adj* (pl vos) your

***vouloir** (voo-*lwaar*) *v* want; *will; **en ~ à** resent; ~ **dire** *mean

vous (voo) *pron* you; yourselves; **vous-même** *pron* yourself; **vousmêmes** *pron* yourselves

voûte (voot) *f* vault, arch

voyage (vwah-ᵞ*aazh*) *m* journey; trip, voyage; ~ **d'affaires** business trip; ~ **de retour** return journey

voyager (vwah-ᵞah-*zhay*) *v* travel; ~ **en auto** motor

voyageur (vwah-ᵞah-*zhurr*) *m*, **-euse** *f* travel(l)er

voyelle (vwah-ᵞ*ehl*) *f* vowel

vrai (vray) *adj* true; very

vraiment (vray-*mahñg*) *adv* really

vraisemblable (vray-sahñg-*blahbl*) *adj* probable

vu (vew) *prep* considering

vue (vew) *f* sight; view; **point de ~** point of view

vulgaire (vewl-*gair*) *adj* vulgar

vulnérable (vewl-nay-*rahbl*) *adj* vulnerable

W

wagon (vah-*gawñg*) *m* carriage; wag(g)on, coach; passenger car *Am*;

wagon-lit sleeping car; **wagon-restaurant** dining car

Y

y (ee) *pron* there; to it

yacht (ˣot) *m* yacht

Z

zèbre (zaibr) *m* zebra
zélé (zay-*lay*) *adj* zealous
zèle (zehl) *m* zeal
zéro (zay-*roa*) *m* zero; nought
zinc (zang̅g̅) *m* zinc
zodiaque (zo-*d*ˣ*ahk*) *m* zodiac

zone (zo̅a̅n) *f* zone; area; ~ **de**
stationnement parking zone; ~
industrielle industrial area
zoo (zoa) *m* zoo
zoom (zoom) *m* zoom lens

Menu Reader
Food

à la, à l', au, aux in the manner of, as in, with

abats, abattis giblets, innards

abricot apricot

agneau lamb

aiglefin haddock

ail garlic

ailloli garlic mayonnaise

airelle a kind of cranberry

alouette sans tête slice of veal rolled and generally stuffed with minced meat, garlic and parsley

(à l')alsacienne usually garnished with sauerkraut, ham and sausages

amande almond

amuse-gueule appetizer

ananas pineapple

anchois anchovy

(à l')ancienne old style; usually with wine-flavoured cream sauce of mushrooms, onions or shallots

(à l')andalouse usually with green peppers, aubergines and tomatoes

andouille a kind of tripe sausage

andouillette smaller kind of tripe sausage

(à l')anglaise 1) usually boiled or steamed vegetables, especially potatoes 2) breaded and fried vegetables, meat, fish or fowl

anguille eel

~ au vert eel braised in a white sauce served with minced parsley and other greens

anis aniseed

artichaut (globe) artichoke

asperge asparagus

assiette plate

~ anglaise cold meat (US cold cuts)

~ de charcuterie assorted pork and other meat products

assorti assorted

aubergine aubergine (US eggplant)

ballottine (de volaille) boned fowl which is stuffed, rolled, cooked and served in gelatine

banane banana

bar bass

barbue brill

basilic basil

béarnaise sauce of egg-yolk, butter, vinegar, shallots, tarragon and white wine

bécasse woodcock

béchamel white sauce

beignet fritter generally filled with fruit, vegetables or meat

(à la) Bercy butter sauce of white wine and shallots

betterave beetroot

beurre butter

~ blanc white butter sauce of shallots, vinegar and white wine

~ maître d'hôtel butter with chopped parsley and lemon juice

~ noir browned butter sauce of vinegar and parsley

bifteck beef steak

(à la) bigarade brown sauce generally with oranges, sugar and vinegar

biscotte rusk (US zwieback)

biscuit biscuit (US cookie)

bisque cream soup of lobster or crayfish (US chowder)

blanc de volaille boned breast of fowl

blanchaille whitebait

blanquette de veau veal stew in white sauce

(au) bleu 1) of fish (usually trout), boiled very fresh 2) of cheese, blue-veined 3) of meat, very underdone (US rare)

bœuf beef

~ **bourguignon** chunks of beef stewed in red wine with onions, bacon and mushrooms

~ **en daube** larded chunks of beef marinated in red wine with vegetables and stewed

~ **miro(n)ton** cold boiled beef or beef stew with onion sauce

~ **mode** larded chunks of beef braised in red wine with carrots and onions

bolet boletus mushroom

bombe glacée moulded ice-cream dessert

(à la) bordelaise red wine sauce with shallots, beef marrow and boletus mushrooms

bouchée à la reine vol-au-vent; puff-pastry shell filled with meat, sweetbreads or seafood and sometimes mushrooms

boudin black pudding (US blood sausage)

bouillabaisse assorted fish and shellfish stewed in white wine, garlic, saffron and olive oil

bouilli 1) boiled 2) boiled beef

bouillon bouillon, broth, stock

(à la) bourguignonne button mushrooms, pearl onions or shallots braised in rich red wine

braisé braised

brandade (de morue) prepared cod with cream, oil and garlic

brie white, mellow cheese

brioche small roll or cake

(à la) broche (on a) spit

brochet pike

(en) brochette (cooked on a) skewer

cabillaud fresh cod

café glacé coffee-flavoured ice-cream dessert

caille quail

camembert soft cheese with a thin white rind and a yellow interior

canard (caneton) duck (duckling)

~ **à l'orange** roast duck braised with oranges and orange liqueur

cannelle cinnamon

cantal smooth, firm cheese not unlike Cheddar

câpre caper

carbonnade charcoal-grilled meat

~ **flamande** beef slices, onions and herbs braised in beer

cardon cardoon (vegetable)

carotte carrot

carottes Vichy steamed carrots

carpe carp

carré loin, rack

~ **de l'Est** usually square-shaped soft, mild, fermented cheese

carrelet plaice

carte des vins wine list

cassis blackcurrant

cassoulet toulousain butter-bean stew of goose or with mutton, pork and sometimes sausage

céleri celery (usually celery root)

~ **en branche** branch celery

~**rave** celeriac, celery root

cèpe boletus mushroom

cerfeuil chervil

cerise cherry

cervelle brains

champignon mushroom

~ **de Paris** button mushroom

chanterelle chanterelle mushroom

charbonnade charcoal-grilled meat

charcuterie various kinds of cold pork products

charlotte fruit dessert (usually apples) made in a deep, round mould

chasse venison

chasseur hunter's style; sauce of mushrooms, tomatoes, wine and garlic herbs

chateaubriand thick slice of beef taken from the fillet

chaud warm

chaudrée fish and seafood stew, often with garlic, herbs, onions and white wine

chausson aux pommes apple dumpling (US turnover)

chevreuil deer

chicorée endive (US chicory)

chou cabbage

  ~ **de Bruxelles** brussels sprouts

  ~ **à la crème** cream puff

  ~**-fleur** cauliflower

  ~ **rouge** red cabbage

choucroute sauerkraut

  ~ **garnie** usually with ham, bacon and sausage

ciboulette chive

citron lemon

civet de lapin (lièvre) jugged rabbit (hare)

clafoutis fruit baked in pancake batter, brandy often added

clémentine pipless (US seedless) tangerine

cochon de lait suck(l)ing pig

(en) cocotte casserole

cœur heart

  ~ **d'artichaut** artichoke heart

(à la) Colbert dipped in egg batter and breadcrumbs, fried

colin hake

concombre cucumber

confit d'oie pieces of goose preserved in its own fat

confiture jam

consommation general word for drinks

consommé clear soup served hot or cold

  ~ **Célestine** with chicken and noodles

  ~ **aux cheveux d'ange** with thin

noodles

  ~ **Colbert** with poached eggs, spring vegetables

  ~ **julienne** with shredded vegetables

  ~ **madrilène** cold and flavoured with tomatoes

  ~ **princesse** with diced chicken and asparagus tips

  ~ **aux vermicelles** with thin noodles

contre-filet sirloin

coq au vin chicken stewed in red wine with mushrooms, bacon, onions and herbs

coquelet cockerel

coquillage shellfish

coquille Saint-Jacques scallop gratinéed in its shell

corbeille de fruits basket of assorted fruit

cornichon small gherkin (US pickle)

côte chop or rib

  ~ **de bœuf** rib of beef

  ~ **de veau** veal chop

côtelette cutlet, chop

  ~ **d'agneau** lamb chop

  ~ **de porc** pork chop

coupe a metal or glass dish usually for individual desserts

  ~ **glacée** ice-cream dessert

courgette a long vegetable with a dark green skin (US zucchini)

couvert cover charge

  ~**, vin et service compris** price includes wine, service and cover charges

crabe crab

crème 1) a dessert with cream or a creamy dessert

  ~ **anglaise** custard

  ~ **caramel** caramel custard

  ~ **Chantilly** whipped cream

  ~ **glacée** ice-cream

crème 2) a creamy soup

crêpe large, paper-thin pancake

~Suzette pancake with orange sauce, flamed with brandy and often orange liqueur

cresson (water)cress

crevette shrimp

croissant crescent-shaped flaky roll (usually served for breakfast)

croque-monsieur grilled or baked ham-and-cheese sandwich

croustade pie, pastry shell filled with fish, seafood, meat or vegetables

(en) croûte (in a) pastry crust

croûton small piece of bread, toasted or fried

cru raw

crudités raw vegetables usually served sliced, grated or diced as an hors d'œuvre

crustacé shellfish

cuisse leg or thigh

cuisses de grenouilles frogs' legs

cuit cooked

bien ~ well-done

cumin caraway, cumin

darne thick fillet of fish, usually of salmon

datte date

daurade gilt-head

déjeuner lunch

délice often used to describe a dessert speciality of the chef

demi half

~-sel soft cream cheese, slightly salty

demoiselle de Cherbourg small rock lobster

(à la) dieppoise garnish of mussels and shrimp served in white-wine sauce

dinde, dindon turkey

dindonneau young turkey

dîner dinner

diplomate moulded custard dessert with crystallized fruit and lined with sponge fingers steeped in liqueur

dodine de canard boned duck, rolled,

stuffed, sometimes served cold in gelatine

(à la) du Barry garnish of cauliflower and cheese sauce, gratinéed

(aux) duxelles with minced mushrooms sautéed with butter, white wine and herbs

échalote shallot

écrevisse (freshwater) crayfish

~ à la nage simmered in white wine, aromatic vegetables and herbs

églefin haddock

émincé slices of cooked meat in gravy or thick cream sauce

endive chicory (US endive)

~ à la bruxelloise steamed chicory rolled in a slice of ham

entrecôte rib-eye steak

entrée dish served between the hors d'oeuvre or soup and the main course; the first course in a smaller dinner (US starter)

entremets small dish served before cheese; today it often means dessert

épaule shoulder

éperlan smelt

épice spice

épicé hot, peppered

épinard spinach

escalope de veau veal scallop, thin slice of veal

escalope viennoise wiener schnitzel; breaded veal cutlet

escargot snail

estouffade braised or steamed in tightly sealed vessel with minimum of cooking liquid

estragon tarragon

étuvé steamed, stewed with minimum of cooking liquid

faisan pheasant

farci stuffed

fenouil fennel

féra dace (fish)

ève broad bean

fïlet meat or fish fillet

~ **de bœuf** fillet of beef (US tenderloin)

~ **mignon** small round veal or pork fillet

~ **de sole** fillet of sole

(à la) **financière** rich sauce of pike dumplings, truffles, mushrooms, Madeira wine, sometimes with olives and crayfish

(aux) **fines herbes** with herbs

(à la) **flamande** Flemish style; usually a garnish of braised potatoes, carrots, cabbage, turnips, bacon and sausage (sometimes simmered in beer)

flambé dish flamed usually with brandy

flétan halibut

foie liver

~ **gras** goose or duck liver

fond d'artichaut artichocke heart (US bottom)

fondue (au fromage) melted-cheese mixture in a pot into which pieces of bread are dipped

fondue bourguignonne bite-size pieces of meat dipped into boiling oil at the table and eaten with a variety of sauces

fondue chinoise paper-thin slices of beef dipped into boiling bouillon and eaten with a variety of sauces

(à la) **forestière** forester's style; generally sautéed in butter with morel mushrooms, potatoes and bacon

(au) **four** baked

frais, fraîche fresh

fraise strawberry

~ **des bois** wild strawberry

framboise raspberry

frappé chilled, iced

friand patty with meat filling

fricandeau braised, larded veal

fricassée browned pieces of meat braised with seasonings and vegetables and served in a thick sauce

frit fried

frites chips (US french fries)

friture (de poisson) fried fish

fromage cheese

~ **frais** fresh curd cheese

~ **de tête** brawn (US headcheese)

fruit confit candied fruit

fruits de mer mussels, oysters, clams

fumé smoked

galette flat, plain cake

garbure thick cabbage soup made of salted pork, spices and *confit d'oie*

garni garnished

(avec) **garniture** (with) vegetables

gâteau cake, flan, tart

gaufre waffle

gaufrette small, crisp, sweet wafer

(en) **gelée** jellied

gélinotte hazel-hen, hazel-grouse (US prairie chicken)

gibelotte de lapin rabbit stew in wine sauce

gibier game

~ **de saison** game in season

gigot d'agneau leg of lamb

girolle chanterelle mushroom

glace ice-cream

~ (à la) **napolitaine** ice-cream layers of different flavours

glacé iced, glazed

goujon gudgeon

gras-double tripe simmered in wine and onions

(au) **gratin** browned with breadcrumbs or cheese

gratin dauphinois sliced potatoes gratinéed in the oven with eggs, cream and cheese

gratin de fruits de mer shellfish in

heavy cream sauce and gratinéed

grillade grilled meat

grillé grilled

grive thrush

groseille à maquereau gooseberry

groseille rouge redcurrant

gruyère a hard cheese rich in flavour

haché minced, hashed

hachis mince, hash

hareng herring

haricot bean

~ **de mouton** stew of mutton with beans and potatoes

~ **vert** French bean (US green bean)

Henri IV artichoke hearts garnished with béarnaise sauce

hollandaise sauce of egg-yolks, butter and lemon juice or vinegar

homard lobster

~ **à l'américaine** (or **à l'armoricaine**) lobster flamed in brandy, simmered in white wine with garlic, tomatoes and herbs

~ **cardinal** flamed in brandy, diced, served in its shell with truffles and chopped mushrooms and gratinéed

~ **Newburg** cut into sections, cooked in brandy and fish stock

~ **Thermidor** simmered in white wine, sautéed in butter with mushrooms, herbs, spices, mustard, flamed in brandy and gratinéed with cheese**huile** oil

huître oyster

~ **belon** flat, pinkish oyster

~ **de claire** similar to bluepoint oyster

~ **portugaise** small, fat oyster

jambon ham

~ **de Bayonne** raw, with a slightly salty flavour

~ **cru** raw, cured

~ **à l'os** baked ham

jardinière cooked assorted vegetables

jarret shank, shin

julienne vegetables cut into fine strips

jus gravy, juice

lamproie lamprey

langouste spiny lobster

langoustine Norway lobster, prawn, crawfish

langue tongue

lapin rabbit

lard bacon

légume vegetable

lentille lentil

levraut young hare, leveret

lièvre hare

limande dab

livarot small, round cheese from Normandy

longe de veau loin of veal

(à la) lorraine usually braised in red wine with red cabbage

loup (de mer) (sea) bass

(à la) lyonnaise generally sautéed with onions

macédoine mixed, diced vegetables or fruit

(au) madère with Madeira wine

maigre lean

maïs maize (US corn)

maître d'hôtel sautéed in butter with chopped parsley and lemon juice

maquereau mackerel

marcassin young boar

marchand de vin red wine sauce seasoned with shallots

mariné marinated

marinière sailor's style; garnish of mussels with other seafood simmered in white wine and spices

marjolaine marjoram

maroilles strong, semi-hard cheese from Picardy

marron chestnut

matelote freshwater-fish stew (especially of eel) with wine, onions, mushrooms médaillon small, round cut of meat

menthe mint

menu in France, generally means *menu à prix fixe*, set meal at a fixed price

merguez very spicy sausage

merlan whiting

merluche dried hake

meunière floured and sautéed in butter with lemon juice and chopped parsley

miel honey

mijoté simmered

millefeuille flaky pastry with cream filling (US napoleon)

(à la) Mirabeau with anchovies, olives, tarragon

mirabelle small yellow plum

(à la) mode in the style (of); often means made according to a local recipe

moelle marrow (bone)

morille morel mushroom

Mornay *béchamel* sauce with cheese

moule mussel

moules marinière mussels simmered in white wine with shallots, thyme and parsley

mousse 1) any frothy cream dish 2) chopped or pounded meat or fish with eggs and cream

mousseline 1) frothy mixture containing cream, usually whipped 2) variation of hollandaise sauce with whipped cream

moutarde mustard

mouton mutton

munster soft cheese with a pungent flavour

mûre mulberry or blackberry

myrtille bilberry (US blueberry)

nature/au naturel plain, without dressing, sauce or stuffing

navarin mutton stew with turnips

navet turnip

(à la/en) neige snow-like; i.e. with beaten egg-whites

(à la) niçoise Riviera style; usually with garlic, anchovies, olives, onions, tomatoes

(à la) nivernaise a garnish of carrots, onions, potatoes

noisette 1) hazelnut 2) boneless round piece of meat usually taken from loin or rib

noix walnut

~ de coco coconut

~ (de) muscade nutmeg

~ de veau pope's eye of veal

(à la) normande usually cooked with gudgeon, shrimps, mushrooms, cream and sometimes truffles

nouilles noodles

œuf egg

~ brouillé scrambled

~ à la coque soft-boiled

~ dur hard-boiled

~ farci stuffed

~ en gelée lightly poached and served in gelatine

~ au jambon ham and eggs

~ au/sur le plat fried

~ poché poached

~ Rossini with truffles and Madeira wine

oie goose

oignon onion

omble-chevalier freshwater fish of the char family

omelette omelet

~ norvégienne ice-cream dessert covered with beaten egg-whites, quickly browned in oven and served flaming (US baked Alaska)

ortolan small game bird like a finch

os bone

~ à moelle marrow bone

oseille sorrel

oursin sea urchin

pain bread

palourde clam

pamplemousse grapefruit

panaché mixed; two or more kinds of something

pané breaded, rolled in breadcrumbs

(en) papillote encased in greased paper and baked

parfait ice-cream dessert

Parmentier containing potatoes

pastèque watermelon

pâté 1) a moulded pastry case which holds meat or fish 2) a thickish paste often of liver (contained in an earthenware dish)

  ~ ardennais a purée of pork and seasonings encased in a loaf of bread, served in slices

  ~ de campagne strongly flavoured with a variety of meat

  ~ en croûte in a pastry crust

  ~ de foie gras goose (or duck) liver paste

pâtes noodles, macaroni, spaghetti

paupiette (de veau) veal bird, thin slice of veal rolled around stuffing

(à la) paysanne country style; usually containing various vegetables

pêche peach

perche perch

perdreau young partridge

perdrix partridge

(à la) périgourdine preparation with truffles

persil parsley

petit small

  ~ déjeuner breakfast

  ~ four small, fancy cake (US fancy cookie)

  ~ pain roll

  ~ pois green pea

  ~ salé (au chou) salt pork (with cabbage)

~suisse a mild-flavoured, double-cream cheese

pied de porc pig's trotter (US pig's foot)

pigeonneau squab

piment pimento

pintade guinea hen

piperade omelet with green peppers, garlic, tomatoes, ham

piquant sharp-tasting, spicy (e.g. of a sauce)

pissaladière onion and anchovy tart with black olives

plat plate

  ~ du jour speciality of the day

  ~ principal main dish

plateau de fromages cheese board

plie plaice

poché poached

(à la) poêle fried

(à) point medium

pointe d'asperge asparagus tip

poire pear

  ~ à la Condé served hot on a bed of vanilla-flavoured rice

  ~ Belle Hélène with vanilla ice-cream and chocolate sauce

poireau leek

pois pea

  ~ chiche chick pea

poisson fish

  ~ d'eau douce freshwater fish

  ~ de mer saltwater fish

poitrine breast

  ~ de bœuf brisket

(au) poivre (with) pepper

poivron sweet pepper

pomme apple

pommes (de terre) potatoes

  ~ allumettes matchstick potatoes

  ~ chips crisps (US potato chips)

  ~ dauphine potatoes mashed in butter and egg-yolks, mixed in seasoned flour and deep-fried

~ duchesse potatoes mashed with butter and egg-yolks

~ en robe des champs potatoes in their jackets

~ frites chips (US french fries)

~ mousseline mashed potatoes

~ nature boiled, steamed potatoes

~ nouvelles new potatoes

~ vapeur steamed, boiled potatoes

pont-l'évêque soft cheese, firmer and yellower than camembert

porc pork

port-salut soft cheese, yellow in colour, mild in taste

potage soup

~ bonne femme potato, leek, mushroom, onion, rice and sometimes bacon

~ cancalais fish consommé (often with oysters or other seafood)

~ Condé mashed red beans

~ Crécy carrots

~ cultivateur mixed vegetables and bacon or pork

~ du Barry cream of cauliflower

~ julienne vegetables

~ Longchamp peas, sorrel and chervil

~ Saint-Germain split-pea, leek and onion

~ soissonnais haricot bean

pot-au-feu 1) stockpot of beef, potatoes and aromatic vegetables 2) stew

potée boiled pork or beef with vegetables, especially cabbage

potiron pumpkin

poularde fat pullet

~ de Bresse grain-fed; reputedly the finest available

~ demi-deuil with truffles inserted under the skin and simmered in broth

poule hen

~ au pot stewed with vegetables

~ au riz stewed in bouillon and served with rice

poulet chicken

~ Marengo sautéed in olive oil, cooked with white wine, tomatoes, garlic, shallots and mushrooms

pourboire tip (but *service* is the percentage added to the bill)

praire clam

pré-salé lamb pastured in the salt meadows on the Atlantic seashore

(à la) printanière with spring vegetables

prix price

~ fixe at a fixed price

profiterole au chocolat puff pastry filled with whipped cream or custard and covered with hot chocolate

(à la) provençale often with garlic, onions, herbs, olives, oil and tomatoes

prune plum

pruneau (blue) plum

~ sec prune

pudding plum pudding

puits d'amour pastry shell filled with liqueur-flavoured custard

purée pulped and strained fruit or vegetables

~ de pommes de terre mashed potatoes

quenelle light dumpling made of fish, fowl or meat

queue tail

quiche flan, open tart with meat or vegetable filling, eggs and cream

~ lorraine tart with cheese, bacon, eggs and cream

râble de lièvre saddle of hare

raclette hot, melted cheese scraped from a block of cheese; accompanied with boiled potatoes and gherkins

radis radish

(en) ragoût stew(ed)

raie skate, ray

raisin grape

~ sec raisin, sultana

ramequin small cheese tart

rascasse a Mediterranean fish, an essential ingredient of *bouillabaisse*

ratatouille Mediterranean stew of tomatoes, peppers, onions, garlic and aubergines, served hot or cold

ravigote vinegar sauce with chopped hard-boiled eggs, capers and herbs

reblochon soft, mild cheese, pale cream colour (Savoy)

(à la) reine with mince meat or fowl

reine-claude greengage

repas meal

rhubarbe rhubarb

(à la) Richelieu garnish of tomatoes, peas, bacon and potatoes

rillettes usually minced pork (sometimes goose or duck) baked in its own fat

ris de veau calf sweetbread

rissole fritter, pasty

riz rice

~ pilaf rice boiled in a bouillon, sometimes with onions

rognon kidney

romarin rosemary

roquefort blue-veined cheese made from ewe's milk; strong, salty with piquant flavour

rosbif roast beef

rôti roast(ed)

rouelle de veau shank of veal (usually a round cut)

roulade 1) a rolled slice of meat or fish with stuffing 2) dessert with cream or jam stuffing (Swiss roll)

sabayon creamy dessert of egg-yolks, sugar and white wine flavoured with a citrus fruit, served warm

safran saffron

saignant underdone (US rare)

saint-pierre John Dory (fish)

salade salad

~ chiffonnade shredded lettuce and sorrel in melted butter, served with a dressing

~ de fruits fruit salad (US fruit cocktail)

~ niçoise lettuce, tomatoes, green beans, hard-boiled eggs, tunny, olives, green pepper, potatoes and anchovies

~ russe cooked vegetables in mayonnaise

~ verte green

salé salted

salmis game or fowl partially roasted, then simmered in wine and vegetable *purée*

salpicon garnish or stuffing of one or various elements held together by sauce

salsifis salsify

sandre pikeperch

sanglier wild boar

sarcelle teal, small freshwater duck

sauce sauce

~ béarnaise vinegar, egg-yolks, butter, shallots and tarragon

~ béchamel white sauce

~ au beurre blanc butter, shallots, vinegar or lemon juice

~ au beurre noir browned butter

~ bordelaise brown sauce with boletus mushrooms, red wine, shallots and beef marrow

~ bourguignonne red wine sauce with herbs, onions and spices (sometimes tarragon)

~ café de Paris cream, mustard and herbs

~ chasseur brown sauce with wine, mushrooms, onions, shallots and herbs

~ **diable** hot, spicy sauce with white wine, herbs, vinegar and cayenne pepper

~ **financière** cream, Madeira wine, herbs, spices, mushrooms, truffles and olives

~ **hollandaise** butter, egg-yolks and vinegar or lemon juice

~ **lyonnaise** onions, white wine and butter

~ **madère** brown sauce with Madeira wine base

~ **Mornay** *béchamel* sauce with cheese

~ **ravigote** vinegar sauce with chopped hardboiled eggs, capers and herbs; served cold

~ **rémoulade** mayonnaise enriched with mustard and herbs

~ **suprême** chicken-stock base, thick and bland, served with fowl

~ **tartare** mayonnaise base with gherkins, chives, capers and olives

~ **vinaigrette** oil, vinegar and herbs (sometimes mustard)

saucisse sausage

~ **de Francfort** frankfurter

saucisson a large sausage

saumon salmon

sauté lightly browned in hot butter, oil or fat, sautéed

savarin sponge cake steeped in rum and usually topped with cream

sel salt

selle saddle

selon grosseur (or **grandeur**) price according to size, e.g. of a lobster, often abbreviated **s.g. service (non) compris** service (not) included

sorbet water ice (US sherbet)

soufflé à la reine soufflé with finely chopped poultry or meat

soufflé Rothschild vanilla-flavoured soufflé with candied fruit

soupe soup

~ **au pistou** vegetables, noodles, garlic, basil and cheese

~ **à l'oignon** onion

~ **à l'oignon gratinée** onion soup topped with toast and grated cheese; gratinéed

spécialité (du chef) (chef's) speciality

steak steak

~ **haché** hamburger

~ **au poivre** broiled with crushed peppercorns (often flamed in brandy)

~ **tartare** minced beef, eaten raw, with sauce of egg-yolks, mustard, capers, onions, oil and parsley

sucre sugar

suprême de volaille boned chicken breast with creamy sauce

sur commande to your special order

(en) sus in addition, additional charge

tarte open(-faced) flan, tart

~ **Tatin** upside-down tart of caramelized apples

tartelette small tart

tendrons de veau breast of veal

(en) terrine a preparation of meat, fish, fowl or game baked in an earthenware dish called a *terrine*, served cold

tête head

thon tunny (US tuna)

(en) timbale meat, fish, seafood, fruit or vegetables cooked in a pastry case or mould

tomate tomato

tomme a mild soft cheese

topinambour Jerusalem artichoke

tortue turtle

tournedos round cut of prime beef

~ **Rossini** garnished with foie gras and truffles, served with Madeira wine sauce

tout compris all-inclusive (price of a

meal)
tranche slice
~ **napolitaine** cassata; slice of layered ice-cream and crystallized fruit
tripes tripe
~ **à la mode de Caen** baked with calf's trotters (US calf's feet), vegetables, apple brandy or cider
truffe truffle
truite trout
vacherin a mellow cheese
~ **glacé** an ice-cream dessert with meringue
vanille vanilla
(à la) vapeur steamed
varié assorted
veau veal
velouté a creamy soup (of vegetables or poultry), thickened with butter

and flour
vert-pré a garnish of cress
viande meat
~ **séchée** dried beef served as hors d'oeuvre in paper-thin slices
viandes froides various cold slices of meat and ham (US cold cuts)
vinaigre vinegar
vinaigrette salad sauce of vinegar, oil, herbs and mustard
volaille fowl
vol-au-vent puff-pastry shell filled with meat, sweetbreads or fish and sometimes mushrooms
waterzoï de poulet chicken poached in white wine and shredded vegetables, cream and egg-yolks
yaourt yoghurt

Drinks

Alsace (93 communes situated on the River Rhine) produces virtually only dry white wine, notably *Gewurztraminer, Riesling, Sylvaner, Traminer*; the terms *grand vin* and *grand cru* are sometimes employed to indicate a wine of exceptional quality
Amer Picon an aperitif with wine and brandy base and quinine flavouring
Anjou a region of the Loire district producing fine rosé and white wine
apéritif often bittersweet, some aperitifs have a wine and brandy base with herbs and bitters (like *Amer Picon, Byrrh, Dubonnet*), others, called *pastis*, have an aniseed base (like *Pernod* or *Ricard*); an aperitif may also be simply vermouth (like *Noilly Prat*) or a liqueur drink like

blanc-cassis
appellation d'origine contrôlée (A.O.C.) officially recognized wines of which there are over 250 in France; standards of quality are rigidly checked by government inspectors
armagnac a wine-distilled brandy from the Armagnac region, west of Toulouse
Beaujolais Burgundy's most southerly and extensive vineyards which produce mainly red wine, e.g., *Brouilly, Chénas, Chiroubles, Côte de Brouilly, Fleurie, Juliénas, Morgon, Moulin-à-Vent*
Belgique Belgium; though the Romans introduced wine-making to Belgium, the kingdom today only incidentally produces wine, primarily

white, sometimes rosé and sparkling wine

bénédictine forest-green liqueur; brandy base, herbs and orange peel, reputedly secret formula

Berry a region of the Loire district producing red, white and rosé wine; e.g., *Châteaumeillant, Menetou-Salon, Quincy, Reuilly, Sancerre, Sauvignon*

bière beer
~ **blonde** light
~ **(en) bouteille** bottled
~ **brune** dark
~ **pression** draught (US draft)
~ **des Trappistes** malt beer brewed by Trappist monks

blanc-cassis white wine mixed with blackcurrant liqueur

Blayais a region of Bordeaux producing mainly red and white wine

boisson drink

Bordeaux divided into several regions: Blayais, Bourgeais, Entre-Deux-Mers, Fronsac, Graves, Médoc, Pomerol, St-Emilion, Sauternais; among the officially recognized wines are 34 reds, 23 whites and two rosés divided into three categories: general (e.g., *Bordeaux* or *Bordeaux supérieur*), regional (e.g., *Entre-Deux-Mers, Graves, Médoc*) and communal (e.g., *Margaux, Pauillac, Sauternes*); Bordeaux red wine is known as claret in America and Britain

Bourgeais a region of Bordeaux producing red and white table wine

Bourgogne Burgundy, divided into five regions: Beaujolais, Chablis, Côte Chalonnaise, Côte d'Or (which comprises the Côte de Beaune and the Côte de Nuits) and Mâconnais; Burgundy counts the largest number

of officially recognized wines of France's wine-growing districts; there are four categories of wine: generic or regional (e.g., *Bourgogne* red, white or rosé), subregional (e.g., *Beaujolais, Beaujolais supérieur, Beaujolais-Villages, Côte de Beaune-Villages, Mâcon, Mâcon supérieur, Mâcon-Villages*), communal (e.g., *Beaune, Chablis, Fleurie, Meursault, Nuits-St-Georges, Volnay*) and vineyard (*climat*) (e.g., *Chambertin, Clos de Vougeot, Musigny*)

brut extra dry, refers to *Champagne*

Byrrh an aperitif with wine base and quinine, fortified with brandy

cacao cocoa

café coffee
~ **complet** with bread, roll, butter and jam; the Continental breakfast
~ **crème** with cream
~ **espresso** espresso
~ **filtre** percolated or dripped through a filter
~ **frappé** iced
~ **au lait** white (with milk)
~ **liégeois** cold with ice-cream, topped with whipped cream
~ **nature, noir** simple, black
~ **sans caféine** caffeine-free

calvados an apple brandy from Normandy

cassis blackcurrant liqueur

Chablis a region of Burgundy noted for its white wine

chambrer to bring wine gently to room (*chambre*) temperature

Champagne district divided into three large regions: Côte des Blancs, Montagne de Reims and Vallée de la Marne with some 200 kilometres (120 miles) of underground caves where the wine ferments; there are ordinary red, white and rosé wines but the production is overwhelmingly centered upon the sparkling white and rosé (usually referred to in English as pink Champagne) for which the region is universally known; vineyards are of little importance in classifying wines from Champagne since, according to tradition, certain varieties of Champagne are produced by blending wine from different vineyards in proportions which are carefully-guarded secrets; sparkling Champagne is sold according to the amount of sugar added: *brut* (extra dry) contains up to 1.5 per cent sugar additive, *extra-sec* (very dry), 1.5–2.5 per cent, *sec* (dry), 2.5–5 per cent, *demi-sec* (slightly sweet), 5–8 per cent and *doux* (sweet), 8–15 per cent

Chartreuse a yellow or green liqueur of herbs and spices produced by monks of Grande Chartreuse in the French Alps

château castle; term employed traditionally in the district of Bordeaux to indicate a wine of exceptional quality; synonyms: *clos, domaine*

chocolat chocolate

cidre cider

citron pressé freshly squeezed lemon juice

citronnade lemon squash (US lemon drink)

claret see *Bordeaux*

clos vineyard; generally indicates a wine of exceptional quality

cognac cognac; the famed winedistilled brandy from the Charente and Charente-Maritime regions

Cointreau orange liqueur

Corse Corsica; this Mediterranean island, a French department, produces fine wine, particularly from the hilly areas and Cape Corsica; red, white and rosé wine is characterized by a rich, full-bodied taste; the best wine, grown near Bastia, is the rosé *Patrimonio*

Côte de Beaune the southern half of Burgundy's celebrated Côte d'Or producing chiefly red wine; e.g., the prestigious *Aloxe-Corton* as well as *Beaune, Blagny, Chassagne-Montrachet, Meursault, Pernand-Vergelesses, Puligny-Montrachet, Santenay, Savigny-lès-Beaune, Volnay*

Côte de Nuits a region of Burgundy especially noted for its red wine, e.g., *Chambolle-Musigny, Fixin, Gevrey-Chambertin, Morey-St-Denis, Nuits-St-Georges, Vosne-Romanée*

Côte d'Or a famed region of Burgundy composed of the Côte de Beaune and de Nuits which is noted for its red and white wine

Côtes du Rhône extend from Vienne to Avignon along the banks of the River Rhone between the Burgundy and Provence wine districts; over a hundred communes offer a wide diversity in white, red and rosé wine of varying character; divided into a northern and southern region with notable wine: *Château-Grillet, Châteauneuf-du-Pape, Condrieu, Cornas, Côte-Rôtie, Crozes-Hermitage, Hermitage, Lirac, St-Joseph, St-Péray, Tavel*

crème 1) cream 2) sweetened liqueur like *crème de menthe, crème de cacao*

cru growth 1) refers to a particular vineyard and its wine 2) a system of grading wine; *premier cru, grand cru, cru classé*

curaçao originally from the name of the island of the Dutch Antilles, now applied to liqueur made from orange peel

cuvée a blend of wine from various vineyards, especially, according to tradition, in the making of Champagne

domaine estate; used on a wine label it indicates a wine of exceptional quality

eau water

~ **gazeuse** fizzy (US carbonated)

~ **minérale** mineral

Entre-Deux-Mers a vast Bordeaux region called "between two seas"—actually it's between two rivers—which produces white and red wine

extra-sec very dry (of Champagne)

framboise raspberry liqueur or brandy

frappé 1) iced 2) milk shake

Fronsac a Bordeaux region producing chiefly red wine

Gueuzelambic a strong Flemish bitter beer brewed from wheat and barley

grand cru, grand vin indicates a wine of exceptional quality

Grand Marnier an orange liqueur

Graves a Bordeaux region especially noted for its white wine but also its red

Jura a six-kilometre- (four-mile-) wide strip which runs 80 kilometres (50 miles) parallel to the western Swiss border and Burgundy; offers white, red, rosé, golden and sparkling wine; there are four formally recognized wines: *Arbois*, *Château-Chalon*, *Côtes du Jura* and *l'Etoile*

kirsch spirit distilled from cherries

Kriekenlambic a strong Brussels bitter beer flavoured with morello cherries

lait milk

~ **écrémé** skimmed

Languedoc district, formerly a French province, to the south-west of the Rhone delta; its ordinary table wine is often referred to as *vin du Midi* but other officially recognized wines, mostly white, are produced, including *Blanquette de Limoux* (sparkling), *Clairette du Languedoc*, *Fitou* and the *Muscats* from Frontignan, Lunel, Mireval and St-Jean-de-Minervois

limonade 1) lemonade 2) soft drink

Loire a district of 200, 000 hectares (80,000 acres) sprawled over the vicinity of France's longest river, the Loire; produces much fine red, white and rosé wine in four regions: Anjou (e.g., *Coteaux-de-l'Aubance*, *Coteaux-du-Layon*, *Coteaux-de-la-Loire*, *Saumur*), Berry and Nivernais (*Menetou-Salon*, *Pouilly-sur-Loire*, *Quincy*, *Reuilly*, *Sancerre*), Nantais (*Muscadet*) and Touraine (*Bourgueil*, *Chinon*, *Montlouis*, *Vouvray*)

Lorraine a flourishing and renowned wine district up to the 18th century, today it is of minor importance; good red, white and rosé wine continue to be produced (e.g., *Vins de la Moselle*, *Côtes-de-Toul*)

Mâcon a region of Burgundy producing basically red wine

marc spirit distilled from grape residue

Médoc a Bordeaux region producing highly reputed red wine including *Listrac*, *Margaux*, *Moulis*, *Pauillac*, *St-Estèphe*, *St-Julien*

mirabelle a brandy made from small yellow plums, particularly produced in the Alsace-Lorraine area

Muscadet a white wine from the Nantes area (Loire)

muscat 1) a type of grape 2) name

given to dessert wine; especially renowned is the muscat from Frontignan (Languedoc)

Nantais a region of the Loire chiefly renowned for its *Muscadet* white wine but offers other wine, e.g., *Coteaux d'Ancenis, Gros-Plant*

Neuchâtel a Swiss region producing primarily white wine (e.g., *Auvernier, Cormondrèche, Cortaillod, Hauterive*)

Noilly Prat a French vermouth

orange pressée freshly squeezed orange juice

pastis aniseed-flavoured aperitif

Pernod an aniseed-flavoured aperitif

pétillant slightly sparkling

Pomerol a Bordeaux region producing red wine (e.g., *Château Pétrus, Lalande-de-Pomerol, Néac*)

Provence France's most ancient wine-producing district; it traces its history back over two-and-a-half milleniums when Greek colonists planted the first vineyards on the Mediterranean coast of Gaul; red, white and rosé wine is produced, e.g., *Bandol, Bellet, Cassis, Coteaux-d'Aix-en-Provence, Coteaux-des-Baux, Coteaux-de-Pierrevert, Côtes-de-Provence, Palette*

quetsche spirit distilled from plums

rancio dessert wine, especially from Roussillon, which is aged in oak casks under the Midi sun

Ricard an aniseed-flavoured aperitif

Roussillon district which was a French province with Perpignan as its capital; its wine is similar in character to that of the Languedoc to the immediate north; good red, white and rosé table wine, e.g., *Corbières du Roussillon* and *Roussillon Dels Aspres*; this region produces three quarters of France's naturally sweet

wine, usually referred to as *rancio*, which is aged in oak casks under the Midi sun; notable examples among them are *Banyuls, Côtes-d'Agly, Côtes-du-Haut-Roussillon, Grand-Roussillon, Muscat de Rivesaltes, Rivesaltes*

St-Emilion a Bordeaux region producing red wine including *Lussac, Montagne, Parsac, Puisseguin, St-Georges*

St-Raphaël a quinine-flavoured aperitif

Sauternais a Bordeaux region noted for its white wine (*Sauternes*), notably the prestigious *Château d'Yquem*

Savoie Savoy; the Alpine district producing primarily dry, light and often slightly acid white wine (e.g., *Crépy, Seyssel*) but also good red, rosé and sparkling wine which is chiefly produced around Chambéry

Sud-Ouest a district in southwestern France producing quite varying types of wine, mostly white but some red and even rosé; the district includes the former province of Aquitaine, Béarn, Basque Country and Languedoc; wines of particular note are *Bergerac, Côtes-de-Duras, Gaillac, Jurançon, Madiran, Monbazillac, Montravel*

Suisse Switzerland; two-thirds of the nation's wine production consists of white wine; some 230 different vineyards are scattered over a dozen of Switzerland's 23 cantons though only four have a special significance: Neuchâtel, Tessin, Valais and Vaud

Suze an aperitif based on gentian

thé tea

Touraine for 14 centuries a celebrated wine district of the Loire producing red, white and rosé wine (e.g.,

Bourgueil, Chinon, Montlouis, St-Nicolas-de-Bourgueil, Vouvray)

Triple Sec an orange liqueur

Valais sometimes referred to as the California of Switzerland, this Swiss region produces nearly a quarter of the nation's wine; the region in the Rhone Valley is noted for providing Switzerland's best red wine (e.g., *Dôle*) and much of its finest white wine (e.g., *Arvine, Ermitage, Fendant, Johannisberg, Malvoisie*)

Vaud a Swiss region producing primarily white wine (e.g., *Aigle, Dézaley, Mont-sur-Rolle, Lavaux, Yvorne*)

V.D.Q.S. (vin délimité de qualité supérieure) regional wine of exceptional quality, produced according to carefully defined specifications and checked by government inspectors

Vieille Cure a wine-distilled liqueur

vin wine

~ **blanc** white

~ **chambré** wine at room temperature

~ **doux** sweet, dessert

~ **gris** pinkish

~ **mousseux** sparkling

~ **ordinaire** table

~ **du pays** local

~ **rosé** rosé (pink in reference to Champagne)

~ **rouge** red

~ **sec** dry

V.S.O.P. (very special old pale) in reference to cognac, indicates that it has been aged at least 5 years

(vin de) xérès sherry

Mini French Grammar

Articles

All nouns in French are either masculine or feminine.

1. Definite article (the):

masc. **le train**	the train		*fem.* **la voiture**	the car

Le and **la** are contracted to **l'** when followed by a vowel or a silent **h***.

l'avion	the plane	**l'hôtel**	the hotel

Plural (masc. and fem.):

les **trains**	*les* **voitures**	*les* **avions**

2. Indefinite article (a/an):

masc. **un timbre**	a stamp		*fem.* **une lettre**	a letter

Plural (masc. and fem.):

des **timbres**	stamps	*des* **lettres**	letters

3. Some/any (partitive)

Expressed by **de, du, de la, de l', des** as follows:

masc. **du** (= **de** + **le**)	**de l'** when followed by a vowel
fem. **de la**	or a silent **h***

Plural (masc. and fem.): **des** (= **de** + **les**)

du **sel**	some salt	*de la* **moutarde**	some mustard
de l' **ail**	some garlic	*des* **oranges**	some oranges

In negatives sentences, **de** is generally used.

Il n'y a pas *de* **taxis.**	There aren't any taxis.
Je n'ai pas *d'* **argent.**	I haven't any money.

Note the contraction **d'** before a vowel.

---

* In French the letter *h* at the beginning of a word is not pronounced. However, in several words the *h* is what is called "aspirate", i.e., no liaison is made with the word preceding it. E.g., *le héros*. See also Guide to Pronunciation, p. 10.

Nouns

. As already noted, nouns are either masculine or feminine. There are no short cuts for determining gender (though, note that most nouns ending in **-e, -té, -tion** are feminine). So always learn a noun together with its accompanying article.

. The plural of the majority of nouns is formed by adding **s** to the singular. (The final **s** is not pronounced.)

. To show possession, use the preposition **de** (of).

a fin *de* la semaine	the end of the week
e début *du* mois	the beginning of the month
e patron *de* l'hôtel	the owner of the hotel
es valises *des* voyageurs	the travellers' luggage

Adjectives

. Adjectives agree with the noun in gender and number. Most of them form the feminine by adding **e** to the masculine (unless the word already ends in **e**). For the plural, add **s**.

a. un grand magasin	a big shop	des grands magasins
b. une auto anglaise	an English car	des autos anglaises

2. As can be seen from the above, adjectives can come (a) before the noun or (b) after the noun. Since it is basically a question of sound and idiom, rules are difficult to formulate briefly; but adjectives more often follow nouns.

3. **Demonstrative adjectives:**

this/that	ce (*masc.*)	these/those	ces (*masc. and fem.*)
	cet (*masc. before a vowel or silent* h)		
	cette (*fem.*)		

4. **Possessive adjectives:** These agree in number and gender with *the noun they modify*, i.e., with the thing possessed and not the possessor.

	masc.	fem.	plur.
my	mon	ma	mes
your	ton	ta	tes
his/her/its	son	sa	ses
our	notre	notre	nos
your	votre	votre	vos
their	leur	leur	leurs

Thus, depending on the context:

son fils	can mean *his* son or *her* son
sa chambre	can mean *his* room or *her* room
ses vêtements	can mean *his* clothes or *her* clothes

Personal pronouns

	Subject	Direct object	Indirect object	After a preposition
I	**je**	**me**	**me**	**moi**
you	**tu**	**te**	**te**	**toi**
he/it (masc.)	**il**	**le**	**lui**	**lui**
she/it (fem.)	**elle**	**la**	**lui**	**elle**
we	**nous**	**nous**	**nous**	**nous**
you	**vous**	**vous**	**vous**	**vous**
they (masc.)	**ils**	**les**	**leur**	**eux**
they (fem.)	**elles**	**les**	**leur**	**elles**

Note: There are two forms for "you" in French: **tu** is used when talking to relatives, close friends and children (and between young people); **vous** is used in all other cases, and is also the plural form of **tu.**

Adverbs

Adverbs are generally formed by adding **-ment** to the feminine form of the adjective.

masc.:	fem.:	adverb:
lent (slow)	**lente**	lentement
sérieux (serious)	**sérieuse**	sérieusement

Verbs

Three regular conjugations appear below, grouped by families according to their infinitive endings, *-er*, *-ir* and *-re*. Verbs with the ending *-er* are considered as the true regular conjugation in French. Verbs which do not follow the conjugations below are considered irregular (see irregular verb list). Note that there are some verbs which follow the regular conjugation of the category they belong to, but present some minor changes in the spelling of the stem. Example: *acheter, j'achète; broyer, je broie.*

		1st conj.	2nd conj.	3rd conj.
Infinitive		**chant er** (*sing*)	**fin ir** (*finish*)	**vend re**[1] (*sell*)
Present	je	chant **e**	fin **is**	vend **s**
	tu	chant **es**	fin **is**	vend **s**
	il	chant **e**	fin **it**	vend
	nous	chant **ons**	fin **issons**	vend **ons**
	vous	chant **ez**	fin **issez**	vend **ez**
	ils	chant **ent**	fin **issent**	vend **ent**
Imperfect	je	chant **ais**	fin **issais**	vend **ais**
	tu	chant **ais**	fin **issais**	vend **ais**
	il	chant **ait**	fin **issait**	vend **ait**
	nous	chant **ions**	fin **issions**	vend **ions**
	vous	chant **iez**	fin **issiez**	vend **iez**
	ils	chant **aient**	fin **issaient**	vend **aient**
Future	je	chant **erai**	fin **irai**	vend **rai**
	tu	chant **eras**	fin **iras**	vend **ras**
	il	chant **era**	fin **ira**	vend **ra**
	nous	chant **erons**	fin **irons**	vend **rons**
	vous	chant **erez**	fin **irez**	vend **rez**
	ils	chant **eront**	fin **iront**	vend **ront**
Conditional	je	chant **erais**	fin **irais**	vend **rais**
	tu	chant **erais**	fin **irais**	vend **rais**
	il	chant **erait**	fin **irait**	vend **rait**
	nous	chant **erions**	fin **irions**	vend **rions**
	vous	chant **eriez**	fin **iriez**	vend **riez**
	ils	chant **eraient**	fin **iraient**	vend **raient**

[1]conjugated in the same way: all verbs ending in *-andre*, *-endre*, *-ondre*, *-erdre*, *-ordre* (except *prendre* and its compounds).

Pres. subj.[2]	je	chant **e**	fin **isse**	vend **e**
	tu	chant **es**	fin **isses**	vend **es**
	il	chant **e**	fin **isse**	vend **e**
	nous	chant **ions**	fin **issions**	vend **ions**
	vous	chant **iez**	fin **issiez**	vend **iez**
	ils	chant **ent**	fin **issent**	vend **ent**
Past part.		chant **é(e)**	fin **i(e)**	vend **u(e)**

[2]French verbs are always preceded by *que* when conjugated in all tenses o subjonctive. Examples: *que je chante, que nous finissions, qu'ils aient.*

Auxiliary verbs

	avoir (*to have*)		**être** (*to be*)	
Present	*Imperfect*	*Present*	*Imperfect*	
j', je	ai	avais	suis	étais
tu	as	avais	es	étais
il	a	avait	est	était
nous	avons	avions	sommes	étions
vous	avez	aviez	êtes	étiez
ils	ont	avaient	sont	étaient
	Future	*Conditional*	*Future*	*Conditional*
j', je	aurai	aurais	serai	serais
tu	auras	aurais	seras	serais
il	aura	aurait	sera	serait
nous	aurons	aurions	serons	serions
vous	aurez	auriez	serez	seriez
ils	auront	auraient	seront	seraient
	Pres. subj.[1]	*Pres. perf*	*Pres. subj.*[1]	*Pres. perf.*
j', je	aie	ai eu	sois	ai été
tu	aies	as eu	sois	as été
il	ait	a eu	soit	a été
nous	ayons	avons eu	soyons	avons été
vous	ayez	avez eu	soyez	avez été
ils	aient	ont eu	soient	ont été

[1]French verbs are always preceded by *que* when conjugated in all tenses of subjonctive. Examples: *que je chante, que nous finissions, qu'ils aient.*

Irregular verbs

Below is a list of the verbs and tenses commonly used in spoken French. In the listing a) stands for the present tense, b) for the imperfect, c) for the future, d) for the conditional, e) for the present subjunctive and f) for the past participle. In the present tense we have given the whole conjugation, for the other tenses the first person singular, as the conjugations for tenses other than present are similar to those used in the regular verbs. Unless otherwise indicated, verbs with prefixes (*ab-*, *ac-*, *com-*, *con-*, *contre-*, *de-*, *dé-*, *dis-*, *é-*, *en-*, *entr(e)-*, *ex-*, *in-*, *o-*, *par-*, *pré-*, *pour-*, *re-*, *ré-*, *sous-*, etc.) are conjugated like the stem verb.

absoudre *absolve*	a) absous, absous, absout, absolvons, absolvez, absolvent; b) absolvais; c) absoudrai; d) absoudrais; e) absolve; f) absous, absoute
accroître *increase*	a) accrois, accrois, accroît, accroissons, accroissez, accroissent; b) accroissais; c) accroîtrai; d) accroîtrais; e) accroisse; f) accru(e)
acquérir *acquire*	a) acquiers, acquiers, acquiert, acquérons, acquérez, acquièrent; b) acquérais; c) acquerrai; d) acquerrais; e) acquière; f) acquis(e)
aller *go*	a) vais, vas, va, allons, allez, vont; b) allais; c) irai; d) irais; e) aille; f) allé(e)
apercevoir *perceive*	→ recevoir
apparaître *appear*	→ connaître
assaillir *assail*	a) assaille, assailles, assaille, assaillons, assaillez, assaillent; b) assaillais; c) assaillirai; d) assaillirais; e) assaille; f) assailli(e)
asseoir *set*	a) assieds, assieds, assied, asseyons, asseyez, asseyent; b) asseyais; c) assiérai; d) assiérais; e) asseye; f) assis(e)
astreindre *compel*	→ peindre
battre *beat*	a) bats, bats, bat, battons, battez, battent; b) battais; c) battrai; d) battrais; e) batte; f) battu(e)
boire *drink*	a) bois, bois, boit, buvons, buvez, boivent; b) buvais; c) boirai; d) boirais; e) boive; f) bu(e)
bouillir *boil*	a) bous, bous, bout, bouillons, bouillez, bouillent; b) bouillais; c) bouillirai; d) bouillirais; e) bouille; f) bouilli(e)
ceindre *gird*	→ peindre
circoncire *circumcise*	→ suffire
circonscrire *limit*	→ écrire

clore	a) je clos, tu clos, il clôt, ils closent; b) –; c) clorai; d) clorais;
close	e) close; f) clos(e)
concevoir	→ recevoir
conceive	
conclure	a) conclus, conclus, conclut, concluons, concluez, concluent;
conclude	b) concluais; c) conclurai; d) conclurais; e) conclue; f)
	conclu(e)
conduire	→ cuire
drive	
connaître	a) connais, connais, connaît, connaissons, connaissez,
know	connaissent; b) connaissais; c) connaîtrai; d) connaîtrais;
	e) connaisse; f) connu(e)
conquérir	→ acquérir
conquer	
construire	→ cuire
build	
contraindre	→ craindre
constrain	
contredire	→ médire
contradict	
coudre	a) couds, couds, coud, cousons, cousez, cousent; b) cousais;
sew	c) coudrai; d) coudrais; e) couse; f) cousu(e)
courir	a) cours, cours, court, courons, courez, courent; b) courais;
run	c) courrai; d) courrais; e) coure; f) couru(e)
couvrir	a) couvre, couvres, couvre, couvrons, couvrez, couvrent;
cover	b) couvrais; c) couvrirai; d) couvrirais; e) couvre; f) couvert(e)
craindre	a) crains, crains, craint, craignons, craignez, craignent;
fear	b) craignais; c) craindrai; d) craindrais; e) craigne; f) craint(e)
croire	a) crois, crois, croit, croyons, croyez, croient; b) croyais;
believe	c) croirai; d) croirais; e) croie; f) cru(e)
croître	a) croîs, croîs, croît, croissons, croissez, croissent; b) croissais;
grow	c) croîtrai; d) croîtrais; e) croisse; f) crû, crue
cueillir	a) cueille, cueilles, cueille, cueillons, cueillez, cueillent;
pick	b) cueillais; c) cueillerai; d) cueillerais; e) cueille; f) cueilli(e)
cuire	a) cuis, cuis, cuit, cuisons, cuisez, cuisent; b) cuisais;
cook	c) cuirai; d) cuirais; e) cuise; f) cuit(e)
décevoir	→ recevoir
deceive	
décrire	→ écrire
describe	
déduire	→ cuire
deduct	
détruire	→ cuire
destroy	

devoir	a) dois, dois, doit, devons, devez, doivent; b) devais;
have to	c) devrai; d) devrais; e) doive; f) dû, due
dire	a) dis, dis, dit, disons, dites, disent; b) disais; c) dirai;
say	d) dirais; e) dise; f) dit(e)
dissoudre	→ absoudre
dissolve	
dormir	a) dors, dors, dort, dormons, dormez, dorment; b) dormais;
sleep	c) dormirai; d) dormirais; e) dorme; f) dormi
échoir	a) il échoit; b) –; c) il échoira; d) il échoirait;
fall to	e) qu'il échoie; f) échu(e)
écrire	a) écris, écris, écrit, écrivons, écrivez, écrivent; b) écrivais;
write	c) écrirai; d) écrirais; e) écrive; f) écrit(e)
élire	→ lire
elect	
émettre	→ mettre
emit	
émouvoir	→ mouvoir; f) ému(e)
affect	
empreindre	→ peindre
imprint	
enduire	→ cuire
coat	
enfreindre	→ craindre
infringe	
envoyer	a) envoie, envoies, envoie, envoyons, envoyez, envoient;
send	b) envoyais; c) enverrai; d) enverrais; e) envoie; f) envoyé(e)
éteindre	→ peindre
switch off	
étreindre	→ peindre
embrace	
exclure	→ conclure
exclude	
faillir	a) –; b) –; c) faillirai; d) faillirais; e) faille; f) failli
fail	
faire	a) fais, fais, fait, faisons, faites, font; b) faisais; c) ferai;
do, make	d) ferais; e) fasse; f) fait(e)
falloir	a) il faut; b) il fallait; c) il faudra; d) il faudrait; e) qu'il faille;
have to	f) il a fallu
feindre	→ peindre
feign	
frire	→ confire
fry	
fuir	a) fuis, fuis, fuit, fuyons, fuyez, fuient; b) fuyais; c) fuirai;
escape	d) fuirais; e) fuie; f) fui

geindre	→ craindre
whine	
haïr	a) hais, hais, hait, haïssons, haïssez, haïssent; b) haïssais;
hate	c) haïrai; d) haïrais; e) haïsse; f) haï(e)
inclure	→ conclure
include	
induire	→ cuire
induce	
inscrire	→ écrire
register	
instruire	→ cuire
instruct	
interdire	→ médire
forbid	
introduire	→ cuire
introduce	
joindre	a) joins, joins, joint, joignons, joignez, joignent;
join	b) joignais; c) joindrai; d) joindrais; e) joigne; f) joint(e)
lire	a) lis, lis, lit, lisons, lisez, lisent; b) lisais; c) lirai;
read	d) lirais; e) lise; f) lu(e)
luire	a) luis, luis, luit, luisons, luisez, luisent; b) luisais;
shine	c) luirai; d) luirais; e) luise; f) lui
maudire	a) maudis, maudis, maudit, maudissons, maudissez, maudis-
curse	sent; b) maudissais; c) maudirai; d) maudirais; e) maudisse;
	f) maudit(e)
médire	a) médis, médis, médit, médisons, médisez, médisent;
speak ill of	b) médisais; c) médirai; d) médirais; e)médise; f) médit(e)
mentir	a) mens, mens, ment, mentons, mentez, mentent; b) mentais;
lie	c) mentirai; d) mentirais; e) mente; f) menti
mettre	a) mets, mets, met, mettons, mettez, mettent; b) mettais;
put	c) mettrai; d) mettrais; e) mette; f) mis(e)
moudre	a) mouds, mouds, moud, moulons, moulez, moulent;
grind	b) moulais; c) moudrai; d) moudrais; e) moule; f) moulu(e)
mourir	a) meurs, meurs, meurt, mourons, mourez, meurent; b)
die	mourais; c) mourrai; d) mourrais; e) meure; f) mort(e)
mouvoir	a) meus, meus, meut, mouvons, mouvez, meuvent; b) mouvais;
set in motion	c) mouvrai; d) mouvrais; e) meuve; f) mû, mue
naître	a) nais, nais, naît, naissons, naissez, naissent; b) naissais;
be born	c) naîtrai; d) naîtrais; e) naisse; f) né(e)
nuire	→ cuire; f) nui
harm	
offrir	→ couvrir
offer	

ouvrir *open*	→ couvrir
paître *graze*	a) pais, pais, paît, paissons, paissez, paissent; b) paissais; c) paîtrai; d) paîtrais; e) paisse; f) –
paraître *appear*	→ connaître
partir *leave*	→ mentir; f) parti(e)
peindre *paint*	a) peins, peins, peint, peignons, peignez, peignent; b) peignais; c) peindrai; d) peindrais; e) peigne; f) peint(e)
percevoir *perceive*	→ recevoir
plaindre *pity*	→ craindre
plaire *please*	a) plais, plais, plaît, plaisons, plaisez, plaisent; b) plaisais; c) plairai; d) plairais; e) plaise; f) plu
pleuvoir *rain*	a) il pleut; b) il pleuvait; c) il pleuvra; d) il pleuvrait; e) qu'il pleuve; f) il a plu
pourvoir *provide*	a) pourvois, pourvois, pourvoit, pourvoyons, pourvoyez, pourvoient; b) pourvoyais; c) pourvoirai; d) pourvoirais; e) pourvoie; f) pourvu(e)
pouvoir *be able to*	a) peux (puis), peux, peut, pouvons, pouvez, peuvent; b) pouvais, c) pourrai; d) pourrais; e) puisse; f) pu
prédire *foretell*	a) prédis, prédis, prédit, prédisons, prédisez, prédisent; b) prédisais; c) prédirai; d) prédirais; e) prédise; f) prédit(e)
prendre *take*	a) prends, prends, prend, prenons, prenez, prennent; b) prenais; c) prendrai; d) prendrais; e) prenne; f) pris(e)
prescrire *prescribe*	→ écrire
prévoir *foresee*	a) prévois, prévois, prévoit, prévoyons, prévoyez, prévoient; b) prévoyais; c) prévoirai; d) prévoirais; e) prévoie; f) prévu(e)
produire *produce*	→ cuire
proscrire *outlaw*	→ écrire
recevoir *receive*	a) reçois, reçois, reçoit, recevons, recevez, reçoivent; b) recevais; c) recevrai; d) recevrais; e) reçoive; f) reçu(e)
requérir *require*	→ acquérir
restreindre *restrict*	→ peindre
rire *laugh*	a) ris, ris, rit, rions, riez, rient; b) riais; c) rirai; d) rirais; e) rie; f) ri

savoir — *know*
a) sais, sais, sait, savons, savez, savent; b) savais; c) saurai; d) saurais; e) sache; f) su(e)

séduire — *seduce*
→ cuire

sentir — *feel*
→ mentir; f) senti(e)

servir — *serve*
a) sers, sers, sert, servons, servez, servent; b) servais; c) servirai; d) servirais; e) serve; f) servi(e)

sortir — *go out*
→ mentir; f) sorti(e)

souffrir — *suffer*
→ couvrir

souscrire — *subscribe*
→ écrire

suffire — *be enough*
a) suffis, suffis, suffit, suffisons, suffisez, suffisent; b) suffisais; c) suffirai; d) suffirais; e) suffise; e) suffi

suivre — *follow*
a) suis, suis, suit, suivons, suivez, suivent; b) suivais; c) suivrai; d) suivrais; e) suive; f) suivi(e)

taire — *be silent*
a) tais, tais, tait, taisons, taisez, taisent; b) taisais; c) tairai; d) tairais; e) taise; f) tu(e)

teindre — *dye*
→ peindre

tenir — *hold*
a) tiens, tiens, tient, tenons, tenez, tiennent; b) tenais; c) tiendrai; d) tiendrais; e) tienne; f) tenu(e)

traduire — *translate*
→ cuire

traire — *milk (cow)*
a) trais, trais, trait, trayons, trayez, traient; b) trayais; c) trairai; d) trairais; e) traie; f) trait(e)

transcrire — *transcribe*
→ écrire

tressaillir — *startle*
→ assaillir

vaincre — *defeat*
a) vaincs, vaincs, vainc, vainquons, vainquez, vainquent; b) vainquais; c) vaincrai; d) vaincrais; e) vainque; f) vaincu(e)

valoir — *be worth*
a) vaux, vaux, vaut, valons, valez, valent; b) valais; c) vaudrai; d) vaudrais; e) vaille; f) valu(e)

venir — *come*
→ tenir

vêtir — *dress*
a) vêts, vêts, vêt, vêtons, vêtez, vêtent; b) vêtais; c) vêtirai; d) vêtirais; e) vête; f) vêtu(e)

vivre — *live*
a) vis, vis, vit, vivons, vivez, vivent; b) vivais; c) vivrai; d) vivrais; e) vive; f) vécu(e)

voir   a) vois, vois, voit, voyons, voyez, voient; b) voyais; c) verrai;
see   d) verrais; e) voie; f) vu(e)

vouloir   a) veux, veux, veut, voulons, voulez, veulent; b) voulais;
want   c) voudrai; d) voudrais; e) veuille; f) voulu(e)

French Abbreviations

ACF	*Automobile-Club de France*	Automobile Association of France
ACS	*Automobile-Club de Suisse*	Swiss Automobile Association
AELE	*Association européenne de libre-échange*	EFTA, European Free Trade Association
apr. J.-C.	*après Jésus-Christ*	A.D.
av. J.-C.	*avant Jésus-Christ*	B.C.
bd	*boulevard*	boulevard
c.-à-d.	*c'est-à-dire*	i.e.
c/c	*compte courant*	current account
CCP	*compte de chèques postaux*	postal account
CFF	*Chemins de fer fédéraux*	Swiss Federal Railways
ch	*chevaux-vapeur*	horsepower
Cie, Co.	*compagnie*	company
CRS	*Compagnies républicaines de sécurité*	French order and riot police
ct	*courant*	of the month
CV	*chevaux-vapeur*	horsepower
EU	*Etats-Unis*	United States
exp.	*expéditeur*	sender
Fs/Fr.s.	*franc suisse*	Swiss franc
h.	*heure*	hour, o'clock
hab.	*habitants*	inhabitants, population
M.	*Monsieur*	Mr.
Me	*Maître*	title for barrister or lawyer
Mgr	*Monseigneur*	ecclesiastic title for the rank of bishop
Mlle	*Mademoiselle*	Miss
MM.	*Messieurs*	gentlemen, Messrs.
Mme	*Madame*	Mrs.
n°	*numéro*	number
ONU	*Organisation des Nations Unies*	UN
OTAN	*Organisation du Traité de l'Atlantique Nord*	NATO, North Atlantic Treaty Organization
PCV	*paiement contre vérification*	reverse-charge call (collect call)
PDG	*président-directeur général*	chairman of the board
p.ex.	*par exemple*	e.g.
PJ	*police judiciaire*	criminal investigation department
p.p.	*port payé*	postage paid

P & T	Postes et Télécommunications	post and telecommunications (France)
PTT	Postes, Télégraphes, Téléphones	Post, Telegraph, Telephone (Belgium and Switzerland)
RATP	Régie autonome des transports parisiens	Parisian transport authority
RF	République française	the French Republic
RN	route nationale	national highway
RP	Révérend Père	Reverend Father
RSVP	répondez, s'il vous plaît	RSVP, please reply
s/	sur	on, at
SA	société anonyme	Ltd., Inc.
S.A.R.L.	société à responsabilité limitée	limited liability company
SE	Son Eminence; Son Excellence	His Eminence; His/Her Excellency
SI	Syndicat d'Initiative	tourist office
SIDA	syndrome immuno-déficitaire acquis	AIDS
SM	Sa Majesté	His/Her Majesty
SNCB	Société nationale des chemins de fer belges	Belgian National Railways
SNCF	Société nationale des chemins de fer français	French National Railways
St, Ste	saint, sainte	saint
succ.	successeur; succursale	successor; branch office
s. v. p.	s'il vous plaît	please
TCB	Touring-Club royal de Belgique	Royal Touring Club of Belgium
TCF	Touring-Club de France	Touring Club of France
TCS	Touring-Club Suisse	Swiss Touring Club
TGV	train à grande vitesse	high-speed train
t. s. v. p.	tournez, s'il vous plaît	please turn over
TVA	taxe à la valeur ajoutée	VAT, value added tax
UE	Union européenne	European Union
Vve	veuve	widow

Numerals

Cardinal numbers		Ordinal numbers	
0	zéro	1er	premier
1	un	2^e	deuxième (second)
2	deux	3^e	troisième
3	trois	4^e	quatrième
4	quatre	5^e	cinquième
5	cinq	6^e	sixième
6	six	7^e	septième
7	sept	8^e	huitième
8	huit	9^e	neuvième
9	neuf	10^e	dixième
10	dix	11^e	onzième
11	onze	12^e	douzième
12	douze	13^e	treizième
13	treize	14^e	quatorzième
14	quatorze	15^e	quinzième
15	quinze	16^e	seizième
16	seize	17^e	dix-septième
17	dix-sept	18^e	dix-huitième
18	dix-huit	19^e	dix-neuvième
19	dix-neuf	20^e	vingtième
20	vingt	21^e	vingt et unième
21	vingt et un	22^e	vingt-deuxième
22	vingt-deux	23^e	vingt-troisième
30	trente	30^e	trentième
40	quarante	40^e	quarantième
50	cinquante	50^e	cinquantième
60	soixante	60^e	soixantième
70	soixante-dix	70^e	soixante-dixième
71	soixante et onze	71^e	soixante et onzième
72	soixante-douze	72^e	soixante-douzième
80	quatre-vingts	80^e	quatre-vingtième
81	quatre-vingt-un	81^e	quatre-vingt-unième
90	quatre-vingt-dix	90^e	quatre-vingt-dixième
100	cent	100^e	centième
101	cent un	101^e	cent unième
230	deux cent trente	200^e	deux centième
1 000	mille	330^e	trois cent trentième
1 107	onze cent sept	1 000^e	millième
2 000	deux mille	1 107^e	onze cent septième
1 000 000	un million	2 000^e	deux millième

Time

Although official time in France is based on the 24-hour clock, the 12-hour system is used in conversation.

If you have to indicate that it is a.m. or p.m., add *du matin*, *de l'après-midi* or *du soir*.

Thus:

huit heures du matin	8 a.m.
deux heures de l'après-midi	2 p.m.
huit heures du soir	8 p.m.

Days of the Week

dimanche	Sunday	*jeudi*	Thursday
lundi	Monday	*vendredi*	Friday
mardi	Tuesday	*samedi*	Saturday
mercredi	Wednesday		

Some Basic Phrases

Please.	S'il vous plaît.
Thank you very much.	Merci beaucoup.
Don't mention it.	Il n'y a pas de quoi.
Good morning.	Bonjour (*matin*).
Good afternoon.	Bonjour (*après-midi*).
Good evening.	Bonsoir.
Good night.	Bonne nuit.
Good-bye.	Au revoir.
See you later.	A bientôt.
Where is/Where are...?	Où se trouve/Où se trouvent...?
What do you call this?	Comment appelez-vous ceci?
What does that mean?	Que veut dire cela?
Do you speak English?	Parlez-vous anglais?
Do you speak German?	Parlez-vous allemand?
Do you speak French?	Parlez-vous français?
Do you speak Spanish?	Parlez-vous espagnol?
Do you speak Italian?	Parlez-vous italien?
Could you speak more slowly, please?	Pourriez-vous parler plus lentement, s'il vous plaît?
I don't understand.	Je ne comprends pas.
Can I have...?	Puis-je avoir...?
Can you show me...?	Pouvez-vous m'indiquer...?
Can you tell me...?	Pouvez-vous me dire...?
Can you help me, please?	Pouvez-vous m'aider, s'il vous plaît?
I'd like...	Je voudrais...
We'd like...	Nous voudrions...
Please give me...	S'il vous plaît, donnez-moi...
Please bring me...	S'il vous plaît, apportez-moi...
I'm hungry.	J'ai faim.
I'm thirsty.	J'ai soif.
I'm lost.	Je me suis perdu.
Hurry up!	Dépêchez-vous!
There is/There are...	Il y a...
There isn't/There aren't...	Il n'y a pas...

Quelques expressions utiles

Arrival

Your passport, please.	Votre passeport, s'il vous plaît.
Have you anything to declare?	Avez-vous quelque chose à déclarer?
No, nothing at all.	Non, rien du tout.

Arrivée

Can you help me with my luggage, please?	Pouvez-vous prendre mes bagages, s'il vous plaît?
Where's the bus to the centre of town, please?	Où est le bus pour le centre de la ville, s'il vous plaît?
This way, please.	Par ici, s'il vous plaît.
Where can I get a taxi?	Où puis-je trouver un taxi?
What's the fare to…?	Quel est le tarif pour…?
Take me to this address, please.	Conduisez-moi à cette adresse, s'il vous plaît.
I'm in a hurry.	Je suis pressé.

Hotel / Hôtel

My name is…	Je m'appelle…
Have you a reservation?	Avez-vous réservé?
I'd like a room with a bath.	J'aimerais une chambre avec bains.
What's the price per night?	Quel est le prix pour une nuit?
May I see the room?	Puis-je voir la chambre?
What's my room number, please?	Quel est le numéro de ma chambre, s'il vous plaît?
There's no hot water.	Il n'y a pas d'eau chaude.
May I see the manager, please?	Puis-je voir le directeur, s'il vous plaît?
Did anyone telephone me?	Y a-t-il eu des appels pour moi?
Is there any mail for me?	Y a-t-il du courrier pour moi?
May I have my bill (check), please?	Puis-je avoir ma note, s'il vous plaît?

Eating out / Restaurant

Do you have a fixed-price menu?	Avez-vous un menu?
May I see the menu?	Puis-je voir la carte?
May we have an ashtray, please?	Pouvons-nous avoir un cendrier, s'il vous plaît?
Where's the toilet, please?	Où sont les toilettes, s'il vous plaît?
I'd like an hors d'uvre (starter).	Je voudrais un hors-d'uvre.
Have you any soup?	Avez-vous du potage?
I'd like some fish.	J'aimerais du poisson.
What kind of fish do you have?	Qu'avez-vous comme poisson?
I'd like a steak.	Je voudrais un steak.
What vegetables have you got?	Quels légumes servez-vous?
Nothing more, thanks.	Je suis servi, merci.
What would you like to drink?	Qu'aimeriez-vous boire?
I'll have a beer, please.	J'aimerais une bière, s'il vous plaît.
I'd like a bottle of wine.	Je voudrais une bouteille de vin.
May I have the bill (check), please?	Puis-je avoir l'addition, s'il vous plaît?
Is service included?	Le service est-il compris?
Thank you, that was a very good meal.	Merci, c'était très bon.

Travelling	**Voyages**
Where's the railway station, please?	Où se trouve la gare, s'il vous plaît?
Where's the ticket office, please?	Où est le guichet, s'il vous plaît?
I'd like a ticket to…	J'aimerais un billet pour…
First or second class?	Première ou deuxième classe?
First class, please.	Première classe, s'il vous plaît.
Single or return (one way or roundtrip)?	Aller simple ou aller et retour?
Do I have to change trains?	Est-ce que je dois changer de train?
What platform does the train for … leave from?	De quel quai part le train pour…?
Where's the nearest underground (subway) station?	Où est la station de métro la plus proche?
Where's the bus station, please?	Où est la gare routière, s'il vous plaît?
When's the first bus to…?	A quelle heure part le premier autobus pour…?
Please let me off at the next stop.	S'il vous plaît, déposez-moi au prochain arrêt.

Relaxing	**Distractions**
What's on at the cinema (movies)?	Que joue-t-on au cinéma?
What time does the film begin?	A quelle heure commence le film?
Are there any tickets for tonight?	Reste-t-il encore des places pour ce soir?
Where can we go dancing?	Où pouvons-nous aller danser?

Meeting people	**Rencontres**
How do you do.	Bonjour, Madame/Mademoiselle/Monsieur.
How are you?	Comment allez-vous?
Very well, thank you. And you?	Très bien, merci. Et vous?
May I introduce…?	Puis-je vous présenter…?
My name is…	Je m'appelle…
I'm very pleased to meet you.	Enchanté de faire votre connaissance.
How long have you been here?	Depuis combien de temps êtes-vous ici?
It was nice meeting you.	Enchanté d'avoir fait votre connaissance.
Do you mind if I smoke?	Est-ce que ça vous dérange que je fume?
Do you have a light, please?	Avez-vous du feu, s'il vous plaît?
May I get you a drink?	Puis-je vous offrir un verre?
May I invite you for dinner tonight?	Puis-je vous inviter à dîner ce soir?
Where shall we meet?	Où nous retrouverons-nous?

Shops, stores and services
Where's the nearest bank, please?

Where can I cash some travellers' cheques?
Can you give me some small change, please?
Where's the nearest chemist's (pharmacy)?
How do I get there?
Is it within walking distance?
Can you help me, please?
How much is this? And that?
It's not quite what I want.
I like it.
Can you recommend something for sunburn?
I'd like a haircut, please.

I'd like a manicure, please.

Street directions
Can you show me on the map where I am?
You are on the wrong road.
Go/Walk straight ahead.
It's on the left/on the right.

Emergencies
Call a doctor quickly.
Call an ambulance.
Please call the police.

Magasins et services
Où se trouve la banque la plus proche, s'il vous plaît?
Où puis-je changer des chèques de voyage?

Pouvez-vous me donner de la monnaie, s'il vous plaît?
Où est la pharmacie la plus proche?

Comment puis-je m'y rendre?
Peut-on y aller à pied?
Pouvez-vous m'aider, s'il vous plaît?
Combien coûte ceci? Et cela?
Ce n'est pas exactement ce que je désire.
Cela me plaît.
Pouvez-vous me conseiller quelque chose contre les coups de soleil?
Je voudrais me faire couper les cheveux, s'il vous plaît.
Je voudrais une manucure, s'il vous plaît.

Directions
Pouvez-vous me montrer sur la carte où je me trouve?
Vous n'êtes pas sur la bonne route.
Continuez tout droit.
C'est à gauche/à droite.

Urgences
Appelez vite un médecin.
Appelez une ambulance.
Appelez la police, s'il vous plaît.

Anglais-Français

English-French

Introduction

Ce dictionnaire a été conçu dans un but pratique. Vous n'y trouverez donc pas d'information linguistique inutile. Les adresses sont classées par ordre alphabétique, sans tenir compte du fait qu'un mot peut être simple ou composé, avec ou sans trait d'union.

Lorsqu'une adresse est suivie d'adresses secondaires (p. ex. expressions usuelles ou locutions), ces dernières sont également rangées par ordre alphabétique sous le mot vedette.

Chaque mot souche est suivi d'une transcription phonétique (voir le Guide de prononciation) et, s'il y a lieu, de l'indication de la catégorie grammaticale (substantif, verbe, adjectif, etc.). Lorsqu'un mot souche peut appartenir à plusieurs catégories grammaticales, les traductions qui s'y réfèrent sont groupées derrière chacune d'elles.

Les pluriels irréguliers des substantifs sont toujours donnés, de même que certains pluriels pouvant prêter à hésitation.

Pour éviter toute répétition, nous avons utilisé un tilde (~) en lieu et place de l'adresse principale.

Dans le pluriel des mots composés, le tiret (-) remplace la partie du mot qui demeure inchangée.

Un astérisque (*) signale les verbes irréguliers. Pour plus de détails, consulter la liste de ces verbes.

Ce dictionnaire tient compte de l'épellation anglaise. Les mots et les définitions des termes typiquement américains ont été indiqués comme tels (voir la liste des abréviations utilisées dans le texte).

Abréviations

adj	adjectif	*num*	numéral
adv	adverbe	*p*	imparfait
Am	américain	*pl*	pluriel
art	article	*plAm*	pluriel (américain)
conj	conjonction	*pp*	participe passé
f	féminin	*pr*	présent
fpl	féminin pluriel	*pref*	préfixe
m	masculin	*prep*	préposition
mpl	masculin pluriel	*pron*	pronom
n	nom	*v*	verbe
nAm	nom (américain)	*vAm*	verbe (américain)

Guide de prononciation

Chaque article de cette partie du dictionnaire est accompagné d'une transcription phonétique qui vous indique la prononciation des mots. Vous la lirez comme si chaque lettre ou groupe de lettres avait la même valeur qu'en français. Au-dessous figurent uniquement les lettres et les symboles ambigus ou particulièrement difficiles à comprendre. *Toutes* les consonnes, y compris celles placées à la fin d'une syllabe ou d'un mot, doivent être prononcées.

Les traits d'union séparent chaque syllabe. Celles que l'on doit accentuer sont imprimées en *italique*.

Les sons de deux langues ne coïncident jamais parfaitement; mais si vous suivez soigneusement nos indications, vous pourrez prononcer les mots étrangers de façon à vous faire comprendre. Pour faciliter votre tâche, nos transcriptions simplifient parfois légèrement le système phonétique de la langue, mais elles reflètent néanmoins les différences de son essentielles.

Consonnes

ð	le **th** anglais de **the**; **z** dit en zézayant
gh	comme **g** dans **g**ai
h	doit être prononcé en expirant fortement; rappelle le **h** de l'interjection **h**ue!
ng/nng	comme dans campi**ng**; ou comme le dernier son de pai**n**, prononcé avec l'accent du Midi
s	toujours comme dans **s**i
θ	le **th** anglais de **th**ink; **s** dit en zézayant
y	toujours comme dans **y**eux

Au début ou à la fin d'un mot anglais, **b, d, v, z** sont moins sonores qu'en français. C'est également le cas avec **gh** et **ð.**

Voyelles et diphtongues

æ	entre **a** et **è**
i	entre **i** et **é**
ii	comme **i** dans l**i**re
o	proche du **o** de p**o**mme, mais avec la langue placée plus bas et plus retirée dans la bouche et avec les lèvres plus arrondies

1) Les voyelles longues sont indiquées par un dédoublement (p.ex. **oo**) ou par un accent circonflexe placé sur le second élément (p.ex. **eû**).

2) Nos transcriptions comprenant un **ï** doivent être lues comme des diphtongues; le **ï** ne doit pas être séparé de la voyelle qui le précède (comme dans tr**ahi**), mais doit se fondre dans celle-ci (comme dans **ail**).

3) Les lettres imprimées en petits caractères et dans une position surélevée doivent être prononcées d'une façon assez faible et rapide (p.ex. ^{ou}**i**, **i**^{eu}).

Prononciation américaine

Notre transcription correspond à la prononciation anglaise habituelle. Si la langue américaine varie grandement d'une région à l'autre, elle présente tout de même quelques différences marquantes par rapport à l'anglais de Grande-Bretagne. Ainsi par exemple:

1) Le **r**, qu'il soit placé devant une consonne ou à la fin d'un mot, se prononce toujours (contrairement à l'habitude anglaise).

2) Le **ââ** devient **ææ** dans certains mots, tels que *ask*, *castle*, *laugh*, etc.

3) Le **o** anglais se prononce **a** ou souvent **oo.**

4) Placé devant **oû,** le son **y** est fréquemment omis (ainsi: *duty*, *tune*, *new*, etc.)

5) Enfin, l'accent tonique de certains mots peut varier considérablement.

a (éï, eu) *art* (an) un *art*

abbey (*æ*-bi) *n* abbaye *f*

abbreviation (eu-brii-vi-*éï*-cheunn) *n* abréviation *f*

ability (eu-*bi*-leu-ti) *n* capacité *f*

able (*éï*-beul) *adj* en mesure; capable; ***be ~ to** *être capable de; *savoir, *pouvoir

aboard (eu-*bood*) *adv* à bord

abolish (eu-*bo*-lich) *v* abolir

abortion (eu-*boo*-cheunn) *n* avortement *m*

about (eu-*baout*) *prep* de; concernant, sur; autour de; *adv* à peu près; autour

above (eu-*bav*) *prep* au-dessus de; *adv* en haut

abroad (eu-*brood*) *adv* à l'étranger

abscess (*æb*-sèss) *n* abcès *m*

absence (*æb*-seunns) *n* absence *f*

absent (*æb*-seunnt) *adj* absent

absolutely (*æb*-seu-loût-li) *adv* absolument

abstain from (eub-*stéïn*) s'*abstenir de

abstract (*æb*-strækt) *adj* abstrait

absurd (eub-*seûd*) *adj* absurde

abundance (eu-*bann*-deunns) *n* abondance *f*

abundant (eu-*bann*-deunnt) *adj* abondant

abuse (eu-*byoûss*) *n* abus *m*

abyss (eu-*biss*) *n* abîme *m*

academy (eu-*kæ*-deu-mi) *n* académie *f*

accelerate (euk-*sè*-leu-réït) *v* accélérer

accelerator (euk-*sè*-leu-réï-teu) *n* accélérateur *m*

accent (*æk*-seunnt) *n* accent *m*

accept (euk-*sèpt*) *v* accepter

access (*æk*-sèss) *n* accès *m*

accessible (euk-*sè*-seu-beul) *adj* accessible

accessories (euk-*sè*-seu-riz) *pl* accessoires *mpl*

accident (*æk*-si-deunnt) *n* accident *m*

accidental (æk-si-*dèn*-teul) *adj* accidentel

accommodate (eu-*ko*-meu-déït) *v* loger

accommodation (eu-ko-meu-*déï*-cheunn) *n* accommodation *f*, logement *m*

accompany (eu-*kamm*-peu-ni) *v* accompagner

accomplish (eu-*kamm*-plich) *v* achever; accomplir

accordance: in ~ with (inn eu-*koo*-deunns ᵒᵘið) conformément à

according to (eu-*koo*-dinng toû) d'après, selon; conformément à

account (eu-*kaount*) *n* compte *m*; récit *m*; **~ for** rendre compte de; **on ~ of** à cause de

accountable (eu-*kaoun*-teu-beul) *adj* responsable

accurate (*æ*-kyou-reut) *adj* précis

accuse (eu-*kyoûz*) *v* accuser

accused (eu-*kyoûzd*) *n* prévenu *m*, -e *f*

accustom (eu-*ka*-steumm) *v* familiariser; **accustomed** accoutumé, habitué

ache (éïk) *v* *faire mal; *n* douleur *f*

achieve (eu-*tchiiv*) *v* *parvenir à; accomplir

achievement (eu-*tchiiv*-meunnt) *n* performance *f*

acid (*æ*-sid) *n* acide *m*

acknowledge (euk-*no*-lidj) *v* *reconnaître; *admettre; confirmer

acne (*æk*-ni) *n* acné *f*

acquaintance (eu-*kouéïn*-teunns) *n* connaissance *f*

acquire (eu-*kouaïeu*) *v* *acquérir
acquisition (æ-k^{ou}i-*zi*-cheunn) *n* acquisition *f*
acquittal (eu-*koui*-teul) *n* acquittement *m*
across (eu-*kross*) *prep* à travers; de l'autre côté de; *adv* de l'autre côté
act (ækt) *n* acte *m*; numéro *m*; *v* agir; se *conduire; jouer
action (*æk*-cheunn) *n* action *f*
active (*æk*-tiv) *adj* actif; animé
activity (æk-*ti*-veu-ti) *n* activité *f*
actor (*æk*-teu) *n* acteur *m*
actress (*æk*-triss) *n* actrice *f*
actual (*æk*-tchou-eul) *adj* véritable, réel
actually (*æk*-tchou-eu-li) *adv* en réalité
acute (eu-*kyoût*) *adj* aigu
adapt (eu-*dæpt*) *v* adapter
add (æd) *v* additionner; ajouter
addition (eu-*di*-cheunn) *n* addition *f*
additional (eu-*di*-cheu-neul) *adj* supplémentaire; accessoire
address (eu-*drèss*) *n* adresse *f*; *v* adresser; s'adresser à
addressee (æ-drè-*sii*) *n* destinataire *m*
adequate (*æ*-di-k^{ou}eut) *adj* adéquat; approprié
adjective (*æ*-djik-tiv) *n* adjectif *m*
adjourn (eu-*djeûnn*) *v* ajourner
adjust (eu-*djast*) *v* ajuster; rectifier; régler
administer (eud-*mi*-ni-steu) *v* administrer
administration (eud-mi-ni-*strèï*-cheunn) *n* administration *f*; gestion *f*
administrative (eud-*mi*-ni-streu-tiv) *adj* administratif; **~ law** droit administratif
admiration (æd-meu-*réï*-cheunn) *n* admiration *f*
admire (eud-*maïeu*) *v* admirer

admission (eud-*mi*-cheunn) *n* admission *f*
admit (eud-*mit*) *v* *admettre; *reconnaître
admittance (eud-*mi*-teunns) *n* accès *m*; **no ~** entrée interdite
adopt (eu-*dopt*) *v* adopter
adoption (eu-*dop*-cheunn) *n* adoption *f*
adorable (eu-*doo*-reu-beul) *adj* adorable
adult (*æ*-dalt) *n* adulte *m*; *adj* adulte
advance (eud-*vââns*) *n* avancement *m*; avance *f*; *v* avancer; **in ~** à l'avance, d'avance
advanced (eud-*vâânst*) *adj* avancé
advantage (eud-*vâân*-tidj) *n* avantage *m*
advantageous (æd-veunn-*téï*-djeuss) *adj* avantageux
adventure (eud-*vèn*-tcheu) *n* aventure *f*
advertise (*æd*-veu-taïz) *v* faire de la réclame (pour), annoncer, faire connaître; insérer une annonce
advertisement (eud-*veû*-tiss-meunnt) *n* annonce *f*; publicité *f*
advertising (*æd*-veu-taï-zinng) *n* publicité *f*
advice (eud-*vaïss*) *n* avis *m*, conseil *m*
advise (eud-*vaïz*) *v* donner des conseils, conseiller
advocate (*æd*-veu-keut) *n* partisan *m*
aerial (*èeu*-ri-eul) *n* antenne *f*
aeroplane (*èeu*-reu-pléïn) *n* avion *m*
affair (eu-*fèu*) *n* affaire *f*; liaison *f*, affaire de cœur
affect (eu-*fèkt*) *v* affecter; toucher
affected (eu-*fèk*-tid) *adj* affecté
affection (eu-*fèk*-cheunn) *n* affection *f*
affectionate (eu-*fèk*-cheu-nit) *adj* affectueux
affiliated (eu-*fi*-li-éï-tid) *adj* affilié
affirm (eu-*feûm*) *v* affirmer, soutenir

affirmative (eu-*feû*-meu-tiv) *adj* affirmatif

afford (eu-*food*) *v* se *permettre

afraid (eu-*frëïd*) *adj* apeuré, effrayé; ***be ~** *avoir peur

Africa (*æ*-fri-keu) Afrique *f*

African (*æ*-fri-keunn) *adj* africain; *n* Africain *m*

after (*ââf*-teu) *prep* après; derrière; *conj* après que

afternoon (ââf-teu-*noûn*) *n* après-midi *m/f*

afterwards (*ââf*-teu-ᵒᵘeudz) *adv* après; par la suite, ensuite

again (eu-*ghèn*) *adv* encore; de nouveau; **~ and again** toujours et encore

against (eu-*ghènst*) *prep* contre

age (éïdj) *n* âge *m*; vieillesse *f*; **of ~** majeur; **under ~** mineur

aged (*éï*-djid) *adj* âgé; vieux

agency (*éï*-djeunn-si) *n* agence *f*; bureau *m*

agenda (eu-*djèn*-deu) *n* ordre du jour

agent (*éï*-djeunnt) *n* agent *m*, représentant *m*

aggressive (eu-*ghrè*-siv) *adj* agressif

ago (eu-*ghôou*) *adv* il y a

agree (eu-*ghrii*) *v* *être d'accord; *consentir; concorder

agreeable (eu-*ghrii*-eu-beul) *adj* agréable

agreement (eu-*ghrii*-meunnt) *n* contrat *m*; accord *m*; entente *f*

agriculture (*æ*-ghri-kal-tcheu) *n* agriculture *f*

ahead (eu-*hèd*) *adv* en avant; **~ of** devant; ***go ~** continuer; **straight ~** tout droit

aid (éïd) *n* aide *f*; *v* assister, aider

aim (éïm) *n* but *m*; **~ at** viser; aspirer à

air (è^eu) *n* air *m*; *v* aérer; **~ conditioning** climatisation *f*

air-conditioned *adj* climatisé

aircraft (*è*eu-krââft) *n* (pl ~) avion *m*; appareil *m*

airfield (*è*eu-fiild) *n* terrain d'aviation

air-filter (*è*eu-fil-teu) *n* filtre à air

airline (*è*eu-laïn) *n* ligne aérienne

airmail (*è*eu-méïl) *n* poste aérienne

airplane (*è*eu-pléïn) *nAm* avion *m*

airport (*è*eu-poot) *n* aéroport *m*

airsickness (*è*eu-sik-neuss) *n* mal de l'air

airtight (*è*eu-taït) *adj* hermétique

airy (*è*eu-ri) *adj* aéré

aisle (aïl) *n* bas-côté *m*; passage *m*

alarm (eu-*lââm*) *n* alerte *f*; *v* alarmer; **~ clock** réveil *m*

album (*æl*-beumm) *n* album *m*

alcohol (*æl*-keu-hol) *n* alcool *m*

alcoholic (æl-keu-*ho*-lik) *adj* alcoolique

ale (éïl) *n* bière *f*

Algeria (æl-*djieu*-ri-eu) Algérie *f*

Algerian (æl-*djieu*-ri-eunn) *adj* algérien; *n* Algérien *m*

alien (*éï*-li-eunn) *n* étranger *m*, -ère *f*; *adj* étranger

alike (eu-*laïk*) *adj* pareil, semblable; *adv* de la même façon

alive (eu-*laïv*) *adj* en vie, vivant

all (ool) *adj* tout; **~ in** tout compris; **~ right!** bien!; **at ~** du tout

allergy (*æ*-leu-dji) *n* allergie *f*

alley (*æ*-li) *n* ruelle *f*

alliance (eu-*laï*-eunns) *n* alliance *f*

Allies (*æ*-laïz) *pl* Alliés

allot (eu-*lot*) *v* assigner

allow (eu-*laou*) *v* autoriser, *permettre; **~ to** autoriser à; ***be allowed** *être autorisé

allowance (eu-*laou*-eunns) *n* allocation *f*

all-round (ool-*raound*) *adj* universel

almond (*ââ*-meunnd) *n* amande *f*

almost (*ool*-môᵒᵘst) *adv* presque; à peu près

alone (eu-*lôoun*) *adv* seul

along (eu-*lonng*) *prep* le long de

aloud (eu-*laoud*) *adv* à haute voix

alphabet (*æl*-feu-bèt) *n* alphabet *m*

already (ool-*rè*-di) *adv* déjà

also (*ool*-sô^ou) *adv* aussi; de même, également

altar (*ool*-teu) *n* autel *m*

alter (*ool*-teu) *v* changer, modifier

alteration (ool-teu-*rêï*-cheunn) *n* changement *m*, modification *f*

alternate (ool-*teû*-neut) *adj* alternatif

alternative (ool-*teû*-neu-tiv) *n* alternative *f*

although (ool-*ðôou*) *conj* quoique, bien que

altitude (*æl*-ti-tyoûd) *n* altitude *f*

alto (*æl*-tô^ou) *n* (pl ~s) contralto *m*

altogether (ool-teu-*ghè*-ðeu) *adv* entièrement; en tout

always (*ool*-^ou éïz) *adv* toujours

am (æm) *v* (pr be)

amaze (eu-*mëïz*) *v* étonner, *surprendre

amazement (eu-*mëïz*-meunnt) *n* étonnement *m*

amazing (eu-*mëï*-zinng) *adj* stupéfiant, étonnant

ambassador (æm-*bæ*-seu-deu) *n* ambassadeur *m*

amber (*æm*-beu) *n* ambre *m*

ambiguous (æm-*bi*-ghyou-euss) *adj* ambigu; équivoque

ambition (æm-*bi*-cheunn) *n* ambition *f*

ambitious (æm-*bi*-cheuss) *adj* ambitieux

ambulance (*æm*-byou-leunns) *n* ambulance *f*

America (eu-*mè*-ri-keu) Amérique *f*

American (eu-*mè*-ri-keunn) *adj* américain; *n* Américain *m*

amid (eu-*mid*) *prep* entre; parmi, au milieu de

ammonia (eu-*môou*-ni-eu) *n* ammoniaque *f*

amnesty (*æm*-ni-sti) *n* amnistie *f*

among (eu-*manng*) *prep* parmi; au milieu de, entre; ~ **other things** entre autres

amount (eu-*maount*) *n* quantité *f*; montant *m*, somme *f*; ~ **to** se monter à

amuse (eu-*myoûz*) *v* divertir, amuser

amusement (eu-*myoûz*-meunnt) *n* amusement *m*, divertissement *m*

amusing (eu-*myoû*-zinng) *adj* plaisant

anaemia (eu-*nii*-mi-eu) *n* anémie *f*

anaesthesia (æ-niss-*θii*-zi-eu) *n* anesthésie *f*

anaesthetic (æ-niss-*θè*-tik) *n* anesthésique *m*

analyse (*æ*-neu-laïz) *v* analyser

analysis (eu-*næ*-leu-siss) *n* (pl -ses) analyse *f*

analyst (*æ*-neu-list) *n* analyste *m/f*; psychanalyste *m/f*

anarchy (*æ*-neu-ki) *n* anarchie *f*

anatomy (eu-*næ*-teu-mi) *n* anatomie *f*

ancestor (*æn*-sè-steu) *n* ancêtre *m/f*

anchor (*æng*-keu) *n* ancre *f*

anchovy (*æn*-tcheu-vi) *n* anchois *m*

ancient (*ëïn*-cheunnt) *adj* vieux, ancien; antique

and (ænd, eunnd) *conj* et

angel (*ëïn*-djeul) *n* ange *m*

anger (*æng*-gheu) *n* colère *f*; fureur *f*

angle (*æng*-gheul) *v* pêcher à la ligne; *n* angle *m*

angry (*æng*-ghri) *adj* en colère

animal (*æ*-ni-meul) *n* animal *m*

ankle (*æng*-keul) *n* cheville *f*

annex[1] (*æ*-nèks) *n* annexe *f*

annex[2] (eu-*nèks*) *v* annexer

anniversary (æ-ni-*veû*-seu-ri) *n* anniversaire *m*

announce (eu-*naouns*) *v* annoncer

announcement (eu-*naouns*-meunnt)

n annonce *f*

annoy (eu-*noï*) *v* agacer, fâcher; ennuyer

annoyance (eu-*noï*-eunns) *n* ennui *m*

annoying (eu-*noï*-inng) *adj* ennuyeux

annual (*æ*-nyou-eul) *adj* annuel; *n* annuaire *m*

annum: per ~ (peur *æ*-neumm) par an

anonymous (eu-*no*-ni-meuss) *adj* anonyme

another (eu-*na*-ðeu) *adj* encore un; un autre

answer (*âân*-seu) *v* répondre à; *n* réponse *f*

ant (*æ*nt) *n* fourmi *f*

antibiotic (*æ*n-ti-baï-*o*-tik) *n* antibiotique *m*

anticipate (*æ*n-*ti*-si-péït) *v* *prévoir, anticiper; *prévenir

antifreeze (*æ*n-ti-friiz) *n* antigel *m*

antipathy (*æ*n-*ti*-peu-θi) *n* antipathie *f*

antique (*æ*n-*tiik*) *adj* antique; *n* antiquité *f*; **~ dealer** antiquaire *m/f*

antiquity (*æ*n-*ti*-k^ou^eu-ti) *n* Antiquité; **antiquities** *pl* antiquités

anxiety (*æ*ng-*zaï*-eu-ti) *n* anxiété *f*

anxious (*æ*ngk-cheuss) *adj* désireux; inquiet

any (*è*-ni) *adj* n'importe quel

anybody (*è*-ni-bo-di) *pron* n'importe qui

anyhow (*è*-ni-haou) *adv* n'importe comment

anyone (*è*-ni-^ou^ann) *pron* chacun

anything (*è*-ni-θinng) *pron* n'importe quoi

anyway (*è*-ni-^ou^éï) *adv* de toute façon

anywhere (*è*-ni-^ou^è^eu) *adv* n'importe où

apart (eu-*pâât*) *adv* à part, séparément; **~ from** abstraction faite de

apartment (eu-*pâât*-meunnt) *nAm* appartement *m*; étage *m*; **~ house**

Am immeuble d'habitation

aperitif (eu-*pè*-reu-tiv) *n* apéritif *m*

apologize (eu-*po*-leu-djaïz) *v* s'excuser

apology (eu-*po*-leu-dji) *n* excuse *f*

apparatus (*æ*-peu-*réï*-teuss) *n* dispositif *m*, appareil *m*

apparent (eu-*pæ*-reunnt) *adj* apparent

apparently (eu-*pæ*-reunnt-li) *adv* apparemment; manifestement

appeal (eu-*piil*) *n* appel *m*

appear (eu-*pieu*) *v* sembler, *paraître; *apparaître; se présenter

appearance (eu-*pieu*-reunns) *n* apparence *f*; aspect *m*; entrée *f*

appendicitis (eu-*pèn*-di-*saï*-tiss) *n* appendicite *f*

appendix (eu-*pèn*-diks) *n* (pl -dices, -dixes) appendice *m*

appetite (*æ*-peu-taït) *n* appétit *m*

appetizer (*æ*-peu-taï-zeu) *n* amusegueule *m*

appetizing (*æ*-peu-taï-zinng) *adj* appétissant

applaud (eu-*plood*) *v* applaudir

applause (eu-*plooz*) *n* applaudissements *mpl*

apple (*æ*-peul) *n* pomme *f*

appliance (eu-*plaï*-eunns) *n* appareil *m*

application (*æ*-pli-*kéï*-cheunn) *n* application *f*; demande *f*; candidature *f*

apply (eu-*plaï*) *v* appliquer; se *servir de; solliciter un emploi; s'appliquer à

appoint (eu-*poïnt*) *v* désigner, nommer

appointment (eu-*poïnt*-meunnt) *n* rendez-vous *m*; nomination *f*

appreciate (eu-*prii*-chi-éït) *v* évaluer; apprécier

appreciation (eu-prii-chi-*éï*-cheunn) *n* appréciation *f*

apprentice (eu-*prèn*-tiss) *n* apprenti

m, -e *f*

approach (eu-*prôoutch*) *v* approcher; *n* approche *f;* accès *m*

appropriate (eu-*prôou*-pri-eut) *adj* juste, approprié, adéquat

approval (eu-*prooû*-veul) *n* approbation *f;* consentement *m,* accord *m;* **on ~** à l'essai

approve (eu-*prooûv*) *v* approuver; **~ of** *être d'accord avec

approximate (eu-*prok*-si-meut) *adj* approximatif

approximately (eu-*prok*-si-meut-li) *adv* à peu près, approximativement

apricot (*éi*-pri-kot) *n* abricot *m*

April (*éi*-preul) avril

apron (*éi*-preunn) *n* tablier *m*

Arab (*æ*-reub) *adj* arabe; *n* Arabe *m/f*

arbitrary (*ââ*-bi-treu-ri) *adj* arbitraire

arcade (ââ-*kéîd*) *n* arcade *f*

arch (ââtch) *n* arche *f;* voûte *f*

arch(a)eologist (ââ-ki-*o*-leu-djist) *n* archéologue *m/f*

arch(a)eology (ââ-ki-*o*-leu-dji) *n* archéologie *f*

archbishop (ââtch-*bi*-cheup) *n* archevêque *m*

arched (ââtcht) *adj* arqué

architect (*ââ*-ki-tèkt) *n* architecte *m/f*

architecture (*ââ*-ki-tèk-tcheu) *n* architecture *f*

archives (*ââ*-kaïvz) *pl* archives *fpl*

are (ââ) *v* (pr be)

area (*èeu*-ri-eu) *n* région *f;* zone *f;* **~ code** indicatif *m*

Argentina (ââ-djeunn-*tii*-neu) Argentine *f*

Argentinian (ââ-djeunn-*ti*-ni-eunn) *adj* argentin; *n* Argentin *m*

argue (*ââ*-ghyoû) *v* argumenter, discuter; disputer

argument (*ââ*-ghyou-meunnt) *n* argument *m;* discussion *f;* dispute *f*

*arise (eu-*raïz*) *v* surgir

arm (ââm) *n* bras *m;* arme *f; v* armer

armchair (*ââm*-tchè^(eu)) *n* fauteuil *m*

armed (ââmd) *adj* armé; **~ forces** forces armées

armour (*ââ*-meu) *n* armure *f*

army (*ââ*-mi) *n* armée *f*

aroma (eu-*rôou*-meu) *n* arôme *m*

around (eu-*raound*) *prep* autour de; *adv* autour

arrange (eu-*réîndj*) *v* classer, arranger; préparer

arrangement (eu-*réîndj*-meunnt) *n* règlement *m*

arrest (eu-*rèst*) *v* arrêter; *n* arrestation *f*

arrival (eu-*raï*-veul) *n* arrivée *f;* venue *f*

arrive (eu-*raïv*) *v* arriver

arrow (*æ*-rô^(ou)) *n* flèche *f*

art (âât) *n* art *m;* habileté *f;* **~ collection** collection d'art; **~ exhibition** exposition d'art; **~ gallery** galerie d'art; **~ history** histoire de l'art; **arts and crafts** arts et métiers; **~ school** académie des beaux-arts

artery (*ââ*-teu-ri) *n* artère *f*

artichoke (*ââ*-ti-tchô^(ou)k) *n* artichaut *m*

article (*ââ*-ti-keul) *n* article *m*

artificial (ââ-ti-*fi*-cheul) *adj* artificiel

artist (*ââ*-tist) *n* artiste *m/f*

artistic (ââ-*ti*-stik) *adj* artistique

as (æz) *conj* comme; aussi; que; puisque, parce que; **~ from** à partir de; **~ if** comme si

asbestos (æz-*bè*-stoss) *n* amiante *m*

ascend (eu-*sènd*) *v* monter; *faire l'ascension de

ascent (eu-*sènt*) *n* montée *f*

ascertain (æ-seu-*téîn*) *v* établir; vérifier

ash (æch) *n* cendre *f*

ashamed (eu-*chéîmd*) *adj* honteux; ***be ~** *avoir honte

ashore (eu-*choo*) *adv* à terre

ashtray (*æch*-tréï) *n* cendrier *m*

Asia (*éï*-cheu) Asie *f*

Asian (*éï*-cheunn) *adj* asiatique; *n* Asiatique *m/f*

aside (eu-*saïd*) *adv* de côté, à part

ask (ââsk) *v* demander; prier

asleep (eu-*sliip*) *adj* endormi

asparagus (eu-*spæ*-reu-gheuss) *n* asperge *f*

aspect (*æ*-spèkt) *n* aspect *m*

asphalt (*æss*-fælt) *n* asphalte *m*

aspire (eu-*spaïeu*) *v* aspirer

aspirin (*æ*-speu-rinn) *n* aspirine *f*

assassination (eu-sæ-si-*néï*-cheunn) *n* assassinat *m*

assault (eu-*soolt*) *v* attaquer; violer

assemble (eu-*sèm*-beul) *v* rassembler; monter, assembler

assembly (eu-*sèm*-bli) *n* réunion *f*, assemblée *f*

assignment (eu-*saïn*-meunnt) *n* tâche assignée

assign to (eu-*saïn*) assigner à; attribuer à

assist (eu-*sist*) *v* assister

assistance (eu-*si*-steunns) *n* secours *m*; aide *f*, assistance *f*

assistant (eu-*si*-steunnt) *n* assistant *m*, -e *f*

associate (eu-*sôou*-chi-eut) *n* partenaire *m/f*, associé *m*, -e *f*; allié *m*; membre *m*; *v* associer; ~ **with** fréquenter

association (eu-sô^{ou}-si-*éï*-cheunn) *n* association *f*

assort (eu-*soot*) *v* classer

assortment (eu-*soot*-meunnt) *n* assortiment *m*

assume (eu-*syoûm*) *v* supposer, présumer

assure (eu-*choueu*) *v* assurer

asthma (*æss*-meu) *n* asthme *m*

astonish (eu-*sto*-nich) *v* étonner

astonishing (eu-*sto*-ni-chinng) *adj* étonnant

astonishment (eu-*sto*-nich-meunnt) *n* étonnement *m*

astronaut (*æss*-treu-noot) *n* astronaute *m/f*

astronomy (eu-*stro*-neu-mi) *n* astronomie *f*

asylum (eu-*saï*-leumm) *n* asile *m*

at (æt) *prep* à, chez; vers

ate (èt) *v* (p eat)

athlete (*æ*θ-liit) *n* athlète *m*

athletics (æθ-*lè*-tiks) *pl* athlétisme *m*

Atlantic (eut-*læn*-tik) Océan Atlantique

atmosphere (*æt*-meuss-fi^{eu}) *n* atmosphère *f*; ambiance *f*

atomic (eu-*to*-mik) *adj* atomique; nucléaire

attach (eu-*tætch*) *v* attacher; fixer; *joindre

attack (eu-*tæk*) *v* attaquer; *n* attaque *f*

attain (eu-*téïn*) *v* *atteindre

attainable (eu-*téï*-neu-beul) *adj* accessible

attempt (eu-*tèmpt*) *v* tenter; essayer; *n* tentative *f*

attend (eu-*tènd*) *v* assister à; ~ **on** *servir; ~ **to** s'occuper de; *faire attention à, prêter attention à

attendance (eu-*tèn*-deunns) *n* assistance *f*

attendant (eu-*tèn*-deunnt) *n* gardien *m*, gardienne *f*

attention (eu-*tèn*-cheunn) *n* attention *f*; **pay** ~ *faire attention

attentive (eu-*tèn*-tiv) *adj* attentif

attest (eu-*tèst*) *v* attester; ~ **to** témoigner de

attic (*æ*-tik) *n* grenier *m*

attitude (*æ*-ti-tyoûd) *n* attitude *f*

attorney (eu-*teû*-ni) *n* avocat *m*, -e *f*

attract (eu-*trækt*) *v* attirer

attraction (eu-*træk*-cheunn) *n*

attraction *f*; attrait *m*

attractive (eu-*træk*-tiv) *adj* séduisant

auction (*ook*-cheunn) *n* vente aux enchères

audible (*oo*-di-beul) *adj* audible

audience (*oo*-di-eunns) *n* public *m*

auditor (*oo*-di-teu) *n* auditeur *m*, -trice *f*

August (*oo*-gheust) août

aunt (âânt) *n* tante *f*

Australia (o-*stréï*-li-eu) Australie *f*

Australian (o-*stréï*-li-eunn) *adj* australien; *n* Australien *m*

Austria (*o*-stri-eu) Autriche *f*

Austrian (*o*-stri-eunn) *adj* autrichien; *n* Autrichien *m*

authentic (oo-*θèn*-tik) *adj* authentique

author (*oo*-θeu) *n* auteur *m*

authoritarian (oo-θo-ri-*tèeu*-ri-eunn) *adj* autoritaire

authority (oo-*θo*-reu-ti) *n* autorité *f*; pouvoir *m*

authorization (oo-θeu-raï-*zéï*-cheunn) *n* autorisation *f*; permission *f*

authorize (*oo*-θeu-raïz) *v* autoriser

automatic (oo-teu-*mæ*-tik) *adj* automatique

automation (oo-teu-*méï*-cheunn) *n* automatisation *f*

automobile (*oo*-teu-meu-biil) *n* auto *f*; ~ **club** club automobile

autonomous (oo-*to*-neu-meuss) *adj* autonome

autumn (*oo*-teumm) *n* automne *m*

available (eu-*véï*-leu-beul) *adj* disponible

avalanche (æ-veu-lâânch) *n* avalanche *f*

avenue (æ-veu-nyoû) *n* avenue *f*

average (æ-veu-ridj) *adj* moyen; *n* moyenne *f*; **on the** ~ en moyenne

averse (eu-*veûss*) *adj* ennemi, peu disposé

aversion (eu-*veû*-cheunn) *n* aversion *f*

avert (eu-*veût*) *v* détourner

avoid (eu-*voïd*) *v* éviter

await (eu-ouéït) *v* attendre

awake (eu-ouéïk) *adj* réveillé

***awake** (eu-ouéïk) *v* réveiller

award (eu-ouood) *n* prix *m*; *v* décerner

aware (eu-ouèeu) *adj* conscient

away (eu-ouéï) *adv* loin; ***go** ~ s'en *aller

awful (*oo*-feul) *adj* terrible

awkward (*oo*-kʰeud) *adj* embarrassant; maladroit

awning (*oo*-ninng) *n* marquise *f*

axe (æks) *n* hache *f*

axle (æk-seul) *n* essieu *m*

B

baby (*béï*-bi) *n* bébé *m*; ~ **carriage** *Am* poussette *f*

babysitter (*béï*-bi-si-teu) *n* baby-sitter *m*

bachelor (*bæ*-tcheu-leu) *n* célibataire *m*

back (bæk) *n* dos *m*; *adv* en arrière; ***go** ~ retourner

backache (*bæ*-kéïk) *n* mal au dos

backbone (*bæk*-bôⁿn) *n* épine dorsale

background (*bæk*-ghraound) *n* fond *m*

backwards (*bæk*-ᵒueudz) *adv* en arrière

bacon (*béï*-keunn) *n* lard *m*

bacterium (bæk-*tii*-ri-eumm) *n* (pl -ria) bactérie *f*

bad (bæd) *adj* mauvais; grave; vilain

bag (bægh) *n* sac *m*; sac à main; valise *f*

baggage (*bæ*-ghidj) *n* bagage *m*; ~ **check** *Am* consigne *f*; **hand** ~ *Am* bagage à main

bail (béïl) *n* caution *f*

bait (béït) *n* amorce *f*

bake (béïk) *v* *cuire au four

baker (*béï*-keu) *n* boulanger *m*

bakery (*béï*-keu-ri) *n* boulangerie *f*

balance (*bæ*-leunns) *n* équilibre *m*; bilan *m*; solde *m*

balcony (*bæl*-keu-ni) *n* balcon *m*

bald (boold) *adj* chauve

ball (bool) *n* ballon *m*, balle *f*; bal *m*

ballet (*bæ*-léï) *n* ballet *m*

balloon (beu-*loûn*) *n* ballon *m*

ballpoint pen (*bool*-poïnt-pèn) *n* stylo à bille

ballroom (*bool*-roûm) *n* salle de bal

bamboo (bæm-*boû*) *n* (pl ~s) bambou *m*

banana (beu-*nââ*-neu) *n* banane *f*

band (bænd) *n* orchestre *m*; lien *m*

bandage (*bæn*-didj) *n* pansement *m*

bandit (*bæn*-dit) *n* bandit *m*

bangle (*bæng*-gheul) *n* bracelet *m*

bank (bængk) *n* rive *f*; banque *f*; *v* déposer en banque; ~ **account** compte en banque

banknote (*bængk*-nô^{ou}t) *n* billet de banque

bank rate (*bængk*-réït) *n* taux d'escompte

bankrupt (*bængk*-rapt) *adj* en faillite

banner (*bæ*-neu) *n* bannière *f*

banquet (*bæng*-k^{ou}it) *n* banquet *m*

baptism (*bæp*-ti-zeumm) *n* baptême *m*

baptize (bæp-*taïz*) *v* baptiser

bar (bââ) *n* bar *m*; barre *f*; barreau *m*

barbecue (*bââ*-bi-kyoû) *n* barbecue *m*; *v* griller au charbon de bois; rôtir tout entier

barber (*bââ*-beu) *n* coiffeur *m*

bare (bè^{eu}) *adj* nu

barely (*bèeu*-li) *adv* à peine

bargain (*bââ*-ghinn) *n* bonne affaire; *v* marchander

baritone (*bæ*-ri-tô^{ou}n) *n* bariton *m*

bark (bââk) *n* écorce *f*; *v* aboyer

barley (*bââ*-li) *n* orge *f*

barman (*bââ*-meunn) *n* (pl -men) barman *m*

barn (bâân) *n* grange *f*

barometer (beu-*ro*-mi-teu) *n* baromètre *m*

baroque (beu-*rok*) *adj* baroque

barracks (*bæ*-reuks) *pl* caserne *f*

barrel (*bæ*-reul) *n* tonneau *m*, baril *m*

barrier (*bæ*-ri-eu) *n* barrière *f*

barrister (*bæ*-ri-steu) *n* avocat *m*

bartender (*bââ*-tèn-deu) *n* barman *m*

base (béïss) *n* base *f*; fondement *m*; *v* baser

baseball (*béïss*-bool) *n* base-ball *m*

basement (*béïss*-meunnt) *n* sous-sol *m*

basic (*béï*-sik) *adj* fondamental

basilica (beu-*zi*-li-keu) *n* basilique *f*

basin (*béï*-seunn) *n* bol *m*, bassin *m*

basis (*béï*-siss) *n* (pl bases) base *f*

basket (*bââ*-skit) *n* panier *m*

bass[1] (béïss) *n* basse *f*

bass[2] (bæss) *n* (pl ~) perche *f*

bastard (*bââ*-steud) *n* bâtard *m*; salaud *m*

batch (bætch) *n* lot *m*

bath (bââθ) *n* bain *m*; ~ **salts** sels de bain; ~ **towel** serviette de bain

bathe (béïð) *v* se baigner

bathing cap (*béï*-ðinng-kæp) *n* bonnet de bain

bathing suit (*béï*-ðinng-soût) *n* maillot de bain

bathing trunks (*béï*-ðinng-tranngks)

n caleçon de bain

bathrobe (*bââθ*-rô^{ou}b) *n* peignoir *m*

bathroom (*bââθ*-roûm) *n* salle de bains

batter (*bæ*-teu) *n* pâte *f*

battery (*bæ*-teu-ri) *n* pile *f*; accumulateur *m*

battle (*bæ*-teul) *n* bataille *f*; lutte, combat *m*; *v* *combattre

bay (béï) *n* baie *f*; *v* aboyer

***be** (bii) *v* *être

beach (biitch) *n* plage *f*; **nudist ~** plage pour nudistes

bead (biid) *n* perle *f*; **beads** *pl* collier *m*; chapelet *m*

beak (biik) *n* bec *m*

beam (biim) *n* rayon *m*; poutre *f*

bean (biin) *n* haricot *m*

bear (bè^{eu}) *n* ours *m*

***bear** (bè^{eu}) *v* porter; tolérer; supporter

beard (bi^{eu}d) *n* barbe *f*

bearer (*bèeu*-reu) *n* porteur *m*

beast (biist) *n* bête *f*; **~ of prey** bête de proie

***beat** (biit) *v* frapper; *battre

beautiful (*byoû*-ti-feul) *adj* beau

beauty (*byoû*-ti) *n* beauté *f*; **~ parlo(u)r** institut de beauté; **~ salon** salon de beauté; **~ treatment** soins de beauté

beaver (*bii*-veu) *n* castor *m*

because (bi-*koz*) *conj* parce que; **~ of** en raison de, à cause de

***become** (bi-*kamm*) *v* *devenir

bed (bèd) *n* lit *m*; **~ and board** pension complète; **~ and breakfast** chambre et petit déjeuner

bedding (*bè*-dinng) *n* literie *f*

bedroom (*bèd*-roûm) *n* chambre à coucher

bee (bii) *n* abeille *f*

beech (bii-tch) *n* hêtre *m*

beef (biif) *n* bœuf *m*

beehive (*bii*-haïv) *n* ruche *f*

been (biin) *v* (pp be)

beer (bi^{eu}) *n* bière *f*

beet (biit) *n* betterave *f*

beetroot (*biit*-roût) *n* betterave *f*

before (bi-*foo*) *prep* avant; devant; *conj* avant que; *adv* d'avance; précédemment, avant

beg (bègh) *v* mendier; supplier; demander

beggar (*bè*-gheu) *n* mendiant *m*, -e *f*

***begin** (bi-*ghinn*) *v* commencer; débuter

beginner (bi-*ghi*-neu) *n* débutant *m*, -e *f*

beginning (bi-*ghi*-ninng) *n* commencement *m*; début *m*

behalf: on ~ of (onn bi-*hââf* ov) au nom de; en faveur de

behave (bi-*héïv*) *v* se comporter

behavio(u)r (bi-*héï*-vyeu) *n* comportement *m*

behind (bi-*haïnd*) *prep* derrière; *adv* en arrière

beige (béïj) *adj* beige

being (*bii*-inng) *n* être *m*

Belgian (*bèl*-djeunn) *adj* belge; *n* Belge *m*

Belgium (*bèl*-djeumm) Belgique *f*

belief (bi-*liif*) *n* croyance *f*

believe (bi-*liiv*) *v* *croire

bell (bèl) *n* cloche *f*; sonnette *f*

bellboy (*bèl*-boï) *n* chasseur *m*

belly (*bè*-li) *n* ventre *m*

belong (bi-*lonng*) *v* *appartenir

belongings (bi-*lonng*-inngz) *pl* affaires *fpl*

beloved (bi-*lavd*) *adj* aimé

below (bi-*lôou*) *prep* au-dessous de; en bas de; *adv* en dessous

belt (bèlt) *n* ceinture *f*

bench (bèntch) *n* banc *m*

bend (bènd) *n* virage *m*, courbe *f*

***bend** (bènd) *v* courber; **~ down** se

pencher

beneath (bi-*niiθ*) *prep* en dessous de; *adv* au-dessous

benefit (*bè*-ni-fit) *n* profit *m*, bénéfice *m*; avantage *m*; *v* profiter

bent (bènt) *adj* (pp bend) tordu

beret (*bè*-réï) *n* béret *m*

berry (*bè*-ri) *n* baie *f*

beside (bi-*saïd*) *prep* à côté de

besides (bi-*saïdz*) *adv* en outre; d'ailleurs; *prep* outre

best (bèst) *adj* le meilleur

bet (bèt) *n* pari *m*

*****bet** (bèt) *v* parier

betray (bi-*tréï*) *v* trahir

better (*bè*-teu) *adj* meilleur

between (bi-*touiin*) *prep* entre

beverage (*bè*-veu-ridj) *n* boisson *f*

beware (bi-*ouèeu*) *v* *prendre garde, *faire attention

bewitch (bi-*ouitch*) *v* ensorceler, enchanter

beyond (bi-*yonnd*) *prep* au delà de; outre; *adv* au delà

bible (*baï*-beul) *n* Bible *f*

bicycle (*baï*-sì-keul) *n* bicyclette *f*; vélo *m*

bid (bid) *v* commander; dire; faire une offre de; **a ~ to** un effort pour

big (bigh) *adj* grand; volumineux; gros; important

bike (baïk) *n* vélo *m*

bile (baïl) *n* bile *f*

bilingual (baï-*linng*-gh^ou eul) *adj* bilingue

bill (bil) *n* facture *f*; addition *f*, note *f*; *v* facturer

billiards (*bil*-yeudz) *pl* billard *m*

billion (*bil*-yeunn) *n* billion *m*, Am milliard *m*

*****bind** (baïnd) *v* lier

binding (*bain*-dinng) *n* reliure *f*

binoculars (bi-*no*-kyeu-leuz) *pl* jumelles *fpl*

biology (baï-*o*-leu-dji) *n* biologie *f*

birch (beûtch) *n* bouleau *m*

bird (beûd) *n* oiseau *m*

Biro (*baï*-rô^ou) *n* crayon à bille *m*

birth (beûθ) *n* naissance *f*

birthday (*beûθ*-déï) *n* anniversaire *m*

biscuit (*biss*-kit) *n* biscuit *m*

bishop (*bi*-cheup) *n* évêque *m*

bit (bit) *n* morceau *m*; peu *m*

bitch (bitch) *n* chienne *f*

bite (baït) *n* bouchée *f*; morsure *f*; piqûre *f*

*****bite** (baït) *v* mordre

bitter (*bi*-teu) *adj* amer

black (blæk) *adj* noir; **~ market** marché noir

blackberry (*blæk*-beu-ri) *n* mûre *f*

blackbird (*blæk*-beûd) *n* merle *m*

blackboard (*blæk*-bood) *n* tableau noir

blackcurrant (blæk-*ka*-reunnt) *n* cassis *m*

blackmail (*blæk*-méïl) *n* chantage *m*; *v* *faire chanter

blacksmith (*blæk*-smiθ) *n* forgeron *m*

bladder (*blæ*-deu) *n* vessie *f*

blade (bléïd) *n* lame *f*; **~ of grass** brin d'herbe

blame (bléïm) *n* blâme *m*; *v* donner la faute à, blâmer

blank (blængk) *adj* blanc

blanket (*blæng*-kit) *n* couverture *f*

blast (blââst) *n* explosion *f*

blazer (*bléï*-zeu) *n* veste de sport, blazer *m*

bleach (bliitch) *v* décolorer

bleak (bliik) *adj* morne; désolé

*****bleed** (bliid) *v* saigner

bless (blèss) *v* bénir

blessing (*blè*-sinng) *n* bénédiction *f*

blind (blaïnd) *n* store *m*, persienne *f*; *adj* aveugle; *v* aveugler

blinker (*blinng*-keu) *n* clignotant *m*

blister (*bli*-steu) *n* ampoule *f*, cloque *f*

blizzard (*bli*-zeud) *n* tempête de neige

block (blok) *v* obstruer, bloquer; *n* bloc *m*; ~ **of flats** immeuble d'habitation

blond(e) (blonnd) *n* blonde *f*

blood (blad) *n* sang *m*; ~ **poisoning** septicémie *f*;~ **pressure** tension artérielle; ~ **vessel** vaisseau sanguin**bloody** (*bla*-di) *adj* ensanglanté; sanguinaire; sacré; vachement

blossom (*blo*-seum) *n* fleur *f*; *v* fleurir

blot (blot) *n* tache *f*; **blotting paper** papier buvard

blouse (blaouz) *n* chemisier *m*

blow (blô^{ou}) *n* claque *f*, coup *m*; coup de vent

***blow** (blô^{ou}) *v* souffler

blowout (*blôou*-aout) *n* éclatement *m*

blue (bloû) *adj* bleu; déprimé

blunt (blannt) *adj* émoussé

blush (blach) *v* rougir

board (bood) *n* planche *f*; tableau *m*; pension *f*; conseil *m*; ~ **and lodging** pension complète

boarder (*boo*-deu) *n* pensionnaire *m/f*

boardinghouse (*boo*-dinng-haouss) *n* pension *f*

boarding school (*boo*-dinng-skoûl) *n* internat *m*

boast (bô^{ou}st) *v* se vanter

boat (bô^{ou}t) *n* navire *m*, bateau *m*

body (*bo*-di) *n* corps *m*

bodyguard (*bo*-di-ghââd) *n* garde du corps

bog (bogh) *n* marais *m*

boil (boïl) *v* *bouillir; *n* furoncle *m*

bold (bô^{ou}ld) *adj* audacieux; effronté, hardi

Bolivia (beu-*li*-vi-eu) Bolivie *f*

Bolivian (beu-*li*-vi-eunn) *adj* bolivien; *n* Bolivien *m*

bolt (bô^{ou}lt) *n* verrou *m*; boulon *m*

bomb (bomm) *n* bombe *f*; *v* bombarder

bond (bonnd) *n* obligation *f*

bone (bô^{ou}n) *n* os *m*; arête *f*; *v* désosser

bonnet (*bo*-nit) *n* capot *m*

book (bouk) *n* livre *m*; *v* *retenir, réserver; *inscrire, enregistrer

booking (*bou*-kinng) *n* réservation *f*

bookseller (*bouk*-sè-leu) *n* libraire *m/f*

bookstand (*bouk*-stænd) *n* stand de livres

bookstore (*bouk*-stoo) *n* librairie *f*

boot (boût) *n* botte *f*; coffre *m*

booth (boûð) *n* échoppe *f*; cabine *f*

border (*boo*-deu) *n* frontière *f*; bord *m*

bore¹ (boo) *v* ennuyer; forer; *n* raseur *m*

bore² (boo) *v* (p bear)

boring (*boo*-rinng) *adj* ennuyeux

born (boon) *adj* né

borrow (*bo*-rô^{ou}) *v* emprunter

bosom (*bou*-zeumm) *n* poitrine *f*; sein *m*

boss (boss) *n* chef *m*, patron *m*

botany (*bo*-teu-ni) *n* botanique *f*

both (bô^{ou}θ) *adj* les deux; **both ... and** aussi bien que

bother (*bo*-ðeu) *v* gêner, tracasser; *n* tracas *m*

bottle (*bo*-teul) *n* bouteille *f*; ~ **opener** ouvre-bouteilles *m*; **hotwater** ~ bouillotte *f*

bottleneck (*bo*-teul-nèk) *n* goulot d'étranglement

bottom (*bo*-teumm) *n* fond *m*; postérieur *m*, derrière *m*; *adj* inférieur

bought (boot) *v* (p, pp buy)

boulder (*bôoul*-deu) *n* rocher *m*

bound (baound) *n* limite *f*; ***be ~ to** *devoir; ~ **for** en route pour

boundary (*baoun*-deu-ri) *n* limite *f*;

frontière f

bouquet (bou-*kéí*) n bouquet m

bourgeois (*boueu*-j^{ou}ââ) adj bourgeois

boutique (bou-*tiik*) n boutique f

bow[1] (baou) v courber

bow[2] (bô^{ou}) n arc m; ~ **tie** nœud papillon

bowels (baou^{eu}lz) pl intestins

bowl (bô^{ou}l) n bol m

bowling (*bôou*-linng) n bowling m; ~ **alley** bowling m

box[1] (boks) v boxer; **boxing match** match de boxe

box[2] (boks) n boîte f

box office (boks-o-fiss) n guichet de location, guichet m

boy (boï) n garçon m; gamin m, gosse m; serviteur m; ~ **scout** scout m

bra (brââ) n soutien-gorge m

bracelet (*bréïss*-lit) n bracelet m

braces (*bréï*-siz) pl bretelles fpl

brain (bréïn) n cerveau m; intelligence f; ~ **wave** idée lumineuse

brake (bréïk) n frein m; ~ **drum** tambour de frein

branch (brâântch) n branche f; succursale f

brand (brænd) n marque f

brand-new (brænd-*nyoû*) adj flambant neuf

brass (brââss) n laiton m; cuivre m, cuivre jaune; ~ **band** n fanfare f

brave (bréïv) adj courageux, brave

Brazil (breu-*zil*) Brésil m

Brazilian (breu-*zil*-yeunn) adj brésilien; n Brésilien m

breach (briitch) n brèche f

bread (brèd) n pain m; **wholemeal** ~ pain complet

breadth (brèdθ) n largeur f

break (bréïk) n fracture f; pause f

*break (bréïk) v rompre, casser; ~ **down** tomber en panne; analyser

breakdown (*bréïk*-daoun) n panne f

breakfast (*brèk*-feust) n petit déjeuner

breast (brèst) n sein m

breaststroke (*brèst*-strô^{ou}k) n brasse f

breath (brèθ) n souffle m

breathe (briið) v respirer

breathing (*brii*-ðinng) n respiration f

breed (briid) n race f; espèce f

*breed (briid) v élever

breeze (briiz) n brise f

brew (broû) v brasser

brewery (*broû*-eu-ri) n brasserie f

bribe (braïb) v *corrompre

bribery (*braï*-beu-ri) n corruption f

brick (brik) n brique f

bricklayer (*brik*-lé^{eu}) n maçon m

bride (braïd) n fiancée f

bridegroom (*braïd*-ghroûm) n marié m

bridge (bridj) n pont m; bridge m

brief (briif) adj bref

briefcase (*briif*-kéïss) n serviette f

briefs (briifs) pl slip m, caleçon m

bright (braït) adj brillant; malin, intelligent

brighten (*braï*-teunn) v faire briller; éclairer; égayer; v s'éclaircir; s'allumer; s'animer

brilliant (*bril*-yeunnt) adj brillant

brim (brimm) n bord m

*bring (brinng) v apporter; amener; ~ **back** rapporter, ramener; ~ **up** élever; soulever

brisk (brisk) adj vif

Britain (*bri*-teunn) Angleterre f

British (*bri*-tich) adj britannique

Briton (*bri*-teunn) n Britannique m; Anglais m

broad (brood) adj large; vaste, étendu

broadcast (*brood*-kââst) n émission f

*broadcast (*brood*-kââst) v *émettre

brochure (*brôou*-chou^{eu}) n brochure f

broke[1] (brô^{ou}k) v (p break)

broke[2] (brô^{ou}k) adj fauché

broken (*brôou*-keunn) *adj* (pp break) cassé, brisé; en dérangement

broker (*brôou*-keu) *n* courtier *m*

bronchitis (bronng-*kaï*-tiss) *n* bronchite *f*

bronze (bronnz) *n* bronze *m*; *adj* en bronze

brooch (brô^{ou}tch) *n* broche *f*

brook (brouk) *n* ruisseau *m*

broom (broûm) *n* balai *m*

brothel (*bro*-œul) *n* bordel *m*

brother (*bra*-ðeu) *n* frère *m*

brother-in-law (*bra*-ðeu-rinn-loo) *n* (pl brothers-) beau-frère *m*

brought (broot) *v* (p, pp bring)

brown (braoun) *adj* brun

bruise (broûz) *n* bleu *m*, contusion *f*; *v* contusionner

brunette (broû-*nèt*) *n* brunette *f*

brush (brach) *n* brosse *f*; pinceau *m*; *v* lustrer, brosser

brutal (*broû*-teul) *adj* brutal

bubble (*ba*-beul) *n* bulle *f*

buck (bak) *m* mâle; *Am colloquial* dollar *m*; chevalet; *v* ruer; ~ **off** jeter, désarçonner; *colloquial* ~ **up** se remuer; prendre courage; résister à, opposer; remonter le moral à

bucket (*ba*-kit) *n* seau *m*

buckle (*ba*-keul) *n* boucle *f*

bud (bad) *n* bourgeon *m*

buddy (*ba*-di) *n* Am colloquial ami *m*; copain *m*

budget (*ba*-djit) *n* budget *m*

buffet (*bou*-fêï) *n* buffet *m*

bug (bagh) *n* punaise *f*; coléoptère *m*; *nAm* insecte *m*

*build (bild) *v* bâtir

building (*bil*-dinng) *n* construction *f*

bulb (balb) *n* bulbe *m*; oignon *m*; **light** ~ ampoule *f*

Bulgaria (bal-*ghèu*-ri-eu) Bulgarie *f*

Bulgarian (bal-*ghèu*-ri-eunn) *adj* bulgare; *n* Bulgare *m*

bulk (balk) *n* masse *f*; majorité *f*

bulky (*bal*-ki) *adj* volumineux

bull (boul) *n* taureau *m*

bullet (*bou*-lit) *n* balle *f*

bulletin (*bou*-li-tinn) *n* bulletin *m*, communiqué *m*; informations *pl*; *Am* **bulletin board** tableau *m* d'affichage

bullfight (*boul*-faït) *n* corrida *f*

bullring (*boul*-rinng) *n* arène *f*

bump (bammp) *v* cogner; tamponner; frapper; *n* coup *m*

bumper (*bamm*-peu) *n* pare-choc *m*

bumpy (*bamm*-pi) *adj* cahoteux

bun (bann) *n* brioche *f*

bunch (banntch) *n* bouquet *m*; bande *f*

bundle (*bann*-deul) *n* paquet *m*; *v* empaqueter, lier ensemble

bunk (banngk) *n* couchette *f*

buoy (boï) *n* bouée *f*

burden (*beû*-deunn) *n* fardeau *m*

bureau (*byoueu*-rô^{ou}) *n* (pl ~x, ~s) bureau *m*; *nAm* commode *f*

bureaucracy (byou^{eu}-*ro*-kreu-si) *n* bureaucratie *f*

burglar (*beû*-ghleu) *n* cambrioleur *m*, -euse *f*

burgle (*beû*-gheul) *v* cambrioler

burial (*bè*-ri-eul) *n* sépulture *f*, enterrement *m*

burn (beûnn) *n* brûlure *f*

*burn (beûnn) *v* brûler

*burst (beûst) *v* éclater

bury (*bè*-ri) *v* enterrer

bus (bass) *n* autobus *m*

bush (bouch) *n* buisson *m*

business (*biz*-neuss) *n* affaires *fpl*, commerce *m*; entreprise *f*, affaire *f*; occupation *f*; ~ **hours** heures d'ouverture, heures de bureau; ~ **trip** voyage d'affaires; **on** ~ pour affaires

businessman (*biz*-neuss-meunn) *n* (pl -men) homme d'affaires

businesswoman (*biz*-neuss-^{ou}ou-meunn) *n* (pl -women) femme d'affaires

bust (bast) *n* buste *m*

bustle (*ba*-seul) *n* remue-ménage *m*

busy (*bi*-zi) *adj* occupé; animé, affairé

but (bat) *conj* mais; cependant; *prep* sauf

butcher (*bou*-tcheu) *n* boucher *m*

butter (*ba*-teu) *n* beurre *m*

butterfly (*ba*-teu-flaï) *n* papillon *m*; ~ **stroke** brasse papillon

buttock (*ba*-teuk) *n* fesse *f*

button (*ba*-teunn) *n* bouton *m*; *v* boutonner

buttonhole (*ba*-teunn-hô^{ou}l) *n* boutonnière *f*

*buy (baï) *v* acheter; *acquérir

buyer (*baï*-eu) *n* acheteur *m*, -euse *f*

buzz (baz) *n* bourdonnement *m*; *Am* ~ **saw** scie *f* circulaire; *colloquial* **give someone a** ~ donner un coup de fil à quelqu'un; bourdonner

by (baï) *prep* par; en; près de

bye-bye (*baï*-baï) *colloquial* au revoir!; adieu!

by-pass (*baï*-pââss) *n* route d'évitement; *v* contourner

C

cab (kæb) *n* taxi *m*

cabaret (*kæ*-beu-réï) *n* cabaret *m*; boîte de nuit

cabbage (*kæ*-bidj) *n* chou *m*

cab driver (*kæb*-draï-veu) *n* chauffeur de taxi

cabin (*kæ*-binn) *n* cabine *f*; cabane *f*

cabinet (*kæ*-bi-neut) *n* cabinet *m*

cable (*kéï*-beul) *n* câble *m*; télégramme *m*

café (*kæ*-féï) *n* café *m*

cafeteria (kæ-feu-*tieu*-ri-eu) *n* cafétéria *f*

caffeine (*kæ*-fiin) *n* caféine *f*

cage (kéïdj) *n* cage *f*

cake (kéïk) *n* gâteau *m*; pâtisserie *f*

calamity (keu-*læ*-meu-ti) *n* calamité *f*, catastrophe *f*

calcium (*kæl*-si-eumm) *n* calcium *m*

calculate (*kæl*-kyou-léït) *v* calculer

calculation (kæl-kyou-*léï*-cheunn) *n* calcul *m*

calculator (*kæl*-kyou-léï-teu) *n* calculatrice *f*

calendar (*kæ*-leunn-deu) *n* calendrier *m*

calf (kââf) *n* (pl calves) veau *m*; mollet *m*; ~ **skin** veau *m*

call (kool) *v* appeler; téléphoner; *n* appel *m*; visite *f*; coup de téléphone; ***be called** s'appeler; ~ **names** injurier; ~ **on** rendre visite à; ~ **up** *Am* téléphoner

calm (kââm) *adj* tranquille, calme; ~ **down** calmer

calorie (*kæ*-leu-ri) *n* calorie *f*

came (kéïm) *v* (p come)

camel (*kæ*-meul) *n* chameau *m*

camera (*kæ*-meu-reu) *n* appareil photographique; caméra *f*; ~ **shop** magasin de photographe

camp (kæmp) *n* camp *m*; *v* camper; ~ **bed** lit de camp

campaign (kæm-*péïn*) *n* campagne *f*

camper (*kæm*-peu) *n* campeur *m*

camping (*kæm*-pinng) *n* camping *m*; ~ **site** terrain de camping

can (kæn) *n* boîte *f*; ~ **opener**

can **194**

ouvreboîte *m*; **canned food** conserves *fpl*

*can (kæn) *v* *pouvoir

Canada (*kæ*-neu-deu) Canada *m*

Canadian (keu-*néï*-di-eunn) *adj* canadien; *n* Canadien *m*

canal (keu-*næl*) *n* canal *m*

canary (keu-*nèeu*-ri) *n* canari *m*

cancel (*kæn*-seul) *v* annuler

cancellation (kæn-seu-*léï*-cheunn) *n* annulation *f*

cancer (*kæn*-seu) *n* cancer *m*

candidate (*kæn*-di-deut) *n* candidat *m*

candle (*kæn*-deul) *n* bougie *f*

candy (*kæn*-di) *nAm* bonbon *m*; confiserie *f*; **~ store** *Am* confiserie *f*

cane (kéïn) *n* canne *f*

canister (*kæ*-ni-steu) *n* boîte métallique

canoe (keu-*noû*) *n* canot *m*

canteen (kæn-*tiin*) *n* cantine *f*

canvas (*kæn*-veuss) *n* grosse toile

cap (kæp) *n* casquette *f*

capable (*kéï*-peu-beul) *adj* capable

capacity (keu-*pæ*-seu-ti) *n* capacité *f*; compétence *f*

cape (kéïp) *n* cape *f*; cap *m*

capital (*kæ*-pi-teul) *n* capitale *f*; capital *m*; *adj* capital, essentiel; **~ letter** majuscule *f*

capitalism (*kæ*-pi-teu-li-zeumm) *n* capitalisme *m*

capitulation (keu-pi-tyou-*léï*-cheunn) *n* capitulation *f*

capsule (*kæp*-syoûl) *n* capsule *f*

captain (*kæp*-tinn) *n* capitaine *m*; commandant *m*

capture (*kæp*-tcheu) *v* *faire prisonnier, capturer; *prendre; *n* capture *f*; prise *f*

car (kââ) *n* voiture *f*; **~ hire** location de voitures; **~ park** parc de stationnement; **~ rental** *Am* location de voitures

caramel (*kæ*-reu-meul) *n* caramel *m*

caravan (*kæ*-reu-væn) *n* caravane *f*; roulotte *f*

carburettor (kââ-byou-*rè*-teu) *n* carburateur *m*

card (kââd) *n* carte *f*; carte postale

cardboard (*kââd*-bood) *n* carton *m*; *adj* en carton

cardigan (*kââ*-di-gheunn) *n* cardigan *m*

cardinal (*kââ*-di-neul) *n* cardinal *m*; *adj* cardinal, principal

care (kèᵉᵘ) *n* soin *m*; souci *m*; **~ about** se soucier de; **~ for** *tenir à; ***take ~ of** *prendre soin de, s'occuper de

career (keu-*rieu*) *n* carrière *f*

carefree (*kèeu*-frii) *adj* insouciant

careful (*kèeu*-feul) *adj* prudent; soigneux, attentif

careless (*kèeu*-leuss) *adj* inattentif, négligent

caretaker (*kèeu*-téï-keu) *n* gardien *m*

cargo (*kââ*-ghôᵘ) *n* (pl ~es) chargement *m*, cargaison *f*

carnival (*kââ*-ni-veul) *n* carnaval *m*

carp (kââp) *n* (pl ~) carpe *f*

carpenter (*kââ*-pinn-teu) *n* menuisier *m*

carpet (*kââ*-pit) *n* tapis *m*

carriage (*kæ*-ridj) *n* wagon *m*; carrosse *m*, voiture *f*

carrot (*kæ*-reut) *n* carotte *f*

carry (*kæ*-ri) *v* porter; *conduire; **~ on** continuer; *poursuivre; **~ out** réaliser

carrycot (*kæ*-ri-kot) *n* berceau de voyage

cart (kâât) *n* charrette *f*

cartilage (*kââ*-ti-lidj) *n* cartilage *m*

carton (*kââ*-teunn) *n* carton *m*; cartouche *f*

cartoon (kââ-*toûn*) *n* dessins animés

cartridge (*kââ*-tridj) *n* cartouche *f*

carve (kââv) *v* découper; entailler, tailler

carving (*kââ*-vinng) *n* gravure *f*

case (kéïss) *n* cas *m*; affaire *f*; valise *f*; étui *m*; **in ~** au cas où; **in ~ of** en cas de

cash (kæch) *n* argent liquide, argent comptant; *v* toucher, encaisser; **~ dispenser** distributeur automatique *m*

cashier (kæ-*chieu*) *n* caissier *m*, caissière *f*

cashmere (*kæch*-mi^eu) *n* cachemire *m*

casino (keu-*sii*-nô^ou) *n* (pl ~s) casino *m*

cask (kââsk) *n* baril *m*, tonneau *m*

cassette (kæ-*sèt*) *n* cassette *f*; **~ player** lecteur *m* de cassettes; **~ recorder** magnétophone *m* à cassettes

cast (kââst) *n* jet *m*

***cast** (kââst) *v* lancer, jeter; **cast iron** fonte *f*

castle (*kââ*-seul) *n* château *m*

casual (*kæ*-jou-eul) *adj* sans façons; fait en passant, fortuit

casualty (*kæ*-jou-eul-ti) *n* victime *f*

cat (kæt) *n* chat *m*

catacomb (*kæ*-teu-kô^ou m) *n* catacombe *f*

catalogue (*kæ*-teu-logh) *n* catalogue *m*

catarrh (keu-*tââ*) *n* catarrhe *m*

catastrophe (keu-*tæ*-streu-fi) *n* sinistre *m*

***catch** (kætch) *v* attraper; saisir; *surprendre; *prendre

category (*kæ*-ti-gheu-ri) *n* catégorie *f*

cathedral (keu-*θii*-dreul) *n* cathédrale *f*

catholic (*kæ*-θeu-lik) *adj* catholique

cattle (*kæ*-teul) *pl* bétail *m*

caught (koot) *v* (p, pp catch)

cauliflower (*ko*-li-flaou^eu) *n* chou-fleur

cause (kooz) *v* causer; provoquer; *n* cause *f*; raison *f*, motif *m*; **~ to** *faire

causeway (*kooz*-^ou éï) *n* chaussée *f*

caution (*koo*-cheunn) *n* prudence *f*; *v* avertir

cautious (*koo*-cheuss) *adj* prudent

cave (kéïv) *n* grotte *f*

cavern (*kæ*-veunn) *n* caverne *f*

caviar (*kæ*-vi-ââ) *n* caviar *m*

cavity (*kæ*-veu-ti) *n* cavité *f*

cd (sii-*dii*) *n* cd *m*; **~ player** lecteur de cd

cease (siiss) *v* cesser

cease-fire (*siiss*-faï^eu) *n* cessez-le-feu *m*

ceiling (*sii*-linng) *n* plafond *m*

celebrate (*sè*-li-bréït) *v* célébrer

celebration (sè-li-*bréï*-cheunn) *n* célébration *f*

celebrity (si-*lè*-breu-ti) *n* célébrité *f*

celery (*sè*-leu-ri) *n* céleri *m*

cell (sèl) *n* cellule *f*

cellar (*sè*-leu) *n* cave *f*

cell phone (sèl-fô^ou n) *n* (téléphone) portable

cement (si-*mènt*) *n* ciment *m*

cemetery (*sè*-mi-tri) *n* cimetière *m*

censorship (*sèn*-seu-chip) *n* censure *f*

center (*sèn*-teu) *n* centre *m*

centigrade (*sèn*-ti-ghréïd) *adj* centigrade

centimetre, *Am* **centimeter** (*sèn*-ti-mii-teu) *n* centimètre *m*

central (*sèn*-treul) *adj* central; **~ heating** chauffage central; **~ station** gare centrale

centralize (*sèn*-treu-laïz) *v* centraliser

centre (*sèn*-teu) *n* centre *m*

century (*sèn*-tcheu-ri) *n* siècle *m*

ceramics (si-*ræ*-miks) *pl* céramique *f*

ceremony (*sè*-reu-meu-ni) *n* cérémonie *f*

certain (*seû*-teunn) *adj* certain

certificate (seu-*ti*-fi-keut) *n* certificat *m*; attestation *f*, document *m*, diplôme *m*

chain (tchéïn) n chaîne f
chair (tchè^eu) n chaise f; siège m
chairman (tchèeu-meunn) n (pl -men)
président m
chalet (chæ-léï) n chalet m
chalk (tchook) n craie f
challenge (tchæ-leunndj) v défier; n
défi m
chamber (tchéïm-beu) n pièce f
champagne (chæm-péïn) n
champagne f
champion (tchæm-pyeunn) n
champion m, -ne f; défenseur m
chance (tchâânss) n hasard m; chance
f, occasion f; risque m; **by ~** par
hasard
change (tchéïndj) v modifier,
changer; se changer; n modification f,
changement m; petite monnaie,
change m
channel (tchæ-neul) n canal m;
English Channel La Manche
chaos (kéï-oss) n chaos m
chaotic (kéï-o-tik) adj chaotique
chap (tchæp) n type m
chapel (tchæ-peul) n église f, chapelle
f
chaplain (tchæ-plinn) n chapelain m
character (kæ-reuk-teu) n caractère
m
characteristic (kæ-reuk-teu-ri-stik)
adj caractéristique; n caractéristique
f; trait de caractère
characterize (kæ-reuk-teu-raïz) v
caractériser
charcoal (tchââ-kô^oul) n charbon de
bois
charge (tchââdj) v demander;
charger; accuser; n prix m; charge f,
chargement m; accusation f, **~ card**
Am carte de crédit; **free of ~** à titre
gracieux; **in ~ of** chargé de; ***take ~ of**
se charger de
charity (tchæ-reu-ti) n charité f

charm (tchââm) n attraits, charme m;
amulette f
charming (tchââ-minng) adj séduisant
chart (tchâât) n tableau m; graphique
m; carte marine; **conversion ~**
tableau de conversions
chase (tchéïss) v pourchasser;
poursuivre, chasser; n chasse f
chasm (kæ-zeumm) n gouffre m,
abîme m
chassis (chæ-si) n (pl ~) châssis m
chaste (tchéïst) adj chaste
chat (tchæt) v bavarder, causer; n
causette f, bavardage m
chatterbox (tchæ-teu-boks) n moulin
à paroles
cheap (tchiip) adj bon marché;
avantageux
cheat (tchiit) v tricher; duper
check (tchèk) v contrôler, vérifier; n
damier m; nAm note f; chèque m;
check! échec!; **~ in** s'*inscrire; **~ out**
*partir
checkbook (tchèk-bouk) nAm carnet
de chèques
checkerboard (tchè-keu-bood) nAm
échiquier m
checkers (tchè-keuz) plAm jeu de
dames
checkroom (tchèk-roûm) nAm
vestiaire m
checkup (tchè-kap) n examen m
cheek (tchiik) n joue f
cheeky (tchii-ki) adj colloquial
insolent, effronté
cheer (tchi^eu) v acclamer; **~ up** égayer
cheerful (tchieu-feul) adj joyeux, gai
cheese (tchiiz) n fromage m
chef (chèf) n chef cuisinier
chemical (kè-mi-keul) adj chimique
chemist (kè-mist) n pharmacien m,
pharmacienne f; **chemist's**
pharmacie f
chemistry (kè-mi-stri) n chimie f

cheque (tchèk) n chèque m

chequebook (tchèk-bouk) n carnet de chèques

chequered (tchè-keud) adj à carreaux, à damiers

cherry (tchè-ri) n cerise f

chess (tchèss) n échecs

chest (tchèst) n poitrine f; coffre m; ~ **of drawers** commode f

chestnut (tchèss-nat) n marron m

chew (tchoú) v mâcher

chewing gum (tchoú-inng-ghamm) n chewing gum m

chicken (tchi-kinn) n poulet m

chickenpox (tchi-kinn-poks) n varicelle f

chief (tchiif) n chef m; adj principal

chieftain (tchiif-teunn) n chef m

child (tchaïld) n (pl children) enfant m

childbirth (tchaïld-beûθ) n accouchement m

childhood (tchaïld-houd) n enfance f

Chile (tchi-li) Chili m

Chilean (tchi-li-eunn) adj chilien; n Chilien m

chill (tchil) n frisson m

chilly (tchi-li) adj frais

chimes (tchaïmz) pl carillon m

chimney (tchimm-ni) n cheminée f

chin (tchinn) n menton m

China (tchaï-neu) Chine f

china (tchaï-neu) n porcelaine f

Chinese (tchaï-niiz) adj chinois; n Chinois m

chip (tchip) n éclat m; jeton m; v tailler, ébrécher; **chips** pommes frites

chives (tchaïvz) pl ciboulette f

chlorine (kloo-riin) n chlore m

chock-full (tchok-foul) adj plein à craquer, bourré

chocolate (tcho-kleut) n chocolat m; praline f

choice (tchoïss) n choix m; sélection f

choir (k^ou aï^eu) n chœur m

choke (tchô^ou k) v étrangler, étouffer; n starter m

*choose (tchoûz) v choisir

chop (tchop) n côte f, côtelette f; v hacher

christen (kri-seunn) v baptiser

christening (kri-seu-ninng) n baptême m

Christian (kriss-tcheunn) adj chrétien; ~ **name** prénom m

Christmas (kriss-meuss) Noël m

chronic (kro-nik) adj chronique

chronological (kro-neu-lo-dji-keul) adj chronologique

chuckle (tcha-keul) v glousser

chunk (tchanngk) n gros morceau

church (tcheûtch) n église f

churchyard (tcheûtch-yââd) n cimetière m

cigar (si-ghââ) n cigare m; ~ **shop** bureau de tabac

cigarette (si-gheu-rèt) n cigarette f; ~ **case** étui à cigarettes; ~ **lighter** briquet m

cinema (si-neu-meu) n cinéma m

cinnamon (si-neu-meunn) n cannelle f

circle (seû-keul) n cercle m; balcon m; v encercler, entourer

circulation (seû-kyou-léï-cheunn) n circulation f

circumstance (seû-keumm-stæns) n circonstance f

circus (seû-keuss) n cirque m

citizen (si-ti-zeunn) n citoyen m, -ne f

citizenship (si-ti-zeunn-chip) n citoyenneté f

city (si-ti) n cité f

civic (si-vik) adj civique

civil (si-veul) adj civil; poli; ~ **law** droit civil; ~ **servant** fonctionnaire m

civilian (si-vil-yeunn) adj civil; n civil m

civilization (si-veu-laï-*zéï*-cheunn) *n* civilisation *f*

civilized (*si*-veu-laïzd) *adj* civilisé

claim (kléïm) *v* revendiquer, réclamer; prétendre; *n* revendication *f*, prétention *f*

clamp (klæmp) *n* mordache *f*; crampon *m*

clap (klæp) *v* applaudir

clarify (*klæ*-ri-faï) *v* éclaircir, clarifier

class (klââss) *n* classe *f*

classical (*klæ*-si-keul) *adj* classique

classify (*klæ*-si-faï) *v* classer

classmate (*klâââss*-méït) *n* camarade de classe

classroom (*klâââss*-roûm) *n* salle de classe

claw (kloo) *n* griffe *f*

clay (kléï) *n* argile *f*

clean (kliin) *adj* pur, propre; *v* nettoyer

cleaning (*klii*-ninng) *n* nettoyage *m*; ~ **fluid** détachant *m*

clear (kli^{eu}) *adj* clair; *v* nettoyer

clearing (*klieu*-rinng) *n* clairière *f*

cleft (klèft) *n* fente *f*

clergyman (*kleû*-dji-meunn) *n* (pl -men) pasteur *m*; ecclésiastique *m*

clerk (klââk) *n* employé(e) de bureau; greffier *m*; secrétaire *m/f*

clever (klè-veu) *adj* intelligent; astucieux, éveillé

click (klik) *n* cliquetis *m*, bruit *m* sec; cliquet *m*; déclic *m*; *v* cliqueter; faire un déclic; *colloquial* become clear; ~ **with** plaire à

client (*klaï*-eunnt) *n* client *m*, -e *f*

cliff (klif) *n* falaise *f*

climate (*klaï*-mit) *n* climat *m*

climb (klaïm) *v* grimper; *n* ascension *f*

cling (klinng) *v* s'accrocher, se cramponner; adhérer (**to** à)

clinic (*kli*-nik) *n* clinique *f*

cloak (klô^{ou}k) *n* manteau *m*

cloakroom (*klôouk*-roûm) *n* vestiaire *m*

clock (klok) *n* horloge *f*; **at ... o'clock** à ... heures

cloister (*kloï*-steu) *n* cloître *m*

close[1] (klô^{ou}z) *v* fermer; **closed** *adj* fermé, clos

close[2] (klô^{ou}ss) *adj* proche

closet (*klo*-zit) *n* placard *m*; *nAm* garde-robe *f*

cloth (kloθ) *n* tissu *m*; chiffon *m*

clothes (klô^{ou}ðz) *pl* habits *mpl*, vêtements *mpl*

clothing (*klôou*-ðinng) *n* habillement *m*

cloud (klaoud) *n* nuage *m*

cloudy (*klaou*-di) *adj* nuageux

clover (*klôou*-veu) *n* trèfle *m*

clown (klaoun) *n* clown *m*

club (klab) *n* club *m*; cercle *m*, association *f*; gourdin *m*, massue *f*

clumsy (*klamm*-zi) *adj* maladroit

clutch (klatch) *n* embrayage *m*; prise *f*

coach (kô^{ou}tch) *n* car *m*; wagon *m*; carrosse *m*; entraîneur *m*

coal (kô^{ou}l) *n* charbon *m*

coarse (kooss) *adj* grossier

coast (kô^{ou}st) *n* côte *f*

coat (kô^{ou}t) *n* pardessus *m*, manteau *m*; ~ **hanger** cintre *m*

cocaine (kô^{ou}-*kéïn*) *n* cocaïne *f*

cock (kok) *n* coq *m*

cocktail (*kok*-téïl) *n* cocktail *m*

coconut (*kôou*-keu-nat) *n* noix de coco

cod (kod) *n* (pl ~) morue *f*

code (kô^{ou}d) *n* code *m*

coffee (*ko*-fi) *n* café *m*

coherence (kô^{ou}-*hieu*-reunns) *n* cohérence *f*

coin (koïn) *n* pièce de monnaie

coincide (kô^{ou}-inn-*saïd*) *v* coïncider

cold (kô^{ou}ld) *adj* froid; *n* froid *m*; rhume *m*; **catch a ~** s'enrhumer

collaborate (keu-*læ*-beu-réït) *v*

collaborer

collapse (keu-*læps*) *v* s'effondrer, s'écrouler

collar (*ko*-leu) *n* collier *m*; col *m*; ~ **stud** bouton de col

collarbone (*ko*-leu-bô^{ou}n) *n* clavicule *f*

colleague (*ko*-liigh) *n* collègue *m*

collect (keu-*lèkt*) *v* rassembler; *prendre; *aller chercher; quêter

collection (keu-*lèk*-cheunn) *n* collection *f*; levée *f*

collective (keu-*lèk*-tiv) *adj* collectif

collector (keu-*lèk*-teu) *n* collectionneur

college (*ko*-lidj) *n* collège *m*

collide (keu-*laïd*) *v* entrer en collision

collision (keu-*li*-jeunn) *n* collision *f*; abordage *m*

colloquial (keu-*lô^{ou}*-k^{ou}i-eul) *adj* familier

Colombia (keu-*lomm*-bi-eu) Colombie *f*

Colombian (keu-*lomm*-bi-eunn) *adj* colombien; *n* Colombien *m*

colonel (*keû*-neul) *n* colonel *m*

colony (*ko*-leu-ni) *n* colonie *f*

colo(u)r (*ka*-leu) *n* couleur *f*; *v* colorer; ~ **film** film en couleurs

colo(u)r-blind (*ka*-leu-blaïnd) *adj* daltonien

colo(u)red (*ka*-leud) *adj* de couleur

colo(u)rful (*ka*-leu-feul) *adj* coloré

column (*ko*-leumm) *n* colonne *f*; rubrique *f*

coma (*kôou*-meu) *n* coma *m*

comb (kô^{ou}m) *v* peigner; *n* peigne *m*

combat (*komm*-bæt) *n* lutte *f*, combat *m*; *v* *combattre, lutter

combination (komm-bi-*néï*-cheunn) *n* combinaison *f*

combine (keumm-*baïn*) *v* combiner

*come (kamm) *v* *venir; ~ **across** rencontrer; trouver

comedian (keu-*mii*-di-eunn) *n* comédien *m*, -ne *f*; comique *m*

comedy (*ko*-meu-di) *n* comédie *f*; **musical** ~ comédie musicale

comfort (*kamm*-feut) *n* bien-être *m*, commodité *f*, confort *m*; réconfort *m*; *v* consoler

comfortable (*kamm*-feu-teu-beul) *adj* confortable

comic (*ko*-mik) *adj* comique

comics (*ko*-miks) *pl* bandes dessinées

coming (*ka*-minng) *n* arrivée *f*

comma (*ko*-meu) *n* virgule *f*

command (keu-*mâând*) *v* commander; *n* ordre *m*

commander (keu-*mâân*-deu) *n* commandant *m*

commemoration (keu-mè-meu-*réï*-cheunn) *n* commémoration *f*

commence (keu-*mèns*) *v* commencer

comment (*ko*-mènt) *n* commentaire *m*; *v* commenter

commerce (*ko*-meûss) *n* commerce *m*

commercial (keu-*meû*-cheul) *adj* commercial; *n* annonce publicitaire; ~ **law** droit commercial

commission (keu-*mi*-cheunn) *n* commission *f*

commit (keu-*mit*) *v* *remettre, confier; *commettre

committee (keu-*mi*-ti) *n* commission *f*, comité *m*

common (*ko*-meunn) *adj* commun; habituel; ordinaire

communicate (keu-*myoû*-ni-kéït) *v* communiquer

communication (keu-myoû-ni-*kêï*-cheunn) *n* communication *f*

communism (*ko*-myou-ni-zeumm) *n* communisme *m*

community (keu-*myoû*-neu-ti) *n* société *f*, communauté *f*

commuter (keu-*myoû*-teu) *n* navetteur *m*

compact (*komm*-pækt) *adj* compact

compact disc (*komm*-pækt disk) *n* compact disc *m*; **~ player** lecteur de compact disc *m*

companion (keumm-*pæ*-nyeunn) *n* compagnon *m*, compagne *f*

company (*kamm*-peu-ni) *n* compagnie *f*; entreprise *f*, société *f*

comparative (keumm-*pæ*-reu-tiv) *adj* relatif

compare (keumm-*pèeu*) *v* comparer

comparison (keumm-*pæ*-ri-seunn) *n* comparaison *f*

compartment (keumm-*pâât*-meunnt) *n* compartiment *m*

compass (*kamm*-peuss) *n* boussole *f*

compel (keumm-*pèl*) *v* *contraindre

compensate (*komm*-peunn-séït) *v* compenser

compensation (komm-peunn-*séï*-cheunn) *n* compensation *f*; indemnité *f*

compete (keumm-*piit*) *v* *concourir

competition (komm-peu-*ti*-cheunn) *n* compétition *f*

competitor (keumm-*pè*-ti-teur) *n* concurrent *m*

compile (keumm-*päïl*) *v* compiler

complain (keumm-*plêïn*) *v* se *plaindre

complaint (keumm-*plêïnt*) *n* plainte *f*; **complaints book** cahier de doléances

complete (keumm-*pliit*) *adj* entier, complet; *v* achever

completely (keumm-*pliit*-li) *adv* entièrement, totalement, complètement

complex (*komm*-plèks) *n* complexe *m*; *adj* complexe

complexion (keumm-*plèk*-cheunn) *n* teint *m*

complicated (*komm*-pli-kéï-tid) *adj* compliqué

compliment (*komm*-pli-meunnt) *n* compliment *m*; *v* complimenter, féliciter

compose (keumm-*pôouz*) *v* composer

composer (keumm-*pôou*-zeu) *n* compositeur *m*, -trice *f*

comprehensive (komm-pri-*hèn*-siv) *adj* étendu

comprise (keumm-*praïz*) *v* *comprendre, *inclure

compromise (*komm*-preu-maïz) *n* compromis *m*

compulsory (keumm-*pal*-seu-ri) *adj* obligatoire

computer (komm-*pyou*-teu) *n* ordinateur *m*; **lap-top ~** ordinateur portable

comrade (*komm*-réïd) *n* camarade *m*

conceal (keunn-*siil*) *v* dissimuler

conceited (keunn-*sii*-tid) *adj* prétentieux

conceive (keunn-*siiv*) *v* *concevoir

concentrate (*konn*-seunn-tréït) *v* concentrer

concentration (konn-seunn-*tréï*-cheunn) *n* concentration *f*

conception (keunn-*sèp*-cheunn) *n* conception *f*

concern (keunn-*seûnn*) *v* regarder, concerner; *n* souci *m*; affaire *f*

concerned (keunn-*seûnnd*) *adj* soucieux; concerné

concerning (keunn-*seû*-ninng) *prep* relatif à, concernant

concert (*konn*-seut) *n* concert *m*; **~ hall** salle de concert

concession (keunn-*sè*-cheunn) *n* concession *f*

concierge (kon-si-*èeuj*) *n* concierge *m*

concise (keunn-*saïss*) *adj* concis

conclusion (keunng-*kloû*-jeunn) *n* conclusion *f*

concrete (*konng*-kriit) *adj* concret; *n*

béton *m*

concussion (keunng-*ka*-cheunn) *n*
commotion cérébrale

condition (keunn-*di*-cheunn) *n*
condition *f*; état *m*/*f*; circonstance *f*

condom (*konn*-dom) *n* préservatif *m*

conduct[1] (*konn*-dakt) *n* conduite *f*

conduct[2] (keunn-*dakt*) *v* *conduire;
diriger

conductor (keunn-*dak*-teu) *n*
conducteur *m*, -trice *f*; chef
d'orchestre

confectioner (keunn-*fèk*-cheu-neu) *n*
confiseur *m*, -seuse *f*

conference (*konn*-feu-reunns) *n*
conférence *f*

confess (keunn-*fèss*) *v* *reconnaître;
confesser; professer

confession (keunn-*fè*-cheunn) *n*
confession *f*

confidence (*konn*-fi-deunns) *n*
confiance *f*

confident (*konn*-fi-deunnt) *adj*
confiant

confidential (konn-fi-*dèn*-cheul) *adj*
confidentiel

confirm (keunn-*feûmm*) *v* confirmer

confirmation (konn-feu-*mëï*-cheunn)
n confirmation *f*

confiscate (*konn*-fi-skéït) *v*
confisquer

conflict (*konn*-flikt) *n* conflit *m*

confuse (keunn-*fyoûz*) *v* confondre;
confused *adj* confus

confusion (keunn-*fyoû*-jeunn) *n*
confusion *f*

congratulate (keunng-*ghræ*-tchou-
léït) *v* congratuler, féliciter

congratulations (keunng-ghræ-
tchou-*léï*-cheunnz) *n* félicitations *fpl*

congregation (konng-ghri-*ghéï*-
cheunn) *n* congrégation *f*

congress (*konng*-ghrèss) *n* congrès *m*

connect (keu-*nèkt*) *v* *joindre;

*mettre en communication; brancher

connection (keu-*nèk*-cheunn) *n*
relation *f*; rapport *m*; communication
f, correspondance *f*

connoisseur (ko-neu-*seû*) *n*
connaisseur *m*

connotation (ko-neu-*tëï*-cheunn) *n*
connotation *f*

conquer (*konng*-keu) *v* *conquérir;
*vaincre

conqueror (*konng*-keu-reu) *n*
conquérant *m*

conquest (*konng*-k^{ou}èst) *n* conquête *f*

conscience (*konn*-cheunns) *n*
conscience *f*

conscious (*konn*-cheuss) *adj*
conscient

consciousness (*konn*-cheuss-neuss)
n conscience *f*

conscript (*konn*-skript) *n* conscrit *m*

consent (keunn-*sènt*) *v* *consentir;
approuver; *n* assentiment *m*,
consentement *m*

consequence (*konn*-si-k^{ou}eunns) *n*
effet *m*, conséquence *f*

consequently (*konn*-si-k^{ou}eunnt-li)
adv par conséquent

conservative (keunn-*seû*-veu-tiv) *adj*
conservateur

consider (keunn-*si*-deu) *v* considérer;
envisager; trouver, estimer

considerable (keunn-*si*-deu-reu-
beul) *adj* considérable; important,
sensible

considerate (keunn-*si*-deu-reut) *adj*
prévenant

consideration (keunn-si-deu-*rëï*-
cheunn) *n* considération *f*; égards
mpl, attention *f*

considering (keunn-*si*-deu-rinng)
prep vu

consignment (keunn-*saïn*-meunnt) *n*
expédition *f*

consist (keunn-*sist*) *v* ~ **in** consister

en; consister à; **~ of** se composer de

conspire (keunn-*spaïeu*) v conspirer

constant (*konn*-steunnt) adj constant

constipation (konn-sti-*péi*-cheunn) n constipation f

constituency (keunn-*sti*-tchou-eunn-si) n circonscription électorale

constitution (konn-sti-*tyoû*-cheunn) n constitution f

construct (keunn-*strakt*) v *construire; bâtir, édifier

construction (keunn-*strak*-cheunn) n construction f; édification f; édifice m

consulate (*konn*-syou-leut) n consulat m

consult (keunn-*salt*) v consulter

consultation (konn-seul-*téï*-cheunn) n consultation f; **~ hours** n heures de consultation

consume (keunn-*syoûm*) v consommer; consumer

consumer (keunn-*syoû*-meu) n utilisateur m, consommateur m, -trice f

contact (*konn*-tækt) n contact m; v contacter; **~ lenses** verres de contact

contagious (keunn-*téï*-djeuss) adj contagieux

contain (keunn-*téïn*) v *contenir; *comprendre

container (keunn-*téï*-neu) n récipient m; conteneur m

contemporary (keunn-*tèm*-peu-reu-ri) adj contemporain; de l'époque; n contemporain m

contempt (keunn-*tèmpt*) n dédain m, mépris m

content (keunn-*tènt*) adj satisfait

contents (*konn*-tènts) pl contenu m

contest (*konn*-tèst) n combat m; concours m

continent (*konn*-ti-neunnt) n continent m

continental (konn-ti-*nèn*-teul) adj continental

continual (keunn-*ti*-nyou-eul) adj continuel

continue (keunn-*ti*-nyoû) v continuer; *poursuivre, durer

continuous (keunn-*ti*-nyou-euss) adj continuel, continu, ininterrompu

contour (*konn*-tou^{eu}) n contour m

contraceptive (konn-treu-*sèp*-tiv) n contraceptif m

contract[1] (*konn*-trækt) n contrat m

contract[2] (keunn-*trækt*) v attraper

contractor (keunn-*træk*-teu) n entrepreneur m

contradict (konn-treu-*dikt*) v *contredire

contradictory (konn-treu-*dik*-teu-ri) adj contradictoire

contrary (*konn*-treu-ri) n contraire m; adj opposé; **on the ~** au contraire

contrast (*konn*-trââst) n contraste m; différence f

contribution (konn-tri-*byoû*-cheunn) n contribution f

control (keunn-*trôoul*) n contrôle m; v contrôler

controversial (konn-treu-*veû*-cheul) adj discuté, controversé

convenience (keunn-*vii*-nyeunns) n commodité f

convenient (keunn-*vii*-nyeunnt) adj pratique; approprié, qui convient, commode

convent (*konn*-veunnt) n couvent m

conversation (konn-veu-*séï*-cheunn) n entretien m, conversation f

convert (keunn-*veût*) v convertir

convict[1] (keunn-*vikt*) v déclarer coupable

convict[2] (*konn*-vikt) n condamné m

conviction (keunn-*vik*-cheunn) n conviction f; condamnation f

convince (keunn-*vinns*) v

*convaincre

convulsion (keunn-*val*-cheunn) *n* convulsion *f*

cook (kouk) *n* cuisinier *m*; *v* *cuire; préparer

cookbook (*kouk*-bouk) *nAm* livre de cuisine

cooker (*kou*-keu) *n* cuisinière *f*; **gas ~** cuisinière à gaz

cookery book (*kou*-keu-ri-bouk) *n* livre de cuisine

cookie (*kou*-ki) *nAm* biscuit *m*

cool (koûl) *adj* frais

cooperation (kô^{ou}-o-peu-*réï*-cheunn) *n* coopération *f*; collaboration *f*

cooperative (kô^{ou}-o-peu-reu-tiv) *adj* coopératif; coopérant; *n* coopérative *f*

coordinate (kô^{ou}-*oo*-di-néït) *v* coordonner

coordination (kô^{ou}-oo-di-*néï*-cheunn) *n* coordination *f*

cope (kô^{ou}p) *v* se débrouiller, s'en tirer, *colloquial* se défendre; **~ with** tenir tête à, faire face à; s'occuper de; venir à bout de

copper (*ko*-peu) *n* cuivre *m*

copy (*ko*-pi) *n* copie *f*; exemplaire *m*; *v* copier; imiter; **carbon ~** copie *f*

coral (*ko*-reul) *n* corail *m*

cord (kood) *n* corde *f*; cordon *m*

cordial (*koo*-di-eul) *adj* cordial

corduroy (*koo*-deu-roï) *n* velours côtelé

core (koo) *n* cœur *m*; trognon *m*

cork (kook) *n* bouchon *m*

corkscrew (*kook*-skroû) *n* tire-bouchon *m*

corn (koon) *n* grain *m*; céréale *f*, blé *m*; durillon *m*, cor au pied; **~ on the cob** maïs en épi

corner (*koo*-neu) *n* coin *m*

cornfield (*koon*-fiild) *n* champ de blé

corpse (koops) *n* cadavre *m*

corpulent (*koo*-pyou-leunnt) *adj* corpulent; gros, obèse

correct (keu-*rèkt*) *adj* juste, correct; *v* corriger

correction (keu-*rèk*-cheunn) *n* correction *f*; rectification *f*

correctness (keu-*rèkt*-neuss) *n* exactitude *f*

correspond (ko-ri-*sponnd*) *v* correspondre; *être conforme

correspondence (ko-ri-*sponn*-deunns) *n* correspondance *f*

correspondent (ko-ri-*sponn*-deunnt) *n* correspondant *m*, -e *f*

corridor (*ko*-ri-doo) *n* corridor *m*

corrupt (keu-*rapt*) *adj* corrompu; *v* *corrompre

corruption (keu-*rap*-cheunn) *n* corruption *f*

corset (*koo*-sit) *n* corset *m*

cosmetics (koz-*mè*-tiks) *pl* cosmétiques *mpl*, produits de beauté

cost (kost) *n* coût *m*; prix *m*

*cost (kost) *v* coûter

cosy (*kôou*-zi) *adj* intime, confortable

cot (kot) *nAm* lit de camp

cottage (*ko*-tidj) *n* villa *f*

cotton (*ko*-teunn) *n* coton *m*; en coton; **~ wool** ouate *f*

couch (kaoutch) *n* canapé *m*

cough (kof) *n* toux *f*; *v* tousser

could (koud) *v* (p can)

council (*kaoun*-seul) *n* conseil *m*

councillor (*kaoun*-seu-leu) *n* conseiller *m*

counsel (*kaoun*-seul) *n* conseil *m*

counsellor (*kaoun*-seu-leu) *n* conseiller *m*

count (kaount) *v* compter; *inclure; *n* comte *m*

counter (*kaoun*-teu) *n* comptoir *m*; barre *f*

counterfeit (*kaoun*-teu-fiit) *v* *contrefaire

counterfoil (*kaoun*-teu-foïl) *n* talon *m*

countess (*kaoun*-tiss) *n* comtesse *f*

country (*kann*-tri) *n* pays *m*; campagne *f*; région *f*; ~ **house** maison de campagne

countryman (*kann*-tri-meunn) *n* (pl -men) **fellow** ~ compatriote *m*

countryside (*kann*-tri-saïd) *n* campagne *f*

county (*kaoun*-ti) *n* comté *m*

couple (*ka*-peul) *n* couple *m*

coupon (*koû*-ponn) *n* coupon *m*

courage (*ka*-ridj) *n* vaillance *f*, courage *m*

courageous (keu-*réï*-djeuss) *adj* brave, courageux

course (kooss) *n* cap *m*; plat *m*; cours *m*; **crash** ~ cours accéléré; **of** ~ évidemment

court (koot) *n* tribunal *m*; cour *f*

courteous (*keû*-ti-euss) *adj* courtois

cousin (*ka*-zeunn) *n* cousine *f*, cousin *m*

cover (*ka*-veu) *v* *couvrir; *n* abri *m*; couvercle *m*; couverture *f*

cow (kaou) *n* vache *f*

coward (*kaou*-eud) *n* lâche *m*

cowardly (*kaou*-eud-li) *adj* lâche

crab (kræb) *n* crabe *m*

crack (kræk) *n* craquement *m*; fissure *f*; *v* craquer; fendre

cracker (*kræ*-keu) *nAm* biscuit *m*

cradle (*kréï*-deul) *n* berceau *m*

cramp (kræmp) *n* crampe *f*

crane (kréïn) *n* grue *f*

crash (kræch) *n* collision *f*; *v* entrer en collision; s'écraser; ~ **barrier** glissière de sécurité

crate (kréït) *n* caisse *f*

crater (*kréï*-teu) *n* cratère *m*

crawl (krool) *v* ramper; *n* crawl *m*

craze (kréïz) *n* rage *f*

crazy (*kréï*-zi) *adj* fou; insensé

creak (kriik) *v* grincer

cream (kriim) *n* crème *f*; crème fraîche; *adj* crème

creamy (*krii*-mi) *adj* crémeux

crease (kriiss) *v* froisser; *n* pli *m*; faux pli

create (kri-*éït*) *v* créer

creative (kri-*éï*-tiv) *adj* créateur, créatif

creature (*krii*-tcheu) *n* créature *f*; être *m*

credible (*krè*-di-beul) *adj* croyable

credit (*krè*-dit) *n* crédit *m*; *v* créditer; ~ **card** carte de crédit

creditor (*krè*-di-teu) *n* créditeur *m*

credulous (*krè*-dyou-leuss) *adj* crédule

creek (kriik) *n* baie *f*, crique *f*

*creep (kriip) *v* ramper

creepy (*krii*-pi) *adj* lugubre, terrifiant

cremate (kri-*méït*) *v* incinérer

crew (kroû) *n* équipage *m*

cricket (*kri*-kit) *n* cricket *m*; grillon *m*

crime (kraïm) *n* crime *m*

criminal (*kri*-mi-neul) *n* délinquant *m*, criminel *m*; *adj* criminel; ~ **law** droit pénal

criminality (kri-mi-*næ*-leu-ti) *n* criminalité *f*

crimson (*krimm*-zeunn) *adj* cramoisi

crippled (*kri*-peuld) *adj* estropié

crisis (*kraï*-siss) *n* (pl crises) crise *f*

crisp (krisp) *adj* croustillant

critic (*kri*-tik) *n* critique *m/f*

critical (*kri*-ti-keul) *adj* critique; précaire, délicat

criticism (*kri*-ti-si-zeumm) *n* critique *f*

criticize (*kri*-ti-saïz) *v* critiquer

crochet (*krôou*-chéï) *v* *faire du crochet

crockery (*kro*-keu-ri) *n* poterie *f*, faïence *f*

crocodile (*kro*-keu-daïl) *n* crocodile *m*

crooked (*krou*-kid) *adj* tordu;

malhonnête

crop (krop) n récolte f

cross (kross) v traverser; adj en colère, fâché; n croix f

cross-eyed (kross-aïd) adj louche

crossing (kro-sinng) n traversée f; croisement m; passage m; passage à niveau

crossroads (kross-rô^{ou}dz) n carrefour m

crosswalk (kross-^{ou}ook) nAm passage pour piétons

crow (krô^{ou}) n corneille f

crowd (kraoud) n masse f, foule f

crowded (kraou-did) adj animé; bondé

crown (kraoun) n couronne f; v couronner

crucifix (kroû-si-fiks) n crucifix m

crucifixion (kroû-si-fik-cheunn) n crucifixion f

crucify (kroû-si-faï) v crucifier

cruel (krou^{eu}l) adj cruel

cruise (kroûz) n croisière f

crumb (kramm) n miette f

crust (krast) n croûte f

crutch (kratch) n béquille f

cry (kraï) v pleurer; crier; appeler; n cri m; appel m

crystal (kri-steul) n cristal m; adj en cristal

Cuba (kyoû-beu) Cuba m

Cuban (kyoû-beunn) adj cubain; n Cubain m

cube (kyoûb) n cube m

cuckoo (kou-koû) n coucou m

cucumber (kyoû-keumm-beu) n concombre m

cuddle (ka-deul) v câliner

cuff (kaf) n manchette f; ~ **links** boutons de manchettes

cuff-links (kaf-linngks) pl boutons de manchettes

cultivate (kal-ti-véït) v cultiver

culture (kal-tcheu) n culture f

cultured (kal-tcheud) adj cultivé

cunning (ka-ninng) adj rusé

cup (kap) n tasse f; coupe f

cupboard (ka-beud) n placard m

curb (keûb) n bord du trottoir; v freiner

cure (kyou^{eu}) v guérir; n cure f; guérison f

curiosity (kyou^{eu}-ri-o-seu-ti) n curiosité f

curious (kyoueu-ri-euss) adj curieux; étrange

curl (keûl) v boucler; friser; n boucle f

curler (keû-leu) n bigoudi m

curly (keû-li) adj bouclé

currant (ka-reunnt) n raisin sec; groseille f

currency (ka-reunn-si) n monnaie f; **foreign** ~ monnaie étrangère

current (ka-reunnt) n courant m; adj courant; **alternating** ~ courant alternatif; **direct** ~ courant continu

curry (ka-ri) n curry m

curse (keûss) v jurer; *maudire; n juron m

curtain (keû-teunn) n rideau m

curve (keûv) n courbe f; tournant m

curved (keûvd) adj courbe, courbé

cushion (kou-cheunn) n coussin m

custody (ka-steu-di) n garde f à vue; garde f

custom (ka-steumm) n coutume f; habitude f

customary (ka-steu-meu-ri) adj usuel, coutumier, ordinaire

customer (ka-steu-meu) n client m

Customs (ka-steummz) pl douane f; ~ **duty** droit de douane; ~ **officer** douanier m

cut (kat) n incision f; coupure f

***cut** (kat) v couper; *réduire; ~ **off** couper; ~ **out** découper

cutlery (kat-leu-ri) n couvert m

cutlet (*kat*-leut) *n* côtelette *f*

cycle (*saï*-keul) *n* vélo *m*; bicyclette *f*; cycle *m*

cyclist (*saï*-klist) *n* cycliste *m*

cylinder (*si*-linn-deu) *n* cylindre *m*; ~ **head** tête de cylindre

cystitis (si-*staï*-tiss) *n* cystite *f*

Czech (tchèk) *adj* tchèque; *n* Tchèque *m*

Czech Republic (tchèk ri-*pa*-blik) République Tchèque

D

dad (dæd) *n* papa *m*

daddy (*dæ*-di) *n* papa *m*

daffodil (*dæ*-feu-dil) *n* jonquille *f*

daily (*déï*-li) *adj* journalier, quotidien; *n* quotidien *m*

dairy (*dèeu*-ri) *n* laiterie *f*

dam (dæm) *n* barrage *m*; digue *f*

damage (*dæ*-midj) *n* dommage *m*; *v* endommager

damn (dæm) *v* condamner; maudire

damned (dæmd) *adj* sacré, fichu

damp (dæmp) *adj* humide; moite; *n* humidité *f*, *v* humidifier

dance (dâans) *v* danser; *n* danse *f*

dandelion (*dæn*-di-laï-eunn) *n* pissenlit *m*

dandruff (*dæn*-dreuf) *n* pellicules

Dane (déïn) *n* Danois *m*

danger (*déïn*-djeu) *n* danger *m*

dangerous (*déïn*-djeu-reuss) *adj* dangereux

Danish (*déï*-nich) *adj* danois

dare (dè^eu) *v* oser

daring (*dèeu*-rinng) *adj* téméraire

dark (dââk) *adj* obscur; *n* obscurité *f*, ténèbres *fpl*

darling (*dââ*-linng) *n* trésor *m*, chéri *m*

darn (dâân) *v* repriser

dash (dæch) *v* se précipiter

dashboard (*dæch*-bood) *n* tableau de bord

data (*déï*-teu) *pl* données *fpl*

date[1] (déït) *n* date *f*; rendez-vous *m*; *v* dater; **out of** ~ démodé

date[2] (déït) *n* datte *f*

daughter (*doo*-teu) *n* fille *f*; **~-in-law** belle-fille *f*

dawn (doon) *n* aube *f*; aurore *f*

day (déï) *n* jour *m*; **by** ~ de jour; ~ **trip** excursion *f*; **per** ~ par jour; **the** ~ **before yesterday** avant-hier

daybreak (*déï*-bréïk) *n* lever du jour

daylight (*déï*-laït) *n* lumière du jour

dead (dèd) *adj* mort; décédé

deaf (dèf) *adj* sourd

deal (diil) *n* transaction *f*, affaire *f*

***deal** (diil) *v* distribuer; ~ **with** *v* s'occuper de; *faire des affaires avec

dealer (*dii*-leu) *n* négociant *m*; marchand *m*, -e *f*

dear (di^eu) *adj* cher

death (dèθ) *n* mort *f*; ~ **penalty** peine de mort

debate (di-*béït*) *n* débat *m*

debit (*dè*-bit) *n* débit *m*

debt (dèt) *n* dette *f*

decaffeinated (dii-*kæ*-fi-néï-tid) *adj* décaféiné

deceit (di-*siit*) *n* tromperie *f*

deceive (di-*siiv*) *v* tromper

December (di-*sèm*-beu) décembre

decency (*dii*-seunn-si) *n* décence *f*

decent (*dii*-seunnt) *adj* décent

decide (di-*saïd*) *v* décider

decision (di-*si*-jeunn) *n* décision *f*

deck (dèk) *n* pont *m*; ~ **cabin** cabine de pont; ~ **chair** chaise longue

declaration (dè-kleu-*réï*-cheunn) *n* déclaration *f*

declare (di-*klèeu*) *v* déclarer; indiquer

decorate (dè-keu-réït) *v* décorer; orner; peindre (et tapisser)

decoration (dè-keu-*réï*-cheunn) *n* décoration *f*

decrease (dii-*kriiss*) *v* *réduire; diminuer; *n* diminution *f*

dedicate (dè-di-kéït) *v* dédier

deduce (di-*dyoûss*) *v* *déduire

deduct (di-*dakt*) *v* *déduire

deed (diid) *n* action *f*, acte *m*

deep (diip) *adj* profond

deep-freeze (diip-*friiz*) *n* congélateur *m*

deer (di^eu) *n* (pl ~) daim *m*

defeat (di-*fiit*) *v* *vaincre; *n* défaite *f*

defective (di-*fèk*-tiv) *adj* défectueux

defence (di-*fèns*) *n* défense *f*

defend (di-*fènd*) *v* défendre

defense Am (di-*fèns*) *n* défense *f*

deficiency (di-*fi*-cheunn-si) *n* déficience *f*

deficit (*dè*-fi-sit) *n* déficit *m*

define (di-*faïn*) *v* définir, déterminer

definite (*dè*-fi-nit) *adj* déterminé

definition (dè-fi-*ni*-cheunn) *n* définition *f*

deformed (di-*foomd*) *adj* contrefait, difforme

degree (di-*ghrii*) *n* degré *m*; grade *m*

delay (di-*léï*) *v* retarder; différer; *n* retard *m*; ajournement *m*

delegate (*dè*-li-gheut) *n* délégué *m*

delegation (dè-li-*ghéï*-cheunn) *n* délégation *f*

deliberate[1] (di-*li*-beu-réït) *v* discuter, délibérer

deliberate[2] (di-*li*-beu-reut) *adj* délibéré

deliberation (di-li-beu-*réï*-cheunn) *n* discussion *f*, délibération *f*

delicacy (*dè*-li-keu-si) *n* délicatesse *f*

delicate (*dè*-li-keut) *adj* délicat; tendre

delicatessen (dè-li-keu-*tè*-seunn) *n* épicerie fine

delicious (di-*li*-cheuss) *adj* exquis, délicieux

delight (di-*laït*) *n* délice *m*, plaisir *m*; *v* enchanter

delightful (di-*laït*-feul) *adj* délicieux, ravissant

deliver (di-*li*-veu) *v* *remettre, livrer; délivrer

delivery (di-*li*-veu-ri) *n* remise *f*, livraison *f*; accouchement *m*; délivrance *f*; ~ **van** camion de livraison

demand (di-*mâând*) *v* exiger, réclamer; *n* demande *f*

democracy (di-*mo*-kreu-si) *n* démocratie *f*

democratic (dè-meu-*kræ*-tik) *adj* démocratique

demolish (di-*mo*-lich) *v* démolir

demolition (dè-meu-*li*-cheunn) *n* démolition *f*

demonstrate (*dè*-meunn-stréït) *v* démontrer; manifester

demonstration (dè-meunn-*stréï*-cheunn) *n* démonstration *f*; manifestation *f*

den (dèn) *n* tanière *f*

Denmark (*dèn*-mââk) Danemark *m*

denomination (di-no-mi-*néï*-cheunn) *n* dénomination *f*

dense (dèns) *adj* dense

dent (dènt) *n* bosse *f*

dentist (*dèn*-tist) *n* dentiste *m*

denture (*dèn*-tcheu) *n* dentier *m*

deny (di-*naï*) *v* nier; dénier, refuser

deodorant (dii-*ôou*-deu-reunnt) *n* désodorisant *m*

depart (di-*pâât*) *v* s'en *aller, *partir; ~

this world trépasser

department (di-*pâât*-meunnt) *n* division *f*, département *m*; **~ store** grand magasin

departure (di-*pââ*-tcheu) *n* départ *m*

depend (di-*pènd*): **~ on** dépendre de

dependent (di-*pèn*-deunnt) *adj* dépendant

deposit (di-*po*-zit) *n* versement *m*; consigne *f*; dépôt *m*; *v* déposer

depository (di-*po*-zi-teu-ri) *n* entrepôt *m*

depot (*dè*-pô^{ou}) *n* dépôt *m*; *nAm* gare *f*

depress (di-*près*) *v* déprimer

depression (di-*prè*-cheunn) *n* dépression *f*

deprive of (di-*praïv*) priver de

depth (dèpθ) *n* profondeur *f*

deputy (*dè*-pyou-ti) *n* député *m/f*; substitut *m*

descend (di-*sènd*) *v* descendre

descendant (di-*sèn*-deunnt) *n* descendant *m*, -e *f*

descent (di-*sènt*) *n* descente *f*

describe (di-*skraïb*) *v* *décrire

description (di-*skrip*-cheunn) *n* description *f*; signalement *m*

desert[1] (*dè*-zeut) *n* désert *m*; *adj* désert

desert[2] (di-*zeût*) *v* déserter; abandonner

deserve (di-*zeûv*) *v* mériter

design (di-*zaïn*) *v* créer; *n* dessein *m*

designate (*dè*-zigh-néït) *v* désigner

desirable (di-*zaïeu*-reu-beul) *adj* désirable

desire (di-*zaïeu*) *n* vœu *m*; envie *f*, désir *m*; *v* *avoir envie de, désirer

desk (dèsk) *n* bureau *m*; pupitre *m*; banc d'école

despair (di-*spèeu*) *n* désespoir *m*; *v* désespérer

despatch (di-*spætch*) *v* expédier

desperate (*dè*-speu-reut) *adj* désespéré

despise (di-*spaïz*) *v* mépriser

despite (di-*spaït*) *prep* malgré

dessert (di-*zeût*) *n* dessert *m*

destination (dè-sti-*néï*-cheunn) *n* destination *f*

destine (*dè*-stinn) *v* destiner

destiny (*dè*-sti-ni) *n* destin *m*, sort *m*

destroy (di-*stroï*) *v* dévaster, *détruire

destruction (di-*strak*-cheunn) *n* destruction *f*; anéantissement *m*

detach (di-*tætch*) *v* détacher

detail (*dii*-téïl) *n* détail *m*

detailed (*dii*-téïld) *adj* détaillé

detect (di-*tèkt*) *v* détecter

detective (di-*tèk*-tiv) *n* détective *m*; **~ story** roman policier

detergent (di-*teû*-djeunnt) *n* détergent *m*

determine (di-*teû*-minn) *v* définir, déterminer

determined (di-*teû*-minnd) *adj* résolu

detest (di-*tèst*) *v* détester

detour (*dii*-tou^{eu}) *n* détour *m*; déviation *f*

devaluation (dii-væl-you-*éï*-cheunn) *n* dévaluation *f*

devalue (dii-*væl*-yoû) *v* dévaluer

develop (di-*vè*-leup) *v* développer

development (di-*vè*-leup-meunnt) *n* développement *m*

deviate (*dii*-vi-éït) *v* dévier

devil (*dè*-veul) *n* diable *m*

devise (di-*vaïz*) *v* *concevoir

devote (di-*vôout*) *v* consacrer

dew (dyoû) *n* rosée *f*

diabetes (daï-eu-*bii*-tiiz) *n* diabète *m*

diabetic (daï-eu-*bè*-tik) *n* diabétique *m/f*

diagnose (daï-eugh-*nôouz*) *v* diagnostiquer

diagnosis (daï-eugh-*nôou*-siss) *n* (pl -ses) diagnostic *m*

diagonal (daï-*æ*-gheu-neul) *n* diagonale *f*; *adj* diagonale

diagram (*daï*-eu-ghræm) *n* diagramme *m*; graphique *m*

dial (daï^{eu}l) *n* cadran *m*; *v* composer, faire

dial(l)ing tone (*daï*-eu-linng-tô^{ou}n) *n* tonalité *f*

dialect (*daï*-eu-lèkt) *n* dialecte *m*

diamond (*daï*-eu-meunnd) *n* diamant *m*

diaper (*daï*-eu-peu) *nAm* couche *f*

diarrh(o)ea (daï-eu-*ri*-eu) *n* diarrhée *f*

diary (*daï*-eu-ri) *n* agenda *m*; journal *m*

dictate (dik-*tèït*) *v* dicter

dictation (dik-*tèï*-cheunn) *n* dictée *f*

dictionary (*dik*-cheu-neu-ri) *n* dictionnaire *m*

did (did) *v* (p do)

die (daï) *v* *mourir

diesel (*dii*-zeul) *n* diesel *m*

diet (*daï*-eut) *n* régime *m*

differ (*di*-feu) *v* différer

difference (*di*-feu-reunns) *n* différence *f*; distinction *f*

different (*di*-feu-reunnt) *adj* différent; autre

difficult (*di*-fi-keult) *adj* difficile

difficulty (*di*-fi-keul-ti) *n* difficulté *f*; peine *f*

*dig (digh) *v* creuser; fouiller

digest (di-*djèst*) *v* digérer

digestible (di-*djè*-steu-beul) *adj* digestible

digestion (di-*djèss*-tcheunn) *n* digestion *f*

digit (*di*-djit) *n* chiffre *m*

dignified (*digh*-ni-faïd) *adj* digne

dignity (*digh*-ni-ti) *n* dignité *f*

dike (daïk) *n* digue *f*

dilapidated (di-*læ*-pi-déï-tid) *adj* délabré

diligence (*di*-li-djeunns) *n* assiduité *f*,

application *f*

diligent (*di*-li-djeunnt) *adj* laborieux, assidu

dilute (daï-*lyoût*) *v* allonger, diluer

dim (dimm) *adj* terne, mat; obscur

dine (daïn) *v* dîner

dinghy (*dinng*-ghi) *n* canot *m*

dining car (*daï*-ninng-kââ) *n* wagon-restaurant

dining room (*daï*-ninng-roûm) *n* salle à manger

dinner (*di*-neu) *n* dîner *m*; **~ jacket** smoking *m*; **~ service** service de table

diphtheria (dif-*θïeu*-ri-eu) *n* diphtérie *f*

diploma (di-*plôou*-meu) *n* diplôme *m*

diplomat (*di*-pleu-mæt) *n* diplomate *m*

direct (di-*rèkt*) *adj* direct; *v* diriger; administrer; *mettre en scène

direction (di-*rèk*-cheunn) *n* direction *f*; instruction *f*; réalisation *f*; **directions for use** mode d'emploi

directive (di-*rèk*-tiv) *n* directive *f*

director (di-*rèk*-teu) *n* directeur *m*, -trice *f*; metteur en scène

directory (di-*rèk*-teu-ri) *n* répertoire *m* d'adresses; annuaire *m* (des téléphones); **~ assistance, ~ enquiry** renseignements *pl*

dirt (deût) *n* saleté *f*

dirty (*deû*-ti) *adj* sale, souillé

disabled (di-*séï*-beuld) *adj* handicapé, invalide

disadvantage (di-seud-*vâân*-tidj) *n* désavantage *m*

disagree (di-seu-*ghrii*) *v* *être en désaccord

disagreeable (di-seu-*ghrii*-eu-beul) *adj* désagréable

disappear (di-seu-*pieu*) *v* *disparaître

disappoint (di-seu-*poïnt*) *v* *décevoir

disappointment (di-seu-*poïnt*-

meunnt) *n* déception *f*

disapprove (di-seu-*proûv*) *v*
désapprouver

disaster (di-*zââ*-steu) *n* désastre *m*;
catastrophe *f*, calamité *f*

disastrous (di-*zââ*-streuss) *adj*
désastreux

disc (disk) *n* disque *m*; **slipped ~**
hernie discale

discard (di-*skââd*) *v* se débarrasser de

discharge (diss-*tchââdj*) *v* décharger;
~ of dispenser de

discipline (*di*-si-plinn) *n* discipline *f*

discolo(u)r (di-*ska*-leu) *v* décolorer

disconnect (di-skeu-*nèkt*) *v*
*disjoindre; débrancher

discontented (di-skeunn-*tèn*-tid) *adj*
mécontent

discontinue (di-skeunn-*ti*-nyoû) *v*
suspendre, cesser

discount (*di*-skaount) *n* réduction *f*,
rabais *m*

discourage (di-*ska*-ridj *v* décourager
(**from** de)

discover (di-*ska*-veu) *v* *découvrir

discovery (di-*ska*-veu-ri) *n*
découverte *f*

discuss (di-*skass*) *v* discuter;
*débattre

discussion (di-*ska*-cheunn) *n*
discussion *f*; conversation *f*,
délibération *f*, débat *m*

disease (di-*ziiz*) *n* maladie *f*

disembark (di-simm-*bââk*) *v*
débarquer

disgrace (diss-*ghréïss*) *n* déshonneur
m

disguise (diss-*ghaïz*) *v* se déguiser; *n*
déguisement *m*

disgust (diss-*ghast*) *n* dégoût *m*;
répugnance *f*; *v* dégoûter

disgusting (diss-*gha*-stinng) *adj*
répugnant, dégoûtant

dish (dich) *n* assiette *f*; plat *m*

dishonest (di-*so*-nist) *adj* malhonnête

dishwasher (*dich*-^{ou}o-cheu) *n* laveur
m de vaisselle; lave-vaisselle *m*

disinfect (di-sinn-*fèkt*) *v* désinfecter

disinfectant (di-sinn-*fèk*-teunnt) *n*
désinfectant *m*

dislike (di-*slaïk*) *v* détester, ne pas
aimer; *n* répugnance *f*, aversion *f*,
antipathie *f*

dislocated (*di*-sleu-kéï-tid) *adj*
disloqué

dismiss (diss-*miss*) *v* *renvoyer

disorder (di-*soo*-deu) *n* désordre *m*;
confusion *f*

dispatch (di-*spætch*) *v* *envoyer,
expédier

display (di-*splêï*) *v* étaler; montrer; *n*
exposition *f*

displease (di-*spliiz*) *v* *déplaire

disposable (di-*spôou*-zeu-beul) *adj* à
jeter

disposal (di-*spôou*-zeul) *n* disposition
f

dispose of (di-*spôouz*) disposer de

dispute (di-*spyoût*) *n* discussion *f*;
querelle *f*, litige *m*; *v* se disputer,
contester

dissatisfied (di-*sæ*-tiss-faïd) *adj*
insatisfait

dissolve (di-*zolv*) *v* *dissoudre, diluer

dissuade from (di-*souéïd*) dissuader

distance (*di*-steunns) *n* distance *f*; **~ in
kilometres,** *Am* **kilometers**
kilométrage *m*

distant (*di*-steunnt) *adj* éloigné

distinct (di-*stinngkt*) *adj* net; distinct

distinction (di-*stinngk*-cheunn) *n*
distinction *f*

distinguish (di-*stinng*-gh^{ou}ich) *v*
distinguer, discerner

distinguished (di-*stinng*-gh^{ou}icht) *adj*
distingué

distress (di-*strèss*) *n* détresse *f*; **~
signal** signal de détresse

distribute (di-*stri*-byoût) *v* distribuer

distributor (di-*stri*-byou-teu) *n* concessionnaire *m*; distributeur *m*

district (*di*-strikt) *n* district *m*; région *f*; quartier *m*

disturb (di-*steûb*) *v* déranger

disturbance (di-*steû*-beunns) *n* dérangement *m*; agitation *f*

ditch (ditch) *n* fossé *m*

dive (daïv) *v* plonger

diversion (daï-*veû*-cheunn) *n* déviation *f*; diversion *f*

divide (di-*vaïd*) *v* diviser; répartir; séparer

divine (di-*vaïn*) *adj* divin

division (di-*vi*-jeunn) *n* division *f*; séparation *f*; département *m*

divorce (di-*vooss*) *n* divorce *m*; *v* divorcer

dizziness (di-*zi*-neuss) *n* vertige *m*

dizzy (*di*-zi) *adj* étourdi

*do (doû) *v* *faire; *suffire

dock (dok) *n* dock *m*; quai *m*; *v* accoster

docker (*do*-keu) *n* docker *m*

doctor (*dok*-teu) *n* médecin *m*, docteur *m*

document (*do*-kyou-meunnt) *n* document *m*

dog (dogh) *n* chien *m*

dogged (*do*-ghid) *adj* obstiné

doll (dol) *n* poupée *f*

dollar (*do*-leu) *n* dollar *m*

dome (dô^{ou}m) *n* dôme *m*

domestic (deu-*mè*-stik) *adj* domestique; intérieur; *n* domestique *m*

domicile (*do*-mi-saïl) *n* domicile *m*

domination (do-mi-*néï*-cheunn) *n* domination *f*

dominion (deu-*mi*-nyeunn) *n* règne *m*

donate (dô^{ou}-*néït*) *v* donner

donation (dô^{ou}-*néï*-cheunn) *n* don *m*, donation *f*

done (dann) *v* (pp do)

donkey (*donng*-ki) *n* âne *m*

donor (*dôou*-neu) *n* donateur *m*

door (doo) *n* porte *f*; **revolving ~** porte tournante; **sliding ~** porte coulissante

doorbell (*doo*-bèl) *n* sonnette *f*

doorkeeper (*doo*-kii-peu) *n* portier *m*

doorman (*doo*-meunn) *n* (pl -men) portier *m*

dormitory (*doo*-mi-tri) *n* dortoir *m*

dose (dô^{ou}ss) *n* dose *f*

dot (dot) *n* point *m*

double (*da*-beul) *adj* double

doubt (daout) *v* douter de, douter; *n* doute *m*; **without ~** sans aucun doute

doubtful (daout-feul) *adj* douteux; incertain

dough (dô^{ou}) *n* pâte *f*

down[1] (daoun) *adv* en bas; vers le bas, par terre; *adj* déprimé; *prep* le long de, en bas de; **~ payment** acompte *m*

down[2] (daoun) *n* duvet *m*

downpour (*daoun*-poo) *n* averse *f*

downstairs (daoun-*stèeuz*) *adv* en bas

downstream (daoun-*striim*) *adv* en aval

downwards (daoun-^{ou}eudz) *adv* vers le bas

dozen (*da*-zeunn) *n* (pl ~, ~s) douzaine *f*

draft[1] (drââft) *n* traite *f*

draft[2] (drââft) *n* courant *m* d'air

drag (drægh) *v* traîner

dragon (*dræ*-gheunn) *n* dragon *m*

drain (dréïn) *v* assécher; drainer; *n* égout *m*

drama (*drââ*-meu) *n* drame *m*; tragédie *f*; théâtre *m*

dramatic (dreu-*mæ*-tik) *adj* dramatique

dramatist (*dræ*-meu-tist) *n* dramaturge *m*

drank (drænngk) *v* (p drink)

drapery (*dréï*-peu-ri) *n* étoffes *fpl*

draught (drââft) *n* courant d'air; **draughts** jeu de dames

draw (droo) *n* tirage *m*

***draw** (droo) *v* dessiner; tirer; ~ **up** rédiger

drawbridge (*droo*-bridj) *n* pont-levis *m*

drawer (*droo*-eu) *n* tiroir *m*; **drawers** caleçon *m*

drawing (*droo*-inng) *n* dessin *m*; ~ **pin** punaise *f*; ~ **room** (*droo*-inng-roûm) *n* salon *m*

dread (drèd) *v* *craindre; *n* crainte *f*

dreadful (*drèd*-feul) *adj* terrible, affreux

dream (driim) *n* rêve *m*

***dream** (driim) *v* rêver, songer

dress (drèss) *v* habiller; se *vêtir, s'habiller, *vêtir; panser; *n* robe *f*

dressing gown (*drè*-sinng-ghaoun) *n* robe de chambre

dressing room (*drè*-sinng-roûm) *n* loge *f*

dressing table (*drè*-sinng-téï-beul) *n* coiffeuse *f*

dressmaker (*drèss*-méï-keu) *n* couturière *f*

drill (dril) *v* forer; entraîner; *n* foreuse *f*

drink (drinngk) *n* apéritif *m*, boisson *f*

***drink** (drinngk) *v* *boire

drinking water (*drinng*-kinng-^(ou)oo-teu) *n* eau potable

drip-dry (drip-*draï*) *adj* qui ne nécessite aucun repassage

drive (draïv) *n* route *f*; promenade en voiture

***drive** (draïv) *v* *conduire

driver (*draï*-veu) *n* conducteur *m*

drizzle (*dri*-zeul) *n* crachin *m*

drop (drop) *v* laisser tomber; *n* goutte *f*

drought (draout) *n* sécheresse *f*

drown (draoun) *v* noyer; ***be drowned** se noyer

drug (dragh) *n* drogue *f*; médicament *m*

drugstore (*dragh*-stoo) *nAm* drugstore *m*

drum (dramm) *n* tambour *m*

drunk (dranngk) *adj* (pp drink) ivre

dry (draï) *adj* sec; *v* sécher; essuyer

dry-clean (draï-*kliin*) *v* nettoyer à sec

dry cleaner's (draï-*klii*-neuz) *n* teinturerie *f*

dryer (*draï*-eu) *n* séchoir *m*

duchess (da-tchiss) *n* duchesse *f*

duck (dak) *n* canard *m*

due (dyoû) *adj* attendu; payable; dû

dues (dyoûz) *pl* droits

dug (dagh) *v* (p, pp dig)

duke (dyoûk) *n* duc *m*

dull (dal) *adj* ennuyeux; terne, mat; émoussé

dumb (damm) *adj* muet; bête

dune (dyoûn) *n* dune *f*

dung (danng) *n* fumier *m*

dunghill (*danng*-hil) *n* tas de fumier

duration (dyou-*réï*-cheunn) *n* durée *f*

during (*dyoueu*-rinng) *prep* durant, pendant

dusk (dask) *n* crépuscule *m*

dust (dast) *n* poussière *f*

dustbin (*dast*-binn) *n* boîte à ordures

dusty (*da*-sti) *adj* poussiéreux

Dutch (datch) *adj* néerlandais, hollandais

duty (*dyoû*-ti) *n* devoir *m*; tâche *f*; droit d'importation; **Customs** ~ droit de douane

duty-free (dyoû-ti-*frii*) *adj* exempt de droits

dwarf (d^(ou)oof) *n* nain *m*

dye (daï) *v* *teindre; *n* teinture *f*

dynamo (*daï*-neu-mô^(ou)) *n* (pl ~s) dynamo *f*

E

each (iitch) *adj* chaque; ~ **other** l'un l'autre

eager (*ii*-gheu) *adj* désireux, impatient

eagle (*ii*-gheul) *n* aigle *m*

ear (i^{eu}) *n* oreille *f*

earache (*ieu*-réïk) *n* mal d'oreille

eardrum (*ieu*-dramm) *n* tympan *m*

earl (eûl) *n* comte *m*

early (*eû*-li) *adj* tôt

earn (eûnn) *v* gagner

earnest (*eû*-nist) *n* sérieux *m*

earnings (*eû*-ninngz) *pl* revenu *m*, gains

earring (*ieu*-rinng) *n* boucle d'oreille

earth (eûθ) *n* terre *f*; sol *m*

earthquake (*eû*θ-k^{ou}éïk) *n* tremblement de terre

ease (iiz) *n* aisance *f*; aise *f*

east (iist) *n* est *m*

Easter (*ii*-steu) Pâques

easterly (*ii*-steu-li) *adj* oriental

eastern (*ii*-steunn) *adj* oriental

easy (*ii*-zi) *adj* facile; commode; ~ **chair** fauteuil *m*

easy-going (*ii*-zi-ghô^{ou}-inng) *adj* décontracté

*eat (iit) *v* manger; dîner

eavesdrop (*iivz*-drop) *v* écouter aux portes

ebony (*è*-beu-ni) *n* ébène *f*

eccentric (ik-*sèn*-trik) *adj* excentrique

echo (*è*-kô^{ou}) *n* (pl ~es) écho *m*

eclipse (i-*klips*) *n* éclipse *f*

economic (ii-keu-*no*-mik) *adj* économique

economical (ii-keu-*no*-mi-keul) *adj* parcimonieux, économe

economist (i-*ko*-neu-mist) *n* économiste *m*

economize (i-*ko*-neu-maïz) *v* économiser

economy (i-*ko*-neu-mi) *n* économie *f*

ecstasy (*èk*-steu-zi) *n* extase *m*

Ecuador (*è*-k^{ou}eu-doo) Equateur *m*

Ecuadorian (*è*-k^{ou}eu-*doo*-ri-eunn) *n* Ecuadorien *m*

eczema (*èk*-si-meu) *n* eczéma *m*

edge (èdj) *n* rebord *m*, bord *m*

edible (*è*-di-beul) *adj* comestible

edit (*è*-dit) *v* éditer; diriger

edition (i-*di*-cheunn) *n* édition *f*; **morning** ~ édition du matin

editor (*è*-di-teu) *n* rédacteur *m*

educate (*è*-djou-kéït) *v* former, éduquer

education (è-djou-*kéï*-cheunn) *n* éducation *f*

eel (iil) *n* anguille *f*

effect (i-*fèkt*) *n* résultat *m*, effet *m*; *v* effectuer; **in** ~ en fait

effective (i-*fèk*-tiv) *adj* efficace, effectif

efficient (i-*fi*-cheunnt) *adj* efficace

effort (*è*-feut) *n* effort *m*

egg (ègh) *n* œuf *m*; ~ **yolk** jaune d'œuf

eggcup (*ègh*-kap) *n* coquetier *m*

eggplant (*ègh*-plâânt) *n* aubergine *f*

ego(t)istic (è-ghô^{ou}-*i*-stik) *adj* égoïste

Egypt (*ii*-djipt) Egypte *f*

Egyptian (i-*djip*-cheunn) *adj* égyptien; *n* Egyptien *m*

eiderdown (*aï*-deu-daoun) *n* édredon *m*

eight (éït) *num* huit

eighteen (*éï*-tiin) *num* dix-huit

eighteenth (*éï*-tiinθ) *num* dix-huitième

eighth (éïtθ) *num* huitième

eighty (*éï*-ti) *num* quatre-vingts

either (*aï*-ðeu) *pron* l'un ou l'autre; **either … or** ou … ou, soit … soit

elaborate (i-*læ*-beu-réït) *v* élaborer

elastic (i-*læ*-stik) *adj* élastique; flexible; élastique *m*

elasticity (è-læ-*sti*-seu-ti) n élasticité f

elbow (*èl*-bô^ou^) n coude m

elder (*èl*-deu) adj plus âgé

elderly (*èl*-deu-li) adj âgé

eldest (*èl*-dist) adj le plus âgé

elect (i-*lèkt*) v *élire

election (i-*lèk*-cheunn) n élection f

electric (i-*lèk*-trik) adj électrique; ~ **razor** rasoir électrique; ~ **wire** fil électrique

electrician (i-lèk-*tri*-cheunn) n électricien m

electricity (i-lèk-*tri*-seu-ti) n électricité f

electronic (i-lèk-*tro*-nik) adj électronique

elegance (*è*-li-gheunns) n élégance f

elegant (*è*-li-gheunnt) adj élégant

element (*è*-li-meunnt) n élément m

elephant (*è*-li-fcunnt) n éléphant m

elevator (*è*-li-véï-teu) nAm ascenseur m

eleven (i-*lè*-veunn) num onze

eleventh (i-*lè*-veunnθ) num onzième

eliminate (i-*li*-mi-néït) v éliminer

else (èls) adv autrement

elsewhere (*èl-soueu*) adv ailleurs

elucidate (i-*loû*-si-déït) v élucider

e-mail (i-méíl) n e-mail m; message électronique

emancipation (i-mæn-si-*péï*-cheunn) n émancipation f

embankment (imm-*bængk*-meunnt) n berge f

embargo (èm-*bââ*-ghô^ou^) n (pl ~es) embargo m

embark (imm-*bââk*) v embarquer

embarkation (èm-bââ-*kéï*-cheunn) n embarquement m

embarrass (imm-*bæ*-reuss) v embarrasser; gêner;

embarrassed (imm-*bæ*-reust) adj confus

embarrassment (imm-*bæ*-reuss-meunnt) n embarras m; gêne f

embassy (*èm*-beu-si) n ambassade f

emblem (*èm*-bleumm) n emblème m

embrace (imm-*bréïss*) v *étreindre; n enlacement m

embroider (imm-*broï*-deu) v broder

embroidery (imm-*broï*-deu-ri) n broderie f

emerald (*è*-meu-reuld) n émeraude f

emergency (i-*meû*-djeunn-si) n cas d'urgence, urgence f; état d'urgence; ~ **exit** sortie de secours

emigrant (*è*-mi-ghreunnt) n émigrant m

emigrate (*è*-mi-ghréït) v émigrer

emigration (è-mi-*ghréï*-cheunn) n émigration f

emotion (i-*môou*-cheunn) n émoi m, émotion f

emotional (i-*môou*-cheu-neul) adj émotionnel; émotif ; qui fait appel aux émotions, touchant, émouvant

emperor (*èm*-peu-reu) n empereur m

emphasize (*èm*-feu-saïz) v souligner

empire (*èm*-pai^eu^) n empire m

employ (imm-*ploï*) v employer; utiliser

employee (èm-ploï-*ii*) n employé m, -e f

employer (imm-*ploï*-eu) n employeur m, -se f

employment (imm-*ploï*-meunnt) n emploi m; ~ **exchange** bureau de l'emploi

empress (*èm*-priss) n impératrice f

empty (*èmp*-ti) adj vide; v vider

enable (i-*néï*-beul) v *permettre

enamel (i-*næ*-meul) n émail m

enamelled (i-*næ*-meuld) adj émaillé

enchanting (inn-*tchâân*-tinng) adj splendide, ravissant

encircle (inn-*seû*-keul) v encercler, entourer

enclose (inng-*klôouz*) v *inclure,

*joindre

enclosure (inng-*klôou*-jeu) *n* pièce jointe

encounter (inng-*kaoun*-teu) *v* rencontrer; *n* rencontre *f*

encourage (inng-*ka*-ridj) *v* encourager

encyclop(a)edia (èn-saï-kleu-*pii*-di-eu) *n* encyclopédie *f*

end (ènd) *n* fin *f*, bout *m*; conclusion *f*; *v* finir

ending (*èn*-dinng) *n* fin *f*

endless (*ènd*-leuss) *adj* infini

endorse (inn-*dooss*) *v* endosser

endure (inn-*dyoueu*) *v* endurer

enemy (*è*-neu-mi) *n* ennemi *m*, -e *f*

energetic (è-neu-*djè*-tik) *adj* énergique

energy (*è*-neu-dji) *n* énergie *f*; puissance *f*

engage (inng-*ghéïdj*) *v* engager; s'engager; **engaged** fiancé; occupé

engagement (inng-*ghéïdj*-meunnt) *n* fiançailles *fpl*; engagement *m*; ~ **ring** bague de fiançailles

engine (*èn*-djinn) *n* machine *f*, moteur *m*; locomotive *f*

engineer (èn-dji-*nieu*) *n* ingénieur *m*

England (*inng*-ghleunnd) Angleterre *f*

English (*inng*-ghlich) *adj* anglais

Englishman (*inng*-ghlich-meunn) *n* (pl -men) Anglais *m*

Englishwoman (*inng*-ghlich-ᵒᵘou-meunn) *n* (pl -women) Anglaise *f*

engrave (inng-*ghréïv*) *v* graver

engraver (inng-*ghréï*-veu) *n* graveur *m*

engraving (inng-*ghréï*-vinng) *n* estampe *f*; gravure *f*

enigma (i-*nigh*-meu) *n* énigme *f*

enjoy (inn-*djoï*) *v* jouir de, *prendre plaisir

enjoyable (inn-*djoï*-eu-beul) *adj* agréable, plaisant; bon

enjoyment (inn-*djoï*-meunnt) *n* plaisir *m*

enlarge (inn-*lââdj*) *v* agrandir; étendre

enlargement (inn-*lââdj*-meunnt) *n* agrandissement *m*

enormous (i-*noo*-meuss) *adj* gigantesque, énorme

enough (i-*naf*) *adv* assez; *adj* suffisant

enquire (inng-*kouaïeu*) *v* s'informer; enquêter

enquiry (inng-*kouaïeu*-ri) *n* information *f*; investigation *f*; enquête *f*

enter (*èn*-teu) *v* entrer; *inscrire

enterprise (*èn*-teu-praïz) *n* entreprise *f*

entertain (èn-teu-*téïn*) *v* divertir, amuser; *recevoir

entertainer (èn-teu-*téï*-neu) *n* animateur *m*

entertaining (èn-teu-*téï*-ninng) *adj* amusant, divertissant

entertainment (èn-teu-*téïn*-meunnt) *n* amusement *m*, divertissement *m*

enthusiasm (inn-*θyoû*-zi-æ-zeumm) *n* enthousiasme *m*

enthusiastic (inn-*θyoû*-zi-æ-stik) *adj* enthousiaste

entire (inn-*taïeu*) *adj* tout, entier

entirely (inn-*taïeu*-li) *adv* entièrement

entrance (*èn*-treunns) *n* entrée *f*; accès *m*; ~ **fee** prix d'entrée

entry (*èn*-tri) *n* entrée *f*; admission *f*; inscription *f*; **no** ~ défense d'entrer

envelop (inn- *vè*-leup) *v* envelopper

envelope (*èn*-veu-lôᵒup) *n* enveloppe *f*

envious (*èn*-vi-euss) *adj* envieux, jaloux

environment (inn-*vaïeu*-reunn-meunnt) *n* environnement *m*; environs *mpl*

envoy (*èn*-voï) *n* envoyé *m*

envy (*èn*-vi) *n* envie *f*; *v* envier

epic (*è*-pik) *n* poème épique; *adj* épique

epidemic (è-pi-*dè*-mik) *n* épidémie *f*

epilepsy (*è*-pi-lèp-si) *n* épilepsie *f*

episode (*è*-pi-sô^{ou}d) *n* épisode *m*

equal (*ii*-k^{ou}eul) *adj* égal; *v* égaler

equality (i-*kouo*-leu-ti) *n* égalité *f*

equalize (*ii*-k^{ou}eu-laïz) *v* égaliser

equally (*ii*-k^{ou}eu-li) *adv* également

equator (i-*kouéï*-teu) *n* équateur *m*

equip (i-*kouip*) *v* équiper

equipment (i-*kouip*-meunnt) *n* équipement *m*

equivalent (i-*koui*-veu-leunnt) *adj* équivalent

eraser (i-*réï*-zeu) *n* gomme *f*

erect (i-*rèkt*) *v* ériger; *adj* debout, droit

err (eû) *v* se tromper, errer

errand (*è*-reunnd) *n* commission *f*

error (*è*-reu) *n* faute *f*, erreur *f*

escalator (*è*-skeu-léï-teu) *n* escalier roulant

escape (i-*skéïp*) *v* échapper; *fuir; n* évasion *f*

escort[1] (*è*-skoot) *n* escorte *f*

escort[2] (i-*skoot*) *v* escorter

especially (i-*spè*-cheu-li) *adv* principalement, spécialement

esplanade (è-spleu-*néïd*) *n* esplanade *f*

essay (*è*-séï) *n* essai *m*; dissertation *f*, composition *f*

essence (*è*-seunns) *n* essence *f*; fond *m*, nature *f*

essential (i-*sèn*-cheul) *adj* indispensable; fondamental, essentiel

essentially (i-*sèn*-cheu-li) *adv* essentiellement

establish (i-*stæ*-blich) *v* établir

estate (i-*stéït*) *n* propriété *f*

esteem (i-*stiim*) *n* respect *m*, estime *f*; *v* estimer

estimate[1] (*è*-sti-méït) *v* évaluer, estimer

estimate[2] (*è*-sti-meut) *n* estimation *f*

estuary (*èss*-tchou-eu-ri) *n* estuaire *m*

etcetera (èt-*sè*-teu-reu) et cætera

etching (*è*-tchinng) *n* eau-forte *f*

eternal (i-*teû*-neul) *adj* éternel

eternity (i-*teû*-neu-ti) *n* éternité *f*

Ethiopia (i-θi-*ôou*-pi-eu) Ethiopie *f*

Ethiopian (i-θi-*ôou*-pi-eunn) *adj* éthiopien; *n* Ethiopien *m*

Euro (*youeu*-reu) *n* euro *m*

Europe (*youeu*-reup) Europe *f*

European (you^{eu}-reu-*pii*-eunn) *adj* européen; *n* Européen *m*

evacuate (i-*væ*-kyou-éït) *v* évacuer

evade (i-*véïd*) *v* éviter, échapper à; éluder

evaluate (i-*væl*-you-éït) *v* évaluer

evaporate (i-*væ*-peu-réït) *v* évaporer

even (*ii*-veunn) *adj* plan, égal; constant; pair; *adv* même

evening (*iiv*-ninng) *n* soir *m*; ~ **dress** tenue de soirée

event (i-*vènt*) *n* événement *m*; cas *m*

eventual (i-*vèn*-tchou-eul) *adj* éventuel

ever (*è*-veu) *adv* jamais; toujours

every (*èv*-ri) *adj* tout, chaque

everybody (*èv*-ri-bo-di) *pron* tout le monde

everyday (*èv*-ri-déï) *adj* quotidien

everyone (*èv*-ri-^{ou}ann) *pron* chacun, tout le monde

everything (*èv*-ri-θinng) *pron* tout

everywhere (*èv*-ri-^{ou}è^{eu}) *adv* partout

evidence (*è*-vi-deunns) *n* preuve *f*

evident (*è*-vi-deunnt) *adj* évident

evil (*ii*-veul) *n* mal *m*; *adj* méchant, mauvais

evolution (ii-veu-*loû*-cheunn) *n* évolution *f*

exact (igh-*zækt*) *adj* juste, exact

exactly (igh-*zœkt*-li) *adv* exactement

exaggerate (igh-*zœ*-djeu-réït) *v* exagérer

exam (igh-*zœm*) *n colloquial* examen *m*

examination (igh-zœ-mi-*néï*-cheunn) *n* examen *m*; interrogatoire *m*

examine (igh-*zœ*-minn) *v* examiner

example (igh-*zâam*-peul) *n* exemple *m*; **for ~** par exemple

exceed (ik-*siid*) *v* excéder; surpasser

excel (ik-*sèl*) *v* exceller

excellent (*èk*-seu-leunnt) *adj* excellent

except (ik-*sèpt*) *prep* excepté

exception (ik-*sèp*-cheunn) *n* exception *f*

exceptional (ik-*sèp*-cheu-neul) *adj* extraordinaire, exceptionnel

excerpt (*èk*-seûpt) *n* extrait *m*

excess (ik-*sèss*) *n* excès *m*

excessive (ik-*sè*-siv) *adj* excessif

exchange (iks-*tchéïndj*) *v* échanger, changer; *n* bourse *f*; **~ office** bureau de change; **~ rate** taux de change

excite (ik-*saït*) *v* exciter

excitement (ik-*saït*-meunnt) *n* agitation *f*, excitation *f*

exciting (ik-*saï*-tinng) *adj* passionnant

exclaim (ik-*skléïm*) *v* exclamer

exclamation (èk-skleu-*méï*-cheunn) *n* exclamation *f*

exclude (ik-*skloûd*) *v* *exclure

exclusive (ik-*skloû*-siv) *adj* exclusif

exclusively (ik-*skloû*-siv-li) *adv* exclusivement, uniquement

excursion (ik-*skeû*-cheunn) *n* excursion *f*

excuse[1] (ik-*skyoûss*) *n* excuse *f*

excuse[2] (ik-*skyoûz*) *v* excuser

execute (*èk*-si-kyoût) *v* exécuter

execution (èk-si-*kyoû*-cheunn) *n* exécution *f*

executive (igh-*zè*-kyou-tiv) *adj* exécutif; *n* pouvoir exécutif; exécutif *m*

exempt (igh-*jèmpt*) *v* dispenser, exempter; *adj* exempt

exemption (igh-*zèmp*-cheunn) *n* exemption *f*

exercise (*èk*-seu-saïz) *n* exercice *m*; *v* exercer

exhale (èks-*héïl*) *v* expirer

exhaust (igh-*zoost*) *n* tuyau d'échappement, échappement *m*; *v* exténuer; **~ gases** gaz d'échappement

exhibit (igh-*zi*-bit) *v* exposer; exhiber

exhibition (èk-si-*bi*-cheunn) *n* exhibition *f*, exposition *f*

exile (*èk*-saïl) *n* exile *m*; exilé *m*

exist (igh-*zist*) *v* exister

existence (igh-*zi*-steunns) *n* existence *f*

exit (*èk*-sit) *n* sortie *f*

exotic (igh-*zo*-tik) *adj* exotique

expand (ik-*spœnd*) *v* étendre; déployer

expansion (ik-*spœn*-cheunn) *n* expansion *f*; dilatation *f*; développement *m*

expect (ik-*spèkt*) *v* attendre

expectation (èk-spèk-*téï*-cheunn) *n* espérance *f*

expedition (èk-speu-*di*-cheunn) *n* expédition *f*

expel (ik-*spèl*) *v* expulser

expenditure (ik-*spèn*-di-tcheu) *n* dépense *f*

expense (ik-*spèns*) *n* dépense *f*; **expenses** *pl* frais *mpl*

expensive (ik-*spèn*-siv) *adj* cher; coûteux

experience (ik-*spieu*-ri-eunns) *n* expérience *f*; *v* éprouver, *vivre, *faire l'expérience de; **experienced** expérimenté

experiment (ik-*spè*-ri-meunnt) *n* épreuve *f*, expérience *f*; *v* expérimenter

expert (*èk*-speût) *n* spécialiste *m*, expert *m*; *adj* compétent

expire (ik-*spaïeu*) *v* *venir à échéance, se terminer, expirer; **expired** périmé

expiry (ik-*spaïeu*-ri) *n* expiration *f*

explain (ik-*splëïn*) *v* expliquer

explanation (èk-spleu-*néï*-cheunn) *n* éclaircissement *m*, explication *f*

explicit (ik-*spli*-sit) *adj* formel, explicite

explode (ik-*splôoud*) *v* exploser

exploit (ik-*sploït*) *v* exploiter

explore (ik-*sploo*) *v* explorer

explosion (ik-*splôou*-jeunn) *n* explosion *f*

explosive (ik-*splôou*-siv) *adj* explosif; *n* explosif *m*

export[1] (ik-*spoot*) *v* exporter

export[2] (*èk*-spoot) *n* exportation *f*

exportation (èk-spoo-*téï*-cheunn) *n* exportation *f*

exports (*èk*-spoots) *n pl* exportation *f*

expose (ik-*spôouz*) *v* exposer; démasquer; dévoiler

exposition (èk-speu-*zi*-cheunn) *n* exposition *f*

exposure (ik-*spôou*-jeu) *n* exposition *f*

express (ik-*sprèss*) *v* exprimer; manifester; *adj* exprès; explicite; ~ **train** rapide *m*

expression (ik-*sprè*-cheunn) *n* expression *f*

exquisite (ik-*skoui*-zit) *adj* exquis

extend (ik-*stènd*) *v* étendre; agrandir

extension (ik-*stèn*-cheunn) *n* prolongation *f*; agrandissement *m*; ligne intérieure; ~ **cord** rallonge *f*

extensive (ik-*stèn*-siv) *adj* considérable; vaste, étendu

extent (ik-*stènt*) *n* dimension *f*

exterior (èk-*stieu*-ri-eu) *adj* extérieur; *n* extérieur *m*

external (èk-*steû*-neul) *adj* extérieur

extinguish (ik-*stinng*-gh^ou ich) *v* *éteindre

extort (ik-*stoot*) *v* extorquer

extortion (ik-*stoo*-cheunn) *n* extorsion *f*

extra (*èk*-streu) *adj* supplémentaire

extract[1] (ik-*strækt*) *v* arracher, *extraire

extract[2] (*èk*-strækt) *n* fragment *m*

extradite (*èk*-streu-daït) *v* extrader

extraordinary (ik-*stroo*-dcunn-ri) *adj* extraordinaire

extravagant (ik-*stræ*-veu-gheunnt) *adj* exagéré, extravagant

extreme (ik-*striim*) *adj* extrême; *n* extrême *m*

exuberant (igh-*zyoû*-beu-reunnt) *adj* exubérant

eye (aï) *n* œil *m*; ~ **shadow** ombre à paupières

eyebrow (*aï*-braou) *n* sourcil *m*; ~ **pencil** crayon pour les yeux

eyelash (*aï*-læch) *n* cil *m*

eyelid (*aï*-lid) *n* paupière *f*

eyewitness (*aï*-^ou it-neuss) *n* témoin oculaire

F

fable (*féï*-beul) *n* fable *f*

fabric (*fæ*-brik) *n* tissu *m*; structure *f*

façade (feu-*sââd*) *n* façade *f*

face (féïss) *n* visage *m*; *v* affronter; ~ **cream** crème de beauté; ~ **massage** massage facial; ~ **pack** masque de

beauté; ~ **powder** poudre de riz;
facing en face de

fact (*fækt*) *n* fait *m*; **in ~** de fait

factor (*fæk-teu*) *n* facteur *m*

factory (*fæk-teu-ri*) *n* usine *f*

factual (*fæk-tchou-eul*) *adj* réel

faculty (*fæ-keul-ti*) *n* faculté *f*; don *m*,
talent *m*, aptitude *f*

fade (*féïd*) *v* se faner, *déteindre

fail (*féïl*) *v* échouer; manquer;
*omettre; **without ~** sans faute

failure (*féil-yeu*) *n* échec *m*

faint (*féïnt*) *v* s'évanouir; *adj* faible,
vague, défaillant

fair (*fèᵉᵘ*) *n* foire *f*; *adj* honnête, juste;
blond; beau

fairly (*fèᵉᵘ-li*) *adv* assez, plutôt

fairy (*fèᵉᵘ-ri*) *n* fée *f*

fairytale (*fèᵉᵘ-ri-téïl*) *n* conte de fées

faith (*féïθ*) *n* foi *f*; confiance *f*

faithful (*féïθ-foul*) *adj* fidèle

fake (*féïk*) *n* falsification *f*

fall (*fool*) *n* chute *f*; *nAm* automne *m*

***fall** (*fool*) *v* tomber

false (*fools*) *adj* faux; ~ **teeth** dentier
m

falter (*fool-teu*) *v* vaciller; balbutier

fame (*féïm*) *n* renommée *f*, célébrité *f*;
réputation *f*

familiar (*feu-mil-yeu*) *adj* familier

family (*fæ-meu-li*) *n* famille *f*; ~ **name**
nom de famille

famous (*féï-meuss*) *adj* fameux

fan (*fæn*) *n* ventilateur *m*; éventail *m*;
fan *m/f*; ~ **belt** courroie de ventilateur

fanatical (*feu-næ-ti-keul*) *adj*
fanatique

fancy (*fæn-si*) *v* aimer, *avoir envie de;
s'imaginer, imaginer; *n* caprice *m*;
imagination *f*

fantastic (*fæn-tæ-stik*) *adj* fantastique

fantasy (*fæn-teu-zi*) *n* fantaisie *f*

far (*fââ*) *adj* loin; *adv* beaucoup; **by ~**
de beaucoup; **so ~** jusqu'à

maintenant

far-away (*fââ-reu-ᵒᵘéï*) *adj* éloigné

fare (*fèᵉᵘ*) *n* prix du voyage; chère *f*,
nourriture *f*

farm (*fââm*) *n* ferme *f*

farmer (*fââ-meu*) *n* fermier *m*;
farmer's wife fermière *f*

farmhouse (*fââm-haouss*) *n* ferme *f*

far-off (*fââ-rof*) *adj* lointain

fascinate (*fæ-si-néït*) *v* fasciner

fascism (*fæ-chi-zeumm*) *n* fascisme *m*

fascist (*fæ-chist*) *adj* fasciste

fashion (*fæ-cheunn*) *n* mode *f*; mode
m

fashionable (*fæ-cheu-neu-beul*) *adj* à
la mode

fast (*fââst*) *adj* prompt, rapide; ferme

fasten (*fââ-seunn*) *v* attacher; fermer

fastener (*fââ-seu-neu*) *n* fermeture *f*

fat (*fæt*) *adj* gras, gros; *n* graisse *f*

fatal (*féï-teul*) *adj* néfaste, mortel,
fatal

fate (*féït*) *n* destin *m*

father (*fââ-ðeu*) *n* père *m*

father-in-law (*fââ-ðeu-rinn-loo*) *n* (pl
fathers-) beau-père *m*

fatness (*fæt-neuss*) *n* obésité *f*

fatty (*fæ-ti*) *adj* gras

faucet (*foo-sit*) *nAm* robinet *m*

fault (*foolt*) *n* faute *f*; imperfection *f*,
défaut *m*

faultless (*foolt-leuss*) *adj* impeccable;
parfait

faulty (*fool-ti*) *adj* imparfait,
défectueux

favo(u)r (*féï-veu*) *n* faveur *f*; *v*
favoriser

favo(u)rable (*féï-veu-reu-beul*) *adj*
favorable

favo(u)rite (*féï-veu-rit*) *n* favori *m*, -te
f; *adj* préféré

fax (*faks*) *n* fax *m*; **send a ~** envoyer un
fax

fear (*fiᵉᵘ*) *n* crainte *f*, peur *f*; *v*

*craindre

feasible (*fii*-zeu-beul) *adj* faisable

feast (fiist) *n* fête *f*

feat (fiit) *n* exploit *m*, prouesse *f*

feather (*fè*-ðeu) *n* plume *f*

feature (*fii*-tcheu) *n* caractéristique *f*; trait du visage

February (*fè*-brou-eu-ri) février

federal (*fè*-deu-reul) *adj* fédéral

federation (fè-deu-*réï*-cheunn) *n* fédération *f*

fee (fii) *n* honoraires *mpl*

feeble (*fii*-beul) *adj* faible

***feed** (fiid) *v* nourrir; **fed up with** dégoûté

***feel** (fiil) *v* *sentir; palper; ~ **like** *avoir envie de

feeling (*fii*-linng) *n* sensation *f*

feet (fiit) *n* (pl foot)

fell (fèl) *v* (p fall)

fellow (*fè*-lôᵘ) *n* gars *m*

felt[1] (fèlt) *n* feutre *m*

felt[2] (fèlt) *v* (p, pp feel)

female (*fii*-méïl) *adj* féminin

feminine (*fè*-mi-ninn) *adj* féminin

fence (fèns) *n* clôture *f*; barrière *f*; *v* *faire de l'escrime

ferment (feû-*mènt*) *v* fermenter

ferry-boat (*fè*-ri-bôᵘt) *n* ferry-boat *m*

fertile (*feû*-taïl) *adj* fertile

festival (*fè*-sti-veul) *n* festival *m*

festive (*fè*-stiv) *adj* de fête

fetch (fètch) *v* apporter; *aller chercher

fever (*fii*-veu) *n* fièvre *f*

feverish (*fii*-veu-rich) *adj* fiévreux

few (fyoû) *adj* peu de

fiancé (fi-*an*-séï) *n* fiancé *m*

fiancée (fi-*an*-séï) *n* fiancée *f*

fibre (*faï*-beu) *n* fibre *f*

fiction (*fik*-cheunn) *n* fiction *f*

field (fiild) *n* champ *m*; domaine *m*; ~ **glasses** jumelles *fpl*

fierce (fiᵉᵘss) *adj* féroce; sauvage, violent

fifteen (fif-*tiin*) *num* quinze

fifteenth (fif-*tiin*θ) *num* quinzième

fifth (fifθ) *num* cinquième

fifty (*fif*-ti) *num* cinquante

fig (figh) *n* figue *f*

fight (faït) *n* lutte *f*, combat *m*

***fight** (faït) *v* se *battre, *combattre

figure (*fi*-gheu) *n* stature *f*, forme *f*; chiffre *m*

file (faïl) *n* lime *f*; dossier *m*

fill (fil) *v* remplir; ~ **in** remplir; **filling station** station-service *f*; ~ **out** *Am* remplir; ~ **up** *faire le plein

filling (*fi*-linng) *n* plombage *m*; farce *f*

film (film) *n* film *m*; pellicule *f*; *v* filmer

filter (*fil*-teu) *n* filtre *m*

filthy (*fil*-θi) *adj* répugnant, sale

final (*faï*-neul) *adj* final

finally (*faï*-neu-li) *adv* enfin; définitivement

finance (faï-*næns*) *v* financer

finances (faï-*næn*-siz) *pl* finances *fpl*

financial (faï-*næn*-cheul) *adj* financier

***find** (faïnd) *v* trouver

fine (faïn) *n* amende *f*; *adj* fin; joli; formidable, merveilleux; ~ **arts** beaux-arts *mpl*

finger (*finng*-gheu) *n* doigt *m*; **little** ~ auriculaire *m*

fingerprint (*finng*-gheu-prinnt) *n* empreinte digitale

finish (*fi*-nich) *v* achever, finir; terminer; *n* fin *f*; ligne d'arrivée

Finland (*finn*-leunnd) Finlande *f*

Finn (finn) *n* Finlandais *m*

Finnish (*fi*-nich) *adj* finlandais

fire (faïᵉᵘ) *n* feu *m*; incendie *m*; *v* tirer; licencier; ~ **alarm** alarme d'incendie; ~ **brigade,** *Am* **fire department** pompiers; ~ **escape** escalier de secours; ~ **extinguisher** extincteur *m*

fireplace (*faïeu*-pléïss) *n* cheminée *f*

fireproof (*faïeu*-proûf) *adj* ignifuge;

qui va au four

firm (feûmm) *adj* ferme; solide; *n* firme *f*

first (feûst) *num* premier; **at ~** d'abord; au début; **~ name** prénom *m*

first aid (feûst-*éïd*) *n* premier secours; **~ kit** trousse de secours; **~ post** poste de secours

first-class (feûst-*klââss*) *adj* de première qualité

first-rate (feûst-*réït*) *adj* de premier ordre, de première qualité

fir tree (*feû*-trii) *n* sapin *m*

fish¹ (fich) *n* (pl ~, ~es) poisson *m*; **~ shop** poissonnerie *f*

fish² (fich) *v* pêcher; **fishing gear** attirail de pêche; **fishing hook** hameçon *m*; **fishing industry** pêche *f*; **fishing licence (license** *Am*) permis de pêche; **fishing line** ligne de pêche; **fishing net** filet de pêche; **fishing rod** canne à pêche; **fishing tackle** attirail de pêche

fishbone (*fich*-bô^ou^n) *n* arête *f*

fisherman (*fi*-cheu-meunn) *n* (pl -men) pêcheur *m*

fist (fist) *n* poing *m*

fit (fit) *adj* convenable; *n* attaque *f*; *v* *convenir; **fitting room** cabine d'essayage

five (faïv) *num* cinq

fix (fiks) *v* réparer

fixed (fikst) *adj* fixe

fizz (fiz) *n* pétillement *m*

flag (flægh) *n* drapeau *m*

flame (fléïm) *n* flamme *f*

flamingo (fleu-*minng*-ghô^ou^) *n* (pl ~s, ~es) flamant *m*

flannel (*flæ*-neul) *n* flanelle *f*

flash (flæch) *n* éclair *m*; **~ bulb** ampoule de flash

flashlight (*flæch*-laït) *n* lampe de poche

flask (flââsk) *n* flacon *m*; **thermos ~** thermos *m*

flat (flæt) *adj* plan, plat; *n* appartement *m*; **~ tire** *Am*, **~ tyre** pneu crevé

flavour (*fléï*-veu) *n* saveur *f*; *v* assaisonner

flee (flii) *v* s'enfuir; fuir

fleet (fliit) *n* flotte *f*

flesh (flèch) *n* chair *f*

flew (floû) *v* (p fly)

flex (flèks) *n* fil souple

flexible (*flèk*-si-beul) *adj* flexible; souple

flight (flaït) *n* vol *m*; **charter ~** vol charter

flint (flinnt) *n* pierre à briquet

float (flô^ou^t) *v* flotter; *n* flotteur *m*

flock (flok) *n* troupeau *m*

flood (flad) *n* inondation *f*; marée haute

floor (floo) *n* sol *m*; étage *m*; **~ show** spectacle de variétés

florist (*flo*-rist) *n* fleuriste *m/f*

flour (flaou^eu^) *n* farine *f*

flow (flô^ou^) *v* s'écouler, couler

flower (flaou^eu^) *n* fleur *f*; **~ shop** fleuriste *m*

flowerbed (*flaoueu*-bèd) *n* plate-bande *f*

flown (flô^ou^n) *v* (pp fly)

flu (floû) *n* grippe *f*

fluently (*floû*-eunnt-li) *adv* couramment

fluid (*floû*-id) *adj* fluide; *n* liquide *m*

flute (floût) *n* flûte *f*

fly (flaï) *n* mouche *f*; braguette *f*

***fly** (flaï) *v* voler

foam (fô^ou^m) *n* mousse *f*, *v* mousser; **~ rubber** caoutchouc mousse

focus (*fôou*-keuss) *n* foyer *m*

fog (fogh) *n* brouillard *m*

foggy (*fo*-ghi) *adj* brumeux

foglamp (*fogh*-læmp) *n* phare antibrouillard

fold (fô^ou^ld) *v* plier; *n* pli *m*

folk (fô^{ou}k) n gens mpl; ~ **dance** danse folklorique; ~ **song** chanson populaire

folklore (fôouk-loo) n folklore m

follow (fo-lô^{ou}) v *suivre; **following** adj prochain, suivant

fond: *be ~ of (bii fonnd ov) aimer

food (foûd) n nourriture f; manger m; ~ **poisoning** intoxication alimentaire

foodstuffs (foûd-stafs) pl aliments mpl

fool (foûl) n idiot m/fou m; v *faire marcher

foolish (foû-lich) adj sot, stupide; absurde

foot (fout) n (pl feet) pied m; ~ **brake** frein à pédale; ~ **powder** poudre pour les pieds; **on ~** à pied

football (fout-bool) n ballon m; ~ **match** match de football

footpath (fout-pâââ) n sentier pour piétons

footwear (fout-^{ou}è^{eu}) n chaussures

for (foo, feu) prep pour; pendant; à cause de, en raison de, par; conj car

***forbid** (feu-bid) v *interdire

force (fooss) v obliger, forcer; n puissance f, force f; **by ~** forcément; **driving ~** force motrice

forecast (foo-kââst) n prévision f; v *prévoir

foreground (foo-ghraound) n premier plan

forehead (fo-rèd) n front m

foreign (fo-rinn) adj étranger

foreigner (fo-ri-neu) n étranger m

foreman (foo-meunn) n (pl -men) contremaître m

foremost (foo-mô^{ou}st) adj premier

forest (fo-rist) n bois m/forêt f

forester (fo-ri-steu) n forestier m

forge (foodj) v falsifier

***forget** (feu-ghèt) v oublier

forgetful (feu-ghèt-feul) adj oublieux

***forgive** (feu-ghiv) v pardonner

fork (fook) n fourchette f; bifurcation f; v bifurquer

form (foom) n forme f; formulaire m; classe f; v former

formal (foo-meul) adj cérémonieux

formality (foo-mæ-leu-ti) n formalité f

former (foo-meu) adj ancien; précédent; **formerly** antérieurement, auparavant

formula (foo-myou-leu) n (pl ~e, ~s) formule f

fortnight (foot-naït) n quinze jours

fortress (foo-triss) n forteresse f

fortunate (foo-tcheu-neut) adj heureux

fortunately (foo-tcheu-neut-li) adv par bonheur, heureusement

fortune (foo-tchoûn) n fortune f; sort m, chance f

forty (foo-ti) num quarante

forward (foo-^{ou}eud) adv en avant; v *faire suivre

foster parents (fo-steu-pè^{eu}-reunnts) pl parents nourriciers

fought (foot) v (p, pp fight)

foul (faoul) adj malpropre; infâme

found[1] (faound) v (p, pp find)

found[2] (faound) v fonder, établir

foundation (faoun-dë̈-cheunn) n fondation f; ~ **cream** fond de teint

fountain (faoun-tinn) n fontaine f; source f; ~ **pen** stylo m

four (foo) num quatre

fourteen (foo-tiin) num quatorze

fourteenth (foo-tiinθ) num quatorzième

fourth (fooθ) num quatrième

fowl (faoul) n (pl ~s, ~) volaille f

fox (foks) n renard m

fraction (fræk-cheunn) n fraction f

fracture (fræk-tcheu) v fracturer; n fracture f

fragile (fræ-djaïl) adj fragile

fragment (*frægh*-meunnt) *n* fragment *m*; morceau *m*

frame (*fréïm*) *n* cadre *m*; monture *f*

France (*frââns*) France *f*

franchise (*fræn*-tchaïz) *n* droit de vote

fraternity (*freu-teû*-neu-ti) *n* fraternité *f*

fraud (frood) *n* fraude *f*

fray (fréï) *v* s'effilocher

free (frii) *adj* libre; gratuit; ~ **of charge** gratuit; ~ **ticket** billet gratuit

freedom (*frii*-deumm) *n* liberté *f*

***freeze** (friiz) *v* geler

freezer (*frii*-zeu) *n* congélateur *m*

freezing (*frii*-zinng) *adj* glacial; ~ **point** point de congélation

freight (fréït) *n* fret *m*, chargement *m*; ~ **train** train de marchandises

French (frèntch) *adj* français

French fries (frèntch-*fraïz*) *nAm* pommes de terre frites *fpl*

frequency (*frii*-k^(ou)eunn-si) *n* fréquence *f*

frequent (*frii*-k^(ou)eunnt) *adj* courant, fréquent

fresh (frèch) *adj* frais; ~ **water** eau douce

friction (*frik*-cheunn) *n* friction *f*

Friday (*fraï*-di) vendredi *m*

fridge (fridj) *n* réfrigérateur *m*, frigo *m*

friend (frènd) *n* ami *m*, -e *f*

friendly (*frènd*-li) *adj* gentil; amical

friendship (*frènd*-chip) *n* amitié *f*

fright (fraït) *n* peur *f*, frayeur *f*

frighten (*fraï*-teunn) *v* effrayer

frightened (*fraï*-teunnd) *adj* effrayé; ***be ~** *être effrayé

frightful (*fraït*-feul) *adj* terrible, affreux

fringe (frinndj) *n* frange *f*

frock (frok) *n* robe *f*

frog (frogh) *n* grenouille *f*

from (fromm) *prep* de; à partir de

front (frannt) *n* face *f*; **in ~ of** devant

frontier (*frann*-ti^(eu)) *n* frontière *f*

frost (frost) *n* gel *m*

froth (froθ) *n* écume *f*

frozen (*frôou*-zeunn) *adj* congelé; ~ **food** aliments surgelés

fruit (froût) *n* fruits; fruit *m*

fry (fraï) *v* *faire sauter; *frire

frying pan (*fraï*-inng-pæn) *n* poêle à frire

fuel (*fyoû*-eul) *n* combustible *m*; essence *f*; ~ **pump** *Am* distributeur d'essence

full (foul) *adj* plein; ~ **board** pension complète; ~ **stop** point *m*; ~ **up** complet

fun (fann) *n* divertissement *m*, plaisir *m*

function (*fanngk*-cheunn) *n* fonction *f*

fund (fannd) *n* fonds *mpl*

fundamental (fann-deu-*mèn*-teul) *adj* fondamental

funeral (*fyoû*-neu-reul) *n* funérailles *fpl*

funnel (*fa*-neul) *n* entonnoir *m*

funny (*fa*-ni) *adj* drôle, amusant; bizarre

fur (feû) *n* fourrure *f*; ~ **coat** manteau de fourrure

furious (*fyoueu*-ri-euss) *adj* furibond, furieux

furnace (*feû*-niss) *n* fournaise *f*

furnish (*feû*-nich) *v* fournir, procurer; installer, meubler; ~ **with** approvisionner en

furniture (*feû*-ni-tcheu) *n* meubles *m*

furrier (*fa*-ri-eu) *n* fourreur *m*

further (*feû*-ðeu) *adj* plus loin; complémentaire

furthermore (*feû*-ðeu-moo) *adv* en outre

furthest (*feû*-ðist) *adj* le plus éloigné

fuse (fyoûz) *n* fusible *m*; mèche *f*

fuss (fass) *n* agitation *f*; embarras *m*, chichi *m*

future (*fyoû*-tcheu) *n* avenir *m*; *adj* futur

G

gable (*ghéï*-beul) *n* pignon *m*

gadget (*ghæ*-djit) *n* gadget *m*

gain (ghéín) *v* gagner; *n* gain *m*

gale (ghéíl) *n* tempête *f*

gall (ghool) *n* bile *f*; ~ **bladder** vésicule biliaire

gallery (*ghæ*-leu-ri) *n* galerie *f*

gallon (*ghæ*-leun) *n* gallon *m*

gallop (*ghæ*-leup) *n* galop *m*

gallstone (*ghool*-stô^{ou}n) *n* calcul biliaire

game (ghéím) *n* jeu *m*; gibier *m*; ~ **reserve** réserve zoologique

gang (ghæng) *n* bande *f*; équipe *f*

gangway (*ghæng*-^{ou}éï) *n* passerelle *f*

gap (ghæp) *n* brèche *f*

garage (*ghæ*-râáj) *n* garage *m*; *v* garer

garbage (*ghââ*-bidj) *n* détritus *m*, ordures *fpl*

garden (*ghââ*-deunn) *n* jardin *m*; **public** ~ jardin public; **zoological gardens** jardin zoologique

gardener (*ghââ*-deu-neu) *n* jardinier *m*, -ière *f*

gargle (*ghââ*-gheul) *v* se gargariser

garlic (*ghââ*-lik) *n* ail *m*

gas (ghæss) *n* gaz *m*; *nAm* essence *f*; ~ **cooker** cuisinière à gaz; ~ **pump** *Am* pompe à essence; ~ **station** *Am* station-service *f*; ~ **stove** fourneau à gaz; ~ **tank** réservoir d'essence

gasoline (*ghæ*-seu-liin) *nAm* essence *f*

gastric (*ghæ*-strik) *adj* gastrique; ~ **ulcer** ulcère à l'estomac

gasworks (*ghæss*-^{ou}eûks) *n* usine à gaz

gate (ghéït) *n* porte *f*; grille *f*

gather (*ghæ*-ðeu) *v* collectionner; se réunir

gauge (ghéïdj) *n* jauge *f*

gave (ghéív) *v* (p give)

gay (ghéí) *adj* gai; éclatant

gaze (ghéíz) *v* fixer

gear (ghi^{eu}) *n* vitesse *f*; équipement *m*; **change** ~ changer de vitesse; ~ **lever** levier de vitesse

gearbox (*ghieu*-boks) *n* boîte de vitesse

geese (ghiiz) *n* (pl goose)

gem (djèm) *n* joyau *m*, pierre précieuse; bijou *m*

gender (*djèn*-deu) *n* genre *m*

general (*djè*-neu-reul) *adj* général; *n* général *m*; ~ **practitioner** médecin généraliste; **in** ~ en général

generate (*djè*-neu-réït) *v* *produire

generation (djè-neu-*réï*-cheunn) *n* génération *f*

generator (*djè*-neu-réï-teur) *n* générateur *m*

generosity (djè-neu-*ro*-seu-ti) *n* générosité *f*

generous (*djè*-neu-reuss) *adj* large, généreux

genital (*djè*-ni-teul) *adj* génital

genius (*djii*-ni-euss) *n* génie *m*

gentle (*djèn*-teul) *adj* doux; léger; délicat

gentleman (*djèn*-teul-meunn) *n* (pl -men) monsieur *m*

genuine (*djè*-nyou-inn) *adj* authentique

geography (dji-*o*-ghreu-fi) *n* géographie *f*

geology (dji-*o*-leu-dji) *n* géologie *f*

geometry (dji-*o*-meu-tri) *n* géométrie *f*

germ (djeûmm) *n* microbe *m*; germe *m*

German (*djeû*-meunn) *adj* allemand; *n* Allemand *m*

Germany (*djeû*-meu-ni) Allemagne *f*

gesticulate (dji-*sti*-kyou-léït) *v* gesticuler

*get (ghèt) *v* *obtenir; *aller prendre; *devenir; ~ **back** retourner; ~ **off** descendre; ~ **on** monter; progresser; ~ **up** se lever

ghost (ghô^{ou}st) *n* fantôme *m*; esprit *m*

giant (*djaï*-eunnt) *n* géant *m*

giddiness (*ghi*-di-neuss) *n* vertige *m*

giddy (*ghi*-di) *adj* étourdi

gift (ghift) *n* don *m*, cadeau *m*; talent *m*

gifted (*ghif*-tid) *adj* doué

gigantic (djaï-*ghæn*-tik) *adj* gigantesque

giggle (*ghi*-gheul) *v* glousser

gill (ghil) *n* branchie *f*

gilt (ghilt) *adj* doré

ginger (*djinn*-djeu) *n* gingembre *m*

girdle (*gheû*-deul) *n* gaine *f*

girl (gheûl) *n* fille *f*; ~ **guide** scout *m*

girlfriend (*gheûl*-frènd) *n* amie *f*; petite amie *f*

*give (ghiv) *v* donner; passer; ~ **away** révéler; ~ **in** céder; ~ **up** renoncer

glacier (*ghlæ*-si-eu) *n* glacier *m*

glad (ghlæd) *adj* joyeux, content; **gladly** avec plaisir, volontiers

gladness (*ghlæd*-neuss) *n* joie *f*

glamorous (*ghlæ*-meu-reuss) *adj* enchanteur, charmant

glamour (*ghlæ*-meu) *n* charme *m*

glance (ghlââns) *n* coup d'œil; *v* jeter un coup d'œil

gland (ghlænd) *n* glande *f*

glare (ghlè^{eu}) *n* éclat *m*; éblouissement *m*

glaring (*ghlèeu*-rinng) *adj* éblouissant

glass (ghlââss) *n* verre *m*; de verre; **glasses** lunettes *fpl*; **magnifying ~** verre grossissant

glaze (ghléïz) *v* vernir

glide (ghlaïd) *v* glisser

glider (*ghlaï*-deu) *n* planeur *m*

glimpse (ghlimmps) *n* aperçu *m*; coup d'œil; *v* entrevoir

global (*ghlô*-beul) *adj* mondial

globe (ghlô^{ou}b) *n* globe *m*

gloom (ghloûm) *n* ténèbres *fpl*

gloomy (*ghloû*-mi) *adj* sombre

glorious (*ghloo*-ri-euss) *adj* splendide

glory (*ghloo*-ri) *n* gloire *f*; honneur *m*, louange *f*

gloss (ghloss) *n* lustre *m*

glossy (*ghlo*-si) *adj* luisant

glove (ghlav) *n* gant *m*

glow (ghlô^{ou}) *v* briller; *n* éclat *m*

glue (ghloû) *n* colle *f*

*go (ghô^{ou}) *v* se rendre, *aller; marcher; *devenir; ~ **ahead** continuer; ~ **away** *partir; ~ **back** retourner; ~ **home** rentrer; ~ **in** entrer; ~ **on** continuer; ~ **out** *sortir; ~ **through** endurer

goal (ghô^{ou}l) *n* objectif *m*, but *m*

goalkeeper (*ghôoul*-kii-peu) *n* gardien de but

goat (ghô^{ou}t) *n* bouc *m*, chèvre *f*

god (ghod) *n* dieu *m*

godfather (*ghod*-fââ-ðeu) *n* parrain *m*

goggles (*gho*-gheulz) *pl* lunettes de plongée

gold (ghô^{ou}ld) *n* or *m*; ~ **leaf** or en feuille

golden (*ghôoul*-deunn) *adj* en or

goldmine (*ghôoul*-maïn) *n* mine d'or

goldsmith (*ghôoul*-smiθ) *n* orfèvre

m

golf (gholf) *n* golf *m*; ~ **course** terrain de golf; ~ **links** terrain de golf

golfclub (*gholf*-klab) *n* club de golf

gondola (*ghonn*-deu-leu) *n* gondole *f*

gone (ghonn) *adv* (pp go) parti

good (ghoud) *adj* bon; sage, brave

goodbye! (ghoud-*baï*) au revoir!

good-humoured (ghoud-*hyoû*-meud) *adj* de bonne humeur

good-looking (ghoud-*lou*-kinng) *adj* joli

good-natured (ghoud-*néï*-tcheud) *adj* de bon caractère

goods (ghoudz) *pl* marchandise *f*, biens *mpl*; ~ **train** train de marchandises

good-tempered (ghoud-*tèm*-peud) *adj* de bonne humeur

goodwill (ghoud-*ouil*) *n* bienveillance *f*

goose (ghoûss) *n* (pl geese) oie *f*; ~ **bumps**, ~ **flesh**, ~ **pimples** chair de poule

gooseberry (*ghouz*-beu-ri) *n* groseille à maquereau

gorge (ghoodj) *n* gorge *f*

gorgeous (*ghoo*-djeuss) *adj* magnifique

gospel (*gho*-speul) *n* évangile *m*

gossip (*gho*-sip) *n* commérage *m*; *v* *faire des commérages

got (ghot) *v* (p, pp get)

gout (ghaout) *n* goutte *f*

govern (*gha*-veunn) *v* gouverner

governess (*gha*-veu-niss) *n* gouvernante *f*

government (*gha*-veunn-meunnt) *n* régime *m*, gouvernement *m*

governor (*gha*-veu-neu) *n* gouverneur *m*

gown (ghaoun) *n* robe *f*

grace (ghréïss) *n* grâce *f*; clémence *f*

graceful (*ghréïss*-feul) *adj* charmant, gracieux

grade (ghréïd) *n* grade *m*; *v* classer

gradient (*ghréï*-di-eunnt) *n* inclinaison *f*

gradual (*ghræ*-djou-eul) *adj* graduel

graduate (*ghræ*-djou-éït) *v* *obtenir un diplôme

grain (ghréïn) *n* grain *m*, blé *m*, céréale *f*

gram (ghræm) *n* gramme *m*

grammar (*ghræ*-meu) *n* grammaire *f*

grammatical (ghreu-*mæ*-ti-keul) *adj* grammatical

grand (ghrænd) *adj* sublime

grandchild (*ghræn*-tchaïld) *n* petit-fils *m*,-fille *f*

granddad (*ghræn*-dæd) *n* grand-papa *m*

granddaughter (*ghræn*-doo-teu) *n* petite-fille *f*

grandfather (*ghræn*-fââ-ðeu) *n* grandpère *m*

grandmother (*ghræn*-ma-ðeu) *n* grand-mère *f*

grandparents (*ghræn*-pè^{eu}-reunnts) *pl* grands-parents *mpl*

grandson (*ghræn*-sann) *n* petit-fils *m*

granite (*ghræ*-nit) *n* granit *m*

grant (ghrâânt) *v* accorder; concéder; *n* subvention *f*, bourse *f*

grapefruit (*ghréïp*-froût) *n* pamplemousse *m*

grapes (ghréïps) *pl* raisin *m*

graph (ghræf) *n* diagramme *m*

graphic (*ghræ*-fik) *adj* graphique

grasp (ghrââsp) *v* saisir; *n* prise *f*

grass (ghrââss) *n* herbe *f*

grasshopper (*ghrââss*-ho-peu) *n* sauterelle *f*

grate (ghréït) *n* grille *f*; *v* râper

grateful (*ghréït*-feul) *adj* reconnaissant

grater (*ghréï*-teu) *n* râpe *f*

gratis (*ghræ*-tiss) *adj* gratuit

gratitude (*ghræ*-ti-tyoûd) *n* gratitude *f*

gratuity (*greu*-*tyoû*-eu-ti) *n* pourboire *m*

grave (*ghréïv*) *n* tombe *f*; *adj* grave

gravel (*ghræ*-veul) *n* gravier *m*

gravestone (*ghréïv*-stô^ou^n) *n* pierre tombale

graveyard (*ghréïv*-yââd) *n* cimetière *m*

gravity (*ghræ*-veu-ti) *n* gravité *f*

gravy (*ghréï*-vi) *n* jus *m*

graze (*ghréïz*) *v* *paître; *n* égratignure *f*

grease (*ghriiss*) *n* graisse *f*; *v* graisser

greasy (*ghrii*-si) *adj* graisseux

great (*ghréït*) *adj* grand; **Great Britain** Grande-Bretagne *f*

Greece (*ghriiss*) *n* Grèce *f*

greed (*ghriid*) *n* cupidité *f*

greedy (*ghrii*-di) *adj* cupide; gourmand

Greek (*ghriik*) *adj* grec; *n* Grec *m*

green (*ghriin*) *adj* vert; ~ **card** carte verte

greengrocer (*ghriin*-ghrô^ou^-seu) *n* marchand de légumes

greenhouse (*ghriin*-haouss) *n* serre *f*

greens (*ghriinz*) *pl* légumes *mpl*

greet (*ghriit*) *v* saluer

greeting (*ghrii*-tinng) *n* salutation *f*

grey (*ghréï*) *adj* gris

greyhound (*ghréï*-haound) *n* lévrier *m*

grief (*ghriif*) *n* chagrin *m*; affliction *f*, douleur *f*

grieve (*ghriiv*) *v* *avoir de la peine

grill (*ghril*) *n* grill *m*; *v* griller

grillroom (*ghril*-roûm) *n* rôtisserie *f*

grim (*ghrimm*) *adj* sinistre; sévère; farouche

grin (*ghrinn*) *n* large sourire

***grind** (*ghraïnd*) *v* *moudre; pulvériser

grip (*ghrip*) *v* saisir; *n* prise *f*, étreinte

f; *nAm* mallette de voyage

grit (*ghrit*) *n* gravillon *m*

groan (*ghrô^ou^n*) *v* gémir

grocer (*ghrôou*-seu) *n* épicier *m*; **grocer's, grocery** épicerie *f*

groceries (*ghrôou*-seu-riz) *pl* articles d'épicerie

groin (*ghroïn*) *n* aine *f*

groom (*ghroûm*) *n* palefrenier *m*; marié *m*; *v* panser; soigner; former, façonner

groove (*ghroûv*) *n* sillon *m*

gross[1] (*ghrô^ou^ss*) *n* (pl ~) grosse *f*

gross[2] (*ghrô^ou^ss*) *adj* grossier; brut

grotto (*ghro*-tô^ou^) *n* (pl ~es, ~s) grotte *f*

ground[1] (*ghraound*) *n* fond *m*, sol *m*; ~ **floor** rez-de-chaussée *m*; **grounds** terrain *m*

ground[2] (*ghraound*) *v* (p, pp grind)

group (*ghroûp*) *n* groupe *m*

grouse (*ghraouss*) *n* (pl ~) grouse *f*

grove (*ghrô^ou^v*) *n* bosquet *m*

***grow** (*ghrô^ou^*) *v* grandir; cultiver

growl (*ghraoul*) *v* grogner

grown-up (*ghrô^ou^n*-ap) *adj* adulte; *n* adulte *m/f*

growth (*ghrô^ou^θ*) *n* croissance *f*; tumeur *f*

grudge (*ghradj*) *v* envier

grumble (*ghramm*-beul) *v* grogner

guarantee (*ghæ*-reunn-*tii*) *n* garantie *f*; caution *f*; *v* garantir

guard (*ghââd*) *n* garde *m*; *v* surveiller

guardian (*ghââ*-di-eunn) *n* tuteur *m*

guess (*ghèss*) *v* deviner; *croire, supposer; *n* conjecture *f*

guest (*ghèst*) *n* hôte *m*, invité *m*; ~ **room** chambre d'ami

guesthouse (*ghèst*-haouss) *n* pension *f*

guide (*ghaïd*) *n* guide *m*; *v* *conduire; ~ **dog** chien d'aveugle

guidebook (*ghaïd*-bouk) *n* guide *m*

guilt (ghilt) *n* culpabilité *f*

guilty (*ghil*-ti) *adj* coupable

guinea pig (*ghi*-ni-pigh) *n* cochon d'Inde

guitar (ghi-*tââ*) *n* guitare *f*

gulf (ghalf) *n* golfe *m*

gull (ghal) *n* mouette *f*

gum (ghamm) *n* gencive *f*; gomme *f*; colle *f*

gun (ghann) *n* fusil *m*, revolver *m*; canon *m*

gunpowder (*ghann*-paou-deu) *n* poudre à canon

gust (ghast) *n* rafale *f*

gusty (*gha*-sti) *adj* venteux

gut (ghat) *n* intestin *m*; **guts** cran *m*

gutter (*gha*-teu) *n* caniveau *m*

guy (ghaï) *n* type *m*

gym (djimm) *n* *colloquial* gymnase *f*; gym(nastique) *f*; de gymnastique; ~ **shoes** tennis *pl*, baskets *pl*

gymnasium (djimm-*néé*-zi-eumm) *n* (pl ~s, -sia) gymnase *m*

gymnast (*djimm*-næst) *n* gymnaste *m*

gymnastics (djimm-*næ*-stiks) *pl* gymnastique *f*

gyn(a)ecologist (ghaï-neu-*ko*-leu-djist) *n* gynécologue *m/f*

H

habit (*hæ*-bit) *n* habitude *f*

habitable (*hæ*-bi-teu-beul) *adj* habitable

habitual (heu-*bi*-tchou-eul) *adj* habituel

had (hæd) *v* (p, pp have)

haddock (*hæ*-deuk) *n* (pl ~) aiglefin *m*

h(a)emorrhage (*hè*-meu-ridj) *n* hémorragie *f*

h(a)emorrhoids (*hè*-meu-roïdz) *pl* hémorroïdes *fpl*

hail (héïl) *n* grêle *f*

hair (hè^eu) *n* cheveu *m*; ~ **cream** crème capillaire; ~ **gel** gel pour les cheveux *m*; ~ **net** résille *f*; ~ **oil** huile capillaire; ~ **piece** postiche *m*; ~ **rollers** bigoudis *mpl*

hairbrush (*hèeu*-brach) *n* brosse à cheveux

haircut (*hèeu*-kat) *n* coupe de cheveux

hairdo (*hèeu*-doû) *n* coiffure *f*

hairdresser (*hèeu*-drè-seu) *n* coiffeur *m*, -se *f*

hairdrier, hairdryer (*hèeu*-draï-eu) *n* sèche-cheveux *m*

hairgrip (*hèeu*-ghrip) *n* pince à cheveux

hairpin (*hèeu*-pinn) *n* épingle à cheveux

hair spray (*hèeu*-spréï) *n* laque capillaire

hairy (*hèeu*-ri) *adj* chevelu

half[1] (hââf) *adj* demi; *adv* à moitié

half[2] (hââf) *n* (pl halves) moitié *f*

half time (hââf-taïm) *n* mi-temps *f*

halfway (hââf-*ouéï*) *adv* à mi-chemin

halibut (*hæ*-li-beut) *n* (pl ~) flétan *m*

hall (hool) *n* vestibule *m*; salle *f*

halt (hoolt) *v* s'arrêter

halve (hââv) *v* diviser en deux

ham (hæm) *n* jambon *m*

hamlet (*hæm*-leut) *n* hameau *m*

hammer (*hæ*-meu) *n* marteau *m*

hammock (*hæ*-meuk) *n* hamac *m*

hamper (*hæm*-peu) *n* panier d'osier

hand (hænd) *n* main *f*; ~ **cream** crème pour les mains; ~ **over** *remettre

handbag (*hænd*-bægh) *n* sac à main

handbook (*hænd*-bouk) *n* manuel *m*

handbrake (*hænd*-bréïk) *n* frein à main

handcuffs (*hænd*-kafs) *pl* menottes *fpl*

handful (*hænd*-foul) *n* poignée *f*

handicap (*hæn*-di-kæp) *n* handicap *m*; *v* handicaper

handicapped (*hæn*-di-kæpt) *adj* handicapé

handicraft (*hæn*-di-krââft) *n* travail manuel; artisanat *m*

handkerchief (*hæng*-keu-tchif) *n* mouchoir *m*

handle (*hæn*-deul) *n* manche *m*, poignée *f*; *v* manipuler; traiter

hand-made (hænd-*méïd*) *adj* fait à la main

handshake (*hænd*-chéïk) *n* poignée de main

handsome (*hæn*-seumm) *adj* beau

handwork (*hænd*-^{ou}eûk) *n* travail artisanal

handwriting (*hænd*-raï-tinng) *n* écriture *f*

handy (*hæn*-di) *adj* commode

***hang** (hæng) *v* suspendre; pendre

hanger (*hæng*-eu) *n* cintre *m*

hangover (*hæng*-ô^{ou}-veu) *n* gueule de bois

happen (*hæ*-peunn) *v* se *produire, arriver

happening (*hæ*-peu-ninng) *n* événement *m*

happiness (*hæ*-pi-neuss) *n* bonheur *m*

happy (*hæ*-pi) *adj* content, heureux

harbo(u)r (*hââ*-beu) *n* port *m*

hard (hââd) *adj* dur; difficile; **hardly** à peine

hardware (*hââd*-^{ou}è^{eu}) *n* quincaillerie *f*; ~ **store** quincaillerie *f*

hare (hè^{eu}) *n* lièvre *m*

harm (hââm) *n* mal *m*; tort *m*; *v* *faire du mal

harmful (*hââm*-feul) *adj* préjudiciable, nuisible

harmless (*hââm*-leuss) *adj* inoffensif

harmony (*hââ*-meu-ni) *n* harmonie *f*

harp (hââp) *n* harpe *f*

harpsichord (*hââp*-si-kood) *n* clavecin *m*

harsh (hââch) *adj* âpre; sévère; cruel

harvest (*hââ*-vist) *n* moisson *f*

has (hæz) *v* (pr have)

haste (héïst) *n* hâte *f*

hasten (*héï*-seunn) *v* se hâter

hasty (*héï*-sti) *adj* précipité

hat (hæt) *n* chapeau *m*; ~ **rack** porte-manteau *m*

hate (héït) *v* détester; *haïr; *n* haine *f*

hatred (*héï*-trid) *n* haine *f*

haughty (*hoo*-ti) *adj* hautain

haul (hool) *v* traîner

***have** (hæv) *v* *avoir; *faire; ~ **to** *devoir

hawk (hook) *n* faucon *m*

hay (héï) *n* foin *m*; ~ **fever** rhume des foins

hazard (*hæ*-zeud) *n* hasard *m*

haze (héïz) *n* brume *f*

hazelnut (*héï*-zeul-nat) *n* noisette *f*

hazy (*héï*-zi) *adj* brumeux; nébuleux

he (hii) *pron* il

head (hèd) *n* tête *f*; *v* diriger; ~ **of state** chef d'Etat; ~ **teacher** directeur d'école; ~ **waiter** maître d'hôtel

headache (*hè*-déïk) *n* mal de tête

heading (*hè*-dinng) *n* titre *m*

headlamp (*hèd*-læmp) *n* phare *m*

headland (*hèd*-leunnd) *n* promontoire *m*

headlight (*hèd*-laït) *n* phare *m*

headline (*hèd*-laïn) *n* manchette *f*

headmaster (hèd-*mââ*-steu) *n* directeur d'école

headquarters (hèd-*kouoo*-teuz) *pl* quartier général

head-strong (*hèd*-stronng) *adj* têtu

heal (hiil) *v* guérir

health (hèlθ) *n* santé *f*; ~ **centre** dispensaire *m*; ~ **certificate** certificat médical

healthy (*hèl*-θi) *adj* sain

heap (hiip) *n* amoncellement *m*, tas *m*

***hear** (hi^{eu}) *v* entendre

hearing (*hieu*-rinng) *n* ouïe *f*

heart (hâât) *n* cœur *m*; **by** ~ par cœur; ~ **attack** crise cardiaque

heartburn (*hâât*-beûnn) *n* brûlures d'estomac

hearth (hââθ) *n* cheminée *f*

heartless (*hâât*-leuss) *adj* insensible

hearty (*hââ*-ti) *adj* cordial

heat (hiit) *n* chaleur *f*; *v* chauffer; **heating pad** coussin chauffant

heater (*hii*-teu) *n* appareil de chauffage; **immersion** ~ thermoplongeur *m*

heath (hiiθ) *n* lande *f*

heathen (*hii*-ðeunn) *n* païen *m*

heather (*hè*-ðeu) *n* bruyère *f*

heating (*hii*-tinng) *n* chauffage *m*

heaven (*hè*-veunn) *n* ciel *m*

heavy (*hè*-vi) *adj* lourd

Hebrew (*hii*-broû) *n* hébreu *m*

hedge (hèdj) *n* haie *f*

hedgehog (*hèdj*-hogh) *n* hérisson *m*

heel (hiil) *n* talon *m*

height (haït) *n* hauteur *f*; sommet *m*, apogée *m*

heir (hè^{eu}) *n* héritier *m* (**to** de); ~ **apparent** héritier *m* présomptif

heir-at-law (*hèeu*-reut-loo) *n* héritier *m* légitime

heiress (*hèeu*-resse) *n* héritière *f*

helicopter (*hè*-li-kop-teu) *n* hélicoptère *m*

hell (hèl) *n* enfer *m*

hello! (hè-*lôou*) bonjour!

helm (hèlm) *n* barre *f*

helmet (*hèl*-mit) *n* casque *m*

help (hèlp) *v* aider; *n* aide *f*

helper (*hèl*-peu) *n* aide *m/f*

helpful (*hèlp*-feul) *adj* serviable

helping (*hèl*-pinng) *n* portion *f*

hem (hèm) *n* ourlet *m*

hemp (hèmp) *n* chanvre *m*

hen (hèn) *n* poule *f*

her (heû) *pron* la *art/pron*, lui; *adj* son

herb (heûb) *n* herbe *f*

herd (heûd) *n* troupeau *m*

here (hi^{eu}) *adv* ici; ~ **you are** voilà

hereditary (hi-*rè*-di-teu-ri) *adj* héréditaire

hernia (*heû*-ni-eu) *n* hernie *f*

hero (*hieu*-rô^{ou}) *n* (*pl* ~es) héros *m*

heron (*hè*-reunn) *n* héron *m*

herring (*hè*-rinng) *n* (*pl* ~, ~s) hareng *m*

herself (heû-*sèlf*) *pron* se; elle-même

hesitate (*hè*-zi-téit) *v* hésiter

heterosexual (hè-teu-reu-*sèk*-chou-eul) *adj* hétérosexuel

hiccup (*hi*-kap) *n* hoquet *m*

hide (haïd) *n* peau *f*

***hide** (haïd) *v* cacher; dissimuler

hideous (*hi*-di-euss) *adj* hideux

hierarchy (*haïeu*-rââ-ki) *n* hiérarchie *f*

high (haï) *adj* haut

highway (*haï*-^{ou}éi) *n* route nationale; *nAm* autoroute *f*

hijack (*haï*-djæk) *v* détourner

hike (haïk) *v* faire des randonnées

hill (hil) *n* colline *f*

hillock (*hi*-leuk) *n* monticule *m*

hillside (*hil*-saïd) *n* coteau *m*

hilltop (*hil*-top) *n* sommet de colline

hilly (*hi*-li) *adj* accidenté

him (himm) *pron* le, lui

himself (himm-*sèlf*) *pron* se; lui-même

hinder (*hinn*-deu) *v* gêner

hinge (hinndj) *n* charnière *f*

hint (hinnt) *n* allusion *f*; signe *m*; *v* suggérer; faire allusion (**at** à)

hip (hip) *n* hanche *f*

hire (haï^{eu}) *v* louer; **for ~** à louer

hire purchase (haï^{eu}-*peû*-tcheuss) *n* achat à tempérament

his (hiz) *adj* son

historian (hi-*stoo*-ri-eunn) *n* historien *m*, -ne *f*

historic (hi-*sto*-rik) *adj* historique

historical (hi-*sto*-ri-keul) *adj* historique

history (*hi*-steu-ri) *n* histoire *f*

hit (hit) *n* succès *m*

*****hit** (hit) *v* frapper; toucher

hitchhike (*hitch*-haïk) *v* *faire de l'auto-stop

hitchhiker (*hitch*-haï-keu) *n* auto-stoppeur *m*, -se *f*

hoarse (hooss) *adj* rauque, enroué

hobby (*ho*-bi) *n* hobby *m*, passetemps *m*

hockey (*ho*-ki) *n* hockey *m*

hoist (hoïst) *v* hisser

hold (hô^{ou}ld) *n* cale *f*

*****hold** (hô^{ou}ld) *v* *tenir; garder; **~ on** s'accrocher; **~ up** *soutenir

hold-up (*hô*oul-dap) *n* attaque *f*

hole (hô^{ou}l) *n* trou *m*

holiday (*ho*-leu-di) *n* vacances; jour de fête; **~ camp** camp de vacances; **on ~** en vacances

Holland (*ho*-leunnd) Hollande *f*

hollow (*ho*-lô^{ou}) *adj* creux

holy (*hô*ou-li) *adj* sacré

homage (*ho*-midj) *n* hommage *m*

home (hô^{ou}m) *n* maison *f*; foyer *m*, demeure *f*; *adv* chez soi; **at ~** à la maison

home-made (hô^{ou}m-*méïd*) *adj* fait à la maison

homesickness (*hôoum*-sik-neuss) *n* mal du pays

homosexual (hô^{ou}-meu-*sèk*-chou-

eul) *adj* homosexuel

honest (*o*-nist) *adj* honnête; sincère

honesty (*o*-ni-sti) *n* honnêteté *f*

honey (*ha*-ni) *n* miel *m*

honeymoon (*ha*-ni-moûn) *n* lune de miel

honk (hanngk) *vAm* klaxonner

hono(u)r (*o*-neu) *n* honneur *m*; *v* honorer, rendre hommage

hono(u)rable (*o*-neu-reu-beul) *adj* honorable; honnête

hood (houd) *n* capuchon *m*; *nAm* capot *m*

hoof (hoûf) *n* sabot *m*

hook (houk) *n* crochet *m*

hoot (hoût) *v* klaxonner

hooter (*hoû*-teu) *n* klaxon *m*

hoover (*hoû*-veu) *v* passer l'aspirateur

hop¹ (hop) *v* sautiller; *n* saut *m*

hop² (hop) *n* houblon *m*

hope (hô^{ou}p) *n* espoir *m*; *v* espérer

hopeful (*hôoup*-feul) *adj* plein d'espoir

hopeless (*hôoup*-leuss) *adj* désespéré

horizon (heu-*raï*-zeunn) *n* horizon *m*

horizontal (ho-ri-*zonn*-teul) *adj* horizontal

horn (hoon) *n* corne *f*; cor *m*; klaxon *m*

horrible (*ho*-ri-beul) *adj* horrible; terrifiant, atroce, horrifiant

horror (*ho*-reu) *n* épouvante *f*, horreur *f*

horse (hooss) *n* cheval *m*

horseman (*hooss*-meunn) *n* (pl -men) cavalier *m*

horsepower (*hooss*-paou^{eu}) *n* chevalvapeur *m*

horserace (*hooss*-réïss) *n* course de chevaux

horseradish (*hooss*-ræ-dich) *n* raifort *m*

horseshoe (*hooss*-choû) *n* fer à cheval

horticulture (*hoo*-ti-kal-tcheu) *n*

horticulture f

hospitable (*ho*-spi-teu-beul) *adj* hospitalier

hospital (*ho*-spi-teul) *n* hôpital *m*

hospitality (ho-spi-*tæ*-leu-ti) *n* hospitalité *f*

host (hôᵘst) *n* hôte *m*

hostage (*ho*-stidj) *n* otage *m*

hostel (*ho*-steul) *n* auberge *f*

hostess (*hôou*-stiss) *n* hôtesse *f*

hostile (*ho*-staïl) *adj* hostile

hot (hot) *adj* chaud

hotel (hôᵘ-*tèl*) *n* hôtel *m*

hot-tempered (hot-*tèm*-peud) *adj* coléreux

hour (aouᵉᵘ) *n* heure *f*

hourly (*aoueu*-li) *adj* toutes les heures

house (haouss) *n* maison *f*; habitation *f*; immeuble *m*; ~ **agent** agent immobilier; ~ **block** *Am* pâté de maisons; **public** ~ café *m*

houseboat (*haouss*-bôᵘt) *n* maisonbateau

household (*haouss*-hôᵘld) *n* ménage *m*

housekeeper (*haouss*-kii-peu) *n* gouvernante *f*

housekeeping (*haouss*-kii-pinng) *n* travaux ménagers, ménage *m*

housemaid (*haouss*-méïd) *n* bonne *f*

housewife (*haouss*-ᵒᵘaïf) *n* ménagère *f*

housework (*haouss*-ᵒᵘeûk) *n* travaux ménagers

how (haou) *adv* comment; que; ~ **many** combien; ~ **much** combien

however (haou-*è*-veu) *conj* pourtant, cependant

hug (hagh) *v* étreindre; *n* étreinte *f*

huge (hyoûdj) *adj* immense, énorme

hum (hamm) *v* fredonner

human (*hyoû*-meunn) *adj* humain; ~ **being** être humain

humanity (hyou-*mæ*-neu-ti) *n* humanité *f*

humble (*hamm*-beul) *adj* humble

humid (*hyoû*-mid) *adj* humide

humidity (hyou-*mi*-deu-ti) *n* humidité *f*

humorous (*hyoû*-meu-reuss) *adj* comique, drôle

humour (*hyoû*-meu) *n* humour *m*

hundred (*hann*-dreud) *n* cent

Hungarian (hanng-*ghèeu*-ri-eunn) *adj* hongrois; *n* Hongrois *m*

Hungary (*hanng*-gheu-ri) Hongrie *f*

hunger (*hanng*-gheu) *n* faim *f*

hungry (*hanng*-ghri) *adj* affamé

hunt (hannt) *v* chasser; *n* chasse *f*; ~ **for** chercher

hunter (*hann*-teu) *n* chasseur *m*

hurricane (*ha*-ri-keunn) *n* ouragan *m*; ~ **lamp** lampe-tempête *f*

hurry (*ha*-ri) *v* se dépêcher, se presser; *n* hâte *f*; **in a** ~ en vitesse

*****hurt** (heût) *v* *faire mal, blesser; offenser

hurtful (*heût*-feul) *adj* nuisible

husband (*haz*-beunnd) *n* époux *m*, mari *m*

hut (hat) *n* hutte *f*

hydrogen (*haï*-dreu-djeunn) *n* hydrogène *m*

hygiene (*haï*-djiin) *n* hygiène *f*

hygienic (haï-*djii*-nik) *adj* hygiénique

hymn (himm) *n* hymne *m*

hyphen (*haï*-feunn) *n* trait d'union

hypocrisy (hi-*po*-kreu-si) *n* hypocrisie *f*

hypocrite (*hi*-peu-krit) *n* hypocrite *m*

hypocritical (hi-peu-*kri*-ti-keul) *adj* hypocrite, fourbe

hysterical (hi-*stè*-ri-keul) *adj* hystérique

I

I (aï) *pron* je

ice (aïss) *n* glace *f*; ~ **bag** sac à glace; ~ **cream** crème glacée, glace *f*

Iceland (aïss-leunnd) Islande *f*

Icelander (aïss-leunn-deu) *n* Islandais *m*

Icelandic (aïss-*læn*-dik) *adj* islandais

icon (aï-konn) *n* icône *f*

idea (aï-*dieu*) *n* idée *f*; pensée *f*; notion *f*, concept *m*

ideal (aï-*dieul*) *adj* idéal; *n* idéal *m*

identical (aï-*dèn*-ti-keul) *adj* identique

identification (aï-dèn-ti-fi-*kéï*-cheunn) *n* identification *f*

identify (aï-*dèn*-ti-faï) *v* identifier

identity (aï-*dèn*-teu-ti) *n* identité *f*; ~ **card** carte d'identité

idiot (*i*-di-eut) *n* idiot *m*

idiotic (i-di-*o*-tik) *adj* idiot

idle (*aï*-deul) *adj* oisif; futile

idol (*aï*-deul) *n* idole *f*

if (if) *conj* si

ignition (igh-*ni*-cheunn) *n* allumage *m*; ~ **coil** bobine d'allumage

ignorant (*igh*-neu-reunnt) *adj* ignorant

ignore (igh-*noo*) *v* ignorer

ill (il) *adj* malade; mauvais; méchant

illegal (i-*lii*-gheul) *adj* illégal

illegible (i-*lè*-djeu-beul) *adj* illisible

illiterate (i-*li*-teu-reut) *n* illettré *m*

illness (*il*-neuss) *n* maladie *f*

illuminate (i-*loû*-mi-néït) *v* illuminer

illumination (i-loû-mi-*néï*-cheunn) *n* illumination *f*

illusion (i-*loû*-jeunn) *n* illusion *f*

illustrate (*i*-leu-stréït) *v* illustrer

illustration (i-leu-*stréï*-cheunn) *n* illustration *f*

image (*i*-midj) *n* image *f*

imaginary (i-*mæ*-dji-neu-ri) *adj* imaginaire

imagination (i-mæ-dji-*néï*-cheunn) *n* imagination *f*

imagine (i-*mæ*-djinn) *v* imaginer; s'imaginer; se figurer

imitate (*i*-mi-téït) *v* imiter

imitation (i-mi-*téï*-cheunn) *n* imitation *f*

immediate (i-*mii*-dyeut) *adj* immédiat

immediately (i-*mii*-dyeut-li) *adv* surle-champ, tout de suite, immédiatement

immense (i-*mèns*) *adj* immense, énorme

immigrant (*i*-mi-ghreunnt) *n* immigrant *m*

immigrate (*i*-mi-ghréït) *v* immigrer

immigration (i-mi-*ghréï*-cheunn) *n* immigration *f*

immodest (i-*mo*-dist) *adj* immodeste

immunity (i-*myoû*-neu-ti) *n* immunité *f*

immunize (*i*-myou-naïz) *v* immuniser

impartial (imm-*pââ*-cheul) *adj* impartial

impassable (imm-*pââ*-seu-beul) *adj* impraticable

impatient (imm-*péï*-cheunnt) *adj* impatient

impede (imm-*piid*) *v* entraver

impediment (imm-*pè*-di-meunnt) *n* entrave *f*

imperfect (imm-*peû*-fikt) *adj* imparfait

imperial (imm-*pi*eu-ri-eul) *adj* impérial

impersonal (imm-*peû*-seu-neul) *adj* impersonnel

impertinence (imm-*peû*-ti-neunns) *n* impertinence *f*

impertinent (imm-*peû*-ti-neunnt) *adj* insolent, effronté, impertinent

implement¹ (*imm*-pli-meunnt) *n*

instrument *m*, outil *m*
implement² (*imm*-pli-mènt) *v* réaliser
imply (imm-*plaï*) *v* impliquer;
comporter
impolite (imm-peu-*laït*) *adj* impoli
import¹ (imm-*poot*) *v* importer
import² (*imm*-poot) *n* importation *f*; ~
duty taxe d'importation
importance (imm-*poo*-teunns) *n*
importance *f*
important (imm-*poo*-teunnt) *adj*
important
importer (imm-*poo*-teu) *n*
importateur *m*
imposing (imm-*pôou*-zinng) *adj*
imposant
impossible (imm-*po*-seu-beul) *adj*
impossible
impotence (*imm*-peu-teunns) *n*
impotence *f*
impotent (*imm*-peu-teunnt) *adj*
impotent
impress (imm-*prèss*) *v* *faire
impression sur, impressionner
impression (imm-*prè*-cheunn) *n*
impression *f*
impressive (imm-*prè*-siv) *adj*
impressionnant
imprison (imm-*pri*-zeunn) *v*
emprisonner
imprisonment (imm-*pri*-zeunn-
meunnt) *n* emprisonnement *m*
improbable (imm-*pro*-beu-beul) *adj*
improbable
improper (imm-*pro*-peu) *adj*
impropre
improve (imm-*proûv*) *v* améliorer
improvement (imm-*proûv*-meunnt) *n*
amélioration *f*
improvise (*imm*-preu-vaïz) *v*
improviser
impudent (*imm*-pyou-deunnt) *adj*
insolent
impulse (*imm*-pals) *n* impulsion *f*;

stimulant *m*
impulsive (imm-*pal*-siv) *adj* impulsif
in (inn) *prep* en; dans, sur; *adv* dedans
inaccessible (i-næk-*sè*-seu-beul) *adj*
inaccessible
inaccurate (i-*næ*-kyou-reut) *adj*
incorrect
inadequate (i-*næ*-di-k°ueut) *adj*
inadéquat
incapable (inng-*kéï*-peu-beul) *adj*
incapable
incense (*inn*-sèns) *n* encens *m*
inch (inntch) *n* pouce *m*; pas *m*; **by
inches** peu à peu, petit à petit;
within an ~ of àdeux doigts de; **inch
one's way** avancer petit à petit
incident (*inn*-si-deunnt) *n* incident *m*
incidental (inn-si-*dèn*-teul) *adj* fortuit
incite (inn-*saït*) *v* inciter
inclination (inng-kli-*néï*-cheunn) *n*
penchant *m*
incline (inng-*klaïn*) *n* pente *f*
inclined (inng-*klaïnd*) *adj* disposé,
enclin; *be ~ to *v* *avoir tendance
include (inng-*kloûd*) *v* *comprendre,
*inclure
inclusive (inng-*kloû*-siv) *adj* compris
income (*inng*-keumm) *n* revenu *m*; ~
tax impôt sur le revenu
incompetent (inng-*komm*-peu-
teunnt) *adj* incompétent
incomplete (inn-keumm-*pliit*) *adj*
incomplet
inconceivable (inng-keunn-*sii*-veu-
beul) *adj* inconcevable
inconspicuous (inng-keunn-*spi*-
kyou-euss) *adj* qui passe inaperçu;
discret
inconvenience (inng-keunn-*vii*-
nyeunns) *n* désagrément *m*,
inconvénient *m*
inconvenient (inng-keunn-*vii*-
nyeunnt) *adj* inopportun; gênant
incorrect (inng-keu-*rèkt*) *adj* incorrect

increase[1] (inng-*kriiss*) v augmenter; s'accumuler, *croître

increase[2] (*inng*-kriiss) n augmentation f; relèvement m

incredible (inng-*krè*-deu-beul) adj incroyable

incurable (inng-*kyoueu*-reu-beul) adj incurable

indecent (inn-*dii*-seunnt) adj indécent

indeed (inn-*diid*) adv en effet

indefinite (inn-*dè*-fi-nit) adj indéfini

indemnity (inn-*dèm*-neu-ti) n dédommagement m, indemnité f

independence (inn-di-*pèn*-deunns) n indépendance f

independent (inn-di-*pèn*-deunnt) adj indépendant; autonome

index (*inn*-dèks) n index m; ~ **finger** index m

India (*inn*-di-eu) Inde f

Indian (*inn*-di-euann) adj indien; n Indien m

indicate (*inn*-di-kéït) v signaler, indiquer

indication (inn-di-*kéï*-cheunn) n signe m, indication f

indicator (*inn*-di-kéï-teu) n clignotant m

indifferent (inn-*di*-feu-reunnt) adj indifférent

indigestion (inn-di-*djèss*-tcheunn) n indigestion f

indignation (inn-digh-*néï*-cheunn) n indignation f

indirect (inn-di-*rèkt*) adj indirect

individual (inn-di-*vi*-djou-eul) adj particulier, individuel; n individu m

Indonesia (inn-deu-*nii*-zi-eu) Indonésie f

Indonesian (inn-deu-*nii*-zi-euann) adj indonésien; n Indonésien m

indoor (*inn*-doo) adj intérieur

indoors (inn-*dooz*) adv à l'intérieur

indulge (inn-*daldj*) v céder

industrial (inn-*da*-stri-eul) adj industriel; ~ **area** zone industrielle

industrious (inn-*da*-stri-euss) adj industrieux

industry (*inn*-deu-stri) n industrie f

inedible (i-*nè*-di-beul) adj immangeable

inefficient (i-ni-*fi*-cheunnt) adj inefficace

inevitable (i-*nè*-vi-teu-beul) adj inévitable

inexpensive (i-nik-*spèn*-siv) adj bon marché

inexperienced (i-nik-*spieu*-ri-eunnst) adj inexpérimenté

infant (*inn*-feunnt) n nourrisson m

infantry (*inn*-feunn-tri) n infanterie f

infect (inn-*fèkt*) v infecter

infection (inn-*fèk*-cheunn) n infection f

infectious (inn-*fèk*-cheuss) adj infectieux

infer (inn-*feû*) v *déduire

inferior (inn-*fieu*-ri-eu) adj moindre, inférieur

infinite (*inn*-fi-neut) adj infini

infinitive (inn-*fi*-ni-tiv) n infinitif m

inflammable (inn-*flæ*-meu-beul) adj inflammable

inflammation (inn-fleu-*méï*-cheunn) n inflammation f

inflatable (inn-*fléï*-teu-beul) adj gonflable

inflate (inn-*fléït*) v gonfler

inflation (inn-*fléï*-cheunn) n inflation f

inflict (inn-*flikt*) v infliger (**on** à)

influence (*inn*-flou-eunns) n influence f; v influencer

influential (inn-flou-*èn*-cheul) adj influent

influenza (inn-flou-*èn*-zeu) n grippe f

inform (inn-*foom*) v informer; *mettre au courant, communiquer

informal (inn-*foo*-meul) adj sans

cérémonie

information (inn-feu-*méï*-cheunn) *n*
information *f*; renseignement *m*,
communication *f*; ~ **office** bureau
des renseignements

infra-red (inn-freu-*rèd*) *adj* infrarouge

infrequent (inn-*frii*-k^{ou}eunnt) *adj* peu
fréquent

ingredient (inng-*ghrii*-di-eunnt) *n*
ingrédient *m*

inhabit (inn-*hæ*-bit) *v* habiter

inhabitable (inn-*hæ*-bi-teu-beul) *adj*
habitable

inhabitant (inn-*hæ*-bi-teunnt) *n*
habitant *m*

inhale (inn-*héïl*) *v* inhaler

inherit (inn-*hè*-rit) *v* hériter

inheritance (inn-*hè*-ri-teunns) *n*
héritage *m*

inhibit (inn-*hi*-bit) *v* empêcher;
inhiber

initial (i-*ni*-cheul) *adj* initial; *n* initiale
f; *v* parapher

initiate (i-*ni*-chi-éït) *v* lancer,
entreprendre; inaugurer; ~ **into**
initier à

initiative (i-*ni*-cheu-tiv) *n* initiative *f*

inject (inn-*djèkt*) *v* injecter

injection (inn-*djèk*-cheunn) *n*
injection *f*

injure (*inn*-djeu) *v* blesser; offenser

injury (*inn*-djeu-ri) *n* blessure *f*; lésion
f

injustice (inn-*dja*-stiss) *n* injustice *f*

ink (inngk) *n* encre *f*

inlet (*inn*-lèt) *n* crique *f*

inn (inn) *n* auberge *f*

inner (*i*-neu) *adj* intérieur; ~ **tube**
chambre à air

innocence (*i*-neu-seunns) *n*
innocence *f*

innocent (*i*-neu-seunnt) *adj* innocent

inoculate (i-*no*-kyou-léït) *v* inoculer

inquire (inng-*kouaïeu*) *v* se

renseigner, s'informer

inquiry (inng-*kouaïeu*-ri) *n* question *f*,
enquête *f*; ~ **office** bureau de
renseignements

inquisitive (inng-*koui*-zeu-tiv) *adj*
curieux

insane (inn-*séïn*) *adj* fou

inscription (inn-*skrip*-cheunn) *n*
inscription *f*

insect (*inn*-sèkt) *n* insecte *m*; ~
repellent insectifuge *m*

insecticide (inn-*sèk*-ti-saïd) *n*
insecticide *m*

insensitive (inn-*sèn*-seu-tiv) *adj*
insensible

insert (inn-*seût*) *v* insérer

inside (inn-*saïd*) *n* intérieur *m*; *adj*
intérieur; *adv* à l'intérieur; dedans;
prep dans, à l'intérieur de; ~ **out** à
l'envers; **insides** ventre *m*

insight (*inn*-saït) *n* compréhension *f*

insignificant (inn-sigh-*ni*-fi-keunnt)
adj insignifiant; sans importance;
futile

insist (inn-*sist*) *v* insister; persister

insolence (*inn*-seu-leunns) *n*
insolence *f*

insolent (*inn*-seu-leunnt) *adj* insolent

insomnia (inn-*somm*-ni-eu) *n*
insomnie *f*

inspect (inn-*spèkt*) *v* inspecter

inspection (inn-*spèk*-cheunn) *n*
inspection *f*; contrôle *m*

inspector (inn-*spèk*-teu) *n* inspecteur
m, -trice *f*

inspire (inn-*spaïeu*) *v* inspirer

insta(l)l (inn-*stool*) *v* installer

installation (inn-steu-*léï*-cheunn) *n*
installation *f*

instal(l)ment (inn-*stool*-meunnt) *n*
versement partiel; **payment by
instalments** paiement échelonné

instance (*inn*-steunns) *n* exemple *m*;
cas *m*; **for** ~ par exemple

instant (*inn*-steunnt) *n* instant *m*

instantly (*inn*-steunnt-li) *adv* instantanément, tout de suite, immédiatement

instead of (inn-*stèd* ov) au lieu de

instinct (*inn*-stinngkt) *n* instinct *m*

institute (*inn*-sti-tyoût) *n* institut *m*; institution *f*; *v* instituer

institution (inn-sti-*tyoû*-cheunn) *n* institution *f*

instruct (inn-*strakt*) *v* *instruire

instruction (inn-*strak*-cheunn) *n* instruction *f*

instructive (inn-*strak*-tiv) *adj* instructif

instructor (inn-*strak*-teu) *n* instructeur *m*

instrument (*inn*-strou-meunnt) *n* instrument *m*; **musical** ~ instrument de musique

insufficient (inn-seu-*fi*-cheunnt) *adj* insuffisant

insulate (*inn*-syou-léït) *v* isoler

insulation (inn-syou-*léï*-cheunn) *n* isolation *f*

insulator (*inn*-syou-léï-teu) *n* isolateur *m*

insult[1] (inn-*salt*) *v* insulter

insult[2] (*inn*-salt) *n* insulte *f*

insurance (inn-*choueu*-reunns) *n* assurance *f*; ~ **policy** police d'assurance

insure (inn-*choueu*) *v* assurer

intact (inn-*tækt*) *adj* intact

integrate (*inn*-ti-ghréït) *v* (s')intégrer

intellect (*inn*-teu-lèkt) *n* intellect *m*, intelligence *f*

intellectual (inn-teu-*lèk*-tchou-eul) *adj* intellectuel

intelligence (inn-*tè*-li-djeunns) *n* intelligence *f*

intelligent (inn-*tè*-li-djeunnt) *adj* intelligent

intend (inn-*tènd*) *v* *avoir l'intention de

intense (inn-*tèns*) *adj* intense; vif

intensify (inn-*tèn*-si-faï) *v* (s')intensifier

intention (inn-*tèn*-cheunn) *n* intention *f*

intentional (inn-*tèn*-cheu-neul) *adj* intentionnel

intercourse (*inn*-teu-kooss) *n* rapports *mpl*

interest (*inn*-treust) *n* intérêt *m*; *v* intéresser

interesting (*inn*-treu-stinng) *adj* intéressant

interfere (inn-teu-*fieu*) *v* *intervenir; ~ **with** se mêler de

interference (inn-teu-*fieu*-reunns) *n* ingérence *f*

interim (*inn*-teu-rimm) *n* intérim *m*

interior (*inn*-tieu-ri-eu) *n* intérieur *m*

interlude (*inn*-teu-loûd) *n* interlude *m*

intermediary (inn-teu-*mii*-dyeu-ri) *n* intermédiaire *m/f*

intermission (inn-teu-*mi*-cheunn) *n* entracte *m*

internal (inn-*teû*-neul) *adj* intérieur, interne

international (inn-teu-*næ*-cheu-neul) *adj* international

interpret (inn-*teû*-prit) *v* interpréter

interpreter (inn-*teû*-pri-teu) *n* interprète *m/f*

interrogate (inn-*tè*-reu-ghéït) *v* interroger

interrogation (inn-tè-reu-*ghéï*-cheunn) *n* interrogatoire *m*

interrogative (inn-teu-*ro*-gheu-tiv) *adj* interrogatif

interrupt (inn-teu-*rapt*) *v* *interrompre

interruption (inn-teu-*rap*-cheunn) *n* interruption *f*

intersection (inn-teu-*sèk*-cheunn) *n* intersection *f*

interval (*inn*-teu-veul) *n* entracte *m*; intervalle *m*

intervene (*inn*-teu-*viin*) *v* *intervenir

interview (*inn*-teu-vyoû) *n* entrevue *f*, interview *f*

intestine (*inn*-*tè*-stinn) *n* intestin *m*

intimate (*inn*-ti-meut) *adj* intime

into (*inn*-tou) *prep* dans

intolerable (inn-*to*-leu-reu-beul) *adj* intolérable

intoxicated (inn-*tok*-si-kéï-tid) *adj* ivre

intrigue (inn-*triigh*) *n* intrigue *f*

introduce (inn-treu-*dyoûss*) *v* présenter; *introduire

introduction (inn-treu-*dak*-cheunn) *n* présentation *f*; introduction *f*

invade (inn-*véïd*) *v* envahir

invalid[1] (*inn*-veu-liid) *n* infirme *m*; *adj* infirme

invalid[2] (inn-*væ*-lid) *adj* nul

invasion (inn-*véï*-jeunn) *n* invasion *f*

invent (inn-*vènt*) *v* inventer

invention (inn-*vèn*-cheunn) *n* invention *f*

inventive (inn-*vèn*-tiv) *adj* inventif

inventor (inn-*vèn*-teu) *n* inventeur *m*

inventory (*inn*-veunn-tri) *n* inventaire *m*

invert (inn-*veût*) *v* intervertir

invest (inn-*vèst*) *v* investir; placer

investigate (inn-*vè*-sti-ghéït) *v* enquêter

investigation (inn-vè-sti-*ghéï*-cheunn) *n* investigation *f*

investment (inn-*vèst*-meunnt) *n* investissement *m*; placement *m*

investor (inn-*vè*-steu) *n* investisseur *m*

invisible (inn-*vi*-zeu-beul) *adj* invisible

invitation (inn-vi-*téï*-cheunn) *n* invitation *f*

invite (inn-*vaït*) *v* inviter

invoice (*inn*-voïss) *n* facture *f*

involve (inn-*volv*) *v* impliquer

inwards (*inn*-[ou]eudz) *adv* vers l'intérieur

iodine (*aï*-eu-diin) *n* iode *m*

Iran (i-*râân*) Iran *m*

Iranian (i-*réï*-ni-eunn) *adj* iranien; *n* Iranien *m*

Iraq (i-*rââk*) Irak *m*

Iraqi (i-*rââ*-ki) *adj* irakien; *n* Irakien *m*

Ireland (*aïeu*-leunnd) Irlande *f*

Irish (*aïeu*-rich) *adj* irlandais

iron (*aï*-eunn) *n* fer *m*; fer à repasser; en fer; *v* repasser

ironical (aï-*ro*-ni-keul) *adj* ironique

irony (*aïeu*-reu-ni) *n* ironie *f*

irregular (i-*rè*-ghyou-leu) *adj* irrégulier

irreparable (i-*rè*-peu-reu-beul) *adj* irréparable

irrevocable (i-*rè*-veu-keu-beul) *adj* irrévocable

irritable (*i*-ri-teu-beul) *adj* irritable

irritate (*i*-ri-téït) *v* agacer, irriter

is (iz) *v* (pr be)

island (*aï*-leunnd) *n* île *f*

isolate (*aï*-seu-léït) *v* isoler

isolation (aï-seu-*léï*-cheunn) *n* isolement *m*; isolation *f*

Israel (*iz*-réïl) Israël *m*

Israeli (iz-*réï*-li) *adj* israélien; *n* Israélien *m*

issue (*i*-choû) *v* distribuer; *n* émission *f*, tirage *m*, édition *f*; question *f*, sujet *m*; issue *f*, résultat *m*, conclusion *f*, fin *f*

it (it) *pron* le

Italian (i-*tal*-yeunn) *adj* italien; *n* Italien *m*

Italy (*i*-teu-li) Italie *f*

itch (itch) *n* démangeaison *f*; *v* démanger

item (*aï*-teumm) *n* article *m*; point *m*

its (its) *adj* son, sa; ses

itself (it-*sèlf*) lui-même, elle-même;

se, soi; **by ~** à part; tout seul; **in ~** en lui-même ; en soi, de soi; **of ~** tout seul; de lui-même, d'elle-même

itinerary (aï-*ti*-neu-reu-ri) n itinéraire

m

ivory (aï-veu-ri) n ivoire m

ivy (aï-vi) n lierre m

J

jack (djæk) n cric m

jacket (*djæ*-kit) n veste f, veston m; jaquette f

jade (djéïd) n jade m

jail (djéïl) n prison f

jam (djæm) n confiture f; embouteillage m

janitor (*djæ*-ni-teu) n concierge m

January (*djæ*-nyou-eu-ri) janvier

Japan (djeu-*pæn*) Japon m

Japanese (djæ-peu-*niiz*) adj japonais; n Japonais m

jar (djââ) n jarre f

jaundice (*djoon*-diss) n jaunisse f

jaw (djoo) n mâchoire f

jealous (*djè*-leuss) adj jaloux

jealousy (*djè*-leu-si) n jalousie f

jeans (djiinz) pl blue-jean m

jelly (*djè*-li) n gelée f

jellyfish (*djè*-li-fich) n méduse f

jersey (*djeû*-zi) n jersey m; chandail m

jet (djèt) n jet m; avion à réaction

jetty (*djè*-ti) n jetée f

Jew (djoû) n juif m, juive f

jewel (*djoû*-eul) n bijou m

jewel(l)er (*djoû*-eu-leu) n bijoutier m

jewellery, Am jewelry (*djoû*-eul-ri) n bijoux; joaillerie f

Jewish (*djoû*-ich) adj juif

job (djob) n boulot m; emploi m, travail m

jobless (*djob*-lèss) adj sans travail

jockey (*djo*-ki) n jockey m

join (djoïn) v *joindre; s'affilier à,

adhérer à; assembler, réunir

joint (djoïnt) n articulation f adj uni, conjoint

jointly (*djoïnt*-li) adv conjointement

joke (djôᵘk) n blague f, plaisanterie f

jolly (*djo*-li) adj gai

Jordan (*djoo*-deunn) Jordanie f

Jordanian (djoo-*déï*-ni-eunn) adj jordanien; n Jordanien m

journal (*djeû*-neul) n périodique m

journalism (*djeû*-neu-li-zeumm) n journalisme m

journalist (*djeû*-neu-list) n journaliste m/f

journey (*djeû*-ni) n voyage m

joy (djoï) n plaisir m, joie f

joyful (*djoï*-feul) adj joyeux

jubilee (*djoû*-bi-lii) n anniversaire m

judge (djadj) n juge m; v juger; apprécier

judgment (*djadj*-meunnt) n jugement m

jug (djagh) n cruche f

Jugoslav (youû-gheu-*slââv*) adj yougoslave; n Yougoslave m

Jugoslavia (youû-gheu-*slââ*-vi-eu) Yougoslavie f

juice (djoûss) n jus m

juicy (*djoû*-si) adj juteux

July (djou-*laï*) juillet

jump (djammp) v sauter; n bond m, saut m

jumper (*djamm*-peu) n chandail m, pull m; Am robe à bretelles

junction (*djanngk*-cheunn) *n* carrefour *m*; jonction *f*
June (djoûn) juin
jungle (*djanng*-gheul) *n* jungle *f*
junior (*djoû*-nyeu) *adj* cadet
junk (djanngk) *n* rebut *m*

jury (*djoueu*-ri) *n* jury *m*
just (djast) *adj* légitime, juste; exact; *adv* à peine; juste
justice (*dja*-stiss) *n* droit *m*; justice *f*
justify (*dja*-sti-faï) *v* justifier
juvenile (*djoû*-veu-naïl) *adj* juvénile

K

kangaroo (kæng-gheu-*roû*) *n* kangourou *m*
keel (kiil) *n* quille *f*
keen (kiin) *adj* passionné; aigu
***keep** (kiip) *v* *tenir; garder; continuer; ~ away from se *tenir éloigné de; ~ off ne pas toucher; ~ on continuer; ~ quiet se *taire; ~ up persévérer; ~ up with *être à la hauteur de
kennel (*kè*-neul) *n* chenil *m*
Kenya (*kè*-nyeu) Kenya *m*
kerosene (*kè*-reu-siin) *n* pétrole *m*
kettle (*kè*-teul) *n* bouilloire *f*
key (kii) *n* clé *f*
keyboard (*kii*-bood) *n* clavier *m*
keyhole (*kii*-hô^ou l) *n* trou de la serrure
khaki (*kââ*-ki) *n* kaki *m*
kick (kik) *v* donner des coups de pied; *n* coup de pied
kickoff (ki-*kof*) *n* coup d'envoi
kid (kid) *n* enfant *m*, gosse *m*; chevreau *m*; *v* taquiner
kidney (*kid*-ni) *n* rein *m*
kill (kil) *v* tuer
kilogram (*ki*-leu-ghræm) *n* kilo *m*
kilometer *Am*, **kilometre** (*ki*-leu-mii-teu) *n* kilomètre *m*
kind (kaïnd) *adj* gentil, aimable; bon; *n* genre *m*

kindergarten (*kinn*-deu-ghââ-teunn) *n* école maternelle
king (kinng) *n* roi *m*
kingdom (*kinng*-deumm) *n* royaume *m*
kiosk (*kii*-osk) *n* kiosque *m*
kiss (kiss) *n* baiser *m*; *v* embrasser
kit (kit) *n* trousseau *m*
kitchen (*ki*-tchinn) *n* cuisine *f*; ~ garden jardin potager, ~ towel torchon *m*
knapsack (*næp*-sæk) *n* havresac *m*
knave (néïv) *n* valet *m*
knee (nii) *n* genou *m*
kneecap (*nii*-kæp) *n* rotule *f*
***kneel** (niil) *v* s'agenouiller
knew (nyoû) *v* (p know)
knife (naïf) *n* (pl knives) couteau *m*
knight (naït) *n* chevalier *m*
***knit** (nit) *v* tricoter
knob (nob) *n* bouton *m*
knock (nok) *v* frapper; *n* coup *m*; ~ against cogner contre; ~ down renverser
knot (not) *n* nœud *m*; *v* nouer
***know** (nô^ou) *v* *savoir, *connaître
knowledge (*no*-lidj) *n* connaissance *f*
knuckle (*na*-keul) *n* jointure *f*

L

label (*léï*-beul) *n* étiquette *f*; *v* étiqueter

laboratory (leu-*bo*-reu-teu-ri) *n* laboratoire *m*

labo(u)r (*léï*-beu) *n* travail *m*, labeur *m*; douleurs; *v* bûcher, peiner; **labor permit** *Am* permis du travail

labo(u)rer (*léï*-beu-reu) *n* travailleur *m*, travailleuse *f*

labo(u)r-saving (*léï*-beu-séï-vinng) *adj* qui économise du travail

labyrinth (*læ*-beu-rinnθ) *n* labyrinthe *m*

lace (léïss) *n* dentelle *f*; lacet *m*

lack (læk) *n* manque *m*; *v* manquer

lacquer (*læ*-keu) *n* vernis *m*

lad (læd) *n* garçon *m*

ladder (*læ*-deu) *n* échelle *f*

lady (*léï*-di) *n* dame *f*; **ladies' room** toilettes pour dames

lagoon (leu-*ghoûn*) *n* lagune *f*

lake (léïk) *n* lac *m*

lamb (læm) *n* agneau *m*

lame (léïm) *adj* paralysé, boiteux

lamentable (*læ*-meunn-teu-beul) *adj* lamentable

lamp (læmp) *n* lampe *f*

lamppost (*læmp*-pôºu*st) *n* lampadaire *m*

lampshade (*læmp*-chéïd) *n* abat-jour *m*

land (lænd) *n* pays *m*, terre *f*; *v* atterrir; débarquer

landlady (*lænd*-léï-di) *n* logeuse *f*

landlord (*lænd*-lood) *n* propriétaire *m*; logeur *m*

landmark (*lænd*-mââk) *n* point de repère

landscape (*lænd*-skéïp) *n* paysage *m*

lane (léïn) *n* ruelle *f*, chemin *m*; voie *f*

language (*læng*-gh^ou idj) *n* langue *f*; **~ laboratory** laboratoire de langues

lantern (*læn*-teunn) *n* lanterne *f*

lap (læp) *n* pan *m*; tour *m* (de piste); *v* laper; envelopper (**in** de); clapoter; **~ of hono(u)r** tour *m* d'honneur; **in** (*or* **on**) **someone's ~** sur les genoux de quelqu'un

lapel (leu-*pèl*) *n* revers *m*

large (lââdj) *adj* vaste; spacieux

largely (*lââdj*-li) *adv* en grande partie

lark (lââk) *n* alouette *f*

laryngitis (læ-rinn-*djaï*-tiss) *n* laryngite *f*

last (lââst) *adj* dernier; précédent; *v* durer; **at ~** enfin; en fin de compte

lasting (*lââ*-stinng) *adj* durable

latchkey (*lætch*-kii) *n* clé de la maison

late (léït) *adj* tard; en retard

lately (*léït*-li) *adv* ces derniers temps, dernièrement, récemment

lather (*lââ*-ðeu) *n* écume *f*

Latin America (*læ*-tinn eu-*mè*-ri-keu) Amérique latine

Latin-American (læ-tinn-eu-*mè*-ri-keunn) *adj* sud-américain

latitude (*læ*-ti-tyoûd) *n* latitude *f*

laugh (lââf) *v* *rire; *n* rire *m*

laughter (*lââf*-teu) *n* rire *m*

launch (loontch) *v* lancer; *n* bateau à moteur

launching (*loon*-tchinng) *n* lancement *m*

launderette (loon-deu-*rèt*) *n* laverie automatique

laundry (*loon*-dri) *n* blanchisserie *f*; lessive *f*

lavatory (*læ*-veu-teu-ri) *n* cabinet *m*

lavish (*læ*-vich) *adj* prodigue

law (loo) *n* loi *f*; droit *m*; **~ court** tribunal *m*

lawful (*loo*-feul) *adj* légal

lawn (loon) *n* gazon *m*, pelouse *f*

lawsuit (*loo*-soût) *n* procès *m*

lawyer (*loo*-yeu) *n* avocat *m*; juriste *m*

laxative (*læk*-seu-tiv) *n* laxatif *m*

*lay (léï) *v* placer, poser; **~ bricks** maçonner

layer (léï^eu) *n* couche *f*

layman (*léï*-meunn) *n* profane *m*

lazy (*léï*-zi) *adj* paresseux

lead¹ (liid) *n* avance *f*; conduite *f*; laisse *f*

lead² (lèd) *n* plomb *m*

*lead (liid) *v* diriger

leader (*lii*-deu) *n* leader *m*, dirigeant *m*

leadership (*lii*-deu-chip) *n* direction *f*

leading (*lii*-dinng) *adj* dominant, principal

leaf (liif) *n* (pl leaves) feuille *f*

league (liigh) *n* ligue *f*

leak (liik) *v* *fuir; *n* fuite *f*

leaky (*lii*-ki) *adj* ayant une fuite

lean (liin) *adj* maigre

*lean (liin) *v* s'appuyer

leap (liip) *n* saut *m*

*leap (liip) *v* bondir

leap year (*liip*-yi^eu) *n* année bissextile

*learn (leûnn) *v* *apprendre

learner (*leû*-neu) *n* débutant *m*

lease (liiss) *n* location *f*; bail *m*; *v* donner en location, louer

leash (liich) *n* laisse *f*

least (liist) *adj* moindre; **at ~** au moins

leather (*lè*-ðeu) *n* cuir *m*; en cuir

leave (liiv) *n* permission *f*

*leave (liiv) *v* *partir, quitter; laisser; **~ out** *omettre

Lebanese (lè-beu-*niiz*) *adj* libanais; *n* Libanais *m*

Lebanon (*lè*-beu-neunn) Liban *m*

lecture (*lèk*-tcheu) *n* cours *m*, conférence *f*

left¹ (lèft) *adj* gauche

left² (lèft) *v* (p, pp leave)

left-hand (*lèft*-hænd) *adj* à gauche, de gauche

left-handed (lèft-*hæn*-did) *adj* gaucher

leg (lègh) *n* pied *m*, jambe *f*

legacy (*lè*-gheu-si) *n* legs *m*

legal (*lii*-gheul) *adj* légitime, légal; juridique

legible (*lè*-dji-beul) *adj* lisible

legitimate (li-*dji*-ti-meut) *adj* légal légitime

leisure (*lè*-jeu) *n* loisir *m*; aise *f*

lemon (*lè*-meunn) *n* citron *m*

lemonade (lè-meu-*néïd*) *n* limonade *f*

*lend (lènd) *v* prêter

length (lèngθ) *n* longueur *f*

lengthen (*lèng*-θeunn) *v* allonger

lengthways (*lèng*θ^ou*éïz*) *adv* en long

lens (lènz) *n* lentille *f*; **telephoto ~** télé-objectif *m*; **zoom ~** zoom *m*

leprosy (*lè*-preu-si) *n* lèpre *f*

less (lèss) *adv* moins

lessen (*lè*-seunn) *v* diminuer

lesson (*lè*-seunn) *n* leçon *f*

*let (lèt) *v* laisser; louer; **~ down** *décevoir

letter (*lè*-teu) *n* lettre *f*; **~ of credit** lettre de crédit; **~ of recommendation** lettre de recommandation; **~ opener** coupe-papier *m*

letterbox (*lè*-teu-boks) *n* boîte aux lettres

lettuce (*lè*-tiss) *n* laitue *f*

level (*lè*-veul) *adj* égal; plat, plan; niveau *m*; *v* égaliser, niveler; **~ crossing** passage à niveau

lever (*lii*-veu) *n* levier *m*

liability (laï-eu-*bi*-leu-ti) *n* responsabilité *f*

liable (*laï*-eu-beul) *adj* responsable; **~ to** sujet à

liar (*laï*-eu) *n* menteur *m*, menteuse *f*

liberal (*li*-beu-reul) *adj* libéral; généreux, large

liberation (li-beu-*réï*-cheunn) *n* libération *f*

Liberia (*laï-bieu-ri-eu*) Libéria *m*
Liberian (*laï-bieu-ri-eunn*) *adj*
  libérien; *n* Libérien *m*
liberty (*li-beu-ti*) *n* liberté *f*
library (*laï-breu-ri*) *n* bibliothèque *f*
licence (*laï-seunns*) *n* licence *f*; permis
  m; **driving ~** permis de conduire
license (*laï-seunns*) *v* autoriser; *nAm*
  licence *f*; permis *m*; **driver's ~** permis
  de conduire; **~ number** numéro
  d'immatriculation; **~ plate** plaque
  d'immatriculation
lick (lik) *v* lécher
lid (lid) *n* couvercle *m*
lie (laï) *v* *mentir; *n* mensonge *m*
*lie (laï) *v* *être couché; **~ down** se
  coucher
life (laïf) *n* (pl lives) vie *f*; **~ insurance**
  assurance-vie *f*
lifebelt (*laïf*-bèlt) *n* bouée de
  sauvetage
lifetime (*laïf*-taïm) *n* vie *f*
lift (lift) *v* soulever, lever; *n* ascenseur
  m
light (laït) *n* lumière *f*; *adj* léger; clair;
  ~ bulb ampoule *f*
*light (laït) *v* allumer
lighter (*laï*-teu) *n* briquet *m*
lighthouse (*laït*-haouss) *n* phare *m*
lighting (*laï*-tinng) *n* éclairage *m*
lightning (*laït*-ninng) *n* éclair *m*
like (laïk) *v* aimer; bien aimer; *adj*
  pareil; *conj* comme
likely (*laï*-kli) *adj* probable
like-minded (laïk-*maïn*-did) *adj* de
  même opinion
likewise (*laïk*-ᵘaïz) *adv* de la même
  manière, également
lily (*li*-li) *n* lis *m*
limb (limm) *n* membre *m*
lime (laïm) *n* chaux *f*; tilleul *m*; limette
  f
limetree (*laïm*-trii) *n* tilleul *m*
limit (*li*-mit) *n* limite *f*; *v* limiter

limp (limmp) *v* boiter; *adj* flasque
line (laïn) *n* ligne *f*; trait *m*; fil *m*;
  rangée *f*; **stand in ~** *Am* *faire la
  queue
linen (*li*-ninn) *n* toile *f*; linge *m*
liner (*laï*-neu) *n* paquebot *m*
lining (*laï*-ninng) *n* doublure *f*
link (linngk) *v* relier; *n* lien *m*; maillon
  m
lion (*laï*-eunn) *n* lion *m*
lip (lip) *n* lèvre *f*
lipstick (*lip*-stik) *n* rouge à lèvres
liqueur (li-*kyoueu*) *n* liqueur *f*
liquid (*li*-kᵒᵘid) *adj* liquide; *n* liquide
  m
liquor (*li*-keu) *n* spiritueux *mpl*; **~
  store** magasin de vins et spiritueux
liquorice (*li*-keu-riss) *n* réglisse *f*
list (list) *n* liste *f*; *v* *inscrire
listen (*li*-seunn) *v* écouter
listener (*liss*-neu) *n* auditeur *m*
liter (*lii*-teu) *nAm* litre *m*
literary (*li*-treu-ri) *adj* littéraire
literature (*li*-treu-tcheu) *n* littérature *f*
litre (*lii*-teu) *n* litre *m*
litter (*li*-teu) *n* détritus *m*; immondices
  fpl; portée *f*
little (*li*-teul) *adj* petit; peu
live¹ (liv) *v* *vivre; habiter
live² (laïv) *adj* vivant
livelihood (*laïv*-li-houd) *n* subsistance
  f
lively (*laïv*-li) *adj* vif
liver (*li*-veu) *n* foie *m*
living (*li*-vinng) *adj* vivant, en vie; *n*
  vie *f*, gagne-pain *m*; **make** (*or* **earn**)
  a ~ gagner sa vie (**by** en); **~ room**
  living *m*, (salle *f* de) séjour *m*; **~
  space** espace *m* vital; **~ standard**
  niveau *m* de vie
lizard (*li*-zeud) *n* lézard *m*
load (lôᵒud) *n* chargement *m*; fardeau
  m; *v* charger
loaf (lôᵘf) *n* (pl loaves) miche *f*

loan 244

loan (lôᵒᵘn) *n* prêt *m*

lobby (*lo*-bi) *n* vestibule *m*

lobster (*lob*-steu) *n* homard *m*

local (*lôou*-keul) *adj* local; ~ **call** communication locale; ~ **train** train local

locality (lôᵒᵘ-*kæ*-leu-ti) *n* localité *f*

locate (lôᵒᵘ-*kéït*) *v* localiser

location (lôᵒᵘ-*kéï*-cheunn) *n* situation *f*

lock (lok) *v* fermer à clé; *n* serrure *f*; écluse *f*; ~ **up** enfermer

locker (*lo*-keu) *n* casier *m*

locomotive (lôᵒᵘ-keu-*môou*-tiv) *n* locomotive *f*

lodge (lodj) *v* loger; *n* pavillon de chasse

lodger (*lo*-djeu) *n* sous-locataire *m*

lodgings (*lo*-djinngz) *pl* logement *m*

log (logh) *n* bûche *f*

logic (*lo*-djik) *n* logique *f*

logical (*lo*-dji-keul) *adj* logique

lonely (*lôoun*-li) *adj* solitaire

long (lonng) *adj* long; ~ **for** désirer; **no longer** ne ... plus

longing (*lonng*-inng) *n* envie *f*

longitude (*lonn*-dji-tyoûd) *n* longitude *f*

look (louk) *v* regarder; sembler; *avoir l'air; *n* coup d'œil, regard *m*; apparence *f*, aspect *m*; ~ **after** s'occuper de, *prendre soin de; ~ **at** regarder; ~ **for** chercher; ~ **out** *prendre garde, *faire attention; ~ **up** chercher

looking-glass (*lou*-kinng-ghlââss) *n* miroir *m*

loop (loûp) *n* boucle *f*

loose (loûss) *adj* lâche

loosen (*loû*-seunn) *v* desserrer

lord (lood) *n* lord *m*

lorry (*lo*-ri) *n* camion *m*

*lose (loûz) *v* perdre

loser (*loû*-zeu) *n* perdant *m*, perdante *f*

loss (loss) *n* perte *f*

lost (lost) *adj* égaré; disparu; ~ **and found** objets trouvés; ~ **property office** bureau des objets trouvés

lot (lot) *n* sort *m*; tas *m*, quantité *f*

lotion (*lôou*-cheunn) *n* lotion *f*; **aftershave** ~ after-shave *m*

lottery (*lo*-teu-ri) *n* loterie *f*

loud (laoud) *adj* fort

loudspeaker (laoud-*spii*-keu) *n* haut-parleur *m*

lounge (laoundj) *n* foyer *m*

louse (laouss) *n* (pl lice) pou *m*

love (lav) *v* aimer; *n* amour *m*; **in** ~ amoureux; ~ **story** histoire d'amour

lovely (*lav*-li) *adj* délicieux, ravissant, beau

lover (*la*-veu) *n* amant *m*

low (lôᵒᵘ) *adj* bas; profond; déprimé; ~ **tide** marée basse

lower (*lôou*-eu) *v* baisser; amener; *adj* inférieur, bas

lowlands (*lôou*-leunndz) *pl* plaine *f*

loyal (*loï*-eul) *adj* loyal

lubricate (*loû*-bri-kéït) *v* huiler, lubrifier

lubrication (loû-bri-*kéï*-cheunn) *n* lubrification *f*; ~ **oil** lubrifiant *m*; ~ **system** système de lubrification

luck (lak) *n* chance *f*; hasard *m*; **bad** ~ malchance *f*

lucky (*la*-ki) *adj* chanceux; ~ **charm** porte-bonheur *m*

ludicrous (*loû*-di-kreuss) *adj* ridicule, grotesque

luggage (*la*-ghidj) *n* bagage *m*; **hand** ~ bagage à main; **left** ~ **office** consigne *f*; ~ **rack** porte-bagages *m*/ filet à bagage; ~ **van** fourgon *m*

lukewarm (*loûk*-ᵒᵘoom) *adj* tiède

lumbago (lamm-*béï*-ghôᵒᵘ) *n* lumbago *m*

luminous (*loû*-mi-neuss) *adj*

lumineux
lump (lammp) *n* morceau *m*, grumeau *m*; bosse *f*; **~ of sugar** morceau de sucre; **~ sum** somme globale
lumpy (lamm-pi) *adj* grumeleux
lunacy (loû-neu-si) *n* folie *f*
lunatic (loû-neu-tik) *adj* fou; *n* aliéné mental

lunch (lanntch) *n* lunch *m*, déjeuner *m*
luncheon (lann-tcheunn) *n* déjeuner *m*
lung (lanng) *n* poumon *m*
luxurious (lagh-*joueu*-ri-euss) *adj* luxueux
luxury (lak-cheu-ri) *n* luxe *m*

M

machine (meu-chiin) *n* appareil *m*, machine *f*
machinery (meu-chii-neu-ri) *n* machinerie *f*; mécanisme *m*
mackerel (mæ-kreul) *n* (pl ~) maquereau *m*
mackintosh (mæ-kinn-toch) *n* imperméable *m*
mad (mæd) *adj* dément, insensé, fou; enragé
madam (mæ-deumm) *n* madame
madness (mæd-neuss) *n* démence *f*
magazine (mæ-gheu-ziin) *n* revue *f*
magic (mæ-djik) *n* magie *f*; *adj* magique
magician (meu-dji-cheunn) *n* prestidigitateur *m*
magistrate (mæ-dji-stréit) *n* magistrat *m*
magnetic (mægh-nè-tik) *adj* magnétique
magneto (mægh-nii-tô^(ou)) *n* (pl ~s) magnéto *f*
magnificent (mægh-ni-fi-seunnt) *adj* magnifique; grandiose, splendide
magnify (mægh-ni-faï) *v* grossir; **magnifying glass** *n* loupe *f*
magpie (mægh-paï) *n* pie *f*
maid (méïd) *n* bonne *f*
maiden name (méï-deunn néïm) nom

de jeune fille
mail (méïl) *n* courrier *m*; *v* *mettre à la poste; **~ order** *Am* mandat-poste *m*
mailbox (méïl-boks) *nAm* boîte aux lettres
main (méïn) *adj* principal; majeur; **~ deck** pont principal; **~ line** ligne principale; **~ road** route principale; **~ street** rue principale
mainland (méïn-leunnd) *n* terre ferme
mainly (méïn-li) *adv* principalement
mains (méïnz) *pl* secteur *m*
maintain (méïn-téïn) *v* *maintenir
maintenance (méïn-teu-neunns) *n* entretien *m*
maize (méïz) *n* maïs *m*
major (méï-djeu) *adj* grand; majeur
majority (meu-djo-reu-ti) *n* majorité *f*
***make** (méïk) *v* *faire, rendre; gagner; réussir; **~ do with** se débrouiller avec; **~ good** compenser; **~ up** dresser
make-up (méï-kap) *n* maquillage *m*
malaria (meu-lèeu-ri-eu) *n* malaria *f*
Malay (meu-léï) *n* Malais *m*
Malaysia (meu-léï-zi-eu) Malaysia *m*
Malaysian (meu-léï-zi-eunn) *adj* malaisien
male (méïl) *adj* mâle
malicious (meu-li-cheuss) *adj* malveillant

malignant (meu-*ligh*-neunnt) *adj* malin

mallet (*mæ*-lit) *n* maillet *m*

malnutrition (mæl-nyou-*tri*-cheunn) *n* dénutrition *f*

mammal (*mæ*-meul) *n* mammifère *m*

man (mæn) *n* (pl men) homme *m*; **men's room** toilettes pour hommes

manage (*mæ*-nidj) *v* diriger; réussir

manageable (*mæ*-ni-djeu-beul) *adj* maniable

management (*mæ*-nidj-meunnt) *n* direction *f*; gestion *f*

manager (*mæ*-ni-djeu) *n* chef *m*, directeur *m*, -trice *f*

mandarin (*mæn*-deu-rinn) *n* mandarine *f*

mandate (*mæn*-déït) *n* mandat *m*

manger (*méïn*-djeu) *n* mangeoire *f*

manicure (*mæ*-ni-kyou^{eu}) *n* manucure *f*; *v* soigner les ongles

manipulate (meu-*ni*-pyou-léït) *v* manipuler ; manœuvrer

mankind (mæn-*kaïnd*) *n* humanité *f*

mannequin (*mæ*-neu-kinn) *n* mannequin *m*

manner (*mæ*-neu) *n* mode *m*, manière *f*; **manners** *pl* savoir-vivre *m*

manor house (*mæ*-neu-haouss) *n* manoir *m*

mansion (*mæn*-cheunn) *n* manoir *m*

manual (*mæ*-nyou-eul) *adj* manuel

manufacture (mæ-nyou-*fæk*-tcheu) *v* fabriquer

manufacturer (mæ-nyou-*fæk*-tcheu-reu) *n* fabricant *m*

manure (meu-*nyoueu*) *n* fumier *m*

manuscript (*mæ*-nyou-skript) *n* manuscrit *m*

many (*mè*-ni) *adj* beaucoup de

map (mæp) *n* carte *f*; plan *m*

maple (*méï*-peul) *n* érable *m*

marble (*mââ*-beul) *n* marbre *m*; bille *f*

March (mââtch) mars

march (mââtch) *v* marcher; *n* marche *f*

mare (mè^{eu}) *n* jument *f*

margarine (mââ-djeu-*riin*) *n* margarine *f*

margin (*mââ*-djinn) *n* marge *f*

maritime (*mæ*-ri-taïm) *adj* maritime

mark (mââk) *v* marquer; caractériser; *n* marque *f*; note *f*; cible *f*

market (*mââ*-kit) *n* marché *m*

marketplace (*mââ*-kit-pléïss) *n* place du marché

marmalade (*mââ*-meu-léïd) *n* marmelade *f*

marriage (*mæ*-ridj) *n* mariage *m*

married (*mæ*-rid) *adj* marié ; conjugal; **~ couple** ménage *m*

marrow (*mæ*-rô^{ou}) *n* moelle *f*

marry (*mæ*-ri) *v* épouser, se marier

marsh (mââch) *n* marais *m*

martyr (*mââ*-teu) *n* martyr *m*

marvel (*mââ*-veul) *n* merveille *f*; *v* s'émerveiller

marvel(l)ous (*mââ*-veu-leuss) *adj* merveilleux

mascara (mæ-*skââ*-reu) *n* cosmétique pour les cils

masculine (*mæ*-skyou-linn) *adj* masculin

mash (mæch) *v* écraser

mask (mââsk) *n* masque *m*

mass^1 (mæss) *n* messe *f*

mass^2 (mæss) *n* masse *f*; **~ production** production en série

massage (*mæ*-sââj) *n* massage *m*; *v* masser

masseur (mæ-*seû*) *n* masseur *m*

massive (*mæ*-siv) *adj* massif

mast (mââst) *n* mât *m*

master (*mââ*-steu) *n* maître *m*; patron *m*; professeur *m*, instituteur *m*; *v* maîtriser

masterpiece (*mââ*-steu-piiss) *n* chef-d'œuvre *m*

mat (mæt) *n* tapis *m*; *adj* mat

match (mætch) *n* allumette *f*; match *m*; *v* s'accorder avec

matchbox (mætch-boks) *n* boîte d'allumettes

material (meu-*tieu*-ri-eul) *n* matériel *m*; tissu *m*; *adj* matériel

mathematical (mæ-θeu-*mæ*-ti-keul) *adj* mathématique

mathematics (mæ-θeu-*mæ*-tiks) *n* mathématiques *fpl*

matrimony (*mæ*-tri-meu-ni) *n* mariage *m*

matter (*mæ*-teu) *n* matière *f*; affaire *f*, question *f*; *v* *avoir de l'importance; **as a ~ of fact** effectivement, en fait

matter-of-fact (mæ-teu-reuv-*fækt*) *adj* réaliste

mattress (*mæ*-treuss) *n* matelas *m*

mature (meu-*tyoueu*) *adj* mûr

maturity (meu-*tyoueu*-reu-ti) *n* maturité *f*

mausoleum (moo-seu-*lii*-eumm) *n* mausolée *m*

mauve (môᵒᵘv) *adj* mauve

May (méï) mai

***may** (méï) *v* *pouvoir

maybe (*méï*-bii) *adv* peut-être

mayor (*mè*ᵉᵘ) *n* maire *m*

maze (méïz) *n* labyrinthe *m*

me (mii) *pron* moi; me

meadow (*mè*-dôᵒᵘ) *n* pré *m*

meal (miil) *n* repas *m*

mean (miin) *adj* mesquin; *n* moyenne *f*

***mean** (miin) *v* signifier; *vouloir dire

meaning (*mii*-ninng) *n* signification *f*

meaningless (*mii*-ninng-leuss) *adj* dénué de sens

means (miinz) *n* moyen *m*; **by no ~** aucunement, en aucun cas

in the meantime (inn ðeu *miin*-taïm) en attendant, entre-temps

meanwhile (*miin*-ᵒᵘaïl) *adv* entretemps

measles (*mii*-zeulz) *n* rougeole *f*

measure (*mè*-jeu) *v* mesurer; *n* mesure *f*

meat (miit) *n* viande *f*

mechanic (mi-*kæ*-nik) *n* monteur *m*, mécanicien *m*

mechanical (mi-*kæ*-ni-keul) *adj* mécanique

mechanism (*mè*-keu-ni-zeumm) *n* mécanisme *m*

medal (*mè*-deul) *n* médaille *f*

media (*mii*-di-eu)*n pl* medias *mpl*

mediaeval (mè-di-*ii*-veul) *adj* médiéval

mediate (*mii*-di-éït) *v* *servir d'intermédiaire

mediator (*mii*-di-éï-teu) *n* médiateur *m*

medical (*mè*-di-keul) *adj* médical

medicine (*mèd*-sinn) *n* médicament *m*; médecine *f*

medieval (mè-di-*ii*-veul) *adj* médiéval

meditate (*mè*-di-téït) *v* méditer

Mediterranean (mè-di-tèu-*réï*-ni-eunn) Méditerranée *f*

medium (*mii*-di-eumm) *adj* moyen

***meet** (miit) *v* rencontrer

meeting (*mii*-tinng) *n* assemblée *f*, réunion *f*; rencontre *f*; **~ place** lieu de rencontre

melancholy (*mè*-leunng-keu-li) *n* mélancolie *f*

mellow (*mè*-lôᵒᵘ) *adj* moelleux

melodrama (*mè*-leu-drââ-meu) *n* mélodrame *m*

melody (*mè*-leu-di) *n* mélodie *f*

melon (*mè*-leunn) *n* melon *m*

melt (mèlt) *v* fondre

member (*mèm*-beu) *n* membre *m*; **Member of Parliament** député *m*

membership (*mèm*-beu-chip) *n* affiliation *f*

memo (*mè*-môᵒᵘ) *n* (pl ~s) mémorandum *m*

memorable (*mè*-meu-reu-beul) *adj*

mémorable

memorial (meu-*moo*-ri-eul) *n* mémorial *m*

memorize (*mè*-meu-raïz) *v* *apprendre par cœur

memory (*mè*-meu-ri) *n* mémoire *f*; souvenir *m*

mend (mènd) *v* réparer

menstruation (mèn-strou-*éï*-cheunn) *n* menstruation *f*

mental (*mèn*-teul) *adj* mental

mention (*mèn*-cheunn) *v* mentionner; *n* mention *f*

menu (*mè*-nyoû) *n* carte *f*, menu *m*

merchandise (*meû*-tcheunn-daïz) *n* marchandise *f*

merchant (*meû*-tcheunnt) *n* commerçant *m*, marchand *m*

merciful (*meû*-si-feul) *adj* miséricordieux

mercury (*meû*-kyou-ri) *n* mercure *m*

mercy (*meû*-si) *n* miséricorde *f*, clémence *f*

mere (mi^{eu}) *adj* pur

merely (*mieu*-li) *adv* seulement

merge (meûdj) *v* fusionner; amalgamer (**with, into** avec); se fondre (**with, into** dans); s'amalgamer

merger (*meû*-djeu) *n* fusion *f*

merit (*mè*-rit) *v* mériter; *n* mérite *m*

merry (*mè*-ri) *adj* joyeux

merry-go-round (*mè*-ri-ghô^{ou}-raound) *n* chevaux de bois

mesh (mèch) *n* maille *f*

mess (mèss) *n* désordre *m*, gâchis *m*; ~ **up** gâcher

message (*mè*-sidj) *n* commission *f*, message *m*

messenger (*mè*-sinn-djeu) *n* messager *m*

metal (*mè*-teul) *n* métal *m*; métallique

meter (*mii*-teu) *n* compteur *m*

method (*mè*-θeud) *n* méthode *f*; ordre

m

methodical (meu-θ-di-keul) *adj* méthodique

metre (*mii*-teu) *n* mètre *m*

metric (*mè*-trik) *adj* métrique

Mexican (*mèk*-si-keunn) *adj* mexicain; *n* Mexicain *m*

Mexico (*mèk*-si-kô^{ou}) Mexique *m*

microphone (*maï*-kreu-fô^{ou}n) *n* microphone *m*

microwave oven (*maï*-kreu-^{ou}éïv a-veunn) *n* four à micro-ondes *m*

midday (*mid*-déï) *n* midi *m*

middle (*mi*-deul) *n* milieu *m*; *adj* du milieu; **Middle Ages** moyen-âge *m*; ~ **class** classe moyenne; **middle-class** *adj* bourgeois

midnight (*mid*-naït) *n* minuit *m*

midsummer (*mid*-sa-meu) *n* milieu *m* de l'été; **in** ~ en plein été

midwife (*mid*-^{ou}aïf) *n* (pl -wives) sage-femme *f*

might (maït) *n* puissance *f*

***might** (maït) *v* *pouvoir

mighty (*maï*-ti) *adj* puissant

mild (maïld) *adj* doux

mildew (*mil*-dyou) *n* moisissure *f*

mile (maïl) *n* mille *m*

mileage (*maï*-lidj) *n* nombre de milles *m*

milepost (*maïl*-pô^{ou}st) *n* poteau indicateur

milestone (*maïl*-stô^{ou}n) *n* borne routière

milieu (*mii*-lyeû) *n* milieu *m*

military (*mi*-li-teu-ri) *adj* militaire; ~ **force** force armée

milk (milk) *n* lait *m*

milkman (*milk*-meunn) *n* (pl -men) laitier *m*

milkshake (*milk*-chéïk) *n* frappé *m*

milky (*mil*-ki) *adj* laiteux

mill (mil) *n* moulin *m*; usine *f*

miller (*mi*-leu) *n* meunier *m*

million (*mil*-yeunn) *n* million *m*

millionaire (mil-yeu-*nèeu*) *n*
millionnaire *m/f*

mince (minns) *v* hacher

mind (maïnd) *n* esprit *m*; *v* prêter
attention à

mine (maïn) *n* mine *f*

miner (*maï*-neu) *n* mineur *m*

mineral (*mi*-neu-reul) *n* minéral *m*; ~
water eau minérale

mingle (*minng*-gheul) *v* (se) mêler
(**with** à); (se) mélanger (**with** avec)

miniature (*minn*-yeu-tcheu) *n*
miniature *f*

minimum (*mi*-ni-meumm) *n*
minimum *m*

mining (*maï*-ninng) *n* exploitation
minière

minister (*mi*-ni-steu) *n* ministre *m*;
pasteur *m*; **Prime Minister** premier
ministre

ministry (*mi*-ni-stri) *n* ministère *m*

minor (*maï*-neu) *adj* petit, menu,
mineur; *n* mineur *m*

minority (maï-*no*-reu-ti) *n* minorité *f*

mint (minnt) *n* menthe *f*

minus (*maï*-neuss) *prep* moins

minute[1] (*mi*-nit) *n* minute *f*; **minutes**
compte rendu

minute[2] (maï-*nyoût*) *adj* minuscule

miracle (*mi*-reu-keul) *n* miracle *m*

miraculous (mi-*ræ*-kyou-leuss) *adj*
miraculeux

mirror (*mi*-reu) *n* miroir *m*

misbehave (miss-bi-*héïv*) *v* se
*conduire mal

miscarriage (miss-*kæ*-ridj) *n* fausse
couche

miscellaneous (mi-seu-*léï*-ni-euss)
adj divers

mischief (*miss*-tchif) *n* espièglerie *f*;
mal *m*, dommage *m*, malice *f*

mischievous (*miss*-tchi-veuss) *adj*
malicieux

miserable (*mi*-zeu-reu-beul) *adj*

misérable, malheureux

misery (*mi*-zeu-ri) *n* détresse *f*, misère
f

misfortune (miss-*foo*-tchèn) *n*
infortune *f*, malheur *m*

mishap (*miss*-hæp) *n* mésaventure *f*;
accident *m*

*mislay** (miss-*léï*) *v* égarer

misplaced (miss-*pléïst*) *adj*
inopportun; mal placé

mispronounce (miss-preu-*naouns*) *v*
mal prononcer

miss[1] (miss) mademoiselle,
demoiselle *f*

miss[2] (miss) *v* manquer

missing (*mi*-sinng) *adj* manquant; ~
person disparu *m*

mist (mist) *n* brume *f*, brouillard *m*

mistake (mi-*stéïk*) *n* méprise *f*, faute *f*,
erreur *f*

*mistake** (mi-*stéïk*) *v* confondre

mistaken (mi-*stéï*-keunn) *adj* erroné;
*be ~ se tromper

mister (*mi*--steu) monsieur *m*

mistress (*mi*-streuss) *n* maîtresse de
maison; patronne *f*, maîtresse *f*

mistrust (miss-*trast*) *v* se méfier de

misty (*mi*-sti) *adj* brumeux

*misunderstand** (mi-sann-deu-
stænd) *v* mal *comprendre

misunderstanding (mi-sann-deu-
stæn-dinng) *n* malentendu *m*

misuse (miss-*yoûss*) *n* abus *m*

mittens (*mi*-teunnz) *pl* moufles *fpl*

mix (miks) *v* mélanger, mêler; ~ **with**
fréquenter

mixed (mikst) *adj* mêlé, mélangé

mixer (*mik*-seu) *n* mixeur *m*

mixture (*miks*-tcheu) *n* mélange *m*

moan (môᵘn) *v* gémir

moat (môᵘt) *n* douve *f*

mobile (*môou*-baïl) *adj* mobile; ~
phone (téléphone) portable;
téléphone mobile

mock (mok) *v* se moquer de

mockery (*mo*-keu-ri) *n* moquerie *f*

model (*mo*-deul) *n* modèle *m*; mannequin *m*; *v* façonner, modeler

moderate (*mo*-deu-reut) *adj* modéré

modern (*mo*-deunn) *adj* moderne

modest (*mo*-dist) *adj* modeste

modesty (*mo*-di-sti) *n* modestie *f*

modify (*mo*-di-faï) *v* modifier

mohair (*môou*-hè^{eu}) *n* mohair *m*

moist (moïst) *adj* mouillé, moite

moisten (*moï*-seunn) *v* humecter

moisture (*moïss*-tcheu) *n* humidité *f*; **moisturizing cream** crème hydratante

molar (*môou*-leu) *n* molaire *f*

moment (*môou*-meunnt) *n* instant *m*, moment *m*

momentary (*môou*-meunn-teu-ri) *adj* momentané

monarch (*mo*-neuk) *n* monarque *m*

monarchy (*mo*-neu-ki) *n* monarchie *f*

monastery (*mo*-neu-stri) *n* monastère *m*

Monday (*mann*-di) lundi *m*

monetary (*ma*-ni-teu-ri) *adj* monétaire; ~ **unit** unité monétaire

money (*ma*-ni) *n* argent *m*; ~ **exchange** bureau de change; ~ **order** mandat-poste *m*

monk (manngk) *n* moine *m*

monkey (*manng*-ki) *n* singe *m*

monologue (*mo*-no-logh) *n* monologue *m*

monopoly (meu-*no*-peu-li) *n* monopole *m*

monotonous (meu-*no*-teu-neuss) *adj* monotone

month (mannθ) *n* mois *m*

monthly (*mann*θ-li) *adj* mensuel; ~ **magazine** revue mensuelle

monument (*mo*-nyou-meunnt) *n* monument *m*

mood (moûd) *n* humeur *f*

moon (moûn) *n* lune *f*

moonlight (*moûn*-laït) *n* clair de lune

moor (mou^{eu}) *n* bruyère *f*, lande *f*

moose (moûss) *n* (pl ~, ~s) élan *m*

moped (*môou*-pèd) *n* vélomoteur *m*

moral (*mo*-reul) *n* morale *f*; *adj* moral; **morals** mœurs *fpl*

morality (meu-*ræ*-leu-ti) *n* moralité *f*

more (moo) *adj* plus; **once** ~ une fois de plus

moreover (moo-*rôou*-veu) *adv* d'ailleurs, de plus

morning (*moo*-ninng) *n* matin *m*; ~ **paper** journal du matin

Moroccan (meu-*ro*-keunn) *adj* marocain; *n* Marocain *m*

Morocco (meu-*ro*-kô^{ou}) Maroc *m*

morphia (*moo*-fi-eu) *n* morphine *f*

morphine (*moo*-fiin) *n* morphine *f*

morsel (*moo*-seul) *n* morceau *m*

mortal (*moo*-teul) *adj* fatal, mortel

mortgage (*moo*-ghidj) *n* hypothèque *f*

mosaic (meu-*zéï*-ik) *n* mosaïque *f*

mosque (mosk) *n* mosquée *f*

mosquito (meu-*skii*-tô^{ou}) *n* (pl ~es) moustique *m*; ~ **net** moustiquaire *f*

moss (moss) *n* mousse *f*

most (mô^{ou}st) *adj* le plus; **at** ~ au maximum, tout au plus; ~ **of all** surtout

mostly (*môoust*-li) *adv* le plus souvent

motel (mô^{ou}-*tèl*) *n* motel *m*

moth (moθ) *n* mite *f*

mother (*ma*-ðeu) *n* mère *f*; ~ **tongue** langue maternelle; ~ **of pearl** nacre *f*

mother-in-law (*ma*-ðeu-rinn-loo) *n* (pl mothers-) belle-mère *f*

motion (*môou*-cheunn) *n* mouvement *m*

motivate (*môou*-ti-véït) *v* motiver

motive (*môou*-tiv) *n* motif *m*

motor (*môou*-teu) *n* moteur *m*; *v* voyager en auto; ~ **body** *Am* carrosserie *f*; **starter** ~ démarreur *m*

motorbike (môou-teu-baïk) *nAm* vélomoteur *m*

motorboat (môou-teu-bô^ou^t) *n* canot automobile

motorcar (môou-teu-kââ) *n* automobile *f*

motorcycle (môou-teu-saï-keul) *n* motocyclette *f*

motorist (môou-teu-rist) *n* automobiliste *m*

motorway (môou-teu-^ou^éï) *n* autoroute *f*

motto (mo-tô^ou^) *n* (pl ~es, ~s) devise *f*

mouldy (môoul-di) *adj* moisi

mound (maound) *n* butte *f*

mount (maount) *v* monter; *n* mont *m*

mountain (maoun-tinn) *n* montagne *f*; ~ **pass** col *m*; ~ **range** chaîne de montagnes

mountaineering (maoun-ti-nieu-rinng) *n* alpinisme *m*

mountainous (maoun-ti-neuss) *adj* montagneux

mourning (moo-ninng) *n* deuil *m*

mouse (maouss) *n* (pl mice) souris *f*

moustache (meu-stââch) *n* moustache *f*

mouth (maouθ) *n* bouche *f*; gueule *f*; embouchure *f*

mouthwash (maouθ-^ou^och) *n* eau dentifrice

movable (môu-veu-beul) *adj* mobile

move (môuv) *v* bouger; déplacer; se *mouvoir; déménager; *émouvoir; *n* tour *m*, pas *m*; déménagement *m*

movement (môuv-meunnt) *n* mouvement *m*

movie (môu-vi) *n* film *m*; **movies** *Am* cinéma *m*; ~ **theatre**, cinéma *m*

much (match) *adj* beaucoup de; *adv* beaucoup; **as** ~ autant

muck (mak) *n* gadoue *f*

mud (mad) *n* boue *f*

muddle (ma-deul) *n* fouillis *m*,

pagaille *f*, confusion *f*; *v* embrouiller

muddy (ma-di) *adj* boueux

muffler (maf-leu) *nAm* silencieux *m*

mug (magh) *n* gobelet *m*, chope *f*

mule (myoûl) *n* mulet *m*, mule *f*

multiplication (mal-ti-pli-kéï-cheunn) *n* multiplication *f*

multiply (mal-ti-plaï) *v* multiplier

mumps (mammps) *n* oreillons *mpl*

municipal (myoû-ni-si-peul) *adj* municipal

municipality (myoû-ni-si-pæ-leu-ti) *n* municipalité *f*

murder (meû-deu) *n* assassinat *m*; *v* assassiner

murderer (meû-deu-reu) *n* meurtrier *m*, -ière *f*

muscle (ma-seul) *n* muscle *m*

muscular (ma-skyou-leu) *adj* musclé

museum (myoû-zii-eumm) *n* musée *m*

mushroom (mach-roûm) *n* champignon *m*

music (myoû-zik) *n* musique *f*; ~ **academy** conservatoire *m*; ~ **hall** music-hall *m*

musical (myoû-zi-keul) *adj* musical; *n* comédie musicale

musician (myoû-zi-cheunn) *n* musicien *m*, -ienne *f*

mussel (ma-seul) *n* moule *f*

***must** (mast) *v* *falloir

mustard (ma-steud) *n* moutarde *f*

mute (myoût) *adj* muet

mutiny (myoû-ti-ni) *n* mutinerie *f*

mutton (ma-teunn) *n* mouton *m*

mutual (myoû-tchou-eul) *adj* mutuel, réciproque

my (maï) *adj* mon

myself (maï-sélf) *pron* me; moi-même

mysterious (mi-stieu-ri-euss) *adj* mystérieux

mystery (mi-steu-ri) *n* énigme *f*, mystère *m*

myth (miθ) *n* mythe *m*

N

nail (néïl) *n* ongle *m*; clou *m*; ~ **file** lime à ongles; ~ **polish** vernis à ongle; ~ **scissors** ciseaux à ongles

nailbrush (néïl-brach) *n* brosse à ongles

naïve (nââ-*iiv*) *adj* naïf

naked (néï-kid) *adj* nu; dénudé

name (néïm) *n* nom *m*; *v* nommer; **in the ~ of** au nom de

namely (néïm-li) *adv* notamment

nap (næp) *n* somme *m*

napkin (næp-kinn) *n* serviette *f*

nappy (næ-pi) *n* couche *f*

narcosis (nââ-*kôou*-siss) *n* (pl -ses) narcose *f*

narcotic (nââ-*ko*-tik) *n* narcotique *m*

narrow (næ-rô^{ou}) *adj* serré, étroit

narrow-minded (næ-rô^{ou}-*maïn*-did) *adj* borné

nasty (nââ-sti) *adj* antipathique, désagréable; méchant

nation (néï-cheunn) *n* nation *f*; peuple *m*

national (næ-cheu-neul) *adj* national; de l'Etat; ~ **anthem** hymne national; ~ **dress** costume national; ~ **park** parc national

nationality (næ-cheu-næ-leu-ti) *n* nationalité *f*

nationalize (næ-cheu-neu-laïz) *v* nationaliser

native (néï-tiv) *n* indigène *m/f*; *adj* indigène; ~ **country** patrie *f*, pays natal; ~ **language** langue maternelle

natural (næ-tcheu-reul) *adj* naturel; inné

naturally (næ-tcheu-reu-li) *adv* bien sûr, naturellement

nature (néï-tcheu) *n* nature *f*

naughty (noo-ti) *adj* polisson, méchant

nausea (noo-si-eu) *n* nausée *f*

naval (néï-veul) *adj* naval

navel (néï-veul) *n* nombril *m*

navigable (næ-vi-gheu-beul) *adj* navigable

navigate (næ-vi-ghéït) *v* naviguer

navigation (næ-vi-*ghéï*-cheunn) *n* navigation *f*

navy (néï-vi) *n* marine *f*

near (ni^{eu}) *prep* près de; *adj* proche, près

nearby (nieu-baï) *adj* proche

nearly (nieu-li) *adv* presque

neat (niit) *adj* soigné; pur

necessary (nè-seu-seu-ri) *adj* nécessaire

necessity (neu-*sè*-seu-ti) *n* nécessité *f*

neck (nèk) *n* cou *m*; **nape of the ~** nuque *f*

necklace (nèk-leuss) *n* collier *m*

necktie (nèk-taï) *n* cravate *f*

need (niid) *v* *falloir, *avoir besoin de; *n* besoin *m*; nécessité *f*; ~ **to** *devoir

needle (nii-deul) *n* aiguille *f*

needlework (nii-deul-^{ou}eûk) *n* travail à l'aiguille

negative (nè-gheu-tiv) *adj* négatif; *n* négatif *m*

neglect (ni-*ghlèkt*) *v* négliger; *n* négligence *f*

neglectful (ni-*ghlèkt*-feul) *adj* négligent

negligee (nè-ghli-jéï) *n* négligé *m*

negotiate (ni-*ghôou*-chi-éït) *v* négocier

negotiation (ni-ghô^{ou}-chi-*éï*-cheunn) *n* négociation *f*

neighbour (néï-beu) *n* voisin *m*, -e *f*

neighbo(u)rhood (néï-beu-houd) *n* voisinage *m*

neighbo(u)ring (néï-beu-rinng) *adj* contigu, avoisinant

neither (naï-ðeu) *pron* ni l'un ni

l'autre; **neither ... nor** ni ... ni

neon (*nii*-onn) *n* néon *m*

nephew (*nè*-fyoû) *n* neveu *m*

nerve (neûv) *n* nerf *m*; audace *f*

nervous (*neû*-veuss) *adj* nerveux

nest (nèst) *n* nid *m*

net (nèt) *n* filet *m*; *adj* net

Netherlands (*nè*-ðeu-leunndz): **the ~** Pays-Bas *mpl*

network (*nèt*-^{ou}eûk) *n* réseau *m*

neuralgia (nyou^{eu}-*ræl*-djeu) *n* névralgie *f*

neurosis (nyou^{eu}-*rôou*-siss) *n* névrose *f*

neuter (*nyoû*-teu) *adj* neutre

neutral (*nyoû*-treul) *adj* neutre

never (*nè*-veu) *adv* ne ... jamais

nevertheless (*nè*-veu-ðeu-*lèss*) *adv* néanmoins

new (nyoû) *adj* nouveau

news (nyoûz) *n* nouvelles, nouvelle *f*; actualités

newsagent (*nyoû*-zéï-djeunnt) *n* marchand de journaux

newspaper (*nyoûz*-péï-peu) *n* journal *m*

newsreel (*nyoûz*-riil) *n* actualités

newsstand (*nyoûz*-stænd) *n* kiosque à journaux

New Year (nyoû yi^{eu}) Nouvel An; **New Year's Eve** la Saint-Sylvestre

New Zealand (nyoû *zii*-leunnd) Nouvelle-Zélande *f*

next (nèkst) *adj* prochain, suivant; **~ to** à côté de

next-door (nèkst-*doo*) *adv* à côté

nice (naïss) *adj* gentil, joli, plaisant; bon; sympathique

nickel (*ni*-keul) *n* nickel *m*

nickname (*nik*-néïm) *n* surnom *m*

nicotine (*ni*-keu-tiin) *n* nicotine *f*

niece (niiss) *n* nièce *f*

Nigeria (naï-*djieu*-ri-eu) Nigeria *m*

Nigerian (naï-*djïeu*-ri-eunn) *adj*

nigérien; *n* Nigérien *m*

night (naït) *n* nuit *f*; soir *m*; **by ~** de nuit; **~ cream** crème de nuit; **~ flight** vol de nuit; **~ rate** tarif de nuit; **~ train** train de nuit

nightclub (*naït*-klab) *n* boîte de nuit

nightdress (*naït*-drèss) *n* chemise de nuit

nightingale (*naï*-tinng-ghéïl) *n* rossignol *m*

nightly (*naït*-li) *adj* nocturne

nightmare (*naït*-mè^{eu}) *n* cauchemar *m*

nil (nil) rien

nine (naïn) *num* neuf

nineteen (naïn-*tiin*) *num* dix-neuf

nineteenth (naïn-*tiin*θ) *num* dix-neuvième

ninety (*naïn*-ti) *num* quatre-vingt-dix

ninth (naïnθ) *num* neuvième

no (nô^{ou}) non; *adj* aucun; **~ one** ne ... personne

nobility (nô^{ou}-*bi*-leu-ti) *n* noblesse *f*

noble (*nô*ou-beul) *adj* noble

nobody (*nôou*-bo-di) *pron* ne ... personne

nod (nod) *n* inclination de la tête; *v* opiner de la tête

noise (noïz) *n* bruit *m*; fracas *m*, vacarme *m*

noisy (*noï*-zi) *adj* bruyant; sonore

nominate (*no*-mi-néït) *v* nommer

nomination (no-mi-*néï*-cheunn) *n* nomination *f*

none (nann) *pron* aucun

nonsense (*nonn*-seunns) *n* sottise *f*

non-smoker (*nonn*-smô^{ou}-keu) *n* non-fumeur *m*

noon (noûn) *n* midi *m*

nor (noo): **neither ~** ni; ne ... pas non plus; **nor do I** (ni) moi non plus

normal (*noo*-meul) *adj* normal

north (nooθ) *n* nord *m*; *adj* septentrional; **North Pole** pôle nord

north-east (nooθ-*iist*) n nord-est m

northerly (noo-ðeu-li) adj du nord

northern (noo-ðeunn) adj
septentrional

north-west (nooθ-*ouèst*) n nord-ouest
m

Norway (noo-^{ou}éï) Norvège f

Norwegian (noo-*ouii*-djeunn) adj
norvégien; n Norvégien m

nose (nô^{ou}z) n nez m

nosebleed (nôou*z*-bliid) n
saignement de nez

nostril (no-stril) n narine f

nosy (nô^{ou}-zi) adj colloquial curieux;
indiscret

not (not) adv ne … pas

notary (nô^{ou}-teu-ri) n notaire m

note (nô^{ou}t) n note f; ton m; v noter;
observer, constater

notebook (nô^{ou}t-bouk) n carnet m

noted (nô^{ou}u-tid) adj illustre

notepaper (nôout-péï-peu) n papier à
lettres

nothing (na-θinng) n rien, ne … rien

notice (nô^{ou}u-tiss) v observer, noter,
remarquer; n avis m, nouvelle f;
attention f

noticeable (nô^{ou}u-ti-seu-beul) adj
perceptible; remarquable

notify (nô^{ou}u-ti-faï) v notifier; avertir

notion (nô^{ou}u-cheunn) n notion f

notorious (nô^{ou}-*too*-ri-euss) adj
notoire

nougat (noû-ghââ) n nougat m

nought (noot) n zéro m

noun (naoun) n nom m, substantif m

nourishing (na-ri-chinng) adj
nourrissant

novel (no-veul) n roman m

November (nô^{ou}-*vèm*-beu) novembre

now (naou) adv maintenant; à l'heure
actuelle; ~ **and then** de temps en
temps

nowadays (naou-eu-déïz) adv
actuellement

nowhere (nô^{ou}u-^{ou}è^{eu}) adv nulle part

nozzle (no-zeul) n bec m

nuance (nyoû-*anss*) n nuance f

nuclear (nyoû-kli-eu) adj nucléaire; ~
energy énergie nucléaire

nucleus (nyoû-kli-euss) n noyau m

nude (nyoûd) adj nu; n nu m

nuisance (nyoû-seunns) n ennui m

numb (namm) adj engourdi

number (namm-beu) n numéro m;
chiffre m, nombre m

numeral (nyoû-meu-reul) n nombre
m

numerous (nyoû-meu-reuss) adj
nombreux

nun (nann) n religieuse f

nunnery (na-neu-ri) n couvent m

nurse (neûss) n infirmière f; bonne
d'enfants; v soigner; allaiter

nursery (neû-seu-ri) n chambre
d'enfants; crèche f; pépinière f

nut (nat) n noix f; écrou m

nutcrackers (nat-kræ-keuz) pl
cassenoix m

nutmeg (nat-mègh) n muscade f

nutritious (nyoû-*tri*-cheuss) adj
nutritif

nutshell (nat-chèl) n coquille de noix

nylon (naï-lonn) n nylon m

O

oak (ô^{ou}k) *n* chêne *m*

oar (oo) *n* rame *f*

oasis (ô^{ou}-*éï*-siss) *n* (pl oases) oasis *f*

oath (ô^{ou}θ) *n* serment *m*

oats (ô^{ou}ts) *pl* avoine *f*

obedience (eu-*bii*-di-euns) *n* obéissance *f*

obedient (eu-*bii*-di-eunt) *adj* obéissant

obey (eu-*béï*) *v* obéir

object¹ (*ob*-djikt) *n* objet *m*; objectif *m*

object² (eub-*djèkt*) *v* objecter; ~ **to** *faire objection à

objection (eub-*djèk*-cheunn) *n* objection *f*

objective (eub-*djèk*-tiv) *adj* objectif; *n* objectif *m*

obligatory (eu-*bli*-gheu-teu-ri) *adj* obligatoire

oblige (eu-*blaïdj*) *v* obliger; *be **obliged to** *être obligé de; *devoir

obliging (eu-*blaï*-djinng) *adj* obligeant

oblong (*ob*-lonng) *adj* oblong; *n* rectangle *m*

obscene (eub-*siin*) *adj* obscène

obscure (eub-*skyoueu*) *adj* vague, sombre, obscur

observation (ob-zeu-*véï*-cheunn) *n* observation *f*

observatory (eub-*zeû*-veu-tri) *n* observatoire *m*

observe (eub-*zeûv*) *v* observer

obsession (eub-*sè*-cheunn) *n* obsession *f*

obstacle (*ob*-steu-keul) *n* obstacle *m*

obstinate (*ob*-sti-neut) *adj* obstiné; opiniâtre

obtain (eub-*téïn*) *v* se procurer, *obtenir

obtainable (eub-*téï*-neu-beul) *adj* disponible

obvious (*ob*-vi-euss) *adj* évident

occasion (eu-*kéï*-jeunn) *n* occasion *f*

occasionally (eu-*kéï*-jeu-neu-li) *adv* de temps en temps

occupant (*o*-kyou-peunnt) *n* occupant *m*

occupation (o-kyou-*péï*-cheunn) *n* occupation *f*

occupy (*o*-kyou-paï) *v* occuper

occur (eu-*keû*) *v* se passer, se *produire, *survenir

occurrence (eu-*ka*-reunns) *n* événement *m*

ocean (ô^{ou}-cheunn) *n* océan *m*

October (ok-*tôou*-beu) octobre

octopus (*ok*-teu-peuss) *n* pieuvre *f*

oculist (*o*-kyou-list) *n* oculiste *m/f*

odd (od) *adj* bizarre; impair

odo(u)r (*ôou*-deu) *n* odeur *f*

of (ov, euv) *prep* de

off (of) *prep* de

offence (eu-*fèns*) *n* infraction *f*; offense *f*, outrage *m*

offend (eu-*fènd*) *v* blesser, offenser; outrager

offense (eu-*fèns*) *nAm* infraction *f*; offense *f*, outrage *m*

offensive (eu-*fèn*-siv) *adj* offensif; grossier; *n* offensive *f*

offer (*o*-feu) *v* *offrir; *n* offre *f*

office (*o*-fiss) *n* bureau *m*; fonction *f*; ~ **hours** heures de bureau

officer (*o*-fi-seu) *n* officier *m*

official (eu-*fi*-cheul) *adj* officiel

off-licence (*of*-laï-seunns) *n* magasin de spiritueux

often (*o*-feunn) *adv* souvent

oil (oïl) *n* huile *f*; pétrole *m*; **fuel** ~ mazout *m*; ~ **filter** filtre à huile; ~ **painting** peinture à l'huile; ~ **pressure** pression d'huile; ~ **refinery** raffinerie de pétrole; ~ **well** gisement de pétrole, puits de pétrole

oily (*oï*-li) *adj* huileux

ointment (*oïnt*-meunnt) *n* onguent *m*

okay! (ô^{ou}-*kéï*) d'accord!

old (ô^{ou}ld) *adj* vieux; ~ **age** vieillesse *f*

old-fashioned (ô^{ou}ld-*fæ*-cheunnd) *adj* démodé

olive (*o*-liv) *n* olive *f*; ~ **oil** huile d'olive

omelette (*omm*-leut) *n* omelette *f*

ominous (*o*-mi-neuss) *adj* sinistre

omit (eu-*mit*) *v* *omettre

omnipotent (omm-*ni*-peu-teunnt) *adj* omnipotent

on (onn) *prep* sur; à

once (^{ou}anns) *adv* une fois; **at ~** immédiatement, tout de suite; **for ~** pour un coup; ~ **more** une fois de plus

oncoming (*onn*-ka-minng) *adj* venant en sens inverse; proche

one (^{ou}ann) *num* un; *pron* on

oneself (^{ou}ann-*sèlf*) *pron* soi-même

onion (*a*-nyeunn) *n* oignon *m*

only (ô^{ou}n-li) *adj* seul; *adv* rien que, seulement; *conj* cependant

onwards (*onn*-^{ou}eudz) *adv* en avant

open (ô*ou*-peunn) *v* *ouvrir; *adj* ouvert; franc

opener (ô*ou*-peu-neu) *n* ouvreur *m*

opening (ô*ou*-peu-ninng) *n* ouverture *f*

opera (*o*-peu-reu) *n* opéra *m*; ~ **house** opéra *m*

operate (*o*-peu-réït) *v* opérer, fonctionner

operation (o-peu-*réï*-cheunn) *n* fonctionnement *m*; opération *f*

operator (*o*-peu-réï-teu) *n* standardiste *m/f*

operetta (o-peu-*rè*-teu) *n* opérette *f*

opinion (eu-*pi*-nyeunn) *n* idée *f*, opinion *f*

opponent (eu-*pôou*-neunnt) *n* adversaire *m/f*

opportunity (o-peu-*tyoû*-neu-ti) *n* occasion *f*

oppose (eu-*pôouz*) *v* s'opposer

opposite (*o*-peu-zit) *prep* en face de; *adj* opposé, contraire

opposition (o-peu-*zi*-cheunn) *n* opposition *f*

oppress (eu-*près*) *v* oppresser, opprimer

optician (op-*ti*-cheunn) *n* opticien *m*, -ienne *f*

optimism (*op*-ti-mi-zeumm) *n* optimisme *m*

optimist (*op*-ti-mist) *n* optimiste *m/f*

optimistic (op-ti-*mi*-stik) *adj* optimiste

optional (*op*-cheu-neul) *adj* facultatif

or (oo) *conj* ou

oral (*o**o*-reul) *adj* oral

orange (*o*-rinndj) *n* orange *f*; *adj* orange

orbit (*oo*-bit) *n* orbite *f*; *v* tourner autour de

orchard (*oo*-tcheud) *n* verger *m*

orchestra (*oo*-ki-streu) *n* orchestre *m*; ~ **seat** *Am* fauteuil d'orchestre

order (*oo*-deu) *v* commander; *n* ordre *m*; commandement *m*; commande *f*; ~ **form** bon de commande; **in ~** en règle; **in ~ to** afin de; **made to ~** fait sur commande; **out of ~** en dérangement; **postal ~** mandat-poste *m*

ordinary (*oo*-deunn-ri) *adj* commun, habituel

ore (oo) *n* minerai *m*

organ (*oo*-gheunn) *n* organe *m*; orgue *m*

organic (oo-*ghæ*-nik) *adj* organique

organization (oo-gheu-naï-*zéï*-cheunn) *n* organisation *f*

organize (*oo*-gheu-naïz) *v* organiser

Orient (*oo*-ri-eunnt) *n* Orient *m*

oriental (oo-ri-*èn*-teul) *adj* oriental

orientate (*oo*-ri-eunn-téït) *v* s'orienter

origin (*o*-ri-djinn) *n* origine *f*; descendance *f*, provenance *f*

original (eu-*ri*-dji-neul) *adj* authentique, original

originally (eu-*ri*-dji-neu-li) *adv* originairement

orlon (*oo*-lonn) *n* orlon *m*

ornament (*oo*-neu-meunnt) *n* ornement *m*

ornamental (oo-neu-*mèn*-teul) *adj* ornemental

orphan (*oo*-feunn) *n* orphelin *m*

orthodox (*oo*-θeu-doks) *adj* orthodoxe

ostrich (*o*-stritch) *n* autruche *f*

other (*a*-ðeu) *adj* autre

otherwise (*a*-ðeu-ᵒᵘaïz) *conj* sinon; *adv* autrement

***ought to** (oot) ***devoir**

ounce (aouns) *n* once *f*

our (aouᵉᵘ) *adj* notre

ours (aouᵉᵘz) le (la) nôtre, les nôtres; à nous; **a ... of ~** un(e) de nos ...

ourselves (aouᵉᵘ-*sèlv*z) *pron* nous; nous-mêmes

out (aout) *adv* dehors, hors; **~ of** en dehors de, de

outbreak (aout-bréïk) *n* déchaînement *m*

outburst (aout-beûst) *n* explosion *f*, éruption *f*

outcome (aout-kamm) *n* résultat *m*

***outdo** (aout-*doû*) *v* surpasser

outdoors (aout-*dooz*) *adv* dehors

outer (*aou*-teu) *adj* extérieur

outfit (*aout*-fit) *n* équipement *m*

outline (*aout*-laïn) *n* contour *m*; *v* esquisser

outlook (*aout*-louk) *n* prévision *f*; point de vue

output (*aout*-pout) *n* production *f*

outrage (*aout*-réïdj) *n* outrage *m*

outside (aout-*saïd*) *adv* dehors; *prep* hors de; *n* extérieur *m*

outsize (aout-*saïz*) *n* hors série

outskirts (*aout*-skeûts) *pl* faubourg *m*

outstanding (aout-*stæn*-dinng) *adj* éminent

outward (*aout*-ᵒᵘeud) *adj* externe

outwards (*aout*-ᵒᵘeudz) *adv* vers l'extérieur

oval (*ôou*-veul) *adj* ovale

oven (*a*-veunn) *n* four *m*

over (*ôou*-veu) *prep* au-dessus de, pardessus; passé; *adv* au-dessus; *adj* fini; **~ there** là-bas

overall (*ôou*-veu-rool) *adj* total

overalls (*ôou*-veu-roolz) *pl* salopette *f*

overcast (*ôou*-veu-kâast) *adj* nuageux

overcoat (*ôou*-veu-kôᵒᵘt) *n* pardessus *m*

***overcome** (ôᵒᵘ-veu-*kamm*) *v* *vaincre

overdo (ôᵒᵘ-veu-*doû*) *v* exagérer; prendre trop de ; excéder; trop cuire

overdraw (ôᵒᵘ-veu-*droo*) *v* exagérer; mettre à découvert

overdue (ôᵒᵘ-veu-*dyoû*) *adj* en retard; arriéré

overgrown (ôᵒᵘ-veu-*ghrôoun*) *adj* couvert de verdure

overhaul (ôᵒᵘ-veu-*hool*) *v* reviser

overhead (ôᵒᵘ-veu-*hèd*) *adv* en haut

overlook (ôᵒᵘ-veu-*louk*) *v* ignorer

overnight (ôᵒᵘ-veu-*naït*) *adv* de nuit

overseas (ôᵒᵘ-veu-*siiz*) *adj* d'outremer

oversight (*ôou*-veu-saït) *n* inadvertance *f*

***oversleep** (ôᵒᵘ-veu-*sliip*) *v* *dormir trop longtemps

overstrung (ôᵒᵘ-veu-*stranng*) *adj* à cordes croisées

***overtake** (ôᵒᵘ-veu-*téïk*) *v* dépasser; **no overtaking** défense de doubler

over-tired (ôᵒᵘ-veu-*taïeud*) *adj* épuisé

overture (*ôou*-veu-tcheu) *n* ouverture *f*

overweight (ôou-veu-^{ou}éït) n
surcharge f
overwhelm (ô^{ou}-veu-ouèlm) v
accabler; écraser
overwork (ô^{ou}-veu-oueûk) v se
surmener
owe (ô^{ou}) v *devoir; **owing to** en
raison de

owl (aoul) n hibou m
own (ô^{ou}n) v posséder; adj propre
owner (ôou-neu) n propriétaire m/f
ox (oks) n (pl oxen) bœuf m
oxygen (ok-si-djeunn) n oxygène m
oyster (oï-steu) n huître f
ozone (ôou-zô^{ou}n) n ozone m

P

pace (péïss) n allure f; pas m; rythme
m
Pacific Ocean (peu-si-fik ôou-
cheunn) Océan Pacifique
pacifism (pæ-si-fi-zeumm) n
pacifisme m
pacifist (pæ-si-fist) n pacifiste m
pack (pæk) v emballer; ~ **up** emballer
package (pæ-kidj) n colis m
packet (pæ-kit) n paquet m
packing (pæ-kinng) n emballage m
pact (pækt) n pacte m, contrat m
pad (pæd) n coussinet m; bloc-notes m
paddle (pæ-deul) n pagaie f
padlock (pæd-lok) n cadenas m
pagan (péï-gheunn) adj païen; n païen
m
page (péïdj) n page f
pageboy (péïdj-boï) n page m
pail (péïl) n seau m
pain (péïn) n douleur f; **pains** peine f
painful (péïn-feul) adj douloureux
painkiller (péïn-ki-leu) n analgésique
m
painless (péïn-leuss) adj sans douleur
paint (péïnt) n peinture f; v *peindre
paintbox (péïnt-boks) n boîte de
couleurs
paintbrush (péïnt-brach) n pinceau m
painter (péïn-teu) n peintre m

painting (péïn-tinng) n peinture f
pair (pè^{eu}) n paire f
Pakistan (pââ-ki-stâân) Pakistan m
Pakistani (pââ-ki-stââ-ni) adj
pakistanais; n Pakistanais m
pal (pæl) n colloquial copain m,
copine f
palace (pæ-leuss) n palais m
pale (péïl) adj pâle
palm (pââm) n palme f; paume f; ~
(**tree**) palmier m
palpitation (pæl-pi-téï-cheunn) n
palpitation f
pan (pæn) n casserole f
pancake (pæn-kéïk) n crêpe f
pane (péïn) n carreau m
panel (pæ-neul) n panneau m
panic (pæ-nik) n panique f
pant (pænt) v haleter
panties (pæn-tiz) pl culotte f
pants (pænts) pl caleçon m; plAm
pantalon m
pant suit (pænt-soût) n ensemble-
pantalon
panty hose (pæn-ti-hô^{ou}z) n collants
mpl
paper (péï-peu) n papier m; journal m;
en papier; **carbon** ~ papier carbone;
~ **bag** sac en papier; ~ **knife** coupe-
papier m; ~ **napkin** serviette de

papier; **typing** ~ papier à machine; **wrapping** ~ papier d'emballage

paperback (*péï*-peu-bæk) *n* livre de poche

parade (peu-*réïd*) *n* parade *f*

paradise (*pæ*-reu-daïs) *n* paradis *m*

paraffin (*pæ*-reu-finn) *n* pétrole *m*

paragraph (*pæ*-reu-ghrââf) *n* paragraphe *m*

parakeet (*pæ*-reu-kiit) *n* perruche *f*

parallel (*pæ*-reu-lèl) *adj* parallèle; *n* parallèle *m*

paralyse, *Am* **paralyze** (*pæ*-reu-laïz) *v* paralyser

parcel (*pââ*-seul) *n* colis *m*, paquet *m*

pardon (*pââ*-deunn) *n* pardon *m*; grâce *f*

parent (*pèeu*-reunnt) *n* père *m*, mère *f*; **parents** *pl* parents *pl*

parents-in-law (*pèeu*-reunnts-inn-loo) *pl* beaux-parents *mpl*

parish (*pæ*-rich) *n* paroisse *f*

park (pââk) *n* parc *m*; *v* se garer

parking (*pââ*-kinng) *n* stationnement *m*; **no** ~ stationnement interdit; ~ **fee** droit de stationnement; ~ **light** feu de position; ~ **lot** *Am* parking *m*; ~ **meter** parcomètre *m*; ~ **zone** zone de stationnement

parliament (*pââ*-leu-meunnt) *n* parlement *m*

parliamentary (pââ-leu-*mèn*-teu-ri) *adj* parlementaire

parrot (*pæ*-reut) *n* perroquet *m*

parsley (*pââ*-sli) *n* persil *m*

parson (*pââ*-seunn) *n* pasteur *m*

parsonage (*pââ*-seu-nidj) *n* presbytère *m*

part (pâât) *n* part *f*, partie *f*; morceau *m*; *v* séparer; **spare** ~ pièce de rechange

partial (*pââ*-cheul) *adj* partiel; partial

participant (pââ-*ti*-si-peunnt) *n* participant *m*, -e *f*

participate (pââ-*ti*-si-péït) *v* participer

particular (peu-*ti*-kyou-leu) *adj* spécial, particulier; exigeant; **in** ~ en particulier

parting (*pââ*-tinng) *n* adieu *m*; raie *f*

partition (pââ-*ti*-cheunn) *n* cloison *f*

partly (*pâât*-li) *adv* en partie, partiellement

partner (*pâât*-neu) *n* partenaire *m/f*; associé *m*

partridge (*pââ*-tridj) *n* perdrix *f*

party (*pââ*-ti) *n* parti *m*; surprise-partie *f*; groupe *m*

pass (pââss) *v* passer, dépasser; réussir; *vAm* doubler; **no passing** *Am* défense de doubler; ~ **by** passer à côté; ~ **through** traverser

passage (*pæ*-sidj) *n* passage *m*; traversée *f*

passenger (*pæ*-seunn-djeu) *n* passager *m*, passagère *f*; ~ **car** *Am* wagon *m*; ~ **train** train de voyageurs

passer-by (*pââ*-seu-*baï*) *n* passant *m*

passion (*pæ*-cheunn) *n* passion *f*; colère *f*

passionate (*pæ*-cheu-neut) *adj* passionné

passive (*pæ*-siv) *adj* passif

passport (*pââss*-poot) *n* passeport *m*; ~ **control** contrôle des passeports; ~ **photograph** photo d'identité

password (*pââss*-[ou]eûd) *n* mot de passe

past (pâast) *n* passé *m*; *adj* passé, dernier; *prep* le long de, au delà de

paste (péïst) *n* pâte *f*; *v* coller

pastime (*pââss*-taïm) *n* passe-temps *m*; distraction *f*

pastry (*péï*-stri) *n* pâtisserie *f*; ~ **shop** pâtisserie *f*

pasture (*pââss*-tcheu) *n* pâture *f*

patch (pætch) *v* rapiécer; ~ **up** réparer

patent (*péï*-teunnt) *n* brevet *m*

path (pââθ) *n* sentier *m*

patience (*péï*-cheunns) *n* patience *f*

patient (*péï*-cheunnt) *adj* patient; *n* patient *m*, -e *f*

patriot (*péï*-tri-eut) *n* patriote *m*

patrol (peu-*trôoul*) *n* patrouille *f*; *v* patrouiller; surveiller

pattern (*pæ*-teunn) *n* motif *m*, dessin *m*

pause (pooz) *n* pause *f*; *v* *faire une pause

pave (péïv) *v* paver

pavement (*péïv*-meunnt) *n* trottoir *m*; pavage *m*

pavilion (peu-*vil*-yeunn) *n* pavillon *m*

paw (poo) *n* patte *f*

pawn (poon) *v* donner en gage, *mettre en gage; *n* pion *m*

pay (péï) *n* salaire *m*, paye *f*

***pay** (péï) *v* payer; ~ **attention to** *faire attention à; ~ **cash** payer comptant; ~ **desk** caisse *f*; **paying** rentable; ~ **off** amortir

payee (péï-*ii*) *n* bénéficiaire *m/f*

payment (*péï*-meunnt) *n* paiement *m*

PC (pii-*sii*) *n* micro *m*; P.C. *m*

pea (pii) *n* pois *m*

peace (piiss) *n* paix *f*

peaceful (*piiss*-feul) *adj* paisible

peach (piitch) *n* pêche *f*

peacock (*pii*-kok) *n* paon *m*

peak (piik) *n* sommet *m*; apogée *m*; ~ **hour** heure de pointe; ~ **season** pleine saison

peanut (*pii*-nat) *n* cacahuète *f*

pear (pè^{eu}) *n* poire *f*

pearl (peûl) *n* perle *f*

peasant (*pè*-zeunnt) *n* paysan *m*

pebble (*pè*-beul) *n* galet *m*

peculiar (pi-*kyoûl*-yeu) *adj* spécial, particulier

peculiarity (pi-kyoû-li-*æ*-reu-ti) *n* particularité *f*

pedal (*pè*-deul) *n* pédale *f*

pedestrian (pi-*dè*-stri-eunn) *n* piéton

m; **no pedestrians** interdit aux piétons; ~ **crossing** passage clouté

peel (piil) *v* peler; *n* pelure *f*

peep (piip) *v* épier

peewit (*pii*-^{ou}it) *n* vanneau *m*

peg (pègh) *n* patère *f*

pelican (*pè*-li-keunn) *n* pélican *m*

pelvis (*pèl*-viss) *n* bassin *m*

pen (pèn) *n* plume *f*

penalty (*pè*-neul-ti) *n* amende *f*; peine *f*; ~ **kick** penalty *m*

pencil (*pèn*-seul) *n* crayon *m*; ~ **sharpener** taille-crayon *m*

pendant (*pèn*-deunnt) *n* pendentif *m*

penetrate (*pè*-ni-tréït) *v* pénétrer

penguin (*pèng*-gh^{ou}inn) *n* pingouin *m*

penicillin (pè-ni-*si*-linn) *n* pénicilline *f*

peninsula (peu-*ninn*-syou-leu) *n* péninsule *f*

penknife (*pèn*-naïf) *n* (pl -knives) canif *m*

penny (*pè*-ni) *n* (pl pence, pennies) penny *m*

pension[1] (pan-si-on) *n* pension *f*

pension[2] (*pèn*-cheunn) *n* pension *f*

Pentecost (*pèn*-ti-kost) *n* Pentecôte *f*

people (*pii*-peul) *pl* gens *mpl/fpl*; *n* peuple *m*

pepper (*pè*-peu) *n* poivre *m*

peppermint (*pè*-peu-minnt) *n* menthe *f*

perceive (peu-*siiv*) *v* *percevoir

percent (peu-*sènt*) *n* pour cent

percentage (peu-*sèn*-tidj) *n* pourcentage *m*

perceptible (peu-*sèp*-ti-beul) *adj* perceptible

perception (peu-*sèp*-cheunn) *n* perception *f*

perch (peûtch) (pl ~) perche *f*

percolator (*peû*-keu-léï-teu) *n* percolateur *m*

perfect (*peû*-fikt) *adj* parfait

perfection (peu-*fèk*-cheunn) *n*

perfection f

perform (peu-*foom*) v accomplir

performance (peu-*foo*-meunns) n
performance f

perfume (*peû*-fyoûm) n parfum m

perhaps (peu-*hæps*) adv peut-être

peril (*pè*-ril) n péril m

perilous (*pè*-ri-leuss) adj périlleux

period (*pieu*-ri-eud) n époque f,
période f; point m

periodical (pi*eu*-ri-*o*-di-keul) n
périodique m; adj périodique

perish (*pè*-rich) v périr

perishable (*pè*-ri-cheu-beul) adj
périssable

perjury (*peû*-djeu-ri) n faux serment

permanent (*peû*-meu-neunnt) adj
durable, permanent; stable, fixe; ~
press pli permanent; ~ **wave**
permanente f

permission (peu-*mi*-cheunn) n
permission f, autorisation f; permis
m, licence f

permit[1] (peu-*mit*) v *permettre

permit[2] (*peû*-mit) n permis m

peroxide (peu-*rok*-saïd) n eau
oxygénée

perpendicular (peû-peunn-*di*-kyou-
leu) adj perpendiculaire

Persia (*peû*-cheu) Perse f

Persian (*peû*-cheunn) adj persan; n
Persan m

person (*peû*-seunn) n personne f; **per**
~ par personne

personal (*peû*-seu-neul) adj
personnel

personality (peû-seu-*næ*-leu-ti) n
personnalité f

personnel (peû-seu-*nèl*) n personnel
m

perspective (peu-*spèk*-tiv) n
perspective f

perspiration (peû-speu-*réï*-cheunn) n
transpiration f, sueur f

perspire (peu-*spaïeu*) v transpirer,
suer

persuade (peu-*souéïd*) v persuader;
*convaincre

persuasion (peu-*souéï*-jeunn) n
conviction f

pessimism (*pè*-si-mi-zeumm) n
pessimisme m

pessimist (*pè*-si-mist) n pessimiste
m/f

pessimistic (pè-si-*mi*-stik) adj
pessimiste

pet (pèt) n animal familier; chouchou
m

petal (*pè*-teul) n pétale m

petition (pi-*ti*-cheunn) n pétition f

petrol (*pè*-treul) n essence f; ~ **pump**
pompe à essence; ~ **station** poste
d'essence; ~ **tank** réservoir d'essence

petroleum (pi-*trôou*-li-eumm) n
pétrole m

petty (*pè*-ti) adj petit, futile,
insignifiant; ~ **cash** petite monnaie

pewter (*pyoû*-teu) n étain m

phantom (*fæn*-teumm) n fantôme m

pharmacist (*fââ*-meu-sist) n
pharmacien m, pharmacienne f

pharmacology (fââ-meu-*ko*-leu-dji)
n pharmacologie f

pharmacy (*fââ*-meu-si) n pharmacie f

phase (féïz) n phase f

pheasant (*fè*-zeunnt) n faisan m

Philippine (*fi*-li-païn) adj philippin

Philippines (*fi*-li-piinz) pl Philippines
fpl

philosopher (fi-*lo*-seu-feu) n
philosophe m

philosophy (fi-*lo*-seu-fi) n
philosophie f

phone (fôoun) n téléphone m; v
téléphoner

phonetic (feu-*nè*-tik) adj phonétique

photo (*fôou*-tôou) n (pl ~s) photo f

photocopy (*fôou*-teu-ko-pi) n

photocopie f; v photocopier

photograph (fôou-teu-ghrââf) n photographie f; v photographier

photographer (feu-to-ghreu-feu) n photographe m

photography (feu-to-ghreu-fi) n photographie f

phrase (fréïz) n locution f; ~ **book** manuel de conversation

physical (fi-zi-keul) adj physique

physician (fi-zi-cheunn) n médecin m

physicist (fi-zi-sist) n physicien m

physics (fi-ziks) n physique f

pianist (pii-eu-nist) n pianiste m

piano (pi-æ-nôou) n piano m; **grand ~** piano à queue

pick (pik) v *cueillir; choisir; n choix m; ~ **up** ramasser; *aller chercher; **pick-up van** camionnette f

pickles (pi-keulz) pl conserves au vinaigre, marinades fpl

picnic (pik-nik) n pique-nique m; v pique-niquer

picture (pik-tcheu) n peinture f; illustration f; image f; ~ **postcard** carte postale, carte postale illustrée; **pictures** cinéma m

picturesque (pik-tcheu-rèsk) adj pittoresque

pie (païe) n pâté m; tourte f

piece (piiss) n morceau m, pièce f

pier (pieu) n jetée f

pierce (pieuss) v percer

pig (pigh) n cochon m

pigeon (pi-djeunn) n pigeon m

pig-headed (pigh-hè-did) adj obstiné

piglet (pigh-leut) n cochon de lait

pigskin (pigh-skinn) n peau de porc

pike (païk) n (pl ~) brochet m

pile (païl) n tas m; v entasser; **piles** pl hémorroïdes fpl

pilgrim (pil-ghrimm) n pèlerin m

pilgrimage (pil-ghri-midj) n pèlerinage m

pill (pil) n pilule f

pillar (pi-leu) n colonne f, pilier m

pillow (pi-lôou) n oreiller m

pillowcase (pi-lôou-kéïss) n taie d'oreiller

pilot (païe-leut) n pilote m

pimple (pimm-peul) n pustule f

pin (pinn) n épingle f; v épingler; **bobby ~** Am pince à cheveux

pincers (pinn-seuz) pl tenailles fpl

pinch (pinntch) v pincer

pineapple (païe-næ-peul) n ananas m

ping-pong (pinng-ponng) n ping-pong m

pink (pinngk) adj rose

pint (païnt) n pinte f

pioneer (païe-eu-nieu) n pionnier m

pious (païe-euss) adj pieux

pip (pip) n pépin m

pipe (païp) n pipe f; tuyau m; ~ **cleaner** cure-pipe m; ~ **tobacco** tabac pour pipe

pipeline (païp-laïn) n pipe-line m

pirate (païe-reut) n pirate m

pistol (pi-steul) n pistolet m

piston (pi-steunn) n piston m; ~ **ring** segment de piston

pit (pit) n fosse f; mine f

pitcher (pi-tcheu) n cruche f

pity (pi-ti) n pitié f; v *avoir pitié de; **what a pity!** dommage!

placard (plæ-kââd) n affiche f

place (pléïss) n place f; v poser, placer; ~ **of birth** lieu de naissance; *take ~ *avoir lieu

plague (pléïgh) n fléau m

plaice (pléïss) (pl ~) plie f

plain (pléïn) adj clair; ordinaire, simple; n plaine f

plan (plæn) n plan m; v planifier

plane (pléïn) adj plat; n avion m; ~ **crash** accident d'avion

planet (plæ-nit) n planète f

planetarium (plæ-ni-tèeu-ri-eumm) n

planétarium *m*

plank (plængk) *n* planche *f*

plant (plâânt) *n* plante *f*; usine *f*; *v* planter

plantation (plæn-*téï*-cheunn) *n* plantation *f*

plaster (*plââ*-steu) *n* plâtre *m*; sparadrap *m*

plastic (*plæ*-stik) *adj* plastique; *n* plastique *m*

plate (pléït) *n* assiette *f*; plaque *f*

plateau (*plæ*-tô°ᵘ) *n* (pl ⁓x, ⁓s) plateau *m*

platform (*plæt*-foom) *n* quai *m*; ⁓ **ticket** billet de quai

platinum (*plæ*-ti-neumm) *n* platine *m*

play (pléï) *v* jouer; *n* jeu *m*; pièce de théâtre; **one-act** ⁓ pièce en un acte; ⁓ **truant** *faire l'école buissonnière

player (pléï°ᵘ) *n* joueur *m*, joueuse *f*

playground (*pléï*-ghraound) *n* terrain de jeux

playing card (*pléï*-inng-kââd) *n* carte de jeu

playwright (*pléï*-raït) *n* dramaturge *m*

plea (plii) *n* plaidoyer *m*

plead (pliid) *v* plaider

pleasant (*plè*-zeunnt) *adj* plaisant, sympathique, agréable

please (pliiz) s'il vous plaît; *v* *plaire; **pleased** content; **pleasing** agréable

pleasure (*plè*-jeu) *n* agrément *m*, divertissement *m*, plaisir *m*

plentiful (*plèn*-ti-feul) *adj* abondant

plenty (*plèn*-ti) *n* abondance *f*

pliers (plaï°ᵘz) *pl* pince *f*

plimsolls (*plimm*-seulz) *pl* chaussures de basket

plot (plot) *n* conspiration *f*, complot *m*; intrigue *f*; lopin *m*

plough (plaou) *n* charrue *f*; *v* labourer

plucky (*pla*-ki) *adj* courageux

plug (plagh) *n* fiche *f*; ⁓ **in** brancher

plum (plamm) *n* prune *f*

plumber (*pla*-meu) *n* plombier *m*

plump (plammp) *adj* potelé

plural (*ploueu*-reul) *n* pluriel *m*

plus (plass) *prep* plus

pneumatic (nyoû-*mæ*-tik) *adj* pneumatique

pneumonia (nyoû-*môou*-ni-eu) *n* pneumonie *f*

poach (pô°ᵘtch) *v* braconner

pocket (po-kit) *n* poche *f*

pocketknife (po-kit-naïf) *n* (pl -knives) couteau de poche

poem (*pôou*-imm) *n* poème *m*

poet (*pôou*-it) *n* poète *m*

poetry (*pôou*-i-tri) *n* poésie *f*

point (poïnt) *n* point *m*; pointe *f*; *v* montrer du doigt; ⁓ **of view** point de vue; ⁓ **out** indiquer

pointed (*poïn*-tid) *adj* pointu

poison (*poï*-zeunn) *n* poison *m*; *v* empoisonner

poisonous (*poï*-zeu-neuss) *adj* vénéneux

Poland (*pôou*-leunnd) Pologne *f*

Pole (pô°ᵘl) *n* Polonais *m*

pole (pô°ᵘl) *n* poteau *m*

police (peu-*liiss*) *pl* police *f*; ⁓ **station** commissariat de police

policeman (peu-*liiss*-meunn) *n* (pl -men) agent de police, policier *m*

policewoman (peu-*liiss*-°ᵘou-meunn) *n* (pl -women) femme policier

policy (*po*-li-si) *n* politique *f*; police *f*

polio (*pôou*-li-ô°ᵘ) *n* poliomyélite *f*

Polish (*pôou*-lich) *adj* polonais

polish (*po*-lich) *v* polir

polite (peu-*laït*) *adj* poli

political (peu-*li*-ti-keul) *adj* politique

politician (po-li-*ti*-cheunn) *n* politicien *m*, politicienne *f*

politics (*po*-li-tiks) *n* politique *f*

poll (pô°ᵘl) *n* vote *m* (par bulletins); scrutin *m*; *v* sonder l'opinion de; réunir; (**opinion**) ⁓ sondage *m*

(d'opinion)

pollution (*peu-loû-cheunn*) *n* pollution *f*

pond (ponnd) *n* étang *m*

pony (*pôou*-ni) *n* poney *m*

pool (poûl) *n* flaque *f* d'eau; mare *f*

poor (pou^{eu}) *adj* pauvre; indigent; piètre

pope (pô^{ou}p) *n* pape *m*

pop music (pop *myoû*-zik) musique pop

poppy (*po*-pi) *n* coquelicot *m*; pavot *m*

popular (*po*-pyou-leu) *adj* populaire

population (po-pyou-*lêï*-cheunn) *n* population *f*

populous (*po*-pyou-leuss) *adj* populeux

porcelain (*poo*-seu-linn) *n* porcelaine *f*

porcupine (*poo*-kyou-païn) *n* porc-épic *m*

pork (pook) *n* porc *m*

port (poot) *n* port *m*; bâbord *m*

portable (*poo*-teu-beul) *adj* portatif

porter (*poo*-teu) *n* porteur *m*; portier *m*

porthole (*poot*-hô^{ou}l) *n* hublot *m*

portion (*poo*-cheunn) *n* portion *f*

portrait (*poo*-trit) *n* portrait *m*

Portugal (*poo*-tyou-gheul) Portugal *m*

Portuguese (poo-tyou-*ghiiz*) *adj* portugais; *n* Portugais *m*

posh (poch) *adj colloquial* chic, chouette

position (peu-*zi*-cheunn) *n* position *f*; situation *f*; attitude *f*

positive (*po*-zeu-tiv) *adj* positif; *n* positif *m*

possess (peu-*zèss*) *v* posséder; **possessed** *adj* possédé

possession (peu-*zè*-cheunn) *n* possession *f*; **possessions** biens *mpl*

possibility (po-seu-*bi*-leu-ti) *n*

possibilité *f*

possible (*po*-seu-beul) *adj* possible; éventuel

post (pô^{ou}st) *n* poteau *m*; poste *m*; poste *f*; *v* poster; ~ **box** boîte *f* postale ~-**office** bureau de poste

postage (*pôou*-stidj) *n* port *m*; ~ **paid** port payé; ~ **stamp** timbre-poste *m*

postcard (*pôoust*-kââd) *n* carte postale

poster (*pôou*-steu) *n* affiche *f*

poste restante (pô^{ou}st rè-*stant*) poste restante

postman (*pôoust*-meunn) *n* (pl -men) facteur *m*

post-paid (pô^{ou}st-*pêïd*) *adj* port payé

postpone (peu-*spôoun*) *v* ajourner, *renvoyer à

pot (pot) *n* pot *m*

potato (peu-*têï*-tô^{ou}) *n* (pl ~es) pomme de terre

pottery (*po*-teu-ri) *n* poterie *f*

pouch (paoutch) *n* pochette *f*

poulterer (*pôoul*-teu-reu) *n* marchand de volaille

poultry (*pôoul*-tri) *n* volaille *f*

pound (paound) *n* livre *f*

pour (poo) *v* verser

poverty (*po*-veu-ti) *n* pauvreté *f*

powder (*paou*-deu) *n* poudre *f*; ~ **compact** poudrier *m*; ~ **room** toilettes pour dames; **talc** ~ talc *m*

power (paou^{eu}) *n* force *f*, puissance *f*; énergie *f*; pouvoir *m*; ~ **station** centrale *f*

powerful (*paoueu*-feul) *adj* puissant; fort

powerless (*paoueu*-leuss) *adj* impuissant

practical (*præk*-ti-keul) *adj* pratique

practically (*præk*-ti-kli) *adv* pratiquement

practice (*præk*-tiss) *n* pratique *f*

practise (*præk*-tiss) *v* pratiquer;

s'exercer

praise (préïz) v louer; n éloge m

pram (præm) n voiture d'enfant

prawn (proon) n crevette f, crevette rose

pray (préï) v prier

prayer (prè^(eu)) n prière f

preach (priitch) v prêcher

precarious (pri-kèeu-ri-euss) adj précaire

precaution (pri-koo-cheunn) n précaution f

precede (pri-siid) v précéder

preceding (pri-sii-dinng) adj précédent

precious (prè-cheuss) adj précieux

precipice (prè-si-piss) n précipice m

precipitation (pri-si-pi-téï-cheunn) n précipitation f

precise (pri-saïss) adj précis, exact; méticuleux

predict (pri-dikt) v *prédire

prefer (pri-feû) v aimer mieux, préférer

preferable (prè-feu-reu-beul) adj préférable

preference (prè-feu-reunns) n préférence f

pregnant (prègh-neunnt) adj enceinte

prejudice (prè-djeu-diss) n préjugé m

preliminary (pri-li-mi-neu-ri) adj préliminaire

premature (prè-meu-tchou^(eu)) adj prématuré

premier (prèm-i^(eu)) n premier ministre

premises (prè-mi-siz) pl locaux mpl

premium (prii-mi-eumm) n prime f

prepaid (prii-péïd) adj payé d'avance

preparation (prè-peu-réï-cheunn) n préparation f

prepare (pri-pèeu) v préparer

prepared (pri-pèeud) adj prêt

preposition (prè-peu-zi-cheunn) n préposition f

prescribe (pri-skraïb) v *prescrire

prescription (pri-skrip-cheunn) n prescription f

presence (prè-zeunns) n présence f

present[1] (prè-zeunnt) n cadeau m; présent m; adj actuel; présent

present[2] (pri-zènt) v présenter

presently (prè-zeunnt-li) adv tout à l'heure

preservation (prè-zeu-véï-cheunn) n conservation f

preserve (pri-zeûv) v conserver; *mettre en conserve

president (prè-zi-deunnt) n président m, -e f

press (prèss) n presse f; v appuyer, presser; repasser; ~ **conference** conférence de presse

pressing (prè-sinng) adj pressant, urgent

pressure (prè-cheu) n pression f; tension f; **atmospheric** ~ pression atmosphérique

prestige (prè-stiij) n prestige m

presumable (pri-zyoû-meu-beul) adj probable

presume (pri-zyoûm) v présumer; prendre des libertés; se permettre (**to** de); ~ (**up**)**on** abuser de

presumptuous (pri-zammp-cheuss) adj présomptueux

pretence (pri-tèns) n prétexte m

pretend (pri-tènd) v *feindre, prétendre

pretext (prii-tèkst) n prétexte m

pretty (pri-ti) adj beau, joli; adv assez, plutôt, passablement

prevent (pri-vènt) v empêcher; *prévenir

preventive (pri-vèn-tiv) adj préventif

preview (prii-vyoû) n avant-première f; aperçu m

previous (prii-vi-euss) adj précédent, antérieur, préalable

pre-war (prii-*ouoo*) *adj* d'avant-guerre

price (praïss) *v* fixer le prix; **~ list** prix courant *m*

priceless (*praïss*-leuss) *adj* inestimable

prick (prik) *v* piquer

pride (praïd) *n* orgueil *m*

priest (priist) *n* prêtre *m*

primary (*praï*-meu-ri) *adj* primaire; premier, primordial; élémentaire

prince (prinns) *n* prince *m*

princess (prinn-*sèss*) *n* princesse *f*

principal (*prinn*-seu-peul) *adj* principal; *n* proviseur *m*, directeur *m*

principle (*prinn*-seu-peul) *n* principe *m*

print (prinnt) *v* imprimer; *n* épreuve *f*; estampe *f*; **printed matter** imprimé *m*

printer (*prinn*-teu) *n* imprimeur *m*; imprimante *f*

prior (praï^{eu}) *adj* antérieur

priority (praï-*o*-reu-ti) *n* priorité *f*

prison (*pri*-zeunn) *n* prison *f*

prisoner (*pri*-zeu-neu) *n* détenu *m*, -e *f*, prisonnier *m*, prisonnière *f*; **~ of war** prisonnier de guerre

privacy (*praï*-veu-si) *n* intimité *f*, vie privée

private (*praï*-vit) *adj* particulier, privé; personnel

privilege (*pri*-vi-lidj) *n* privilège *m*

prize (praïz) *n* prix *m*; récompense *f*

probable (*pro*-beu-beul) *adj* vraisemblable, probable

probably (*pro*-beu-bli) *adv* probablement

problem (*pro*-bleumm) *n* problème *m*; question *f*

procedure (preu-*sii*-djeu) *n* procédure *f*

proceed (preu-*siid*) *v* procéder

process (*prôou*-sèss) *n* processus *m*,

procédé *m*; procès *m*

procession (preu-*sè*-cheunn) *n* procession *f*, cortège *m*

proclaim (preu-*klêim*) *v* proclamer

produce[1] (preu-*dyoûss*) *v* *produire

produce[2] (*prod*-yoûss) *n* produit *m*

producer (preu-*dyoû*-seu) *n* producteur *m*

product (*pro*-dakt) *n* produit *m*

production (preu-*dak*-cheunn) *n* production *f*

profession (preu-*fè*-cheunn) *n* métier *m*, profession *f*

professional (preu-*fè*-cheu-neul) *adj* professionnel

professor (preu-*fè*-seu) *n* professeur *m*

profit (*pro*-fit) *n* bénéfice *m*, profit *m*; avantage *m*; *v* profiter

profitable (*pro*-fi-teu-beul) *adj* profitable

profound (preu-*faound*) *adj* profond

programme (*prôou*-ghræm) *n* programme *m*

progress[1] (*prôou*-ghrèss) *n* progrès *m*

progress[2] (preu-*ghrèss*) *v* avancer

progressive (preu-*ghrè*-siv) *adj* progressif

prohibit (preu-*hi*-bit) *v* *interdire

prohibition (prô^{ou}-i-*bi*-cheunn) *n* interdiction *f*

prohibitive (preu-*hi*-bi-tiv) *adj* inabordable

project (*pro*-djèkt) *n* plan *m*, projet *m*

promenade (pro-meu-*nââd*) *n* promenade *f*

promise (*pro*-miss) *n* promesse *f*; *v* *promettre

promote (preu-*môout*) *v* *promouvoir

promotion (preu-*môou*-cheunn) *n* promotion *f*

prompt (prommpt) *adj* instantané, prompt

pronounce (preu-*naouns*) *v*

prononcer

pronunciation (preu-nann-si-*éï*-cheunn) *n* prononciation *f*

proof (proûf) *n* preuve *f*

propel (preu-*pèl*) *v* propulser

propeller (preu-*pè*-leu) *n* hélice *f*

proper (*pro*-peu) *adj* juste; convenable, pertinent, adéquat, approprié

property (*pro*-peu-ti) *n* propriété *f*

proportion (preu-*poo*-cheunn) *n* proportion *f*

proportional (preu-*poo*-cheu-neul) *adj* proportionnel

proposal (preu-*pôou*-zeul) *n* proposition *f*

propose (preu-*pôouz*) *v* proposer

proposition (pro-peu-*zi*-cheunn) *n* proposition *f*

proprietor (preu-*praï*-eu-teu) *n* propriétaire *m/f*

prospect (*pro*-spèkt) *n* perspective *f*

prospectus (preu-*spèk*-teuss) *n* prospectus *m*

prosperity (pro-*spê*-reu-ti) *n* prospérité *f*

prosperous (*pro*-speu-reuss) *adj* prospère

prostitute (*pro*-sti-tyoût) *n* prostituée *f*

protect (preu-*tèkt*) *v* protéger

protection (preu-*tèk*-cheunn) *n* protection *f*

protest[1] (*prôou*-tèst) *n* protestation *f*

protest[2] (preu-*tèst*) *v* protester

Protestant (*pro*-ti-steunnt) *adj* protestant

proud (praoud) *adj* fier; orgueilleux

prove (proûv) *v* démontrer, prouver; se révéler

proverb (*pro*-veûb) *n* proverbe *m*

provide (preu-*vaïd*) *v* fournir; **provided that** pourvu que

province (*pro*-vinns) *n* province *f*

provincial (preu-*vinn*-cheul) *adj* provincial

provisional (preu-*vi*-jeu-neul) *adj* provisoire

provisions (preu-*vi*-jeunnz) *pl* provision *f*

prune (proûn) *n* pruneau *m*

psychiatrist (saï-*kaï*-eu-trist) *n* psychiatre *m*

psychic (*saï*-kik) *adj* psychique

psychological (saï-ko-*lo*-dji-keul) *adj* psychologique

psychologist (saï-*ko*-leu-djist) *n* psychologue *m*

psychology (saï-*ko*-leu-dji) *n* psychologie *f*

pub (pab) *n* bistrot *m*

public (*pa*-blik) *adj* public; général; *n* public *m*; **~ garden** jardin public; **~ house** café *m*

publication (pa-bli-*kéï*-cheunn) *n* publication *f*

publicity (pa-*bli*-seu-ti) *n* publicité *f*

publish (*pa*-blich) *v* publier

publisher (*pa*-bli-cheu) *n* éditeur *m*, éditrice *f*

puddle (*pa*-deul) *n* flaque *f*

pull (poul) *v* tirer; **~ out** *partir; **~ up** s'arrêter

Pullman (*poul*-meunn) *n* voiture Pullman

pullover (*pou*-lô^ou-veu) *n* pull-over *m*

pulpit (*poul*-pit) *n* pupitre *m*, chaire *f*

pulse (pals) *n* pouls *m*

pump (pammp) *n* pompe *f*; *v* pomper

pun (pann) *n* jeu *m* de mots

punch (panntch) *v* donner des coups de poing; *n* coup de poing

punctual (*panngk*-tchou-eul) *adj* ponctuel

puncture (*panngk*-tcheu) *n* crevaison *f*

punctured (*panngk*-tcheud) *adj* crevé

punish (*pa*-nich) *v* punir

punishment (*pa-nich-meunnt*) *n* punition *f*

pupil (*pyoû-peul*) *n* élève *m/f*

puppet-show (*pa-pit-chô*ᵒᵘ) *n* théâtre de marionnettes

purchase (*peû-tcheuss*) *v* acheter; *n* acquisition *f*, achat *m*; **~ price** prix d'achat

purchaser (*peû-tcheu-seu*) *n* acheteur *m*, acheteuse *f*

pure (*pyou*ᵉᵘ) *adj* pur

purple (*peû-peul*) *adj* pourpre

purpose (*peû-peuss*) *n* intention *f*, but *m*; **on ~** intentionnel

purse (*peûss*) *n* bourse *f*, porte-monnaie *m*

pursue (*peu-syoû*) *v* *poursuivre; aspirer à

pus (*pass*) *n* pus *m*

push (*pouch*) *n* poussée *f*, coup *m*; *v* pousser

***put** (*pout*) *v* placer, poser, *mettre; **~ away** ranger; **~ off** ajourner; **~ on** *mettre; **~ out** *éteindre

puzzle (*pa-zeul*) *n* casse-tête *m*; énigme *f*; *v* embarrasser; **jigsaw ~** puzzle *m*

puzzling (*paz-linng*) *adj* embarrassant

pyjamas (*peu-djââ-meuz*) *pl* pyjama *m*

Q

quail (*k*ᵒᵘ*éïl*) *n* (pl ~, ~s) caille *f*

quaint (*k*ᵒᵘ*éïnt*) *adj* étrange; vieillot

qualification (*k*ᵒᵘ*o-li-fi-kéï-cheunn*) *n* qualification *f*, réserve *f*, restriction *f*

qualified (*kouo-li-faïd*) *adj* qualifié; compétent

qualify (*kouo-li-faï*) *v* *être qualifié

quality (*kouo-leu-ti*) *n* qualité *f*; caractéristique *f*

quantity (*kouonn-teu-ti*) *n* quantité *f*; nombre *m*

quarantine (*kouo-reunn-tiin*) *n* quarantaine *f*

quarrel (*kouo-reul*) *v* se disputer; *n* querelle *f*

quarry (*kouo-ri*) *n* carrière *f*

quarter (*kouoo-teu*) *n* quart *m*; trimestre *m*; quartier *m*; **~ of an hour** quart d'heure

quarterly (*kouoo-teu-li*) *adj* trimestriel

quay (*kii*) *n* quai *m*

queen (*k*ᵒᵘ*iin*) *n* reine *f*

queer (*k*ᵒᵘ*i*ᵉᵘ) *adj* étrange; drôle

query (*kouieu-ri*) *n* question *f*; *v* s'informer; *mettre en doute

question (*kouèss-tcheunn*) *n* question *f*; problème *m*; *v* interroger; *mettre en doute; **~ mark** point d'interrogation

queue (*kyoû*) *n* queue *f*; *v* *faire la queue

quick (*k*ᵒᵘ*ik*) *adj* rapide

quick-tempered (*k*ᵒᵘ*ik-tèm-peud*) *adj* irascible

quiet (*kouaï-eut*) *adj* paisible, calme, tranquille; *n* silence *m*, tranquillité *f*

quilt (*k*ᵒᵘ*ilt*) *n* courtepointe *f*

quit (*k*ᵒᵘ*it*) *v* cesser

quite (*k*ᵒᵘ*aït*) *adv* entièrement, tout à fait; assez, plutôt

quiz (*k*ᵒᵘ*iz*) *n* (pl ~zes) jeu concours *m*

quota (*kouôou-teu*) *n* quote-part *f*

quotation (*k*ᵒᵘ*ôou-téï-cheunn*) *n* citation *f*; **~ marks** guillemets *mpl*

quote (*k*ᵒᵘ*ôou*t) *v* citer

R

rabbit (*ræ*-bit) *n* lapin *m*

rabies (*réï*-biz) *n* rage *f*

race (réïss) *n* course *f*

racecourse (*réïss*-kooss) *n* champ de courses, hippodrome *m*

racehorse (*réïss*-hooss) *n* cheval de course

racetrack (*réïss*-træk) *n* piste de courses

racial (*réï*-cheul) *adj* racial

racket (*ræ*-kit) *n* vacarme *m*; raquette *f*

radiator (*réï*-di-éï-teu) *n* radiateur *m*

radical (*ræ*-di-keul) *adj* radical

radio (*réï*-di-ô*ou*) *n* radio *f*

radish (*ræ*-dich) *n* radis *m*

radius (*réï*-di-euss) *n* (pl radii) rayon *m*

raft (rââft) *n* radeau *m*

rag (rægh) *n* chiffon *m*

rage (réïdj) *n* fureur *f*, rage *f*; *v* rager, sévir

raid (réïd) *n* raid *m*

rail (réïl) *n* balustrade *f*, barre *f*

railing (*réï*-linng) *n* rampe *f*

railroad (*réïl*-rô*ou*d) *nAm* voie ferrée, chemin de fer

railway (*réïl*-*ou*éï) *n* chemin de fer, voie ferrée

rain (réïn) *n* pluie *f*; *v* *pleuvoir

rainbow (*réïn*-bô*ou*) *n* arc-en-ciel *m*

raincoat (*réïn*-kô*ou*t) *n* imperméable *m*

rainproof (*réïn*-proûf) *adj* imperméable

rainy (*réï*-ni) *adj* pluvieux

raise (réïz) *v* élever; relever; cultiver; *nAm* augmentation de salaire

raisin (*réï*-zeunn) *n* raisin sec

rake (réïk) *n* râteau *m*

rally (*ræ*-li) *n* rassemblement *m*

ramp (ræmp) *n* pente *f*

rancid (*ræn*-sid) *adj* rance

rang (ræng) *v* (p ring)

range (réïndj) *n* gamme *f*

rank (rængk) *n* grade *m*; rang *m*

ransom (*ræn*-seumm) *n* rançon *f*

rape (réïp) *v* violer

rapid (*ræ*-pid) *adj* rapide

rapids (*ræ*-pidz) *pl* rapide *m*

rare (rè*eu*) *adj* rare

rarely (*rèeu*-li) *adv* rarement

rascal (*rââ*-skeul) *n* coquin *m*, fripon *m*

rash (ræch) *n* éruption *f*; *adj* imprudent, inconsidéré

raspberry (*rââz*-beu-ri) *n* framboise *f*

rat (ræt) *n* rat *m*

rate (réït) *n* tarif *m*; vitesse *f*; **at any ~** de toute façon, quoiqu'il en soit; **~ of exchange** cours du change

rather (*rââ*-ðeu) *adv* assez, passablement, plutôt

ration (*ræ*-cheunn) *n* ration *f*

rattan (*ræ*-*tæn*) *n* rotin *m*

raven (*réï*-veunn) *n* corbeau *m*

raw (roo) *adj* cru; **~ material** matière première

ray (réï) *n* rayon *m*

razor (*réï*-zeu) *n* rasoir *m*; **~ blade** lame de rasoir

reach (riitch) *v* *atteindre; *n* portée *f*

react (ri-*ækt*) *v* réagir

reaction (ri-*æk*-cheunn) *n* réaction *f*

***read** (riid) *v* *lire

reader (*rii*-deu) *n* lecteur *m*, lectrice *f*; maître *m* de conférences; livre *m* de lecture

reading (*rii*-dinng) *n* lecture *f*; **~ lamp** lampe de travail; **~ room** salle de lecture

ready (*rè*-di) *adj* prêt

ready-made (rè-di-*méïd*) *adj* de confection

real (ri^{eu}l) *adj* réel
reality (ri-*æ*-leu-ti) *n* réalité *f*
realizable (*rieu*-laï-zeu-beul) *adj* réalisable
realize (*rieu*-laïz) *v* se rendre compte; réaliser
really (*rieu*-li) *adv* vraiment, réellement; en réalité
rear (ri^{eu}) *n* arrière *m*; *v* élever; **~ light** feu arrière
reason (*rii*-zeunn) *n* cause *f*, raison *f*; sens *m*; *v* raisonner
reasonable (*rii*-zeu-neu-beul) *adj* raisonnable; équitable
reassure (rii-eu-*choueu*) *v* rassurer
rebate (*rii*-béït) *n* réduction *f*, rabais *m*
rebellion (ri-*bèl*-yeunn) *n* révolte *f*, rébellion *f*
recall (ri-*kool*) *v* se rappeler; rappeler; révoquer
receipt (ri-*siit*) *n* reçu *m*; réception *f*
receive (ri-*siiv*) *v* *recevoir
receiver (ri-*sii*-veu) *n* combiné *m*
recent (*rii*-seunnt) *adj* récent
recently (*rii*-seunnt-li) *adv* l'autre jour, récemment
reception (ri-*sèp*-cheunn) *n* réception *f*; accueil *m*; **~ office** réception *f*
receptionist (ri-*sèp*-cheu-nist) *n* hôtesse *f*
recipe (*rè*-si-pi) *n* recette *f*
recital (ri-*saï*-teul) *n* récital *m*
reckon (*rè*-keunn) *v* calculer; estimer; supposer
recognition (rè-keugh-*ni*-cheunn) *n* reconnaissance *f*
recognize (*rè*-keugh-naïz) *v* *reconnaître
recollect (rè-keu-*lèkt*) *v* se *souvenir
recommence (rii-keu-*mèns*) *v* recommencer
recommend (rè-keu-*mènd*) *v* recommander; conseiller
recommendation (rè-keu-mèn-*déï*-cheunn) *n* recommandation *f*

reconciliation (rè-keunn-si-li-*éï*-cheunn) *n* réconciliation *f*
record[1] (*rè*-kood) *n* disque *m*; record *m*; dossier *m*; **long-playing ~** microsillon *m*; **~ player** tourne-disque *m*
record[2] (ri-*kood*) *v* enregistrer
recorder (ri-*koo*-deu) *n* magnétophone *m*
recording (ri-*koo*-dinng) *n* enregistrement *m*
recover (ri-*ka*-veu) *v* récupérer; se *remettre, guérir
recovery (ri-*ka*-veu-ri) *n* guérison *f*
recreation (rè-kri-*éï*-cheunn) *n* récréation *f*; **~ centre** centre de loisirs; **~ ground** terrain de jeux
rectangle (*rèk*-tæng-gheul) *n* rectangle *m*
rectangular (rèk-*tæng*-ghyou-leu) *adj* rectangulaire
rector (*rèk*-teu) *n* pasteur *m*, recteur *m*
rectory (*rèk*-teu-ri) *n* presbytère *m*
red (rèd) *adj* rouge
redeem (ri-*diim*) *v* racheter, compenser
reduce (ri-*dyoûss*) *v* *réduire, diminuer
reduction (ri-*dak*-cheunn) *n* rabais *m*, réduction *f*
redundant (ri-*dann*-deunnt) *adj* superflu
reed (riid) *n* roseau *m*
reef (riif) *n* récif *m*
referee (rè-feu-*rii*) *n* arbitre *m*; *v* arbitrer; *v* être arbitre, faire fonction d'arbitre
reference (*rèf*-reunns) *n* référence *f*; rapport *m*; **with ~ to** relatif à
refer to (ri-*feû*) *renvoyer à
refill (*rii*-fil) *n* recharge *f*
refinery (ri-*faï*-neu-ri) *n* raffinerie *f*
reflect (ri-*flèkt*) *v* refléter

reflection (ri-*flèk*-cheunn) n reflet m

reflector (ri-*flèk*-teu) n réflecteur m

reformation (rè-feu-*méï*-cheunn) n réforme f

refresh (ri-*frèch*) v rafraîchir

refreshment (ri-*frèch*-meunnt) n rafraîchissement m

refrigerator (ri-*fri*-djeu-réï-teu) n frigidaire m, réfrigérateur m

refugee (rè-fyoû-*djii*) n réfugié m, réfugiée f

refund[1] (ri-*fannd*) v rendre, rembourser

refund[2] (*rii*-fannd) n remboursement m

refusal (ri-*fyoû*-zeul) n refus m

refuse[1] (ri-*fyoûz*) v refuser

refuse[2] (*rè*-fyoûss) n rebut m

regard (ri-*ghâad*) v considérer; n respect m; **as regards** quant à, concernant, en ce qui concerne

regarding (ri-*ghââ*-dinng) prep en ce qui concerne, concernant; à propos de

régime (réï-*jiim*) n régime m

region (*rii*-djeunn) n région f

regional (*rii*-djeu-neul) adj régional

register (*rè*-dji-steu) v s'*inscrire; recommander; **registered letter** lettre recommandée

registration (rè-dji-*stréï*-cheunn) n inscription f, **~ form** formulaire d'inscription; **~ number** numéro d'immatriculation; **~ plate** plaque d'immatriculation

regret (ri-*ghrèt*) v regretter; n regret m

regular (*rè*-ghyou-leu) adj régulier; ordinaire, normal

regulate (*rè*-ghyou-léït) v régler

regulation (rè-ghyou-*léï*-cheunn) n règlement m

rehabilitation (rii-heu-bi-li-*téï*-cheunn) n rééducation f

rehearsal (ri-*heû*-seul) n répétition f

rehearse (ri-*heûss*) v répéter

reign (réïn) n règne m; v régner

reimburse (rii-imm-*beûss*) v restituer, rembourser

reject (ri-*djèkt*) v refuser, rejeter

relate (ri-*léït*) v relater

related (ri-*léï*-tid) adj apparenté

relation (ri-*léï*-cheunn) n rapport m, relation f; parent m

relationship (ri-*léï*-cheunn-chip) n rapport m; parenté f

relative (*rè*-leu-tiv) n parent m; adj relatif

relax (ri-*læks*) v se détendre

relaxation (ri-læk-*séï*-cheunn) n détente f

reliable (ri-*laï*-eu-beul) adj digne de confiance

relic (*rè*-lik) n relique f

relief (ri-*liif*) n soulagement m; soutien m; relief m

relieve (ri-*liiv*) v soulager; relayer

religion (ri-*li*-djeunn) n religion f

religious (ri-*li*-djeuss) adj religieux

rely on (ri-*laï*) compter sur

remain (ri-*méïn*) v rester

remainder (ri-*méïn*-deu) n restant m, reste m

remaining (ri-*méï*-ninng) adj restant

remark (ri-*mââk*) n remarque f; v remarquer

remarkable (ri-*mââ*-keu-beul) adj remarquable

remedy (*rè*-meu-di) n remède m

remember (ri-*mèm*-beu) v se rappeler; *retenir

remembrance (ri-*mèm*-breunns) n souvenir m

remind (ri-*maïnd*) v rappeler

remit (ri-*mit*) v *remettre

remittance (ri-*mi*-teunns) n versement m

remnant (*rèm*-neunnt) n reste m, restant m

remote (ri-*môout*) adj éloigné, lointain

removal (ri-*moû*-veul) n déplacement m

remove (ri-*moûv*) v enlever

remunerate (ri-*myoû*-neu-réït) v rémunérer

remuneration (ri-myoû-neu-*réï*-cheunn) n rémunération f

renew (ri-*nyoû*) v renouveler

rent (rènt) v louer; n loyer m

repair (ri-*pèeu*) v réparer; n réparation f

reparation (rè-peu-*réï*-cheunn) n réparation f

*repay (ri-*péï*) v rembourser

repayment (ri-*péï*-meunnt) n remboursement m

repeat (ri-*piit*) v répéter

repellent (ri-*pè*-leunnt) adj écœurant, répugnant

repentance (ri-*pèn*-teunns) n repentir m

repertory (*rè*-peu-teu-ri) n répertoire m

repetition (rè-peu-*ti*-cheunn) n répétition f

replace (ri-*pléïss*) v remplacer

reply (ri-*plaï*) v répondre; n réponse f; in ~ en réponse

report (ri-*poot*) v relater; rapporter; se présenter; n compte rendu, rapport m

reporter (ri-*poo*-teu) n reporter m

represent (rè-pri-*zènt*) v représenter

representation (rè-pri-zèn-*téï*-cheunn) n représentation f

representative (rè-pri-*zèn*-teu-tiv) adj représentatif

reprimand (*rè*-pri-mâând) v réprimander

reproach (ri-*prôoutch*) n reproche m; v reprocher

reproduce (rii-preu-*dyoûss*) v *reproduire

reproduction (rii-preu-*dak*-cheunn) n reproduction f

reptile (*rèp*-taïl) n reptile m

republic (ri-*pa*-blik) n république f

republican (ri-*pa*-bli-keunn) adj républicain

repulsive (ri-*pal*-siv) adj repoussant

reputation (rè-pyou-*téï*-cheunn) n réputation f

request (ri-*kouèst*) n requête f; demande f; v *requérir

require (ri-*kouaïeu*) v exiger

requirement (ri-*kouaïeu*-meunnt) n exigence f

requisite (*rè*-k^{ou}i-zit) adj requis

rescue (*rè*-skyoû) v sauver; n sauvetage m

research (ri-*seûtch*) n recherche f

resemblance (ri-*zèm*-bleunns) n ressemblance f

resemble (ri-*zèm*-beul) v ressembler à

resent (ri-*zènt*) v s'offenser de, en *vouloir à

reservation (rè-zeu-*véï*-cheunn) n réservation f

reserve (ri-*zeûv*) v réserver; *retenir; n réserve f

reserved (ri-*zeûvd*) adj réservé

reservoir (*rè*-zeu-v^{ou}ââ) n réservoir m

reside (ri-*zaïd*) v résider

residence (*rè*-zi-deunns) n résidence f; ~ permit permis de séjour

resident (*rè*-zi-deunnt) n résident m; adj domicilié; interne

resign (ri-*zaïn*) v démissionner

resignation (rè-zigh-*néï*-cheunn) n démission f

resin (*rè*-zinn) n résine f

resist (ri-*zist*) v résister

resistance (ri-*zi*-steunns) n résistance f

resolute (*rè*-zeu-loût) adj résolu, déterminé

respect (ri-*spèkt*) n respect m; estime f, considération f; v respecter

respectable (ri-*spèk*-teu-beul) adj honorable, respectable

respectful (ri-*spèkt*-feul) adj respectueux

respective (ri-*spèk*-tiv) adj respectif

respiration (rè-speu-*réï*-cheunn) n respiration f

respite (*rè*-spaït) n répit m

responsibility (ri-sponn-seu-*bi*-leu-ti) n responsabilité f

responsible (ri-*sponn*-seu-beul) adj responsable

rest (rèst) n repos m; reste m; v se reposer; **~ home** maison de repos; **~ room** toilettes

restaurant (*rè*-steu-ron) n restaurant m

restful (*rèst*-feul) adj reposant

restless (*rèst*-leuss) adj agité; inquiet

restrain (ri-*strèïn*) v *contenir, *retenir

restriction (ri-*strik*-cheunn) n restriction f

result (ri-*zalt*) n résultat m; effet m; v résulter

resume (ri-*zyoûm*) v *reprendre

résumé (*rè*-zyou-méï) n résumé m; Am curriculum vitae m; C.V. m

retail (*rii*-téïl) v détailler; **~ trade** commerce de détail

retailer (*rii*-téï-leu) n détaillant m, -e f

retina (*rè*-ti-neu) n rétine f

retired (ri-*taïeud*) adj retraité

return (ri-*teûnn*) v *revenir, retourner; n retour m; **~ flight** vol de retour; **~ journey** voyage de retour

reunite (rii-you-*naït*) v réunir

reveal (ri-*viil*) v révéler

revelation (rè-veu-*léï*-cheunn) n révélation f

revenge (ri-*vèndj*) n vengeance f

revenue (*rè*-veu-nyoû) n recettes, revenu m

reverse (ri-*veûss*) n contraire m; revers m; marche arrière; revirement m; adj inverse; v *faire marche arrière

review (ri-*vyoû*) n critique f; revue f

revise (ri-*vaïz*) v reviser

revision (ri-*vi*-jeunn) n révision f

revival (ri-*vaï*-veul) n reprise f

revolt (ri-*vôoult*) v se révolter; n rébellion f, révolte f

revolting (ri-*vôoul*-tinng) adj dégoûtant, révoltant, répugnant

revolution (rè-veu-*loû*-cheunn) n révolution f; rotation f

revolver (ri-*vol*-veu) n revolver m

revue (ri-*vyoû*) n revue f

reward (ri-*ouood*) n récompense f; v récompenser

rheumatism (*roû*-meu-ti-zeumm) n rhumatisme m

rhinoceros (raï-*no*-seu-reuss) n (pl ~, ~es) rhinocéros m

rhubarb (*roû*-bââb) n rhubarbe f

rhyme (raïm) n rime f

rhythm (*ri*-ðeumm) n rythme m

rib (rib) n côte f

ribbon (*ri*-beunn) n ruban m

rice (raïss) n riz m

rich (ritch) adj riche

riches (*ri*-tchiz) pl richesse f

rid (rid) v débarrasser (**of** de); **get ~ of** se débarrasser de

riddle (*ri*-deul) n énigme f

ride (raïd) n course f

***ride** (raïd) v aller; monter à cheval

rider (*raï*-deu) n cavalier m

ridge (ridj) n arête f

ridicule (*ri*-di-kyoûl) v ridiculiser

ridiculous (ri-*di*-kyou-leuss) adj ridicule

riding (*raï*-dinng) n équitation f; **~ school** manège m

rifle (*raï*-feul) v fusil m

right (raït) *n* droit *m*; *adj* correct, juste; droit; équitable; **all ~!** d'accord!; ***be ~** *avoir raison; **~ of way** priorité de passage

righteous (raï-tcheuss) *adj* juste

right-hand (raït-hænd) *adj* à droite, de droite

rightly (raït-li) *adv* justement

rim (rimm) *n* jante *f*; rebord *m*

ring (rinng) *n* bague *f*; cercle *m*; piste *f*

*ring (rinng) *v* sonner; **~ up** téléphoner

rinse (rinns) *v* rincer; *n* rinçage *m*

riot (raï-eut) *n* émeute *f*

rip (rip) *v* déchirer

ripe (raïp) *adj* mûr

rise (raïz) *n* augmentation de salaire, augmentation *f*; élévation *f*; montée *f*; essor *m*

*rise (raïz) *v* se lever; monter

rising (raï-zinng) *n* insurrection *f*

risk (risk) *n* risque *m*; danger *m*; *v* risquer

risky (ri-ski) *adj* dangereux, risqué

rival (raï-veul) *n* rival *m*, -e *f*; concurrent *m*, -e *f*; *v* rivaliser

rivalry (raï-veul-ri) *n* rivalité *f*; concurrence *f*

river (ri-veu) *n* fleuve *m*; **~ bank** rive *f*

riverside (ri-veu-saïd) *n* bord de la rivière

roach (rôᵘtch) *n* (pl ~) gardon *m*

road (rôᵘd) *n* rue *f*, route *f*; **~ fork** bifurcation *f*; **~ map** carte routière; **~ system** réseau routier; **~ up** attention travaux

roadhouse (rôᵘd-haouss) *n* auberge *f*

roadside (rôᵘd-saïd) *n* bord de la route; **~ restaurant** auberge *f*

roadway (rôᵘd-ᵒᵘéï) *n Am* chaussée *f*

roam (rôᵘm) *v* vagabonder

roar (roo) *v* mugir, rugir; *n* rugissement *m*, grondement *m*

roast (rôᵘst) *v* griller, rôtir

rob (rob) *v* voler

robber (ro-beu) *n* voleur *m*

robbery (ro-beu-ri) *n* vol *m*

robe (rôᵘb) *n* robe *f*

robin (ro-binn) *n* rouge-gorge *m*

robust (rôᵘ-bast) *adj* robuste

rock (rok) *n* rocher *m*; *v* balancer

rocket (ro-kit) *n* fusée *f*

rocky (ro-ki) *adj* rocheux

rod (rod) *n* barre *f*, tige *f*

roe (rôᵘ) *n* œufs de poisson, laitance *f*

role, rôle (rôᵘl) *n* rôle *m*

roll (rôᵘl) *v* rouler; *n* rouleau *m*; petit pain

roller-skating (rôᵘou-leu-skéï-tinng) *n* patinage à roulettes

Roman Catholic (rôᵘou-meunn kæ-œu-lik) catholique

romance (reu-mæns) *n* idylle *f*

romantic (reu-mæn-tik) *adj* romantique

roof (rôᵘf) *n* toit *m*; **thatched ~** toit de chaume *m*

room (rôᵘm) *n* pièce *f*, chambre *f*; espace *m*, place *f*; **~ and board** pension complète; **~ service** service d'étage; **~ temperature** température ambiante

roomy (rôᵘ-mi) *adj* spacieux

root (rôût) *n* racine *f*

rope (rôᵘp) *n* corde *f*

rosary (rôᵘou-zeu-ri) *n* rosaire *m*

rose (rôᵘz) *n* rose *f*; *adj* rose

rotten (ro-teunn) *adj* pourri

rouge (rôûj) *n* rouge *m*

rough (raf) *adj* rugueux

roulette (roû-lèt) *n* roulette *f*

round (raound) *adj* rond; *prep* autour de; *n* reprise *f*; **~ trip** *Am* aller et retour

roundabout (raoun-deu-baout) *n* rond-point *m*

rounded (raoun-did) *adj* arrondi

route (roût) n route f
routine (roû-*tiin*) n routine f
row[1] (rô^{ou}) n rang m; v ramer
row[2] (raou) n querelle f
rowdy (*raou*-di) adj tapageur
rowing boat (*rô^{ou}*-inng-bô^{ou}t) n
  bateau à rames
royal (*roï*-eul) adj royal
rub (rab) v frotter
rubber (*ra*-beu) n caoutchouc m;
  gomme f; ~ **band** élastique m
rubbish (*ra*-bich) n détritus m;
  radotage m, sottise f; ~ **bin** poubelle f;
  talk ~ baratiner
rucksack (*rak*-sæk) n sac à dos
rudder (*ra*-deu) n gouvernail m
rude (roûd) adj grossier
rug (ragh) n tapis m
ruin (*roû*-inn) v ruiner; n ruine f
rule (roûl) n règle f; régime m,
  gouvernement m, règne m; v régner,
  gouverner; **as a** ~ généralement, en
  général
ruler (*roû*-leu) n monarque m,
dirigeant m; règle f
Rumania (roû-*mêï*-ni-eu) Roumanie f
Rumanian (roû-*mêï*-ni-eunn) adj
  roumain; n Roumain m
rumo(u)r (*roû*-meu) n rumeur f
*run (rann) v *courir; ~ **into**
  rencontrer
runaway (*ra*-neu-^{ou}éï) n fugitif m
rung (rann) v (pp ring)
runner (*ra*-neu) n coureur m,
  coureuse f; patin m; coulisseau m
runway (*rann*-^{ou}éï) n piste de
  décollage
rural (*roue*-reul) adj rural
ruse (roûz) n ruse f
rush (rach) v se presser; n jonc m; ~
  hour heure de pointe
Russia (*ra*-cheu) Russie f
Russian (*ra*-cheunn) adj russe; n
  Russe m
rust (rast) n rouille f
rustic (*ra*-stik) adj rustique
rusty (*ra*-sti) adj rouillé

S

sack (sæk) n sac m
sacred (*sêï*-krid) adj sacré
sacrifice (*sæ*-kri-faïss) n sacrifice m; v
  sacrifier
sacrilege (*sæ*-kri-lidj) n sacrilège m
sad (sæd) adj triste; malheureux,
  affligé
saddle (*sæ*-deul) n selle f
sadness (*sæd*-neuss) n tristesse f
safe (sêïf) adj sûr; n coffre-fort
safety (*sêïf*-ti) n sécurité f; ~ **belt**
  ceinture de sécurité; ~ **pin** épingle de
  sûreté
sail (sêïl) v naviguer; n voile f

sailing boat (*sêï*-linng-bô^{ou}t) n bateau
  à voiles
sailor (*sêï*-leu) n marin m
saint (sêïnt) n saint m
salad (*sæ*-leud) n salade f; ~ **oil** huile
  de table
salary (*sæ*-leu-ri) n paie f, salaire m
sale (sêïl) n vente f; **clearance** ~
  soldes; **for** ~ à vendre; **sales** soldes
saleable (*sêï*-leu-beul) adj vendable
salesgirl (*sêïlz*-gheûl) n vendeuse f
salesman (*sêïlz*-meunn) n (pl -men)
  vendeur m
salmon (*sæ*-meunn) n (pl ~) saumon

m

salon (*sæ*-lon) *n* salon *m*

saloon (seu-*loûn*) *n* café *m*

salt (soolt) *n* sel *m*; ~ **cellar**, *Am* ~ **shaker** salière *f*

salty (*sool*-ti) *adj* salé

salute (seu-*loût*) *v* saluer

salve (sââv) *n* onguent *m*

same (séïm) *adj* même

sample (*sââm*-peul) *n* échantillon *m*

sanatorium (sæ-neu-*too*-ri-eumm) *n* (pl ~s, -ria) sanatorium *m*

sand (sænd) *n* sable *m*

sandal (*sæn*-deul) *n* sandale *f*

sandpaper (*sænd*-péï-peu) *n* papier de verre

sandwich (*sæn*-ᵒᵘidj) *n* sandwich *m*; tartine *f*

sandy (*sæn*-di) *adj* sableux

sanitary (*sæ*-ni-teu-ri) *adj* sanitaire; ~ **towel** (*Am* ~ **napkin**) serviette hygiénique

sardine (sââ-*diin*) *n* sardine *f*

satchel (*sæ*-tcheul) *n* cartable *m*

satellite (*sæ*-teu-laït) *n* satellite *m*

satin (*sæ*-tinn) *n* satin *m*

satisfaction (sæ-tiss-*fæk*-cheunn) *n* satisfaction *f*

satisfactory (sæ-tiss-*fæk*-teu-ri) *adj* satisfaisant

satisfy (*sæ*-tiss-faï) *v* *satisfaire

Saturday (*sæ*-teu-di) samedi *m*

sauce (sooss) *n* sauce *f*

saucepan (*sooss*-peunn) *n* poêle *f*

saucer (*soo*-seu) *n* soucoupe *f*

Saudi Arabia (saou-di-eu-*réï*-bi-eu) Arabie Séoudite

sauna (*soo*-neu) *n* sauna *m*

sausage (*so*-sidj) *n* saucisse *f*

savage (*sæ*-vidj) *adj* sauvage

save (séïv) *v* sauver; épargner

savings (*séï*-vinngz) *pl* économies; ~ **bank** caisse d'épargne

savio(u)r (*séï*-vyeu) *n* sauveur *m*

savo(u)ry (*séï*-veu-ri) *adj* savoureux; piquant

saw¹ (soo) *v* (p see)

saw² (soo) *n* scie *f*

sawmill (*soo*-mil) *n* scierie *f*

***say** (séï) *v* *dire

scaffolding (*skæ*-feul-dinng) *n* échafaudage *m*

scale (skéïl) *n* échelle *f*; gamme *f*; écaille *f*; **scales** *pl* balance *f*

scandal (*skæn*-deul) *n* scandale *m*

Scandinavia (skæn-di-*néï*-vi-eu) Scandinavie *f*

Scandinavian (skæn-di-*néï*-vi-eunn) *adj* scandinave; *n* Scandinave *m*

scapegoat (*skéïp*-ghôᵘt) *n* bouc émissaire

scar (skââ) *n* cicatrice *f*

scarce (skeᵘss) *adj* rare

scarcely (*skèeu*-sli) *adv* à peine

scarcity (*skèeu*-seu-ti) *n* pénurie *f*

scare (skèᵘ) *v* effrayer; *n* panique *f*

scarf (skââf) *n* (pl ~s, scarves) écharpe *f*

scarlet (*skââ*-leut) *adj* écarlate

scary (*skèeu*-ri) *adj* inquiétant

scatter (*skæ*-teu) *v* disperser

scene (siin) *n* scène *f*

scenery (*sii*-neu-ri) *n* paysage *m*

scenic (*sii*-nik) *adj* pittoresque

scent (sènt) *n* parfum *m*

schedule (*chè*-dyoûl) *n* horaire *m*

scheme (skiim) *n* plan *m*; projet *m*

scholar (*sko*-leu) *n* érudit *m*; élève *m*/*f*

scholarship (*sko*-leu-chip) *n* bourse d'études

school (skoûl) *n* école *f*

schoolboy (*skoûl*-boï) *n* écolier *m*

schoolgirl (*skoûl*-gheûl) *n* écolière *f*

schoolmaster (*skoûl*-mââ-steu) *n* instituteur *m*, maître d'école

schoolteacher (*skoûl*-tii-tcheu) *n* instituteur *m*, institutrice *f*

science (*saï*-eunns) *n* science *f*

scientific (saï-eunn-*ti*-fik) *adj* scientifique

scientist (*saï*-eunn-tist) *n* savant *m*

scissors (*si*-zeuz) *pl* ciseaux *mpl*

scold (skô^{ou}ld) *v* gronder; insulter

scooter (*skoû*-teu) *n* scooter *m*; patinette *f*

score (skoo) *n* nombre de points; *v* marquer

scorn (skoon) *n* dédain *m*, mépris *m*; *v* mépriser

Scot (skot) *n* Ecossais *m*

Scotch (skotch) *adj* écossais; **scotch tape** ruban adhésif

Scotland (*skot*-leunnd) Ecosse *f*

Scottish (*sko*-tich) *adj* écossais

scout (skaout) *n* scout *m*

scrap (skræp) *n* morceau *m*

scrapbook (*skræp*-bouk) *n* album de collage

scrape (skréïp) *v* racler

scratch (skrætch) *v* érafler, gratter; *n* rayure *f*, égratignure *f*

scream (skriim) *v* hurler, crier; *n* cri *m*

screen (skriin) *n* écran *m*

screw (skroû) *n* vis *f*

screwdriver (*skroû*-draï-veu) *n* tournevis *m*

scrub (skrab) *v* frotter; *n* buisson *m*

sculptor (*skalp*-teu) *n* sculpteur *m*

sculpture (*skalp*-tcheu) *n* sculpture *f*

sea (sii) *n* mer *f*; ~ **urchin** oursin *m*; ~ **water** eau de mer

seabird (*sii*-beûd) *n* oiseau de mer

sea-coast (*sii*-kô^{ou}st) *n* littoral *m*

seafood (*sii*-foûd) *n* fruits *mpl* de mer

seagull (*sii*-ghal) *n* mouette *f*, goéland *m*

seal (siil) *n* sceau *m*; phoque *m*

seam (siim) *n* couture *f*

seaman (*sii*-meunn) *n* (pl -men) marin *m*

seamless (*siim*-leuss) *adj* sans couture

seaport (*sii*-poot) *n* port de mer

search (seûtch) *v* chercher; fouiller; *n* fouille *f*

searchlight (*seûtch*-laït) *n* projecteur *m*

seascape (*sii*-skéïp) *n* marine *f*

seashell (*sii*-chèl) *n* coquillage *m*

seashore (*sii*-choo) *n* bord de la mer

seasick (*sii*-sik) *adj* souffrant du mal de mer

seasickness (*sii*-sik-neuss) *n* mal de mer

seaside (*sii*-saïd) *n* bord de la mer; ~ **resort** station balnéaire

season (*sii*-zeunn) *n* saison *f*; **high** ~ pleine saison; **low** ~ morte-saison *f*; **off** ~ hors saison; ~ **ticket** carte d'abonnement

seat (siit) *n* siège *m*; place *f*; ~ **belt** ceinture de sécurité

second (*sè*-keunnd) *num* deuxième; *n* seconde *f*; instant *m*

secondary (*sè*-keunn-deu-ri) *adj* secondaire; ~ **school** école secondaire

second-hand (sè-keunnd-*hænd*) *adj* d'occasion

secret (*sii*-kreut) *n* secret *m*; *adj* secret

secretary (*sè*-kreu-tri) *n* secrétaire *f*; secrétaire *m*

section (*sèk*-cheunn) *n* section *f*; case *f*, service *m*

secure (si-*kyoueu*) *adj* sûr; *v* s'assurer de

security (si-*kyoueu*-reu-ti) *n* sécurité *f*; caution *f*

sedative (*sè*-deu-tiv) *n* sédatif *m*

seduce (si-*dyoûss*) *v* *séduire

***see** (sii) *v* *voir; *comprendre, se rendre compte; ~ **to** s'occuper de

seed (siid) *n* semence *f*

***seek** (siik) *v* chercher

seem (siim) *v* *paraître, sembler

seen (siin) *v* (pp see)

seesaw (*sii*-soo) *n* balançoire *f*

seize (siiz) *v* saisir

seldom (*sèl*-deumm) *adv* rarement

select (si-*lèkt*) *v* sélectionner, choisir; *adj* exquis, choisi

selection (si-*lèk*-cheunn) *n* choix *m*, sélection *f*

self (sèlf) (*pl* selves) **the ~** le moi

self-... (sèlf) *pref* de soi; auto-; automatique(ment)

self-centered *Am*, **self-centred** (sèlf-*sèn*-teud) *adj* égocentrique

self-employed (sèl-fimm-*ploïd*) *adj* indépendant

self-evident (sèl-*fè*-vi-deunnt) *adj* évident

self-government (sèlf-*gha*-veu-meunnt) *n* autonomie *f*

selfish (*sèl*-fich) *adj* égoïste

selfishness (*sèl*-fich-neuss) *n* égoïsme *m*

self-service (sèlf-*seû*-viss) *n* libre-service *m*

*sell (sèl) *v* vendre

semblance (*sèm*-bleunns) *n* apparence *f*

semi- (*sè*-mi) semi-

semicircle (*sè*-mi-seû-keul) *n* demicercle *m*

semicolon (sè-mi-*kôou*-leunn) *n* point-virgule *m*

senate (*sè*-neut) *n* sénat *m*

senator (*sè*-neu-teu) *n* sénateur *m*

*send (sènd) *v* expédier, *envoyer; **~ back** *renvoyer; **~ for** *faire venir; **~ off** expédier

sender (*sèn*-deu) *n* expéditeur *m*, expéditrice *f*

senile (*sii*-naïl) *adj* sénile

senior (*sii*-nyeu) *adj* aîné; plus âgé (**to** que); supérieur (**to** à); premier; **~ citizens** *pl* personnes *pl* âgées; **~ partner** associé *m* principal; aîné *m*,

aîné *f*; le plus ancien *m*, la plus ancienne *f*; supérieur *m*, supérieure *f*

sensation (sèn-*séï*-cheunn) *n* sensation *f*

sensational (sèn-*séï*-cheu-neul) *adj* spectaculaire, sensationnel

sense (sèns) *n* sens *m*; bon sens, raison *f*; signification *f*; *v* *percevoir; **~ of honour** sens de l'honneur

senseless (*sèns*-leuss) *adj* insensé

sensible (*sèn*-seu-beul) *adj* raisonnable

sensitive (*sèn*-si-tiv) *adj* sensible

sentence (*sèn*-teunns) *n* phrase *f*; jugement *m*; *v* condamner

sentimental (sèn-ti-*mèn*-teul) *adj* sentimental

separate[1] (*sè*-peu-réït) *v* séparer

separate[2] (*sè*-peu-reut) *adj* distinct, séparé

separately (*sè*-peu-reut-li) *adv* à part

September (sèp-*tèm*-beu) septembre

septic (*sèp*-tik) *adj* septique; ***become ~** s'infecter

sequel (*sii*-kᵒᵘeul) *n* suite *f*

sequence (*sii*-kᵒᵘeunns) *n* succession *f*; série *f*

serene (seu-*riin*) *adj* serein; clair

serial (*sieu*-ri-eul) *n* feuilleton *m*

series (*sieu*-riiz) *n* (*pl* ~) suite *f*, série *f*

serious (*sieu*-ri-euss) *adj* sérieux

seriousness (*sieu*-ri-euss-neuss) *n* sérieux *m*

sermon (*seû*-meunn) *n* sermon *m*

serum (*sieu*-reumm) *n* sérum *m*

servant (*seû*-veunnt) *n* domestique *m*

serve (seûv) *v* *servir

service (*seû*-viss) *n* service *m*; **~ charge** service *m*; **~ station** station-service *f*

serviette (seû-vi-*èt*) *n* serviette *f*

session (*sè*-cheunn) *n* séance *f*

set (sèt) *n* jeu *m*

*set (sèt) *v* poser; **~ menu** menu fixe; **~**

out *partir

setting (*sè*-tinng) *n* cadre *m*; ~ **lotion** fixateur *m*

settle (*sè*-teul) *v* régler, arranger; ~ **down** s'établir

settlement (*sè*-teul-meunnt) *n* règlement *m*, arrangement *m*, accord *m*

seven (*sè*-veunn) *num* sept

seventeen (*sè*-veunn-*tiin*) *num* dixsept

seventeenth (*sè*-veunn-*tiin*θ) *num* dix-septième

seventh (*sè*-veunnθ) *num* septième

seventy (*sè*-veunn-ti) *num* soixantedix

several (*sè*-veu-reul) *adj* divers, plusieurs

severe (si-*vieu*) *adj* violent, sévère, grave

sew (sô^{ou}) *v* *coudre

sewer (soû-eu) *n* égout *m*

sewing machine (*sôou*-inng-meu-chiin) *n* machine à coudre

sex (sèks) *n* sexe *m*

sexual (*sèk*-chou-eul) *adj* sexuel

sexuality (sèk-chou-*æ*-leu-ti) *n* sexualité *f*

shade (chéïd) *n* ombre *f*; nuance *f*

shadow (*chæ*-dô^{ou}) *n* ombre *f*

shady (*chéï*-di) *adj* ombragé

***shake** (chéïk) *v* secouer

***shall** (chæl) *v* *devoir

shallow (*chæ*-lô^{ou}) *adj* peu profond

shame (chéïm) *n* honte *f*; déshonneur *m*; **shame!** quelle honte!

shampoo (chæm-*poû*) *n* shampooing *m*

shamrock (*chæm*-rok) *n* trèfle *m*

shape (chéïp) *n* forme *f*; *v* former

share (chè^{eu}) *v* partager; *n* part *f*; action *f*

shark (chââk) *n* requin *m*

sharp (chââp) *adj* aigu

sharpen (*chââ*-peunn) *v* affiler, aiguiser

shave (chéïv) *v* se raser

shaver (*chéï*-veu) *n* rasoir électrique

shaving brush (*chéï*-vinng-brach) *n* blaireau *m*

shaving cream (*chéï*-vinng-kriim) *n* crème à raser

shaving soap (*chéï*-vinng-sô^{ou}p) *n* savon à barbe

shawl (chool) *n* châle *m*

she (chii) *pron* elle

shed (chèd) *n* réduit *m*

***shed** (chèd) *v* verser; répandre

sheep (chiip) *n* (pl ~) mouton *m*

sheer (chi^{eu}) *adj* absolu, pur

sheet (chiit) *n* drap *m*; feuille *f*; plaque *f*

shelf (chèlf) *n* (pl shelves) étagère *f*

shell (chèl) *n* coquille *f*

shellfish (*chèl*-fich) *n* crustacé *m*

shelter (*chèl*-teu) *n* abri *m*; *v* abriter

shepherd (*chè*-peud) *n* berger *m*

shift (chift) *n* équipe *f*

***shine** (chaïn) *v* briller; resplendir

ship (chip) *n* navire *m*; *v* expédier; **shipping line** compagnie de navigation

shipowner (*chi*-pô^{ou}-neu) *n* armateur *m*

shipyard (*chip*-yâåd) *n* chantier naval

shirt (cheût) *n* chemise *f*

shiver (*chi*-veu) *v* trembler, frissonner; *n* frisson *m*

shock (chok) *n* choc *m*; *v* choquer; ~ **absorber** amortisseur *m*

shocking (*cho*-kinng) *adj* choquant

shoe (choû) *n* chaussure *f*; **gym shoes** chaussures de gymnastique; ~ **polish** cirage *m*; ~ **shop** magasin de chaussures

shoelace (*choû*-léïss) *n* lacet *m*

shoemaker (*choû*-méï-keu) *n* cordonnier *m*

shook (chouk) v (p shake)

*shoot (choût) v tirer

shop (chop) n boutique f; v *faire des achats; **~ assistant** vendeur m, vendeuse f

shopping (cho-pinng) n achats pl; **go ~** *faire des achats; **~ bag** sac à provisions; **~ centre** centre commercial

shopkeeper (chop-kii-peu) n commerçant m, commerçante f

shopwindow (chop-ouinn-dôou) n vitrine f

shore (choo) n rive f, rivage m

short (choot) adj court; petit; **~ circuit** court-circuit m

shortage (choo-tidj) n carence f, manque m

shorten (choo-teunn) v raccourcir

shortly (choot-li) adv sous peu, prochainement, bientôt

shorts (choots) pl short m; plAm caleçon m

short-sighted (choot-saï-tid) adj myope

shot (chot) n coup de feu; piqûre f; prise de vue

*should (choud) v *devoir

shoulder (chôoul-deu) n épaule f

shout (chaout) v crier; n cri m

shovel (cha-veul) n pelle f

show (chôou) n représentation f, spectacle m; exposition f

*show (chôou) v montrer; exposer; démontrer

showcase (chôou-kéïss) n vitrine f

shower (chaoueu) n douche f; averse f

showroom (chôou-roûm) n salle d'exposition

shriek (chriik) v pousser des cris; n cri aigu

shrimp (chrimmp) n crevette f

shrine (chraïn) n sanctuaire m

*shrink (chrinngk) v rétrécir

shrinkproof (chrinngk-proûf) adj irrétrécissable

shrub (chrab) n arbuste m

shudder (cha-deu) n frisson m

shuffle (cha-feul) v *battre

*shut (chat) v fermer; **shut** clos, fermé; **~ in** enfermer

shutter (cha-teu) n persienne f, volet m

shy (chaï) adj farouche, timide

shyness (chaï-neuss) n timidité f

Siamese (saï-eu-miiz) adj siamois; n Siamois m

sick (sik) adj malade; ayant mal au cœur

sickness (sik-neuss) n maladie f; mal au cœur

side (saïd) n côté m; parti m; **onesided** adj unilatéral; **~ street** rue transversale

sideburns (saïd-beûnnz) pl favoris

sidelight (saïd-laït) n lumière latérale

sidewalk (saïd-ouook) nAm trottoir m

sideways (saïd-ouéïz) adv de côté

siege (siidj) n siège m

sieve (siv) n passoire f; v tamiser

sift (sift) v tamiser

sight (saït) n vue f; spectacle m; curiosité f

sightseeing (saït-sii-inng) n visite f (de la ville)

sign (saïn) n marque f, signe m; geste m; v signer

signal (sigh-neul) n signal m; signe m; v signaler

signature (sigh-neu-tcheu) n signature f

significant (sigh-ni-fi-keunnt) adj significatif

signpost (saïn-pôoust) n poteau indicateur

silence (saï-leunns) n silence m; v *faire taire

silencer (saï-leunn-seu) n silencieux

m

silent (*saï*-leunnt) *adj* silencieux; ***be ~**
se *taire

silk (silk) *n* soie *f*

silly (*si*-li) *adj* bête, sot

silver (*sil*-veu) *n* argent *m*; en argent

silversmith (*sil*-veu-smiθ) *n* orfèvre *m*

silverware (*sil*-veu-ᵒᵘèᵉᵘ) *n* argenterie
f

similar (*si*-mi-leu) *adj* analogue,
similaire

similarity (si-mi-*læ*-reu-ti) *n*
similitude *f*

simple (*simm*-peul) *adj* ingénu,
simple; ordinaire

simply (*simm*-pli) *adv* simplement

simulate (*si*-myou-léit) *v* simuler

simultaneous (si-meul-*téï*-ni-euss)
adj simultané

sin (sinn) *n* péché *m*

since (sinns) *prep* depuis; *adv* depuis;
conj depuis que; comme

sincere (sinn-*sieu*) *adj* sincère; **Yours
sincerely** sincères salutations;
veuillez agréer, chère Madame / cher
Monsieur, l'expression de mes
sentiments distingués

sinew (*si*-nyoû) *n* tendon *m*

*sing (sinng) *v* chanter

singer (*sinng*-eu) *n* chanteur *m*,
chanteuse *f*

single (*sinng*-gheul) *adj* seul;
célibataire

singular (*sinng*-ghyou-leu) *n* singulier
m; *adj* singulier

sinister (*si*-ni-steu) *adj* sinistre

sink (sinngk) *n* évier *m*

*sink (sinngk) *v* s'enfoncer

sip (sip) *n* gorgée *f*

sir (seû) monsieur *m*

siren (*saïeu*-reunn) *n* sirène *f*

sister (*si*-steu) *n* sœur *f*

sister-in-law (*si*-steu-rinn-loo) *n* (pl
sisters-) belle-sœur *f*

*sit (sit) *v* *être assis; **~ down**
s'*asseoir

site (saït) *n* site *m*

sitting room (*si*-tinng-roûm) *n* salon
m

situated (*si*-tchou-éï-tid) *adj* situé

situation (si-tchou-*éï*-cheunn) *n*
situation *f*

six (siks) *num* six

sixteen (siks-*tiin*) *num* seize

sixteenth (siks-*tiin*θ) *num* seizième

sixth (siksθ) *num* sixième

sixty (*siks*-ti) *num* soixante

size (saïz) *n* taille *f*, mesure *f*;
dimension *f*, grandeur *f*; format *m*

skate (skéït) *v* patiner; *n* patin *m*

skating (*skéï*-tinng) *n* patinage *m*; **~
rink** patinoire *f*

sketch (skètch) *n* dessin *m*, esquisse *f*;
v dessiner, esquisser

ski¹ (skii) *v* skier

ski² (skii) *n* (pl ~, ~s) ski *m*; **~ boots**
chaussures de ski; **~ jump** saut à ski; **~
lift** téléski *m* **~ pants** pantalon de ski;
~ poles *Am* bâtons de ski; **~ sticks**
bâtons de ski

skid (skid) *v* déraper

skier (*skii*-eu) *n* skieur *m*, skieuse *f*

skiing (*skii*-inng) *n* ski *m*

skil(l)ful (*skil*-feul) *adj* habile, adroit

skill (skil) *n* habileté *f*

skilled (skild) *adj* habile; expert

skin (skinn) *n* peau *f*; **~ cream** crème
de beauté

skip (skip) *v* sautiller; sauter

skirt (skeût) *n* jupe *f*

skull (skal) *n* crâne *m*

sky (skaï) *n* ciel *m*; air *m*

skyscraper (*skaï*-skréï-peu) *n*
gratteciel *m*

slack (slæk) *adj* lâche; faible

slacks (slæks) *pl* pantalon *m*

slam (slæm) *v* claquer

slander (*slâân*-deu) *n* calomnie *f*

slang (slæng) *n* argot *m*

slant (slâânt) *v* s'incliner

slanting (*slâân*-tinng) *adj* oblique, en pente, incliné

slap (slæp) *v* *battre; *n* claque *f*

slate (sléït) *n* ardoise *f*

slave (sléïv) *n* esclave *m*

sledge (slèdj) *n* luge *f*, traîneau *m*

sleep (sliip) *n* sommeil *m*

*sleep (sliip) *v* *dormir

sleeping bag (*slii*-pinng-bægh) *n* sac de couchage

sleeping car (*slii*-pinng-kââ) *n* wagonlit

sleeping pill (*slii*-pinng-pil) *n* somnifère *m*

sleepless (*sliip*-leuss) *adj* sans sommeil

sleepy (*slii*-pi) *adj* somnolent

sleeve (sliiv) *n* manche *f*; housse *f*

sleigh (sléï) *n* luge *f*, traîneau *m*

slender (*slèn*-deu) *adj* svelte

slice (slaïss) *n* tranche *f*

slide (slaïd) *n* glissade *f*; toboggan *m*; diapositive *f*

*slide (slaïd) *v* glisser

slight (slaït) *adj* léger; faible

slim (slimm) *adj* mince; *v* maigrir

slip (slip) *v* déraper, glisser; s'échapper; *n* faux pas; combinaison *f*

slipper (*sli*-peu) *n* pantoufle *f*

slippery (*sli*-peu-ri) *adj* glissant

slope (slô^ou^p) *n* versant *m*; *v* décliner

sloping (*slôou*-pinng) *adj* en pente

sloppy (*slo*-pi) *adj* négligé

slot (slot) *n* fente *f*; ~ **machine** appareil à jetons

slovenly (*sla*-veunn-li) *adj* mal soigné

slow (slô^ou^) *adj* lent; ~ **down** ralentir; freiner

sluice (sloûss) *n* écluse *f*

slum (slamm) *n* bas quartier

slump (slammp) *n* baisse des prix

slush (slach) *n* boue *f*

sly (slaï) *adj* malin

smack (smæk) *v* donner une claque; *n* claque *f*

small (smool) *adj* petit; faible

smallpox (*smool*-poks) *n* variole *f*

smart (smâât) *adj* élégant; adroit, alerte

smash (smæch)*v* (se)briser, (se) fracasser; *n* fracas *m*; coup *m* (violent); collision *f*, ~ **hit** succès *m*

smell (smèl) *n* odeur *f*

*smell (smèl) *v* *sentir; *sentir mauvais

smelly (*smè*-li) *adj* malodorant

smile (smaïl) *v* *sourire; *n* sourire *m*

smith (smiθ) *n* forgeron *m*

smog (smoog) *n* smog *m*

smoke (smô^ou^k) *v* fumer; *n* fumée *f*; **no smoking** défense de fumer

smoker (*smôou*-keu) *n* fumeur *m*; compartiment fumeurs

smoking compartment (*smôou*-kinng-keumm-pâât-meunnt) *n* compartiment fumeurs

smooth (smoûð) *adj* uni, plat, lisse; doux

smuggle (*sma*-gheul) *v* passer en contrebande

snack (snæk) *n* casse-croûte *m*; ~ **bar** snack-bar *m*

snail (snéïl) *n* escargot *m*

snake (snéïk) *n* serpent *m*

snapshot (*snæp*-chot) *n* instantané *m*

sneakers (*snii*-keuz) *plAm* chaussures de gymnastique

sneeze (sniiz) *v* éternuer

snooty (*snoû*-ti) *adj* snob

snore (snoo) *v* ronfler

snorkel (*snoo*-keul) *n* tube de plongée

snout (snaout) *n* museau *m*

snow (snô^ou^) *n* neige *f*; *v* neiger

snowstorm (*snôou*-stoom) *n* tempête de neige

snowy (*snôou*-i) *adj* neigeux

so (sô^{ou}) *conj* donc; *adv* ainsi; tellement, si; **and ~ on** et ainsi de suite; **~ far** jusqu'à présent; **~ that** de manière que, pour que, afin que

soak (sô^{ou}k) *v* tremper

soap (sô^{ou}p) *n* savon *m*; **~ powder** savon en poudre

sober (sôou-beu) *adj* sobre; sérieux, posé

so-called (sôou-koold) *adj* soi-disant

soccer (so-keu) *n* football *m*; **~ team** équipe *f*

social (sôou-cheul) *adj* social

socialism (sôou-cheu-li-zeumm) *n* socialisme *m*

socialist (sôou-cheu-list) *adj* socialiste; *n* socialiste *m*

society (seu-*saï*-eu-ti) *n* société *f*; association *f*; compagnie *f*

sock (sok) *n* chaussette *f*

socket (so-kit) *n* douille *f*

soda water (sôou-deu-^{ou}oo-teu) *n* eau de Seltz

sofa (sôou-feu) *n* canapé *m*

soft (soft) *adj* mou; **~ drink** boisson non alcoolisée

soften (so-feunn) *v* adoucir

software (soft- ouèeu) *n* logiciel *m*

soil (soïl) *n* sol *m*; terroir *m*, terre *f*

soiled (soïld) *adj* souillé

solar (sôou-leu) *adj* solaire; **~ cell** cellule *f* photovoltaïque; **~ eclipse** éclipse *f* du soleil; **~ plexus** plexus *m* solaire

sold (sô^{ou}ld) *v* (p, pp sell); **~ out** épuisé

soldier (sôoul-djeu) *n* soldat *m*

sole[1] (sô^{ou}l) *adj* unique

sole[2] (sô^{ou}l) *n* semelle *f*; sole *f*

solely (sôoul-li) *adv* exclusivement

solemn (so-leumm) *adj* solennel

solicitor (seu-*li*-si-teu) *n* avoué *m*, avocat *m*

solid (so-lid) *adj* robuste, solide; massif; *n* solide *m*

soluble (so-lyou-beul) *adj* soluble

solution (seu-*loû*-cheunn) *n* solution *f*

solve (solv) *v* *résoudre

somber *Am*, **somber** (somm-beu) *adj* sombre

some (samm) *adj* quelques; *pron* certains, quelques; un peu; **~ day** un jour ou l'autre; **~ more** encore un peu; **~ time** une fois

somebody (samm-beu-di) *pron* quelqu'un

somehow (samm-haou) *adv* d'une manière ou d'une autre

someone (samm-^{ou}ann) *pron* quelqu'un

something (samm-θïnng) *pron* quelque chose

sometimes (samm-taïmz) *adv* parfois

somewhat (samm-^{ou}ot) *adv* quelque peu

somewhere (samm-^{ou}è^{eu}) *adv* quelque part

son (sann) *n* fils *m*

song (sonng) *n* chanson *f*

son-in-law (*sa*-ninn-loo) *n* (pl sons-) gendre *m*

soon (soûn) *adv* rapidement, sous peu, prochainement, bientôt; **as ~ as** dès que

sooner (soû-neu) *adv* plutôt

sore (soo) *adj* douloureux; *n* plaie *f*; **~ throat** mal de gorge

sorrow (so-rô^{ou}) *n* tristesse *f*, douleur *f*, chagrin *m*

sorry (so-ri) *adj* désolé; **sorry!** excusez-moi!, pardon!

sort (soot) *v* classer, ranger; *n* catégorie *f*, sorte *f*; **all sorts of** toutes sortes de

soul (sô^{ou}l) *n* âme *f*; esprit *m*

sound (saound) *n* son *m*; *v* sonner; *adj* solide

soundproof (saound-proûf) *adj*

insonorisé

soup (soûp) *n* soupe *f*

sour (saou^eu^) *adj* aigre

source (sooss) *n* source *f*

south (saouθ) *n* sud *m*; **South Pole** pôle sud

South Africa (saouθ æ-fri-keu) Afrique du Sud

South America (saouθ eu-mè-ri-keu) Amérique du Sud

southeast (saouθ-*iist*) *n* sud-est *m*

southerly (*sa*-ðeu-li) *adj* méridional

southern (*sa*-ðeunn) *adj* méridional

southwest (saouθ-*ouèst*) *n* sud-ouest *m*

souvenir (*soû*-veu-ni^eu^) *n* souvenir *m*

sovereign (*sov*-rinn) *n* souverain *m*

***sow** (sô^ou^) *v* semer

spa (spââ) *n* station thermale

space (spéïss) *n* espace *m*; distance *f*, intervalle *m*; *v* espacer

spacious (*spéï*-cheuss) *adj* spacieux

spade (spéïd) *n* bêche *f*, pelle *f*

Spain (spéïn) Espagne *f*

Spanish (*spæ*-nich) *adj* espagnol

spanking (*spæng*-kinng) *n* fessée *f*

spanner (*spæ*-neu) *n* clé à écrous

spare (spè^eu^) *adj* de réserve, disponible; *v* se passer de; ~ **part** pièce détachée; ~ **room** chambre d'ami; ~ **time** temps libre; ~ **tyre** (*Am* **tire**) pneu de rechange; ~ **wheel** roue de secours

spark (spââk) *n* étincelle *f*

sparking plug (*spââ*-kinng-plagh) *n* bougie d'allumage

sparkle (*spââ*-keul) *v* briller

sparkling (*spââ*-klinng) *adj* scintillant; mousseux

sparrow (*spæ*-rô^ou^) *n* moineau *m*

***speak** (spiik) *v* parler

speaker (*spii*-keu) *n* parleur *m*, parleuse *f*; haut-parleur *m*

spear (spi^eu^) *n* lance *f*

special (*spè*-cheul) *adj* particulier, spécial; ~ **delivery** exprès

specialist (*spè*-cheu-list) *n* spécialiste *m/f*

speciality (spè-chi-æ-leu-ti) *n* spécialité *f*

specialize (*spè*-cheu-laïz) *v* se spécialiser

specially (*spè*-cheu-li) *adv* particulièrement

species (*spii*-chiiz) *n* (pl ~) espèce *f*

specific (speu-*si*-fik) *adj* spécifique

speck (spèk) *n* tache *f*

spectacle (*spèk*-teu-keul) *n* spectacle *m*; **spectacles** lunettes *fpl*

spectator (spèk-*téï*-teu) *n* spectateur *m*, spectatrice *f*

speculate (*spè*-kyou-léït) *v* spéculer

speech (spiitch) *n* parole *f*; allocution *f*, discours *m*

speechless (*spiitch*-leuss) *adj* interloqué

speed (spiid) *n* vitesse *f*; rapidité *f*, hâte *f*; **cruising** ~ vitesse de croisière; ~ **limit** limite de vitesse, limitation de vitesse

***speed** (spiid) *v* foncer; rouler trop vite

speeding (*spii*-dinng) *n* excès de vitesse

speedometer (spii-*do*-mi-teu) *n* indicateur de vitesse

spell (spèl) *n* enchantement *m*

***spell** (spèl) *v* épeler

spelling (*spè*-linng) *n* orthographe *f*

***spend** (spènd) *v* dépenser; employer

sphere (sfi^eu^) *n* sphère *f*

spice (spaïss) *n* épice *f*

spiced (spaïst) *adj* épicé

spicy (*spaï*-si) *adj* épicé

spider (*spaï*-deu) *n* araignée *f*; **spider's web** toile d'araignée

***spill** (spil) *v* répandre

***spin** (spinn) *v* filer; tourner

spinach (*spi*-nidj) *n* épinards *mpl*

spine (spaïn) *n* épine dorsale

spinster (*spinn*-steu) *n* vieille fille

spire (spaï^{eu}) *n* aiguille *f*

spirit (*spi*-rit) *n* esprit *m*; humeur *f*; **spirits** boissons alcoolisées, spiritueux *mpl*; moral *m*; ~ **stove** réchaud à alcool

spiritual (*spi*-ri-tchou-eul) *adj* spirituel

spit (spit) *n* crachat *m*, salive *f*; broche *f*

*spit (spit) *v* cracher

spite: in ~ of (inn spaït ov) en dépit de, malgré

spiteful (spaït-feul) *adj* malveillant

splash (splæch) *v* éclabousser

splendid (*splèn*-did) *adj* magnifique, splendide

splendo(u)r (*splèn*-deu) *n* splendeur *f*

splint (splinnt) *n* éclisse *f*

splinter (*splinn*-teu) *n* écharde *f*

*split (split) *v* fendre

*spoil (spoïl) *v* gâter

spoke[1] (spô^{ou}k) *v* (p speak)

spoke[2] (spô^{ou}k) *n* rayon *m*

sponge (spanndj) *n* éponge *f*

spook (spoûk) *n* spectre *m*, fantôme *m*

spool (spoûl) *n* bobine *f*

spoon (spoûn) *n* cuillère *f*

spoonful (*spoûn*-foul) *n* cuillerée *f*

sport (spoot) *n* sport *m*

sports car (*spoots*-kââ) *n* voiture de sport

sports jacket (*spoots*-djæ-kit) *n* veston sport

sportsman (*spoots*-meunn) *n* (pl -men) sportif *m*

sportswear (*spoots*-^{ou}è^{eu}) *n* vêtements de sport

spot (spot) *n* tache *f*; lieu *m*, endroit *m*

spotless (*spot*-leuss) *adj* immaculé

spotlight (*spot*-laït) *n* projecteur *m*

spotted (*spo*-tid) *adj* tacheté

spout (spaout) *n* jet *m*

sprain (spréïn) *v* fouler; *n* foulure *f*

spray (spréï) *n* spray *m*, aérosol *m*; *v* vaporiser; arroser

*spread (sprèd) *v* étendre

spring (sprinng) *n* printemps *m*; ressort *m*; source *f*

springtime (*sprinng*-taïm) *n* printemps *m*

sprouts (spraouts) **Brussels ~** *pl* choux de Bruxelles

spy (spaï) *n* espion *m*

square (sk^{ou}è^{eu}) *adj* carré; *n* carré *m*; square *m*, place *f*

squash (sk^{ou}och) *n* sirop *m*; *Am* courgette

squeeze (sk^{ou}iiz) *v* serrer; presser; extorquer (**from** à); ~ **out** exprimer

squirrel (*sk^{ou}i*-reul) *n* écureuil *m*

squirt (sk^{ou}eût) *n* jet *m*

stable (*stéï*-beul) *adj* stable; *n* étable *f*

stack (stæk) *n* pile *f*

stadium (*stéï*-di-eumm) *n* stade *m*

staff (stââf) *n* personnel *m*

stage (stéïdj) *n* scène *f*; phase *f*, étape *f*

stain (stéïn) *v* tacher; *n* tache *f*; **stained glass** verre de couleur; ~ **remover** détachant *m*

stainless (*stéïn*-leuss) *adj* immaculé; ~ **steel** acier inoxydable

staircase (*stèeu*-kéïss) *n* escalier *m*

stairs (stè^{eu}z) *pl* escalier *m*

stale (stéïl) *adj* rassis

stall (stool) *n* étal *m*; **seat in the stalls** fauteuil d'orchestre

stamp (stæmp) *n* timbre *m*; *v* affranchir; piétiner; ~ **machine** distributeur de timbres

stand (stænd) *n* stand *m*; tribune *f*

*stand (stænd) *v* se *tenir debout

standard (*stæn*-deud) *n* norme *f*; standard; ~ **of living** niveau de vie

stanza (*stæn*-zeu) *n* strophe *f*

staple (stéï-peul) n agrafe f

star (stââ) n étoile f

starboard (stââ-beud) n tribord m

stare (stè^{eu}) v fixer

starling (stââ-linng) n étourneau m

start (stâât) v commencer; n début m

starting point (stââ-tinng-poïnt) n point de départ

state (stéït) n Etat m; état m; v déclarer; **the States** les Etats-Unis

statement (stéït-meunnt) n déclaration f

statesman (stéïts-meunn) n (pl -men) homme d'Etat

station (stéï-cheunn) n gare f; poste m

stationary (stéï-cheu-neu-ri) adj stationnaire

stationer's (stéï-cheu-neuz) n papeterie f

stationery (stéï-cheu-neu-ri) n papeterie f

statistics (steu-ti-stiks) pl statistique f

statue (stæ-tchoû) n statue f

stay (stéï) v rester; séjourner; n séjour m

steadfast (stèd-fââst) adj ferme

steady (stè-di) adj ferme

steak (stéïk) n bifteck m

*steal (stiil) v voler

steam (stiim) n vapeur f

steamer (stii-meu) n bateau à vapeur

steel (stiil) n acier m

steep (stiip) adj abrupt, escarpé

steeple (stii-peul) n clocher m

steering column (stieu-rinng-koleumm) n colonne de direction

steering wheel (stieu-rinng-^{ou}iil) n volant m

stem (stèm) n tige f

step (stèp) n pas m; marche f; v marcher

stepchild (stèp-tchaïld) n (pl -children) enfant d'un autre lit

stepfather (stèp-fââ-ðeu) n beau-père

m

stepmother (stèp-ma-ðeu) n belle-mère f

stereo (stè-ri-ô^{ou}) n stéréo f

sterile (stè-raïl) adj stérile

sterilize (stè-ri-laïz) v stériliser

stern (steûn) adj sévère

steward (styoû-eud) n steward m

stewardess (styoû-eu-dèss) n hôtesse de l'air

stick (stik) n bâton m

*stick (stik) v coller

sticky (sti-ki) adj gluant

stiff (stif) adj raide

still (stil) adv encore; toutefois; adj tranquille

stimulant (sti-myou-leunnt) n stimulant m

stimulate (sti-myou-léït) v stimuler

sting (stinng) n piqûre f

*sting (stinng) v piquer

stingy (stinn-dji) adj mesquin

*stink (stinngk) v puer

stir (steû) v bouger; remuer

stitch (stitch) n point m, point de côté; suture f

stock (stok) n stock m; v *avoir en stock; **~ exchange** bourse des valeurs, bourse f; **~ market** marché des valeurs; **stocks and shares** actions

stocking (sto-kinng) n bas m

stole¹ (stô^{ou}l) v (p steal)

stole² (stô^{ou}l) n étole f

stomach (sta-meuk) n estomac m; **~ ache** mal au ventre, mal d'estomac

stone (stô^{ou}n) n pierre f; pierre précieuse; noyau m; en pierre; **pumice ~** pierre ponce

stood (stoud) v (p, pp stand)

stop (stop) v arrêter; cesser; n arrêt m; **stop!** stop!

stopper (sto-peu) n bouchon m

storage (stoo-ridj) n emmagasinage m

store (stoo) *n* provision *f*; magasin *m*; *v* emmagasiner; **~ house** magasin *m*

stor(e)y (*stoo*-ri) *n* étage *m*

stork (stook) *n* cigogne *f*

storm (stoom) *n* tempête *f*

stormy (*stoo*-mi) *adj* orageux

story (*stoo*-ri) *n* histoire *f*

stout (staout) *adj* gros, obèse, corpulent

stove (stô^{ou}v) *n* fourneau *m*; cuisinière *f*

straight (stréit) *adj* droit; *adv* directement; **~ ahead** tout droit; **~ away** directement, tout de suite; **~ on** tout droit

strain (stréïn) *n* effort *m*; tension *f*; *v* forcer

strainer (*stréï*-neu) *n* passoire *f*

strange (stréïndj) *adj* étrange; bizarre

stranger (*stréïn*-djeu) *n* étranger *m*; inconnu *m*

strangle (*stræng*-gheul) *v* étrangler

strap (stræp) *n* courroie *f*

straw (stroo) *n* paille *f*

strawberry (*stroo*-beu-ri) *n* fraise *f*

stream (striim) *n* ruisseau *m*; courant *m*; *v* couler

street (striit) *n* rue *f*

streetcar (*striit*-kââ) *nAm* tram *m*

strength (strèngθ) *n* vigueur *f*, force *f*

stress (strèss) *n* tension *f*; accent *m*; *v* souligner

stretch (strètch) *v* tendre; *n* section *f*

strict (strikt) *adj* sévère

strike (straïk) *n* grève *f*

*strike (straïk) *v* frapper; *faire grève; amener

striking (*straï*-king) *adj* frappant, remarquable

string (strinng) *n* ficelle *f*; corde *f*

strip (strip) *n* bande *f*

stripe (straïp) *n* raie *f*

striped (straïpt) *adj* rayé

stroke (strô^{ou}k) *n* attaque *f*

stroll (strô^{ou}l) *v* flâner; *n* promenade *f*

strong (stronng) *adj* fort; puissant

stronghold (*stronng*-hô^{ou}ld) *n* place forte

structure (*strak*-tcheu) *n* structure *f*

struggle (*stra*-gheul) *n* combat *m*, lutte *f*; *v* lutter

stub (stab) *n* souche *f*

stubborn (*sta*-beunn) *adj* têtu

student (*styoû*-deunnt) *n* étudiant *m*; étudiante *f*

study (*sta*-di) *v* étudier; *n* étude *f*; cabinet *m*

stuff (staf) *n* substance *f*; fatras *m*

stuffed (staft) *adj* farci

stuffing (*sta*-finng) *n* farce *f*

stuffy (*sta*-fi) *adj* mal aéré

stumble (*stamm*-beul) *v* trébucher

stung (stanng) *v* (p, pp sting)

stupid (*styoû*-pid) *adj* stupide

style (staïl) *n* style *m*

stylish (*staï*-lich) *adj* élégant; chic; à la mode

subject[1] (*sab*-djikt) *n* sujet *m*; **~ to** sujet à

subject[2] (seub-*djèkt*) *v* *soumettre

submarine (sab-meu-*riin*) *n* sous-marin *m*

submit (seub-*mit*) *v* se *soumettre

subordinate (seu-*boo*-di-neut) *adj* subordonné; secondaire

subscriber (seub-*skraï*-beu) *n* abonné *m*

subscription (seub-*skrip*-cheunn) *n* abonnement *m*

subsequent (*sab*-si-k^{ou}eunnt) *adj* postérieur

subsidy (*sab*-si-di) *n* subvention *f*

substance (*sab*-steunns) *n* substance *f*

substantial (seub-*stæn*-cheul) *adj* matériel; réel; substantiel

substitute (*sab*-sti-tyoût) *v* substituer; *n* substitut *m*

subtitle (*sab*-taï-teul) *n* sous-titre *m*

subtle (*sa*-teul) *adj* subtil

subtract (seub-*træ*kt) *v* *soustraire

suburb (*sa*-beûb) *n* banlieue *f*, faubourg *m*

suburban (seu-*beû*-beunn) *adj* suburbain

subway (*sab*-^{ou}éï) *nAm* métro *m*

succeed (seuk-*siid*) *v* réussir; succéder

success (seuk-*sèss*) *n* succès *m*

successful (seuk-*sèss*-feul) *adj* réussi

succumb (seu-*kamm*) *v* succomber

such (satch) *adj* tel; *adv* tellement; ~ **as** tel que

suck (sak) *v* sucer

sudden (*sa*-deunn) *adj* soudain

suddenly (*sa*-deunn-li) *adv* soudain

suede (s^{ou}éïd) *n* daim *m*

suffer (*sa*-feu) *v* *souffrir; subir

suffering (*sa*-feu-rinng) *n* souffrance *f*

suffice (seu-*faïss*) *v* *suffire

sufficient (seu-*fi*-cheunnt) *adj* adéquat, suffisant

suffrage (*sa*-fridj) *n* droit de vote, suffrage *m*

sugar (*chou*-gheu) *n* sucre *m*

suggest (seu-*djèst*) *v* suggérer

suggestion (seu-*djèss*-tcheunn) *n* suggestion *f*

suicide (*soû*-i-saïd) *n* suicide *m*

suit (soût) *v* *convenir; adapter à; bien *aller; *n* complet *m*

suitable (*soû*-teu-beul) *adj* qui convient, approprié

suitcase (*soût*-kéïss) *n* valise *f*

suite (s^{ou}iit) *n* appartement *m*

sum (samm) *n* somme *f*

summary (*sa*-meu-ri) *n* sommaire *m*, résumé *m*

summer (*sa*-meu) *n* été *m*; ~ **time** heure d'été

summit (*sa*-mit) *n* sommet *m*

sun (sann) *n* soleil *m*

sunbathe (*sann*-béïð) *v* *prendre un bain de soleil

sunburn (*sann*-beûnn) *n* coup de soleil

Sunday (*sann*-di) dimanche *m*

sunglasses (*sann*-ghlââ-siz) *pl* lunettes de soleil

sunlight (*sann*-laït) *n* lumière du soleil

sunny (*sa*-ni) *adj* ensoleillé

sunrise (*sann*-raïz) *n* lever du soleil

sunset (*sann*-sèt) *n* coucher du soleil

sunshade (*sann*-chéïd) *n* parasol *m*

sunshine (*sann*-chaïn) *n* soleil *m*

sunstroke (*sann*-strô^{ou}k) *n* insolation *f*

suntan oil (*sann*-tæn-oïl) huile solaire

super (*soû*-peu) *adj colloquial* super

superb (sou-*peûb*) *adj* grandiose, superbe

superficial (soû-peu-*fi*-cheul) *adj* superficiel

superfluous (sou-*peû*-flou-euss) *adj* superflu

superior (sou-*pieu*-ri-eu) *adj* supérieur, majeur

supermarket (*soû*-peu-mââ-kit) *n* supermarché *m*

superstition (soû-peu-*sti*-cheunn) *n* superstition *f*

supervise (*soû*-peu-vaïz) *v* superviser

supervision (soû-peu-*vi*-jeunn) *n* supervision *f*, surveillance *f*

supervisor (*soû*-peu-vaï-zeu) *n* surveillant *m*

supper (*sa*-peu) *n* souper *m*

supple (*sa*-peul) *adj* souple

supplement (*sa*-pli-meunnt) *n* supplément *m*

supply (seu-*plaï*) *n* fourniture *f*; stock *m*; offre *f*; *v* fournir

support (seu-*poot*) *v* supporter, *soutenir; *n* soutien *m*; ~ **hose** bas élastiques

supporter (seu-*poo*-teu) *n* supporter *m*

suppose (seu-*pôouz*) *v* supposer;
  supposing that en admettant que

suppository (seu-*po*-zi-teu-ri) *n*
  suppositoire *m*

suppress (seu-*près*) *v* réprimer

surcharge (*seû*-tchââdj) *n*
  supplément *m*

sure (chou^{eu}) *adj* sûr

surely (*chou*eu-li) *adv* sûrement

surface (*seû*-fiss) *n* surface *f*

surgeon (*seû*-djeunn) *n* chirurgien *m*;
  veterinary ~ vétérinaire *m*

surgery (*seû*-djeu-ri) *n* opération *f*;
  cabinet de consultations

surname (*seû*-néïm) *n* nom de famille

surplus (*seû*-pleuss) *n* surplus *m*

surprise (seu-*praïz*) *n* surprise *f*; *v*
  *surprendre

surrender (seu-*rèn*-deu) *v* se rendre; *n*
  reddition *f*

surround (seu-*raound*) *v* entourer

surrounding (seu-*raoun*-dinng) *adj*
  environnant

surroundings (seu-*raoun*-dinngz) *pl*
  alentours *mpl*

survey (*seû*-véï) *n* résumé *m*

survival (seu-*vaï*-veul) *n* survie *f*

survive (seu-*vaïv*) *v* *survivre

suspect[1] (seu-*spèkt*) *v* soupçonner;
  suspecter

suspect[2] (*sa*-spèkt) *n* suspect *m*, -e *f*

suspend (seu-*spènd*) *v* suspendre

suspenders (seu-*spèn*-deuz) *plAm*
  bretelles *fpl*

suspension (seu-*spèn*-cheunn) *n*
  suspension *f*; **~bridge** pont suspendu

suspicion (seu-*spi*-cheunn) *n* soupçon
  m; soupçons *mpl*

suspicious (seu-*spi*-cheuss) *adj*
  suspect; soupçonneux, méfiant

sustain (seu-*stéïn*) *v* endurer

swallow (*souo*-lô^{ou}) *v* avaler; *n*
  hirondelle *f*

swam (s^{ou}æm) *v* (p swim)

swamp (s^{ou}ommp) *n* marais *m*

swan (s^{ou}onn) *n* cygne *m*

swap (s^{ou}op) *v* troquer

***swear** (s^{ou}è^{eu}) *v* jurer

sweat (s^{ou}èt) *n* sueur *f*; *v* suer

sweater (*souè*-teu) *n* chandail *m*

Swede (s^{ou}iid) *n* Suédois *m*

Sweden (*souii*-deunn) Suède *f*

Swedish (*souii*-dich) *adj* suédois

***sweep** (s^{ou}iip) *v* balayer

sweet (s^{ou}iit) *adj* sucré; gentil; *n*
  bonbon *m*; dessert *m*; **sweets**
  douceurs *fpl*, bonbons

sweeten (*souii*-teunn) *v* sucrer

sweetheart (*souiit*-hâât) *n* mon
  amour, chéri *m*

sweetshop (*souiit*-chop) *n* confiserie *f*

swell (s^{ou}èl) *adj* formidable

***swell** (s^{ou}èl) *v* enfler

swelling (*souè*-linng) *n* enflure *f*

swift (s^{ou}ift) *adj* rapide

***swim** (s^{ou}imm) *v* nager

swimmer (*soui*-meu) *n* nageur *m*,
  nageuse *f*

swimming (*soui*-minng) *n* natation *f*;
  ~ pool piscine *f*

swimmingtrunks (*soui*-minng-
  tranngks) *n* caleçon de bain

swimsuit (*souimm*-soût) *n* maillot de
  bain

swindle (*souinn*-deul) *v* escroquer; *n*
  escroquerie *f*

swindler (*souinn*-dleu) *n* escroc *m*

swing (s^{ou}inng) *n* balançoire *f*

***swing** (s^{ou}inng) *v* balancer

Swiss (s^{ou}iss) *adj* suisse; *n* Suisse *m*

switch (s^{ou}itch) *n* commutateur *m*; *v*
  changer; **~ off** *éteindre; **~ on**
  allumer

switchboard (*souitch*-bood) *n* tableau
  de distribution

Switzerland (*souit*-seu-leunnd) Suisse
  f

sword (sood) *n* épée *f*

swum (s^{ou}amm) *v* (pp swim)

syllable (*si*-leu-beul) *n* syllabe *f*

symbol (*simm*-beul) *n* symbole *m*

sympathetic (simm-peu-*θè*-tik) *adj* compatissant, de sympathie

sympathy (*simm*-peu-θi) *n* sympathie *f*, compassion *f*

symphony (*simm*-feu-ni) *n* symphonie *f*

symptom (*simm*-teumm) *n* symptôme *m*

synagogue (*si*-neu-ghogh) *n* synagogue *f*

synonym (*si*-neu-nimm) *n* synonyme *m*

synthetic (sinn-*θè*-tik) *adj* synthétique

syphon (*saï*-feunn) *n* siphon *m*

Syria (*si*-ri-eu) Syrie *f*

Syrian (*si*-ri-eunn) *adj* syrien; *n* Syrien *m*

syringe (*si*-rinndj) *n* seringue *f*

syrup (*si*-reup) *n* sirop *m*

system (*si*-steumm) *n* système *m*; **decimal ~** système décimal

systematic (si-steu-*mæ*-tik) *adj* systématique

T

table (*téï*-beul) *n* table *f*; **~ of contents** table des matières; **~ tennis** ping-pong *m*

tablecloth (*téï*-beul-kloθ) *n* nappe *f*

tablespoon (*téï*-beul-spoûn) *n* cuillère *f*

tablet (*tæ*-blit) *n* tablette *f*

taboo (teu-*boû*) *n* tabou *m*

tactics (*tæk*-tiks) *pl* tactique *f*

tag (tægh) *n* étiquette *f*

tail (téïl) *n* queue *f*

taillight (*téïl*-laït) *n* feu arrière

tailor (*téï*-leu) *n* tailleur *m*

tailor-made (*téï*-leu-méïd) *adj* fait sur mesure

***take** (téïk) *v* *prendre; saisir; *conduire; **~ away** emporter; enlever; **~ off** décoller; **~ out** ôter; **~ over** *reprendre; **~ place** *avoir lieu; **~ up** occuper

take-off (*téï*-kof) *n* décollage *m*

tale (téïl) *n* conte *m*, récit *m*

talent (*tæ*-leunnt) *n* don *m*, talent *m*

talented (*tæ*-leunn-tid) *adj* doué

talk (took) *v* parler; *n* conversation *f*

talkative (*too*-keu-tiv) *adj* bavard

tall (tool) *adj* haut; grand

tame (téïm) *adj* domestiqué, apprivoisé; *v* apprivoiser

tampon (*tæm*-peunn) *n* tampon *m*

tangerine (tæn-djeu-*riin*) *n* mandarine *f*

tangible (*tæn*-dji-beul) *adj* tangible

tank (tængk) *n* réservoir *m*

tanker (*tæng*-keu) *n* bateau-citerne *m*

tanned (tænd) *adj* hâlé

tap (tæp) *n* robinet *m*; coup *m*; *v* frapper

tape (téïp) *n* bande *f*, ruban *m*; **adhesive ~** ruban adhésif; **~ recorder** magnétophone *m*

tar (tââ) *n* goudron *m*

target (*tââ*-ghit) *n* objectif *m*, cible *f*

tariff (*tæ*-rif) *n* taux *m*

task (tââsk) *n* tâche *f*

taste (téïst) *n* goût *m*; *v* *avoir goût de; goûter

tasteless (*téïst*-leuss) *adj* insipide

tasty (*téï*-sti) *adj* succulent, savoureux

taught (toot) *v* (p, pp teach)

tavern (*tæ*-veunn) *n* taverne *f*

tax (tæks) *n* impôt *m*; *v* imposer

tax-free (*tæks*-frii) *adj* exempt d'impôts

taxi (*tæk*-si) *n* taxi *m*; ~ **driver** chauffeur de taxi; ~ **rank** station de taxis; ~ **stand** *Am* station de taxis

taximeter (*tæk*-si-mii-teu) *n* taximètre *m*

tea (tii) *n* thé *m*; ~ **set** service à thé; ~ **towel** torchon *m*

teach (tiitch) *v* *apprendre, enseigner

teacher (*tii*-tcheu) *n* professeur *m*, maître *m*; instituteur *m*, institutrice *f*, maître d'école

teachings (*tii*-tchinngz) *pl* enseignements

teacup (*tii*-kap) *n* tasse à thé

team (tiim) *n* équipe *f*

teapot (*tii*-pot) *n* théière *f*

tear¹ (ti^{eu}) *n* larme *f*

tear² (tè^{eu}) *n* déchirure *f*; *tear *v* déchirer

tear-jerker (*tieu*-djeû-keu) *n* mélo *m*

tease (tiiz) *v* taquiner

teashop (*tii*-chop) *n* pâtisserie-salon de thé

teaspoon (*tii*-spoûn) *n* cuillère à thé

teaspoonful (*tii*-spoûn-foul) *n* cuillerée à thé

technical (*tèk*-ni-keul) *adj* technique

technician (tèk-*ni*-cheunn) *n* technicien *m*

technique (tèk-*niik*) *n* technique *f*

technology (tèk-*no*-leu-dji) *n* technologie *f*

teenager (*tii*-néï-djeu) *n* adolescent *m*, -e *f*

teetotaller (tii-*tôou*-teu-leu) *n* antialcoolique *m*

telegram (*tè*-li-ghræm) *n* télégramme *m*

telephone (*tè*-li-fô^{ou}n) *n* téléphone *m*; ~ **book** *Am* annuaire téléphonique; ~ **booth** cabine téléphonique; ~ **call** coup de téléphone, appel téléphonique; ~ **directory** annuaire téléphonique, bottin *m*; ~ **exchange** central téléphonique

television (*tè*-li-vi-jeunn) *n* télévision *f*; ~ **set** télévision *f*; **cable** ~ télévision par câble; **satellite** ~ télévision par satellite

telex (*tè*-lèks) *n* télex *m*

tell (tèl) *v* *dire; raconter

telly (*tè*-li) *n colloquial* télé *f*

temper (*tèm*-peu) *n* colère *f*

temperature (*tèm*-preu-tcheu) *n* température *f*

tempest (*tèm*-pist) *n* tempête *f*

temple (*tèm*-peul) *n* temple *m*; tempe *f*

temporary (*tèm*-peu-reu-ri) *adj* provisoire, temporaire

tempt (tèmpt) *v* tenter

temptation (tèmp-*téï*-cheunn) *n* tentation *f*

ten (tèn) *num* dix

tenant (*tè*-neunnt) *n* locataire *m*

tend (tènd) *v* *avoir tendance; soigner; ~ **to** tendre à

tendency (*tèn*-deunn-si) *n* inclination *f*, tendance *f*

tender (*tèn*-deu) *adj* tendre, délicat

tendon (*tèn*-deunn) *n* tendon *m*

tennis (*tè*-niss) *n* tennis *m*; ~ **court** court de tennis; ~ **shoes** chaussures de tennis

tense (tèns) *adj* tendu

tension (*tèn*-cheunn) *n* tension *f*

tent (tènt) *n* tente *f*

tenth (tènθ) *num* dixième

tepid (*tè*-pid) *adj* tiède

term (teûmm) *n* terme *m*; période *f*; condition *f*

terminal (*teû*-mi-neul) *n* terminus *m*

terrace (tè-reuss) n terrasse f
terrain (tè-réïn) n terrain m
terrible (tè-ri-beul) adj épouvantable, terrible
terrific (teu-ri-fik) adj formidable
terrify (tè-ri-faï) v terrifier
territory (tè-ri-teu-ri) n territoire m
terror (tè-reu) n terreur f
terrorism (tè-reu-ri-zeumm) n terrorisme m
terrorist (tè-reu-rist) n terroriste m/f
test (tèst) n test m, épreuve f; v essayer, éprouver
testify (tè-sti-faï) v témoigner
text (tèkst) n texte m
textbook (tèks-bouk) n manuel m
textile (tèk-staïl) n textile m
Thai (taï) adj thaïlandais; n Thaïlandais m
Thailand (taï-lænd) Thaïlande f
than (ðæn) conj que
thank (θængk) v remercier; ~ you merci
thankful (θængk-feul) adj reconnaissant
that (ðæt) adj ce; pron celui-là, cela; qui; conj que
thaw (θoo) v dégeler, fondre; n dégel m
the (ðeu, ði) art le art; **the ... the** plus ... plus
theater Am, **theatre** (θieu-teu) n théâtre m
theft (θèft) n vol m
their (ðè^eu) adj leur
them (ðèm) pron les; leur
theme (θiim) n thème m, sujet m
themselves (ðeumm-sèlvz) pron se; eux-mêmes
then (ðèn) adv alors; ensuite, puis
theology (θi-o-leu-dji) n théologie f
theoretical (θi^eu-rè-ti-keul) adj théorique
theory (θieu-ri) n théorie f

therapy (θè-reu-pi) n thérapie f
there (ðè^eu) adv là
therefore (ðèeu-foo) conj donc
thermometer (θeu-mo-mi-teu) n thermomètre m
thermostat (θê-meu-stæt) n thermostat m
these (ðiiz) adj ces
thesis (θii-siss) n (pl theses) thèse f
they (ðéï) pron ils
thick (θik) adj gros; épais
thicken (θi-keunn) v épaissir
thickness (θik-neuss) n épaisseur f
thief (θiif) n (pl thieves) voleur m, voleuse f
thigh (θaï) n cuisse f
thimble (θimm-beul) n dé m
thin (θinn) adj mince; maigre
thing (θinng) n chose f
*****think** (θinngk) v penser; réfléchir; ~ of penser à; songer à; ~ over réfléchir à
third (θûd) num troisième
thirst (θûst) n soif f
thirsty (θû-sti) adj assoiffé
thirteen (θû-tiin) num treize
thirteenth (θû-tiinθ) num treizième
thirtieth (θû-ti-euθ) num trentième
thirty (θû-ti) num trente
this (ðiss) adj ce; pron ceci
thistle (θi-seul) n chardon m
thorn (θoon) n épine f
thorough (θʌ-reu) adj minutieux, soigné
thoroughfare (θʌ-reu-fè^eu) n route principale, artère f
those (ðô^ouz) adj ces; pron ceux-là
though (ðô^ou) conj bien que, encore que, quoique; adv pourtant
thought¹ (θoot) v (p, pp think)
thought² (θoot) n pensée f
thoughtful (θoot-feul) adj pensif; prévenant
thousand (θʌou-zeunnd) num mille

thread (θrèd) *n* fil *m*; *v* enfiler

threadbare (θrèd-bè^{eu}) *adj* usé

threat (θrèt) *n* menace *f*

threaten (θrè-teunn) *v* menacer;
  threatening menaçant

three (θrii) *num* trois

three-quarter (θrii-*kouoo*-teu) *adj*
  trois quarts

threshold (θrè-chô^{ou}ld) *n* seuil *m*

threw (θroû) *v* (p throw)

thrifty (θrif-ti) *adj* parcimonieux

throat (θrô^{ou}t) *n* gorge *f*

throne (θrô^{ou}n) *n* trône *m*

through (θroû) *prep* à travers

throughout (θroû-*aout*) *adv* partout

throw (θrô^{ou}) *n* lancement *m*

***throw** (θrô^{ou}) *v* jeter, lancer

thrush (θrach) *n* grive *f*

thumb (θamm) *n* pouce *m*

thumbtack (θamm-tæk) *nAm* punaise
  f

thump (θammp) *v* marteler

thunder (θann-deu) *n* tonnerre *m*; *v*
  tonner

thunderstorm (θann-deu-stoom) *n*
  orage *m*

thundery (θann-deu-ri) *adj* orageux

Thursday (θûz-di) *n* jeudi *m*

thus (ðass) *adv* ainsi

thyme (taïm) *n* thym *m*

tick (tik) *n* coche *f*; **~ off** pointer

ticket (ti-kit) *n* billet *m*; contravention
  f; **~ collector** contrôleur *m*; **~**
  machine distributeur de billets

tickle (ti-keul) *v* chatouiller

tide (taïd) *n* marée *f*; **high ~** marée
  haute; **low ~** marée basse

tidy (taï-di) *adj* ordonné; **~ up** ranger

tie (taï) *v* nouer, attacher; *n* cravate *f*

tiger (taï-gheu) *n* tigre *m*

tight (taït) *adj* serré; étroit, juste; *adv*
  fortement

tighten (taï-teunn) *v* serrer; resserrer;
  se resserrer

tights (taïts) *pl* collants *mpl*

tile (taïl) *n* carreau *m*; tuile *f*

till (til) *prep* jusqu'à; *conj* jusqu'à ce
  que

timber (timm-beu) *n* bois d'œuvre

time (taïm) *n* temps *m*; fois *f*; **all the ~**
  continuellement; **in ~** à temps; **~ of**
  arrival heure d'arrivée; **~ of**
  departure heure de départ

time-saving (taïm-séï-vinng) *adj* qui
  fait gagner du temps

timetable (taïm-téï-beul) *n* horaire *m*

timid (ti-mid) *adj* timide

timidity (ti-*mi*-deu-ti) *n* timidité *f*

tin (tinn) *n* étain *m*; boîte *f*; **~ opener**
  ouvreboîte *m*; **tinned food** conserves
  fpl

tinfoil (*tinn*-foïl) *n* papier d'étain

tiny (taï-ni) *adj* minuscule

tip (tip) *n* bout *m*; pourboire *m*

tire^1 (taï^{eu}) *n* pneu *m*; **~ pressure**
  pression des pneus

tire^2 (taï^{eu}) *v* fatiguer

tired (taï^{eu}d) *adj* fatigué; **~ of** las de

tiring (taïeu-rinng) *adj* fatigant

tissue (ti-choû) *n* tissu *m*; mouchoir
  de papier

title (taï-teul) *n* titre *m*

to (toû) *prep* jusque; à, pour, chez; afin
  de

toad (tô^{ou}d) *n* crapaud *m*

toadstool (*tôoud*-stoûl) *n*
  champignon *m*

toast (tô^{ou}st) *n* toast *m*

tobacco (teu-*bæ*-kô^{ou}) *n* (pl ~s) tabac
  m; **~ pouch** blague à tabac

tobacconist (teu-*bæ*-keu-nist) *n*
  débitant de tabac; **tobacconist's**
  bureau de tabac

today (teu-*déï*) *adv* aujourd'hui

toddler (tod-leu) *n* bambin *m*

toe (tô^{ou}) *n* orteil *m*

toffee (to-fi) *n* caramel *m*

together (teu-*ghè*-ðeu) *adv* ensemble

toilet (*toï*-leut) n toilettes *fpl*; **~ case** nécessaire de toilette; **~ paper** papier hygiénique

toiletry (*toï*-leu-tri) n articles de toilette

token (*tôou*-keunn) n signe m; jeton m

told (tô°uld) v (p, pp tell)

tolerable (*to*-leu-reu-beul) adj tolérable

toll (tô°ul) n péage m

tomato (teu-*mââ*-tô°u) n (pl ~es) tomate f

tomb (toûm) n tombe f

tombstone (*toûm*-stô°un) n pierre tombale

tomorrow (teu-*mo*-rô°u) adv demain

ton (tann) n tonne f

tone (tô°un) n ton m; timbre m

tongs (tonngz) pl pince f

tongue (tanng) n langue f

tonic (*to*-nik) n tonique m

tonight (teu-*naït*) adv cette nuit, ce soir

tonsillitis (tonn-seu-*laï*-tiss) n amygdalite f

tonsils (*tonn*-seulz) pl amygdales *fpl*

too (toû) adv trop; aussi

took (touk) v (p take)

tool (toûl) n instrument m, outil m; **~ kit** boîte à outils

toot (toût) vAm klaxonner

tooth (toûθ) n (pl teeth) dent f

toothache (*toû*-θéïk) n mal aux dents

toothbrush (*toûθ*-brach) n brosse à dents

toothpaste (*toûθ*-péïst) n pâte dentifrice

toothpick (*toûθ*-pik) n cure-dent m

toothpowder (*toûθ*-paou-deu) n poudre dentifrice

top (top) n sommet m; dessus m; couvercle m; supérieur; **on ~ of** au-dessus de; **~ side** haut m

topic (*to*-pik) n sujet m

topical (*to*-pi-keul) adj actuel

torch (tootch) n torche f; lampe de poche

torment¹ (too-*mènt*) v tourmenter

torment² (*too*-mènt) n tourment m

torture (*too*-tcheu) n torture f; v torturer

toss (toss) v lancer

tot (tot) n bambin m

total (*tôou*-teul) adj total; complet, absolu; n total m

totalitarian (tô°u-tæ-li-*tèeu*-ri-eunn) adj totalitaire

touch (tatch) v toucher; n contact m, attouchement m; toucher m

touching (*ta*-tchinng) adj touchant

tough (taf) adj coriace

tour (tou°u) n excursion f

tourism (*tou°eu*-ri-zeumm) n tourisme m

tourist (*tou°eu*-rist) n touriste m/f; **~ class** classe touriste; **~ office** syndicat d'initiative

tournament (*tou°eu*-neu-meunnt) n tournoi m

tow (tô°u) v remorquer

towards (teu-*ou°oodz*) prep vers; envers

towel (taou°ul) n serviette f

towel(l)ing (*taou°eu*-linng) n tissu-éponge m

tower (taou°u) n tour f

town (taoun) n ville f; **~ centre** centre de la ville; **~ hall** hôtel de ville

townspeople (*taounz*-pii-peul) pl citadins mpl

toxic (*tok*-sik) adj toxique

toy (toï) n jouet m

toyshop (*toï*-chop) n magasin de jouets

trace (tréïss) n trace f; v tracer, retracer

track (træk) n voie f; piste f

tractor (*træk*-teu) n tracteur m

trade (tréïd) n commerce m; métier m;

v *faire du commerce; ~ **union**
syndicat *m*

trademark (*tréïd*-mââk) *n* marque de
fabrique

trader (*tréï*-deu) *n* commerçant *m*, -e *f*

tradesman (*tréïdz*-meunn) *n* (pl -men)
marchand *m*

tradition (treu-*di*-cheunn) *n* tradition *f*

traditional (treu-*di*-cheu-neul) *adj*
traditionnel

traffic (*træ*-fik) *n* circulation *f*; ~ **jam**
embouteillage *m*; ~ **light** feu de
circulation

tragedy (*træ*-djeu-di) *n* tragédie *f*

tragic (*træ*-djik) *adj* tragique

trail (tréïl) *n* piste *f*, sentier *m*

trailer (*tréï*-leu) *n* remorque *f*; *nAm*
caravane *f*

train (tréïn) *n* train *m*; *v* dresser,
former; **slow** ~ omnibus *m*; **through**
~ train direct; ~ **ferry** ferry-boat *m*

trainee (tréï-*nii*) *n* apprenti *m*, e *f*;
stagiaire *m,f*

trainer (*tréï*-neu) *n* entraîneur *m*,
entraîneuse *f*; dresseur *m*, dresseuse *f*

training (*tréï*-ninng) *n* entraînement
m

trait (tréït) *n* trait *m*

traitor (*tréï*-teu) *n* traître *m*

tram (træm) *n* tram *m*

tramp (træmp) *n* chemineau *m*,
vagabond *m*; *v* vagabonder

tranquil (*træng*-k^{ou}il) *adj* tranquille

tranquillizer (*træng*-k^{ou}i-laï-zeu) *n*
calmant *m*

transaction (træn-*zæk*-cheunn) *n*
transaction *f*

transatlantic (træn-zeut-*læn*-tik) *adj*
transatlantique

transfer (træns-*feû*) *v* transférer

transform (træns-*foom*) *v* transformer

transformer (træns-*foo*-meu) *n*
transformateur *m*

transition (træn-*si*-cheunn) *n*

transition *f*

translate (træns-*léït*) *v* *traduire

translation (træns-*léï*-cheunn) *n*
traduction *f*

translator (træns-*léï*-teu) *n* traducteur
m, traductrice *f*

transmission (trænz-*mi*-cheunn) *n*
émission *f*

transmit (trænz-*mit*) *v* *émettre

transmitter (trænz-*mi*-teu) *n* émetteur
m

transparent (træn-*spèeu*-reunnt) *adj*
transparent

transport[1] (*træn*-spoot) *n* transport *m*

transport[2] (træn-*spoot*) *v* transporter

transportation (træn-spoo-*téï*-
cheunn) *n* transport *m*

trap (træp) *n* piège *m*

trash (træch) *n* ordures *fpl*; ~ **can** *Am*
boîte à ordures

travel (*træ*-veul) *v* voyager; ~ **agency**
bureau de voyages; ~ **agent** agent de
voyages; ~ **insurance** assurance
voyages *f*; **travelling expenses** frais
de voyage

travel(l)er (*træ*-veu-leu) *n* voyageur *m*,
voyageuse *f*; **traveler's check** *Am*,
traveller's cheque chèque de
voyage

tray (tréï) *n* plateau *m*

treason (*trii*-zeunn) *n* trahison *f*

treasure (*trè*-jeu) *n* trésor *m*

treasury (*trè*-jeu-ri) *n* Trésor *m*

treat (triit) *v* traiter

treatment (*triit*-meunnt) *n* traitement
m

treaty (*trii*-ti) *n* traité *m*

tree (trii) *n* arbre *m*

tremble (*trèm*-beul) *v* frissonner,
trembler; vibrer

tremendous (tri-*mèn*-deuss) *adj*
énorme

trendy (*trèn*-di) *adj* à la (dernière)
mode, dernier cri; dans le vent

trespass (*trèss*-peuss) *v* empiéter

trespasser (*trèss*-peu-seu) *n* intrus *m*

trial (traï^[eul]) *n* procès *m*; essai *m*

triangle (*traï*-æng-gheul) *n* triangle *m*

triangular (traï-*æng*-ghyou-leu) *adj* triangulaire

tribe (traïb) *n* tribu *f*

tributary (*tri*-byou-teu-ri) *n* affluent *m*

tribute (*tri*-byoût) *n* hommage *m*

trick (trik) *n* truc *m*

trigger (*tri*-gheu) *n* gâchette *f*

trim (trimm) *v* tailler

trip (trip) *n* excursion *f*, voyage *m*

triumph (*traï*-eummf) *n* triomphe *m*; *v* triompher

triumphant (traï-*amm*-feunnt) *adj* triomphant

troops (troûps) *pl* troupes *fpl*

tropical (*tro*-pi-keul) *adj* tropical

tropics (*tro*-piks) *pl* tropiques *mpl*

trouble (*tra*-beul) *n* ennui *m*, peine *f*, dérangement *m*; *v* déranger

troublesome (*tra*-beul-seumm) *adj* gênant

trousers (traou-zeuz) *pl* pantalon *m*

trout (traout) *n* (pl ~) truite *f*

truck (trak) *nAm* camion *m*

true (troû) *adj* vrai; réel; loyal, fidèle

trumpet (*tramm*-pit) *n* trompette *f*

trunk (tranngk) *n* malle *f*; tronc *m*; *nAm* coffre *m*; **trunks** *pl* slip de bain

trunk-call (*tranngk*-kool) *n* appel interurbain

trust (trast) *v* *faire confiance; *n* confiance *f*

trustworthy (*trast*-^[ou]eû-ði) *adj* digne de confiance

truth (troûθ) *n* vérité *f*

truthful (*troûθ*-feul) *adj* véridique

try (traï) *v* essayer; tenter, s'efforcer; *n* tentative *f*; ~ **on** essayer

tube (tyoûb) *n* tuyau *m*, tube *m*

tuberculosis (tyoû-beû-kyou-*lôou*-siss) *n* tuberculose *f*

Tuesday (*tyoûz*-di) mardi *m*

tug (tagh) *v* remorquer; *n* remorqueur *m*; à-coup *m*

tuition (tyoû-*i*-cheunn) *n* enseignement *m*

tulip (*tyoû*-lip) *n* tulipe *f*

tumbler (*tamm*-bleu) *n* gobelet *m*

tumo(u)r (*tyoû*-meu) *n* tumeur *f*

tuna (*tyoû*-neu) *n* (pl ~, ~s) thon *m*

tune (tyoûn) *n* air *m*; *v* accorder

tuneful (*tyoûn*-feul) *adj* harmonieux

tunic (*tyoû*-nik) *n* tunique *f*

Tunisia (tyoû-*ni*-zi-eu) Tunisie *f*

Tunisian (tyoû-*ni*-zi-eunn) *adj* tunisien; *n* Tunisien *m*

tunnel (*ta*-neul) *n* tunnel *m*

turbine (*teû*-baïn) *n* turbine *f*

Turk (teûk) *n* Turc *m*

Turkey (*teû*-ki) Turquie *f*

turkey (*teû*-ki) *n* dinde *f*

Turkish (*teû*-kich) *adj* turc; ~ **bath** bain turc

turn (teûnn) *v* tourner; retourner, virer; *n* revirement *m*, tour *m*; tournant *m*; ~ **back** retourner; ~ **down** rejeter; ~ **into** changer en; ~ **off** fermer; ~ **on** allumer; *ouvrir; ~ **over** retourner; ~ **round** retourner; se retourner

turning (*teû*-ninng) *n* virage *m*; ~ **point** tournant *m*

turnover (*teû*-nôou-veu) *n* chiffre d'affaires; ~ **tax** impôt sur le chiffre d'affaires

turnpike (*teûnn*-païk) *nAm* route à péage

turpentine (*teû*-peunn-taïn) *n* térébenthine *f*

turtle (*teû*-teul) *n* tortue *f*

tutor (*tyoû*-teu) *n* tuteur *m*

tuxedo (tak-*sii*-dô^[ou]) *nAm* (pl ~s, ~es) smoking *m*

TV (tii-*vii*) *n* télévision *f*

tweed (t^[ou]iid) *n* tweed *m*

tweezers (*touii*-zeuz) *pl* pince *f*
twelfth (t^{ou}èlfθ) *num* douzième
twelve (t^{ou}èlv) *num* douze
twentieth (*touèn*-ti-euθ) *num* vingtième
twenty (*touèn*-ti) *num* vingt
twice (t^{ou}aïss) *adv* deux fois
twig (t^{ou}igh) *n* rameau *m*; branche *f*
twilight (*touaï*-laït) *n* crépuscule *m*
twine (t^{ou}aïn) *n* ficelle *f*
twins (t^{ou}innz) *pl* jumeaux *mpl*; **twin beds** lits jumeaux
twist (t^{ou}ist) *v* tordre; *n* torsion *f*

two (toû) *num* deux
two-piece (toû-*piiss*) *adj* deux-pièces *m*
type (taïp) *v* taper à la machine, dactylographier; *n* type *m*
typewriter (*taïp*-raï-teu) *n* machine à écrire
typhoid (*taï*-foïd) *n* typhoïde *f*
typical (*ti*-pi-keul) *adj* caractéristique, typique
typist (*taï*-pist) *n* dactylo *f*
tyre (taï^{eu}) *n* pneu *m*; ~ **pressure** pression des pneus

U

ugly (*a*-ghli) *adj* laid
ulcer (*al*-seu) *n* ulcère *m*
ultimate (*al*-ti-meut) *adj* ultime
ultraviolet (al-treu-*vaïeu*-leut) *adj* ultra-violet
umbrella (amm-*brè*-leu) *n* parapluie *m*
umpire (*amm*-paï^{eu}) *n* arbitre *m*
unable (a-*néï*-beul) *adj* incapable
unacceptable (a-neuk-*sèp*-teu-beul) *adj* inacceptable
unaccountable (a-neu-*kaoun*-teu-beul) *adj* inexplicable
unaccustomed (a-neu-*ka*-steummd) *adj* inhabitué
unanimous (yoû-*næ*-ni-meuss) *adj* unanime
unanswered (a-*nâân*-seud) *adj* sans réponse
unauthorized (a-*noo*-θeu-raïzd) *adj* illicite
unavoidable (a-neu-*voï*-deu-beul) *adj* inévitable
unaware (a-neu-*ouèeu*) *adj* inconscient

unbearable (ann-*bèeu*-reu-beul) *adj* insupportable
unbreakable (ann-*bréï*-keu-beul) *adj* incassable
unbroken (ann-*brôou*-keunn) *adj* intact
unbutton (ann-*ba*-teunn) *v* déboutonner
uncertain (ann-*seû*-teunn) *adj* incertain
uncle (*anng*-keul) *n* oncle *m*
unclean (ann-*kliin*) *adj* malpropre
uncomfortable (ann-*kamm*-feu-teu-beul) *adj* inconfortable
uncommon (ann-*ko*-meunn) *adj* inhabituel, rare
unconditional (ann-keunn-*di*-cheu-neul) *adj* inconditionnel
unconscious (ann-*konn*-cheuss) *adj* inconscient
uncork (ann-*kook*) *v* déboucher
uncover (ann-*ka*-veu) *v* *découvrir
uncultivated (ann-*kal*-ti-véï-tid) *adj* inculte
under (*ann*-deu) *prep* en bas de, sous

undercurrent (*ann*-deu-ka-reunnt) *n* courant *m*

underestimate (ann-deu-*rè*-sti-méït) *v* sous-estimer

underground (*ann*-deu-ghraound) *adj* souterrain; *n* métro *m*

underline (ann-deu-*laïn*) *v* souligner

underneath (ann-deu-*niiθ*) *adv* dessous

underpants (*ann*-deu-pænts) *plAm* caleçon *m*

undershirt (*ann*-deu-cheût) *n* tricot de corps

***understand** (ann-deu-*stænd*) *v* *comprendre

understanding (ann-deu-*stæn*-dinng) *n* compréhension *f*

understatement (ann-deu-*stéït*-meunnt) *n* affirmation *f* qui reste au-dessous de la vérité; amoindrissement *m*

***undertake** (ann-deu-*téïk*) *v* *entreprendre

undertaking (ann-deu-*téï*-kinng) *n* entreprise *f*

underwater (*ann*-deu-^{ou}oo-teu) *adj* sous-marin

underwear (*ann*-deu-^{ou}è^{eu}) *n* sous-vêtements *mpl*

undesirable (ann-di-*zaïeu*-reu-beul) *adj* indésirable

***undo** (ann-*doû*) *v* *défaire

undoubtedly (ann-*daou*-tid-li) *adv* sans aucun doute

undress (ann-*drèss*) *v* se déshabiller

unearned (a-*neûnnd*) *adj* immérité

uneasy (a-*nii*-zi) *adj* mal à l'aise

uneducated (a-*nè*-dyou-kéï-tid) *adj* ignorant

unemployed (a-nimm-*ploïd*) *adj* en chômage

unemployment (a-nimm-*ploï*-meunnt) *n* chômage *m*

unequal (a-*nii*-k^{ou}eul) *adj* inégal

uneven (a-*nii*-veunn) *adj* inégal, accidenté; irrégulier

unexpected (a-nik-*spèk*-tid) *adj* imprévu, inattendu

unfair (ann-*fèeu*) *adj* inéquitable, injuste

unfaithful (ann-*féïθ*-feul) *adj* infidèle

unfamiliar (ann-feu-*mil*-yeu) *adj* inconnu

unfasten (ann-*fââ*-seunn) *v* détacher

unfavo(u)rable (ann-*féï*-veu-reu-beul) *adj* défavorable

unfit (ann-*fit*) *adj* impropre

unfold (ann-*fôould*) *v* déplier

unfortunate (ann-*foo*-tcheu-neut) *adj* malheureux

unfortunately (ann-*foo*-tcheu-neut-li) *adv* hélas, malheureusement

unfriendly (ann-*frènd*-li) *adj* froid; hostile

ungrateful (ann-*ghréït*-feul) *adj* ingrat

unhappy (ann-*hæ*-pi) *adj* malheureux

unhealthy (ann-*hèl*-θi) *adj* malsain

unhurt (ann-*heût*) *adj* indemne

uniform (*yoû*-ni-foom) *n* uniforme *m*; *adj* uniforme

unimportant (a-nimm-*poo*-teunnt) *adj* insignifiant

uninhabitable (a-ninn-*hæ*-bi-teu-beul) *adj* inhabitable

uninhabited (a-ninn-*hæ*-bi-tid) *adj* inhabité

unintentional (a-ninn-*tèn*-cheu-neul) *adj* involontaire

union (*yoû*-nyeunn) *n* union *f*; ligue *f*

unique (yoû-*niik*) *adj* unique

unit (*yoû*-nit) *n* unité *f*

unite (yoû-*naït*) *v* unir

United States (yoû-*naï*-tid stéïts) Etats-Unis

unity (*yoû*-neu-ti) *n* unité *f*

universal (yoû-ni-*veû*-seul) *adj* général, universel

universe (*yoû*-ni-veûss) *n* univers *m*

university (yoû-ni-*veû*-seu-ti) *n* université *f*

unjust (ann-*djast*) *adj* injuste

unkind (ann-*kaïnd*) *adj* désagréable, peu aimable

unknown (ann-*nôoun*) *adj* inconnu

unlawful (ann-*loo*-feul) *adj* illicite

unleaded (ann-*lèd*-id) *adj* sans plomb

unlearn (ann-*leûnn*) *v* *désapprendre

unless (eunn-*lèss*) *conj* à moins que

unlike (ann-*laïk*) *adj* dissemblable, différent

unlikely (ann-*laï*-kli) *adj* improbable

unlimited (ann-*li*-mi-tid) *adj* illimité

unload (ann-*lôoud*) *v* décharger

unlock (ann-*lok*) *v* *ouvrir

unlucky (ann-*la*-ki) *adj* infortuné

unnecessary (ann-*nè*-seu-seu-ri) *adj* superflu

unoccupied (a-*no*-kyou-païd) *adj* vacant

unpack (ann-*pæk*) *v* déballer

unpleasant (ann-*plè*-zeunnt) *adj* ennuyeux, déplaisant; désagréable, antipathique

unpopular (ann-*po*-pyou-leu) *adj* peu aimé, impopulaire

unprotected (ann-preu-*tèk*-tid) *adj* non protégé

unqualified (ann-*kouo*-li-faïd) *adj* incompétent

unreal (ann-*rieul*) *adj* irréel

unreasonable (ann-*rii*-zeu-neu-beul) *adj* déraisonnable

unreliable (ann-ri-*laï*-eu-beul) *adj* douteux

unrest (ann-*rèst*) *n* agitation *f*; inquiétude *f*

unsafe (ann-*sèïf*) *adj* dangereux

unsatisfactory (ann-sæ-tiss-*fæk*-teu-ri) *adj* insatisfaisant

unscrew (ann-*skroû*) *v* dévisser

unselfish (ann-*sèl*-fich) *adj* désintéressé

unskilled (ann-*skild*) *adj* non qualifié

unsound (ann-*saound*) *adj* malsain

unstable (ann-*stèï*-beul) *adj* instable

unsteady (ann-*stè*-di) *adj* branlant, instable

unsuccessful (ann-seuk-*sèss*-feul) *adj* infructueux

unsuitable (ann-*soû*-teu-beul) *adj* inadéquat

unsurpassed (ann-seu-*pââst*) *adj* sans pareil

untidy (ann-*taï*-di) *adj* désordonné

untie (ann-*taï*) *v* dénouer

until (eunn-*til*) *prep* jusqu'à

untrue (ann-*troû*) *adj* faux

untrustworthy (ann-*trast*-ᵒᵘeû-ði) *adj* sujet à caution

unusual (ann-*yoû*-jou-eul) *adj* inhabituel, insolite

unwell (ann-*ouèl*) *adj* indisposé

unwillingly (ann-*oui*-linng-li) *adv* à contrecœur

unwise (ann-*ouaïz*) *adj* imprudent

unwrap (ann-*ræp*) *v* déballer

up (ap) *adv* vers le haut, en haut

upholster (ap-*hôoul*-steu) *v* capitonner

upkeep (*ap*-kiip) *n* entretien *m*

uplands (*ap*-leunndz) *pl* hautes terres

upon (eu-*ponn*) *prep* sur

upper (*a*-peu) *adj* supérieur

upright (*ap*-raït) *adj* droit; *adv* droit

upset (ap-*sèt*) *v* déranger; *adj* bouleversé

upside-down (ap-saïd-*daoun*) *adv* sens dessus dessous

upstairs (ap-*stèeuz*) *adv* en haut

upstream (ap-*striim*) *adv* en amont

upwards (ap-ᵒᵘeudz) *adv* vers le haut

urban (*eû*-beunn) *adj* urbain

urge (eûdj) *v* exhorter; *n* impulsion *f*

urgency (*eû*-djeunn-si) *n* urgence *f*

urgent (*eû*-djeunnt) *adj* urgent

urine (*youeu*-rinn) *n* urine *f*

Uruguay (*youeu*-reu-gh^{ou}aï) Uruguay *m*

Uruguayan (you^{eu}-reu-*ghouaï*-eunn) *adj* uruguayen; *n* Uruguayen *m*

us (ass) *pron* nous

usable (*yoû*-zeu-beul) *adj* utilisable

usage (*yoû*-zidj) *n* usage *m*

use¹ (yoûz) *v* employer; *be used to* *être habitué à; ~ up user

use² (yoûss) *n* emploi *m*; utilité *f*; *be of ~* *servir

useful (*yoûss*-feul) *adj* utile

useless (*yoûss*-leuss) *adj* inutile

user (*yoû*-zeu) *n* usager *m*

usher (*a*-cheu) *n* ouvreur *m*

usherette (a-cheu-*rèt*) *n* ouvreuse *f*

usual (*yoû*-jou-eul) *adj* ordinaire

usually (*yoû*-jou-eu-li) *adv* habituellement

utensil (yoû-*tèn*-seul) *n* outil *m*, ustensile *m*

utility (yoû-*ti*-leu-ti) *n* utilité *f*

utilize (*yoû*-ti-laïz) *v* utiliser

utmost (*at*-mô^{ou}st) *adj* extrême

utter (*a*-teu) *adj* complet, total; *v* *émettre

V

vacancy (*véï*-keunn-si) *n* vacance *f*

vacant (*véï*-keunnt) *adj* vacant

vacate (veu-*kéït*) *v* quitter

vacation (veu-*kéï*-cheunn) *n* congé *m*

vaccinate (*væk*-si-néït) *v* vacciner

vaccination (væk-si-*néï*-cheunn) *n* vaccination *f*

vacuum (*væ*-kyou-eumm) *n* vide *m*; *vAm* passer l'aspirateur; **~ cleaner** aspirateur *m*; **~ flask** thermos *m*

vague (véïgh) *adj* vague

vain (véïn) *adj* vaniteux; vain; **in ~** inutilement, en vain

valid (*væ*-lid) *adj* valable

valley (*væ*-li) *n* vallée *f*

valuable (*væ*-lyou-beul) *adj* de valeur, précieux; **valuables** *pl* objets de valeur

value (*væ*-lyoû) *n* valeur *f*, *v* estimer

valve (vælv) *n* soupape *f*

van (væn) *n* fourgon *m*

vanilla (veu-*ni*-leu) *n* vanille *f*

vanish (*væ*-nich) *v* *disparaître

vapo(u)r (*véï*-peu) *n* vapeur *f*

variable (*vèeu*-ri-eu-beul) *adj* variable

variation (vè^{eu}-ri-*éï*-cheunn) *n* variation *f*; changement *m*

varied (*vèeu*-rid) *adj* varié

variety (veu-*raï*-eu-ti) *n* variété *f*; **~ show** spectacle de variétés; **~ theatre** (*Am* **theater**) théâtre de variétés

various (*vèeu*-ri-euss) *adj* divers

varnish (*vââ*-nich) *n* laque *f*, vernis *m*; *v* vernir

vary (*vèeu*-ri) *v* varier; changer; différer

vase (vââz) *n* vase *m*

vaseline (*væ*-seu-liin) *n* vaseline *f*

vast (vââst) *adj* immense, vaste

vault (voolt) *n* voûte *f*; chambre forte

veal (viil) *n* veau *m*

vegetable (*vè*-djeu-teu-beul) *n* légume *m*; **~ merchant** marchand de légumes

vegetarian (vè-dji-*tèeu*-ri-eunn) *n* végétarien *m*, végétarienne *f*

vegetation (vè-dji-*téï*-cheunn) *n* végétation *f*

vehicle (*vii*-eu-keul) *n* véhicule *m*

veil (véïl) *n* voile *m*

301   **vocalist**

vein (véïn) *n* veine *f*; **varicose ~** varice
  f
velvet (vèl-vit) *n* velours *m*
velveteen (vèl-vi-tiin) *n* velvet *m*
venerable (vè-neu-reu-beul) *adj*
  vénérable
venereal disease (vi-nieu-ri-eul di-
  ziiz) maladie vénérienne
Venezuela (vè-ni-zouéï-leu) •
  Venezuela *m*
Venezuelan (vè-ni-zouéï-leunn) *adj*
  vénézuélien; *n* Vénézuélien *m*
ventilate (vèn-ti-léït) *v* ventiler; aérer
ventilation (vèn-ti-léï-cheunn) *n*
  ventilation *f*; aération *f*
ventilator (vèn-ti-léï-teu) *n*
  ventilateur *m*
venture (vèn-tcheu) *v* risquer
veranda (veu-ræn-deu) *n* véranda *f*
verb (veûb) *n* verbe *m*
verbal (veû-beul) *adj* verbal
verdict (veû-dikt) *n* sentence *f*, verdict
  m
verge (veûdj) *n* bord *m*
verify (vè-ri-faï) *v* vérifier
verse (veûss) *n* vers *m*
version (veû-cheunn) *n* version *f*
versus (veû-seuss) *prep* contre
vertical (veû-ti-keul) *adj* vertical
very (vè-ri) *adv* très; *adj* même,
  justement; tout
vessel (vè-seul) *n* vaisseau *m*;
  récipient *m*
vest (vèst) *n* chemise *f*, *nAm* gilet *m*
veterinary surgeon (vè-tri-neu-ri seû-
  djeunn) vétérinaire *m/f*
via (vaï^eu) *prep* via
vibrate (vaï-bréït) *v* vibrer
vibration (vaï-bréï-cheunn) *n*
  vibration *f*
vicar (vi-keu) *n* vicaire *m*
vice president (vaïss-prè-zi-deunnt) *n*
  vice-président *m*
vicinity (vi-si-neu-ti) *n* alentours *mpl*,

voisinage *m*
vicious (vi-cheuss) *adj* vicieux
victim (vik-timm) *n* victime *f*; dupe *f*
victory (vik-teu-ri) *n* victoire *f*
video camera (vi-di-ô^ou kæ-meu-reu)
  n caméra vidéo *f*
video recorder (vi-di-ô^ou ri-koo-deu)
  n magnétoscope *m*
view (vyoû) *n* vue *f*; point de vue,
  opinion *f*; *v* contempler
viewfinder (vyoû-faïn-deu) *n* viseur *m*
vigilant (vi-dji-leunnt) *adj* vigilant
villa (vi-leu) *n* villa *f*
village (vi-lidj) *n* village *m*
vine (vaïn) *n* vigne *f*
vinegar (vi-ni-gheu) *n* vinaigre *m*
vineyard (vinn-yeud) *n* vignoble *m*
vintage (vinn-tidj) *n* vendange *f*
violation (vaï^eu-léï-cheunn) *n*
  violation *f*
violence (vaïeu-leunns) *n* violence *f*
violent (vaïeu-leunnt) *adj* violent
violet (vaïeu-leut) *n* violette *f*; *adj*
  violet
violin (vaï^eu-linn) *n* violon *m*
VIP (vii-aï-pii) *n* V.I.P. *m*
virgin (veû-djinn) *n* vierge *f*
virtue (veû-tchoû) *n* vertu *f*
visa (vii-zeu) *n* visa *m*
visibility (vi-zeu-bi-leu-ti) *n* visibilité *f*
visible (vi-zeu-beul) *adj* visible
vision (vi-jeunn) *n* vision *f*
visit (vi-zit) *v* visiter; *n* visite *f*;
  visiting card carte de visite;
  visiting hours heures de visite
visitor (vi-zi-teu) *n* visiteur *m*, -euse *f*,
  invité *m*, -e *f*
vital (vaï-teul) *adj* vital
vitamin (vi-teu-minn) *n* vitamine *f*
vivid (vi-vid) *adj* vif
vocabulary (veu-kæ-byou-leu-ri) *n*
  vocabulaire *m*
vocal (vôou-keul) *adj* vocal
vocalist (vôou-keu-list) *n* chanteur *m*

voice (voïss) *n* voix *f*

void (voïd) *adj* nul

volcano (vol-kéï-nô^{ou}) *n* (pl ~es, ~s) volcan *m*

volt (vô^{ou}lt) *n* volt *m*

voltage (vôoul-tidj) *n* voltage *m*

volume (vo-lyoum) *n* volume *m*; tome *m*

voluntary (vo-leunn-teu-ri) *adj* volontaire

volunteer (vo-leunn-*tieu*) *n* volontaire *m*

vomit (vo-mit) *v* vomir

vote (vô^{ou}t) *v* voter; *n* vote *m*

voter (vôou-teu) *n* votant *m*, votante *f*; électeur *m*, électrice *f*

voucher (vaou-tcheu) *n* reçu *m*, bon *m*

vow (vaou) *n* vœu *m*, serment *m*; *v* jurer

vowel (vaou^{eu}l) *n* voyelle *f*

voyage (voï-idj) *n* voyage *m*

vulgar (*val*-gheu) *adj* vulgaire, grossier

vulnerable (*val*-neu-reu-beul) *adj* vulnérable

vulture (*val*-tcheu) *n* vautour *m*

W

wade (^{ou}éïd) *v* patauger

wafer (ouéï-feu) *n* gaufrette *f*

waffle (ouo-feul) *n* gaufre *f*

wages (ouéï-djiz) *pl* gages *mpl*

wag(g)on (ouæ-gheunn) *n* wagon *m*

waist (^{ou}éïst) *n* taille *f*

waistcoat (ouéïss-kô^{ou}t) *n* gilet *m*

wait (^{ou}éït) *v* attendre; **~ on** *v* servir

waiter (ouéï-teu) *n* garçon *m*

waiting (ouéï-tinng) *n* attente *f*; **~ list** liste d'attente; **~ room** salle d'attente

waitress (ouéï-triss) *n* serveuse *f*

***wake** (^{ou}éïk) *v* réveiller; **~ up** s'éveiller, se réveiller

walk (^{ou}ook) *v* marcher; se promener; *n* promenade *f*; démarche *f*; **walking** à pied

walker (ouoo-keu) *n* promeneur *m*

walking stick (ouoo-kinng-stik) *n* canne *f*

wall (^{ou}ool) *n* mur *m*; cloison *f*

wallet (ouo-lit) *n* portefeuille *m*

wallpaper (ouool-péï-peu) *n* papier peint

walnut (ouool-nat) *n* noix *f*

waltz (^{ou}ools) *n* valse *f*

wander (ouonn-deu) *v* errer

want (^{ou}onnt) *v* *vouloir; désirer; *n* besoin *m*; carence *f*, manque *m*

war (^{ou}oo) *n* guerre *f*

warden (ouoo-deunn) *n* surveillant *m*, gardien *m*

wardrobe (ouoo-drô^{ou}b) *n* garde-robe *f*

warehouse (ouèeu-haouss) *n* magasin *m*, dépôt *m*

wares (^{ou}è^{eu}z) *pl* marchandise *f*

warm (^{ou}oom) *adj* chaud; *v* chauffer

warmth (^{ou}oomθ) *n* chaleur *f*

warn (^{ou}oon) *v* *prévenir, avertir

warning (ouoo-ninng) *n* avertissement *m*

wary (ouèeu-ri) *adj* prudent

was (^{ou}oz) *v* (p be)

wash (^{ou}och) *v* laver; **~ and wear** sans repassage; **~ up** *faire la vaisselle

washable (ouo-cheu-beul) *adj* lavable

washbasin (ouoch-béï-seunn) *n*

lavabo *m*

washing (*ouo*-chinng) *n* lavage *m*;
lessive *f*; ~ **machine** machine à laver;
~ **powder** lessive

washroom (*ouoch*-roûm) *nAm*
toilettes *fpl*

wasp (^{ou}osp) *n* guêpe *f*

waste (^{ou}éïst) *v* gaspiller; *n* gaspillage
m; *adj* en friche

wasteful (*ouéïst*-feul) *adj* gaspilleur

wastepaper basket (^{ou}éïst-*péï*-peu-
bââ-skit) *n* corbeille à papier

watch (^{ou}otch) *v* regarder, observer;
surveiller; *n* montre *f*; ~ **for** guetter; ~
out *prendre garde

watchmaker (*ouotch*-méï-keu) *n*
horloger *m*, horlogère *f*

watchstrap (*ouotch*-stræp) *n* bracelet
pour montre

water (*ouoo*-teu) *n* eau *f*; **iced** ~ eau
glacée; **running** ~ eau courante; ~
pump pompe à eau; ~ **ski** ski
nautique; ~ **softener** adoucisseur
d'eau

watercolo(u)r (*ouoo*-teu-ka-leu) *n*
couleur à l'eau; aquarelle *f*

watercress (*ouoo*-teu-krèss) *n* cresson
m

waterfall (*ouoo*-teu-fool) *n* cascade *f*

watermelon (*ouoo*-teu-mè-leunn) *n*
pastèque *f*

waterproof (*ouoo*-teu-proûf) *adj*
imperméable

waterway (*ouoo*-teu-^{ou}éï) *n* voie d'eau

watt (^{ou}ot) *n* watt *m*

wave (^{ou}éïv) *n* ondulation *f*, vague *f*; *v*
*faire signe

wavelength (*ouéïv*-lèngθ) *n* longueur
d'onde

wavy (*ouéï*-vi) *adj* ondulé

wax (^{ou}æks) *n* cire *f*

waxworks (*ouæks*-^{ou}eûks) *pl* musée
des figures de cire

way (^{ou}éï) *n* manière *f*, façon *f*; voie *f*;

côté *m*, direction *f*; distance *f*; **by the**
~ à propos; **one-way traffic** sens
unique; **out of the** ~ écarté; **the other**
~ **round** en sens inverse; **the back**
~ chemin du retour; ~ **in** entrée *f*; ~ **out**
sortie *f*

wayside (*ouéï*-saïd) *n* bord de la route

we (^{ou}ii) *pron* nous

weak (^{ou}iik) *adj* faible; léger

weakness (*ouiik*-neuss) *n* faiblesse *f*

wealth (^{ou}èlθ) *n* richesse *f*

wealthy (*ouèl*-θi) *adj* riche

weapon (*ouè*-peunn) *n* arme *f*

***wear** (^{ou}è^{eu}) *v* porter; ~ **out** user

weary (*ouieu*-ri) *adj* las, fatigué

weather (*ouè*-ðeu) *n* temps *m*; ~
forecast bulletin météorologique

***weave** (^{ou}iiv) *v* tisser

wedding (*ouè*-dinng) *n* mariage *m*; ~
ring alliance *f*

web (^{ou}èb) *n* tissu *m*; toile *f*; **the Web**
le Web, la Toile

wedge (^{ou}èdj) *n* cale *f*

Wednesday (*ouènz*-di) mercredi *m*

weed (^{ou}iid) *n* mauvaise herbe

week (^{ou}iik) *n* semaine *f*

weekday (*ouiik*-déï) *n* jour de la
semaine

weekly (*ouii*-kli) *adj* hebdomadaire

***weep** (^{ou}iip) *v* pleurer

weigh (^{ou}éï) *v* peser

weighing machine (*ouéï*-inng-meu-
chiin) *n* bascule *f*

weight (^{ou}éït) *n* poids *m*

welcome (*ouèl*-keumm) *adj* bienvenu;
n accueil *m*; *v* *accueillir

weld (^{ou}èld) *v* souder

welfare (*ouèl*-fè^{eu}) *n* bien-être *m*

well¹ (^{ou}èl) *adv* bien; *adj* sain; **as** ~
également, aussi bien; **as** ~ **as** aussi
bien que; **well!** bien!

well² (^{ou}èl) *n* source *f*, puits *m*

well-founded (^{ou}èl-*faoun*-did) *adj*
bien fondé

well-known (ouèl-nô^{ou}n) adj connu

well-to-do (^{ou}èl-teu-doû) adj aisé

went (^{ou}ènt) v (p go)

were (^{ou}eû) v (p be)

west (^{ou}èst) n occident m, ouest m

westerly (ouè-steu-li) adj occidental

western (ouè-steunn) adj occidental

wet (^{ou}èt) adj mouillé; humide

whale (^{ou}éïl) n baleine f

wharf (^{ou}oof) n (pl ~s, wharves) quai m

what (^{ou}ot) pron quoi; ce que; ~ **for** pourquoi

whatever (^{ou}o-tè-veu) pron tout ce que

wheat (^{ou}iit) n blé m

wheel (^{ou}iil) n roue f

wheelbarrow (ouiil-bæ-rô^{ou}) n brouette f

wheelchair (ouiil-tchè^{eu}) n fauteuil roulant

when (^{ou}èn) adv quand; conj quand, lorsque

whenever (^{ou}è-nè-veu) conj n'importe quand

where (^{ou}è^{eu}) adv où; conj où

wherever (^{ou}è^{eu}-rè-veu) conj partout où

whether (ouè-ðeu) conj si; **whether ... or** si ... ou

which (^{ou}itch) pron quel; qui

whichever (^{ou}i-tchè-veu) adj n'importe quel

while (^{ou}aïl) conj tandis que; n moment m

whilst (^{ou}aïlst) conj tandis que

whim (^{ou}imm) n lubie f, caprice m

whip (^{ou}ip) n fouet m; v fouetter

whiskers (oui-skeuz) pl favoris

whisper (oui-speu) v chuchoter; n chuchotement m

whistle (oui-seul) v siffler; n sifflet m

white (^{ou}aït) adj blanc

whiting (ouaï-tinng) n (pl ~) merlan m

Whitsun (ouit-seunn) Pentecôte f

who (hoû) pron qui

whole (hô^{ou}l) adj complet, entier; intact; n ensemble m

wholesale (hôoul-séïl) n vente en gros; ~ **dealer** grossiste m

wholesome (hôoul-seumm) adj sain

wholly (hôoul-li) adv entièrement

whom (hoûm) pron à qui

whore (hoo) n putain f

whose (hoûz) pron dont; de qui

why (^{ou}aï) adv pourquoi

wicked (oui-kid) adj mauvais

wide (^{ou}aïd) adj vaste, large

widen (ouaï-deunn) v élargir

widow (oui-dô^{ou}) n veuve f

widower (oui-dô^{ou}-eu) n veuf m

width (^{ou}idθ) n largeur f

wife (^{ou}aïf) n (pl wives) épouse f, femme f

wig (^{ou}igh) n perruque f

wild (^{ou}aïld) adj sauvage; féroce

will (^{ou}il) n volonté f; testament m

***will** (^{ou}il) v *vouloir

willing (oui-linng) adj disposé

willingly (oui-linng-li) adv volontiers

willpower (ouil-paou^{eu}) n volonté f

***win** (^{ou}inn) v gagner

wind (^{ou}innd) n vent m

***wind** (^{ou}aïnd) v serpenter; enrouler; ~ **up** remonter

winding (ouaïn-dinng) adj serpentant

windmill (ouinnd-mil) n moulin à vent

window (ouinn-dô^{ou}) n fenêtre f

windowsill (ouinn-dô^{ou}-sil) n rebord de fenêtre

windscreen (ouinnd-skriin) n pare-brise m; ~ **wiper** essuie-glace m

windshield (ouinnd-chiild) nAm parebrise m; ~ **wiper** Am essuie-glace m

windy (ouinn-di) adj venteux

wine (^{ou}aïn) n vin m; ~ **cellar** cave f; ~ **list** carte des vins; ~ **merchant** négociant en vins

wine-waiter (*ouaïn-*ᵒᵘ*éï-teu*) *n* sommelier *m*

wing (ᵒᵘinng) *n* aile *f*

winkle (*ouinng-keul*) *n* bigorneau *m*

winner (*oui-neu*) *n* vainqueur *m*

winning (*oui-ninng*) *adj* gagnant; **winnings** *pl* gains

winter (*ouinn-teu*) *n* hiver *m*; ~ **sports** sports d'hiver

wipe (ᵒᵘaïp) *v* ôter, essuyer

wire (ᵒᵘaïᵉᵘ) *n* fil *m*; fil de fer

wireless (*ouaïeu-leuss*) *n* radio *f*

wisdom (*ouiz-deumm*) *n* sagesse *f*

wise (ᵒᵘaïz) *adj* sage

wish (ᵒᵘich) *v* désirer, souhaiter; *n* désir *m*, souhait *m*

witch (ᵒᵘitch) *n* sorcière *f*

with (ᵒᵘið) *prep* avec; chez; de

*****withdraw** (ᵒᵘið-*droo*) *v* retirer

within (ᵒᵘi-*ðinn*) *prep* dans; *adv* à l'intérieur

without (ᵒᵘi-*ðaout*) *prep* sans

witness (*ouit-neuss*) *n* témoin *m*

wit (ᵒᵘit) *n* esprit *m*; intelligence *f*

wits (ᵒᵘits) *pl* raison *f*

witty (*oui-ti*) *adj* spirituel

wolf (ᵒᵘoulf) *n* (pl wolves) loup *m*

woman (*ouou-meunn*) *n* (pl women) femme *f*

won (ᵒᵘann) *v* (p, pp win)

wonder (*ouann-deu*) *n* miracle *m*; étonnement *m*; *v* se demander

wonderful (*ouann-deu-feul*) *adj* splendide, merveilleux; délicieux

wood (ᵒᵘoud) *n* bois *m*

wooded (*ouou-did*) *adj* boisé

wooden (*ouou-deunn*) *adj* en bois; ~ **shoe** sabot *m*

woodland (*ououd-leunnd*) *n* pays boisé

wool (ᵒᵘoul) *n* laine *f*; **darning** ~ laine à repriser

wool(l)en (*ouou-leunn*) *adj* en laine

word (ᵒᵘeûd) *n* mot *m*

wore (ᵒᵘoo) *v* (p wear)

work (ᵒᵘeûk) *n* travail *m*; activité *f*; *v* travailler; fonctionner; **working day** jour ouvrable; ~ **of art** œuvre d'art; ~ **permit** permis de travail

worker (*oueû-keu*) *n* ouvrier *m*, ouvrière *f*

working (*oueû-kinng*) *n* fonctionnement *m*

workman (*oueûk-meunn*) *n* (pl -men) ouvrier *m*

works (ᵒᵘeûks) *pl* usine *f*

workshop (*oueûk-chop*) *n* atelier *m*

world (ᵒᵘeûld) *n* monde *m*; ~ **war** guerre mondiale

world-famous (ᵒᵘeûld-*féï-meuss*) *adj* de renommée mondiale

world-wide (*oueûld-*ᵒᵘaïd) *adj* mondial

worm (ᵒᵘeûmm) *n* ver *m*

worn (ᵒᵘoon) *adj* (pp wear) usé

worn-out (ᵒᵘoon-*aout*) *adj* usé

worried (*oua-rid*) *adj* soucieux

worry (*oua-ri*) *v* s'inquiéter; *n* souci *m*, inquiétude *f*

worse (ᵒᵘeûss) *adj* pire; *adv* pire

worship (*oueû-chip*) *v* adorer; *n* culte *m*

worst (ᵒᵘeûst) *adj* le plus mauvais; *adv* le pire

worth (ᵒᵘeûθ) *n* valeur *f*; *****be** ~ **valoir**; *****be worth-while** *valoir la peine

worthless (*oueûθ-leuss*) *adj* sans valeur

worthy of (*oueû-ði euv*) digne de

would (ᵒᵘoud) *v* (p will) *avoir l'habitude de

wound¹ (ᵒᵘoûnd) *n* blessure *f*; *v* offenser, blesser

wound² (ᵒᵘaound) *v* (p, pp wind)

wrap (ræp) *v* envelopper

wreck (rèk) *n* épave *f*; *v* *détruire

wrench (rèntch) *n* clé *f*; mouvement *m* violent de torsion; *v* tordre

wrinkle (*rinng*-keul) *n* ride *f*

wrist (rist) *n* poignet *m*

wristwatch (rist-^{ou}otch) *n* braceletmontre *m*

***write** (raït) *v* *écrire; **in writing** par écrit; ~ **down** noter

writer (*raï*-teu) *n* écrivain *m*

writing pad (*raï*-tinng-pæd) *n* bloc-notes *m*

writing paper (*raï*-tinng-péï-peu) *n* papier à lettres

written (*ri*-teunn) *adj* (pp write) par écrit

wrong (ronng) *adj* impropre, incorrect; *n* tort *m*; *v* *faire tort à; ***be ~ ***avoir tort

wrote (rô^{ou}t) *v* (p write)

X

Xmas (*kriss*-meuss) Noël

X-ray (*èks*-réï) *n* radiographie *f*; *v* radiographier

Y

yacht (yot) *n* yacht *m*; ~ **club** yacht-club *m*

yachting (*yo*-tinng) *n* yachting *m*

yard (yââd) *n* cour *f*

yarn (yâân) *n* fil *m*

yawn (yoon) *v* bâiller

year (yi^{eu}) *n* année *f*

yearly (*yieu*-li) *adj* annuel

yeast (yiist) *n* levure *f*

yell (yèl) *v* hurler; *n* cri *m*

yellow (yè-lô^{ou}) *adj* jaune

yes (yèss) oui

yesterday (*yè*-steu-di) *adv* hier

yet (yèt) *adv* encore; *conj* pourtant, cependant

yield (yiild) *v* rendre; céder

yoke (yô^{ou}k) *n* joug *m*

yolk (yô^{ou}k) *n* jaune d'œuf

you (yoû) *pron* tu; te; vous

young (yanng) *adj* jeune

your (yoo) *adj* votre; ton; vos

yours (yooz) le tien, la tienne, les tiens, les tiennes; à toi; le (la) vôtre, les vôtres; à vous

yourself (yoo-*sèlf*) *pron* te; toi-même; vous-même

yourselves (yoo-*sèlvz*) *pron* vous; vous-mêmes

youth (yoûθ) *n* jeunesse *f*; ~ **hostel** auberge de jeunesse

Z

zap (zæp) *colloquial* v zapper;
agresser; assommer; détruire, filer (à
toute allure); n vigueur f, énergie f,
entrain m

zeal (ziil) n zèle m

zealous (zè-leuss) *adj* zélé

zebra (zii-breu) n zèbre m

zenith (zè-niθ) n zénith m; apogée m

zero (zieu-rô^{ou}) n (pl ~s) zéro m

zest (zèst) n entrain m

zinc (zinngk) n zinc m

zip (zip) n fermeture éclair; ~ **code**
Am code postal

zipper (zi-peu) n fermeture éclair

zodiac (zôou-di-æk) n zodiaque m

zone (zô^{ou}n) n zone f; région f

zoo (zoû) n (pl ~s) zoo m

Lexique gastronomique

Mets

almond amande

anchovy anchois

angel food cake gâteau aux blancs d'œufs

angels on horseback huîtres enrobées de lard, grillées et servies sur toast

appetizer amuse-gueule

apple pomme

~ dumpling sorte de chausson aux pommes

~ sauce compote de pommes

Arbroath smoky églefin fumé

artichoke artichaut

asparagus asperge

~ tip pointe d'asperge

assorted varié

avocado (pear) avocat

bacon lard à griller

~ and eggs œufs au lard

bagel petit pain en forme de couronne

baked au four

~ Alaska omelette norvégienne

~ beans haricots blancs dans une sauce tomate

~ potato pomme de terre en robe des champs cuite au four

Bakewell tart gâteau aux amandes et à la confiture

banana banane

~ split banane coupée en tranches, servie avec de la glace et des noix, arrosée de sirop ou de crème au chocolat

barbecue 1) hachis de bœuf dans une sauce relevée aux tomates, servi dans un petit pain 2) repas en plein air

~ sauce sauce aux tomates très relevée

barbecued grillé au charbon de bois

basil basilic

bass bar

bean haricot, fève

beef bœuf

~ olive paupiette de bœuf

beefburger bifteck haché, grillé et servi dans un petit pain

beet, beetroot betterave rouge

bilberry myrtille

bill addition

~ of fare carte des mets, menu

biscuit 1) petit gâteau sec, biscuit (GB) 2) biscuit sec (US)

black pudding boudin noir

blackberry mûre

blackcurrant cassis

bloater hareng saur

blood sausage boudin noir

blueberry myrtille

boiled bouilli

Bologna (sausage) sorte de mortadelle

boloney sorte de mortadelle

bone os

boned désossé

Boston baked beans haricots blancs au lard et à la mélasse dans une sauce tomate

Boston cream pie tourte à la crème en couches superposées, glacée au chocolat

brains cervelle

braised braisé

bramble pudding pudding aux mûres (souvent servi avec des pommes)

braunschweiger saucisson au foie fumé

bread pain

breaded pané

breakfast petit déjeuner

bream brème (poisson)

breast poitrine, blanc de volaille

brisket poitrine de bœuf

broad bean grosse fève

broth bouillon

brown Betty sorte de charlotte aux pommes et aux épices recouverte de chapelure

brunch repas qui tient lieu de petit déjeuner et de déjeuner

Brussels sprouts choux de Bruxelles

bubble and squeak sorte de galette de pommes de terre et choux, parfois accompagnés de morceaux de bœuf

bun 1) petit pain au lait avec des fruits secs 2) sorte de petit pain (US)

butter beurre

buttered beurré

cabbage chou

Caesar salad salade verte, ail, anchois, croûtons et fromage râpé

cake gâteau

cakes pâtisseries

calf veau

Canadian bacon carré de porc fumé, coupé en fines tranches

caper câpre

capercaillie, capercailzie grand coq de bruyère

carp carpe

carrot carotte

cashew noix de cajou

casserole en cocotte

catfish poisson-chat

catsup ketchup

cauliflower chou-fleur

celery céleri

cereal céréale, cornflakes

hot ~ porridge

check addition

Cheddar (cheese) fromage à pâte dure au goût légèrement acide

cheese fromage

~ **board** plateau de fromages

~ **cake** gâteau au fromage double crème

cheeseburger bifteck haché, grillé avec une tranche de fromage, servi dans un petit pain

chef's salad salade de jambon, poulet, œufs durs, tomates, laitue et fromage

cherry cerise

chestnut marron

chicken poulet

chicory 1) endive (GB) 2) (e)scarole, chicorée (US)

chili con carne hachis de bœuf aux haricots rouges et aux piments rouges

chili pepper piment rouge

chips 1) pommes frites (GB) 2) pommes chips (US)

chitt(er)lings tripes de porc

chive ciboulette

chocolate chocolat

choice premier choix

chop côtelette

~ **suey** émincé de porc ou de poulet, de riz et de légumes

chopped émincé, haché

chowder bisque

Christmas pudding cake anglais aux fruits secs, parfois flambé; très nourrissant et servi à Noël

chutney condiment indien épicé à saveur aigre-douce

cinnamon cannelle

clam palourde

club sandwich double sandwich au *bacon*, poulet, tomate, salade et mayonnaise

cobbler tourte aux fruits

cock-a-leekie soup crème de volaille et de poireaux

coconut noix de coco

cod cabillaud

Colchester oyster huître anglaise très

renommée

cold cuts/meat assiette anglaise, viandes froides

coleslaw salade de chou cru

cooked cuit

cookie biscuit

corn 1) blé (GB) 2) maïs (US)

~ **on the cob** épi de maïs

cornflakes flocons de maïs

cottage cheese fromage blanc égoutté

cottage pie hachis de viande aux oignons recouvert de purée de pommes de terre

course plat

cover charge prix du couvert

crab crabe

cracker biscuit salé, craquelin

cranberry canneberge

~ **sauce** sauce à la canneberge

crawfish, crayfish 1) écrevisse 2) langouste (GB) 3) langoustine (US)

cream 1) crème 2) velouté (potage) 3) crème (dessert)

~ **cheese** fromage double crème

~ **puff** chou à la crème

creamed potatoes pommes de terre coupées en dés dans une sauce béchamel

creole mets très relevé, préparé avec des tomates, des poivrons et des oignons, servi avec du riz blanc

cress cresson

crisps pommes chips

crumpet petite crêpe épaisse servie chaude et beurrée

cucumber concombre

Cumberland ham jambon fumé très réputé

Cumberland sauce sauce aigredouce; vin, jus d'orange, zeste de citron, épices et gelée de groseilles

cupcake petit gâteau

cured salé et parfois fumé

currant 1) raisin de Corinthe 2) groseille

curried au curry

custard crème anglaise, flan

cutlet sorte d'escalope, fine tranche de viande, côtelette

dab limande

Danish pastry pâtisserie ou gâteau riche en levure

date datte

Derby cheese fromage à pâte molle et au goût piquant, de couleur jaune pâle

devilled à la diable; assaisonnement très relevé

devil's food cake tourte au chocolat

devils on horseback pruneaux cuits dans du vin rouge et farcis d'amandes et d'anchois, enrobés de lard et grillés

Devonshire cream double crème, très épaisse

diced coupé en dés

diet food aliment diététique

dill aneth

dinner dîner, repas du soir

dish plat, assiette, mets

donut, doughnut beignet en forme d'anneau

double cream double crème, crème entière

Dover sole sole de Douvres, très réputée

dressing 1) sauce à salade 2) farce pour la volaille (US)

Dublin Bay prawn langoustine

duck canard

duckling caneton

dumpling boulette de pâte

Dutch apple pie tarte aux pommes saupoudrée de cassonade ou nappée de mélasse

eel anguille

egg œuf

boiled ~ à la coque

fried ~ au plat
hard-boiled ~ dur
poached ~ poché
scrambled ~ brouillé
soft-boiled ~ mollet
eggplant aubergine
endive 1) (e)scarole, chicorée (GB) 2) endive (US)
entrée 1) entrée (GB) 2) plat principal (US)
fennel fenouil
fig figue
fillet filet de viande ou de poisson
finnan haddock églefin fumé
fish poisson
~ **and chips** filets de poisson frits et pommes frites
~ **cake** galette de poisson et de pommes de terre
flan tarte
flapjack matefaim, crêpe épaisse
flounder flet, plie
forcemeat farce, hachis
fowl volaille
frankfurter saucisse de Francfort
French bean haricot vert
French bread baguette
French dressing 1) vinaigrette (GB) 2) sauce à salade crémeuse assaisonnée de ketchup (US)
French fries pommes frites
French toast croûte dorée
fresh frais
fried frit, grillé
fritter beignet
frogs' legs cuisses de grenouilles
frosting glaçage
fry friture
game gibier
gammon jambon fumé
garfish aiguille de mer
garlic ail
garnish garniture
gherkin cornichon

giblets abats, abattis
ginger gingembre
goose oie
~ **berry** groseille à maquereau
grape raisin
~ **fruit** pamplemousse
grated râpé
gravy jus de viande épaissi
grayling omble
green bean haricot vert
green pepper poivron vert
green salad laitue, salade verte
greens garniture de légumes verts
grilled grillé
grilse saumoneau
grouse petit coq de bruyère
gumbo 1) gombo (légume d'origine africaine) 2) plat créole à base d'*okra*, de viande, de poisson ou de fruits de mer et de légumes
haddock églefin
haggis panse de mouton farcie aux flocons d'avoine
hake colin
half moitié, demi
halibut flétan
ham jambon
~ **and eggs** œufs au jambon
hare lièvre
haricot bean haricot blanc
hash 1) émincé 2) hachis de bœuf recouvert de pommes de terre
hazelnut noisette
heart cœur
herb herbe aromatique
herring hareng
home-made fait maison
hominy grits bouillie de maïs, sorte de polenta
honey miel
~ **dew melon** variété de melon très doux à la chair vert-jaune
horse-radish raifort
hot 1) chaud 2) épicé

~ **cross bun** brioche aux raisins (se mange pendant le Carême)

~ **dog** hot-dog, saucisse chaude dans un petit pain

huckleberry myrtille

hush puppy beignet de farine de maïs

ice-cream glace

iced glacé

icing glaçage

Idaho baked potato pomme de terre en robe des champs cuite au four

Irish stew ragoût de mouton aux oignons et aux pommes de terre

Italian dressing vinaigrette

jam confiture

jellied en gelée

Jell-O dessert à la gélatine

jelly gelée de fruits

Jerusalem artichoke topinambour

John Dory Saint-Pierre (poisson)

jugged hare civet de lièvre

juice jus

juniper berry baie de genièvre

junket lait caillé sucré

kale chou frisé

kedgeree miettes depoisson au riz, aux œufs et au beurre

kidney rognon

kipper hareng fumé

lamb agneau

Lancashire hot pot ragoût de côtelettes, de rognons d'agneau, de pommes de terre et d'oignons

larded lardé

lean maigre

leek poireau

leg gigot, cuisse

lemon citron

~ **sole** limande-sole

lentil lentille

lettuce laitue, salade verte

lima bean fève

lime lime, citron vert

liver foie

loaf pain, miche

lobster homard

loin filet, carré

Long Island duck canard de Long Island, très réputé

low-calorie pauvre en calories

lox saumon fumé

lunch déjeuner, repas de midi

macaroon macaron

mackerel maquereau

maize maïs

mandarin mandarine

maple syrup sirop d'érable

marinated mariné

marjoram marjolaine

marmalade confiture d'orange ou d'autres agrumes, marmelade

marrow moelle

~ **bone** os à moelle

marshmallow bonbon à la guimauve

marzipan pâte d'amandes

mashed potatoes purée de pommes de terre

meal repas

meat viande

~ **ball** boulette de viande

~ **loaf** rôti haché

medium (done) à point

melted fondu

Melton Mowbray pie croustade de viande

milk lait

mince hachis

~ **pie** tartelette aux fruits confits et aux épices

minced haché

~ **meat** viande hachée

mint menthe

mixed mélangé, panaché

~ **grill** assortiment de grillades

molasses mélasse

morel morille

mulberry mûre

mullet mulet

mulligatawny soup potage au poulet, très épicé, d'origine indienne

mushroom champignon

muskmelon sorte de melon

mussel moule

mustard moutarde

mutton mouton

noodle nouille

nut noix

oatmeal (porridge) porridge, bouillie d'avoine

oil huile

okra pousse de *gumbo* généralement utilisée pour lier les potages et les ragoûts

omelet omelette

onion oignon

ox tongue langue de bœuf

oyster huître

pancake crêpe

parsley persil

parsnip panais (racine comestible)

partridge perdrix

pastry pâtisserie

pasty pâté, chausson, rissole

pea petit pois

peach pêche

peanut cacahuète

~ **butter** beurre de cacahuètes

pear poire

pearl barley orge perlé

pepper poivre

peppermint menthe (poivrée)

perch perche

persimmon kaki

pheasant faisan

pickerel brocheton (poisson)

pickle 1) légume ou fruit au vinaigre 2) cornichon (US)

pickled en saumure, au vinaigre

pie tarte, recouverte le plus souvent d'une couche de pâte, farcie ou garnie de viande, de légumes, de fruits ou de crème anglaise

pig porc

pike brochet

pineapple ananas

plaice plie, carrelet

plain nature

plate plat, assiette

plum 1) prune 2) pruneau 3) raisin sec

~ **pudding** cake anglais aux fruits secs, parfois flambé; très nourrissant et servi à Noël

poached poché

popcorn grains de maïs éclatés

popover petit pain au lait

pork porc

porterhouse steak épaisse tranche de filet de bœuf

pot roast bœuf braisé aux légumes

potato pomme de terre

~ **chips** 1) pommes frites (GB) 2) pommes chips (US)

~ **in its jacket** pomme de terre en robe des champs

potted shrimps crevettes au beurre épicé (fondu et refroidi)

poultry volaille

prawn grosse crevette rose

prune pruneau

ptarmigan perdrix des neiges

pudding pudding (mou ou consistant) à base de farine, garni de viande, de poisson, de légumes ou de fruits

pumpernickel paim de seigle complet

pumpkin potiron, courge

quail caille

quince coing

rabbit lapin

radish radis

rainbow trout truite arc-en-ciel

raisin raisin sec

rare saignant

raspberry framboise

raw cru

red mullet rouget

red (sweet) pepper poivron rouge

redcurrant groseille rouge

relish condiment fait de légumes émincés au vinaigre

rhubarb rhubarbe

rib (of beef) côte (de bœuf)

rib-eye steak entrecôte

rice riz

rissole croquette de viande ou de poisson

river trout truite de rivière

roast(ed) rôti(e)

Rock Cornish hen variété de poulet de grain

roe œufs de poisson

roll petit pain

rollmop herring filet de hareng mariné au vin blanc, enroulé sur un cornichon

round steak quasi de bœuf

Rubens sandwich corned-beef sur toast, avec choucroute, emmenthal et sauce à salade, servi chaud

rumpsteak rumsteak

rusk biscotte

rye bread pain de seigle

saddle selle

saffron safran

sage sauge

salad salade

  ~ bar choix de salades

  ~ cream sauce à salade crémeuse, légèrement sucrée

  ~ dressing sauce pour salade

salmon saumon

  ~ trout truite saumonée

salt sel

salted salé

sauerkraut choucroute

sausage saucisse, saucisson

sauté(ed) sauté

scallop 1) peigne (coquille Saint-Jacques 2) escalope de veau

scone petit pain tendre à base de farine de blé ou d'orge

Scotch broth soupe à base d'agneau ou de bœuf et de légumes

Scotch woodcock toast avec œufs brouillés et beurre d'anchois

sea bass loup de mer

sea kale chou marin

seafood poissons et fruits de mer

(in) season (en) saison

seasoning assaisonnement

service charge montant à payer pour le service

service (not) included service (non) compris

set menu menu fixe

shad alose (sorte de sardine)

shallot échalote

shellfish crustacé

sherbet sorbet

shoulder épaule

shredded wheat croquettes de froment (servies au petit déjeuner)

shrimp crevette

silverside (of beef) gîte (de bœuf)

sirloin steak steak d'aloyau

skewer brochette

slice tranche

sliced coupé en tranches

sloppy Joe hachis de bœuf dans une sauce relevée aux tomates, servi dans un petit pain

smelt éperlan

smoked fumé

snack casse-croûte

soup potage, soupe

sour aigre

soused herring hareng au vinaigre et aux épices

spare rib côte de porc grillée

spice épice

spinach épinard

spiny lobster langouste

(on a) spit (à la) broche

sponge cake gâteau mousseline

sprat harenguet

squash courge

starter hors-d'œuvre

steak and kidney pie croustade de viande de bœuf et de rognons

steamed cuit à la vapeur

stew ragoût

Stilton (cheese) fromage anglais réputé (blanc ou à moisissures bleues)

strawberry fraise

string bean haricot vert

stuffed farci, fourré

stuffing farce

suck(l)ing pig cochon de lait

sugar sucre

sugarless sans sucre

sundae coupe de glace aux fruits, noix, crème Chantilly et parfois sirop

supper souper, léger repas du soir

swede rutabaga

sweet 1) doux 2) dessert

~ **corn** maïs jaune

~ **potato** patate douce

sweetbread ris de veau

Swiss cheese emmenthal

Swiss roll biscuit roulé à la confiture

Swiss steak tranche de bœuf braisée avec des légumes et des épices

T-bone steak morceau de contrefilet et de filet séparés par un os en forme de T

table d'hôte repas à prix fixe

tangerine mandarine

tarragon estragon

tart tarte (généralement aux fruits)

tenderloin filet (de viande)

Thousand Island dressing mayonnaise aux piments ou au ketchup, avec des poivrons, des olives et des œufs durs

thyme thym

toad-in-the-hole morceaux de viande ou de saucisse briochés

toasted grillé

~ **cheese** toast au fromage

tomato tomate

tongue langue

treacle mélasse

trifle sorte de charlotte russe à l'eau-de-vie avec amandes, confiture, crème Chantilly et crème anglaise

trout truite

truffle truffe

tuna, tunny thon

turkey dinde

turnip navet

turnover chausson

turtle tortue

underdone saignant

vanilla vanille

veal veau

~ **bird** paupiette de veau

vegetable légume

~ **marrow** courge

venison gros gibier

vichyssoise soupe froide aux poireaux, pommes de terre et crème

vinegar vinaigre

Virginia baked ham jambon cuit au four, piqué de clous de girofles, garni de tranches d'ananas, de cerises et glacé avec le jus des fruits

wafer gaufrette

waffle sorte de gaufre, chaude

walnut noix

water ice sorbet

watercress cresson de fontaine

watermelon pastèque

well-done bien cuit

Welsh rabbit/rarebit croûte au fromage

whelk buccin (mollusque)

whipped cream crème Chantilly

whitebait blanchaille

Wiener Schnitzel escalope viennoise

wine list carte des vins

woodcock bécasse

Worcestershire sauce condiment

liquide piquant, à base de vinaigre, de soja et d'ail

yoghurt yaourt

York ham jambon (fumé) d'York

Yorkshire pudding sorte de pâte à choux cuite et servie avec le rosbif

zucchini courgette

zwieback biscotte

Boissons

ale bière brune, légèrement sucrée, fermentée à haute température

bitter ~ brune, amère et plutôt lourde

brown ~ brune en bouteille, légèrement sucrée

light ~ blonde en bouteille

mild ~ brune à la pression, au goût prononcé

pale ~ blonde en bouteille

angostura essence aromatique amère ajoutée aux cocktails

applejack eau-de-vie de pomme

Athol Brose boisson écossaise composée de whisky, de miel, d'eau et parfois de flocons d'avoine

Bacardi cocktail cocktail au rhum avec du gin, du sirop de grenadine et du jus de lime (citron vert)

barley water boisson rafraîchissante à base d'orge et aromatisée de citron

barley wine bière brune très alcoolisée

beer bière

bottled ~ en bouteille

draft, draught ~ à la pression

bitters apéritifs et digestifs à base de racines, d'écorces ou d'herbes

black velvet champagne additionné de *stout* (accompagne souvent les huîtres)

bloody Mary vodka, jus de tomate et épices

bourbon whisky américain, à base de maïs

brandy 1) appellation générique désignant les eaux-de-vie de vin ou de fruit 2) cognac

~ Alexander mélange d'eau-de-vie, de crème de cacao et de crème fraîche

British wines vins «anglais» faits de raisins (ou de jus de raisin) importés en Grande-Bretagne

cherry brandy liqueur de cerise

chocolate chocolat

cider cidre

~ cup mélange de cidre, d'épices, de sucre et de glace

claret vin rouge de Bordeaux

cobbler *long drink* glacé à base de fruits, auquel on ajoute du vin ou une liqueur

coffee café

~ with cream crème

black ~ noir

caffeine-free ~ décaféiné

white ~ au lait

cordial liqueur

cream crème

cup boisson rafraîchissante composée de vin glacé, d'eau gazeuse, d'un spiritueux et décorée d'une tranche d'orange, de citron ou de concombre

daiquiri cocktail au rhum, au jus de lime et d'ananas

double double dose

Drambuie liqueur à base de whisky et de miel

dry martini 1) vermouth sec (GB) 2) cocktail au gin avec un peu de vermouth sec (US)

egg-nog boisson faite de rhum ou d'un autre alcool fort avec des jaunes d'œufs battus et du sucre

gin and it mélange de gin et de vermouth italien

gin-fizz gin avec jus de citron, sucre et soda

ginger ale boisson sans alcool, parfumée à l'essence de gingembre

ginger beer boisson légèrement alcoolisée, à base de gingembre et de sucre

grasshopper mélange de crème de menthe, de crème de cacao et de crème fraîche

Guinness (stout) bière brune légèrement sucrée, au goût très prononcé et à forte teneur en malt et houblon

half pint environ 3 décilitres

highball eau-de-vie ou whisky allongé d'eau gazeuse ou de *ginger ale*

iced glacé

Irish coffee café sucré, arrosé de whisky irlandais et nappé de crème Chantilly

Irish Mist liqueur irlandaise à base de whisky et de miel

Irish whiskey whisky irlandais, moins âpre que le *scotch*; outre l'orge, il contient du seigle, de l'avoine et du blé

juice jus

lager bière blonde légère, servie très fraîche

lemon squash citronnade

lemonade limonade

lime juice jus de lime (citron vert)

liquor spiritueux

long drink alcool allongé d'eau ou d'une boisson gazeuse, avec des glaçons

madeira madère

Manhattan whisky américain, vermouth et *angostura*

milk lait

~ **shake** frappé

mineral water eau minérale

mulled wine vin chaud aux épices

neat sans glace ni sans eau, sec, pur

old-fashioned whisky, *angostura*, cerises au marasquin et sucre

on the rocks avec des glaçons

Ovaltine Ovomaltine

Pimm's cup(s) boisson alcoolisée mélangée à du jus de fruit ou du soda

~ **No. 1** à base de gin

~ **No. 2** à base de whisky

~ **No. 3** à base de rhum

~ **No. 4** à base d'eau-de-vie

pink champagne champagne rosé

pink lady mélange de blanc d'œuf, de Calvados, de jus de citron, de grenadine et de gin

pint environ 6 décilitres

port (wine) porto

porter bière brune et amère

quart 1,14 litre (US 0,95 litre)

root beer boisson gazeuse sucrée, aromatisée d'herbes et de racines

rum rhum

rye (whiskey) whisky de seigle, plus lourd et plus âpre que le *bourbon*

scotch (whisky) whisky écossais, généralement fait d'une combinaison de whisky d'orge et de whisky de blé

screwdriver vodka et jus d'orange

shandy *bitter ale* mélangée à une limonade ou une *ginger beer*

sherry xérès

short drink tout alcool non dilué

shot dose de spiritueux

sloe gin-fizz liqueur de prunelle avec soda et jus de citron

soda water eau de Seltz

soft drink boisson sans alcool
spirits spiritueux
stinger cognac et crème de menthe
stout bière brune fortement
  houblonnée et alcoolisée
straight alcool bu sec, pur
tea thé
toddy grog
Tom Collins gin, jus de citron, sucre,
  eau gazeuse
tonic (water) eau gazéifiée,

aromatisée de quinine
water eau
whisky sour whisky, jus de citron,
  sucre et soda
wine vin
  dry ~ sec
  red ~ rouge
  sparkling ~ mousseux
  sweet ~ doux (de dessert) **white** ~
  blanc

Mini-grammaire anglaise

L'article

L'article défini (le, la, les) a une seule forme: *the*.

the room, the rooms   la chambre, les chambres

L'article indéfini (un, une, des) a deux formes: *a* s'emploie devant une consonne, *an* devant une voyelle ou un «h» muet.

a coat	un manteau
an umbrella	un parapluie
an hour	une heure

Some indique une quantité ou un nombre indéfini.

I'd like some water, please.   Je voudrais de l'eau, s.v.p.

Any s'emploie dans les phrases négatives et différents types d'interrogatives.

There isn't any soap.	Il n'y a pas de savon.
Do you have any stamps?	Avez-vous des timbres?

Le nom

Le pluriel de la plupart des noms se forme par l'addition de *-(e)s* au singulier.

cup – cups (tasse – tasses)   **dress – dresses** (robe – robes)

Note: Si un nom se termine par *-y* précédé d'une consonne, le pluriel se termine par *-ies*; si le *-y* est précédé d'une voyelle, il n'y a pas de changement.

lady – ladies (dame – dames)   **key – keys** (clef – clefs)

Quelques pluriels irréguliers:

man – men (homme – hommes)	**foot – feet** (pied – pieds)
woman – women (femme – femmes)	**tooth – teeth** (dent – dents)
child – children (enfant – enfants)	**mouse – mice** (souris – souris)

Le complément du nom (génitif)

1. Le possesseur est une personne: si le nom ne se termine pas par *-s*, on ajoute *'s*.

the boy's room	la chambre du garçon
the children's clothes	les vêtements des enfants

Si le nom se termine par *s*, on ajoute l'apostrophe (').

the boys' room   la chambre des garçons

2. Le possesseur n'est pas une personne: on utilise la préposition *of*:

the key of the door   la clef de la porte

L'adjectif

Les adjectifs se placent normalement avant le nom.

a large brown suitcase   une grande valise brune

Il y a deux façons de former le comparatif et le superlatif des adjectifs:

1. Les adjectifs d'une syllabe et de nombreux adjectifs de deux syllabes prennent la terminaison -*(e)r* et -*(e)st*.

small (petit) – **smaller** – **smallest**   pretty (joli) – **prettier** – **prettiest***

2. Les adjectifs de trois syllabes et plus, et certains de deux (en particulier ceux qui se terminent par -*ful* et -*less*) forment leurs comparatifs et superlatifs avec *more* et *most*.

expensive (cher) – **more expensive** – **most expensive**

Le pronom

		Sujet	Complément (dir./indir.)	Possessif 1	2
Singulier					
1re personne		**I**	**me**	**my**	**mine**
2e personne		**you**	**you**	**your**	**yours**
3e personne	(m)	**he**	**him**	**his**	**his**
	(f)	**she**	**her**	**her**	**hers**
	(n)	**it**	**it**	**its**	–
Pluriel					
1re personne		**we**	**us**	**our**	**ours**
2e personne		**you**	**you**	**your**	**yours**
3e personne		**they**	**them**	**their**	**their**

Note: L'anglais ignore le tutoiement. La forme *you* signifie donc «tu» et «vous».

Le cas complément s'emploie aussi après les prépositions.

Give it to me.   Donnez-le-moi.

La forme 1 du possessif correspond à «mon», «ton», etc., la forme 2 à «le mien», «le tien», etc.

Where's my key? Où est ma clef?   **That's not mine.** Ce n'est pas la mienne.

---

* L'«y» se change en «i» lorsqu'il est précédé d'une consonne.

Verbes auxiliaires

a. **to be** (être)

	Forme contractée	Négatif – formes contractées	
I am	**I'm**		**I'm not**
you are	**you're**	**you're not** ou	**you aren't**
he is	**he's**	**he's not**	**he isn't**
she is	**she's**	**she's not**	**she isn't**
it is	**it's**	**it's not**	**it isn't**
we are	**we're**	**we're not** ou	**we aren't**
they are	**they're**	**they're not**	**they aren't**

Interrogatif: **Am I? Are you? Is he?** etc.

b. **to have** (avoir)

	Contraction		Contraction
I have	**I've**	**we have**	**we've**
you have	**you've**	**you have**	**you've**
he/she/it has	**he/she/it's**	**they have**	**they've**

Négation: **I have not (I haven't)**
Interrogation: **Have you? – Has he?**

c. **to do** (faire)

	Négatif contracté		Négatif contracté
I do	**I don't**	**we do**	**we don't**
you do	**you don't**	**you do**	**you don't**
he/she/it does	**he/she/it doesn't**	**they do**	**they don't**

Interrogation: **Do you? Does he/she/it?**

Autres verbes

L'infinitif est utilisé pour toutes les personnes du présent; on ajoute simplement
-(*e*)*s* à la 3ᵉ personne du singulier.

	(to) love (aimer)	**(to) come** (venir)	**(to) go** (aller)
I	love	come	go
you	love	come	go
he/she/it	loves	comes	goes
we	love	come	go
they	love	come	go

La négation se forme au moyen de l'auxiliaire *do/does* + *not* + infinitif du verbe.

We do not (don't) like this hotel.   Nous n'aimons pas cet hôtel.

L'interrogation se forme aussi avec l'auxiliaire *do* + sujet + infinitif.

Do you like her?   L'aimez-vous?

Verbes irréguliers

L'imparfait et le participe passé des verbes réguliers se forment en ajoutant -(e)d à l'infinitif. La liste suivante vous donne les verbes irréguliers anglais. Les verbes composés ou précédés d'un préfixe se conjuguent comme les verbes principaux: p.ex. *withdraw* se conjugue comme *draw* et *mistake* comme *take*.

Infinitif	Imparfait	Participe passé	
arise	arose	arisen	*(se) lever*
awake	awoke	awoken	*(se) réveiller*
be	was	been	*être*
bear	bore	borne	*porter*
beat	beat	beaten	*battre*
become	became	become	*devenir*
begin	began	begun	*commencer*
bend	bent	bent	*plier*
bet	bet	bet	*parier*
bid	bade/bid	bidden/bid	*ordonner*
bind	bound	bound	*attacher*
bite	bit	bitten	*mordre*
bleed	bled	bled	*saigner*
blow	blew	blown	*souffler*
break	broke	broken	*briser*
breed	bred	bred	*élever*
bring	brought	brought	*apporter*
build	built	built	*bâtir*
burn	burnt/burned	burnt/burned	*brler*
burst	burst	burst	*éclater*
buy	bought	bought	*acheter*
can*	could	–	*pouvoir*
cast	cast	cast	*jeter*
catch	caught	caught	*attraper*
choose	chose	chosen	*choisir*
cling	clung	clung	*se cramponner*
clothe	clothed/clad	clothed/clad	*vêtir*
come	came	come	*venir*
cost	cost	cost	*coter*
creep	crept	crept	*ramper*
cut	cut	cut	*couper*
deal	dealt	dealt	*conclure (marché)*
dig	dug	dug	*creuser*
do (he does)	did	done	*faire*

---

* présent de l'indicatif

draw	drew	drawn	*dessiner*
dream	dreamt/dreamed	dreamt/dreamed	*rêver*
drink	drank	drunk	*boire*
drive	drove	driven	*conduire (auto)*
dwell	dwelt	dwelt	*habiter*
eat	ate	eaten	*manger*
fall	fell	fallen	*tomber*
feed	fed	fed	*nourrir*
feel	felt	felt	*ressentir*
fight	fought	fought	*combattre*
find	found	found	*trouver*
flee	fled	fled	*fuir*
fling	flung	flung	*lancer*
fly	flew	flown	*voler*
forsake	forsook	forsaken	*abandonner*
freeze	froze	frozen	*geler*
get	got	got	*obtenir*
give	gave	given	*donner*
go	went	gone	*aller*
grind	ground	ground	*moudre*
grow	grew	grown	*croître*
hang	hung	hung	*pendre*
have	had	had	*avoir*
hear	heard	heard	*entendre*
hew	hewed	hewed/hewn	*couper*
hide	hid	hidden	*cacher*
hit	hit	hit	*frapper*
hold	held	held	*tenir*
hurt	hurt	hurt	*blesser*
keep	kept	kept	*garder*
kneel	knelt	knelt	*s'agenouiller*
knit	knitted/knit	knitted/knit	*tricoter/unir*
know	knew	known	*savoir*
lay	laid	laid	*étendre, placer*
lead	led	led	*guider*
lean	leant/leaned	leant/leaned	*s'appuyer*
leap	leapt/leaped	leapt/leaped	*sauter*
learn	learnt/learned	learnt/learned	*apprendre*
leave	left	left	*quitter*
lend	lent	lent	*prêter*
let	let	let	*permettre*
lie	lay	lain	*être couché*
light	lit/lighted	lit/lighted	*allumer*
lose	lost	lost	*perdre*

make	made	made	*faire*
may*	might	–	*pouvoir*
mean	meant	meant	*signifier*
meet	met	met	*rencontrer*
mow	mowed	mowed/mown	*faucher*
must*	–	–	*falloir*
ought (to)*	–	–	*devoir*
pay	paid	paid	*payer*
put	put	put	*mettre*
read	read	read	*lire*
rid	rid	rid	*débarrasser*
ride	rode	ridden	*monter (à cheval)*
ring	rang	rung	*sonner*
rise	rose	risen	*se lever*
run	ran	run	*courir*
saw	sawed	sawn	*scier*
say	said	said	*dire*
see	saw	seen	*voir*
seek	sought	sought	*chercher*
sell	sold	sold	*vendre*
send	sent	sent	*envoyer*
set	set	set	*poser*
sew	sewed	sewed/sewn	*coudre*
shake	shook	shaken	*secouer*
shall*	should	–	*devoir*
shed	shed	shed	*verser*
shine	shone	shone	*briller*
shoot	shot	shot	*tirer*
show	showed	shown	*montrer*
shrink	shrank	shrunk	*rétrécir*
shut	shut	shut	*fermer*
sing	sang	sung	*chanter*
sink	sank	sunk	*couler*
sit	sat	sat	*s'asseoir*
sleep	slept	slept	*dormir*
slide	slid	slid	*glisser*
sling	slung	slung	*jeter*
slink	slunk	slunk	*s'esquiver*
slit	slit	slit	*fendre*
smell	smelled/smelt	smelled/smelt	*sentir (odeur)*
sow	sowed	sown/sowed	*semer*
speak	spoke	spoken	*parler*

---

* présent de l'indicatif

speed	sped/speeded	sped/speeded	*accélérer*
spell	spelt/spelled	spelt/spelled	*épeler*
spend	spent	spent	*dépenser*
spill	spilt/spilled	spilt/spilled	*renverser*
spin	spun	spun	*filer*
spit	spat	spat	*cracher*
split	split	split	*fendre, séparer*
spoil	spoilt/spoiled	spoilt/spoiled	*gâter*
spread	spread	spread	*répandre, enduire*
spring	sprang	sprung	*jaillir*
stand	stood	stood	*se tenir debout*
steal	stole	stolen	*dérober*
stick	stuck	stuck	*coller*
sting	stung	stung	*piquer*
stink	stank/stunk	stunk	*empester*
strew	strewed	strewed/strewn	*joncher*
stride	strode	stridden	*marcher à grands pas*
strike	struck	struck/stricken	*frapper*
string	strung	strung	*ficeler*
strive	strove	striven	*s'efforcer*
swear	swore	sworn	*jurer*
sweep	swept	swept	*balayer*
swell	swelled	swollen	*enfler*
swim	swam	swum	*nager*
swing	swung	swung	*se balancer*
take	took	taken	*prendre*
teach	taught	taught	*enseigner*
tear	tore	torn	*déchirer*
tell	told	told	*dire*
think	thought	thought	*penser*
throw	threw	thrown	*jeter*
thrust	thrust	thrust	*pousser*
tread	trod	trodden	*piétiner*
wake	woke/waked	woken/waked	*(se) réveiller*
wear	wore	worn	*porter (habit)*
weave	wove	woven	*tisser*
weep	wept	wept	*pleurer*
will*	would	–	*vouloir*
win	won	won	*gagner*
wind	wound	wound	*enrouler*
wring	wrung	wrung	*tordre*
write	wrote	written	*écrire*

* présent de l'indicatif

Abréviations anglaises

AA	*Automobile Association*	Automobile Club de Grande-Bretagne
AAA	*American Automobile Association*	Automobile Club des Etats-Unis
ABC	*Amercican Broadcasting Company*	société privée de radio-diffusion et de télévision (US)
A.D.	*anno Domini*	apr. J.-C.
AIDS	*acquired immune deficiency syndrome*	SIDA
Am.	*America; American*	Amérique; américain
a.m.	*ante meridiem (before noon)*	du matin (de minuit à midi)
Amtrak	*American railroad corporation*	société privée des chemins de fer américains
AT & T	*American Telephone and Telegraph Company*	compagnie privée des télé-phones et télégraphes (US)
Ave.	*avenue*	avenue
BBC	*British Broadcasting Corporation*	société britannique de radio-diffusion et de télévision
B.C.	*before Christ*	av. J.-C.
bldg.	*building*	immeuble
Blvd.	*boulevard*	boulevard
B.R.	*British Rail*	chemins de fer britanniques
Brit.	*Britain; British*	Grande-Bretagne; britannique
Bros.	*brothers*	frères
¢	*cent*	1/100 de dollar
Can.	*Canada; Canadian*	Canada; canadien
CBS	*Columbia Broadcasting System*	société privée de radiodiffu-sion et de télévision (US)
CID	*Criminal Investigation Department*	police judiciaire (GB)
CNN	*Cable News Network*	société privée de télévision
CNR	*Canadian National Railway*	société nationale des chemins de fer canadiens
c/o	*(in) care of*	p.a., aux bons soins de
Co.	*company*	compagnie
Corp.	*corporation*	type de société
CPR	*Canadian Pacific Railways*	société privée des chemins de fer canadiens
D.C.	*District of Columbia*	District de Columbia (Washington, D.C.)

DDS	*Doctor of Dental Science*	dentiste
dept.	*department*	département
e.g.	*for instance*	par exemple
Eng.	*England; English*	Angleterre; anglais
EU	*European Union*	UE
excl.	*excluding; exclusive*	non compris, exclu
ft.	*foot/feet*	pied/pieds (30,5 cm)
GB	*Great Britain*	Grande-Bretagne
H.E.	*His/Her Excellency;*	Son Excellence;
	His Eminence	Son Eminence
H.H.	*His Holiness*	Sa Sainteté
H.M.	*His/Her Majesty*	Sa Mejesté
H.M.S.	*Her Majesty's ship*	bâtiment de la marine royale
		de Grande-Bretagne
hp	*horsepower*	chevaux-vapeur
i.e.	*that is to say*	c'est-à-dire
in.	*inch*	pouce (2,54 cm)
Inc.	*incorporated*	type de société anonyme
		américaine
incl.	*including, inclusive*	compris, inclus
£	*pound sterling*	livre sterling
L.A.	*Los Angeles*	Los Angeles
Ltd.	*limited*	type de société anonyme
		britannique
M.D.	*Doctor of Medicine*	médecin
M.P.	*Member of Parliament*	membre du Parlement
		britannique
mph	*miles per hour*	miles à l'heure
Mr	*Mister*	Monsieur
Mrs	*Missis*	Madame
Ms	*Missis/Miss*	Madame/Mademoiselle
nat.	*national*	national
NBC	*National Broadcasting*	société privée de radiodiffu-
	Company	sion et de télévision (US)
No.	*number*	numéro
N.Y.C.	*New York City*	ville de New York
O.B.E.	*Officer (of the Order)*	Officier de l'Ordre de l'Empire
	of the British Empire	britannique
p.	*page; penny/pence*	page; 1/100 de livre sterling
p.a.	*per annum*	par an, annuel
Ph.D.	*Doctor of Philosophy*	docteur en philosophie
p.m.	*post meridiem*	de l'après-midi/du soir
	(after noon)	(de midi à minuit)
PO	*Post Office*	bureau de poste

P.T.O.	*please turn over*	tournez, s'il vous plaît
RAC	*Royal Automobile Club*	Automobile Club de Grande-Bretagne
RCMP	*Royal Canadian Mounted Police*	police royale montée canadienne
Rd.	*road*	route, rue
ref.	*reference*	voir, comparer
Rev.	*reverend*	pasteur dans l'Eglise anglicane
RFD	*rural free delivery*	distribution du courrier à la campagne
RR	*railroad*	chemin de fer
RSVP	*please reply*	répondez, s'il vous plaît
$	*dollar*	dollar
soc.	*society*	société
St.	*saint; street*	saint; rue
STD	*Subscriber Trunk Dialling*	téléphone automatique
UK	*United Kingdom*	Royaume-Uni
UN	*United Nations*	Nations Unies
UPS	*United Parcel Service*	service d'expédition de colis (US)
US	*United States*	Etats-Unis
USS	*United States Ship*	bâtiment de la marine de guerre américaine
VAT	*value added tax*	TVA
VIP	*very important person*	personne jouissant de privilèges particuliers
Xmas	*Christmas*	Noël
yd.	*yard*	yard (91,44 cm)
YMCA	*Young Men's Christian Association*	Union Chrétienne de Jeunes Gens
YWCA	*Young Women's Christian Association*	Union Chrétienne de Jeunes Filles
ZIP	*ZIP code*	code postal

Nombres

Nombres cardinaux

0	zero
1	one
2	two
3	three
4	four
5	five
6	six
7	seven
8	eight
9	nine
10	ten
11	eleven
12	twelve
13	thirteen
14	fourteen
15	fifteen
16	sixteen
17	seventeen
18	eighteen
19	nineteen
20	twenty
21	twenty-one
22	twenty-two
23	twenty-three
24	twenty-four
25	twenty-five
30	thirty
40	forty
50	fifty
60	sixty
70	seventy
80	eighty
90	ninety
100	a/one hundred
230	two hundred and thirty
500	five hundred
1,000	a/one thousand
10,000	ten thousand
100,000	a/one hundred thousand
1,000,000	a/one million

Nombres ordinaux

1st	first
2nd	second
3rd	third
4th	fourth
5th	fifth
6th	sixth
7th	seventh
8th	eighth
9th	ninth
10th	tenth
11th	eleventh
12th	twelfth
13th	thirteenth
14th	fourteenth
15th	fifteenth
16th	sixteenth
17th	seventeenth
18th	eighteenth
19th	nineteenth
20th	twentieth
21st	twenty-first
22nd	twenty-second
23rd	twenty-third
24th	twenty-fourth
25th	twenty-fifth
26th	twenty-sixth
27th	twenty-seventh
28th	twenty-eighth
29th	twenty-ninth
30th	thirtieth
40th	fortieth
50th	fiftieth
60th	sixtieth
70th	seventieth
80th	eightieth
90th	ninetieth
100th	hundredth
230th	two hundred and thirtieth
500th	five hundredth
1,000th	thousandth

L'heure

Les Britanniques et les Américains utilisent le système des douze heures. L'expression *a.m.* (*ante meridiem*) désigne les heures précédant midi, *p.m.* (*post meridiem*) celles de l'après-midi et du soir (jusqu'à minuit).
Toutefois, en Grande-Bretagne, les horaires sont progressivement libellés sur le modèle continental.

I'll come at seven a.m. — Je viendrai à 7 h. du matin.
I'll come at one p.m. — Je viendrai à 1 h. de l'après-midi.
I'll come at eight p.m. — Je viendrai à 8 h. du soir.

Les jours de la semaine

Sunday	dimanche	*Thursday*	jeudi
Monday	lundi	*Friday*	vendredi
Tuesday	mardi	*Saturday*	samedi
Wednesday	mercredi		

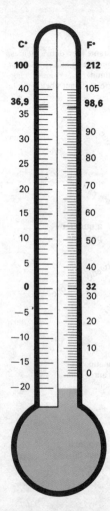

C°	F°
100	212
40	105
36,9	98,6
35	
30	90
25	80
20	70
15	60
10	50
5	40
0	32
	30
−5	20
−10	10
−15	
	0
−20	

Conversion tables/
Tables de conversion

Metres and feet

The figure in the middle stands for both metres and feet, e.g. 1 metre = 3.281 ft. and 1 foot = 0.30 m.

Mètres et pieds

Le chiffre du milieu représente à la fois des mètres et des pieds. Par ex.: 1 mètre = 3,281 pieds et 1 pied = 0,30 m.

Metres/ Mètres		Feet/Pieds
0.30	**1**	3.281
0.61	**2**	6.563
0.91	**3**	9.843
1.22	**4**	13.124
1.52	**5**	16.403
1.83	**6**	19.686
2.13	**7**	22.967
2.44	**8**	26.248
2.74	**9**	29.529
3.05	**10**	32.810
3.66	**12**	39.372
4.27	**14**	45.934
6.10	**20**	65.620
7.62	**25**	82.023
15.24	**50**	164.046
22.86	**75**	246.069
30.48	**100**	328.092

Temperature

To convert Centigrade to Fahrenheit, multiply by 1.8 and add 32.
To convert Fahrenheit to Centigrade, subtract 32 from Fahrenheit and divide by 1.8.

Température

Pour convertir les degrés centigrades en degrés Fahrenheit, multipliez les premiers par 1,8 et ajoutez 32 au total obtenu.